Piero di Lorenzo de' Medici and the Crisis of Renaissance Italy

Following the life of one man, Piero de Medici, Lorenzo the Magnificent's son, Alison Brown sheds new light on several of the most important themes of Renaissance history and culture by combining political history, the history of ideas and cultural history. This interdisciplinary study weaves together an understudied period of crisis in Italy that brought down three leading dynasties, the revolution that in turn led to the new political realism of writers like Machiavelli, Guicciardini and Francesco Vettori, and, finally, the transition from the civic culture of the early Renaissance to the courtly or princely culture of the Cinquecento. Focusing on Piero's full life and colourful character, Brown grants us a unique and contextualised insight into the patronage, culture and politics of Renaissance Italy, whilst grounding broader trends within the lived experience of Florence's most famous ruling family.

ALISON BROWN is Emeritus Professor of History at Royal Holloway, University of London, having been a British Academy Exchange Fellow at the Newberry Library, Chicago, and an Invited Visiting Professor and Fellow at the Harvard University Center for Italian Renaissance Studies at the Villa I Tatti, Florence. She is the author of the biography *Bartolomeo Scala 1430–1497, Chancellor of Florence*, which won the Premio Arnolfo in Colle Val d'Elsa in 1979, and *The Return of Lucretius to Renaissance Florence* (2010).

Piero di Lorenzo de' Medici and the Crisis of Renaissance Italy

Alison Brown

Royal Holloway, University of London

CAMBRIDGE
UNIVERSITY PRESS

Shaftesbury Road, Cambridge CB2 8EA, United Kingdom

One Liberty Plaza, 20th Floor, New York, NY 10006, USA

477 Williamstown Road, Port Melbourne, VIC 3207, Australia

314–321, 3rd Floor, Plot 3, Splendor Forum, Jasola District Centre, New Delhi – 110025, India

103 Penang Road, #05–06/07, Visioncrest Commercial, Singapore 238467

Cambridge University Press is part of Cambridge University Press & Assessment, a department of the University of Cambridge.

We share the University's mission to contribute to society through the pursuit of education, learning and research at the highest international levels of excellence.

www.cambridge.org
Information on this title: www.cambridge.org/9781108746571

DOI: 10.1017/9781108783798

© Alison Brown 2020

This publication is in copyright. Subject to statutory exception and to the provisions of relevant collective licensing agreements, no reproduction of any part may take place without the written permission of Cambridge University Press & Assessment.

First published 2020
First paperback edition 2023

A catalogue record for this publication is available from the British Library

Library of Congress Cataloging-in-Publication data
Names: Brown, Alison, 1934- author.
Title: Piero di Lorenzo de' Medici and the Crisis of Renaissance Italy / Alison Brown.
Description: Cambridge, United Kingdom ; New York, NY : Cambridge University Press, 2020. | Includes bibliographical references and index.
Identifiers: LCCN 2019038166 (print) | LCCN 2019038167 (ebook) | ISBN 9781108489461 (hardback) | ISBN 9781108746571 (paperback) | ISBN 9781108783798 (epub)
Subjects: LCSH: Medici, Piero di Lorenzo de', 1472-1503. | Florence (Italy)–Biography. | Florence (Italy)–Politics and government–1421-1737.
Classification: LCC DG737.95 .B76 2020 (print) | LCC DG737.95 (ebook) | DDC 945/.505092 [B]–dc23
LC record available at https://lccn.loc.gov/2019038166
LC ebook record available at https://lccn.loc.gov/2019038167

ISBN   978-1-108-48946-1   Hardback
ISBN   978-1-108-74657-1   Paperback

Cambridge University Press & Assessment has no responsibility for the persistence or accuracy of URLs for external or third-party internet websites referred to in this publication and does not guarantee that any content on such websites is, or will remain, accurate or appropriate.

For Ros

Contents

Acknowledgements	*page* ix
List of Abbreviations	xii
Introduction	1

Part I The Early Years

1	Piero's Childhood	9
2	Family Backgrounds	16
3	Education under Poliziano's Tutelage	26
4	Political Tyro at Home and Abroad, 1484–1486	39
5	Marrying into the Roman Aristocracy, 1487–1488	52
6	The Choice of Hercules: Between Duty and Pleasure, 1488–1489	71
7	Piero as Lorenzo's Deputy in 1490	88

Part II Between Republicanism and Princely Rule

8	Cultural Patronage and Sportsmanship	107
9	Ruling as Patrons in Florence's Dominion and Beyond	123

Part III Piero in Power

10	Lorenzo's Death and Its Aftermath, 1492	149
11	Balancing Power in Italy, 1493	168
12	'The Viper with Its Tail in Florence', 1493–1494	180
13	The Crux, 1494	190

14 The French Descent	198
15 Revolution in Florence	214

Part IV Piero in Exile

16 Perambulating Italy, 1494–1497	231
17 'Contamination in the Labyrinth': Networking in Exile	254
18 The Last Years, 1498–1503	271
19 Piero's Burial and Legacy	292

Conclusion

20 Power and Legitimacy in Renaissance Italy	301
Bibliography	308
Index	325

Acknowledgements

First of all, my warmest thanks and gratitude are owed to the wide *brigata* of friends and colleagues who have long supported me with their interest, advice and information, and helped in so many different ways to bring this project to fruition. Among them are friends who have given me specific information about Piero and generously shared with me their own research – even directing it towards subjects that they knew would help my project on its way (thinking here especially of Lorenzo Fabbri, Francesco Guidi Bruscoli and Eckart Marchant). Some time ago, Alison Wright told me that Piero was buried in Montecassino, and more recently Mario Casari and Camilla Russell took me there on a memorable trip from Rome. Mario transcribed the inscription on Piero's tomb atop a high ladder and provided me with a copy of Caravita's account of Montecassino. Camilla and my daughter Charlotte photographed the tomb and they have both helped me in innumerable other ways. Charles Robertson provided me with invaluable suggestions and models for the tomb. Letizia Panizza has advised me on Piero's poems and David Rosenthal on networking. Carla Darista gave me invaluable information about the Pucci family, Marcello Simonetta gave me an early transcript of Lorenzo Guiducci's *Diario* and Blake Wilson a copy of his 'Sound Patrons' before its publication.

For help in reading and interpreting documents, I owe special thanks to Francesco Guidi, who helped me to interpret the account book of the Medici Bank in Pisa (Ginori Conti 5), also to Richard Goldthwaite, who discussed these accounts with me and much else. Andrea Guidi, Giovanni Ciappelli and Sergio Nelli gave me help in reading and locating documents, and in Rome Cristina Falcucci gave me generous help in consulting the Orsini papers in the Capitoline Library.

I owe a special debt of gratitude to the friendship and support of librarians and archivists at the Warburg Institute and the British Library in London, and at the Biblioteca Laurenziana , the Biblioteca Nazionale and the private Guicciardini and Niccolini family archives in Florence – above all to Rita Romanelli, archivist in the Niccolini archives, who very recently showed me an important filza of Piero's letters that I have been able to refer to in my text, albeit at a late stage. Without the warm support and friendship of everyone in the Archivio di Stato in Florence, this book would never have been written. The staff there have borne the brunt of my researches and helped me with great generosity in innumerable ways – in the late stages, especially Pietro Marchi, Orsola Gori and Francesca Klein. Francesca was not only responsible for supervising the digitalisation of the *Mediceo avanti il Principato fondo*, on which my research so largely relied, but she has shared my interest in Piero's life, suggesting to me relevant material and also giving me invaluable help in translating difficult Italian words and expressions.

Some debts are very long-standing and can't be easily expressed. One is to the late Bill Kent. Although his biography of Lorenzo de' Medici was unfinished when he died, I have profited from his rich work on the Medici (now edited and republished by Carolyn James in *The Princely Citizen*, Brepols, 2013), as well as from his draft volume on *The Young Lorenzo*, which I read in typescript and which contributed to my early chapters on Piero's childhood. Carolyn James herself has helped me with advice and material. So has David Chambers, who read and commented on an early draft of the book and gave me copies of all of Piero's letters in the Mantuan state archives, as well as alerting me to other relevant material. Riccardo Fubini and Maria Leuzzi Fubini have shared their work with me and offered me warm hospitality, and it is my great regret that Riccardo is no longer alive to read and offer me his invaluable comments on this book.

There are two people to whom my debt is greatest and who need special acknowledgement: John Najemy and Ros Pesman Cooper, both colleagues in the Renaissance field and long-standing friends. If John has helped to bring this book into the world as one of its readers and then nurtured it with exceptional care and understanding, Ros has been its godmother in providing its name, or title, after reading and improving two earlier drafts at a very difficult time for her. I dedicate it to her in acknowledgement of her contribution to Renaissance history before she expanded into other fields (and in gratitude to her for returning to it now). I have enjoyed discussions with both Ros and John about Florence's republicanism and the 'cadre of public officials' – Ros's term – that contributed to it. They (and the anonymous second reader) have greatly improved the book's scope and argument and have saved me from all too many errors – if not from the official axe that, alas, felled many of the footnotes with their transcriptions of letters translated in the text, and ruled out the illustrations I had hoped to include.

This, for me, has been a lateish-life project that I am delighted to have completed, thanks in no small part to the interest and support of all the friends mentioned here, as well as many others, including the editorial team at Cambridge University Press. Still believing (as I once put it) that biographies can 'give coherence to the interpretation of ideas', I have tried to avoid the polarising language of the 'republican-signorial' debate about Medici power - used at the time and now - in order to explain Piero's life as part of the complex and contested years of change in Italy, during which early communes like Florence were gradually transformed into territorial states and principates.

List of Abbreviations

Acq. Doni	Acquisti e Doni, fondi in ASF and the Bibl. Laurenziana, Florence
AS	Archivio di Stato
ASF	Archivio di Stato, Florence
ASI	*Archivio storico italiano*
BNCF	Biblioteca Nazionale Centrale, Florence
Brown, *Florence* (2011)	A. Brown, *Medicean and Savonarolan Florence*, 2011
Can	Canestrini G.-Desjardins, A., *Négotiations diplomatiques de la France avec la Toscane*
Corrispondenza 3, 5, 7	*Corrispondenza degli ambasciatori fiorentini a Napoli*, 3 (di Bernardo Rucellai, 1486–87, ed. Meli); 5 (di Paolo Antonio Soderini, 1489–90, ed. Trapani); 7 (di Piero Alamanni, 1492–93, and Bartolomeo Ugolini [1–18 aprile 149, ed. B. Figliuolo, 2012])
CS	Carte strozziane in ASF
DBI	*Dizionario biografico degli Italiani*, Rome: Treccani
Dovizi	ser Piero Dovizi, not his brothers Bernardo (later Cardinal Bibbiena) and Antonio, both of whom also worked as secretaries for the Medici
GC	Ginori Conti fondo in BNCF
Guicciardini, *Storie*	F. Guicciardini, *Storie fiorentine*
JWCI	*Journal of the Warburg and Courtauld Institutes*
Lorenzo, *Lettere* 1–12, 15–16	Lorenzo de' Medici, *Lettere* 1–2 (ed. Fubini), 3–4 (ed. Rubinstein), 5–7 (ed. Mallett), 8–9 (ed. Butters), 12 (ed. Pellegrini), 15–16 (ed. Böninger)
MAP	Mediceo avanti il Principato fondo in ASF
Mitteilungen	*Mitteilungen des Kunsthistorischen Institutes in Florenz*

Najemy, *A History*   J. Najemy, *A History of Florence, 1200–1575*
Piero   Piero de' Medici
SSX8LCMR   ASF Signori, Dieci, Otto, Legazione e Commissarie, Missive e Responsive

Abbreviated References to *fondi* in the Archivio di Stato, Florence

    Notarile ante cos<imiano>
    Otto di Guardia rep<ublicano>
    Otto di Pratica, Delib<erazioni>
    Otto <di Pratica> Respons<ive>
    Provv<isioni> 186
    Signori, Coll<egi>, Cond<otte> e Stanz<iamenti>
    Signori, Delib<erazioni> ord<inaria> aut<orità>
    Signori, Leg<azioni> e Comm<issarie>. Elez<ioni>, Istruz<ioni> e Lett<ere>
    Signori Respons<ive> 11
    SSX8LCMR, see above

Introduction

Piero de' Medici's life remains unstudied, despite being pivotal to the crisis faced by Italian states in the late fifteenth century. Following the French invasion in 1494, Piero was not only driven out of Florence but spent the remainder of his life in exile, drowning in 1503 in an overladen baggage train while fighting with the French in southern Italy against Spain. As Lorenzo il Magnifico's eldest son and heir, he also experienced the problems of all Italy's communal regimes as they transformed themselves into territorial states in the fourteenth and fifteenth centuries. Since Florence was still nominally a republic, many of its citizens were alienated by the way Lorenzo – and his son Piero – were treated by other rulers as de facto princes and as the 'idols' of their adherents in Florence, and they later blamed Piero for the regime's collapse in 1494.[1] This created great ambivalence towards him during his years in Florence and hostility afterwards. Yet as the narrative of his life will show, he was more intelligent and talented than his critics suggest, and he provides an invaluable prism through which to view these confused years of crisis for Florence and for Italy.

Born in 1472, Piero was educated from the age of three by the humanist Angelo Poliziano, and in his youth he was praised for his precocious learning, his sportsmanship and his intelligence. But the clever and beautiful child with whom passers-by loved to converse became the man who, according to his frustrated widow Alfonsina Orsini, kept her and their son Lorenzo out of power for nearly twenty years. Why this happened is the puzzle underlying the story of his life and his short time in power, for as Renaissance historians were well aware, differing versions of events are given by winners and losers – and some losers risked disappearing from the narrative of their times altogether, as Piero

---

[1] On Lorenzo as 'de facto prince', Najemy, *A History*, p. 344; as *idolo*, Lorenzo, *Lettere* 7, p. 157 (intro. n.) and pp. 159–60 in this volume.

has done.² To see how quickly his reputation was blackened before suffering this fate, we have only to compare Bartolomeo Cerretani's account of him as Lorenzo's 'warrior' son with Marin Sanudo's version, according to which Piero is the mad and bad son compared with his brothers, the 'good' Giovanni and the 'wise' Giuliano.³ Because Piero died in exile, he never returned to share his brothers' rehabilitation as princes in the new social order – one a pope, the other a duke. Instead, he remained in people's memory as Machiavelli's 'great rebel' who, as a twenty-two-year old, had apparently failed both his family and his city by not responding adequately to the international crisis of 1494.

In fact, his heritage would never have been easy, thanks to his father Lorenzo's dominant personality and the rivalries within the ruling class. Lorenzo had himself faced a series of crises similar to Piero's on the death of his sickly father in 1469, when he, too, was only twenty. Initially supported by the leading families in Florence, he had quickly faced a rebellion in the subject-city Volterra, and six years after it was put down with force, he was threatened far more seriously by the so-called Pazzi conspiracy of 1478, when he was wounded and his brother Giuliano 'cut to pieces' during the celebration of mass in Florence's cathedral. Although Lorenzo emerged from the ensuing war with strengthened powers that ensured his future success, he and his family were left with a legacy of fear and distrust, reflected not only in the paintings he and Piero commissioned, but in the savage imagery of his son's later poems.⁴ If Lorenzo, with all his foresight and authority, had scarcely been able to control his factious rivals (one Florentine reflected on Lorenzo's death), what hope was there for the young Piero, who soon after his father's death faced the rebellion of his cousins, Lorenzo and Giovanni di Pierfrancesco, and then the French invasion that overthrew his regime?⁵

Piero also suffered a Buddenbrooks fate as the third-generation heir to banking wealth. His great-grandfather, the usurious merchant banker Cosimo, had been famous as one of the richest men in Italy, and already the cultured lifestyles of his gout-ridden son Piero and his grandson, the magnificent Lorenzo, were eating away at the family's wealth, which the

---

² Ianziti, *Humanistic Historiography*, p. 57, citing G. A. Campana: 'aliter ab his qui vicerunt, aliter qui victi sunt, proferuntur'; Fournel, 'L'ennemi dans l'histoire florentine', esp. p. 39.
³ Cerretani, *Storia fiorentina*, p. 186; Sanudo, *Diarii* 24, 90; Pieraccini, *Stirpe*, 1, pp. 169–70, and recently Simonetta, *Volpi e Leoni*, pp. 27–57, 277 ('il Pazzo Piero', 'detto il Fatuo').
⁴ p. 110 in this volume. On Lorenzo and the Medici regime, Najemy, *A History*, pp. 278–374; Fubini, *Politica e pensiero politico*, esp. pp. 187–203; Rubinstein, *Government*; Brown, 'Between Constitution and Government'.
⁵ Parenti, *Storia* 1, p. 25.

Introduction 3

younger Piero in his turn did little to preserve. He must have been in Francesco Guicciardini's mind when he commented in one of his maxims on the proverb that the third generation can never enjoy its ill-gotten gains.[6] Rejecting his father Piero Guicciardini's explanation – that since no one was totally bad, God allowed some of the money to be enjoyed before eventually punishing the family – Francesco said that it was, among other reasons, because the founder of the family's wealth knew how to preserve as well as earn money, whereas his heirs, raised in wealth, had never learnt how to earn it, and through overspending and carelessness they had unsurprisingly lost it. This is what happened to Piero and it, too, contributes to the story of his life.

Above all, Piero and his siblings suffered 'the double bind' of labouring under their father's domination while trying to fulfil their family's expectations.[7] For them, this meant behaving as republicans in Florence while being thrust into a courtly lifestyle abroad as a result of the ambitious marriages and careers engineered for them by Lorenzo. Lorenzo is the key to understanding Piero, for the father and son not only shared many characteristics but also conducted the same double-level politics that are difficult to detect without close reading of their private as well as their public letters. The ongoing edition of Lorenzo's letters is only now beginning to reveal the extent of his father's 'acrobatic' politics that we shall see Piero imitating in his attempt to become, like Lorenzo, the 'needle' balancing power in Italy. Lorenzo left a difficult act to follow, all the more so because the French king was blaming his putative invasion on Lorenzo even before Lorenzo's death. So the young Piero was left facing a crisis that even his father might have been unable to resolve, let alone the twenty-year-old Piero.[8]

The contrasting influences on Piero's life were reflected in his temperament, which combined an extrovert personality as a sportsman and champion jouster with an underlying vein of depression, unhappiness and fear, movingly expressed in letters and poems. His love of playing football in the streets during Lorenzo's absences from Florence encouraged his father's friends in 1489 to take his political education in hand, in order to ensure he succeeded his father as an equally effective 'master of the workshop'. As a result, we find Piero left in charge during Lorenzo's prolonged absence at the baths the following summer, when his frequent autograph letters to his father throw revealing light on the

---

[6] *Ricordi*, C 33, ed. Spongano, pp. 39–40. Francesco's father Piero quotes St. Augustine.
[7] Denis Feeney in *London Review of Books,* 15 June 2017, p. 42.
[8] Brown, 'Piero in Power', p. 118, citing Lorenzo Spinelli's probably unread letter to Lorenzo of 30 March 1492.

wide range of activities that he undertook on Lorenzo's behalf. Although much of the daily burden was borne by his secretaries, his diplomatic activities gave him standing with Italy's other rulers, and so did his sportsmanship and his cultural patronage as a talented musician and poet like his father. They were all facets of the soft power that was becoming a feature of Renaissance rulers, not only in Italy but in England, under the young king Henry VIII, and in France under Francis I.

So, too, was the patronal influence exerted by Piero over clients in Florence's dominion, where it was easier to play the prince than in the mercantile city itself, with its family rivalries and republican tradition. The bonds he established with these clients linked him to old Guelf networks that in turn helped to support him and his brothers in exile. The failure of Piero's four attempts to return to Florence after 1494 – most spectacularly in 1497, when five of his leading partisans and relatives were executed – fatally weakened his support base in Florence, but he nevertheless remained a serious threat to the city by attaching himself to Florence's external enemies, especially Cesare Borgia and the Vitelli, making his story part of the wider narrative of Italy's turmoil in these years.

Italy had frequently been subjected to barbarian invasions – from the Vandals, Huns and Ostrogoths in the fifth century AD to the Angevins in the thirteenth century – but nothing prepared Renaissance Italy for 'the flame and the scourge' of Charles VIII's polyglot army in 1494, which not only 'overthrew states' (according to Francesco Guicciardini) but also 'changed their forms of government and their methods of warfare'.[9] Charles VIII also changed the carefully calibrated balance of power in Italy. From the mid-fifteenth century, after the pope and emperor had ceased to compete for overall authority in Italy in divisive Guelf–Ghibelline conflicts, power was balanced between its five leading states according to a series of agreements and alliances that the Florentines liked to conceptualise in mathematical terms, as triangles of almost equidistant cities, each counterbalancing the power of the others. After 1494, one Florentine attributed the breakdown of this system to everyone playing with the abacus 'in his own way, without following the rule of counterbalancing Venice' (the only state unaffected by the French invasion until its defeat in 1509).[10]

---

[9] Guicciardini, *Storie*, p. 92: 'una fiamma ed una peste che non solo mutò gli stati, ma e' modi ancora del governargli ed e' modi delle guerre'; Santoro, *Fortuna, ragione e prudenza*, pp. 11–21.
[10] Anon. letter from Rome to the Signoria, April 1497, pp. 245–6, n. 55 in this volume.

Although Florence was smaller than the other powers, the city had been able to punch above its weight (the Florentine ambassador in Rome declared in 1500) because it had always been 'the nerve of Italy', and if not 'first or equal in terms of power', 'it's been considered the first for anticipating events and providing adequate remedies better and more quickly than anyone else'; for this reason, he said, the other princes of Italy had always vied for its friendship and alliance.[11] He must have been referring to the years between 1470 and 1492, when Lorenzo acted as the needle of the balance in the Triple Alliance with Milan and Naples, and later as the mediator between the pope and his recalcitrant vassal King Ferrante of Naples.[12] Although Piero was blamed for no longer acting as Italy's fulcrum, in fact – as his allies acknowledged – he attempted to continue his father's role in acting as mediator between the powers until the balance was destroyed by the French alliance with Milan, which led to the collapse of the two remaining allies, the Medici in Florence and King Alfonso in Naples.

This was the immediate crisis faced by Italian states, since it resulted in successive foreign invasions and wars that continued until 1559.[13] Underlying it was the more fundamental problem of how these newly consolidated territories could give themselves 'an aura of legitimacy' to justify their control of previously self-governing communes within their dominion. This has given rise to the still unresolved debate about whether to contrast signorial regimes as 'despotisms' or 'tyrannies' compared with self-governing 'republican' communes, or whether these traditional and value-laden terms are inadequate to describe the new territorial states emerging from both lordships and republics.[14] Piero encapsulates the problem of defining the status and power of these new states according to the old terminology, for once he had been condemned as a tyrant by his republican critics, it has been difficult to view his life dispassionately. But from the wider perspective of his

---

[11] Antonio Malegonnelle in Rome to the Signoria, 10 January 1500, Signori respons. 11, fols. 2v-3r, 'il nervo de Italia ... la prima di antivedere le cose e di fare e' rimedii sufficienti e presti più che tucte l'altre'.

[12] Gentile Becchi (24 November 1470, MAP 61, 30): 'examen della bilancia', Bernardo Rucellai, *De bello italico*, p. 4: 'examine aequo penderent', Santoro, *Fortuna*, p. 151; Guicciardini, *Storie*, p. 72, 'quasi una bilancia di tutta Italia', v. Fubini, 'The Italian League and the Balance of Power'.

[13] Aubert, *La crisi degli antichi stati italiani*, I, pp. 1, 61–91; *The Italian Wars*, ed. Mallett and Shaw, esp. pp. 1–5, *Italy and the European Powers*, ed. Shaw, esp. 3–21; Pepper, 'Castles and cannon in the Naples campaign'.

[14] Chittolini, 'Dominant Cities', p. 18 and Varanini, 'Medicean Florence and Beyond'; essays in *Communes and Despots*, ed. Law and Paton, esp. Philip Jones, pp. 3–24, and in *The Origins of the State in Italy, 1300–1600*, ed. Kirshner, esp. Schiera, 'Legitimacy, Discipline and Institutions', pp. 11–33.

influence outside Florence – as patronal boss in Florence's territory (the subject of Chapter 9) and as an ally and arbiter of the Italian powers (Chapter 11) – he was already enjoying the role of an early modern sovereign rather than that of a tyrant. The old terminology would soon be made irrelevant by the pragmatism of political thinkers like Machiavelli in the wake of the foreign invasions, after Piero's death. But even before then, the terms used by Florentines to describe his role – as an 'idol', 'a more than citizen' or city 'boss' – suggest he may have represented for them the pragmatic sovereignty that people wanted from their secular head of state, that is, not legitimacy *ex titulo* (as Bartolus defined it) but an elevated status (to command respect) combined with patronal power and protection.[15]

To reconstruct Piero's life from the traces he left behind nevertheless presents a challenge – to the reader as well as to his biographer – especially in view of the Medici henchmen's constant refrain, 'cover the tracks' (*nettare i segni*). For the devil lies in the detail, and it is only through the close reading of letters and other evidence that we can detect the double politics and manipulations of the Medici regime, which used many of the same techniques as late republican Rome to transform the constitution and its position in Italy. The contemporary histories of the Florentine citizens Piero Parenti and Bartolomeo Cerretani also contribute valuable evidence, for although they are critical of Piero, they are less biased than the writings of the better-known Francesco Guicciardini, who has long shaped our view of Piero's 'tyrannical and arrogant' nature. In acknowledging the difficulties he faced, his contemporaries show him trapped in the dilemma described by his old tutor, Gentile Becchi, who told Piero on the eve of his exile how difficult it was 'to play the role of prince in a republic unless you appear to be a wholehearted republican in the eyes of the people'.[16] Neither one nor the other, Piero could, perhaps, have provided Florence with a figurehead without a princely title had he not been faced with the crisis of the French invasion.

---

[15] Cf. Brown, 'Piero in Power', pp. 124–5, and Chapter 20 in this volume.
[16] Brown, ibid., p. 114, n. 2.

Part I

The Early Years

1   Piero's Childhood

Lorenzo de' Medici's marriage to Clarice Orsini in June 1469 had created a precedent, for it was the first time that the Florentine mercantile and banking family had married out of Tuscany and into a family of long-established Roman aristocrats. The Milanese ambassador predicted at the time that it would give 'the populace, as well as some of the leading citizens, plenty to talk about', and so, too, did the lengthy wedding ceremonies.[1] Only six months later, Lorenzo's father Piero died, plunging the twenty-year-old Lorenzo into a political crisis, as he 'hoisted his sails' to secure his primacy in Florence, and all too soon – before the end of his first decade in power – he was at war with the pope and the king of Naples following his brother's murder in 1478.[2]

It was during this decade, from 1469 to 1479, that all Lorenzo and Clarice's seven children were born: Lucrezia, the eldest child, in August 1470, followed quickly by the miscarriage of twin boys; then, on 15 February 1472, Piero was born, baptised Piero Giovanni et Romolo a day later.[3] In these circumstances, it was the cause for great celebration. One faithful supporter congratulated Lorenzo for securing the succession by extending the Medici line from Cosimo to Piero, from Piero to Lorenzo and now beyond – while the famous captain and ruler Federigo da Montefeltro envied Lorenzo and Clarice for having produced a son so quickly, since his own wife had given birth to eight girls before his son finally arrived.[4] Other intimates were delighted by the

---

[1] Brown, *Medici in Florence*, p. 87, n. 57; on the wedding, Kent, *Princely Citizen*, pp. 37–8, Parenti, *Lettere*, Appendix, pp. 247–50, and Trexler, *Public Life*, pp. 433–5.
[2] Brown, *Scala*, pp. 61–9 (n. 3: 'troppo alza le vele per bonaza'); Najemy, *A History*, pp. 344–52.
[3] Florence, Opera del Duomo, Registri battesimali, 3, p. 224: 'Piero Giovanni et Romolo di Lorenzo di Piero di Cosimo de' Medici ... nacque dì 15 a hore 10, ba<ptezza>to a dì 16'. On 'Romolo', Klapisch-Zuber, 'San Romolo'. On the miscarriage, Luigi Pulci to Lorenzo, 27 March 1471, *Morgante e Lettere*, ed. De Robertis, p. 969.
[4] Benedetto Colucci to Lorenzo, 10 March 1472, *Scritti inediti*, ed. Frugoni , p.74; Federigo to Lorenzo, 25 February 1472, ed. P. Viti, 'Lettere familiari', pp. 481–2. Cf. ser Francesco Dovizi to Lorenzo, 16 February 1472, Moncallero, *Il Cardinale*, pp. 23–4.

news for 'the public good' as well as for their own personal benefit, like the captain in Pisa Giovanni Aldobrandini, who told Lorenzo to wish Clarice 'all the best and say that I'm greatly indebted to her for her work', while from Venice Giovanni Lanfredini and his wife also wished her well and sent sweetmeats for her 'convalescence and swift recovery'.[5] So in narrating the story of Piero's early years, it is the children's apparent security and happiness that is striking. For although their father was often absent, they enjoyed the care of exceptionally strong and loving women who were all drawn from old Italian families and helped to provide the security that was lacking in their political environment.

Following the traditional practice of nearly all Tuscan families, Piero was nourished by a wet nurse who would have been carefully chosen for her temperament and quality, hence his parents' dismay when the six-month-old baby developed a little fever – infected, his grandmother Lucrezia Tornabuoni supposed, by the wet nurse. Since she was with Piero and his nurse in Florence while his parents were in their villa at Cafaggiolo, she found herself responsible for replacing the nurse two days later with another young woman 'of good quality and happy'.[6] Two months later his mother left Florence to visit her family in Rome, but she was kept well informed about 'la Lucrezia' and 'Piero mio' while absent from Florence – and we know from the letters of the humanist Luigi Pulci (who accompanied her) that they hoped to be back in Florence for the San Giovanni celebrations in late June, 'drawn like magnets' to 'the little Lucrezia and baby Piero'.[7] She was certainly back in Florence by July, when she received a warm letter from the wife of the manager of the Medici Bank in Rome asking her 'to kiss your children a hundred times on my behalf, who I hear are becoming good, one as beautiful as the other'.[8]

Employing a wet nurse not only gave the mother greater freedom but also enabled her to bear children at closer intervals, enhancing her status 'as a fertile and prolific' wife.[9] After Lucrezia and Piero, Clarice gave birth to another daughter, Maddalena, in 1473, followed by Giovanni in

---

[5] Aldobrandini in Pisa to Lorenzo, 18 February 1472, MAP 23, 321; Lanfredini in Venice to Clarice, 22 February, MAP 85, 38.

[6] Lucrezia Tornabuoni, *Lettere*, ed. Salvadori, pp. 72–3 (to Lorenzo and to Clarice, 28 and 30 August 1472), Lorenzo, *Lettere*, I, p. 392 (postscript) and n. 6 (to Michelozzi, 28 August 1472).

[7] Clarice in Cortona to Lorenzo, 24 April 1472 (MAP 42, 212, ed. De Robertis, 'Supplementi', p. 556, n. 1); Luigi Pulci in Rome to Lorenzo, 6 May, *Morgante e Lettere*, p. 979: 'come calamita'. Cf. p. 22 in this volume.

[8] Francesca Tornabuoni to Clarice (31 July 1472), MAP 28, 339.

[9] Klapisch-Zuber, *Women, Family and Ritual*, ch. 6, esp. pp. 135–40, 158–9; Gavitt, *Charity and Children*, pp. 226–43, esp. 237.

1475, then (yearly from 1477 to 1479) Luisa, Contessina and Giuliano. So when Poliziano wrote to Clarice from Pisa in 1475, 'according to our agreement', he hoped to find her well 'and with a child around your neck'.[10] By then she was fully involved in the upbringing and care of the children, especially in the long months after the Pazzi conspiracy when she was left to manage the household in the Mugello, what Lorenzo's sister Bianca called the 'brigata di Mugello'. When forced by the threat of plague to move from Cafaggiolo to the more remote town of Gagliano – 'where, as you know, there is nothing apart from the walls' – Clarice asked Lucrezia to send her lots of pairs of sheets from Florence, as well as tablecloths and twenty yards of linen cloth, so she could make shirts for the children.[11] Letters to Lorenzo in Florence tell us about their life in the country. When the newly born Giuliano was ill, Clarice told Lorenzo that 'apart from his illness, he's very well, that is, he's a fine little fellow … and I will look after him, as a mother should'.[12] And in a loving letter to her grandmother Lucrezia Tornabuoni, her namesake, Piero's seven-year-old sister Lucrezia told her that 'all of us children are here at Careggi with madonna Clarice, together with mona Bartolomea and all her band'.[13] When separated from the children by her prolonged treatment at the baths at Bagno a Morbo in 1480, Clarice asked her mother-in-law Lucrezia to tell Lorenzo that she would like to stay in the villa at Poggio a Caiano by preference, with her children, 'for it seems like a thousand years since I saw them. Tell me often how they are, and especially Giuliano, and you others', for hearing about them 'is my solace in my solitude here'.[14]

After Clarice, it was Lucrezia Tornabuoni who played the most important part in the children's upbringing, looking after the baby Piero during his early illness and reporting 'Pierino's recovery' from another upset in 1474; when parted from them three years later, she wrote that getting news of the children was her only solace, such was her 'great love' and longing for them that every day without them 'seems like a thousand

---

[10] Poliziano in Pisa to Clarice, 1 December 1475, MAP 137, 363: 'con un bambino in collo' (Giovanni was born ten days later). On the children, Lorenzo, 1480 Catasto (1016, fol. 475v), Pieraccini, *Stirpe*, I, pp. 197–232.
[11] Tornabuoni, *Lettere*, cit., pp. 160–1 and 156–7 (15 July and 2 June 1479): 'nonn è se non le mura'. On the Medici's 'chasa vecchia' and 'chasa grande' in Gagliano, Nanni, *Lorenzo Agricoltore*, pp. 34–5.
[12] Clarice in Cafaggiolo to Lorenzo, 25 April 1479, MAP 37, 263: 'è buon fanciullozo'.
[13] Tornabuoni, *Lettere*, pp. 144–5 (24 May 1477). On Bartolomea (Baccia) Minerbetti, who tended Clarice in Rome in 1487–88 and Maddalena as midwife in 1489, pp. 65 and 86 in this volume.
[14] Clarice in Bagno to Lucrezia Tornabuoni in Florence, 24 June 1480, GC 29, 38 bis, fol. 34: 'questo è'l mio refrigerio in questa mia solitudine'.

years'.¹⁵ The great-grandmothers – Contessina Bardi, Cosimo's widow, and Ginevra Cavalcanti, his brother Lorenzo's widow – contributed to the affectionate atmosphere in which the children were raised by having them for visits to the Mugello. It was during a visit to Contessina in September 1473, without their parents or grandmother Lucrezia, that we hear the voice of the eighteen-month-old Piero for the first time. Going frequently to the gate and calling out to everyone, he said, 'Grandma and daddy, mama'; 'it would make you laugh if you were here', the priest Cristofano wrote to Lucrezia. He also reported that Piero was healthy, lively and happy, while his sister was obedient, 'like the clever little child she is' – in contrast to their cousin Cosimo di Bernardo Rucellai, whom Contessina wasn't pleased with (as we shall see, Cosimo later opposed Piero in the events of 1494). Cosimo was the grandson of Lorenzo's sister Nannina, who was also staying there with another sister, Bianca Pazzi and her children, and Lorenzo's brother Giuliano. On this occasion, Piero's sister Maddalena (born in July) remained in Florence with her wet nurse, as Piero had done the previous summer.¹⁶

Piero's first surviving letter was sent to his grandmother Lucrezia in August 1476 from Trebbio, the Medici villa that now belonged to the younger branch of the family descended from Cosimo's brother Lorenzo and his wife Ginevra Cavalcanti. Their sole son and heir, Pierfrancesco, had died only a month earlier, leaving two sons, Lorenzo and Giovanni, then aged thirteen and nine. Piero was staying in Trebbio with the seventy-six-year-old Ginevra, who – he wrote – was spoiling them all. Although penned in a secretarial hand, his letter has the importunate tone of a four-year-old, anxious for treats from his grandmother in Careggi to compete with Ginevra's: 'Send us some of those figs that I liked, I mean those Borgiotto figs. And send us some of those peaches with the nut, and some of the other things that you know we like, sweetmeats and cakes and other little things you think of'.¹⁷ The same is true of his next surviving letter, also in a secretarial hand, which listed more desiderata sought from his father in Pisa, whom he assured, 'I'm well and I feel fine', and so, too, were Clarice, Lucretia (his grandmother), Giuliano (his uncle) and his siblings, 'Lucretia, Maddalena,

---

¹⁵ Tornabuoni, *Lettere*, pp. 79 and 85 (Kent, *Princely Citizen*, p. 85); cf. Clarice to Lorenzo 16 March, MAP 30, 155.

¹⁶ Cristofano d'Antonio di Maso in Florence to Lucrezia in Pisa, 25 September 1473, ed. Gori, *Una donna del Rinascimento*, pp. 126–7; Tornabuoni, *Lettere*, pp. 123–4: 'Nona et babo, mama' (tr. Ross, *Lives*, pp. 172–3). Cosimo (b. 1468) was betrothed in 1477 to a daughter of Gabriele Malaspina, lord of Fosdinovo (Tornabuoni, *Lettere*, pp. 146–7).

¹⁷ Piero in Trebbio to Lucretia in Careggi, 16 August 1476, MAP 85, 173. Ginevra was born in 1400, according to Lorenzo's 1469 Catasto, 924, fol. 325r.

Giovanni and Luisa' (the latest baby, born in January that year): 'we are all well, well – as I hope you are'. Only Lorenzo di Pierfrancesco was ill, 'perhaps with the chickenpox that I had'.[18]

This reference to Piero's cousin – and Piero's visit to Trebbio – shows that the children's early years were spent together. Their families had shared a common home in Via Larga until Cosimo's new adjacent palace was completed in the mid-1450s, but resentment between the two branches of the family had already begun to show itself following the death of Pierfrancesco's father in 1440, when, as his uncle Cosimo's ward, Pierfrancesco had been prevented from sharing in the Medici Bank's swelling profits. In the settlement of 1451, when Pierfrancesco was twenty-one, he was awarded the villa of Trebbio, but while he enjoyed his half-share of the Medici inheritance undivided, Cosimo's children, Piero and Giovanni, in turn were rankled at having to divide their share, 'giving him a gross advantage over us and all the best items' (Lorenzo il Magnifico later complained).[19] Pierfrancesco's marriage in 1456 to the daughter of Angelo Acciaiuoli, one of the Medici's opponents ten years later, caused further resentments that – as we shall see – had serious repercussions for Piero after his father's death.[20] Despite this, it seems that both branches of the family lived happily enough together during their childhood years.

The last snapshot of the family in Piero's letters is in 1479, when the children were isolated with Clarice and their tutor Angelo Poliziano in Cafaggiolo. Regretting that his pony had not yet returned from Florence, Piero went on to describe his siblings, who now included the newly born Giuliano: 'Giovanni is beginning to spell ... for Giuliano, laughing is enough; as for my sisters, Lucrezia sews, sings and reads; Maddalena knocks her head against the wall but without harming herself; Luisa is already talking quite a lot, and Contessina fills the whole house with her noise'. The letter itself, Piero told his father, was evidence of his own progress – though also showing Poliziano's influence – and it provides a lively and convincing account of the children at their various stages of development, first the boys and then the girls in order of age.[21]

---

[18] Piero in Florence to Lorenzo in Pisa, 3 March 1477, MAP 33, 144, asking for 'palle pisane, parechi nichi' and some 'alesine'; 'io sono sano e sto bene'. Lorenzo and Giovanni di Pierfrancesco were in fact Piero's second cousins once removed.
[19] Brown, *Medici in Florence*, pp. 73–102 at 77–8; Gori, *Contessina*, pp. 7–11.
[20] On the Pitti conspiracy, Gori, 'Crisi del regime mediceo'; Rubinstein, *Government*, pp. 183–92; Najemy, *A History*, pp. 298–306; Ganz, 'Paying the price'.
[21] Piero to Lorenzo in Florence, recd. 27 May 1479, MAP 22, 466, Miglio, *Governare l'alfabeto*, p. 88; tr. Ross, *Lives*, pp. 219–20.

Lorenzo himself was often absent, especially in these years, but he was much missed by the children. In 1478 the three-year-old Giovanni continually asked for news of Lorenzo 'and says, "When will Loencio come?"' Five years later, when Lorenzo was absent at the Diet of Cremona, it was the four-year-old Giuliano who was aggrieved not to find Lorenzo at the table on Friday, and 'got very angry that there was no one to give him fruit or anything else'.[22] He insisted on coming to the table and it was then a great business to get him down again. He kept everyone entertained – as ser Pace Bambello put it, 'he'd keep a city in festivity, always wanting arms and especially a helmet; he'd like Lorenzo back tomorrow and says he'll tell Lorenzo about every minor injury done to him'. Giovanni, by contrast, was 'all wisdom and speaks like an old man and seems desperate to please Lorenzo over the affairs of Poggio'. Piero is unmentioned – perhaps he was with his tutor Poliziano in Fiesole – but, in ser Pace's eyes, they were, in intelligence and manners, 'quite different from the children of your other citizens'.[23]

Two years later, Matteo Franco provides another vivid picture of the children rushing to welcome their mother home from Bagno a Morbo (while Lorenzo went on to Pisa), the little Giuliano still bewailing the absence of his father: '"O o o o, where is Lorenzo?"', he asked, 'with a long O', and when told that he had gone to Poggio to meet them, replied, 'almost in tears, "he's never here": you never saw anything more moving', Franco wrote. Whereas Piero had become a most beautiful young man and Giovanni had a fine face with not much colour, the little Giuliano at six was 'alive and fresh as a rose ... and as clean as a little mirror'.[24]

This was the environment in which Piero was born and brought up, surrounded by an apparently close and loving family. The family secretaries and intimates were, of course, prejudiced in their affectionate description of the children, but in one sense ser Pace was right in calling

---

[22] Clarice in Pistoia to Lorenzo, 30 August 1478, MAP 31, 231: '"Quando verrà Loencio?"', Kent, *Princely Citizen*, p. 57, 17 February 1483, MAP 38, 400: 'non vi trovando, sta tucto adirato che non v'è chi li dia fructe né altro'.
[23] Clarice to Michelozzi in Cremona, 28 February 1483, GC 29, 38 bis, fol. 33: 'è poi una festa a rimenarlo in giù'; ser Pace to the same, 25 February, ivi, 29, 84, fol. 22; Brown, *Florence* (2011), p. 53, n. 54 (and 39–61 on ser Pace's role as Michelozzi's secretary in the Wool Guild [cf. Najemy, *A History*] and frequent stand-in for him with the Medici family).
[24] Franco, *Lettere*, p. 83: 'Disse el gentile Giulianino con uno "O" lungho: "O o o o dove è Lorenzo? ... E' mai no<n> è"'; 'vivolino e freschellino com'una rosa ... e nettolino come uno spechio'.

them quite different from the children of other citizens. For although the Medici themselves were bankers and merchants like 'other citizens', they had married into noble families, especially the Orsini, who, as we shall see in the following chapter, regarded themselves as 'more than citizens', as it was feared Piero did, too, shortly before he died.[25]

[25] Marco Parenti, 'animo sopra cittadino', p. 21, n. 21 in this volume; on Piero as 'plus quam civis', p. 281 in this volume.

2 Family Backgrounds

The social disparity between the Medici and the families they married into was not evident in the children's early years. The Medici lacked noble status and came originally from the Mugello – the area north of Florence in the foothills of the Apennines, where they always retained possessions. Although some of the family were to be found in Florence in the thirteenth and fourteenth centuries, they were there as moneylenders, participating in the city's government as members of the Cambio, or Moneychangers' Guild. Only a few members of the clan became wealthy – messer Averardo (called Bicci) in the first half of the fourteenth century and Veri di Cambio in the latter half of the century – and despite making good marriages, many of the family retreated to the Mugello after the economic downturn in the mid-fourteenth century. Those who remained became overbearing and litigious, including messer Salvestro de' Medici, Veri's cousin, who happened to be Gonfalonier of Justice at the beginning of the Ciompi uprising in 1378. Cosimo and his cousin Averardo descended from two sons of Bicci, Giovanni and his elder brother Francesco. Because Francesco died in 1402 when Giovanni was first elected a prior, Giovanni and his descendants were able to overtake Averardo politically, even though as cousins Averardo and Cosimo remained close allies. Giovanni worked for Veri di Cambio in Rome until 1397, when he returned to Florence to establish his own banking company.[1]

Cosimo's prudence and discretion had enabled him to avoid the factionalism and arrogance that had weakened the family in the later fourteenth century, but his family lacked the lustre enjoyed by the ancient nobility and the long-established merchant ruling elite. This is what they gained by marrying into Florence's oldest and most distinguished families, like the Bardi, the Tornaquinci – from whom the Tornabuoni were descended – and the Cavalcanti, all of whom provided spouses for

---

[1] Brucker, 'Medici in the Fourteenth Century'; Arrighi and Klein, 'Strategie familiari', pp. 243–6; D. Kent, 'I Medici in esilio' (on Averardo).

the children and descendants of the modest banker Giovanni di Bicci. These families, or clans, had been disfranchised after the 1280–90s as a result of their magnate status, before reenfranchising themselves a century and more later by opting for popular status and sometimes by changing their name as well, as the Tornabuoni did in 1393.[2] As a result, they all not only became richer and more powerful through losing the stigma of magnate status, but by their skilful use of heraldry and the choice of new family names redolent of their chivalric past they managed at the same time to retain the aura and influence of their ancient nobility.[3]

Cosimo's wife, Contessina de' Bardi, was descended from the Bardi di Vernio and, on her mother's side, from the Sienese noble family of Pannochieschi, both powerful feudal houses that enabled the Medici to fraternise with other such families in Siena and also in Pistoia, whose territory abutted the county of Vernio.[4] In addition, Contessina was related to the banking Bardi, who had been partners in the Medici Bank from the time of Cosimo's father Giovanni and his cousin Averardo.[5] But it was the Vernio branch that proved most useful to the Medici, thanks to the position and status of Vernio as an imperial fief. By acquiring it in 1332, a decade before their bank crashed in 1343, the Bardi were able to transform themselves from rich international bankers into owners of a feudal state placed strategically along the route from Prato to Bologna in the Apennines, north of Florence. Owing allegiance to the emperor, not to Florence, they were independent enough to boast in 1349 that despite the system of justice that prevailed in Florence, 'here in the countryside we are the ones who exercise justice according to our own understanding of it'.[6] By the fifteenth century, Gualterotto Bardi's prowess as a military captain made him and his strategically placed fief invaluable to the Medici, as well as to their regime. Not only did he send armed men to Florence to support Cosimo's son Piero and his grandson Lorenzo

---

[2] Klapisch-Zuber, *Retour à la Cité*, pp. 88, 92–4, and the tables on pp. 216, 362–5, 454, 456–7, on the Tornaquinci/Tornabuoni, pp. 257–60; Pampaloni, 'I Tornaquinci'. On their banking links to the Medici, de Roover, *Banco Medici*, pp. 313–21, Bullard, *Lorenzo*, pp. 119–20, 155–7.
[3] As Klapisch-Zuber so well describes, *Retour*, pp. 82–3: 'la stratégie de communication visuelle qui tendait á suggérer la puissance inébranlable d'une vieille famille de la cité'.
[4] Gori, *Una donna del Rinascimento*, pp. 4–6, 26–8, citing the Sienese Pannocchieschi, Malavolti and Salimbeni, and from Pistoia the Panciatichi (28); Tomas, *Medici Women*, *ad indicem*.
[5] Gori, *Una donna*, p. 5; de Roover, *Banco Medici*, pp. 54–62 *et passim*; on the Bardi bank and its crash, ibid., pp. 113–15.
[6] Klapisch-Zuber, *Retour*, p. 122 ('seigneurs-brigands du haut de leur montagne'), 139, n. 81: 'faremo al nostro senno'; on Vernio, also Gori, 'Per un contributo', pp. 301–2.

(il Magnifico) during the political crises of 1465–66 and 1478 at their request, but he also responded to the government's request for troops in 1458 and 1467, helping to guard the public square during the crucial pro-Medici *parlamento* of 1458 and to fight against its exiles in 1467.[7]

In 1466, as we know from Gualterotto's recently discovered letters, Piero di Cosimo played a much more active role in events than was suggested at the time, not merely reacting against a possible attack by his enemies but seizing the initiative by galvanising military help from outside. In contravention of the Signoria's orders to both sides to disarm, Gualterotto responded to Piero's two appeals for help on 27 and 31 August, first sending soldiers to protect the Medici palace in Via Larga and to Cafaggiolo to protect the northern approaches to the city, and then arriving himself the next day with four hundred men to help to guard the piazza for the plebiscite that marked Piero's victory. With them was the seventeen-year-old Lorenzo, wearing shining armour for this civic event, although dismounted from his metal-plated charger. This suggested to one diarist that the Bardi 'had been chosen by order of the said Piero rather than by the wishes of the Signoria'.[8]

The same is probably true of the other occasions when Gualterotto Bardi was asked to serve Florence as a soldier – in 1472, in the war against Volterra, and again in 1478–79, in the war that followed the Pazzi conspiracy, when he was immediately asked by the government to help. In July 1478 Gualterotto asked Lorenzo if he should replace the men fighting in Volterra with his own trusted soldiers, and the following year, after the fall of the fortress of Poggio Imperiale, when the government was unable to pay for the troops he had raised in Firenzuola, he offered to pay them himself, 'because being mine, they are also yours'.[9] After Gualterotto's death in 1483, his son Tommaso continued to support Lorenzo and then his children, especially in their attempts to return to Florence after being exiled in 1494 – for which he shared their fate in being declared a rebel and exiled from Vernio until his cousins' return to power in 1512.[10] As well as supplying the Medici with a personal fighting force, the Bardi also enmeshed them in a web of patronal relationships and gift exchanges that extended their influence well beyond the walls of Florence. So, although the young Piero was only eighteen months old

---

[7] Gori, ibid., esp. pp. 284–6, 366–9, Gori, *Una donna del Rinascimento*, pp. 27–9.
[8] Gori, 'La crisi del regime mediceo', esp. 812–22 (citing Alamanno Rinuccini on 820), 823 (Append. I–II), and n. 7 in this chapter.
[9] Gori, 'Per un contributo', pp. 279–85, 362, 364–5 ('che sendo miei sono tutti vostri', 18 November 1479) and 367 (citing his letter to Lorenzo of 24 July 1478).
[10] Ibid., pp. 295–6.

when his great-grandmother Contessina died in October 1473, her family exercised greater influence on his life than we have until now appreciated.[11]

Ginevra Cavalcanti, the grandmother of Piero's second cousins, was of equally distinguished magnate ancestry. On her marriage to Cosimo's brother Lorenzo in 1416, she had been praised by the humanist Francesco Barbaro as 'a young, virtuous, beautiful, honourable woman, with a noble lineage and very great wealth'.[12] When the four-year-old Piero and his siblings visited her in Trebbio after her son Pierfrancesco's death, she was still fully involved in family and estate affairs despite her age, as we can see from two surviving letters written in October that year: one sent to her from the factor at Trebbio, listing payments and receipts from the estate; the other sent by Ginevra herself to Lorenzo il Magnifico, about a farm given by his mother Lucrezia to Francesca di Giovenco, who wished to sell it – unless Lorenzo wanted it, Ginevra would like to use its revenue for charitable purposes. Despite the fact that Lucrezia was still alive, Ginevra's letter makes her own views clearly felt while at the same time acknowledging that, after her own son Pierfrancesco's recent death, Lorenzo was now the oldest member of the family and its undisputed head, for whom 'we will do whatever you want to be done'.[13]

Ginevra lived until at least 1480, two years before Lucrezia Tornabuoni herself died, when Piero was ten years old. Inevitably Lucrezia exercised a greater influence on him than the great-grandparents – and, as we have seen, she was the person to whom he addressed his first surviving letter at the age of four. As spouses of the heads of the family, she and Contessina also acted as 'incorporated wives' in enjoying a specific social role by entertaining visiting dignitaries to the palace and acting as intermediaries for favours and patronage.[14] But unlike Contessina, who could read but not write, and who never accompanied her husband Cosimo on diplomatic missions outside Florence, Lucrezia was better educated and played a fuller part in her husband's life, even being accused of overplaying her role when accompanying him to Rome in

---

[11] Ibid., pp. 263–5.
[12] Francesco Barbaro, *Uxoria*, cited by Tomas, *Medici Women*, p. 14; on Ginevra and her family, Zervas and Preyer, 'Donatello's "Nunziata del Sasso"', esp. p. 154; on her birth, evidently in 1400, p. 12, n. 17 in this volume.
[13] Dino in Prato to Ginevra in Trebbio, 7 October 1476, MAP 10, 601; Ginevra in Trebbio to Lorenzo in Poggio a Caiano, 'tanquam filii dilectissime', 20 October 1476, MAP 33, 868: 'tutto faremo secondo che parrà a tte'. On 5 September 1480, Clarice wrote to Michelozzi about a visit with Ginevra (to messer Carlo [de' Medici?]), GC 29, 38 bis, fol. 12.
[14] The term is Natalie Tomas's, *Medici Women*, pp. 29–32; cf. Bryce, 'Performing for Strangers', esp. pp. 1079–83.

1467. She could write, read widely from the many books in her study, composed poems and formed part of a literary circle that included the humanists Luigi Pulci and Angelo Poliziano. In addition, she also enjoyed a certain amount of independence as a businesswoman, buying property in Pisa and elsewhere and establishing the baths at Bagno a Morbo as a commercial enterprise.[15]

Lucrezia's mother was a Guicciardini, one of the old merchant elite, and her father, Francesco di Simone Tornabuoni, was a rich banker whose son Giovanni made his fortune by entering the Medici Bank aged fifteen (in the same year in which his sister Lucrezia married Piero di Cosimo de' Medici), then rising to become head of the Rome branch of the bank in 1465. But it would be a mistake to define her origins as mercantile rather than feudal, since the Tornabuoni in fact descended from a magnate family – the Tornaquinci – that was as ancient as the Bardi and the Cavalcanti.[16] Changing their name in 1393, the Tornabuoni under Simone became the richest members of the lineage from which Lucrezia and her brother Giovanni were descended, the owners of a large palace in the street that still bears their name and the patrons of the famous Ghirlandaio fresco cycle in S. Maria Novella in Florence that celebrated the whole Tornaquinci clan.[17] So despite not being feudal warriors, the Tornabuoni bestowed on the Medici the lustre of an ancient clan that had played a distinguished public role in the city since the beginning of the fourteenth century. They paid a heavier price than the Bardi for their loyalty to the Medici, not simply by exile but with a life – for in 1497 Lorenzo Tornabuoni, Giovanni's rich and cultured heir, was put to death together with four other Florentines for being involved in Piero's failed attempt to return to the city.[18]

Despite their former magnate status, the Bardi and the Tornabuoni were dwarfed in importance by the Orsini family, which was one of the oldest and most powerful Roman clans, rich in land and military expertise. Clarice herself united two branches of the family, the Monte Rotondo and the Bracciano branches, which together owned large estates in and around Rome as well as in southern Tuscany and the kingdom of Naples. They provided Florence with two of the most outstanding *condottieri* of the day, Virginio from the Bracciano branch and Niccolò,

---

[15] Kent, *Princely Citizen*, pp. 67–103, esp. 74–5, Salvadori, ed. Lucrezia Tornabuoni, *Lettere*, pp. 3–45. On her bad handwriting, however, Miglio, *Governare*, pp. 94–6.

[16] On the Tornabuoni, n. 2 in this chapter.

[17] Simons, 'Patronage in the Tornaquinci Chapel', esp. 221–2; Simons, 'Giovanna and Ginevra', pp. 106–8; on the palace, Preyer, 'Palazzo Tornabuoni'.

[18] On Lorenzo, Simons, 'Giovanna and Ginevra', pp. 106–7; Preyer, 'Palazzo Tornabuoni', pp. 54, 60–1.

count of Pitigliano in Tuscany – as well as with an archbishop, Clarice's brother Rinaldo Orsini – names that will frequently recur in Piero de' Medici's life.[19] Rinaldo, together with Giovanni Tornabuoni, was put in charge of the young Piero on his first visit to Rome in 1484, when Lorenzo instructed his son to repay their family's debt to the Orsini by offering his lifelong service to the head of the family, Cardinal Giovan Battista.[20] The Orsini, as the Florentine citizen and chronicler Piero Parenti said, were 'lords who rated themselves as more than citizens (*sopra cittadino*)'.[21] Although the rivalry between Virginio and Niccolò Orsini in the 1480s caused Lorenzo considerable problems, the Orsini in turn suffered from supporting the Medici after 1494 by losing their employment as Florence's military captains, although they were kept busy by helping Piero's abortive attempts to return to Florence.[22] When Piero's brothers did return after 1512, their Orsini upbringing must have helped to prepare them for their new status as ecclesiastical and secular princes.

From a Florentine perspective, Clarice was not in a class with her Tuscan counterparts as far as looks and sexuality went. Lucrezia Tornabuoni had described her future daughter-in-law as a somewhat timorous girl, 'extremely modest', who should 'quickly be made to adapt to our ways', 'her head not erect like ours but a bit poking forward, as if she was ashamed of herself ... far from ordinary but not to be compared to Maria, Lucrezia and Bianca' (her own daughters).[23] Clarice also apparently lacked the physical appeal that Florentine girls like Lucretia Donati held for Lorenzo, nor did she offer him the intellectual companionship of his mother, whom Lorenzo described on her death as 'the irreplaceable refuge from my many troubles'.[24] Unsurprisingly, perhaps, Clarice was diffident about writing to a spouse she had not yet met after their proxy wedding in Rome in December 1468. When she was eventually persuaded to write by Francesco Tornabuoni, cousin of Giovanni, the manager of the Medici Bank in Rome, her gesture of wifely

---

[19] Tomas, *Medici Women*, pp. 18–19; Kent, *Princely Citizen*, p. 55; Shaw, 'Lorenzo ... and Virginio' and 'Lorenzo ... and Niccolò', esp. pp. 261–2, 265, and in general, Shaw, *The Political Role of the Orsini Family*.
[20] Lorenzo to Piero, 26 November 1484, *Lettere* 8, p. 75, and p. 40 in this volume.
[21] Parenti, *Ricordi storici*, p. 141: 'signori che già haveva l'animo sopra cittadino ... assai et antichi signori in Italia et nobili capitani'.
[22] See especially Carlo Orsini's letter to Piero on 25 December 1498, p. 275 below.
[23] Lucrezia in Rome to Piero, 28 March 1467, *Lettere*, pp. 62–3; cf. Tomas, *Medici Women*, p. 18; Kent, *Princely Citizen*, pp. 76–7.
[24] Kent, ibid., pp. 67, 86–7 and on Lorenzo's 'love of women', pp. 41–66, esp. 50–3; Del Lungo, *Gli amori*, pp. 15–108 (31–91 on Clarice).

devotion was made in her own well-formed, semi-humanist cursive hand, to which Lorenzo – also at Francesco's urging – responded in kind.[25] We know from Francesco that Clarice (unlike Alfonsina Orsini, Piero's future wife) was preparing herself for her new life in Florence by learning to dance: 'she learns a new one every day, and she knows it just as soon as she is shown it'. She was also touchingly concerned about Lorenzo's fate in the joust that prevented him from seeing his bride in Rome, regarding his victory as an answer to her prayers.[26] So despite her aristocratic upbringing in 'strictly clerical surroundings', she was less austere than she has been portrayed, though clearly – as the people of Colle Val d'Elsa were to discover – quite acerbic, too. As Luigi Pulci inimitably put it when riding with her to Rome in 1472, she was 'not tired, not boring, not annoying like our ladies but happy, adroit and as a delicate as a thousand cheese-graters'.[27]

Once in Florence and united with her husband in June 1469, Clarice seems to have established a certain independence from her Roman family. She did not hurry to write to them about her new life or respond immediately to their letters bombarding her with advice and requests for patronage and assistance.[28] She soon proved as adept as Lorenzo in playing the patronage game, and also became 'another Lorenzo' in representing him on visits to Florence's subject cities. Three years after her marriage, aged only twenty-two, she was entertained and honoured by them en route to visit her family in Rome, dining with the government of Castiglione and even staying with the captain of Cortona. In 1485 she similarly found herself having to stand in for Lorenzo when he went off to Pisa instead of returning home with her from Bagno a Morbo.[29]

---

[25] Francesco Tornabuoni to Lorenzo, 4 January 1469, tr. Ross, *Lives*, pp. 122–3; Clarice to Lorenzo, same day, MAP 34, 450, cf. 28 January, MAP 20, 450 (both autogr.) and n. 26 in this chapter. On the protocol of marital letters, James, 'Marriage by Correspondence', pp. 325–8, esp. 326; cf. Miglio, *Governare l'alfabeto*, pp. 90–3 at 90 and 146–9).

[26] Francesco to Lorenzo, 4 January 1469, tr. Ross, *Lives*, p. 122. On dancing in Florence, Bryce, 'Performing for Strangers'. On the joust, Clarice to Lorenzo, 25 February, MAP 20, 457 (autogr.), ed. Miglio, *Governare*, p. 268, tr. Ross, *Lives*, pp. 125–6.

[27] Pulci in San Polo to Lorenzo, 29 April 1472, ed. De Robertis, 'Supplementi', p. 560: 'lieta, dextra, galante quanto mille grattuge'.

[28] Caterina Sanseverino, her mother, and her sister Gracellina to Clarice, 21 May and 26 July 69, MAP 24, 7 and 21, 137, Miglio, *Governare*, p. 91; her brother Rinaldo Orsini to Clarice, 28 June, MAP 21, 127 and Pierangelo Orsini, 12 July, MAP 21, 133, etc. On her patronage, Tomas, *Medici Women*, pp. 44, 59–62 and n. 33 in this chapter, Kent, *Princely Citizen*, pp. 55–8.

[29] Tomas, *Medici Women*, pp. 31–2; Matteo Franco to ser Piero Dovizi, 12 May 1485, *Lettere*, pp. 79–85; tr. Ross, *Lives*, pp. 267–73; Del Lungo, *Florentia*, pp. 422–5 and Pieraccini, *Stirpe*, I, p. 164. On Franco as among the 'prime e care creature di casa mia', Kent, *Princely Citizen*, pp. 196, 219, 258, 313; cf. Poliziano to Piero (*Opera*, I, pp. 144–5): 'noster Matteus Francus, homo (ut scis) mihi amicissimus'.

The Medici intimate Matteo Franco provides a vivid picture of her party gaily setting out before being challenged outside Montecastelli: 'Who goes there?' On replying 'Palle, Palle!!' (the Medici's emblem of pawnbrokers' balls), the cry went up in reply, 'Palle! Palle! Orso! Orso!' – the first of many such battle cries we will encounter that showed the Medici being treated on a par with other feudal families outside Florence, linking the Medici's 'balls' with the Orsini 'bears'. Without stopping at Casale to see Lorenzo's sister Nannina (to the regret of both sisters-in-law), they finally reached the dangerously crumbling town of Colle (its old walls ruined after the recent bombardment during the Pazzi war), where they spent the night. Before supper, Clarice was presented with various gifts that were intended for Lorenzo, she was told, but 'since he hadn't come, they were presented to her, as if she were another Lorenzo'. Her reply was diplomatic if astringent: 'On one hand you grieve and ask me to tell Lorenzo about your poverty and your needs, and then you spend money on these things. I accept them all and give them back to you, since you're needier than me'.[30] After supper, Clarice and Lorenzo's secretary spent half an hour with an ambassador from Siena, and the following day they moved on to Passignano, the Vallombrosan abbey recently seized for messer Giovanni on the death of its incumbent.[31] The following morning they received a message from little Piero asking what route they were taking, eventually meeting him and his male siblings (messer Giovanni, Giuliano and their cousin Giulio) near the Certosa outside Florence. As soon as they espied their mother (Matteo Franco reported), they threw themselves down from their horses and rushed to embrace her, with great happiness and kisses.[32]

So Clarice was evidently a loved and loving mother and also a devoted spouse, operating as shrewdly as her husband in the field of patronage and politics.[33] Like her response to the Colligiani, a letter she wrote to Lorenzo in 1478 combines humanity with trenchancy, in urging that Lorenzo should forgive his servant 'either for his proven fidelity, or for compassion for his mother, or for his disposition, or for my intercession'.[34] She also enjoyed warm relationships with

---

[30] Franco, *Lettere*, p. 81: 'come a uno altro lui'. Clarice kept four *fiaschi* of wine and a cake, and returned the rest.
[31] Brown, *Scala*, pp. 111–12.
[32] Franco, *Lettere*, p. 83: 'con tanta allegreza e baci e gloria'.
[33] Kent, *Princely Citizen*, p. 55, referring to Tomas, *Medici Women* (see pp. 86–7 on Clarice's religious patronage); James, 'Florence and Ferrara', p. 375; on Clarice, also Cortese, 'Noterelle Medicee', esp. p. 535; Picotti, *Ricerche*, p. 40.
[34] Clarice in Cafaggiolo to Lorenzo, 13 December 1478, MAP 36, 1359, *manu* Poliziano (in Miglio, *Governare*, p. 161 (IXa), cf. 148). Other letters of recommendation include MAP 37: 237 and 261 (18 and 24 April 1479).

Lorenzo's secretaries, each of whom had his own arrangement, or 'pact' (as Poliziano called it), to communicate with her during Lorenzo's absences – every eight days in the case of Gentile Becchi, when he wrote to her in 1469 after what he called 'the first octave'.[35] Writing from Rome to Lorenzo's newly appointed secretary, Niccolò Michelozzi, in 1472, Clarice tells him how pleased she is to have had his newsy letter from Florence, and after urging him to 'persevere' in reporting 'how things are going day by day', she ends by asking him to 'give kisses to my children from me'.[36] When Niccolò was away with Lorenzo in Cremona in 1483, negotiating a treaty to end the war of Ferrara, his place was taken by ser Pace Bambello, who wrote letters for her and joked with her about Niccolò's 'beloved' (whoever she was).[37] Although Clarice claimed not to understand politics, these letters suggest that she was kept fully abreast of what was going on in her husband's absence. In 1483 she told Lorenzo's secretaries, ser Niccolò and ser Piero Dovizi, through ser Pace, that the leading citizens thought Lorenzo would be more helpful to the league if he were in Florence rather than in Cremona, and although 'I don't understand these things, nevertheless, according to my poor judgement, I agree with them'.[38] A year later even the overweening Piero Dovizi entrusted her with a full account of the forthcoming Treaty of Bagnolo, which she was to confide in no one.[39]

The letters to these secretaries, especially to Niccolò Michelozzi, show Clarice's constant concern for Lorenzo's health and safety, although they could be astringent, too, when she was promised a visit that never materialized.[40] Shortly before she died in July 1488, a surviving letter to her 'dearest consort' from Rome shows her shrewdly discussing with him financial and diplomatic matters relating to her family. She had stayed on in Rome after Piero's betrothal to Alfonsina was celebrated in Bracciano, and as well as having a private audience with the pope

---

[35] Poliziano in Pisa to Clarice, 1 December 1475, MAP 137, 363: 'per observare con voi e' patti'; Becchi in Serezzana to Clarice, 18 July 1469, MAP 21, 135: 'satisfare alla prima octava'.

[36] Clarice in Rome to Niccolò Michelozzi in Florence, 'cancellario Magnifici Laurentii de Medicis', 15 May 1472, GC 29, 38 bis, fol. 1: 'e baciate e' miei fanciulli per mia parte'. Cf. the same, 20 September 1478, ibid., fol. 2.

[37] On her relationship with ser Pace, Brown, *Florence* (2011), p. 52.

[38] Clarice in Florence to Michelozzi and 'Piero da Bibbiena [Dovizi], cancellieri di Lorenzo ... in Cremona', 21 February 1483, GC 29, 38, fol. 31: 'io non m'intendo di queste cose ma secondo il mio povero giudicio a me pare quello medesimo'.

[39] Dovizi in Florence to Clarice in Cafaggiolo, 29 July 1484, MAP 39, 26. He also reported 'a queste sere una cometa grande uno braccio et mezo'.

[40] E.g. Clarice to Michelozzi in GC 29, 38 bis, fols. 2 (20 September 1478), 5 (7 September 1479), 36 and 21 (5 April and 17 September 1485); and on Lorenzo's promised visit, ibid., fol. 19 (16 August 1482).

(together with her daughter Maddalena, by then the pope's daughter-in-law), she was involved in discussions about securing the payment of Alfonsina's dowry and about her brother Rinaldo's wish to be a cardinal. Both were problematic, and although she proposed that the matter of the dowry should be put into Lorenzo's hands, she had been asked for her own opinion in Bracciano and showed herself to be well in command of the situation when discussing it with Virginio Orsini (Alfonsina's uncle), and her mother, Caterina of Sanseverino, 'the countess'.[41] Despite her illness – 'this blessed tribulation of the stomach that leaves me, as usual, neither well nor its opposite' – she remained in Rome until after Piero's wedding, dying in Florence on 30 July, not long after the death of her third daughter, Luisa.[42]

So Clarice devoted her last months to the affairs and marriages of Piero and Maddalena with the same mixture of maternal care and aristocratic authority that she had exercised since their birth. It was this that seems to have caused her well-known falling-out with Poliziano, Piero's tutor, who – after his mother and grandmother – was probably the most important influence on Piero's early years, as we shall see.

---

[41] Clarice in Rome to Lorenzo, 'consorti carissimo', 9 April 1488, MAP 40, 253. On Alfonsina's dowry, Lorenzo, *Lettere* 12, pp. 192–3, n. 22, and 206, n. 16; Reiss, 'Widow, Mother, Patron of Art', pp. 125–6; on Rinaldo, *Lettere* 12, pp. 22–3, and on the audience with the pope, ibid., p. 275, n. 12. On Maddalena's marriage contract, p. 65 in this volume.

[42] MAP 40, 253: 'Io mi sto ad l'usato, sempre infra due quando bene et quando el contrario', 'questa benedecta tibulatione dello stomaco che poco mi lassa riposare'; Lorenzo, *Lettere* 12, pp. 206, n. 17, 317, n. 19, 474, 488.

3   Education under Poliziano's Tutelage

Piero was only three years old when he was entrusted to the care of Angelo Poliziano in 1475 – two years after Poliziano entered the Medici household – and he remained close to him until Poliziano's death in 1494.[1] The tutor, who became one of Italy's most outstanding humanists, was a precocious but impecunious youth from the provinces when he first met Lorenzo de' Medici. He had been sent to Florence to be educated at the university not long after his father's murder in Montepulciano, when Angelo was ten. Three years after openly asking for Lorenzo's help in continuing his studies and completing his Latin translation of the second book of Homer's *Iliad* in 1470 (which he dedicated to Lorenzo), he was invited to join the Medici household.[2] Perhaps Lorenzo already saw Poliziano as a promising, avant-garde teacher for his very young son, as well as a stimulating companion for himself on his trips outside Florence, especially to the Pisan countryside, where he hunted and hawked while working to establish a new university in Pisa. But in promising Lorenzo great success as Piero's tutor in return for patronage, Poliziano was signing a Faustian pact that may have exaggerated Piero's achievements and compromised himself.[3]

It was an established practice in Florence for rich families to employ private tutors for their children who also doubled as secretaries for their patrons. Although Lorenzo had seconded Niccolò Michelozzi from the state chancery to be his private secretary in 1471, he still needed the help of other letter writers, especially when he was away from Florence, and so we find Poliziano writing not only to Clarice and Lucrezia Tornabuoni

---

[1] Poliziano in Mantua to Lorenzo, 'Apologia', 20 March [13 kal. apr.] 1480, ed. Picotti but dated 19 March), *Ricerche*, doc. 5, pp. 73–82, at 76: 'Trimulum accepi tuum Petrum … septuennem reddidi'. Cf. Lorenzo, *Lettere* 1, p. 516, n. 3.
[2] Ed. Del Lungo, *Florentia*, p. 119, tr. Ross, pp. 156–7; on his education, see his letter of 20 March 1480, n. 1, p. 74.
[3] Poliziano to Lorenzo, 'patrono meo', 3 July 1477, ed. Picotti, *Ricerche*, doc. I, p. 70: 'iam me totum ad Petrulum, ad studia, ad te ornandum extollendumque convertam'.

about the children's health and studies, but also to Lorenzo.⁴ In March 1476, for instance, he described how 'Piero is chatting away to me, as usual. Today I took him with me to see the execution of the man from Lastro', and a year later he wrote about the baby Giovanni and 'our little Piero' (*Petrulus noster*), to whose education he was devoting himself.⁵ In return for being given a benefice in Florence – the priory of San Paolo, income 100 florins a year for practically no work, he said – he again promised to repay his debt with 'the fruits reaped from Piero, who would stand as a witness before everyone of my gratitude'.⁶ His promise not to bother Lorenzo again was short-lived, since the following year he found himself appealing to Lorenzo to save his cousin Tommaso in return for his own devotion to Lorenzo and 'the hope you have in your – and my – Piero'.⁷

To be the bond for these favours to Poliziano must have been an oppressive burden for the young Piero and, unsurprisingly perhaps, he became less than the model student Poliziano had promised his father. Marooned in the countryside with Clarice and the children after the Pazzi conspiracy, while Lorenzo stayed with his mother and Niccolò Michelozzi in Florence, Poliziano was also deprived of Lorenzo's companionship. 'I wanted and believed I was going to be with you', Poliziano wrote miserably to him in late August 1478, 'but since you, or rather my unhappy fortune, has assigned me this position, I will tolerate it'; two days later he repeated that, despite his devotion to Piero, he had hoped to be useful to Lorenzo 'in something greater'. Piero, meanwhile, had given up studying hard and was enjoying himself in the countryside, while Clarice, unhappy herself, was beginning to criticise Poliziano. Quoting Virgil's *Aeneid* ('because of you the Libyan lords detest me'), Poliziano asked Lorenzo to ensure he retained his authority as Piero's tutor, such as it was, so he could do his duty by the boy and carry out his office in a fit and proper way.⁸

---

⁴ Lorenzo, *Lettere* 1, pp. 389–90, n. 1; Kent, *Princely Citizen*, p. 141; Tomas, *Medici Women*, pp. 61–2. Poliziano to Clarice and to Lucrezia, 1 December 1475, 8, 19 April 1476, 31 May 1477, ed. Del Lungo, *Prose*, pp. 45–50; tr. Ross, *Lives*, pp. 177–8, 181–2.
⁵ Poliziano to Michelozzi, 30 March 1476, and to Lorenzo, 24 February 1477, ed. Campana, 'Per il carteggio', pp. 462–8, at 464 and 468.
⁶ Poliziano to Lorenzo, 3 July 1477, the same 19 October, ed. Del Lungo, *Prose*, p. 55. On the priory (which had been offered to the nephew of Giovanni Tornabuoni), Picotti, *Ricerche*, pp. 33–5, 83–4.
⁷ Poliziano to Lorenzo, received on 11 July 1478, ed. Del Lungo, *Prose*, pp. 56–7; the letter ends by requesting Lorenzo to destroy it. On Lorenzo's help in saving his cousin's life, Poliziano, 'Apologia', ed. Picotti, *Ricerche*, p. 75.
⁸ Poliziano to Lorenzo, 24 and 26 August 1478, ed. Del Lungo, *Prose*, at pp. 58 (quoting Virg. *Aen* IV, 320, and Horace *Odes*, I. 24: '*durum: sed levius fit patientia*') and 59, tr. Ross, *Lives*, pp. 208–10. Poliziano's *Latini* are discussed later in this chapter.

28   The Early Years

Clarice herself was fearful of a possible miscarriage, as well as of the dangers faced by Lorenzo in Florence and the family in Pistoia, and she asked for the companionship of her husband's uncle, Giovanni Tornabuoni, who was back in Florence after the Medici Bank had been expelled from Rome and the Papal State in the aftermath of the Pazzi conspiracy.[9] Giovanni did come to support Clarice in Pistoia, and in early September it was he who helped Piero perform his first public engagement: a little speech honouring Florence's newly appointed captain, Ercole d'Este. Composed on Lorenzo's instruction – doubtless by Poliziano – the six-year-old Piero delivered the opening words 'very well' before being lifted by Ercole on to his horse for their entry together into Pistoia.[10]

It was while they were in Pistoia that Poliziano told Lorenzo, 'Piero never leaves me nor I him'. Difficult though he found this period of enforced exile – especially during the winter in Cafaggiolo, when rain forced him to entertain the children by playing ball with them indoors instead of hunting in the countryside – he promised Lorenzo to do his best, and it may have been now that he bonded with his special charge.[11] He got a local writing master to teach Piero to write in only fifteen days, while he himself taught him Virgil and Theodore of Gaza's Greek grammar – as Piero proudly told his father, in the first, well-formed letter that he penned himself. Six months later, in April 1479, aged seven, Piero not only wrote the letter to his father but also composed it himself, in one sitting, unlike his previous letters (Poliziano said), which he had copied at Poliziano's suggestion.[12]

As Piero's tutor, Poliziano followed the pattern established by famous humanists like Vittorino da Feltre and Guarino Guarini at the beginning of the century, teaching spelling and vocabulary through learning classical texts by rote, and alternating mental exercises in the mornings and evenings with physical sport in the afternoons. Reading Livy when he was four, a Greek fable (probably Aesop) and 'so much Dante it's amazing' aged five, Piero then embarked on the first book of Theodore

---

[9] Poliziano to Lorenzo, 26 August 1478, p. 59, tr. Ross, pp. 209–10; on the expulsion of 'tutti gli compagni et ministri del banco de' Medici a Roma', Lorenzo, *Lettere* 3, p. 160, n. 2; cf. Bullard, *Lorenzo*, p. 135.
[10] Poliziano in Pistoia to Lorenzo, 7 September 1478, ed. Fabroni, *Laurentii ... vita*, 2, pp. 184–5, Del Lungo, *Prose*, p. 63, tr. Ross, *Lives*, pp. 211–12.
[11] Poliziano in Pistoia to Lorenzo, 26 August 1478: 'Piero non si spicca mai da me, o io da lui. Vorrei potere esservi a proposito in maggior cosa; ma poi che mi tocca questo, lo farò volentieri'; the same in Cafaggiolo to Lucrezia Tornabuoni, 18 December, ed. Del Lungo, *Prose*, pp. 59, 68–9, tr. Ross, *Lives*, pp. 209–10, 213–14.
[12] Poliziano to Lorenzo, 21 September 1478, ed. Del Lungo, *Prose*, p. 65 and 16 April 1479, ed. Picotti, *Ricerche*, doc. 3, p.71, tr. Ross, pp. 212–13, 216–17.

of Gaza's Greek grammar and a lot of Virgil, which he learnt by heart aged six.[13] Poliziano's description of what he taught Piero in his self-justificatory letter to Lorenzo in March 1480 (after he had been sacked by Clarice) is much fuller: Cicero, Homer and Isocrates 'and other Greek and Latin, as well as Etruscan [Italian] writers', Greek and Latin grammars, including the whole of Gaza, from which Piero learnt declension and syntax. As well as creating a 'treasury' of useful moral excerpts for the boy to memorize, Poliziano also narrated to him passages from Virgil's *Aeneid*, Statius's *Achilleis* and Aesop's *Fables*, which 'so scented and rubbed off on him that they became part, not so much of his memory, as of his intelligence itself'.[14] We know this teaching was novel from what Poliziano told Lorenzo when brooding on the reasons for his dismissal in March 1480. He then admitted that he had been criticised for teaching Piero Greek before he had completely grasped Latin; he had also distracted him with too much variety and, 'perversely', he had taught him literature by narrating the story before turning to the themes. Comparing himself to Apelles, who finished only the head and shoulders of his statue of Venus and left no one capable of completing her, Poliziano feared that, having built Piero's foundations, no one would be able to complete the building process: not, he said, that others weren't more learned than himself, but they lacked his industry and diligence.[15]

In the event, Poliziano was allowed to complete the foundations of Piero's education, although he was never readmitted to the Medici household. The friction between Poliziano and Clarice had been building up for some time, but it was his influence on Piero's younger brother Giovanni's reading, not Piero's, that was the immediate cause of his dismissal at the end of April 1479. Writing to Lorenzo on 16 April to describe Piero's prowess in writing a letter on his own, he continued: 'as for Giovanni, his mother has taken it upon herself to change his course of reading to the Psalter, a thing I did not approve of'. In her absence, he continued, Giovanni had made great progress, selecting without his help 'all the letters and syllables in his exercise in composition'. Three weeks later, Poliziano found himself seeking refuge in the Medici villa in Careggi, 'having left Cafaggiuolo by command of Madonna Clarice'.[16]

---

[13] Verde, *Lo Studio*, 3, 2, p. 799 (extract from Poliziano's letter of 11 July 1476; on its date, Picotti, *Ricerche*, p. 27, n. 2); Michelozzi to Lorenzo, 17 April 1477. On these teachers, Grendler, *Schooling*, pp. 125–32.

[14] 'Apologia', ed. Picotti, *Ricerche*, p. 76: '... ita undique olfaciebat itaque etiam atque etiam conterebat ut non tam in memoriam quam etiam in ingenium abire possent'.

[15] Ibid., p. 77.

[16] Letters of 16 April 1479, ed. Picotti, *Ricerche*, p. 71, and 6 May, ed. Del Lungo, *Prose*, p.70, Lorenzo, *Lettere*, p. 80, n. 1; both tr. Ross, *Lives*, pp. 216 (6 April), 217.

Despite the attempts of Lorenzo and Niccolò Michelozzi to negotiate his return – Lorenzo asking her to treat him well while he was there (in Careggi), 'so that Piero doesn't lose what he's acquired with considerable effort', since she knew the benefit Piero had derived from him – she was adamant, writing to Lorenzo on 28 May that Poliziano 'shouldn't be able to say that he'll live in your house whether I like it or not and that you've put him in your room at Fiesole'; it was true she had said that if this was what Lorenzo wanted, she would accept it, but, patient though she was, having suffered a thousand insults, she couldn't believe he did want it.[17]

Although Poliziano retained his friendship with Lorenzo, his pleas to be allowed to accompany him on his peace-seeking mission to Naples in December went unheard and he was even refused permission to see Lorenzo before he left Florence. So the long letter, or 'Apologia', he wrote Lorenzo from Mantua on 11 March 1480 represented his attempt to return to favour after his self-imposed exile. After Lorenzo's departure, Poliziano himself left for an extended visit to cities in north-eastern Italy – Venice, Padua, Verona and Mantua – which served not only to make his name as a scholar outside Florence, but also to publicise his defence of Lorenzo in his *Commentary on the Pazzi Conspiracy*.[18] His letter has been said to highlight his relationship with Lorenzo as one of 'vassalage or clientelage, if not total servitude', but inevitably there was a price to be paid for the 'leisure, freedom and tender love' that Lorenzo had supplied him with, that is – as he so often repeated – the task of 'making your children worthy of you through my work, learning and diligence'.[19]

In Poliziano's absence from Florence, Piero and his siblings were taught by several tutors who were more compatible with Clarice's tastes. One of them was Gentile Becchi, the bishop of Arezzo and Lorenzo's former tutor – an appointment that delighted Marsilio Ficino, who believed, like Plato, that a future statesman should learn the principles

---

[17] Lorenzo 'a meza via' to Clarice in Cafaggiolo to Lorenzo [after 6 May 1479], *Lettere* 4, p. 80 (and n. 1 on Clarice's letter of 28 May to Lorenzo, ed. Fabroni, *Laurentii ... Vita*, 2, p. 288, Roscoe, *Life*, 2, Append. no. LXI, pp. 54, and 128, tr. Ross, *Lives*, pp. 218–19). Cf. her trenchant letter to Michelozzi (28 [May], GC 29, 38bis, fol. 29r) regretting returning the books, which – if it was Michelozzi's suggestion – was a battle that 'per oportunità m'avete vinto'. Cf. Tomas, *Medici Women*, pp. 24–5, James, 'Florence and Ferrara', p. 375.

[18] On these events, Picotti, *Ricerche*, pp. 54–69, *Coniurationis pactianae commentarium* (Florence: [Nicolaus Laurentii], 1478), ed. Perosa, *Della Congiura*, text and Ital. tr. in *La congiura della verità*, ed. Simonetta.

[19] Poliziano to Lorenzo, 20 March 1480 (n. 1 in this chapter), pp. 74–5, Martelli, *Poliziano*, pp. 32–4, at 34, and similarly Orvieto, *Poliziano*, pp. 97–8.

of governing from an early age.[20] Becchi had evidently been living in Cafaggiolo with the family in the winter of 1478, and he may still have been there when Poliziano left. A much younger tutor who briefly taught Piero at this time was Clarice's protégé, Martino della Commedia, whom she described as 'a good young man, also – they say – learned and very needy'. She had already set him up in Bernardetto de' Medici's family, and when Lorenzo refused to give him one of the Medici family's shared chapels in San Lorenzo as Clarice wanted, the young Piero protested to his father on his tutor's behalf.[21] Martino soon returned to Bernardetto's family and was replaced by another Medici dependent, Bernardo Michelozzi, brother of Lorenzo's secretary Niccolò. Although he did not teach Piero for long, he was evidently regarded as a doctrinally safe pair of hands for Giovanni as he embarked on his ecclesiastical career.[22]

Piero's letters to his father in this interim period suggest that his education continued smoothly, despite reversing Poliziano's priorities. Martino's influence can be seen in the seven-year-old's somewhat pretentious comparison between his father's travailles in the Pazzi war and those of Scipio fighting Hannibal in Carthage, made in the same letter in which Piero also wrote that Martino was helping to improve his Latin while not letting him forget his Greek ('as for Greek, Martino helps to keep me exercised rather than to progress', he wrote in an earlier letter).[23] This suggests that Poliziano, though unmentioned, was not forgotten by Piero. Nevertheless, the children were clearly thriving in their different ways. Piero and his eldest sister, Lucrezia, were vying with each other to see who could write better, the winner being rewarded with what they had requested – Lucrezia from her grandmother and Piero from his father. Since Piero had written in Latin and had not obtained the horse Lorenzo had promised him, everyone – he told his father – was laughing at him; and when it still failed to arrive, despite Piero's hard labours, he could think of nothing, day and night, but the horse. So when it finally arrived, he was filled with delight at hearing its 'joyous neighs'

---

[20] Ficino to Becchi, *Epistolae*, bk. VI in *Opera*, pp. 863–4, tr. in *Letters*, 5, p. 65.
[21] Clarice to Lorenzo, 24 April 1479, MAP 37, 261: 'è buon giovane et, secondo dicono, ancora docto et molto bisognoso'; Piero to Lorenzo (received 26 May), cf. n. 23 in this chapter.
[22] Picotti, *Giovinezza*, pp. 12–16. As a cleric, Bernardo received a doctorate in canon law in 1482, later becoming secretary to Giovanni as cardinal, ibid., p. 520; Verde, *Lo Studio*, 4, 3, pp. 1369–70.
[23] Piero to Lorenzo, received 26 May 1479, the same, received 27 May: 'nam graeca, adiutore Martino, servo magis quam augeam in presentia', Verde, *Studio*, 3.1, p. 474, Picotti, *Ricerche*, p. 52, n. 2.

reverberating in the countryside and promised his father that he would try with all his heart to 'become what you wish'.[24]

After a year or two of this reward-based tutelage, Piero returned to the care of Poliziano as his teacher. The so-called *Latini* that Poliziano prepared as exercises in translation for Piero around 1481 throw interesting light on their relationship, as well as on Piero's character. Although Poliziano refers to them as fables (*favole*), their free-flowing comments on politics and people, especially Piero, are a strange mixture of shrewd realism and fantasy – suggesting that through this stream of consciousness, Poliziano was expressing his own pent-up feelings, as well as manipulating his somewhat distanced patron through his son.[25] It seems that in two years Piero had become not only 'lightweight and disobedient' but also lazy and given to daydreaming instead of concentrating on his verbs; he made rude gestures with his fingers (a trait that continued into adulthood), and unless he could be weaned from his pleasures in time, he would endanger all his parents' hopes.[26] It is possible that the *Latini* were intended as moral homilies to exhort Piero rather than criticise his actual behaviour, yet Poliziano's imagined response to Piero's invitation to 'choose what you would like as a present' for the holidays was remarkably perceptive, in view of Piero's later success as a champion jouster, his bedroom filled with arms and trophies: Piero, he suggested, would choose a Spanish horse with a golden saddle and tasselled reins, not the gelded and more manageable horse he imagined for himself, nor Giovanni's pony or colt to have fun with.[27] Equally perceptive was the fable telling Piero that he was confident Piero would repay his debt to him, 'but if you deceive me, I deceive your father, who, when he sees he has been deceived of the hope he placed in me, won't consider me the same Angelo but a changed person'.[28] The danger for Poliziano of Piero behaving badly and not fulfilling his parents' hopes was real enough. From now on, succeeding as Piero's tutor became crucial to Poliziano's own success, since it was through Piero that

---

[24] Piero to Lorenzo, received 27 May (p. 13, n. 21 in this volume), and from Gagliano, n.d., tr. Ross, *Lives*, p. 221.
[25] 'Latini dettati a Piero de Medici [1481]', ed. Del Lungo, *Prose*. Cf. Orvieto, *Poliziano*, p. 99: 'lascia scorrere i suoi pensieri, a ruota libera'; Garin, 'L'ambiente del Poliziano', p. 35: 'curiosi pensieri'. As a teaching method, Black, *Humanism and Education*, p. 136, n. 405.
[26] Ed. Del Lungo, *Prose*, p. 28, no. X: 'formare castelli in aria', 'la vostra leggerezza vi caccia a gambe in grembo a quella pigrizia, la quale ogni virtu da voi esclude'; 30, no. XII: 'fare sempre con le dita cotesti tua attucci'), etc.
[27] Ibid., p. 22, no. V: 'tu, Piero, eleggeresti un giannetto con una sella dorata e con la briglia piena di frappe'.
[28] Ibid., p. 30, no. XII.

Education under Poliziano's Tutelage 33

Poliziano was able to remain close to Lorenzo as his friend and the curator of his library.

The practical basis of this relationship emerges from the exchange of letters between Poliziano and Lorenzo about Tommaso, the cousin who had avenged the death of Poliziano's father and was now threatened with a death sentence himself. In July 1478 Poliziano begged Lorenzo to save his cousin's life and not alienate him, on account of 'the hope you have in your – and my – Piero'. Five years later, when Tommaso needed more help, Piero was still caught up in the web of obligation, since he was asked by his father to thank Jacopo Guicciardini for helping Tommaso, whereby (Lorenzo explained) his friends – Angelo, whom he loved as the teacher of his children, and Tommaso as Angelo's cousin – became Guicciardini's friends too.[29] When, a year earlier, Piero had asked his father, through Michelozzi, to help the husband of his sister Lucrezia's nurse, he carefully explained that he didn't like to disappoint anyone, but he also didn't want to err by 'doing things which are above me'. So at an early age Piero found himself playing the role of *mezzadro*, patronal go-between, that would become a predominant theme of his later letters and friendships.[30]

Poliziano was now firmly back in control of Piero's education, once again teaching him Greek. Piero ended his letter to Michelozzi on 27 July 1482 by asking him 'to tell Lorenzo that I'm very well and I'm not wasting time'; two days later he wrote again to ask Michelozzi for a copy of the Greek comic writer Aristophanes, whom Poliziano wanted to expound to him.[31] In a letter (in Latin) to his brother Giovanni, he agreed to commend him to Poliziano as requested: 'it's nothing, for I am your brother. Whatever you ask, I have passed on to him'. Perhaps Giovanni was missing the teaching and company of Poliziano that Piero was enjoying in Fiesole, while he was spending the summer with his mother in Cafaggiolo.[32]

Piero returned to Florence in September, where an amusing incident took place in the office of the Dieci di Balìa (in the government palace). Entering it with Piero, Lorenzo failed to see ser Pace, who was standing

---

[29] Poliziano to Lorenzo, recd. 11 July 1478 (n. 7 in this chapter), the same, 20 March 1480, p. 75; Lorenzo to Jacopo Guicciardini, 25 March 1483, *Lettere* 7, pp. 211–12; Piero to the same, 9 July 1483, Florence, Arch. Guicciardini, LC V, 54.
[30] Piero in Fiesole to Michelozzi, 27 July 1482, ed. De Marinis and Perosa, *Nuovi documenti*, p. 74: 'pure non vorrei errare in fare *quae supra me sint*'; also the same, 26 September 1480, GC 29, 35, fol. 2. On Lorenzo, Kent, *Princely Citizen*, pp. 26–7.
[31] Letters of 27 July 1482, p. 74 ('Dite a Lorenzo come io sto molto bene et non perdo tempo') and 29 July, ibid.
[32] Piero in Fiesole to Giovanni in Cafaggiolo, 28 July 1482, autogr., ed. Picotti, *Giovinezza*, p. 648: 'nihil est; tuus enim sum frater'.

in as the Dieci's secretary while Niccolò Michelozzi was absent in Milan. When he did notice him, he joked that he had appointed another secretary in Niccolò's place – his son Piero. Writing to Niccolò, Lorenzo told him that 'because of the dearth of secretaries, this letter will be in Piero's hand, so you needn't return for this reason'.[33] This may have been the occasion when the ten-year-old Piero formally met the head of the chancery, Bartolomeo Scala, for two years later he asked Scala to inscribe the dedication copy of the Latin translation he had made of Leonardo Bruni's Greek treatise *On the Constitution of Florence*. Bruni was a former head of the chancery when he wrote this treatise for the benefit of the Greek delegates to the Council of Florence in 1439. As Piero explained to his father, his eye had fallen on it by chance when he happened to be in Fiesole without his books; with nothing else to do, he started to translate it into Latin as an exercise, and when his tutor Poliziano saw what he had done, he told him to send it to his father. It was this dedication copy, in the hand of one of Florence's leading calligraphers, Antonio Sinibaldi, that Scala inscribed for Piero, 'in my little old hand, as you wanted', regretting on the one hand that Bruni hadn't written more in Greek for Piero to improve, and on the other urging him 'not only to conserve but add lustre to the glory of your parent(s) and family'.[34] Since Sinibaldi also copied the volume of Scala's own fables that he had dedicated to Lorenzo in 1481, Piero's volume may have resulted from a collaboration between Scala and Poliziano that usefully flattered Lorenzo and his son and also served a didactic purpose.

Piero's Adolescence

Piero was in the company of both Poliziano and Scala when he went on his first visit to Rome at the end of 1484, since Scala had been chosen to deliver the oration congratulating and offering obedience to the new pope, Innocent VIII, as one of the embassy of six Florentine citizens. Piero was too young to be an ambassador himself, but it marked a new phase in his life, as we shall see, and was the first of several visits he made

---

[33] Lorenzo to Niccolò Michelozzi, 12 September 1482, *Lettere* 7, p. 84 (Piero's autogr. but signed and addressed by ser Pace, n. 23 in this volume, cf. Brown, *Florence* (2011), p. 52, n. 51). Piero also wrote Lorenzo's letter to Michelozzi from Poggio a Caiano on 29 September, *Lettere* 7, pp. 109–11.

[34] BNF, MS. Panciatichi 126, fols. 1r–8v, dedication (fol. 1r) ed. Verde, *Lo Studio*, 3, 2, p. 802, Scala's inscription (fol. 9r) ed. Brown in Scala, *Writings*, pp. 154–5. On the treatise (ed. Moulakis in *Rinascimento*, 26, tr. Griffiths, *Humanism of Bruni*, pp. 171–4), Moulakis, 'Civic Humanism', pp. 203–4 and below; on All Souls' Day 1492 Scala sent Piero a fable and a distich commemorating Lorenzo's death, *Writings*, pp. 170, 393, 453. On Piero's later criticism of Scala, n. 50 in this chapter.

to Rome with his friends and his tutor Poliziano, who returned with him in 1487 for his betrothal to Alfonsina Orsini and for his marriage to her the following May.[35]

The betrothal and wedding lay in the future, however, and for the present Piero continued his education with Poliziano in the countryside, evidently disgruntled in the autumn of 1485 to be excluded from the important affairs that were occupying Lorenzo in Florence, with nothing to write to him about – he said – but Homer and Virgil's *Eclogues* that he was teaching to his young brother Giovanni.[36] As well as translating Greek and teaching his brother Latin, we know he was also playing the lyre, going on country walks with Poliziano around Fiesole – or, as Poliziano described it in a poem, 'scrambling up the mountainside' ahead of his breathless tutor – and attending with Matteo Franco the ceremony awarding Poliziano a doctorate in canon law.[37] Poliziano had succeeded in stimulating Piero's interest in books and ancient objects, and later they worked together on acquiring books for the Medici library. When the great bibliophile King Matthias Corvinus of Hungary died in April 1490, Piero wrote to tell his father a month later that he was 'a bit behind' in his work on the library because of the king's death, but 'the part of the library that's my responsibility is being carried out, with many books finished, others begun and almost finished'. And although he couldn't make any decision about the king's books until he had seen them all and their quality, in order not to duplicate them, 'I and messer Agnolo of Montepulciano hope to be done in two or three days'.[38] Two days later Piero (in his father's absence) famously invited the Venetian humanist Ermolao Barbaro to dinner in the Medici palace, together with Poliziano, Ficino, Pico and his brother-in-law Bernardo Rucellai, later demonstrating his knowledge and appreciation of the family treasures when he took his distinguished visitor on a tour of the palace.[39]

---

[35] Verde, 'Un terzo soggiorno'. On the oration and its six editions (1484–90), Scala, *Writings*, ed. Brown, pp. xxxiv, 224–31, cf. p. 42, n. 12, in this volume.

[36] pp. 49–50 in this volume.

[37] Poliziano, *Nutricia*, ed. Bausi, *Poesie*, pp. 756–8, ll. 776–90 ('arrampicandosi sul monte et me che ansimo incalza, già quasi mi procede'); Verde, *Studio*, 2, p. 738, n. 49; Franco, *Lettere*, p. 35. On the Dio Cassio, p. 50, n. 43, in this volume.

[38] Piero in Florence to Lorenzo in Bagno a Morbo, 8 May 1490, MAP 42, 57 (autogr), fol. 57v: 'spero fra dua o tre dì esserne fuora'. He continues: 'et in tanto gli scriptori si riducono a migliore pregio che non possono havere faccienda da altri'; cf. Dillon Bussi 'Biblioteca medicea', p. 136; de la Mare, 'New Research', pp. 468–70.

[39] Piero to Lorenzo, 10 May 1490, ed. Fabroni, *Laurentii ... Vita*, 2, pp. 377–9, with an extract and full bibliography in Fusco and Corti, ed. *Lorenzo de' Medici*, p. 315, doc. 137, discussed more fully in Chapter 8 in this volume.

What is less clear is the impact of Poliziano's teaching on Piero's mental outlook and behaviour. If, as Poliziano said, he had impregnated Piero's mind with the scent of Virgil, Statius and Aesop, how did they make their influence felt? He rarely quoted them, but perhaps Virgil's epic story of Aeneas influenced him more subtly. And what was the effect on him of translating Bruni's treatise *On the Constitution of Florence*, which was more relevant to the political role he was beginning to play in the city? The treatise was strongly influenced by Aristotle's *Politics*, which Bruni had translated a few years earlier, and it opens by describing Florence's constitution as a mixture of aristocracy and democracy.[40] It was democratic in excluding the ancient aristocracy, or magnates, from office and in having short-term offices chosen by lot, and it was aristocratic in excluding the lowest classes from office and in not allowing the popular council to discuss anything not previously approved by the chief magistrates or emend the laws put before them. So far, then, it would have provided Piero with a balanced view of Florence's republican constitution that allowed little room for the Medici's creeping control. Its final paragraph, however, did acknowledge the Medici's route to power during Bruni's lifetime, by showing how the replacement of militias by paid mercenaries transferred power from the people to 'the best and the richest, who contribute most to the public good'.[41] Piero would have been familiar with Roman republicanism from his reading of Livy, and through Bruni's treatise on Florence's constitution, he would have known about the city's much-vaunted republican origins as a Roman colony, founded around 82 BC by the dictator Sulla 'with best Roman stock'.[42]

Although this account had been accepted by Poliziano himself when dedicating his translation of the *Iliad* to Lorenzo in 1472, he had then discovered in the Medici's own library, in 'an extremely old' manuscript (the *Libri regionum*, which he misattributed to Frontinus), that Florence – 'the city in which you rightly occupy the place of preeminence that your family has long held' – had been founded by 'three emperors' or generals – 'Gaius Caesar, later called Augustus, the greatest of all', Marcus Antonius and Marcus Lepidus, the 'high priest' – who, he told Piero, were Florence's first citizens and all unconquerable.[43] Perhaps by

---

[40] Griffiths, *Humanism of Bruni*, pp. 115–16, 171–4.   [41] Ibid., p. 174.
[42] Ibid., Rubinstein, 'Poliziano e la questione', pp. 101–2.
[43] Poliziano to Piero, *Opera*, I, pp. 2–4, letter 2, '*De civitatis Florentiae origine*' (which he said Piero had asked him to write about), *Letters*, ed. and tr. Butler, pp. 8–17, 320–1 (nn. 2 and 4); cf. Rubinstein, 'Poliziano e la questione', and n. 1, dating the letter 'dopo la morte di Lorenzo' (8 April 1492). Officially the first triumvirate, it is now known as the second.

then Poliziano's triumphalist account of Florence's origins reflected Piero's own view of his family's changing position, as Florence was transformed from a guild-based commune to an oligarchy dominated by his own increasingly princely family.[44] After Lorenzo's death on 8 April 1492, Poliziano responded with one last act of loyalty, an edition of his own letters that served as propaganda to bolster Piero and his family.

In the dedication of his *Libro delle epistole* to his 'dear Piero', Poliziano claimed that he had collected the letters at Piero's suggestion, with no attempt at completeness or consistency; rather they represented a haphazard assortment of what he happened to have at hand. Despite this, they were seemingly selected as 'political propaganda' for Piero and his family in the uneasy years that followed Lorenzo's death in April 1492.[45] The first letter after the dedication was Poliziano's letter to Piero 'on the origins of Florence', which, as we have seen, opened by referring to Florence as 'the city in which you rightly occupy the place of preeminence that your family has long held', and ended by thanking the Medici for adopting Poliziano himself into their city, thereby enabling him to extol the fame and distinction of its citizens, who had been 'until now, an object of ignorance for so many centuries'.[46] As well as including Poliziano's long letter to Jacopo Antiquario describing Lorenzo's death (with its emphasis on Piero's worthiness as his heir), the collection also included Poliziano's letters to Pico della Mirandola describing the victories of Piero and Lorenzo Tornabuoni in the joust on 14–15 July 1493, and Piero's exemplary behaviour after the discovery of his cousins' conspiracy against him in April 1494 – on this occasion going so far as to call him 'almost divine' in forgiving his cousins.[47]

Only four months after sending this edition of his letters to Piero on 23 May 1494, Poliziano was dead. Despite Piero's best efforts on his behalf, he had failed to become either a cardinal or the Vatican librarian, and on his death, according to one Florentine chronicler, he was vituperated thanks to Piero's unpopularity.[48] Yet the two men had remained

---

[44] Najemy, *A History*, pp. 250–86 (v. 280–6), 341–74; Rubinstein, *Government*, passim, cf. Guicciardini, *Storie*, p. 71.
[45] Poliziano, *Opera*, I, p. 1, *Letters*, ed. Butler, pp. 2–3; Martelli, 'Il *Libro delle Epistole*', esp. pp. 189 ('scopo di propaganda politico'), 193, etc. Printed in 1498 by the Aldine Press, Poliziano completed it by 23 May 1494, when he told Piero that Becchi thought it 'molto a vostro proposito' (ed. Del Lungo, *Prose*, p. 85).
[46] *Opera* I, pp. 2–4, *Letters*, ed. Butler, pp. 8–9, 14–17.
[47] Poliziano in Fiesole to Jacopo Antiquario, 18 May 1492, *Letters*, pp. 226–51; to Pico, undated, *Opera*, I, pp. 167–8, and 20 May 1494, Martelli, 'Il *Libro delle Epistole*', pp. 188–9, 191–3.
[48] Parenti, *Storia*, I, p. 100; cf. Godman, *From Poliziano*, p. 141, cf. 124–5.

close to each other. At the end of January that year Piero had apparently urged Poliziano to write to Pontano on Ferrante's death, and Poliziano in turn thanked Piero for adopting and supporting Matteo Franco.[49] The extent of Piero's loyalty to Poliziano and his understanding of him are shown by the two autograph letters Piero drafted after Poliziano's death to his own long-term supporters, Bartolomeo Scala and ser Piero Dovizi, angrily denouncing them both for attacking and misrepresenting his old teacher and friend. Taking up Poliziano's criticism of Scala's literary style (in their famous epistolary dispute in 1493–94), the letter to Scala demonstrates Piero's own learning (owed to Poliziano) by being drafted entirely in Latin and ending in Greek.[50] By contrast, only the opening sentence of his letter to Dovizi is in Latin, before continuing in pungent and demotic Italian that is equally revealing of Piero's character and relationship with Dovizi. What amazed him, he continued, was how little Dovizi understood 'messer Angelo and me', since he knew what they were like and should have recognised Poliziano's volatile nature, 'jumping up and shouting back when shouted at, even if he was in the wrong'. During his father's lifetime, Poliziano was always 'kicking against the pricks', as Piero put it, yet he could never get angry with him, 'since from my earliest days he always gave me licence to say what I wanted'.[51] This freedom seems to have ensured the lifelong friendship of these two difficult and not dissimilar men throughout the years of Piero's political apprenticeship and his two years in power. It remains to be seen how well it equipped Piero for the future. For if, on the one hand, Poliziano helped to make him a discerning scholar and patron of the arts by forcing him to serve as hostage for his teacher's and his father's ambition, he may also have contributed to Piero's own recalcitrance and later unhappiness.

---

[49] Poliziano, *Opera*, I, pp. 22–3; Verde, *Studio*, 3, 2, p. 802.

[50] Piero, draft autogr. letter to Scala, MAP 72, 88, ed. Del Lungo, 'Tra lo Scala e il Poliziano', pp. 179–80; on Scala's and Poliziano's epistolary dispute, Brown, *Scala*, pp. 213–19.

[51] Piero to Dovizi, ditto, MAP 72, 89, fol. 103r–v, ed. Picotti, *Ricerche*, pp. 123–4 (29 September–26 October 1494), 'che sapete *eius est contra stimulum calcitare* ... et infine io non mi posso adirare con lui', cf. p. 197 in this volume.

4 Political Tyro at Home and Abroad, 1484–1486

Piero's life has so far been described through the fond eyes of his family and his tutor Poliziano, who protected his childhood years with loving care. In 1484, however, Piero left Florence for his first semi-official mission abroad when he went with the Florentine embassy to Rome to congratulate and offer obedience to the new pope, Innocent VIII. Aged twelve, he was four years younger than his father had been when sent on his first 'quasi-diplomatic mission' to Milan in 1465, but unlike Lorenzo he was not on a solo visit but merely one of several young men accompanying the six ambassadors.[1] It was a suitable occasion to launch him on the political scene not only because of the presence there of so many of his Orsini relatives, including his uncle Rinaldo who was put in charge of him, but also because Florence's official delegation included his great-uncle, Giovanni Tornabuoni, as well as the chancellor Bartolomeo Scala, both sound mentors for Piero's first diplomatic venture.[2]

On the day before they all left, on 27 November 1484, Lorenzo wrote a long letter of 'instructions' for Piero, just as he did for Giovanni, when he left for Rome as a very young cardinal eight years later.[3] After describing the people he was to visit in Siena en route, Lorenzo expressed his concern that Piero should not seem 'too learned' when he was there, but talk with the Sienese leaders and everyone else in a 'natural, sweet and serious manner'. And similarly, he was not to pull rank over the other young men accompanying the ambassadors:

---

[1] Quoting Kent, *Princely Citizen*, p. 24, to Milan in 1465. On the 1484 embassy, Lorenzo, *Lettere* 8, intro. n., pp. 56–68, esp. 65–8.
[2] On Scala, p. 34 in this volume. The other ambassadors included one knight (Antonio Canigiani), two lawyers (Guidantonio Vespucci, the resident ambassador, and Agnolo Niccolini), and Bishop Francesco Soderini.
[3] Lorenzo to Piero, 26 November 1484, *Lettere* 8, pp. 68–79; tr. Ross, *Lives*, pp. 260–5 (for Lorenzo's letter to Giovanni in March 1492, Fabroni, *Laurentii ... Vita*, 2, pp. 308–12; Roscoe, *Life*, 2, Append. lxvi, pp. 64–7).

Behave gravely and politely and with humanity towards your equals, and be careful not to take precedence over them if they are older than you; because as my son you are no more than a citizen of Florence, just like them.[4]

The principal purpose of Piero's visit was to offer personal obedience to the new pope in his father's name, since Lorenzo was unable to do so himself – as he had in 1471, on the election of Sixtus IV. After the pope, Piero was to visit all the cardinals and be guided by Tornabuoni about whether to show them Lorenzo's letters of credence or not. Picking out various cardinals for special messages, Lorenzo focused on Cardinal Giovan Battista Orsini as head of the family, to whom Piero was to show himself ready to repay his lifelong debt of gratitude to the Orsini, 'which cannot be greater, since you owe your existence to them'. After acknowledging in this way Piero's Roman blood, Lorenzo told his son he could be less formal with all his other Orsini relatives, whom he should visit and offer his devotion as their son and servant. His uncle Rinaldo, archbishop of Florence, should be shown his instructions, which were not to be acted on without Rinaldo's advice, being 'better informed and more prudent' than Piero; if he suggested visiting any of the family outside Rome, Piero could do so.[5]

Although Lorenzo had been annoyed that Rinaldo had not written to him at once about Sixtus IV's death on 12 August and the election of Innocent VIII seventeen days later, he must have been pleased to learn that, because of Rinaldo's 'familiarity with His Holiness' while he was in minor orders, he had quickly been able to enjoy a long audience with Innocent, and by 'testing the waters' discover that the new pope was favourably disposed towards Lorenzo. It emerged from Rinaldo's second, fuller letter to Lorenzo on 7 September that he had discussed not only the Medici Bank with the pope but also the conflict between Florence and Genoa, so he was evidently involved in current affairs and a useful guide for his young nephew, sharing responsibility for him with Giovanni Tornabuoni.[6]

Giovanni Tornabuoni was not only older than Rinaldo but a far more experienced player in Rome as former head of the Medici Bank there, although not part of the papal curia.[7] He had helped to complete Piero's little speech to Ercole d'Este in 1478, when he came to keep Clarice

---

[4] Lorenzo, *Lettere* 8, p. 70.   [5] Ibid., pp. 75–6; cf. Kent, *Princely Citizen*, p. 228.
[6] Rinaldo Orsini to Lorenzo, 30 August 1484 ('per testare el guado') and 7 September, MAP 39, 305 and 313. On Lorenzo's trust in Rinaldo and initial attempt to make him a cardinal, Lorenzo, *Lettere* 8, p. 77, n. 25.
[7] De Roover, *Banco Medici*, pp. 315–21 and *ad ind.*, Bullard, *Lorenzo*, pp. 156–7, etc., and n. 8 following.

company in the countryside, and, as Piero's great-uncle, he was the person, Lorenzo told Piero,

whom you must obey in everything, nor presume to do anything without him, behaving modestly towards him and humanely towards everyone, and above all behaving with gravity, all of which requires much greater effort at your age – for the honours and flattery you will receive would be a great danger to you unless you restrain yourself and remember who you are.

If Guglielmo de' Pazzi or his sons and nephews paid him a visit – that is, Lorenzo's brother-in-law, who, though not directly involved in the Pazzi conspiracy himself, had been exiled with all his male relations for their role in it – he was to welcome them, 'but with restraint, showing you have compassion for their condition and urging them to behave well and be hopeful if they do so'.[8]

Despite telling Piero that his instructions were 'quite brief, in view of your age', the task Lorenzo set his son was more complicated than it might seem. Florence's relationship with Rome – that 'sink of iniquity', as Lorenzo called it when writing to Giovanni in 1492 – was soured by the recently concluded peace at Bagnolo, as well as by continuing resentment over the Pazzi conspiracy and war.[9] The reason why Lorenzo was unable to come to Rome himself, Piero had to explain to the pope, was because he no longer had a brother to stand in for him in his absence (due to Giuliano's murder in 1478, it would be well understood, at the hands of the former pope, among others). This was followed by a similarly veiled allusion to the conspiracy when Lorenzo promised absolute devotion to the Holy See in view of the damage he had suffered, 'through no fault of my own'. After this somewhat barbed introduction, Piero was then to commend his brother Giovanni, 'whom I have made a priest', Lorenzo wrote, and now needed benefices.[10] No easy mission for the twelve-year-old Piero then, and it was not surprising that Lorenzo stressed the important role Tornabuoni and the archbishop were to play in his audiences.

---

[8] *Lettere* 8, p. 77; on Tornabuoni, p. 70, n. 7 and p. 28 in this volume. The Pazzi terms of exile are listed by Brown, 'Insiders and Outsiders': 'A list of Florentine Exiles, 1433–1494', pp. 377–8.

[9] The peace, concluded on 7 August, five days before Sixtus's death, left Florence's fortress of Serezzana in the hands of Genoa, the new pope's home town, which was still at war with Florence, Lorenzo, *Lettere* 8, pp. 56–65, 71–2. On Rome as 'sentina di tutti i mali', Lorenzo to Giovanni (n. 3 in this chapter).

[10] Lorenzo, *Lettere* 8, pp. 71–2, 'senza mia colpa' (alluding to the closure of the bank and the attempt to overturn the Medici regime, n. 12), 73: 'il quale io ho fatto prete' (on the benefices, ibid., nn. 13 and 14).

Tornabuoni's initial comments on Piero in his letters to Lorenzo were quite brief. On 9 December, he reported that the Florentine embassy had been welcomed on its arrival in Rome, 'and similarly your Piero, who has behaved, and is behaving, very well, and he does me so much honour with his company that I can't find words to thank you enough'.[11] A week later, after the formal ceremony offering obedience to the pope on the 15th, Tornabuoni and Florence's resident ambassador in Rome, Guidantonio Vespucci, had a private audience with him to discuss the Medici's affairs – during which Innocent, having cherished Piero in the public audience, said he wanted to see him more privately – 'I hope tomorrow' – and asked how best he could please Piero. 'Not knowing at that moment what else to reply', Tornabuoni wrote to Lorenzo, 'I said I was sure Piero would be more than satisfied by being in his good graces'. This was evidently the meeting referred to by Vespucci on the 17th, when he told Lorenzo that 'your Piero and Giovanni [Tornabuoni]' had been summoned to an audience with the pope that day and that 'the son seems worthy of the father', adding only that 'Scala has been highly praised by all'.[12]

There was no more formal business during the Christmas festival – apart from the ceremony of Scala's knighthood in St. Peter's on Christmas Day itself, unmentioned by either Tornabuoni or Vespucci. But Tornabuoni was kept busy with other matters – the reopening of the Medici Bank, benefices for Giovanni, and Lorenzo's cultural commissions: a window in St. Peter's, the Phaeton cornelian that Piero was to bring back with him (although it took two more years to buy it from the Roman dealer Ciampolini), as well as something from Carlo Martelli, 'a beautiful modern object rather than an ancient one'.[13] Piero had his own work to do in discussing a canonry with Guglielmo (Capponi), whom he found 'very tough'.[14] And Poliziano was busy winning from the pope a commission to translate Herodian's *Lives of the Caesars* (completed three

---

[11] Giovanni Tornabuoni, 'orator', to Lorenzo, 9 December 1484, MAP 39, 399: 'se è portato et porta molto bene et fammi tanto honore con la sua compagnia'.
[12] The same, 17 December 1484, MAP 39, 405, fol. 456r: 'Piero nostro fu molto carezato da nostro Signore in la audientia publica'; Vespucci to Lorenzo, 17 December, MAP 39, 406r: 'Lo Schala *summe* è stato commendato da tutti'.
[13] Tornabuoni to Lorenzo, 28 December 1484 and 10 January 1485, MAP 39, 415 and 58, Fusco and Corti, *Lorenzo de' Medici*, pp. 17–18, 23–4, docs. 55, 70, and pl. 4.
[14] Tornabuoni to Lorenzo, 17 December 1484: 'molto duro'. On Guglielmo Capponi, grand master of the hospital at Altopascio, *DBI*, 19, 1976 (M. Luzzati). In 1486 he gave Lorenzo as an exchange (and then in emphyteusis to his sons) the villas of Spedaletto and Agnano (pp. 138–9 in this volume).On his imprisonment by Lucca in May 1494, Piero to Dovizi, 29 May 1494, MAP 73, 81; Anziani of Lucca to Piero, same day, ATL, 536, reg. 47, fol. 61.

years later) and discussing Rome's antiquities with the dignitaries he visited with Piero.[15] Lorenzo had written to Tornabuoni before Christmas about Piero's return, perhaps worried that all the excitement was going to his head, but Tornabuoni replied on 28 December that he shouldn't worry that flattery would make Piero insolent: 'he's too intelligent to be led astray so easily'; what was more likely, he thought, was that the experience had brought him on more quickly than would ordinarily have happened:

And certainly everyone with one voice speaks marvellously well of him and praises your prudence in choosing the best occasion and time to send him to Rome. Rest assured that although I have the greatest love for him, I'm not deceiving myself ...[16]

This makes what he says five days later about Piero all the more convincing, especially as it confirms other accounts of Piero's appealing way of talking that was both modest and spirited. In the visitations they made together, Tornabuoni told Lorenzo, not only were his responses 'natural', but 'they arose extempore and were to the point':

And what amazes me and others is that one can't tell which is stronger in him, modesty or spirit, because he tempers and seasons that innate ardour of his with discretion and reverence, leaving everyone with the highest opinion of him and hope that he will become a person of great worth.[17]

There were other reasons, however, for Lorenzo wanting Piero back home, apart from worry about success going to his head. Despite the apparent harmony of his visits to all the Orsini relatives, two of them, the cardinal and Giulio, were now threatening to join Roberto Sanseverino in attacking Siena, and possibly also Bologna, against the wishes of Florence and the league.[18] So after two more letters from Lorenzo about Piero's return, there was a change of plan. Instead of travelling to Florence via the Orsini castle of Monte Rotondo (to the north-east of Rome) and Perugia as originally planned, Rinaldo now suggested he should return via Monte Rotondo and Viterbo, to avoid encountering Fregoso (on his way from Genoa to visit the pope) and the need for

---

[15] Del Lungo, *Florentia*, pp. 240–6; Lorenzo to Lanfredini, 22 July 1487, *Lettere* 10, p. 454 and n. 6.
[16] Tornabuoni to Lorenzo, 28 December, 'non dubiti ... che le careze facteli l'habbino a fare insolente, che non ha ingegno da smarrirsi così facilmente'.
[17] The same, 2 January 1485, MAP 39, 59, partly cit. Lorenzo, *Lettere*, 8, p. 77, n. 27: 'le risposte sue sono naturali et nascono *extempore* e a proposito ... sì bene temporisce e condisce un certo innato ardire con la discretione et reverentia'.
[18] Lorenzo, *Lettere* 8, intro., pp. viii, 182–3, and 194, n. 6; Shaw, 'Lorenzo ... and Niccolò Orsini', pp. 265–6.

formal visitations in Perugia. Piero had done his final rounds and had taken an affectionate leave of the pope on 7 January and would leave the next day for Monte Rotondo.[19] But once more the plans had to be changed due to a new danger anticipated by the archbishop Rinaldo Orsini: now it was Civita Castellana and the Savelli lands to the north of Rome that had to be avoided because of constant friction with the neighbouring Orsini.[20] So Piero made a separate visit to Monte Rotondo on Sunday the 10th, 'a beautiful day', returning secretly to Rome on Monday evening. The following day at dawn he finally set out for home by taking a north-westerly route via Bracciano, where Virginio had prepared a great festivity for him. Spending two nights there, Piero left for Viterbo 'in high spirits' (according to Baccio Ugolini, who had accompanied him so far), then on to Acquapendente and to Montepulciano on Saturday. There Piero would be safely within Florentine territory, and since Montepulciano was also the home town of his tutor and companion Poliziano, their return schedule to Florence via Arezzo and Cortona could be more flexible.[21]

On his return from Rome, Dovizi found Piero transformed, 'filled out, blooming, taller and now handsome, enjoying the favour of the pope and others'.[22] Keen though Lorenzo had been for his return, he would have seen little of his son that spring, when he was frequently away from Florence, taking the waters at Porretta and then at Bagno a Morbo to cure one of his periodic bouts of sickness. Lorenzo was in Bagno with Clarice when Niccolò Michelozzi wrote to him towards the end of March, asking him 'to tell Clarice that Piero and all the boys are extremely well – as well as I've ever seen them, and so I hope they'll remain'; if Lorenzo got better and came home quickly completely cured, everything else would be fine.[23] Evidently the boys were in the charge of Niccolò's brother Bernardo, since Clarice wrote to him at the beginning of April to find out how he was getting on with 'the brigade', asking him

---

[19] Tornabuoni to Lorenzo, 7 January 1485, MAP 39, 55: 'una vostra breve ... sollicita el mandare Piero senza indugio', 'Questa mutatione se è facta per consiglio di Mons. l'arcivescovo et mio, perché s'intende che il Fregoso viene per la via di lá'.

[20] Civita Castellana belonged to the Savelli before Sixtus IV gave it to Roderigo Borgia; their lands around Rome intermingled with the Orsini's, Shaw, *Political Role*, p. 99; Shaw, 'Lorenzo ... and Niccolò Orsini', pp. 263–4.

[21] Lorenzo, *Lettere* 8, p. 78, n. 29 (citing Tornabuoni's letters of 10 and 13 January 1485, MAP 38: 58 and 61, fol. 68v) and 202, n. 1, n. 5.

[22] Dovizi to Niccolò Michelozzi, 22 January 1485, GC 29, 72, fol. 20, Brown, *Florence* (2011), p. 70, n. 14.

[23] Michelozzi in Florence to Lorenzo in Bagno a Morbo, 24 March 1485, MAP 39, 74: 'Piero e tutti i fanciulli stanno benissimo quanto li vedessi mai' (and similarly, he heard, 'le fanciulle', the same, 26 March, MAP 39, 11). On Lorenzo's illness since January, *Lettere* 8, pp. 127–8, n. 3.

to go and see the girls sometimes, to see how they were and to tell them that their father was getting better day by day; if Giuliano (now aged six) was giving him more trouble than the others, Bernardo must control him by degrees and remind those who were looking after him what they had to do.²⁴ A month later, however, it was Piero who was giving concern. 'As to Piero', Lorenzo wrote to Niccolò, 'I've nothing more to say to you. It seems he needs my presence. In the meantime, advise him, admonish him as you think fit and try to see that he behaves well when messer Giovanni comes.'²⁵

Messer Giovanni (Bentivoglio) was passing through Florence from Rome on hearing that Sanseverino might be planning to attack Bologna, as well as reinstate the exiles in Siena. After being welcomed in Pisa by the Florentine commissary and rectors and spending the night in the Medici house there, he was to proceed via Lucca and Pistoia to Prato, where Piero and his cousin Lorenzo di Pierfrancesco would meet him, with other citizens, and accompany him honourably to Florence.²⁶ Lorenzo must already have complained to Michelozzi about Piero and his worry that he would dress too grandly when he went to welcome Giovanni. For Niccolò had admitted to him that, like Dovizi, he had found Piero transformed by his visit to Rome; and although it was true he needed Lorenzo's bridle, Niccolò couldn't lay down the law to someone who was his patron, nor did he know whether or not Piero's long purple gown was made from the forbidden crimson cloth. When Michelozzi passed on Lorenzo's message to his son, Piero burst into tears and said, 'ser Niccolò, I don't know how I can live, I have nothing to wear in order to appear anywhere, not even anything made of cloth'. He had been allowed by Lorenzo to wear a crimson silk garment when accompanying the dauphin and the cardinal Balue because he had nothing else, and Clarice had allowed him to wear it on other occasions. For this reason he had had a garment made of damask to honour Bentivoglio and it would be the best possible allowed by the statutes (which prohibited the use of the luxury cloth made of kermis): 'I feel sorry for him', Michelozzi told his father, 'because he hasn't anything to wear, I've seen all his clothes'.²⁷

---

²⁴ Clarice in Bagno to Bernardo Michelozzi in Florence, 5 April 1495, GC 29, 38 bis, fol. 36: 'et se Giuliano vi da più briga che tutti gli altri bisogna a pocho a pocho lo riduc<iete>'.
²⁵ Lorenzo to Niccolò Michelozzi, 29 April 1485, *Lettere* 8, p. 179.
²⁶ The same, 19 April 1485, *Lettere* 8, pp. 172–3, also 157–60 (intro. n.) and 173, n. 15 (Michelozzi to Lorenzo, 26 April). On Bentivoglio's visit, the same, 28 April 1485, MAP 39, 430, Pierfilippo Pandolfini to Lorenzo, 3 May, MAP 26, 360v.
²⁷ Michelozzi in Florence to Lorenzo in Bagno, 26 and 28 April 1485, MAP 39: 425 and 430, partly cit. in Lorenzo. *Lettere* 8, pp. 179–80, n. 9; Martelli (*Studi laurenziani*, p. 200) finds Piero's behaviour 'profondamente antipatico' and Michelozzi ironic. On Lorenzo's

An equally engaging account of Piero at this time comes from the priest ser Matteo Franco – 'our Franco', Lorenzo called him, who was 'among the first and dearest creatures of my family'. Although it was little Giuliano, 'as fresh as a rose', who won Franco's sentimental heart when describing how the boys had greeted their mother on her return from the baths in May, in fact he devoted much of his letter to Piero, who had become 'the most beautiful young man, the most charming thing you ever saw'. He had grown quite a bit, had an angelic profile, his hair was quite long and his body more filled out than before.[28]

Piero was also witty, as Franco demonstrates in a postscript describing 'Two sayings of Piero' (*Due motti di Piero*), one made on a visit to Franco's home, the second walking through Florence. The first describes how Piero stopped at Franco's house for some refreshment after returning together from a service in the Carmine. Putting on his coat before leaving, he was asked by Franco if he wanted any more to drink; '"yes", Piero replied, having put his coat on, "another bit, not to smell of overcoat (*catelano*)", which made everyone laugh'. In the second, they were passing by Santa Maria Novella together when Franco saw a carpenter in the doorway of a house, formerly ser Francesco's school for children, where wood was now piled up.

"Oh dear me", Franco exclaimed, "ser Francesco who kept the school must be dead!" – "Yes", the carpenter replied – "The devil, that makes me feel bad", said Franco, at which Piero asked, "Why, 'the devil'? Did you want him to outlive the span of his life? He must have been eighty years old." At which everyone laughed all the way to the Piazza di Madonna. "I thought he was repeating what he'd heard said", Franco commented, "but looking him in the face and seeing him burst out laughing, I realized he said it purposely as a joke."[29]

Franco was not the only person to appreciate Piero's wit and affability – even though, interestingly, there are no examples of his witticisms in Poliziano's omnigathering of *Detti piacevoli*.[30] After describing these two sayings, Franco went on to describe how Piero couldn't go outdoors 'without all Florence falling on him, and it's the same in the house. They've tried and try all sorts of tricks to get him to perform – although

---

strictures on his children's clothes, Guicciardini, *Dialogue*, pp. 59–60, tr. Brown, 57–8 and n. 167.

[28] Franco to Dovizi, 12 May 1485, *Lettere*, pp. 79–85 at 83; tr. Ross, *Lives*, pp. 267–73 at 271: 'con certo profilo di viso che pare un agnolo', cf. pp. 14 and 23 in this volume.

[29] Franco to Dovizi, pp. 84–5. Frosini (ivi, p. 245, 'Glossario') suggests 'forse usata in riferimento a qualche taccia che avevano i Catalani'; Ross (*Lives*, p. 272) suggests the joke may be a simple play on words: overcoat (*catelano*) and Catalonian.

[30] Angelo Poliziano's *Detti piacevoli* refer to him once, playing a game of *palmate* (slap hands?) with Ginevra Benci, before going to his room to write (no. 323, p. 99).

within the limits of decency, on which he sets much store.' People couldn't be held back, and although Lorenzo was unhappy about it and didn't want Piero to be impeded, he would have to lock him in a cupboard if he didn't want him hearing questions for him to answer: 'I can't tell you how charming he is, he captivates everyone who talks to him for a while.'[31]

Franco was, of course, biased, like all the intimates of the Medici family, but others commented on Piero's special way of talking. The republican exile Jacopo Nardi also described Piero's 'sweet and serious and pleasing way of speaking', unlike his father, who because of his restricted nose 'always sounded hoarse'.[32] Although Nardi wrote his history at the end of his long life, with help from other historians, his memory for telling details such as this is striking. In referring to Piero's 'quick and ready tongue', being both very learned and inclined to declaim in verse unexpectedly, and also by nature very scornful and choleric, quick to charm and equally quick to anger, he may be referring to the characteristics that Giovanni Tornabuoni hinted at in referring to Piero's 'innate enthusiasm' and 'spirit'.[33]

So Lorenzo was worried not only by Piero's clothing but also by his popularity with people in the street, from whom he wanted to shield him. Perhaps he already saw his younger son, the pale and serious Giovanni – who in 1483 spoke like an old man and was desperate to please his father – as a more stable focus for his ambitions. A letter from Clarice to Giovanni (written probably a year later) makes it clear how much store his parents were setting on the cleric's future success. In it, she told him to cherish and honour his tutor, Bernardo Michelozzi, by learning and studying hard:

if you do, you'll attain a position where your virtues will be seen and recognized by the whole of Italy; if not, you will be known for your ignorance, *for a city that is built on a hill cannot be hidden.*

She went on to say she was telling Giovanni this because his father was continually thinking about his interests and soon they were hoping to send him something to his benefit (*un buon pro ti faccia*), worth four or five thousand ducats a year; she could almost tell him now, but to be on the safe side, since it wasn't yet finalised, she wouldn't; nevertheless, he should begin to rejoice with them and ensure that such things were a spur

---

[31] Franco, *Lettere*, p. 85.
[32] Nardi, *Istorie* 1, p. 21: 'd'una certa dolce e grave e grata pronunzia'. [33] Ibid.

to virtue.³⁴ Clarice was probably referring to the wealthy benefice of Passignano, which Giovanni had been promised but did not finally obtain for another two years – unless they already had Montecassino in their sights, for which Lorenzo was negotiating the following year.³⁵ The question of a cardinalate for Giovanni had also been in the air since Piero's visit to Rome in 1484–85, and although the pope firmly refused to consider it at that time, he did promise it in the future.³⁶ For now, Clarice encouraged Giovanni to go outside and enjoy himself like his brother Piero, who was too busy playing 'a game of skirmishing with clods of mud and water' to be given Giovanni's message that day: 'tell messer Bernardo to take you out sometimes', she wrote to him, suggesting that, despite her homily, she thought life should not be all work and no play, even for Giovanni.³⁷

For the remainder of that year, 1485, Piero reverted to his status of a teenager, being educated with Giovanni by tutors in Florence and in their country villas. Lorenzo had returned to Florence by late May and spent the summer there, heavily involved in events in Siena (threatened by the return of its exiles) and Genoa (which still refused to return Serezzana to Florence). In early September a new danger loomed in the threatened uprising of Neapolitan nobles against King Ferrante. What began as an internal revolt rapidly spiralled into a war between Ferrante and the pope (quick to profit from the chance of curbing the power of his recalcitrant vassal) before drawing in the rest of Italy. Florentines found it difficult to understand why Lorenzo de' Medici wanted them to support Ferrante against the church, 'especially as this war had nothing to do with us' (the chemist Luca Landucci commented in his diary). It not only detracted from Florence's attempt to recover Serezzana and incurred vast new expenses that the city could ill afford, it also set back Lorenzo's own attempt to unfreeze relations with Rome

---

³⁴ Clarice in Bagno a Morbo to 'reverendo Iuveni Messer Giovanni di Lorenzo de' Medici, figluolo karissimo in Firence', 1[0] May 1485 (on the date, n. 37 in this chapter), GC 29, 38 bis, fol. 35, qu. Matth. 5: 14.
³⁵ On Passignano, whose abbot had died on 1 March 1485, Picotti, *Giovinezza*, pp. 89–90; Brown, *Scala*, pp. 111–12; on Lorenzo and Montecassino in 1486, *Lettere* 9, pp. 307 and n. 13, 370–1, nn. 2 and 4; p. 57, n. 17 in this volume.
³⁶ On the Medici's 'antica voluntà' for a cardinalate, Lorenzo to Sixtus IV, 15 November 1472, *Lettere* 1, pp. 400–1, and 398–400 (intro. n.); Picotti, *Giovinezza*, pp. 161–5 and ff., Chambers, 'A Cardinal in Rome'; on Giovanni's cardinalate, Tornabuoni to Lorenzo, 13 and 22 January 1485, MAP 39: 61 and 69.
³⁷ Letter of 1[0] May, n. 34 in this chapter; cf. Brown, *Florence* (2011), pp. 72–3. The date is uncertain because Franco and Clarice left Bagno on 9–10 May, when Piero was evidently in Florence (Lorenzo, *Lettere* 8, p. 194 and Franco, *Lettere*, p. 79).

after the glacial Sistine years post-1478.[38] Moreover, it also divided the Orsini family, who found themselves on opposing sides in the conflict. For although Niccolò, count of Pitigliano, had been employed by Florence since 1483 and had been its captain general since May 1485, Giulio in Monte Rotondo had opposed Florence and the league since the beginning of 1485, and in July both Giulio and Virginio in Bracciano signed military contracts with the pope.[39] In this situation, it was Lorenzo's personal achievement to reunite the family. Although he was by then again unwell and taking the waters at Bagno a Filippo, he summoned both men there to make them understand that, 'to take the side of the pope is the death of them and others, the side of the king is their salvation', while to his secretaries he explained that if the church acquired the kingdom of Naples, it would possess 'perhaps two-thirds of Italy' and rule as lord of Bologna, Perugia and other church states.[40] So the military *condotta* with Florence and Milan that Virginio, Giulio and Gian Paolo Orsini all agreed to on 2 November was what has been called 'a great coup' for Lorenzo, whose crucial role in hiring them was acknowledged by both Ferrante and Milan. Although it led to the alienation of Niccolò Orsini as Florence's captain general, it nevertheless contributed to the success of the war against the pope and the rebel barons in August 1486.[41]

Perhaps it was not surprising that Piero sounded somewhat excluded from these events when he wrote to his father at the baths in September 1485. He had, after all, been the centre of attention in Rome at the beginning of the year, when he had been 'greatly admired by everyone with one voice' and entertained by both the Monte Rotondo and the Bracciano branches of the Orsini family (as well as by the pope). He may have been hoping to see his Orsini hosts again when they visited his father, instead of being marooned in the family villa at Poggio a Caiano, labouring on Homer and teaching his brother to read Virgil's *Eclogues*:

---

[38] On the war, Butters, 'Florence, Milan and the Barons' War' (citing Landucci, *Diario*, p. 51, on p. 290); on Florence's finances, 289.

[39] Shaw, 'Lorenzo ... and Niccolò Orsini', pp. 261, 264–5; Lorenzo, *Lettere* 8, p. 234, n. 2, cf. p. 303, n. 4; on Giulio, also n. 18 in this chapter; Montecatini to Ercole d'Este, 17 May and 24 June 1485, ed. Cappelli, 'Lettere', pp. 270, 271.

[40] Lorenzo to Michelozzi, 28 and 19 September 1485, repeated to (Francesco Gaddi on 14 October), *Lettere* 8, pp. 304 and 289, *Lettere* 9, pp. 7–8; cf. Butters, 'Florence, Milan and the Barons' War', p. 306.

[41] Ibid., p. 292; Rome, Arch. Capit., Orsini, ser. I, 101, fols. 91, 92 (Dieci in Florence and G. A. Vespucci in Rome to Virginio, 3 and 8 November 1485); Shaw, 'Lorenzo ... and Niccolò Orsini', pp. 262–3; Montecatini to Ercole, 1 and 11 November 1485, ed. Cappelli, 'Lettere', p. 273.

Nothing is harder work, father, than finding something to write to you about when I'm afraid there is nothing to tell you, since – as you know – I obviously know nothing about the affairs of greater importance. So I beg you again and again to write something to me in your name that I can use as a model of writing.[42]

The following year his father wrote to Ercole d'Este to procure a copy of Dio Cassius's 'very rare' *History of Rome* in Greek for Piero. In fact, this was the second time Lorenzo had asked Ercole if he could borrow the history, perhaps encouraged by Pico della Mirandola, who knew it was in Ercole's library (despite Ercole's claim that he had returned it to the Doge of Venice without copying it). This time Lorenzo told Ercole that both he and his son greatly wanted to see it – he because of his love of history and Piero because he could read some Greek and knew it was very rare. It proved to be a long saga. Unwilling to send his copy to Lorenzo, despite Lorenzo's repeated requests for it, Ercole instead allowed him to send a scribe to transcribe the Greek volume in Ferrara, which makes it, perhaps, one of Piero's first acquisitions for the library to which he later devoted much care and attention.[43]

Lorenzo would have had little time to read Dio Cassius until the Barons' War was finally over the following August. Although May found him back in Bagno a Morbo – to avoid the French ambassadors then passing through Florence in support of the Angevin claim to Naples – he remained indirectly involved in the peace negotiations that dragged on until 11 August.[44] The wealthy benefice of Montecassino formed part of these negotiations, and although Lorenzo disclaimed 'being by nature ambitious or ever having dared to ask for a cardinal's hat', it seems that both Giovanni's cardinalate and the benefice of Montecassino were now back in play.[45]

The war and the peace negotiations also opened new possibilities for Piero. Profiting from the arrival of Neapolitan galleys in Porto Pisano in

---

[42] Piero in Poggio a Caiano to Lorenzo in Bagno a Filippo, 11 September 1485, autogr., in Latin, MAP 26, 421, ed. Fabroni, *Laurentii ... Vita* 2, p. 298. Cf. Lorenzo, *Lettere* 8, pp. 243–55 and n. 6.

[43] Ercole did send Lorenzo his copy of a translation of the history, with the proviso he neither made it public nor printed it. On the saga, Del Piazzo, *Carteggio Medici-Este*, pp. 53, 55, n. 5 (5 June 1484 and 5 February 1486); Lorenzo to Ercole d' Este, 5 February 1486, ed. *Lettere* 9, pp. 165–6, and nn. 1–3; Aldovrandino Guidoni to Ercole, 27 September 1488 and his reply, 19 November, ed. Cappelli, 'Lettere', pp. 304–5).

[44] Lorenzo to Michelozzi, 13 May 1486, *Lettere* 9, pp. 286–7, and intro. n.; Gentile Becchi to Lorenzo, 30 April, MAP 39, 475.

[45] Lorenzo to Jacopo Guicciardini, 10 July 1486, *Lettere* 9, p. 370 and nn. 2 and 4; cf. pp. 307, n. 13, 414–15, n. 10. On Montecassino in the peace negotiations, ibid., pp. 311, n. 10 and intro. n. at 361.

June to send Francesco Gaddi with arms and money to the league camp, Lorenzo added his own private instructions to the Dieci's instructions, telling Gaddi to negotiate 'with signor Virginio Orsino to give Alfonsina, daughter of cavaliere Orsino, to Piero as his wife' – if necessary going to Naples to discuss it with Ferrante, too.[46] In Pisa, however, Gaddi found that neither the ships nor their captain could be trusted with a cargo of arms and money, so he was ordered by the Dieci to return home. When he arrived in Florence eleven days later, he found Lorenzo angered by his failure to carry out his private commission, and even more enraged when Gaddi refused to return to Pisa because he was suffering from dysentery. On the same day, Lorenzo ordered his son Piero to visit Gaddi at home, 'to ask me' (Gaddi wrote in his diary) 'to return both my written commission and the special cipher Lorenzo and I had made together secretly. So I handed both of them over to him.'[47] Despite having to perform this tasteless task for his father, Piero came to depend heavily on Gaddi, who continued to work for Piero as he had done for his father, although never failing to distinguish his private commissions from his public work as a chancery secretary and emissary. Piero's personal relationship with Gaddi lay in the future, like his marriage, which opened a new, more independent chapter in his life.

---

[46] Gaddi, *Ricordi*, Bibl. Laur. MS. Acq. e Doni 213, fols. 93 left–xciii right (12 June 1486), Lorenzo to Gaddi, 15 June, *Lettere* 9, pp. 327–30, and nn. 1–2. On Gaddi, Klein, *Scritture e governo dello stato*, pp. 163–5; Brown, *Florence* (2011), pp. 99–100.

[47] Gaddi, *Ricordi* , fol. xciii right (21 July 1485): 'così li consegnai l'una cosa e l'altra', Brown, *Florence*, p. 99, n. 44.

5 Marrying into the Roman Aristocracy, 1487–1488

Although Lorenzo had been planning Piero's marriage to Alfonsina Orsini since the summer of 1486, he was unable to carry the plan forward until November, after the conclusion of the Barons' War. He described it to Francesco Gonzaga the following March as a gift from Ferrante to Piero, 'to whom it pleased him to give the daughter of the late illustrious Orsini knight'. With its huge dowry of 12,000 ducats, the marriage clearly represented a gesture of gratitude to Lorenzo for contributing to their victory in the war, in which the Orsini had played a crucial part in supporting Ferrante, not the pope. Virginio was Alfonsina's guardian after the death of her father, Roberto, Count of Tagliacozzo and Alba, who had been a favourite condottiere of Ferrante's. So the marriage served to confirm and consolidate the Medici's bonds with both the Orsini and Ferrante – although initially risking the loss of his hard-won friendship with the pope.[1]

In the event, Piero's marriage was contracted – coincidentally – on the same day, 25 February 1487, as his sister Maddalena's to the pope's son Franceschetto Cibo.[2] Together, they marked a milestone in the family's advance towards princely status. Both were the result of Lorenzo's political ambition that succeeded in transforming his own position in Italy, although at some cost to the children themselves, as well as to the Medici Bank. Piero's part in these events is interesting for the contrasting impact these marriages had on him, on one hand flowering as a cousin of the Orsini barons in their castles and as Franceschetto's brother-in-law, and on the other suffering as the butt of the jokes of his witty Florentine companions on his visits to Rome, who offered a foretaste of how his new status would go down when he returned home.

---

[1] Lorenzo to Francesco Gonzaga, Marchese of Mantua, 4 March 1487, *Lettere* 10, p. 143. On the marriage, Tomas, *Medici Women*, pp. 20 and 36, n. 59; Reiss, 'Widow, Mother, Patron of Art'.

[2] Lorenzo, *Lettere* 10, 'Excursus', pp. 481–92; Scarton, *Lanfredini*, p. 275; Guidi-Bruscoli, '1487 Medici-Cybo Marriage'.

Once again, Lorenzo used a relative to further his plans, this time not his Tornabuoni uncle but his brother-in-law, Bernardo Rucellai, who was married to his sister Nannina. During Piero's childhood, both families had been close and Bernardo was one of the few people who continued to address Lorenzo with the familiar *tu* after Lorenzo assumed political control, instead of with the respectful *voi* used by nearly everyone else. He was a man of wit and learning, although politically 'restless', according to Francesco Guicciardini; despite being a valued contributor to public *consulte*, and listened to as though he was a siren, he was critical of all political regimes in Florence – including Piero's – and as a historian and intellectual, he later founded the famous cultural gatherings in his gardens, the Orti Oricellari.[3] He had already been employed as Florentine ambassador to Milan and his appointment as ambassador to Naples in October 1486 provided Lorenzo with the mediator he needed for his plans. En route, Rucellai stayed in Rome, where he talked at length with Rinaldo Orsini about many things, 'but about that matter of yours, I learned no more than what you told me in Florence, because signor Virginio – with whom we have to negotiate – was not there'.[4] Although oblique, this must be a reference to the plans for Piero's marriage, which became more overt a month later when Lorenzo shared them with Rucellai and the Florentine emissary to the allied camp (where Virginio Orsini would be found). Only six days after this, Rucellai sent Lorenzo, 'separately, as you ordered', a detailed appraisal of Alfonsina, for which he had laboured so hard among these young maidens, 'you'd have thought I'd become several years younger'.[5]

Rucellai's depiction of Alfonsina was nevertheless as unsentimental as his mother-in-law's description of Clarice had been: 'nothing special, either good or bad. I'm only somewhat offended by her throat, which seems to me a little thick seen from the front, which wouldn't bother me overall if it was in proportion.' According to the merchant friend who had arranged the sighting, it hadn't been like that as a child and he would

---

[3] Guicciardini, *Oratio accusatoria*, cit. Comanducci, 'Impegno politico', p. 155: 'come una sirena', ead. in *DBI* 89 (2017), s.v.; *Corrispondenza ... a Napoli* 3, esp. pp. ix–x; Gilbert, 'Bernardo Rucellai'; on his influence, Nardi, *Istorie*, I, p. 153: 'si dilettava con le ragioni aprire nelle consulte le menti deli uditori'; Fachard, 'Dietro le quinte', pp. 273–4. On the use of *tu*, Kent, *Princely Citizen*, pp. 217–18.

[4] Rucellai in Rome to Lorenzo in Florence, 18 October 1486, MAP 49, 51; cf. Lorenzo, *Lettere* 10, pp. 3–4.

[5] Lorenzo to Rucellai, 19 November 1486, *Lettere* 10, p. 14, cf. pp. 62, n. 2 and 63, intro. n. (the emissary was Baccio Ugolini); Rucellai to Lorenzo, 25 November, MAP 49, 60, ed. Verde *Lo Studio*, 3, 2, pp. 802–3. Rucellai and Rinaldo Orsini were made procuratores 'et ad anuli dationem' on 8 November, ASF Notarile antecos. 10200, fols. 268r, 270r–271r.

find out if there was a reason for it, because he too thought she was rather thick in front of the gullet.

Otherwise, she doesn't displease me because of her size, which doesn't seem small – if she's no more than 14 years old, according to this friend – although, as you know, one can be deceived. But her arms, which are usually an indication of the legs, are just right, like her hands. She seems upright, although I'll be more precise about this and her size another time. The skin is beautiful and has a good natural colour. White eyes but reasonable and not unseemly. Fine nose and mouth, although a little thick, but not enough to make her unpleasing.

Writing again about her at the end of the year, when he saw her standing up instead of sitting down, he no longer thought her mouth was too thick but sharp, her nose he thought was just a little bit snub and her size the result of her age – and if her windpipe was rather thick, it was a common defect around here, due, they say, to the local water (and not, Lorenzo would understand, to her heredity).[6]

What Piero thought of his prospective bride, we don't know, nor was he present at the betrothal ceremony the following year, when Bernardo Rucellai acted as his proxy. Although both Lorenzo and Virginio were keen to conclude the contract in early February, Rucellai urged caution, since 'carrying it out is easy but going back on it is impossible', and in fact it was he who criticised the contract.[7] He nevertheless thought the proxy marriage should go ahead despite his reservations, in order to avoid alienating Virginio by not meeting his deadline, which would have 'created enmity in the place of affinity'.[8] Telescoping the first two stages of the traditional marriage procedure, both the contract signing (or betrothal) and the festive *matrimonium* (or exchange of rings) took place on the same day (25 February), the latter in the great hall of Castelnuovo in Naples; and in the evening the wedding feast was hosted in 'the house of lord Virginio'.[9] Rucellai was delighted with the warmth shown towards

---

[6] Letters of 25 November, cit., 31 December 1486, MAP 49, 73, 'dicono nasce *dall'acqua*' (decoded), ed. Verde, *Lo Studio*, 3, ii, p. 803 (not noting decoded passages and omitting '[*la bocha*] astuto'); cf. Lorenzo, *Lettere* 10, pp. 131–5 (intro. n.).

[7] Rucellai to Lorenzo, 6 February 1487, MAP 49, 82: 'lo exeguire è facile ma el tornare in drieto è impossibile', 13 February, MAP 49, 84. Rucellai criticised not only details of the dowry but the five-year wait for it to be paid.

[8] Rucellai to Lorenzo, 13 February 1487, MAP 49, 84, and 24 February, MAP 49, 87, fols. 143r ('*inimicitia* in luogo *di affinità*' [decoded]). For the contracts, Notarile antecos. 10200, fol. 250r–v, MAP 89, 93, MAP 137,1006 and MAP 148, 26. On Alfonsina's dowry of 12,000 ducats (with an *antefato* of 4000 ducats), Tomas, *Medici Women*, pp. 20, 113–14. On its ratification and the Roman contract ('falsamente rogato'), n. 52 in this chapter.

[9] On the wedding, Rucellai to Lorenzo, 24 February 1487, fols. 143r–144v and bis (25 February), cf. Lorenzo, *Lettere* 10, p. 132. On the triptych of the marriage ritual, Klapisch-Zuber, *Women, Family and Ritual*, pp. 183–7.

Lorenzo and Virginio by the king and all the royal family. The following day he visited Alfonsina and her mother, the countess of Tagliacozzo, for although they had both participated in all the ceremonies, he 'wanted to see them at home and savour them better'; the countess he found to be 'knowledgeable and a woman of worth' and Alfonsina 'a charming maiden who should provide contentment, as I pray God she will'. Promising to go again, he asked Lorenzo to tell him if he should say or do anything else, and if not, 'I shall ask Piero, whom I want to satisfy no less than you'.[10]

Piero was still an absent presence in the proceedings, as he remained until the end of the year, and it was even longer before he completed the third stage of the marriage ritual, the bedding of his wife. In the meantime, as Baccio Ugolini put it, 'it's good she enjoys the liberty that her home territory and time allow her'. Virginio did not recommend giving her any heavy jewelry as part of her marriage gifts – just a charming little ring, perhaps, but nothing not allowed by the sumptuary laws – but because it would be some time before Piero led her home, he thought some beautiful brocades would be a very fitting present, so she could dress as she liked while still at home before having to conform to Florentine restrictions.[11]

In the same letter in which Baccio talked about Piero and Alfonsina's marriage, he also refers to another marriage, 'il parentado nuovo'. At the time, Lorenzo had 'many rivals' in Rome, who 'spoke openly against him'. Resentments had continued to smoulder after the end of the Barons' War. Florence refused to ratify the peace settlement because the return of Serezzana was not included in it, and when Lorenzo heard the pope was planning a separate alliance with Venice, he was speechless with rage, saying – when he had recovered his voice – that he could believe every evil of the pope and that 'this ecclesiastical state has always been the ruin of Italy'.[12] He was equally disparaging about the pope's divisive marriage strategy in offering his son to competitive bidders, calling him 'this whore' who 'has offered himself to everyone like a bitch on heat'.[13] So there was general surprise when it was learnt that Lorenzo

---

[10] Rucellai to Lorenzo, 2 March 1487, MAP 49, 88: 'e se ti rincrescerà, lo commetterai a Piero, al quale io vedrò di satisfare non manco che a te'; on his later visit, ibid. (13 and 20 March), cf. Lorenzo, *Lettere* 10, pp. 132–3.

[11] Baccio Ugolini in Naples to Lorenzo, 21 March 1487, MAP 138, 230, cf. *Lettere* 10, p. 133.

[12] Antonio Alabanti to Michelozzi, 24 December 1486, Brown, *Florence* (2011), p. 270, n. 20; Guidoni to Ercole d'Este, 20 November 1486, in Lorenzo, *Lettere* 10, p. 18, n. 6. In general, ibid., pp. v–ix, 481–92 (Excursus), and n. 13 following.

[13] Lorenzo to Piero Alamanni, 31 December 1486, *Lettere* 10, p. 86: 'questa puttana se è offerta a ciascuno come la bracie'.

himself was among the suitors for the pope's favour. He had been told in late November, via Rinaldo Orsini, that the pope wanted a marriage relationship with him, but despite procrastinating for a long time over the suitability of the dissolute Franceschetto as a husband for his young daughter, Lorenzo was finally persuaded that it was in the interests of 'the city and himself' (for the pope wanted 'to rest the papacy' on Lorenzo, Pierfilippo Pandolfini told him two days later, 'so in effect you should count on being pope yourself').[14] Thereafter, things moved to a rapid conclusion. Lorenzo made Rinaldo Orsini his procurator to sign the agreement on 17 February, it arrived in Rome on the 21st and, delayed by a storm, it was concluded on the 25th, the day on which Piero's marriage was also being celebrated in Naples.[15]

Unlike Piero's celebration, Maddalena's marriage was to be kept secret under pain of excommunication, but the news quickly leaked out. Lorenzo had been careful to consult the Otto di Pratica and its coopted members in Florence before signing the contract, and shortly afterwards he announced the engagements of two of his other daughters to Florentine citizens, Luisa to Giovanni di Pierfrancesco de' Medici (although she died in 1488 before it took place), and Contessina to Piero di Niccolò Ridolfi. Like the betrothal of his eldest daughter, Lucrezia, to Jacopo Salviati, Luisa's betrothal was in fact as strategic as the 'foreign' marriages, since the Salviati and the children of Pierfrancesco needed reconciling after the Pazzi conspiracy; but as Lorenzo explained to Piero Alamanni in Milan:

I thought I had to do it, because having made these other [marriages] outside Florence, I don't want these citizens to think that I want to forget them or don't deem them worthy, and in this way I'll mitigate somewhat the blame I might receive from these others and escape from this madness for ever.[16]

A week later, after obtaining the commend of the Abbey of Montecassino for Giovanni (which formed part of the marriage negotiations), Lorenzo rejoiced that 'what with Piero's marriage and this abbey, it's a long time since our family – and all our friends – were so happy'. If overoptimistic

---

[14] Pandolfini in Rome to Lorenzo, 4 February 1487, MAP 51, 379, fol. 498r, and 6 February, MAP 53, 35, fol. 35r: 'su voi si voleva posare il papato ... che facciate conto di essere papa voi' (Bullard, *Lorenzo*, p. 139). On Franceschetto (who was at least twenty-four years older than Maddalena), Lorenzo, *Lettere* 10, pp. 489–90; 11, p. 317, n. 16; and p. 72, n. 4 in this volume.
[15] Lorenzo, *Lettere* 12, pp. 488–91. On the role of Antonio Alabanti, General of the Servites, in the negotiations, Brown, *Florence* (2011), pp. 271–2.
[16] Lorenzo to Piero Alamanni, 11 March 1487, *Lettere* 10, p. 157; Bullard, *Lorenzo*, p. 140, n. 25; cf. Tomas, *Medici Women*, p. 21. On Luisa and Contessina, Pieraccini, *Stirpe*, I, pp. 231–3.

in being as certain as he was 'of dying' that the pope would pose him no further risk, it is true that from this time until his death, Lorenzo's and his family's position in Italy was transformed by these events.[17]

Piero's Triumphal Return to Rome

Although Maddalena was inevitably the main focus of attention, the impact of the Roman visit on Piero was equally important. After the success of his first visit as a boy, he had returned to a quiet life in Florence, completing his education with Poliziano, occasionally dressing up to meet visiting dignitaries – like Giovanni Bentivoglio in 1485, or Giuliano della Rovere and Giacomo Trivulzio as they passed through Florence in September 1487 – and exercising minor acts of patronage.[18] Even after his betrothal to Alfonsina, he remained under Poliziano's tutelage, relatively uninvolved in the politics that absorbed his father's time and interest. It was in late October 1487 that the visit to Rome was first broached, after it was learnt that Maddalena was eagerly awaited there. Since Lorenzo thought she would go more readily if Piero went too, he was included in the trip, 'to see the woman' (his betrothed, Alfonsina).[19] We know he was writing letters to Alfonsina and in September had ordered some brocade – for himself, or possibly as the gift to Alfonsina that he and his father had already been told would be welcome – so he may have been happier than his sister at the prospect of going to Rome to meet their spouses.[20]

The party of six – Clarice, Maddalena and Piero, their brother-in-law Jacopo Salviati, Gentile Becchi and Poliziano – eventually left Florence on 5 November.[21] Letters exchanged between Florence and Rome reveal

---

[17] Lorenzo to Ugolini, 17 March 1487, *Lettere* 10, pp. 165, 167. On Montecassino or 'la Badia di San Germano' (the town below the monastery), Picotti, *Giovinezza*, pp. 97–106; Bullard, *Lorenzo*, p. 149, n. 37, and p. 48, n. 35 in this volume.

[18] Lorenzo, *Lettere* 11, intro. n., p. 162 (the 'Lorenzino' mentioned as part of the reception party was not, however, Piero's as yet unborn son but his cousin Lorenzo di Pierfrancesco); Piero in Fiesole to Michelozzi, 12 October 1486, GC 29, 35, fol. 4. On 18 October 1487 Poliziano wrote to Francesco di Giuliano de' Medici that 'Piero, anchora, come buon discepolo mi aiuterà a paghare questo obligho con Vostro Signore', ed. A. Campana, *La Rinascita* 6 (1943), pp. 471–2.

[19] Lorenzo to Lanfredini in Rome, 21–22 October 1487, *Lettere* 11, pp. 317–18: 'per vedere la donna'; on their hesitations and Clarice as the excuse for going, pp. 367–8, n. 12 and 387.

[20] Lorenzo to Michelozzi and G. A. d'Arezzo, 2 October 1487, *Lettere* 11, p. 248, Piero to Michelozzi, 22 September 1487, GC 29, 35, fol. 5.

[21] Guidoni to Ercole d'Este, 4 November 1487, *Lettere*, ed. Cappelli, p. 296: 'et similiter Pietro, per visitare sua mogliera che non vide mai'; the same 24 November, reporting the papal banquet and gifts for Maddalena, p. 297.

that many difficulties still remained, not just over the dowries but about where they were to stay. The pope wanted them all near to him and Franceschetto, in the quarters vacated by the recent death of the queen of Cyprus, whereas Clarice wanted to stay in Paolo Orsini's apartment in the Orsini compound at Monte Giordano on the other side of the Tiber. When a compromise was suggested whereby Clarice and Maddalena would stay at Monte Giordano and Piero and his brother-in-law with Franceschetto, Lorenzo wasn't happy about Piero staying with Cibo, since he was 'coming in his mother's company and should stay with her continually'. This and the fact that Lorenzo wanted the ambassador Lanfredini to help and advise Piero in Rome suggests he may have been as worried about Franceschetto's influence on Piero as about him marrying Maddalena. Meanwhile, Franceschetto had unexpectedly left Rome for Cerveteri and Viterbo, 'to get a bit of air', and had to be recalled by his father, the pope, who was awaiting the Florentines in great expectation and offered to pay all their expenses as they travelled through papal territory.[22]

The party's first stop was Siena, where Piero told his father they had been 'very lovingly and honourably' received. Piero had already visited Siena on his way to Rome three years earlier, when his father had given him detailed instructions about whom to visit, how to speak ('not too learnedly, but naturally, sweetly and seriously') and what to say in support of their regime, but since July the regime had changed: the popular philo-Florentine regime had been expelled by the returning exiles and replaced by the Noveschi, who smoothed the way for the rise of Pandolfo Petrucci. Since the new government was not ratified until December, the visit was limited to formalities – to Lorenzo's regret, he told the government – but it may nevertheless have helped to lay the foundations of Piero's close relationship with the Petrucci in the 1490s.[23] After Siena, they travelled to Pitigliano for three or four days, bolstering Niccolò Orsini's relationship with Florence at a time when he was becoming increasingly jealous of Virginio's growing influence and seeking to change his *condotta*.[24] Thence to Viterbo, where it was hoped Franceschetto would arrive in time to greet them, and on to Virginio's

---

[22] Lorenzo to Lanfredini, 4 and 10 November, *Lettere* 11, pp. 379, 400–1; 366–7, n. 11 (on the journey), and 374, n. 7 (on Franceschetto's gambling).

[23] Lorenzo to the Ufficiali di Balia di Siena, 10 November 1487, *Lettere* 11, pp. 407–8 and n. 1, citing Malavolti, *Lettere* 12, intro., p. xiv; on Pandolfo, Jackson, *Pandolfo Petrucci*; Shaw, *Popular Government*, pp. 96–100; Hicks, 'The Sienese Oligarchy', esp. p. 1052. On Piero's 1484 visit, pp. 39–40, 132 in this volume.

[24] Lorenzo, *Lettere* 11, p. 367, n. 11; on Niccolò, ibid., pp. 363–4. nn. 2, 3; Shaw, 'Lorenzo ... and Niccolò Orsini', pp. 269–70.

castle at Bracciano for two or three days (Rinaldo Orsini predicted), further delaying their arrival in Rome.[25] It was in Bracciano, in Virginio's elegant Renaissance castle beside the lake, that Piero's famous encounter with the powerful condottiere took place. Immortalised in the grandiose fresco that once greeted visitors under an arch on entering the palace (but now safely indoors, on the walls of the audience chamber), it serves to mark the young Piero's transition into the world of the Roman aristocracy.

Shortly before sunset on 11 November, the party reached Rome six days after setting out. Maddalena was now the main focus of attention as she entered the city 'with her mother and many women and servants'. The papal master of ceremonies, Johan Burchard, describes how they were met and accompanied in an orderly procession to the gate of the Borgo: the retinues of the prelates and ambassadors who first greeted them were followed by those of the Medici (where Becchi and Poliziano would have found themselves); then Franceschetto on horseback between Piero on his right and Jacopo Salviati on his left; behind them, Maddalena with Niccolò Bucciardi Cibo, Archbishop of Cosenza (a relative and a favourite of the pope) on her right and Antoniotto Pallavicino, the datary, on her left; and finally Clarice, flanked by the Milanese ambassador (Giacomo Botta, Bishop of Tortona) on her right and Francesco Soderini, Bishop of Volterra, on her left, with a middle-ranking collection of prelates and women bringing up the rear. After suppering at Franceschetto's house in the Borgo, the party crossed the Tiber to Paolo Orsini's house in the family enclave of Monte Giordano, where they were all comfortably lodged 'according to your plan', Lorenzo was told.[26]

The following day the family had a protracted audience of several hours with Pope Innocent, who received them very affectionately. The pope 'couldn't have enough of madonna Maddalena, who could not have pleased and satisfied him more', and similarly his son, Franceschetto, who was unable to spend an hour without going to where she was – despite the fact, Nofri Tornabuoni told Lorenzo, that until he saw her, 'I can't say how unhappy he was about it'. Jacopo Salviati reported that Maddalena was 'especially happy to have her signor Francesco here, whom she likes a lot, as he seems to like her', and so it continued.[27]

---

[25] Lanfredini to Lorenzo, 10 November 1487, MAP 40, 161: 'siche la giunta loro fia più tardi stando cosi', cf. *Lettere* 11, p. 367, n. 11.
[26] Lorenzo, *Lettere* 11, pp. 415–16, intro. n., citing Burchard and the letters of Nofri Tornabuoni, Salviati and Lanfredini (16 November). On Botta, Milan's ambassador in Rome from August 1487, ivi, p. 78, n. 3, *DBI* 13, 1971 (U. Rozzo).
[27] Lorenzo, *Lettere* 11, pp. 416–17, citing Nofri's and Jacopo's letters on 417.

A week after their arrival, the pope 'wanted her to supper in the palace and to participate himself. Nevertheless his Beatitude ate at his table alone, near to that of the bride. He provided a great festivity of songs, music and dancing.'[28] He also gave Maddalena costly jewelry on behalf of his son, and hopes were high that she would continue to have a good effect on her betrothed (who had already chased a groom out of his house) and that he would be given lands and a military position to sustain his future role.[29]

Although somewhat outshone by his sister, Piero also made a good impression in Rome. He did the rounds of cardinals, accompanied by his great-uncle Giovanni Tornabuoni (his mentor on his first visit to Rome) and Giovanni Lanfredini, and both – predictably – reported well on his behaviour. 'He's done a fine thing. We've begun to visit the cardinals,' Tornabuoni wrote on the 16th; 'he'll follow through to the end and he couldn't behave better'. On the same day Lanfredini agreed that Piero had behaved very appropriately in everything he did with them. His twenty-seven-year-old brother-in-law, Jacopo Salviati, also agreed, telling Niccolò Michelozzi that Piero was deporting himself fearlessly in all his engagements – kissing the cardinals' 'fat cheeks', as instructed by Michelozzi – and his sister, too, was proving to be most admirable.[30] Jacopo was in Rome 'to keep Piero company ... not for any other reason', he told Michelozzi. He had been betrothed to Piero's eldest sister, Lucrezia, in 1481 (as a political gesture after the hanging of two of his uncles for their part in the Pazzi conspiracy), although he did not marry her for another five years, after Piero's marriage. Despite the age gap (he was eleven years older than Piero), he was much closer to him in age than Piero's other mentors and his letters provide a correspondingly livelier account of events in Rome.[31]

Impressed by the warm reception given to them, Jacopo reported on 24 November the entry of the Venetian ambassadors to Rome, 'with the greatest triumph, that seemed to me one of the most beautiful things I've seen': more than two thousand people, the retinues of the gentlemen, the cardinals and the pope, following them the lords and gentlemen, among

---

[28] Nofri Tornabuoni to Lorenzo, 19 November 1487, MAP 52, 59: 'mangiò Sua Beatitudine a la tavola sua solo apresso a quella della sposa. Fecesi buona gala di chanti, suoni e balli', Lorenzo, *Lettere* 11, p. 418.

[29] Ibid. (16 November): 'Quello [triste] che menò costì la cchinea' (the white horse presented by Naples to the pope annually). On the jewelry, Salviati on the 18th to Francesco Baroni, MAP 102, 24 and to Michelozzi, GC 29, 91, fol. 28.

[30] Salviati to Michelozzi, 18 November 1487, Brown, Florence (2011), p. 72, n. 24, cf. Lorenzo, *Lettere* 10, p. 418. Cf. n. 47 in this chapter.

[31] Hurtubise, *Une famile-Témoin*, pp. 59–61, 80, n. 36.

the last of whom (by order of the pope) were Signor Franceschetto on the right hand and Piero on the left, then the prelates and the other ambassadors.[32] He also reported Franceschetto's assiduous visits to Maddalena, always twice a day, each day eating either lunch or supper with them. Franceschetto in turn took them out and about for pleasure in the mornings and evenings, and one day they even played ball (*palla pichola*). On the 23rd the party went after lunch to the Castel Sant'Angelo, Clarice having invited the wives of various nobles and relatives to accompany them, which they were happy to do. The men – that is, Piero, Jacopo, Franceschetto and Girolamo d'Éstouteville – enjoyed hearty meals together, music, dancing and a trip to Ostia, where even the constant rain failed to dampen their spirits.[33]

The Florentines' life in Rome also revealed the hazards of encountering *persone non grate* (people unwelcome to the Medici), like exiles and the former student in Florence Alessandro Cortesi, who had now fallen out of Lorenzo's favour. Piero was annoyed when Cosimo Pazzi and Cortesi insisted on accompanying him and Jacopo Salviati, in view of Lorenzo's instructions not to go about with other people. Jacopo, however, felt less constrained than Piero. He was willing to commend Cortesi to ser Francesco Baroni in Florence and would have even visited Cortesi (he told ser Francesco) if he hadn't had 'to go about continually with Piero, so the only time I have to write even a short letter is when he is in bed'. Jacopo also corresponded with Giovanni di Pierfrancesco de' Medici. So although he was in Rome as Piero's companion, as a Salviati he was linked to wider circles than those prescribed by Lorenzo, which meant, as we shall see, that he could report more openly on events in Rome.[34]

It was Jacopo who reported Piero's and Alfonsina's first meeting to Niccolò Michelozzi in Florence, since he knew that his 'fastidiousness' and unwillingness to speak of things other than as he saw them would make his account more trustworthy than the many others Niccolò would receive.[35] In fact, their meeting was delayed by Alfonsina's and her mother's difficulty in leaving the kingdom of Naples.[36] Initially the plan

---

[32] Salviati to ser Francesco, 24 November 1487, MAP 102, 25, fol. 27v; cf. Lorenzo, *Lettere* 11, p. 394, n. 5; the same, 15 November, MAP 102, 23: 'per una gita io non potevo fare la più bella né in migliore tempo'.

[33] The same, 24 November 1487, cit. On Jérome, natural son of the late cardinal of Rouen, Guillaume d'Éstouteville, Lorenzo, *Lettere* 11, p. 317, n. 16, and 12, pp. 173–4, n. 15.

[34] The same, 24 November 1487, fol. 27r: 'non ho non che altro tempo a scrivere una letteruza se non quando è al letto'. On Cortesi, *DBI* 29, 1983 (G. Ballistreri), Brown, *Medici in Florence*, pp. 247–62, esp. 248–53.

[35] The same, 12 December 1487, GC 29, 91, fol. 31.

[36] Lorenzo, *Lettere* 11, pp. 232 and 318, n. 18.

was for Piero and Jacopo to meet them at Vicovaro, an Orsini castle to the east of Rome, but in the end the meeting took place in the Orsini palace in Monte Rotondo, where the Florentine party passed the time before they arrived hunting and bird catching, taking little game 'in order to create more expenses for Signore Organtino [Piero's uncle], who is paying for us', Jacopo joked to Michelozzi.[37] When the betrotheds finally met two days later, Piero couldn't have been happier or more satisfied, Jacopo reported, and so was everyone else at being 'relieved of a great worry'.[38] When the party moved on to Virginio Orsini's castle at Bracciano, the happy couple continued to be delighted by each other's company and spent the whole day together, from morning to evening, enjoying 'the greatest intimacy in the world and so many discussions that I don't know where they draw them from'. Piero was behaving correctly and not embarrassingly, the countess was indeed a woman of worth (as Bernardo Rucellai had said), and as for 'this wife of Piero's, she is the most pleasing and happy girl and of such spirit that I have rarely experienced, so I think Lorenzo will be no less satisfied by her than Piero – so far as one can see up to now'.[39]

Piero had told Jacopo not to write about Alfonsina to ser Francesco Baroni, since it was for him to do so, not Jacopo.[40] So when Jacopo did write to ser Francesco about her, his letters – though no less flattering to Alfonsina – present a rather different picture of events, adding 'a few details' that he thought Piero would understandably have omitted. These included the small but revealing contretemps when Alfonsina and her party finally arrived at Monte Rotondo on 12 December in drenching rain. When their horses appeared in sight, it was raining so hard that only Jacopo and Piero mounted their horses to meet them, preceded by Golpino (later one of Piero's bodyguards) and followed by Piero's household servants, grooms and everyone else. Dressed in purple damask with a red cap, Golpino, rather than Piero, was to exchange words with Alfonsina, but when Virginio got wind of the plan, he commanded that

---

[37] Salviati to Michelozzi, 29 November (in Rome) and 10 December (in Monte Rotondo) 1487, GC 29, 91, fols. 29 and 30 ('e pigliano poche fiere per dare maggiore spesa al Signore Organtino che ci fa le spese'); Lorenzo, *Lettere* 11, p. 386, n. 9.

[38] The same, 12 December 1487, cit.

[39] The same, Bracciano, 21 December, GC 29, 91, fol. 32: 'tanti ragionamenti che non so donde segli cavino', 'Piero si porta costumatamente, non però in un modo che si facci vergognia.'

[40] Salviati to ser Francesco, 12 and 14 December 1487, MAP 102: 21 and 22, fol. 23v; cf. n. 46 in this chapter.

he alone was to speak and no one else, so Golpino was silent, and as they retreated no one spoke to Piero either, in case it wasn't him.[41]

Their arrival was followed by two and a half days of celebrations, for which all the Orsini clan arrived 'to welcome our Piero'. Organtino was joined by Giulio and Paolo Orsini (who stayed two miles away at Mentana), then one of the Savelli, with heads of squadrons and crossbowmen; Franceschetto Cibo arrived with his friends, Galeazzo, lord of Correggio, Girolamo d'Éstouteville, messer Giorgio of Santa Croce and many others, and finally Cardinal Giovan Battista and Napoleone Orsini.[42] Even now there was a hitch, because 'the woman [Alfonsina] doesn't dance', so those among the many guests who wanted to play and sing had to celebrate secretly. Piero's party loyally preferred to stay with Alfonsina, and Piero never left her side, so that even such an expert in protocol as Franceschetto thought Piero would shame no one, he'd been 'so diligent and perfect in this art'. 'Piero and his wife', Jacopo concluded, 'demonstrate so much love to each other that we're all astonished' – even her mother the countess was surprised and delighted by the speed with which this had happened.[43] Clarice was equally delighted by her daughter-in-law when she wrote to Michelozzi from Rome on 18 December (having left the rest of the party to continue their festivities in Virginio's newly embellished castle in Bracciano, where the housing and everything else was expected to be better than in the austere palace in Monte Rotondo): 'My Alfonsina', she told Michelozzi, 'has satisfied me so much that I pray to God she will satisfy all of you in Florence.'[44]

These letters reveal how apprehensive the family must have felt about Piero's reaction to Alfonsina. Jacopo's account of their quick rapport and long discussions together is consistent with what we know about Piero's learning and engaging way of talking to people, but we know virtually nothing of his attitude to women before his marriage and little to reassure us afterwards. He had been educated almost exclusively by his homoerotic tutor Poliziano and seems to have shared none of the hedonistic

---

[41] Ibid., 14 December, fols. 23v. In 1492, Golpino was one of Piero's retinue, 'for the mules', in Rome and in November 1493 one of his bodyguard of eighteen, p. 162 and n. 51 in this volume, Otto di Guardia rep. 96, fol. 1v.

[42] Salviati to ser Francesco, 20 December 1487, MAP 102, 45. On Girolamo, n. 33 in this chapter, and on Giorgio di Paolo Santacroce, Lorenzo, *Lettere* 12, pp. 337–8, n. 28.

[43] The same, 14 December, 1487, fols. 23v–24r: '(la) donna, che non fa a ballare. Piero non si spichò mai punto dalla sua et sono dimestichi insieme a maraviglia ... tanto è diligente et perfecto in questa arte ... veramente è tanta l'amore che mostrono Piero et la donna di porttarsi che ognuno di noi ne resta stupefatto.'

[44] Clarice to Michelozzi, 18 December 1487, GC 29, 38 bis, fol. 26. On Bracciano and its frescoes, Cantone, 'Il Castello Orsini di Bracciano', and Cavallaro, 'Musica, danza e svaghi di corte'.

adolescence enjoyed by his father Lorenzo. So to hear how easily Piero fell into an intimate and 'domestic' relationship with Alfonsina must have been a relief to all the friends and family in Florence. The letters explain, too, Piero's nervousness about how things were reported back home, especially to ser Francesco, who must have spread Jacopo's account of Piero's initial reception in Monte Rotondo.[45] Had he known how ser Francesco responded to Piero's order to Jacopo by quoting Aulus Gellius on the back of Jacopo's letter, he would have been even more upset. On the reverse side of Jacopo's brief note to him of 12 December, he wrote, 'Publius Crassus thought that the authority of a commander would be totally destroyed if his orders weren't obeyed.'[46] This mocking comment on Piero's authoritarian order as a sign of weakness explains Piero's nervousness about how things were reported to Florence. Whereas he was 'more affectionate' towards Michelozzi than towards anyone else, Jacopo said, ser Francesco was another matter, and Jacopo himself could be equally barbed, describing Poliziano – otherwise unmentioned in the festivities – as 'too experienced a jouster' in the art of winning patronage and profligate in 'consuming' what little paper there was in Bracciano.[47]

Piero was back in Florence in early January without waiting to celebrate Maddalena's quiet marriage to Franceschetto in Monte Giordano on 20 January 1488, where of the original party only Clarice, Maddalena and Gentile Becchi were present.[48] Negotiations continued over Franceschetto's settlement and over Alfonsina's dowry, which Clarice had stayed on in Rome to conclude, despite her growing illness.[49] The countess, Caterina Sanseverino Orsini, was due to return to Bracciano from Rome with Alfonsina on 5 April, accompanied by Baccio Ugolini, who had been toing and froing between Rome and Bracciano to complete the settlement.[50] On the 7th, however, he wrote to Lorenzo to postpone Piero's 'mission', since it seemed that the guarantee being offered by Virginio for the payment of Alfonsina's dowry (the *obligatione*

---

[45] Salviati to ser Francesco, 22 December 1487, MAP 102, 33r.
[46] The same, 12 December 1487, n. 40 in this chapter ('... però allui mi riferischo per ubidire'), citing on the *verso* (in ser Francesco's hand) Aulus Gellius, *Noctium Atticarum*, I, xiii, 13.
[47] Salviati to Michelozzi, 29 November, 1487; to ser Francesco, 7 December, MAP 102, 20 ('troppo praticho giostrante') and 21 December ('s'à consumato Messer Angnolo').
[48] Verde, 'Un terzo soggiorno romano', p. 262 (that he was back by 9 January, v. MAP 57, 6); on the marriage, Lorenzo, *Lettere* 11, p. 600, n. 15, citing Gentile Becchi (MAP 26, 510, 1 February). Registered on 20 January, its 'consumatione ... et perfecto compimento de le noze' was reported by Cibo to Lorenzo on 19 February, *Lettere* 12, p. 45, n. 1.
[49] Clarice to Lorenzo, 9 April 1488, cf. p. 25, n. 41 in this volume.
[50] Baccio Ugolini to Lorenzo, 3 April 1488, MAP 40, 239, fol. 254 bis; Clarice to Lorenzo, 9 April, P. A. Soderini to Lorenzo, 3 September 1489 and 31 March 1490, *Corrispondenza* 5, pp. 132, 249. On Caterina, Lorenzo, *Lettere* 15, pp. 411–12, n. 2.

Virginiana) was insufficient. The negotiations that followed between Baccio, Clarice and Nofri Tornabuoni required 'a little guile' to avoid the embarrassment of not seeming to trust Virginio, and until they got a good notary (Niccolò da Castello) to redraft the document for Lorenzo to ratify, Piero was told not to move but only 'prepare himself' for the journey to Rome.[51] Despite this, the document ratified in Florence on 24 April had been drawn up nine days earlier by ser Giovanni da Pescia, one of the two notaries who were later said to have 'falsely rogated' the contract that was later the subject of great contention.[52] Meanwhile, Alfonsina had been struck down with a fever, coughing and sneezing, at first thought to be the result of the vile weather on her visit to Rome and return to Bracciano, but which turned out to be German measles. So Piero's arrival in Rome – eagerly awaited by the countess and by Baccio, who thought 'the best doctor' for Alfonsina 'would be Piero' – was delayed still further.[53]

No less eager to see 'my Piero' was the ailing Clarice, 'well one day, ill the next', who was in the care of Madonna Bartolomea Minerbetti.[54] Although Clarice's illness wasn't new to Lorenzo, he was upset to hear this and said she should return to Florence now if she wanted to, despite preferring her to return with Alfonsina and Maddalena, who was 'still no more than a child' and needed respite from Franceschetto's disorderly household.[55] Finally the contract arrived and Piero was able to leave for Rome at the end of April to complete the final instalment of his long drawn-out marriage.

Piero's Marriage in Rome

Piero departed for Rome in high spirits. Eating well and singing May Day songs en route, he and his companions reached Acquapendente, via Montepulciano, on the evening of 1 May, where they discovered that the songs being sung there *alla Romanesca* were amazingly novel, both for

---

[51] Ugolini to Lorenzo, 6, 7, 13 April 1488, MAP 40: 246, 249, 264. According to Clarice (to Lorenzo, 9 April), the trouble lay with 'queste Sanseverinesche'.
[52] Lorenzo, *Lettere* 12, pp. 206, n. 16 and 275, n. 11; ASF Notarile antecos. 10200, fols. 299r–300v. According to Lamberto dell'Antella (*Processo*, ed. Villari, p. xi), ser 'Francesco' da Pescia and ser Marco da Bracciano drew up the contract in Rome 'falsamente' (I could find no traces of it in AS Rome; cf. Bullard, *Lorenzo*, p. 138, n. 14).
[53] The same, 16 April 1488, MAP 40, 268, fol. 283v, cf. 17 April, MAP 40, 269.
[54] Lanfredini to Lorenzo, 12 April 1488, MAP 58, 30: 'uno dì bene e 2 indisposta', Lorenzo, *Lettere* 12, p. 206, n. 17, and on Minerbetti, ivi, n. 18.
[55] Lorenzo to Lanfredini, 10 April 1488, *Lettere* 12 (1199), pp. 189–90, and to Bernardo Dovizi (late April), ibid., p. 275.

their words and for their music. The next day they reached Viterbo, thence, via Bracciano, to Rome, where 'the happy party' arrived on Monday 6 May.[56] This time Piero was accompanied not only by Jacopo Salviati and Poliziano but also by Giovanni Serristori and the young Bernardo Dovizi (shortly to join his elder brother as one of Piero's secretaries), whose presence makes it clear the trip involved business as well as pleasure. Serristori was there to help Piero settle the dispute over the Vallombrosan Abbey of Monte Scalari involving his family, Piero's mother and Giuliano della Rovere, who were ranged against the general of the Vallombrosan Order and eventually the pope.[57] Bernardo was there to help write letters and carry out the tasks outlined in Lorenzo's letter of instruction to him, in which – as we shall see – Piero was included.

Most of these tasks were straightforward, if time-consuming: discussion of the alum mines, interviews with the cardinals San Giorgio, San Marco and Vincula, the ratification of Alfonsina's dowry and the return of Maddalena to Florence.[58] The first task outlined was not straightforward, however, as Lorenzo's blunt opening indicates:

> As the ambassador will tell you, the pope has had it planted in his head that it's impossible to place firm reliance on this city and me because in matters of state we follow our own interests without any respect for his Holiness, and for this reason he spat out something to the ambassador about needing some separate guarantee to reassure him.

Once Lorenzo knew what Innocent wanted in order to ensure his and Florence's good faith in the face of these 'diabolical suggestions', the letter continued, he would immediately send the pope 'my daughter, you and my other sons and, if necessary, even I will come in person to make sure everyone is completely clear' – in this way showing that the instructions were intended for Piero as well as for ser Bernardo.[59] This in turn suggests – importantly, for Piero's future behaviour – that Piero must have already been privy to (and surely influenced by) his father's double-dealing politics that were upsetting the pope.

---

[56] Poliziano in Acquapendente to Lorenzo, 2 May 1488, MAP 40, 313, ed. Del Lungo, *Prose*, pp. 74–5; tr. Ross, *Lives*, p. 288; cf. Lorenzo, *Lettere* 12, p. 262, n. 15; Lanfredini to Lorenzo, 3 May 1488, MAP 40, 315; Matteo Franco to ser Piero Dovizi, 7 May 1488, *Lettere*, ed. Frosini, p. 92: 'et io in questo bordello [in Stignano]'.

[57] On Monte Scalari, Lorenzo to Lanfredini, 19 January 1488, *Lettere* 11, pp. 602–4 and n. 20; and 16 and 30 April, *Lettere* 12, pp. 202–3, 265 (and n. 26 on Giovanni Serristori).

[58] Lorenzo, 'Instructio' to Bernardo Dovizi (April 1488), *Lettere* 12, pp. 269–75; on Maddalena, p. 275 and Lorenzo to Lanfredini, 2 May, ibid., p. 287, n. 10.

[59] Lorenzo, 'Instructio', pp. 270, 273 (my underlining); on Bernardo, 269–70.

What they were emerged from the Florence ambassador, Lanfredini, who had been told that Piero would inform him about 'the little clause' that was causing papal umbrage. The *capitoletto* concerned the pope's demand for a written guarantee of Lorenzo's part in the secret agreement with Venice – no small matter.[60] This was one of Lorenzo's secret and mutually incompatible deals that were upsetting Italian rulers at this time. His secret agreement with Venice upset Ferrante, who was also threatened by Lorenzo's equally secret promise to accept Lodovico as heir to the duchy of Milan. And although Ferrante may have welcomed Lorenzo's and Virginio Orsini's reconciliation with Giuliano della Rovere ('il Vincula'), which upset Rinaldo and Cardinal Giovan Battista Orsini in the curia, he and Virginio in turn were both upset by Lorenzo's secret agreement with the pope to share half of Niccolò Orsini's new *condotta*. So although Lorenzo's precarious acrobatics may have helped to 'balance power' in Italy, they also contributed to the problems that faced Piero on his return to Rome – and even more so after his father's death.[61]

The moment for Piero's wedding could not have been less auspicious. Not only was the pope, his new *parente*, deeply suspicious of his father, but his mother was dying and her family in Monte Rotondo was in conflict with Virginio, the head of the Bracciano branch of the family. So whereas in early April Virginio had been planning a ceremonious wedding for Alfonsina, with his son Gian Giordano Orsini accompanying the bride *et pompa assai*, now Baccio Ugolini suggested something simpler, the consummation of the marriage at Bracciano and sending the bride 'without so many things'.[62] Planned for Friday 8 May, the wedding took place two days later in order to accommodate Alfonsina and 'some devotion of hers'. The party had been received very honourably in Rome by Franceschetto before going back to Bracciano together with Maddalena.[63] Jacopo Salviati again provides an amused insider's view of the proceedings for the benefit of ser Francesco:

---

[60] Lorenzo to Lanfredini, 30 April 1488, *Lettere* 12, p. 261: 'Pure, a questa parte Piero vi raguaglerà', and n. 14; cf. 439–40 (intro. n.); Lanfredini to Lorenzo, 3 May.

[61] Lorenzo to Lanfredini, 10 and 30 April, *Lettere* 12, pp. 186, 463 and n. 2; Bartolomeo da Bracciano to Virginio Orsini, MAP 40, 234, 31 March. Cf. Lorenzo, *Lettere* 8, pp. viii–xvii, 189, n. 13, 252–5 (254 on Lorenzo's 'acrobazie politiche', cf. Pellegrini, *Congiure di Romagna*, p. 148: 'funambolica tattica').

[62] Ugolini in Bracciano to Lorenzo, 6 April 1488, MAP 40, 246.

[63] Lanfredini to Lorenzo, 10 May 1488, MAP 40, 324; Dovizi to Lorenzo, 13 and 15 May, MAP 56, 25 and 15 (Piero had married on Saturday [9th] and would leave on Monday [11th] but 'qui siamo al buio').

Signor Virginio didn't want Piero on any account to touch her [Alfonsina] until three hours after sunset, and so he didn't. And I can tell you that he wasn't there for the rest of the time. She burst out crying when she went to hear the wedding mass (*la messa del congiunto*), but no squabbling at the bedding ceremony, because of our annoyance at the first outburst.

On going to mass, Alfonsina was accompanied by Virginio's sons, Gian Giordano and Carlo, and on her return by Piero, Giovanni (Serristori) and Jacopo, 'with so many trumpets that the world turned upside down'. To celebrate, all the Orsini were there (except for Rinaldo and the cardinal): Virginio, Organtino (Clarice's brother), Paolo, Virginio's two sons and a bastard son of *cavaliere* Orsino, then the Roman contingent, Franceschetto and Marco Cibo, Girolamo d'Éstouteville, Giorgio di Santa Croce and a lot of other gentlemen. Jacopo also enjoyed reporting a fracas between the notary – who hoped to take the money for saying the mass, leaving only some bread and a bottle of wine behind for the parish – and the parish priest, who beat him to it and took the lot, only to have Virginio step in to adjudicate. Promising to add more on his return to Florence, Jacopo told ser Francesco they were leaving Bracciano the next day and would return via Siena (hoping to receive there some of his letters that they all enjoyed so much).[64]

Approaching Florence in high spirits on 24 May, later than expected, they received the tragic news that Piero's sister Luisa had died unexpectedly two days earlier – perhaps from tuberculosis, like her mother – which cast the wedding party into sudden gloom. Piero had been very anxious for news from home as they travelled to Rome, and after being reassured to hear that Luisa was well, he must have been stricken that their delay had prevented them from seeing her before she died.[65] A ceremony had been planned to greet the newly-weds on their return to honour to the countess and her daughter, for which Lorenzo had returned early from his cure at the baths near Spedaletto – after pressure from Virginio Orsini's secretary to be present for this ceremony, 'which only happens once'.[66] Now Lorenzo prevented the wedding party from entering Florence and sent them to the Medici villa in Poggio a Caiano

---

[64] Salviati to ser Francesco, 11 May 1488, MAP 102, 35: 'per rispecto di certa sua divotione', etc. Cf. Stefano Maldei in Florence to Michelozzi in Spedaletto, 15 May 1488, GC 29, 27, fol. 107.

[65] Salviati in Rome to ser Francesco, 7 May 1488, MAP 102,34 (and that Piero was also concerned about events in Forlì after Riario's murder); the same, 11 May; Maldei to Michelozzi, 13 May, GC 29, 27, fol. 105 ('Luizia è guarita'), cf. 15th. On the party's grief on Luisa's death, Del Lungo, *Florentia*, p. 430.

[66] Lorenzo, *Lettere* 12, intro. n., pp. 289–90; Dovizi to Lorenzo, 15 May 1488, MAP 56, 15. On their dismay at Piero's delay, 'per rispecto di Lorenzo', Maldei to Michelozzi, 16 May, GC 29, 27, fol. 108.

for the brief eight-day period of mourning, 'to save having to reclothe them'.[67]

So instead of being welcomed home with a fitting ceremony, Piero and his bride had to wait in the countryside before being offered an official dinner in the Medici place on Sunday 31 May, to which all the resident ambassadors were invited.[68] It was a quiet affair compared with Franceschetto's joyous *entrée* in June, who had arrived in time to join his bride for the San Giovanni festivities celebrating Florence's patron saint. Even that was not unproblematic, thanks to Franceschetto's difficult character and extravagance. He refused to allow Matteo Franco to accompany Maddalena – his entourage was too large for the Pazzi palace acquired for him from the d'Éstoutevilles – forcing Lorenzo to rent rooms in a nearby palace, and by changing his route to Florence he failed to encounter Piero as planned, forcing Lorenzo with his other sons, Giovanni and Giuliano, to do the honours in his place.[69]

Five days after his entry into Florence, Franceschetto was treated to the *coup de théâtre* celebrating the feast day of the city's patron saint, San Giovanni, in which he took pride of place among all the other distinguished visitors from abroad. On the morning of the 24th itself he was offered hospitality by the Signoria, as well as by Lorenzo's relatives (the Tornabuoni, Rucellai and Lorenzo di Pierfrancesco) and other citizens. By making his offering in his local *gonfalone* 'as a private citizen', he also pleased the Florentines, who accepted him as one of themselves – and so did the crowds of people (including peasants from the countryside) who had flocked to the city for the festival. When asked why they had come, they shouted back, 'We've come to the city to see the son of the Pope!'[70] The contrast with the celebration for Piero and his new bride could not have been more marked. Yet even Franceschetto's welcome remained a civic event that enabled Lorenzo to reciprocate the elaborate ritual with which the pope received his children in Rome, without seeming to overdo it.

At the end of this momentous period, on 11 July, Lorenzo finally emancipated the sixteen-year-old Piero from his control as *pater*

---

[67] G. A. d'Arezzo to Lanfredini in Rome, 25 May 1488, MAP 59, 159 (cf. Del Lungo, *Florentia*, p. 430): 'per non havere a rivestirgle'. According to Guidoni, they initially stayed at Careggi (*Lettere*, ed. Cappelli, 22 May, p. 301), cf. Lorenzo, *Lettere* 12, p. 317, n. 19; Pieraccini, *Stirpe*, I, pp. 231–2.

[68] Guidoni to Ercole, 29 May 1488, *Lettere*, ed. Cappelli, p. 30.

[69] Franco to Piero Dovizi, 6 May 1488, *Lettere*, ed. Frugoni, pp. 88–9, Frosini, 'Honore et utile', pp. 5–6, and Del Lungo, *Florentia*, pp. 429–33; Lorenzo, *Lettere* 12, pp. 425, n. 20; 428–9, nn. 1 and 2; and 462 (intro. n.).

[70] Dovizi to Lanfredini, 26 June 1488, MAP 59, 179, ed. Fabroni, *Laurentii ... Vita*, 2, pp. 386–88; Lorenzo, *Lettere* 12, pp. 460–2.

familias.⁷¹ Scarcely three weeks later Clarice died, supported by her children but not by Lorenzo, who was away in Lucca and then at the baths, preoccupied as ever with political concerns and his own ill health.⁷² The Ferrarese ambassador in Florence did not think her death important enough to report to Ercole until the day of her public requiem, 'according to the custom here', which was held three days after her death and burial 'without any show or ceremony'. Before attending the requiem, to which all the ambassadors were invited, Guidoni and the Milanese ambassador had gone together to the Medici palace on behalf of their rulers to condole with 'Piero, the magnificent Lorenzo's eldest son on the death of his mother'.⁷³ Piero's emancipation and his mother's death together symbolised his rite of passage from boyhood to his future as Lorenzo's heir. His marriage to Alfonsina had apparently launched him on the path to social success following his entry into the princely Roman aristocracy. Even so, he had met with rebuffs – on the occasion of his first meeting with Alfonsina and on their return from Rome, when the happy occasion was marred by Luisa's death, followed by that of his mother. Florence was not Rome and the years that followed would show how difficult it was – as Becchi had said – to combine the roles of prince and citizen.

---

[71] ASF Notarile antecos. 10200, fol. 302r-v, confirmed on 303r: Lorenzo 'emancipavit ... Petrum suum filium'.

[72] Lorenzo to Lanfredini, 30 June and 3 July, *Lettere* 12, pp. 474, 488–9 and n. 3. The pope allowed Maddalena to stay on in Florence but sent Franceschetto to Perugia to suppress an uprising of the faction favoured by the Medici.

[73] Guidoni to Ercole d'Este, 1 August 1488, ed. Cappelli, 'Lettere', pp. 302–3, cf. Kent, *Princely Citizen*, pp. 57–8; Strocchia, 'Death Rites', esp. p. 124.

6   The Choice of Hercules
Between Duty and Pleasure, 1488–1489

The year that followed Piero's and Maddalena's high-ranking marriages in 1488 saw Piero faced with a choice between two different ways of life. On one hand, he had to play his part in the civic life of Florence and learn the political role that he would inherit from Lorenzo. On the other, he had been seduced by his reception in Rome and by the courtly pleasures he had experienced there with Franceschetto and his curial friends. Its impact on him became clear when, at the end of that year, he demanded two of Franceschetto's men to accompany him to Milan for Gian Galeazzo Sforza's wedding, 'because here it's impossible to find men who are their equal'.[1] Like Hercules approaching the crossroads as a young man (according to the well-known tale told by Prodicus), he seemed to be faced by a choice between a rocky uphill path and an easy downhill one.[2]

Florentines were used to visiting royal and ducal courts in Italy as ambassadors, dressing up grandly and behaving as courtiers – as Angelo Acciaiuoli did in Milan, for instance – before casting off their 'masks' and rich apparel in order to return to Florence as 'the men they were before'. Piero had already been to Rome in 1484, but then he had been carefully chaperoned by his great-uncle Giovanni Tornabuoni and his maternal uncle Rinaldo Orsini, his dress strictly monitored by his father to conform to Florentine republican standards. Outside Florence, the Medici remained tainted as 'ignoble merchants', a label that was revived just before Piero's wedding in May, when Ferrante criticised Lodovico Sforza for talking badly of Lorenzo, since it would make him 'return to being a *vile mercatante*'.[3] So his children's triumphant entry into Rome in 1487 as the siblings of the pope's new daughter-in-law transformed their status in Italy. They were met and accompanied into Rome in great splendour, and Piero and Franceschetto were included in the great *entrée* of the

---

[1] Brown, *Florence* (2011), p. 73, n. 29: 'de' simili suoi pari' (22 December 1488).
[2] Mommsen, 'Petrarch and the Story of the Choice of Hercules'.
[3] Piero Alamanni to Lorenzo, 7 May 1488, Lorenzo, *Lettere* 12, p. 433, n. 9.

Venetian ambassador to Rome shortly afterwards. They dined intimately with the pope and visited the Castel Sant'Angelo, and later they were received by the whole Orsini clan. Piero and Jacopo also spent time enjoying themselves with the gambler and womaniser Franceschetto and his friend Girolamo d'Éstouteville.[4] Little wonder he was torn between the desire to be honoured for his new status and fear of being mocked for it. Although in the year after his return from Rome Piero seemed able to balance his duties and pleasures – he made diplomatic visits to Virginio Orsini and the Sforza in Milan and also developed his skills as a sportsman – things came to a head in July 1489 when his lifestyle was challenged by his father's closest colleagues: a choice, they suggested, had to be made.

Piero in Florence and Pisa

To the approval of his intimates, Piero began to be involved in politics in the autumn following Clarice's death in July 1488, when Lorenzo returned to his villa in Spedaletto. In September, he was responsible for seeing that his Orsini cousin Franciotto got paid for his *condotta* and he 'behaved very well' when visiting fra Francesco d'Aragona, sent by Ferrante to get Lorenzo to mediate between him and the pope.[5] Piero's close friends were greatly cheered 'to see him in the public arena' on his frequent visits to the chancery to collect Franciotto's money from the tough but low-born controller of finance, Antonio di Bernardo Dini, who had apparently treated Piero very well, 'and used very loving and suitable words towards him'.[6]

A month later Piero spent a week in Pisa with Alfonsina and his siblings, the ten-year-old Contessina and nine-year-old Giuliano, the two youngest members of his now diminished family *brigata*, after the deaths of his mother and his sister Luisa in the summer. We know he was a member of a hunt of young Florentines called La Ruota, and, like his father, he enjoyed hunting in the countryside around Pisa (where Lorenzo was developing the villas of Agnano and Spedaletto). But this time he – and Alfonsina – had more serious business to do in Pisa as

---

[4] On Franceschetto's womanising and gambling, Lorenzo, *Lettere* 11, pp. 317, n. 16, 374–5, n. 7, Guidi-Bruscoli, '1487 Medici-Cybo Marriage', pp. 73, 76, and Nofri Tornabuoni in Rome to Lorenzo, 13 January 1487 (decoded), MAP 52, 22. On d'Éstouteville, p. 61, n. 33 in this volume.

[5] Dovizi to Lorenzo in Spedaletto, 16 September 1488, MAP 56, 30. On Franciotto and fra Francesco, Lorenzo, *Lettere* 12, pp. 308–9, n. 4, and 398, n. 13.

[6] Dovizi to Lorenzo, 16 September; on Dini, proveditor of the Monte, Guicciardini, *Dialogue*, tr. Brown, p. 72, n. 206.

Lorenzo's emissaries to Virginio Orsini, who was there as captain general of Florence's army protecting the Lunigiana. The day after Piero arrived on 22 October, he visited Virginio to carry out his father's commission 'as well as I knew how', and later in the day Alfonsina, too, visited him to perform the rest of the commission (following Piero's instructions). Apart from discussing his mother-in-law's difficulty in being allowed to leave Naples, which Piero told his father he had dealt with 'dexterously in the way you told me to', the main business concerned Virginio's response to the letter Lorenzo had sent him on 6 October and his fear that Lorenzo's diplomatic acrobatics since the summer would leave both Ferrante and himself, as his great constable, dangerously exposed.[7] After reading the letter from Lorenzo that Piero brought him, Virginio told Piero that he wanted Lorenzo to get closer to Ferrante as protection against Lodovico Sforza, to which Piero responded firmly that he didn't think it was up to Lorenzo to act, since he was doing (and had done) everything to demonstrate his loyalty towards Ferrante. Virginio replied he knew that very well, but 'these are people who need to be served at their convenience and according to their own way of doing things'; when Piero was silent, Virginio continued by saying that the king would curse God at hearing the thing hadn't succeeded – perhaps referring to Lorenzo's failure to reestablish the old alliance between Naples, Florence and Milan.[8]

Piero's visit to Virginio touched obliquely on several issues that Lorenzo was juggling with at the time, especially concerning Naples and Genoa. Ever since the crisis precipitated by the murders in the Romagna in the summer, Lorenzo had been playing a dangerous game by deceptively supporting rival alliances, the old Triple Alliance with Naples and Milan, and a new secret alliance with Venice and the pope – with the wild card, Lodovico Sforza, like Lorenzo, moving between both but kept in check by Lorenzo's secret promise to protect his position as ruler of Milan in return for Lodovico's help against Genoa.[9] So Piero's meeting with Virginio throws interesting light on some of the tensions in the delicate diplomatic network in which his father was enmeshed,

---

[7] Piero to Lorenzo, 23 October 1488, MAP 50, 12 (autogr.): 'el meglio che io seppi', 'nel modo che voi dicesti destramente'. In his letter of 6 October, Lorenzo had sought Virginio's opinion about a recent letter from Naples (which he enclosed) and thanked him for his advice concerning 'le cose della contes<s>a', in Lorenzo, *Lettere* 13, forthcoming.

[8] Piero to Lorenzo, 23 October: 'bisogna servire a loro posta et a loro modo'. Other topics concerned Genoa and Milan.

[9] Pellegrini, *Congiure di Romagna*, pp. 148 ('una fragilissima, funambolica tattica dell'*appeasement*'), 171, esp. 160–1; cf. Lorenzo, *Lettere* 12, pp. xv–xvii and 344–7, 353, n. 1, and on Genoa 208–9, nn. 23, 24; also *Lettere* 13, forthcoming (Lorenzo to Lanfredini, 31 October, 2 November 1488).

especially concerning his and Virginio's relationship with Ferrante, and Lodovico's role in Genoa and the Lunigiana at this time, all of which would be highlighted when Piero visited Milan for Duke Gian Galeazzo's marriage to Isabella of Aragon in January 1489.

The following month saw Piero back in Florence, asking Francesco Gonzaga for a gift of some peregrine falcons, which he said would be as welcome to him as two of Francesco's best horses (for which the Gonzaga stables were renowned). On receiving only one moulted falcon, Piero intrepidly asked for one of the two falcons Gonzaga's man had just received in Florence, which would make him indebted to him for 'the whole of my life, because of my dedicated pursuit and love of hawking'.[10] As well as interchanging falcons and horses, the Gonzaga were also closely involved with the Medici as *condottieri* and art collectors. A few weeks earlier Giovanni Tornabuoni had returned to the family from the bank all the cameos held as surety for the deceased cardinal Francesco's large debts, but the Medici still held some of the late cardinal's objects (from which Piero tried to raise money when in exile).[11] At this time he was asked by the Bolognese humanist Giovanni Sabbadino degli Arienti to free from prison Marco Vespucci, whose father had been involved in the Pazzi conspiracy. His letter, sent via Benedetto Dei, suggests that Piero already formed part of the patronage network of the northern courts.[12]

In the middle of the following month, Piero and three of Florence's leading citizens (Jacopo Guicciardini, Pierfilippo Pandolfini and Pagolantonio Soderini) were elected by the Otto di Pratica to welcome Isabella of Aragon in their name when she arrived in Livorno and Pisa en route to her marriage in Milan – and 'to keep them company', Alfonsina and Lucrezia (by now married to Jacopo Salviati) were to accompany them.[13] Then Piero received an invitation to attend Isabella's marriage in Milan, which was regarded as an even greater honour, especially in view of Lodovico Sforza's recent hostility towards Lorenzo and Florence. As Piero Dovizi told Niccolò Michelozzi (who was in Perugia), the invitation 'seems to us full of love and faith and very contrary to the outcry you are

---

[10] Piero to Francesco Gonzaga, 3 and 21 November, Mantua AS, Busta 1085, 245 and 246; Gonzaga's reply on 11 November is ed. Vatovec, 'Lorenzo il Magnifico e i Gonzaga', doc. 2, p. 94.

[11] Chambers, *A Renaissance Cardinal*, pp. 126–7, and n. 170 citing Lorenzo to Lanfredini, 14 October 1488; on Lorenzo in Mantua, Kent, *Lorenzo de' Medici*, p. 35.

[12] Degli Arienti in Bologna to Dei in Florence, 23 November 1488, *Letters*, ed. James, pp. 108–9 (on Arienti and Dei, 39–47) on Piero Vespucci, now a high-ranking official in Lombardy, Gentile, 'Tuscans and Lombards', pp. 106–10.

[13] Otto di Pratica, Delib, Partiti, Condotte e Stanziamenti, 2, fol. 58r (18 December 1488); Jacopo Salviati to Michelozzi in Perugia, 20 December 1488, GC 29, 58, fol. 1v.

hearing there, which you can refute'. So Piero went north to Milan instead of to Livorno and Pisa, travelling not with Alfonsina but with two young friends, Alessandro Nasi and Pierantonio Carnesecchi.[14]

When Dovizi next wrote to Michelozzi on 31 December, he said Alfonsina and Piero's sister Lucrezia had already set off for Pisa and Livorno, now accompanied by Giovanni (di Pierfrancesco de' Medici) and Franciotto Orsini, although because of Isabella's delay they were still in Florence ten days later.[15] Piero, too, set off later than planned, on 7 January, with his friends and ser Stefano Maldei from Castrocaro as his secretary, who was evidently a rising star in the competitive secretarial world.[16] Dovizi was sorry Michelozzi was not back in Florence in time to be chosen instead, since he would have been better, as an old hand in Milan, than the rising star, and he would have enjoyed this hardship, 'if hardship it is, since to me it seems, and would seem, like going to paradise' (Dovizi, unlike the other secretaries, was rooted in Florence throughout the Medici years, apart from visits to the baths with Lorenzo and his solo visit to Milan in July–August 1493).[17]

Thanks to his absence in Milan, Piero was able to avoid the embarrassment suffered by his colleagues of having to investigate the misconduct of Virginio Orsini's men in Pisa (they were accused of abducting a young girl and stealing some money), as well as the aftermath of a political scandal in Florence over the sacking of two members of the colleges for hunting with Piero's Ruota hunt after Christmas.[18] Delayed by bad weather in Gaeta and Livorno, Isabella and her very large entourage were finally welcomed in Pisa in mid-January, with 'great honour and at immeasurable expense', by the ambassadors and the youthful Medici party. Alfonsina, Lucrezia and Giovanni di Pierfrancesco were now joined by Piero's siblings Giuliano and Contessina, who were perhaps

---

[14] Dovizi to Michelozzi in Perugia, 23 [December 1488] (recd. 25th), GC 29, 62, fol. 42r: 'quelle vociferationi'. In 1485 the duke of Mantua had presented Piero and his friends wih 'tre belli pugnali' (Jacopo Acciaiuoli to Francesco Gonzaga, 26 September 1485, ed. Vatovec, 'Lorenzo de' Medici e i Gonzaga', doc. 8, p. 97). Their visit to Rome is discussed in ch. 10

[15] Dovizi to Michelozzi, 31 December 1488, GC 29, 62, fol. 45r, and 10 January 1489, GC 29, 64, fol. 47r.

[16] The same, 10 January 1489, and 31 December: 'et qui sapete come possa solo satisfare'. On Maldei, Lorenzo, *Lettere* 16, p. 58, n. 1, citing Verde, *Studio* 3, 1, pp. 477–8; Parenti, *Storia* 2, p. 38.

[17] Dovizi to Michelozzi, 31 December: 'vegho che non vi sarebbe suto ingrata questa fatica, se fatica è, benché a me paia et parebbe ire in paradyso', etc.

[18] Otto di Pratica to Guicciardini, Pandolfini and Soderini, 'legatis Pisis', 2 and 5 January 1489, Otto Missive 11, fols. 171r–v, 172v–173v (to Livorno); cf. Guicciardini, *Storie fiorentine*, pp. 69–70; Cambi, *Istorie*, pp. 38–47, esp. 40 and 44; and Brown, 'Between the Palace and the Piazza', pp. 39–41.

deemed more suitable companions for the young Isabella on her tour of the city (at her request) than their sickly father Lorenzo (who was in fact then in Pisa with Poliziano to regain his health) or the two young clerics Giovanni and Giulio, who remained at home with Dovizi until Lorenzo's return on 22 January.[19]

Piero in Milan

It was after receiving his invitation to attend Gian Galeazzo's wedding that Piero requested two of Franceschetto's retainers to accompany him to Milan because no one was good enough in Florence. Although Lorenzo had wanted Piero to accompany Isabella to Milan, her delayed arrival changed their plans and Piero instead travelled overland via Fivizzano in the Lunigiana (within Florentine territory), whereas Isabella travelled from Pisa to Genoa, presumably by sea and on to Tortona on 25 January, where she was awaited by the Sforza and Piero. Until two days before his arrival in Milan on 17 January, no one knew where Piero was – to Lodovico's dismay, since he had wanted to honour his arrival by meeting him perhaps even as far away as Parma. It was then decided that Piero would be met by two ducal chamberlains at Lodi, and after lunching en route he would be received honourably on entering Milan by twelve gentlemen (as well as by the Florentine ambassador Piero Alamanni) and taken to stay in the Sforza castle. According to Dovizi, Florence was sending a wedding present of eighty yards of brocade but no new ambassadors (the Milanese had told the resident ambassador that 'the usual things' were to be sent), in this way making it clear that Piero was there by invitation of the Sforza and not as Florence's special envoy.[20]

As a result, Piero's period in Milan shows him juggling his private activities as the Sforza's guest with his more public engagements as his father's representative. Having failed to communicate with either Lorenzo or Lodovico en route for want of a courier, Piero left his secretary to describe to Lorenzo their arrival on the 17th 'with the greatest honour', and wrote himself to his father about his meeting with the ambassador Alamanni. Since he was awaiting them at the gate,

---

[19] Landucci, *Diario*, p. 56; Dovizi to Lorenzo, 22 January 1489, GC 29, 62, fol. 49v.
[20] Piero Alamanni to Lorenzo, 10 January 1489, MAP 59, 99, fol. 107 biš: 'Credo che si farà per il S. Lodovico *quanto desiderate* [decoded] verso Piero', etc.; the same, 14 and 15 January, MAP 26, 512 and 40, 197; Dovizi, 10 January (fol. 47r). On Alamanni, Lorenzo, *Lettere* 10, p. 35 (intro. n.) and p. 157 and n. 33 in this volume.

I couldn't follow your instructions to go at once to find him secretly since he didn't think it appropriate, wanting me instead to visit him openly today, which I did to obey you and him.

Alamanni approved his commission, and with his permission Piero decided to accept Lodovico's and Duke Gian Galeazzo's invitation to go with them to Tortona to meet the bride, warning his father that it would be difficult to write from there without any couriers, although he would 'force himself' to do his duty if necessary.[21]

This laconic letter typifies Piero's approach to his ill-defined duties in Milan. That Lorenzo wanted Piero's initial meeting with the ambassador Alamanni to be secret suggests he had a private diplomatic agenda for Piero in Milan that Alamanni perhaps discouraged. Since bad weather had aborted an invitation to go hunting with Lodovico, Piero had his first audience with him at court on 22 January, in the company of the young duke, Gian Galeazzo, messer Galeotto della Mirandola and signor Alessandro Sforza, Lodovico's illegitimate brother. After Piero had presented his credential letters and explained that his embassy was to acknowledge their 'ancient bonds of servitude', it was Lodovico who responded by saying he had invited Piero to the wedding to show that he loved Lorenzo and Piero more than any of his friends and relations. Then, turning to Gian Galeazzo (who had simply welcomed Piero as a brother), Lodovico urged him to get on well with the Florentines, especially Lorenzo and Piero, since past events had shown Florence to be the most stable and natural investment they could have; certainly, Milan had also done something to help Florence, but if goodwill and force were needed to help the republic, now was the moment when nothing was lacking – and if anything should happen, despite God's protection, the whole of Italy would know that this lord valued Florence as much as his own state. Responding in turn to this grandiose – and in the event deceptive – offer of help, Piero neatly picked up Lodovico's reference to his 'goodwill and force' by saying that 'if this lord did not lack goodwill and force, then Florence too did not lack hope'.[22]

Piero told his father, when writing to him the following day, that Lodovico 'wanted you as his brother and me as his son', noting that he had said this not to win Piero's favour but for its effect on others, and that Lodovico didn't want to take a step without him and was always accompanied by 'Terzago [his secretary] or by gentlemen'. Since Piero had

---

[21] Piero in Milan to Lorenzo, 18 January 1489, MAP 50, 14 (autogr.), Brown, *Florence* (2011), p. 75, n. 33.
[22] Maldei to Lorenzo, 22 January, MAP 50, 23, Brown, *Florence* (2011), p. 74, n. 31. See also the following note.

been unable to complete his commission on the 22nd – because Lodovico had wanted to 'talk about horses and other pleasant matters' before departing for lunch – he returned the next day to discuss the rest of his commission. Here it is interesting to see Piero transmitting Lodovico's responses to Lorenzo without knowing enough to be able to pursue them, referring, for example, to:

> the – I don't know what – restitution and the other matters about which I am not informed, but [Lodovico] told me, "I give you my word that I will at any rate settle them, and write that to Lorenzo", so I have told you exactly the words he used to me about this matter. [23]

Concerning the pope, Piero said Lodovico was happy for Lorenzo to try everything and trusted him, knowing that Lorenzo and the pope 'would skilfully govern and rule the whole of Italy as long as you were both friends'. And because Alamanni had told Lodovico he was doing something about 'the business of the Orsini', Piero would leave that until his return to Milan and had nothing more to report for now. As for the duke, he had tried his best to carry out Lorenzo's commission, but Gian Galeazzo had said nothing in his reply that he could understand. Annibale Bentivoglio wanted to visit him but hadn't 'taken it at all badly' that Piero had beaten him to it by meeting him as he returned from Genoa. Lorenzo's more recent commission to see Guidantonio Arcimboldo and Belpiatto he would try to carry out on returning to Milan.[24]

The letter suggests Piero had meticulously carried out his father's instructions, even if without great enthusiasm. Ser Stefano told Lorenzo that on leaving Piero's first public audience, Galeotto della Mirandola stopped by with a message for Lorenzo that his son was becoming 'more than mature' and if – as he'd heard it said – Pierfrancesco's father used to say that he'd pay 4000 ducats not to be recognised in Italy, Piero's father should pay 8000 ducats to ensure Piero was recognised all over Italy, so that everyone could know, considering his age, how admirable he was.[25] Two days later ser Stefano noted that in all the ceremonies Lodovico had paid more attention to Piero than to all the others, always wanting him to be treated as an equal of the duke and himself, and offering to show him, after the others had left, 'the castle in Milan and perhaps Pavia', as well as

---

[23] Piero in Tortona to Lorenzo, 23 January 1489, MAP 50, 16, fol. 17r-v (autogr.): 'si era indugiata non so che restituzione et le altre pratiche di che non sono informato ... Sichè vi ho riferite le parole apunto che e' mi dixe circa questo'.
[24] Ibid., fol. 17v: 'non lo habbi havuto punto per male'.
[25] Maldei to Lorenzo, 22 January: 'più che vechio'.

all his hunts in Pavia and Vigevano.[26] And although Alamanni (who was knighted on this occasion) was more measured in his praise of Piero than ser Stefano, even he reported that Piero was getting better all the time and that it seemed a marvel to the Lombards, and even to the ambassadors, that for someone as young as he was, 'his behaviour and his replies are so good and that he argues so well about everything'.[27]

Despite this, Piero was anxious to return home. In a much shorter letter to ser Piero Dovizi, he asked to be excused for not writing more since he had just written at such length to Lorenzo that he had 'worn out his finger', but he wanted to ask for two favours: first, that Dovizi write him a letter he could use as an excuse not to stay on after the celebrations, 'since every hour seems like a thousand years'; and second, to see that they returned via Pontremoli to avoid having their necks broken by 'those drunkards' (in Fivizzano), for if they returned the way they had come, they would never make it home to see them again – a plea ser Stefano repeated in asking Lorenzo to think carefully about their return. Annibale Bentivoglio had twice asked Piero to return via Bologna, and any route but the one they took going to Milan, he wrote, 'would seem easy'. The words with which Piero then signed his letter to Dovizi – 'to you, my good and beautiful and useful ser Piero, I am totally yours' – presage his later dependent and exploitative relationship with his father's secretary.[28]

The encounter with Isabella finally took place on 25 January, when 'in the greatest triumph and pomp' she went to meet the duke, who looked like a St. George in his short robe of white damask, his most beautiful necklace and no *corsiere*: 'it was a splendid sight'. However, ser Stefano was as keen as Jacopo Salviati had been to read as an omen the initial meeting of young betrotheds, and on this occasion it appeared that the signs were not good: the duke had intimated that the duchess didn't greatly please him, and on dismounting, he didn't want to touch her, whether from embarrassment or for some other reason.[29] They were all to meet up again for the nuptial mass in Milan the following week (Piero going to Vigevano, where 'no one for twenty-five years had been made

---

[26] Maldei in Tortona to Lorenzo, 25 January 1489, MAP 50, 24: 'ha tenuto più conto di Piero solo che di tucti li altri'.
[27] Alamanni to Lorenzo, 31 January 1489, MAP 59, 110, Brown, *Florence* (2011), pp. 74–5, n. 32.
[28] Piero to Dovizi, 23 January 1489, MAP 124, 15, Brown, *Florence* (2011), pp. 75–6 and n. 35; Maldei to Lorenzo, 25 and 27 January, MAP 50: 24, 25.
[29] Maldei in Vigevano to Lorenzo, 25 January 1489, MAP 50, 24: 'che pareva uno San Giorgio ... qualche segno che la Duchessa non li sia molto piaciuta et ... non l'à voluto a faticha toccare, non so se el viene d vergogna o pure da altro.'

such a fuss of'), and then the duke would go to Pavia and get rid of Isabella's mother and her huge entourage that was not at all popular in Milan.[30] In the event, ser Stefano was overwhelmed by the wedding in Milan on 2 February: the grandeur of Isabella's entry on the 1st, her beauty and extravagant adornment, the white damask *baldachino* in which she and Gian Galeazzo were borne to the cathedral by forty doctors wearing scarlet silk gowns and berets, the ceremony itself and the singing, then the knighting of the Florentine ambassador Alamanni and the Milanese secretary Bartolomeo Calchi, and the compensatory gift to Piero of a rich gown of gold brocade. Despite the immense crowds, there was no whiff of trouble thanks to the shut-off access points, the armed soldiers and the care taken to disarm the populace, including the Florentines, who were used to carrying arms everywhere.[31]

Although Piero could not hope to rival the duke with his diamonds and huge pearls, ser Stefano loyally thought Piero's gown with the family emblem of the *broncone* 'beat everyone else's', and the following day everyone wanted to see and admire it. Before the wedding, Lodovico had shown Piero his vases and given him an enamelled historiated silver cup that by connoisseurs was considered beautiful, 'worth more than a hundred ducats', and he was so admired and honoured by everyone that he was becoming the paragon of all the others.[32] Apologising for this 'confused and disordered letter', written hurriedly before going riding with Piero, ser Stefano promised Lorenzo to fill it out at greater leisure on his return home. It nevertheless provides a revealing picture of the courtly world Piero had reentered and yet was anxious to leave, in order to return home to his own, then pregnant, bride, to whom he had sent special greetings in his long letter to his father on 23 January.[33]

Before he left Milan, Piero had one more meeting with Lodovico and Alamanni about Genoa, the pope and Virginio Orsini, which reinforces this picture of Piero as a competent if unenthusiastic stand-in for Lorenzo.[34] Alamanni had hoped Piero would initiate this meeting

---

[30] The same, 27 January 1489, MAP 50, 25; the same, 25 January, 'tucti male visti, *pro reddere vices* di quello è suto facto alli loro a Napoli'.

[31] The same, 2 February 1489, MAP 50, 27, fol. 29v: 'per farle porre giù a ogni persona, dalli nostri in fuori che sempre l'hanno portate per tucto'.

[32] Ibid., fol. 29 bis^r; the same, 1 February, MAP 50, 26, fol. 28r ('una taza d'argento smaltata con arte historya et da questi intendenti è tenuta bella'), Bullard, *Lorenzo*, pp. 53–4, n. 36.

[33] Dovizi to Michelozzi, 14 February 1489, GC 29, 62, fol. 50: 'Alfonsina continua nella grosseza.'

[34] Alamanni to Lorenzo, 10 February 1489, MAP 50, 148, fol. 151 bis; on the still-unpaid dowry, Piero's special concern, Lorenzo to Lanfredini, 23 June, *Lettere* 15, p. 292 and n. 4 (and *Lettere* 12, pp. 192–3, n. 22, 206, n. 16 , 275, n. 11).

himself, but when nothing happened he organised it with Piero in attendance. If, as he told Lorenzo, 'your Piero is improving all the time as he gains experience', he was at same time becoming spoilt by the unbounded admiration of Lodovico and the Milanese, as well as all the ambassadors in Milan. Lodovico liked to say that he had never seen two sons resemble their fathers more than messer Annibale and Piero, but he showed his preference by seating Piero beside himself on a bench with Gian Galeazzo Sforza and the papal, Venetian, Florentine and Ferrarese ambassadors, while Annibale sat with Galeotto della Mirandola and Ridolfo Gonzaga. For Alamanni, this meant that if Lodovico became intimate with the Florentines, as he seemed to be doing (through Piero), Giovanni Bentivoglio, Annibale's father, would also revert to his former friendship with Florence before the events in Forlì and Faenza.[35] Towards the end of January Lorenzo told his ambassador in Rome, Giovanni Lanfredini – despite wishing that Lanfredini had heard it from others, not himself – that Lodovico had bestowed such honour and affection on 'my Piero', 'it seems excessive'.[36]

As well as consolidating the Medici's old friendship with Lodovico and the Bentivoglio, the other, unstated achievement of Piero's visit to Milan may have been the support he gave indirectly to his brother's cardinalate, which was becoming pressing at the time – needing 'profit rather than loss', as Dovizi put it, especially from cardinals like Ascanio Sforza and Giovan Battista Orsini.[37] A month before Giovanni's youthful appointment as a cardinal became known, Lanfredini had suggested that a message should be sent to Milan in secret, to 'your Piero or the ambassador, better your Piero', to forewarn Lodovico that Giovanni's cardinalate was – as ser Piero put it – entirely due to Ascanio's efforts.[38] Whether or not Piero received this message before leaving (he arrived home on 18 February), he was then proposed as an appropriate emissary to Rome to thank the pope, 'now that the thing is here', as Lorenzo wrote to Lanfredini on 14 March.[39] However, the pope thought this would be over-celebrating what was meant to be a secret, and although in early

---

[35] Alamanni to Lorenzo, 31 January 1489, MAP 59, 11, fol. 120v, cf. Pellegrini, *Congiure*, esp. pp. 143–71. On Lodovico's comment, Brown, *Florence* (2011), p. 77.

[36] Lorenzo to Lanfredini in Rome, 26 January 1489, MAP 59, 104, fol. 113r: 'ho più caro le intendiate da altri che da me'.

[37] Dovizi to Michelozzi, 22 January 1489, GC 29, 62, fol. 49r: 'più tosto guadagno che perdita'.

[38] Lanfredini to Lorenzo, 11 February 1489 and Dovizi to Michelozzi, 10 March 1489, Brown, *Florence* (2011), pp. 77–8, n. 40 (also citing Pellegrini and Picotti).

[39] On Piero's return, Dovizi to Michelozzi, 15, 19 February 1489, GC 29, 62, fols. 50r, 51r; Lorenzo to Lanfredini, 14 March 1489, *Lettere* 15, p. 7 and n. 8 ('poi che la cosa è qui'); cf. Dovizi to Michelozzi in Pitigliano, same day, GC 29, 62, fol. 55r.

April Lorenzo was still talking about sending Piero, or even visiting Rome himself in order to help prepare the bull, five days later Piero's trip was off and Giovanni was later sent to Rome instead.[40]

Once again events had conspired to prevent Piero from enjoying the limelight in Rome as in Florence, but since he had been anxious to return home to his pregnant wife, he was perhaps pleased on this occasion to be able to remain in Florence with 'Madonna, madonna', who 'never puts on weight!' (as Dovizi described Alfonsina to Michelozzi at the beginning of March).[41] We know that in April the son of Count Niccolò Orsini of Pitigliano stayed *en famille* with Piero, Giovanni and Giuliano in the Medici palace, as a hostage for the return of the Castle of Monteaguto the Orsini had taken from the Sienese. For once, Lorenzo was in Florence until mid-July, apart from a brief visit to Pisa in April to discuss Virginio Orsini's wish to terminate his *condotta* with Florence.[42] Preoccupied with the problem of replacing both Virginio and Niccolò with other military leaders without offending the pope, Lodovico or Ferrante, Lorenzo seems to have left Piero free to pursue his own interests, which included organising a new play to celebrate Pentecost, gaming with new sparrowhawks and partridges from Faenza, using his influence to release some cherrywood (*corniuole*) from the customs for Caradosso (an engraver travelling to Hungary), sending the present of a cloak and hose for Annibale Bentivoglio's newborn son, entertaining (with his brother Giuliano) Paolo Orsini on Lorenzo's behalf and especially preparing for his forthcoming joust – a list that was insufficient for a person of Piero's age and intelligence, according to leading members of the regime, who at the end of July brought the simmering crisis of Piero's lifestyle to a head.[43]

Piero at the Crossroads

The summer had begun with Piero organising a new play, the *Festa del miracolo dello Spirito Santo*, to be performed in the Carmine to celebrate Pentecost, using the equipment of the company of Sant. Agnese. He had been admitted as a member of the company in January 1488 (though

---

[40] Dovizi to Michelozzi, 19 March 1489, ibid., fol. 57v, Lorenzo to Lanfredini, 4 April, *Lettere* 15, p. 55.

[41] The same, 6 March 1489, GC 29, 62, fol. 53r: 'Madonna, Madonna, non fa mai grossa' (she was then scarcely three months pregnant, cf. n. 33 in this chapter).

[42] Lorenzo to Michelozzi, 4 April 1489, *Lettere* 15, pp. 60–1 and n. 3; to Lanfredini,14 April, pp. 84–5 (intro. n.) and viii–x.

[43] Maldei in Florence to Michelozzi in Spedaletto, 21, 22, 25, 29 July, GC 29, 27, fols. 113–15, 111, n. 51 in this chapter; Dovizi in Florence to Lorenzo, 24 July, CS I, 3, fol. 138r. On Paolo, Lorenzo, *Lettere* 15, pp. 329, n. 13, 338, n. 13.

underage) and now he wanted to use the Carmine equipment – its castle of Jerusalem, Mount of Olives, Heaven and Paradise – for the Pentecost play traditionally held in S. Spirito before its destruction by fire in 1471.[44] According to Tribaldo de' Rossi, 'it was done at the wish of the young lad Piero di Lorenzo de' Medici and it pleased no one, or not most people' – and when he went on to allude to the 'fine joust held in the Piazza of Santa Croce on 31 August', he failed to mention that it, too, had been organised by Piero.[45] Piero had invited Galeazzo Sanseverino to his joust when in Milan at the beginning of the year. Galeazzo promised to come if Piero was jousting too, so in July Piero began to prepare himself by riding a horse belonging to his cousin Giovanni di Pierfrancesco. 'He broke two lances on the wall', ser Stefano reported; 'he's good on a horse and shows signs of being quite skilled and experienced'; provided the horse could withstand blows, things couldn't be better, and the two beautiful steeds Galeazzo Sanseverino had sent would be tried out every day to see how good they were. The armed men already arriving in Florence were offered stabling and fodder by the government but had to provide the rest themselves, and by early August 'these jousters of Piero's are beginning to delight the people', Dovizi told Lorenzo; 'twice they have made a try and broken several lances quite well'.[46]

Jousting had long been a popular sport in Florence to celebrate feast days, like the one held shortly before Piero's, on 20 August, to celebrate the feast of San Bernardo, with funds contributed by the communal Monte. Even Lorenzo had turned out to watch it, on horseback because of the crippling pain in his feet that had impeded his writing and talking for some days – despite 'the feet being far removed from the tongue' (he wittily wrote).[47] Piero's joust was to be more elitist than popular, however. For although he had initially planned to hold it on the Feast of San Bartolomeo on 24 August, the day when the confraternity traditionally celebrated the feast day with a play in the Piazza of Santa Croce, it was postponed until the end of the month to allow certain important

---

[44] Newbigin, *Feste d'Oltrarno*, I, pp. 147, 151, 206 (summarising the play, published by Libri, 1485–93), 2, pp. 652–3 (appendix); Newbigin, 'Piety and Politics', p. 26 and nn. 24–7.

[45] Rossi, *Ricordanze*, p. 276; Newbigin, *Piety and Politics*, p. 27, n. 28; recorded among events in 1491–92, the comment may reflect his later view of Piero.

[46] Maldei to Michelozzi in Pisa, 'o dove fussi', 29 July 1489, fol. 111v; Alamanni, postscript to Dovizi, 22 July 1489, MAP 50, 156, fol. 160 ter^r; Dovizi to Lorenzo, 3 August 1489, MAP 56, 12.

[47] Lorenzo to Lanfredini in Rome, 20 August 1489, *Lettere* 15, pp. 397, 404 ('in frecta, perché siamo su una giostra').

people to participate, like Franceschetto Cibo and Annibale Bentivoglio. Drawn by the rich prizes as well as by the pope's son, the joust was clearly intended to be a great success.[48]

There was nothing remarkable, either, about Piero's other summer pastime, hunting and hawking in the countryside – except (as with the joust) for its timing. For he left to try out some new sparrowhawks in Careggi on the very day that his siblings had gathered in the Medici palace to dine together, perhaps to commemorate Clarice's death before the boys left for the countryside. The ten-year-old Contessina had been recalled from a visit to her future in-laws, the Ridolfi, in order to keep the pregnant Alfonsina company. She was evidently unhappy to do this on her own, and after her brothers and cousin left to escape the heat in Passignano and Coltibuono, she asked the secretary ser Stefano 'a hundred times' when Lorenzo was returning and then sent for Giuliano to come and have supper with her.[49] Lorenzo promised his 'dear little Contessina' (*Contessinuccia mia*), to return soon, and in the meantime urged her to spoil Alfonsina and 'the [as yet unborn] baby'.[50] Perhaps it was a woman's job to keep the pregnant Alfonsina company, but Lorenzo clearly thought his younger sons and nephew should have helped – if not her husband Piero, who was busy not only with his sparrowhawks but also duly honouring Florence's *condottiere* (his relation by marriage), Paolo Orsini, in Florence and Careggi.[51]

However, Piero's activities were becoming a cause for concern to the ruling elite during Lorenzo's absence in Spedaletto. On 24 July, two of the regime's most respected members, Jacopo Guicciardini and Pierfilippo Pandolfini, summoned his secretary Piero Dovizi to meet them in the piazza. There they told him that for some time they and other friends of Lorenzo had been discussing Piero, either together or separately, and their message to Lorenzo was, in Dovizi's words:

since your Piero is now a man, so to speak, as he is about to have children and is singularly intelligent, they thought it would be extremely necessary and useful – to the city, to Piero, and to themselves, for the public good and theirs, and to make Piero fully competent – that you should begin to give him reputation and involve him in some important affair, no matter what, that would give him

---

[48] Ibid., pp. 395–6 (intro. n.), 404, n. 20, and pp. 117–18 in this volume.
[49] Maldei to Michelozzi in Spedaletto, 21 and 22 July, 1489, fols. 113, 114.
[50] Lorenzo in Spedaletto to Contessina, 31 July 1489, *Lettere* 15, pp. 360–1. The baby (Clarice), born on 14 September (n. 56 in this chapter), was not the 'unnamed son ... born in mid 1489' referred to by Tomas (*Medici Women*, p. 119, n. 21).
[51] Maldei to Michelozzi in Spedaletto, GC 29, 27, fols. 113–15 (21–25 July 1489) and Fusco-Corti, *Lorenzo de' Medici*, p. 312 (doc. 127).

authority and credit, and let him join them in their secret consultations and get involved in their business affairs, which produce all the above benefits and especially the security of their regime in every eventuality.

After Lorenzo's departure for the country a week earlier, they had debated whether to write to him about their concern or await his return; and since Lorenzo was now not returning for some days, they finally decided that Dovizi should write to him, and if Lorenzo agreed, he could send Piero some commission and they could discuss the matter with other close friends, to whom, apart from messer Angelo (Niccolini), they hadn't yet mentioned it, since they wanted to be sure it was well founded and that Piero would be happy to go ahead. They could not have spoken more effectively or lovingly, Dovizi concluded, nor with words of greater tenderness, for which he thanked them as Lorenzo's servant.[52]

When Dovizi met Pierfilippo Pandolfini three days later about other business, he found Pierfilippo even more convinced that Piero should work with the leading citizens. He had not yet talked to Jacopo Guicciardini, who was with some other leading citizens at 'the Mammola' (a festive company associated with Ficino that included Lorenzo, among others).[53] A day after Jacopo's return, on 31 July, Dovizi duly reported that Jacopo and Pierfilippo had summoned a meeting in the latter's house, where 'what they thought about the matter of Piero caused by Lorenzo's absence was discussed very skilfully':

And having seen Piero in these days with nothing to do, and appearing in public so idle for his age, presence and intelligence, it seemed their duty to record that now if ever it would be very useful to give him some occupation, which they not only encouraged but pressed and importuned you to do.

Jacopo in particular was very willing to take this on, for he had done the same with Piero's father Lorenzo, with great success because he had begun early, and now he wanted to do the same for Piero, who showed great promise – saying, Dovizi added, many things in his praise. The others agreed, and arguing to and fro they saw only two disadvantages: one, the responsibility involved; the other, removing Piero from his pleasures, if not totally then at least partially. After two hours of discussion, during which they admitted their status in the city depended – as much as Lorenzo's and his descendants' did – on the Medici's public and

---

[52] Dovizi to Lorenzo, 24 July 1489, CS I, 3, fol. 138v, Rubinstein, *Government*, p. 265 (that in view of subsequent meetings, Lorenzo must have given his consent).
[53] The same, 27 July, MAP 56, 35; on the Mammola, Comanducci, 'B. R. e l' "Accademia Neoplatonica"', pp. 236–9.

private morality and lifestyle, they agreed they should urge Lorenzo to let them introduce Piero to all their private secrets and do everything to enhance his reputation and authority. Afterwards, both Pandolfini and messer Agnolo confirmed how important they thought this was. So Dovizi concluded his letter by telling Lorenzo that it was now up to him: 'with your honour you can and should, in my opinion, honour your son'.[54]

These letters dramatically illustrate the crux of Piero's situation: he was clever ('of singular intelligence') but idle. But instead of the choice of which path to follow lying with Piero, or his father, it was the ruling elite who took the decision into their own hands, in order to protect themselves and the regime. This suggests Lorenzo may have been responsible for the paradoxical situation in which, far from it being him pressing his competitive peers and elders to accept Piero as his successor, it was they who were pressing the reluctant father to accept his son in this role. Piero's own laconic distancing of himself from the political fray contributed to this crisis within the elite, who may have underestimated the second drawback: removing him from his pleasures. For the following year he was still to be found playing football in the street, and in 1493 he spent two days on end playing 'with a wretched Spaniard, who won from him perhaps fifty ducats'.[55]

Nevertheless, the elder statesmen, and especially Jacopo Guicciardini, did succeed in getting Piero to play a fuller role in politics, especially during Lorenzo's prolonged absence from Florence at the baths the following year, when we will see him increasingly acting as his father's deputy. Before then, Piero became not only a father but also an uncle, when the birth of his daughter Clarice ('la Cice') on 14 September was followed by that of his sister Maddalena's daughter in mid-December. After his second granddaughter was born, Lorenzo 'modestly but lovingly' reminded Pope Innocent what he (the pope) had said after la Cice's birth two months earlier – that 'such births to princes are usually happy and fortunate'. Yet he himself chided Maddalena's midwife two days later for not having brought forth 'a male child'.[56] Was he worried

---

[54] Dovizi to Lorenzo, 31 July 1489, MAP 56, 37r-v; cf. Picotti, *Giovinezza*, pp. 392–3, n. 33.
[55] Alessandro Alessandri to Piero, 4 May 1490, MAP 18, 15 and p. 175, n. 29 in this volume.
[56] Lorenzo to Alamanni, 14 September 1489, to Michelozzi and Giovantonio d'Arezzo, 15 and 17 December, *Lettere* 16, p. 32 and n. 9 (quoting Lodovico Sforza), 231, 248–9. On Baccia Minerbetti, p. 65, n. 54 in this volume.

about his succession, now that Giovanni (and his nephew Giulio) were both clerics and his youngest son Giuliano still unwed? If so, the birth of Piero's son Lorenzo in 1492 would have comforted him in providing him with an heir who – but for his early death in 1519 – would probably have become Florence's first hereditary ruler, an honour that was won, instead, by the rival younger branch of the family.

7 Piero as Lorenzo's Deputy in 1490

The interest of the two months from late April to late June 1490 lies in the light they throw on Piero's active involvement in politics, as well as on his more hidden role as Lorenzo's stand-in, collaborating with the friends in the Otto di Pratica (the all-important foreign affairs magistracy) to ensure that Lorenzo got his way. He already enjoyed a close relationship with Niccolò Michelozzi, the principal secretary who remained in Florence, and neither Michelozzi nor Piero Dovizi (with Lorenzo at the baths) found much to add – they said – to Piero's letters at this time. Michelozzi only once added a paragraph in his own hand to one of them, and on 9 May he told Lorenzo he was letting Piero communicate with him, since he 'writes and behaves most diligently, as you have seen'. And Dovizi told Michelozzi that he rarely wrote to him any longer: 'writing to Piero, as one is doing, there's very little or nothing to say to you'.[1]

Even before Lorenzo left for the baths in late April, Piero was being given more political responsibilities as a result of the friends' intervention the previous year – causing his brother-in-law Jacopo Salviati to comment, with his usual facetiousness, that 'the father is giving him as many prestigious jobs to do as he can, so flies have no time to settle on him', which he, if not Piero, was delighted about.[2] Piero wrote a letter concerning the Cittadella Vecchia in Pisa, and he was also involved in the trouble that broke out in Pistoia in March 1490, when he met with five of the men Dovizi defined as his father's intimates (*questi vostri*) to advise what should be done.[3] With Pierfilippo Pandolfini absent as Florence's ambassador in Rome, the most important of these intimates

---

[1] Michelozzi to Lorenzo, 9 May 1490, MAP 42, 58; Dovizi to Michelozzi, 2 June, GC 29, 62, fol. 74.

[2] Jacopo Salviati to Michelozzi, 30 January 1490, GC 29, 58, fol. 2: 'non se gli posa le mosche adosso', also telling him that Piero 'non ha bisognio che voi gli siate ricordato, che continuamente va nel quore'.

[3] Lorenzo, *Lettere* 16, p. 148 (intro. and n. 16) and on 'questi vostri', n. 5 in this chapter. On Pistoia, Dovizi to Lorenzo, 15 March 1490, MAP 56, 42, Dovizi to Piero, 7 April, MAP 56, 18, Milner, 'Lorenzo and Pistoia', esp. p. 237, n. 9, and p. 126 in this volume.

was Jacopo Guicciardini, who as a member of the Otto di Pratica would have introduced Piero to its work and given him support and guidance, which Piero reciprocated by repeatedly visiting the dying Jacopo and condoling with his son immediately after Jacopo died on 17 May.[4] The other intimates named by Dovizi (together with 'your Piero') were the lawyers Angelo Niccolini and Giovanni Serristori, Piero's relatives by marriage Bernardo Rucellai and Niccolò Ridolfi, and also Francesco Dini, Bernardo del Nero and Antonio di Bernardo Dini, the last two lower-class men who had become important factotums in the regime.[5] Although these men were often ill or away from the city, they were Piero's link to the Otto until he became an *aggiunto*, or one of its coopted members, after Jacopo's death.[6]

The Otto di Pratica, with its six-monthly terms of office, served as a revolving door through which the constantly changing but circumscribed group of friends entered and left office as the caucus or inner circle at the heart of the regime. As Dovizi put it when describing one 'new' member of the Otto in January 1492, 'the others are those you know, for one office is exchanged for the other'.[7] Nevertheless, after Jacopo's death and Francesco Valori's departure as ambassador to Milan, Lorenzo found it difficult to replace them with the men he wanted – Domenico Pandolfini and the lawyer Guidantonio Vespucci – because, as Piero reminded his father, they were already members of the financial magistracy of twelve procurators (also drawn from the Seventy). The law seemed 'difficult to accommodate, since it says the opposite of what you write we should do', Piero wrote to his father towards the end of May, so the *brigata* was 'trying to split hairs to get round it, and if we can't twist it at all, we'll do what we can without telling you'. As both men were chosen as replacements for the missing members on 12 June, Piero's and his friends' 'twisting' and 'splitting hairs' evidently succeeded in getting round the law.[8]

---

[4] Piero to Lorenzo in Bagno, 1–3, 6, 8, 14, 18 May 1490, MAP 42: 49, 54, 57 (fol. 57v), 65, 55 ('Jacopo "come piaqque a Dio hieri a hore xvii morì quasi favellando con tucti e" sagramenti et con optimo sentimento').

[5] Dovizi to Lorenzo, 14 May 1490, MAP 56, 41, cf. Martines, *Lawyers*, pp. 63–4, 492, 497–8; Guicciardini, *Dialogue*, ed. Brown, pp. 72, n. 206, 180–1, and pp. 154–9 in this volume.

[6] Discussed later. On their illnesses, Piero to Lorenzo in Bagno, 1–3 May, MAP 42, fol. 49r and 8 May, fol. 57r.

[7] Dovizi to Michelozzi in Rome, 18 January 1492, GC 29, 62, fol. 91r; on the Otto, drawn from the Seventy, Ricchioni, *La costituzione politica*, p. 174, Rubinstein, *Government*, pp. 229–30, 262, 373–4; cf. Otto, Delib. 3, fols. 1r, 30 and 53r.

[8] Piero to Lorenzo, 27 May 1490, MAP 42, 73, fol. 74r: '[la legge] denota de darecto el contrario di quello voi scrivete si faccia', Otto di Pratica, Delib. 3, fol. 30v (12 June 1490).

So although Lorenzo may have been slow to act after Guicciardini's and Pandolfini's intervention the previous summer, his sickness forced him to do what otherwise he seemed reluctant to do in letting Piero act as his deputy. Quite exceptionally, no letters at all are recorded in Lorenzo's letter book from late April until mid-June 1490, when he and his secretary Piero Dovizi were at the baths at Vignone and San Filippo near Mount Amiata, south of Siena, leaving Piero (with Niccolò Michelozzi) in charge in Florence.[9] No wonder his friend Alessandro Alessandri teased him for having to forgo his pleasures, 'because of the burdens placed on your back': 'be patient about labouring' – he wrote – 'so we [he was at the baths with Lorenzo] can relax and enjoy ourselves'.[10] Since Dovizi was also with Lorenzo at the baths, we can for once be sure the lengthy autograph letters that Piero sent his father are his own and reflect his own experience of his father's double politics as he acted as the link between his father at the baths and 'the friends' in the piazza and the palace.[11]

Piero in Loco Parentis

Among Piero's responsibilities during his father's absence, diplomacy was foremost, thanks to the continuing friction between the pope and his vassal, Ferrante of Naples, and between their two competing *condottieri*, Niccolò and Virginio Orsini. However, when Piero was summoned to see Ferrante's resident ambassador in Florence, Marino Tomacelli, on 27 April, it was not to discuss politics but to be informed that Ferrante's son-in-law, Gian Galeazzo Sforza, had finally consummated his marriage on the 25th – welcome news, since it might provide an heir to bolster his claims on Milan against his ambitious uncle Lodovico.[12] Piero also sent Lorenzo an extract from a letter he was shown by the Ferrarese ambassador about events in Hungary, and a message to Bernardo del Nero from someone from Faenza: the first not important, but Lorenzo needed to be told so he could reply – if, indeed, he thought of replying.[13] Faenza, however, was important, and like Forlì under 'Madonna'

---

[9] There is a hiatus between 26 April and 24 July, *Protocolli*, ed. Del Piazzo, p. 416, and Böninger, ed., Lorenzo, *Lettere* 16, doc. 1, p. 148.
[10] Alessandro in Bagno to Piero, 4 May 1490, MAP 18, 15, also 8 May, MAP 18, 390 on his devotion to Piero.
[11] E.g. Piero in Lorenzo in Bagno, 8 May 1490, MAP 42, 57r: 'quelli che trovai in piaza et in palagio degli amici'.
[12] Piero to Lorenzo in Bagno a Vignone, 27 April 1490, MAP 42, 44r; cf. Piero Dovizi to Michelozzi in Rome, 11 January, GC 29, 62, fol. 64.
[13] Letter of 27 April: 'quello vi pare di risponderli, se vi pare da rispondere nulla'.

(the redoubtable Caterina Sforza), it remained a source of concern to Lorenzo after his intervention following the murders of their rulers in 1488. The friends didn't think the situation there was as urgent as Lorenzo did, and they took nearly a week to meet and discuss his 'long paragraph' (*capitolone*) about Faenza in early May. They did then agree 'to castigate, etc.', as Lorenzo wanted, although they also wanted him to know that objections had been raised, especially against the Florentine commissary (the Medici intimate Dionigi Pucci), who should be replaced.[14] The outcome was nevertheless what Lorenzo wanted, because the friends were unable to agree on a replacement and Pucci was reappointed.[15]

There was friction in Pistoia, too, where the commissaries were unhappy about a decision to withdraw nearly all the soldiers (apart from a few crossbowmen) sent to deal with the trouble that had broken out in March.[16] They were also upset that the Otto di Guardia in Florence was attempting to suspend the death sentence they had imposed on one of the troublemakers, a cobbler, to which Lorenzo then added his own pressure for them to rescind their sentence.[17] When Piero, too, attempted to intervene in their execution of justice in Pistoia, the two men, Piero Vettori and Giovanbattista Ridolfi (later republican opponents of Piero's), delayed exiling a culprit, in order not to 'upset' Piero, but warned him that if the man remained unpunished, it would set a bad example and people had already been to them to complain.[18] This lesson to the young Piero on the exercise of public office reflects Francesco Valori's veiled criticism of Bernardo Ricci for playing a double role as his publicly appointed secretary (when he was ambassador in Milan) and as Piero's 'creature'.[19] So although these ambassadors and commissaries worked closely with the Medici as part of the regime, their letters to Piero

---

[14] Piero to Lorenzo in Bagno, 8 and 14 May 1490, MAP 42, 57, and 42, 65, fol. 65r.
[15] Lorenzo, *Lettere* 16, pp. 19–20 and n. 6; Piero to Lorenzo in Bagno, 18 May 1490 (MAP 42, 55, fol. 55v): 'et Bernardo del Nero mi dixe "scrivi a Lorenzo che voi non harete mai a Faenza commissario che sia forte se voi non lo fate di qua"'. Otto di Pratica Delib. 4, fols. 2v, 4r (1 and 15 July); Dionigi Pucci in Modigliana to Lorenzo, 10 and 14 July 1490 (MAP 54, 116–17, 119) and in Faenza, 26 July (MAP 54,120); cf. Piero di Lutozzo Nasi (the departing commissary), 13 July, MAP 54, 118.
[16] Piero to Lorenzo, 14 May 1490; on the earlier disturbances, n. 3 in this chapter and Milner, 'Lorenzo and Pistoia', esp. pp. 243–4.
[17] Vettori and Ridolfi in Pistoia to Piero, 16 May 1490, MAP 25, 602; Piero to Lorenzo in Bagno San Filippo, 18 May; Lorenzo to the commissaries, 21 May, MAP 43, 58 (tr. Ross, *Lives*, p. 317), Milner, 'Lorenzo and Pistoia', p. 243, n. 37: 'facta fuit executio'.
[18] Vettori and Ridolfi in Pistoia to Piero, 3 July 1490, MAP 18, 34; Brown, *Florence* (2011), p. 152. Cf. Jacopo Conte in Pistoia to Piero, 17 April, MAP 18, 7 ('me doglio non posere satisfare ad li domandi di Quella').
[19] Francesco Valori in Milan to Piero, [7–8] May 1490, MAP 14, 234: 'sì per le qualità sua sì ancora per essere tua creatura'. On Ricci, pp. 171–3 in this volume.

at this time foreshadow the later conflict that developed between 'the duties of government' and 'the bonds of clientage', from which these early critics of Piero emerged as republicans committed to fight against Piero's return.[20]

Piero's other diplomatic duties involved meeting and entertaining visiting ambassadors, such as messer Camillo Scorciati (originally sent by Ferrante to Milan to find out if the duke was indeed *frigidissimo* as alleged, a mission hastily transformed into congratulating the happy pair). Piero greeted him outside Florence, visited him while he was in the city and then accompanied him when he left.[21] He was also closely involved in the visit to Florence of the eminent Venetian scholar and diplomat Ermolao Barbaro, en route to Rome via a brief visit to Lorenzo at the baths. Barbaro's visit is famous as a cultural event (described more fully in the following chapter), but of course it had a political dimension, too. As Sante Vittorini (Virginio Orsini's man in Florence) describes it, the honour shown to Barbaro was measured by the size of the reception committee: four members of the Otto di Pratica, twelve other leading citizens (unnamed) and two secretaries of the Signoria, 'that is, messer Bartolomeo Scala and messer Cristoforo Landino', with all the servants of the Signoria, who then threw a public dinner for him in advance of a private dinner organised by Piero in the Medici palace. In Piero's account, this civic event is contrasted unfavourably with his own, for near the end of the public dinner the Gonfalonier of Justice, Bartolomeo Pucci, broke wind, causing embarrassment to some of Piero's friends, even though Barbaro laughed about it. And it is the private dinner, attended by Florence's famous humanists, for which Barbaro's visit is now remembered.[22]

Piero was also involved in shipping and in banking affairs. He promised his father on one occasion to do as ordered concerning 'the things of the ship' and also to pass on Lorenzo's memoranda to Giovannbattista (Bracci, codirector of the bank in Florence), who would deal with the rest, since he, and not Piero, understood them. It was at this time that a trading ship despatched to the Barbary Coast was referred to as 'your [Piero's] galley', with an employee on board from the Pisa branch of the bank, Francesco Naldini, who clearly knew the way to his patron's heart

---

[20] Gentile, 'Tuscans and Lombards', pp. 104–5.
[21] Manfredi in Florence to Ercole in Ferrara, 4 May 1490, *Lettere*, ed. Cappelli, pp. 307–8; Piero to Lorenzo in Bagno, 1–3 May 1490, Map 42, 49, fol. 49v, also 5 May, MAP 42, 52. On Scorciati, Lorenzo, *Lettere* 16, p. 350, n. 7, and *Corrispondenza* 5, pp. 64–6, 270–5, 277–8, 286 (4, 14, 15, 22 May and 14 June 1490).
[22] Rome, Capit. Arch. Orsini, 1st ser. 102 (1), fols, 165–6, Sante Vittorini to Virginio Orsini, 11 May 1490; and pp. 114–15 in this volume.

by offering to bring him horses and falcons back from Africa.²³ Piero also had to keep his father informed about ongoing family lawsuits and arbitrations. Initially, he was unable to tell Lorenzo much about the Pucci settlement (of Antonio Pucci's estate) because they hadn't yet agreed who the arbiters were to be – and when they still failed to agree, he later reported that they had decided to follow Lorenzo's suggestion and appoint Antonio Dini (the tough finance minister) to arbitrate.²⁴ Although Dovizi claimed it was 'beneath Piero's dignity' to deal with money matters, he nevertheless told Michelozzi to go ahead and use Piero's authority with Dini if he wanted, and if Dini procrastinated he should go to 'your Bartolini'.²⁵

Inevitably patronage was another area in which Piero was expected to get involved (as he had been for some time). Lorenzo's departure was followed by a series of appeals for Piero's help from devoted clients, 'in the absence of the Magnificent Lorenzo', as well as from Lorenzo himself, who asked Piero to deal with someone he knew nothing about, so 'he'll know I'm getting him off my back'.²⁶ In early May Piero received a letter from the Gonfalonier of Arezzo recalling his long devotion to the Medici – to Cosimo, Piero, Lorenzo and now to Lorenzo's son Piero, who two years earlier had been given a house in Arezzo to enable him to visit and see for himself the servitude to which his most affectionate people had been reduced. Now it was payback time. Asking Piero to help three close friends of his who were supported by 'all citizens of standing, true Guelfs and your servants', he ended by reminding him that

---

²³ Piero to Lorenzo, 1–3 May, 1490: 'del resto ... lascierò governare a lui che se ne intende et io no' (on Bracci, director general after Lorenzo's death, De Roover, *Banco Medici*, pp. 126, 343, Tewes, *Kampf um Florenz*, pp. 163–73); Maldei in Pisa to Piero, 13 May, MAP 18, 23 (postscript), Francesco Naldini in Pisa to Piero, 3 and [8?] May (recd. 10th), MAP 18, 4 and 389 ('de' chavalli e falchoni volete avere da Barberia'), cf. the same, 4 May, 18, 387. On Francesco di Domenico Naldini, Tewes, *Kampf um Florenz*, pp. 167–8.

²⁴ Letters in MAP 42 of 1–3, 6 and 14 May 1490, fols. 49r–v, 54r and 65r; Dionigi Pucci told Dovizi on 15 June 1494 (MAP 19, 588, fol. 655r), there would soon be agreement if 'e' figluoli d'Antonio [his nephews] mi verranno per fratello et per compagno al traffico, et non per factorino'.

²⁵ Dovizi in Bagno to Michelozzi, 18 May 1490, GC 29, 62, fol. 71. On Antonio Dini's 'hardness' and on the Bartolini as the Medici's bankers, Brown, *Florence* (2011), pp. 3, 28–9.

²⁶ Ottaviano Manfredi in Pisa to Piero, 13 May 1490, MAP 18, 12; Lorenzo in Bagno to Piero, 4 May 1490, MAP 18, 14, Kent, *Princely Citizen*, p. 214 (and 199–25). On Piero as patron, Chapter 9 in this volume.

'every uprising causes the greatest disturbance, especially over the taxes'.[27] Taxes had long been a bone of contention between Florence and the Aretines, who relied on the Medici to mitigate gabelles, taxation and lump-sum contributions to the Florentine fisc to which they were subjected. Although Lorenzo had gratified them in 1488 (hence the house given to Piero), new rates of taxation two years later renewed the pressure on the Medici to act, and in early June two Florentine commissaries were sent to quell the trouble.[28]

Lorenzo's 'Shady' Power in the Face of Danger

More revealing of the Medici's double politics was Piero's role during three dangerous incidents that occurred in 1490: two when Lorenzo was absent at the baths in May and June, one in November after his return but when he was in his villa at Agnano. Shortly before the first incident in May, Dovizi had written to Michelozzi that it would be necessary to think about the future, 'because Lorenzo won't survive for ever'.[29] This must have been a thought shared by many Florentines at the time, not only because of Lorenzo's ill health but because of the danger of assassination. When Lorenzo departed for the baths at Bagno a Vignone in late April, he was escorted by eight squadrons of lances and five hundred paid soldiers provided by the Sienese government in recognition of the danger he faced in the countryside.[30] After the attempt on his life at Poggio a Caiano in 1480 (two years after the murder of his brother) and another plot to kill him the following year, Lorenzo was always protected by a body of armed guards when he went to stay in his villas and the baths in the countryside.[31] Despite this, his friends and intimates pleaded with him in 1488 'not to go any more to Poggio a Caiano, because they say its

---

[27] Francesco Gozarius, Vexillifer in Arezzo to Piero, 3 May 1490, MAP 18, 11: 'che ogni novità dà alterazione grandissima, maxime cerca le graveze'; Black, 'Arezzo, the Medici', pp. 305, cf. 301–3.

[28] Map 41, 504 (5 June 1490), Black, 'Lorenzo and Arezzo', p. 231, n. 128. On Piero's recommendations of friends for offices in Arezzo and also in San Gemignano in 1490–91, ibid., p. 221, Piero to the priors of S. Gimignano, 7 March 1491, ASF, Acq. e Doni MS. 59, ins. 3; also Angelo Niccolini to Piero, 14 August 1490, Florence, Niccolini Archives, 14: ins. 44.

[29] Dovizi in Bagno San Filippo to Michelozzi, 22 May 1490, GC 29, 62, fol. 73: 'Lorenzo non reggerà sempre'. On 'il dominio larvato dei Medici', 'che è un circolo chiuso, anzi un circolo vizioso', Anzilotti, *Crisi costituzionale*, pp. 23–38, at 31.

[30] Tribaldo de' Rossi, *Ricordanze*, p. 251. A *squadra* consisted of 75 men (25 *lancie* of three men) increasing to 150, commanded by a constable, Barsacchi, *Cacciate Lorenzo!*, p. 17; Clough, 'The Romagna Campaign', pp. 205–6.

[31] Landucci, *Diario*, pp. 36–8; Lorenzo, *Lettere* 5, pp. 227–8 (nn. 12, 13); Walter, *Lorenzo il Magnifico*, pp. 185–6.

situation makes it easy for Giovanni [Bentivoglio] or anyone who wants to bump him off to do so'.[32] So rumours of an attack on Lorenzo's life by two Neapolitans in April 1490, planned for the anniversary of Giuliano's murder on the 26th, provided Piero with the first of several tests of his authority that also throw revealing light on how the regime operated under pressure.[33]

The rumour, reported by Ercole d'Este's ambassador in Florence on 18 May, was that two men, Raimo da Gaeta and Vincenzo Ragonoro, 'wanted to come here to go the baths where Lorenzo is at present in order to poison or murder him'. The immediate reaction of Piero and the Dovizi secretaries was to scotch it by saying (probably on the basis of Piero's letter to Lorenzo on the 13th) that it was Vincenzio Pappacoda, Piero's fencing master, and his brother Antonio whom they planned to assassinate, not Lorenzo, and that the police magistracy of the Otto di Guardia was holding the culprits and torturing them with fourteen pulls of the rope until the Pappacoda reached safety.[34] A day later ser Piero similarly told Michelozzi in Florence not to listen to the rumours nor to worry about their safety, since they were very well protected at the baths, but that Piero should ride outside Florence with his vaulting master Vincenzio 'as little as possible'.[35] In the letter Piero sent his father by despatch rider on 13 May, he explained that Antonio Pappacoda had escaped the intended ambush by returning from France, not via Bologna as expected but via Pontremoli (and Pisa, where Naldini, the Medici Bank employee, had given him a letter for Piero); and since one of the conspirators was in Florence and wanted to meet the other near Firenzuola, Piero asked his father if they should be captured, and if so, secretly or openly? He had 'secretly' sent his father's letter to ser Zanobi del Pace (the Otto di Guardia's chancellor), by someone trustworthy who wouldn't arouse suspicion.[36]

---

[32] Guidoni to Ercole, 17 August, 1488, *Lettere*, ed. Cappelli, p. 303; Lorenzo, *Lettere* 8, pp. 240–2 (3 September 1485); Piero Capponi to Lorenzo in Bagno a Morbo, 15 May 1486, MAP 39, 499, fols. 552v–553r: 'ingegniatevi di fare buona guardia al Bagnio'.
[33] Manfredo Manfredi (the new Este ambassador) to Ercole, 18 May 1490, ed. Cappelli, 'Lettere', p. 308, named as Raymo da Gaeta and Vincenzo Capezza da Napoli in Otto di Guardia rep. 85, fol. 130r–v.
[34] Manfredi to Ercole, 18 May 1490, p. 308; Bernardo Dovizi in Bagno S. Filippo to Andrea da Foiano in Siena, 21 May 1490, ed. Moncallero, I, pp. 5–6 (on Bernardo, Brown, *Florence* [2011], p. 36).
[35] Piero Dovizi to Michelozzi, 22 May 1490, fol. 73r: 'insomma curate pocho, come facciamo noi, el dire populare … Noi qui stiamo con una buona et grande securtà …'
[36] Piero to Lorenzo in Bagno, 13 May 1490, MAP 42, 63r (autogr.): 'se voi volete … si faccino piglare o no, o se vi curate si facci segreto o no'; Naldini in Pisa to Piero, 4 May, MAP 18, 387.

The secrecy emphasized by Piero – despite the involvement of Florence's criminal justice magistracy – is the first indication of the double level on which he and his father were operating. The following day (14 May), Piero acted immediately on Lorenzo's response to this letter by ordering ser Zanobi to do what was necessary and if Raimo (*colui*) came, they would have him in their hands; all that had been missing was the 'yes' or 'no', which they now had.[37] So it was the absent Lorenzo who authorised the Otto di Guardia's chancellor to capture Raimo and bring him to Florence by night to prevent rumours circulating that 'he had come to do what we feared'.[38] Despite this, news leaked out and when it reached the ears of the Neapolitan ambassador, Marino Tomacelli, he was told it was the Otto di Guardia's affair, and 'we pretended' (Piero told his father) 'we knew from them that they had acted on account of messer Vincenzio without our involvement'. The 'friends' thought two of them should examine Raimo, so it was Bernardo del Nero and Niccolò Ridolfi – members of the inner circle, but neither of them members either of the Otto di Guardia nor of the Otto di Pratica at the time – who examined them on two consecutive evenings, only on the second evening applying 'fourteen pulls of the rope' – but torture revealed nothing more than they knew already.[39] Piero had been absent in Poggio a Caiano for the weekend when the men were captured, and when he attempted to discuss Raimo with the Otto di Pratica five days later, he was unable to assemble more than four of 'the friends', since three of them were ill or had other excuses, but they would give their opinion on what Lorenzo had written when they could.[40] According to one chronicler, this private interrogation caused much talk at the time because one of the prisoners was a man of standing whose orders must have come from high up, and the prisoners were quickly released without people ever knowing what

---

[37] The same, 14 May 1490, MAP 42, 65r (autogr.): 'solo mancava el sì o no che hora habbiamo'.

[38] Piero in Poggio to Michelozzi in Florence, 16 May 1490, GC 29, 35, fol. 6 (autogr.) and to Lorenzo in Bagno, 18 May 1490, MAP 42, 55, fol. 55r (autogr): 'fingemo sapere da loro che questo era facto ... sanza altra nostra participatione'; cf. Alfonso Pitti, vicar in Firenzuola, to Piero, 15 May, MAP 18, 24.

[39] Piero to Lorenzo in Bagno, 18 May: 'Parve qui agl'amici che vi andassi dua di loro a examinargli et vi è ito dua sere alla fila', etc. Manfredi (to Ercole, 18 May) names as interrogators Michelozzi and two members of the Otto di Pratica, Giovanni Serristori and Bernardo Rucellai (called by Tribaldo, p. 252, 'Bernardo del Nero', who was not then in the Otto).

[40] Piero to Lorenzo in Bagno, 23 May 1490, MAP 42, 7: 'messer Agnolo ha mal di fianco, Niccolò Ridolfi male di un piè ... A Bernardo del Nero è morta la suocera ...' As well as Serristori and Rucellai, the Otto also included Piero Alamanni and Antonio Dini, Otto, Delib. 3, fol. 30r.

they had confessed.⁴¹ Although the friends had been authorised to do what they thought best – and had freed Raimo as the law demanded – Piero went on to tell Lorenzo he would let this happen, 'to disguise the fact that anything has been done with your consent'.⁴² Piero's 'disguises' and 'pretences' show not only that he was fully involved in his father's subterfuges, but that the whole incident had been dealt with unconstitutionally – the men's capture, their torture by non-judicial interrogators and their release all ostensibly decided by the Otto di Pratica but in fact with Lorenzo's consent. Within Medici circles, it was clear the attack was aimed principally at the Medici rather than the Pappacoda, and the fact that Dovizi warned Piero of the danger of riding outside Florence with his vaunting master suggests he was no less at risk than his father.⁴³

Hardly had this danger been averted than Piero had to deal with a different threat to his father and the regime. In this case, it was the Medici's reputation that was threatened, not their lives, but the choreography was the same, with the same obfuscation and triangular interplay between Lorenzo, Piero and the friends. At the beginning of June Piero was told that his father was implicated in a conspiracy against the government of Lucca by offering (through his factor in Pisa Francesco Fracassini), a reward of golden ducats to one of the conspirators.⁴⁴ Although the conspirator then retracted his confession, Fracassini was publicly summonsed and, to Lorenzo's 'considerable displeasure', the whole of Lucca was talking about it.⁴⁵ On this occasion, the inner cabal of friends took action by sending Piero Corsini as public ambassador to Lucca (rather than as a private envoy), who promised Lorenzo he would report fully to him on his return, knowing 'how many doubts you

---

[41] Tribaldo de' Rossi, *Ricordanze*, pp. 252–3; Manfredi to Ercole, 29 May 1490, *Lettere*, ed. Cappelli, p. 309 (that Raimo was 'molto passionato e afflitto' after 'circa a 18 tratti di corda'). On Lorenzo's tricky relationship with Naples at the time, *Lettere* 16, pp. 342–3, and Dovizi to Michelozzi, 22 May, GC 29, 62, fol. 73.

[42] Piero to Lorenzo, 27 May 1490, MAP 42, 73, fol. 74r (autogr.): 'così *disponunt iura* ... lascierò seguire per non monstrare che nulla si sia facto vostro *consensu* et non aspectare di costì risposta'.

[43] On 19 May Maldei wrote from Pisa to Michelozzi (GC 29, 27, fol. 117r): 'Qui è divulgato per tucta la terra com'è stati presi due a Firenzuola, e' quali venivano per fare dispiacere a Lorenzo.'

[44] Cambi in Pisa to Piero, recd. 2 June 1490, MAP 42, 79, Piero to Lorenzo in Bagno, 3 June, MAP 42, 83, fol. 84r (autogr.). On Cambi, p. 139, n. 70 in this volume, and on Fracassini, initially the Medici's factor in Cafaggiolo, Kent, *Princely Citizen*, p. 255.

[45] Tommasi, *Sommario della storia di Lucca*, pp. 341–2; Bratchel, *Lucca*, pp. 75–6; Martelli, *Studi laurenziani*, pp. 207–8, nn. 104, 105 (citing Dovizi to Michelozzi, 2 June) and Brown, Florence (2011), pp. 80–1.

entertain in this affair and the many thoughts you may be having about it'.[46] Piero was involved when accosted in the piazza by the Milanese ambassador (messer Branda da Castiglione) demanding Fracassini's imprisonment; finding it difficult to refuse him, Piero begged his father to reply for him by sending a response he could show messer Branda.[47] Otherwise, he served as the hub of an information network that spread between Florence, Bagno a San Filippo, Lucca and Pisa, forwarding letters and writing them himself. On 9 June he told his father he had little to add to Corsini's immense letter – what Corsini called a 'Pliny' compared with Piero's 'Bible' to his father – 'and here there's nothing else at all that's important enough to write about'.[48]

Piero, however, faced one more crisis on his father's behalf – also involving messer Branda – that again highlights the choreography of the regime under pressure. On 3 November 1490, when Lorenzo was absent in his villa at Agnano, a Florentine citizen was savagely attacked and robbed by two Milanese criminals, and since it was the third or fourth time this had happened, 'the friends' reacted badly to the incident (especially when the victim, Benedetto Calderini, died a few days later), saying it was something unheard of for several years and a bad example.[49] Four months later, in late March 1491, two men (nicknamed Colombano and Mezzatesta) were put to death by hanging from the windows of the Bargello, following a spate of attacks by a gang of men who seized the clothes of their victims to divide up among themselves.[50] What was exceptional about this quotidian hanging was the widely held opinion it revealed among people of every condition – high and low, including some of Lorenzo's own friends (according to Dovizi) – that 'our Piero' had been responsible for Calderini's murder the previous November. Fortunately Dovizi remembered that Piero was at Poggio on the day Calderini was attacked, and now everyone was saying, 'So, you see, it wasn't Piero who did it!'[51] Three days earlier Dovizi had informed Lorenzo that the culprits had been captured; nor was he surprised, he

---

[46] Piero to Lorenzo, 3 June 1490, fol. 84r; Otto di Pratica to Lorenzo, 3 June, MAP 42, 84r, and Corsini to Lorenzo, 8 June, MAP, 42, 92, fol. 93 ter^r. On Corsini, later Piero's nemesis, Lorenzo, *Lettere* 16, p. 340, n. 1, Chapters 16 and 18 in this volume.
[47] Piero to Lorenzo, 3 June and 23 May (fol. 71r). On messer Branda, *DBI* 22, 1979 (D. Girgensohn).
[48] The same, 9 August, MAP 42, 95r (autogr.); Corsini to Lorenzo, 8 June, Brown, *Florence* (2011), p. 81, n. 52.
[49] Dovizi in Florence in Lorenzo in Agnano, 6 November 1490, MAP 56, 47.
[50] Otto di Guardia rep. 88, fols. 28v (31 March 1491, referring to Joamantonio Marci al. Mezatesta and Ghaspare di Gabriele Ghuenzi al. Colombano, both from Milan), 134r (payment for hanging them 'alle finestre del Bargello').
[51] Dovizi to Lorenzo in Agnano, 30 March 1491, Brown, *Florence* (2011), p. 82, n. 54.

said, that they were messer Branda da Castiglione's men, since he had always been suspicious of them. His letter shows the regime using the same secret procedures as the previous summer. For when the chief minister of the Otto della Guardia, ser Zanobi del Pace, learnt who the assassins were, he talked with Ruggieri (Corbinelli) alone; Ruggieri talked to Giovanni Serristori; Giovanni then immediately got together with the leading citizens, except for messer Agnolo (Niccolini) and Pierfilippo (Pandolfini), who couldn't be found until the morning, when they drew in Piero and Dovizi to discuss *quid agendum*.

And the opinions were so varied and so fought over ... that a decision was deferred till this morning and ser Zanobi was ordered to watch the offender and be on the alert ... If you want to tell me what you think about this, do so. Your Piero raises his hands to heaven, and with good reason, he's behaved very seriously.[52]

Lorenzo would not have been pleased about messer Branda's and Milan's involvement, in view of his secret support for Lodovico in Milan, and advised that because of 'the enormity of the excesses', the two assassins should be put to death as 'the friends' and the people wanted, and the others – one of whom was a blood relative of messer Brando – should secretly be saved.[53] By not publishing it, this verdict would simultaneously protect the friends' favour with Lorenzo and Lorenzo's with Lodovico, who professed not to be upset by the executions – suggesting again that law was being administered by the inner circle in its own interests.[54] And although everyone initially jumped to conclusions about Piero's involvement in the attack – perhaps because he was involved in street violence at the time or because his footballing with foreigners in the streets encouraged rumours about his behaviour – he evidently behaved responsibly and with his customary composure when drawn back into the centre of power in his father's absence.

The same is true of Piero's one recorded contribution to a debate in the Otto di Pratica that also involved Milan and showed how concerned the Medici were not to offend Lodovico. This was only the second

---

[52] The same, 27 March 1491, MAP 56, 48 ('Et i pareri furono tanto varii et tanto dibattiti vi si feciono ... che a stamane si differì la cosa') and on Piero, Brown, *Florence* (2011), p. 82, n. 54. Corbinelli and Serristori were members respectively of the Otto di Guardia and Otto di Pratica.

[53] p. 73 in this volume and n. 47 in this chapter. On messer Branda's involvement in Forlì in 1488 and Lorenzo's subsequent 'intelligenza segreta' with Lodovico, Pellegrini, *Congiure in Romagna*, pp. 61, 109 (n. 37), 121, 168–9 and n. 42.

[54] Dovizi to Lorenzo, 30 March 1491, fol. 51r–v ('ma questo secreto non si publicherà, et loro si serveranno per gratificarsene con Lorenzo'), 3 April, MAP 26, 565r; Valori in Milan to the Otto, 11 April 1491 Otto Respons. 8, fol. 26r–v.

occasion on which Piero had been invited to join the Otto as a coopted member (*arroto*), and his intervention provides a rare example of how he spoke and interacted with other leading citizens in a public forum.[55] The meeting called on 21 July was to discuss whether Florence should accept in its dominion two Lunigiana towns – Malgra (now Malgrate) and Filetto – that had been offered to them by their envoys. Lying on the disputed frontier between Florence, Lucca and Milan, their ownership had wide ramifications, since they were in the possession of the Marchese Gabriele Malaspina, who was not only intermarried with several Florence families but had offered the towns to Milan.[56] Piero entered the debate after two opposing arguments had been set out: first, that Florence should acquire the towns as a matter of honour and to increase Florence's territory (although only after their envoys had returned with a formal mandate), and second, that it would be better to wait to see if the Milanese accepted the marchese's offer of the towns to them before doing anything.[57] Piero's concise and well-articulated intervention then followed, that:

> it seemed to him there were two things to be taken into consideration in this matter, one concerning Marchese Gabrielle, since the issue of Malgra had been his concern, the other signor Lodovico. So he thought that the places should be well provisioned, in order to be safe for a few days before deciding or concluding anything, and Pietro Tornabuoni [his relative, and Florence's captain and commissary in Sarzana] should be told to provision the places well. No decision should be taken or ruled out with those men, and for now they should only be given good words.[58]

It already demonstrated what became a familiar characteristic of Piero's, to balance the arguments *in utramque partem* without coming down on either side – or as he put it, doing nothing and ruling nothing out. The chairman, the lawyer Guidantonio Vespucci, then shrewdly concluded the debate by saying that the towns should be accepted immediately while Milan was preoccupied in Savoy and Genoa. When the same members reconvened after the summer break, however, the opposite decision was taken – as a result, we must assume, of Lorenzo's unrecorded intervention – that the towns were to be restored, provided their

---

[55] Otto di Pratica Delib. 4, fol. 4v (21 July 1490). On the Otto, n. 7 in this chapter, Rubinstein, *Palazzo Vecchio*, pp. 34 (n. 254), 36.

[56] Meli, 'Un episodio dell' espansione fiorentina'; on conflict over Massa and Lorenzo's firm support of its marchese in October 1487, Lorenzo, *Lettere* 11, pp. 348–9 and n. 1.

[57] The first speaker was Florence's hard-headed finance minister Antonio Dini, the second Bernardo Rucellai, one of the *voci più accreditate* in Consulte e pratiche debates, Fachard, 'Dietro le quinte', pp. 273–4.

[58] Otto, Delib. 4, fols. 4v–6r, citing Piero on 5v.

men could be protected.⁵⁹ As mastermind of Florence's high-risk diplomacy, Lorenzo must have rated the hostile reaction of Milan and Gabriele Malaspina more highly than Florence's territorial gain, despite the dismay of the commissary.⁶⁰ So Piero's intervention would have served to keep all options open for his father to make the ultimate decision.

'Going Off to Enjoy Myself': Piero's Life After His Father's Return

When Piero received a letter from his father in mid-June to say he was returning home – taking a long route in order to see Maddalena and Franceschetto in Montepulciano, visiting Pienza and Monte Uliveto and perhaps his son messer Giovanni's benefice at Coltibuono – Piero immediately decided to go off to enjoy himself.⁶¹ As he told Michelozzi, he had left early, 'to escape anything that would annoy me', and after spending the night at Careggi, he would return for a meeting in the Duomo with the Medici 'about that business', which Michelozzi was to arrange.⁶² This suggests he was looking forward to his father's return in order to revert to an eighteen-year-old's life of sport, fun and music making. Not that his two months in control had deprived him entirely of his pleasures, as we shall see in Chapter 8, but such an immediate response to his father's return is a sign that he was still torn between the lives of pleasure and duty, despite applying himself more vigorously to politics than his father and elders may have expected.

Horses were his first concern after his father's return. On 28 June, he replied to the marquis of Mantua's request for some horses to race in Mantua: Lorenzo, he told him, would be happy to send them provided the horses weren't riderless, otherwise not, so if Francesco could assure him that they would have jockeys, he was happy to obey and send 'a few good horses' – an offer that the marquis accepted quickly, in order to give

---

[59] Ibid., fol. 7v (1 September 1490): 'per obviare ad qualche scandolo di mala natura ... pareva loro detto castello di Malgra si dovessi restituire ...'
[60] On Lorenzo and Milan, p. 73 in this volume; on the importance of Malgra 'et quanto egli è bello', Piero Tornabuoni in Sarzana to ser Francesco Baroni, 24 August 1490, MAP 102, 73r.
[61] Lorenzo in Bagno to Piero, 'filio meo charissimo', in Florence, 13 June 1490, MAP 18, 32. fol. 33r–v, adding on fol. 34r that having heard nothing more from Piero, their doctor, Pier Leone, should be allowed to return to Rome.
[62] Piero to Michelozzi in Florence, 15 June 1490, GC 29, 35, fol. 7, autogr.: 'Io me ne sono ito stamani a spasso ... Sonmi fuggito a buona hora perché non mi venissi cosa mi dessi noia idol.'

Lorenzo time to prepare them.⁶³ This year, the Feast of San Giovanni on 24 June was celebrated with great splendour by the Florentine community in Rome, perhaps to celebrate the badly kept secret of Giovanni de' Medici's cardinalate, but in the joust held in Florence in late August, Piero's jouster had no success, unlike the previous year when Piero had organised his own prestigious joust.⁶⁴ Around this time, when Lorenzo was suffering from gout again and about to leave for Spedaletto and both Piero's brothers and his cousin Giulio were ill with fever, Piero paid a visit to his brother-in-law Franceschetto in the loggia of the Pazzi palace (where Franceschetto lived in Florence).⁶⁵ On 1 September he attended his last meeting as an *aggiunto* of the Otto di Pratica, and by the middle of the month he was off to visit his now convalescent brother Giovanni in the Medici villa of Montepaldi.⁶⁶ Back in Florence in early October, he wrote to Niccolò Michelozzi in Rome, asking him to get the groom to send him Franceschetto's horse, then set off for Pisa, where Jacopo Salviati found him 'well and handsome, as usual'.⁶⁷ Normally Jacopo would see Piero in Florence, but because of meeting him in Pisa where Jacopo was convalescing until the end of the year, he told ser Francesco Baroni he didn't need to return to Florence and instead asked ser Francesco to commend him to his patron Piero on his behalf.⁶⁸

The scarcity of references to politics, and Piero's absence from meetings of the Otto di Pratica from the beginning of September until the end of 1491, suggest that Lorenzo reassumed the reins of power after his return, despite his growing illness and frequent sojourns in his villas outside Florence. He was appointed a member of the Seventeen Reformers from 15 July 1490 until 15 July 1491, an all-powerful commission that instituted a series of reforms, many of them directly benefiting Lorenzo himself.⁶⁹ And when its authority came to an end, he was appointed a member of the Otto di Pratica until January 1492, in

---

⁶³ Piero to Francesco Gonzaga, 28 June 1490, Mantua AS. busta 1085, no. 24, Francesco's reply on 5 July, MAP 18, 35.

⁶⁴ Pierfil. Pandolfini to ser Andrea d Foiano, 28 August 1490, MAP 76, 188 ('mi duole che il giostrante di Piero non habbia havuto honore'). On the Florentine celebrations in Rome for their patron saint, Bartolomeo da Bracciano to Virginio Orsini, 24 June, *Lettres*, ed. Broüard, pp. 291–3.

⁶⁵ Manfredi to Ercole d'Este, 31 August 1491, *Lettere*, ed. Cappelli, p. 309; Sante Vittorini to Virginio, 25 August, Rome, Capit., Orsini, ser. 1, 102 (2), fol. 318.

⁶⁶ Dovizi, note to Lorenzo, 17 September 1490, MAP 56, 14.

⁶⁷ Dovizi to Michelozzi in Rome, 8 October 1491, GC 29, 62, fol. 81; Salviati in Pisa to ser Francesco in Florence, 13 October 1490, MAP 102, 38.

⁶⁸ The same, 20 October 1491 ('nostro comune patrone'), MAP 102, 39, and to ser Francesco, 11 December (MAP 102, 44): 'Dite a Giovanni di Pierfrancesco che in qualunche grado io mi ritroverrò, sarò sempre tutto suo.'

⁶⁹ Brown, *Medici in Florence*, pp. 151–211, esp. 166–77.

which – to judge from his four periods as its elected chairman – he was still actively involved in its work.[70] Nevertheless, Piero was by now said to be 'applying himself hard to the affairs of state, and especially in the Company of the Magi, it seems that the regime [*stato*] already rests almost entirely on his shoulders'.[71] He was also fulfilling many of the social duties he had performed during Lorenzo's absence in 1490. He met dignitaries passing through Florence, conducted others to Poggio a Caiano to be astounded by the villa under construction – including messer Branda, as we shall see.[72] And if many of his letters were written on his behalf by Dovizi – especially about the exchange and gifts of horses and falcons – he wrote himself to his father about events in Siena.[73] Procurators were appointed in Milan to fight Genoa's sentence against his bank in Pisa and to represent him for his godson's christening, and in Lyon to support the Medici Bank there; and at the end of December, on his father's last day in office as chairman of the Otto di Pratica, the Otto requested Piero to decide how much tax his brother-in-law Franceschetto ('nephew' of the pope) was to pay for safe conduct for men and goods from Genoa to Rome.[74]

There are hints, perhaps, of Piero's growing sensuality in the 'little pot of pomade' Matteo Franco sent him from Rome in December 1491, with more from a parfumier who hoped for Piero's patronage – for 'despite making perfumes', the parfumier was 'a learned and experienced courtier' and former notary who now wanted to come and 'repose under the

---

[70] Lorenzo, *Protocolli*, ed. del Piazzo, pp. 416–90 (cf. *Censimento*, pp. 178–89), listing, e.g., more than eighty letters to Alamanni as ambassador in Rome, July 1491–March 1492 (usually 'dictated by Lorenzo' and copied by his secretaries), with a gap from 28 August to 16 September when he was at Spedaletto.

[71] Piero Pucci in Florence to Giannozzo Pucci in Rome, 30 December 1491, ASF Acq. Doni, 301, ins.1, fol. 155v–156r (cf. Rubin, *Images and Identity*, p. 302, n. 5): 'Parmi che lo stato si riposi già quasi tutto in sulle sue spalle'; cf. n. 73 in this chapter. On the Magi, Parenti, *Storia*, I, pp. 24, 27, and p. 121 in this volume.

[72] Dovizi to Lorenzo in Agnano, 21, 24, 26 May 1491, MAP 56: 52, 49, 11, see pp. 115–16 in this volume.

[73] Dovizi to Lorenzo, 21 May (referring to news in Siena of the 'partita da Napoli di Neri Placidi, come vi scrive Piero di Lorenzo'), 26 May ('Al Bentivoglo risponderò come mi dirà messer Agnolo in nome di Piero'); Lorenzo, *Protocolli*, ed. Del Piazzo, pp. 466, 470, 478, 482, 484, 487 (26 July, 23 August, 25 November 1491, 10, 27 January, 8, 17 February 1492).

[74] Notarile antecos. 10200, fols. 326r–v (8 July 1491), 332r–v (22 August), 340r–341v (7–8 November and 13 December), and 343r–344r (14 March 1492, also Valori to the Otto, June 1491, Otto Responsive 8, fol. 106) on the bank in Lyon, ibid., fols. 336–7 (20 September); on the baptism, ibid., fol. 348r (21 May 1492, also Dovizi to Michelozzi in Rome, 16 September 1491, GC 29, 62, fol.77r). On Franceschetto, esp. pp. 142–3 in this volume.

shadow of [Piero's] wings', making for him all sorts of little things, 'soaps, pomades, oils of every kind, and powder'.[75]

Earlier that year Piero had written a tormented poem – admired by Poliziano – about being torn between 'the false shadow of hope' and the true good, suggesting that he may already have been tempted by the love affair on which he embarked a year later.[76] But in December it was his father's impending death that must have weighed most heavily on him. At the beginning of December, Gentile Becchi, his father's tutor and devoted family friend, assured Piero, in response to 'that last testament you whispered in my ear', that he would stand by him, as he always stood by his father, 'because if the trunk is sound, the branches will be too'.[77] The image reflects not only Lorenzo's insignia of the sprouting laurel branch, the *broncone*, but also Piero's own insignia of flaming green shoots that Baccio Ugolini referred to five days before Lorenzo's death: referring to Piero as 'the blessing and honour of the commune', he hoped his 'real live embers' might help him more than 'the smoke' he found in San Germano, from where he administered Cardinal Giovanni's benefice of Montecassino.[78]

Piero's years of apprenticeship before his father's death provide insight into his years in power, in which business was still combined with pleasure. For although learning about politics in Florence was central to his training, Piero's cultural life and pastimes were also important, and so were his patronal relationships in Florence's dominion and beyond, both of which added to his prestige and prepared him for the role his father had pioneered as Renaissance ruler of a growing territorial state.

---

[75] Matteo Franco in Rome to Piero, 20 December 1491, *Lettere*, ed. Frosini, p. 106; Giuliano and Lorenzo Ridolfi in Naples to Piero, 18 May 1493 and 17 January 1494, MAP 14, 352 and 18, 81 ('una ampolla di olio di mongivi'); cf. GC 5 (Pisa account book of Piero de' Medici & Co.), fol. 236 left.

[76] Ed. Del Lungo, *Florentia*, pp. 253–4, cf. pp. 116–17 in this volume.

[77] Becchi to Piero, recd. 2 December 1491, MAP 19, 187: 'quello ultimo testamento mi facesi nell'orechio ... perché salvo il pedale si salvono e' rami'. On Becchi, *DBI* 7, 1970 (C. Grayson), Picotti, *Giovinezza*, pp. 254–63, esp. 257; Simonetta, *Congiura della verità*, pp. 17–24.

[78] Ugolini in San Germano to Michelozzi in Naples, 3 April 1492, GC 29, 18, fol. 34: 'bracia caldissimo et vera' (the same, 23 March, fol. 30: Lorenzo has taught 'se et i suoi a stimare le brace et non el fumo'). On Piero's insignia and Poliziano's motto for him, Centanni, *Fantasmi del'antico*, pp. 478–9. On Baccio, pp. 168–9, n. 2, 207 in this volume.

Part II

Between Republicanism and Princely Rule

8 Cultural Patronage and Sportsmanship

Although Piero was criticised for his love of sports and footballing in the streets, sportsmanship – like cultural patronage – contributed to the soft power increasingly enjoyed by Renaissance rulers. Visits to the antiquities in the Medici palace and to the model farm at Poggio a Caiano formed part of diplomats' tours of Florence, while the sports of horse racing and falconry provided invaluable items for gift exchanges with other rulers. So too did Piero's famous Spanish runner Garzerano, who was regarded as a trophy ('like some prince', in the eyes of the royal court) when borrowed by Alfonso of Naples for his son.[1] So if Piero's sporting activities were unappreciated at home, they gave him more standing outside Florence than his critics may have realised.

When left in charge during his father's absence at the baths near Siena in 1490, Piero was teased by his friends, as we saw, for having to work so they could relax and enjoy themselves. Alessandro Alessandri was with Lorenzo at the baths, and the carefully selected topics he chose to write about to Piero provide our best evidence of what Piero's interests were at the time, especially footballing, duelling and hunting, but also books and singing. Warning him 'to be careful not to harm yourself playing ball in these times' and not to become 'so good that I can't play with you any more', Alessandro then referred to the missals Piero was to choose for Lorenzo at the baths, and to the two pairs of good bloodhounds Lorenzo also wanted, since the ones already sent were only good for raising hares, and then he told Piero that Bevilaqua was going to fight with cloak and dagger against 'that Jacopo del Pio' in Santa Fiore the following day, 'pray God he wins'.[2] Four days later, he reported on the fight, on the missal that had been brought by Francesco degli Organi and on Piero's message to Lorenzo about Lascaris, the Greek scholar then busy hunting

---

[1] On Garzerano, n. 67 in this chapter.
[2] Alessandri to Piero, 4 May 1490, MAP 18, 15 (cf. p. 90, n. 10 in this volume). A year later, Piero sent Alexo to Siena under his protection, 'che è come vedrete quello ragazo di Bevilacqua' (to Andrea da Foiano, 7 June 1491, MAP 76, 293).

for books for the Medici library. On the 12th, after more about the dogs, he told Piero how pleased he was to hear that he hadn't forgotten how to sing *improviso* at night, and that he wasn't surprised to hear that Piero had been awarded 'the Crown of Reciters'.[3]

Piero's Talents and Cultural Patronage

Alessandro's letters reveal how wide Piero's interests were, but music was especially important. He won the award of 'Crown of Reciters' for his impromptu singing with friends, which Poliziano told Lorenzo he admired for its fluency and for Piero's clearly enunciated witticisms and retorts; they reminded him, he said, of Lorenzo, but they were also the same qualities that people had admired in Piero as a boy, when they were so captivated by his witticisms they would not let him go unless he performed for them.[4] Music had played an important part in the Medici children's upbringing from at least the time of Piero's grandparents. They were all taught to dance and sing – both of Lorenzo's sisters performed for members of the papal court returning from the congress at Mantua in 1460, and Lorenzo and all his siblings were offered dancing lessons before Lorenzo's wedding in 1469 (while Clarice prepared herself by having dancing lessons in Rome).[5] Piero and his companions danced and played music with Franceschetto Cibo in Rome before his betrothal in 1488, and on their way to the wedding ceremony the following year they sang May Day songs and were delighted to learn ones with new words and music when they reached Acquapendente – even though Alfonsina herself didn't dance and, unlike Clarice, evidently made no attempt to learn.[6]

Piero not only sight-read music and played musical instruments but, like his father, he also kept a number of northern singers in his household, including Heinrich Isaac, with two viola accompanists, one of whom, Cardiere, used to play for Piero 'almost every evening, after supper'; and he knew enough about their repertoire to be able to provide Isabella d'Este in 1493 with copies of polyphonic masses that were being

---

[3] The same, 8 and 12 May 1490, MAP 18: 390 and 22 ('Padrone mio caro ... vegho non avete dimenticato lo stare a cantare la nocte inproviso ... v'è dato la Corona de' dicitori'), cf. Poliziano to Lorenzo, 5 June, on hearing 'Piero nostro cantar improviso', ed. Fabroni, *Laurentii. ...Vita*, 2, p. 295, discussed by d'Accone, 'Lorenzo and Music', pp. 278–9.
[4] Poliziano to Lorenzo, 5 June, 1490, and pp. 46–7, n. 31 in this volume.
[5] Bryce, 'Performing for Strangers', esp. pp. 1081, 1094.   [6] pp. 61, 65–6 in this volume.

performed in Mantua.[7] Although to have a private chapel and singers was – like the library – a sign of princely status, the decision to import northern polyphonic singers to Florence had been taken by Cosimo as a communal gesture to keep Florence abreast of developments elsewhere in Italy, and once there, they worked freelance – as stand-up improvisers in public squares and as performers for confraternities and private banquets. Even when patronised by the Medici, someone like Isaac did not lose his freedom as he would have done in a court. But it is interesting that when he wrote a long and expensive composition to celebrate Florence's capture of Sarzanello in 1487, it was feared it would not be produced unless Piero returned from Rome (where he was celebrating his betrothal to Alfonsina) and bankrolled it, 'because it is a matter for which some expenditure is needed'.[8] Was it Piero's commission rather than Lorenzo's, as an Orsini now perhaps regarded as a more generous and 'courtly' patron than his father? Although Giovanni, after he became pope, took the courtly route by establishing a private chapel in Rome, it seems clear that the early tradition of improvised vernacular singing survived in Florence – without Piero – to create the new form of madrigal singing in the early academies, not the court.[9]

As well as singing, Piero also wrote poetry, although not as prolifically as his father. All that survives is a sonnet sent by Poliziano in April 1491 to another former pupil of his, Bernardo Ricci, and twenty or so mostly unpublished poems written during his exile and contained in a volume with many of Lorenzo's poems.[10] The 1491 sonnet discusses the dilemma of whether to follow the true good, which is unattainable in life, or desert it for vain hope, and despite finding it difficult to understand, Poliziano deemed it 'beautiful and very acute' and wanted Ricci to show it to the poet Bernardo Bellincioni at Lodovico's court for his opinion. It is unclear whether Piero's dilemma concerns the love affair on which he embarked a year later (spooking him with its false shadow of hope, as in his father's poem on fortune), or a spiritual dilemma similar to his father's in his questing poem on the vicious circle, 'Lo spirito talora

---

[7] d'Accone, 'Lorenzo and Music', pp. 278–80, and nn. 54, 55; on the *rimatore* Jacopo Corsi, see p. 175, n. 30 in this volume.
[8] Wilson, 'Sound Patrons', pp. 276–7 and n. 35, citing Kent (now in *Princely Citizen*, pp. 182–3).
[9] Wilson, p. 272; d'Accone, p. 265.
[10] Poliziano to Ricci, 23 April 1491, ed. Del Lungo, *Florentia*, pp. 253–4 (including the poem); Laur. 41, 38, 'Laurentii et Petri Mediceorum Carmina', discussed by Zanato, Lorenzo, *Canzoniere*, I, pp. 29–30 and by Brown, forthcoming in a volume in honour of Letizia Panizza. Cf. Del Corno Branca, *Sulla tradizione*, p. 38, n. 21; Bandini, *Catalogus* 5, cols. 155–8, citing nos. 1 and 2 (fol. 68r-v, no. 1 ed. Pieraccini, *Stirpe*, I, p. 169, no. 2 ed. and tr. Roscoe, *Life*, 1, pp. 274–5).

a sè redutto' (which comes first, saving grace or the will to be saved?), which Piero would have known as the subject of a debate transferred from the cathedral to the Medici palace in 1489.[11] It is nevertheless revealing of his mental world and conflicted feelings – like the poems he wrote in exile. Although many of the love poems follow his father and Poliziano in using well-worn Dantesque and Petrarchan imagery, one or two are strikingly original in adopting the still unfamiliar philosophy of Empedocles to express the idea of strife and love as alternating forces in the universe. So, too, is the third poem, which expresses the horror and bitterness of exile through images that seem to be drawn from Seneca's *Medea* and *Thyestes* – reflecting in them the same violence that is expressed in the Laocoön fresco (begun by Lorenzo but completed by Piero) in the villa at Poggio a Caiano.[12]

Piero had been closely involved in his father's cultural patronage and his acquisition of antiquities since his first visit to Rome in 1484, and he quickly became a noted patron himself, as well as a lover of books and paintings. His own room in the Medici palace has been said to show 'considerable refinement' that belies his reputation for being uninterested in art. It contained several bronzes, including a figure mounted on a horse by Filarete (identified as Marcus Aurelius), a centaur by Bertoldo, and a Pallas with shield and spear by Botticelli (now lost). It also contained two religious paintings, an *Annunciation* (from his grandfather's collection) and a *Christ on Mount Olive*.[13] In Piero's *anticamera*, among various furnishings and objects – a fine carpet, a Flemish tapestry and a St. Francis – there was a *Christ on the Cross* by fra Angelico, a naturalistic portrait of Alfonsina's head, and above the bed a *Fortune* by Botticelli or his school, which it has been suggested may be an exceptional early example of an erotic painting.[14] And although there were no portraits of Hercules in Piero's rooms, Antonio Pollaiuolo's famous paintings of his *Labours* in the main *sala* of the palace were cited by Antonio as evidence of his attachment to the Medici when, in July 1494, he asked Virginio Orsini to allow him, 'for my love of Piero de'

---

[11] Lorenzo, *Canzoniere*, ed. Zanato, 2, nos. 29, 'Fortuna come suol' (tr. Dempsey, *Portrayal of Love*, p. 104) and 74, 'Lo spirito talora' (discussed by Zanato in I, pp. 294–9); on the debate, Kraye, 'Lorenzo and the Philosophers', pp. 151–7, and Orvieto, 'Religion and Literature', esp. pp. 200–3.

[12] Laur. 41, 38, esp. nos. 3, 20 and 21 (fols. 68v, 74v–75v), cf. n. 41 in this chapter and Brown, 'Piero's Poems', forthcoming.

[13] Ciardi Dupré Dal Poggetto, 'I dipinti di Palazzo Medici', pp. 157–8: 'una notevole raffinatezza', Spallanzani and Bertelà, *Libro d'Inventario*, pp. 80–1. The passage leading to his room had two paintings, Starnina's *Tebaide* (Uffizi), from Cosimo's time, and 'una storia di fauni e altre figure' by Desiderio da Settignano, ivi, p. 80, Dal Poggetto, p. 157.

[14] Nelson, 'Leonardo e la reinvenzione', p. 15, n. 54, citing Everett Fahy.

Medici', to return to his property 'between Poggio a Caiano and the city of Pistoia'.[15]

Piero also showed personal interest in the growing taste for Florentine primitives by offering to buy a Cimabue he had heard was in a Benedictine monastery outside Florence, which the abbot then tactfully gave him as a personal gift.[16] It has recently been suggested he was also interested in Signorelli's paintings, which he would have got to know through the Vitelli (to whom he was related by marriage) when he visited them in Città di Castello in the 1490s.[17] He continued his father's patronage of Michelangelo, whose close attachment to the Medici household is shown by the 'compelling' and 'playful' conceit of the snow sculpture – possibly a recumbent Goliath beneath Donatello's *David* – that Piero in 1494 asked Michelangelo to make for him in the middle of the courtyard of their palace in Via Larga.[18] Piero consulted Michelangelo when he wanted to acquire ancient cameos and gems and he commissioned sculptures from him, perhaps the early *Madonna of the Stairs* and the *Battle of the Centaurs*, as well as the colossal Hercules that later belonged to Filippo Strozzi.[19] Piero may have introduced him to the prior of Santo Spirito (for whom he made a wooden crucifix), since Piero was elected as an *operaio* to Santo Spirito's board of works in July 1492, when he inherited his father's interest in the sacristy and the vault of its vestibule.[20] Like many other posthumous accounts of Piero, Condivi's account of his patronage of Michelangelo seems to have been coloured by later events, although what he says about Piero being upset by Michelangelo's silent flight from Florence in 1494 is evidently supported by contemporary evidence.[21] Piero also patronised Michelangelo's friend Tanaglia, who helped him to buy gems and three marble heads, and the

---

[15] Antonio del Pollaiuolo in Roma to Virginio Orsini, 13 July 1494, Rome, Archivio Capitolino, Orsini Ms 102, fol. 305, Wright, *The Pollaiuolo Brothers*, pp. 3–4, 425, n. 7. On Piero's involvement in Filippino Lippi's frescoes at Poggio a Caiano, n. 41 in this chapter.

[16] Ciardi Dupré Dal Poggetto, 'I dipinti di Palazzo Medici', pp. 148–9.

[17] Mazzalupi, 'Signorelli, i Vitelli e i Medici.'

[18] Marchand, 'Materials of Ephemeral Sculpture', pp. 261–3.

[19] Hirst, *Michelangelo*, pp. 18–22 (cf. Hirst, *Young Michelangelo*, pp. 17, 35, pls. 7 and 8); Vasari, *Le Vite* and Condivi, *Vita*, partly ed. Fusco and Corti, *Lorenzo de' Medici*, pp. 345 (doc. 222), and 350 (doc. 228 [5]); Elam, 'Lorenzo's sculpture garden', pp. 58–60 and nn. 126, 127; Wright, 'Myth of Hercules', p. 334.

[20] On 20 May 1493 it was agreed the vault in front of the sacristy was to be made according to the model and 'quello che più paresse a Piero di Lorenzo', Botto, 'L'edificazione', p. 36, Belluzzi, 'Chiese a pianta centrale', pp. 399–400 and n. 57, 403 and n. 70.

[21] Botto, 'L'edificazione', p. 36, n. 1 (his letters suggest he was later ready to work for Piero in Rome, although let down by him); Hirst, *Michelangelo*, pp. 19–22, at 21–22 (on the dream of the musician Johannes Cordier, who also went with him to Rome in 1492).

goldsmith Michelangelo di Viviani, who made a necklace for his embassy to Rome in 1492 and mounted other gems for him.[22]

So Piero's interest in art and sculpture seems to have been genuine and not simply a dutiful fulfilment of his father's legacy. Although he had been brought up by his father and Poliziano to value and enjoy the Medici mirabilia – the paintings and the ancient sculptures, cameos and goblets now incised forever with his father's name – his especial love was the books in the Medici library. In the same letter of 8 May in which he described to Lorenzo his visit to Poggio a Caiano, Piero immediately turned from talking about the farm and the breeding pigeons to the library:

> The library, in what concerns me, has been done. I have already finished many books, begun and nearly finished others. What holds me up now is this death of the king of Hungary, and although it creates an abundance of scribes ... until I see all his books and their quality, I can do nothing in order not to replicate them, but I hope in two or three days messer Angelo da Montepulciano and I will be on top of it, and meanwhile the scribes are coming down in price since they can't get work from others.[23]

Two days later, after describing at length Ermolao Barbaro's visit to Florence, he added that he was no further forward with the library because of this visit. But despite his many other preoccupations at this time, Piero did acquire some of Matthias Corvinus's library for the Medici library, which was being created at the same time and used many of the same scribes.[24]

Based on the dated inscriptions and the emblems, seventeen manuscripts in the Medici library were acquired for and by Piero, nearly all richly decorated by the miniaturist Attavante. Moreover, he (together with Poliziano), rather than his father, was probably responsible for the accession of many of the much larger group of sixty-four manuscripts that were 'paid for by Lorenzo' or were 'for Lorenzo and his heirs' – only five of which specifically mention Lorenzo.[25] The same is true of most of the two hundred Greek manuscripts that Janus Lascaris claimed he had

---

[22] p. 162, n. 51 in this volume on the 'Ritratto della ispeza' in Rome'; on the jeweler Piero Maria Serbaldi, Fusco and Corti, *Lorenzo de' Medici*, pp. 137, 184, 267 (n. 32) and 321 (doc. 158).

[23] Piero to Lorenzo, 8 May 1490, MAP 42, 57v, cf. Dillon Bussi and Fantoni, 'Biblioteca', p. 136.

[24] De la Mare, 'New Research', p. 468 (on three of his manuscripts with Medici bindings or arms).

[25] Dillon Bussi and Fantoni, 'Biblioteca', pp. 137–9 and the lists on 140–7, esp. 2 (144–50); Dillon Bussi, 'Le biblioteche di Mattia Corvino', pp. 233, 250–2; de la Mare 'New Research', p. 469.

acquired for the Medici library in his 1494 preface to Piero of his *Greek Anthology*, in which he also praised Piero as a collector of classical texts.[26] For although Lascaris embarked on his two book hunts in the east under Lorenzo's aegis in 1490, most of the books arrived back in Florence after Lorenzo's death, when the library was reorganised with a new system of numeration. This makes their accession to the library Piero's (and Poliziano's) responsibility; a later note listing thirty-one Greek books in it specifically states that Piero paid for the 'beautifully written' manuscript.[27] The Syrianus is dated September 1492, 'a spese di Piero', and is one of four Greek manuscripts in Dillon Bussi's list of seventeen 'Codici per Piero di Lorenzo' (with a Eusebius, a Galen and a Damascius, the last head of Plato's academy in Athens); the others include a Plato translated by Ficino, a commentary by Calcidius on Plato's *Timaeus*, and a Bede; the rest were Church Fathers: Ambrose, Augustine, Gregory and Jerome.[28]

The library also contained books dedicated to Piero and just one or two that contained his own writings, including the poems referred to earlier.[29] If it reveals less about Piero's taste than about Lorenzo's and that of his friends, the humanists Poliziano, Pico and Giorgio Benigno Salviati, two of them were in fact Piero's teachers, as was the Franciscan Giovanni da Prato, who just after Lorenzo's death had proposed a nurturing reading list for Piero that 'tempered some ancients with the modern' (as Giovanni put it): a mixture of historians (Diodorus Siculus, Strabo, Livy, Caesar and Justinus) and Cicero's *De officiis* and the 'modern' Aquinas.[30] So we can assume the library was intended for scholars, as well as being a status symbol – like the Medici's other

---

[26] Wright, 'Myth of Hercules', pp. 338–9.
[27] Syrianus, Proclus's teacher, Laur. plut. 85, 25. ASF Acq. e Doni 142, ins. 8, no. 2 (24 September 1492); the 'sirianus' is one of the eighty-five Greek manuscripts 'in domo Petri' on 31 October 1495, *Inventario*, ed. Piccolomini, pp. 83–6, at 86; cf. Piero to Lorenzo 6 May 1490 (MAP 42, 54r); Gentile, 'Lorenzo e Giano Lascaris' at pp. 190–2.
[28] Dillon Bussi and Fantoni, 'Biblioteca', pp. 144–5, 137; cf. Fryde, 'Lorenzo's Greek Manuscripts', pp. 99, 101–3, de la Mare, 'New Research', pp. 469–70.
[29] Eg. Giovanni Nesi's *De moribus* (1484), pl. 77, 24; Sigismondo de Sigismondis, *Epistolae*, pl. 43, 25 (de la Mare, 'New Research', p. 473, 481, Bandini, *Catalogus*, 5, 220–1); Poliziano, *Liber Epigrammatum Graecorum* (pl. 55, 18, ed. Pontani, pp. l–li). Both Landino's printed Virgil commentary and Filippo Redditi's *Exhortatio* were dedicated to Piero, (Fubini, 'Lorenzo il Magnifico's Regime', pp. 78–9), also Marullo's *Hymni naturales*, bk. 3 (McGann, 'Medicean dedications'), and Benigno Salviati's *Dialectica nova*, pr. Florence, 1499 (and to Giovanni, Kraye, 'Lorenzo and the Philosophers', p. 154, n. 18). On his Bruni translation, pp. 34 and 36 in this volume; he also may have translated a treatise by Plutarch on conjugal love.
[30] Giovanni da Prato to Piero, recd. 13 April 1492, MAP 15, 82, ed. Verde, *Lo Studio* 2, pp. 370–1. On Benigno Salviati as Piero's teacher, Vasoli, *Profezia*, pp. 39, 45, 52–7; Kraye, 'Lorenzo and the Philosophers', p. 154.

collections – that competed with the royal and ducal libraries then being created by King Matteus Corvinus and the duke of Urbino. It was even referred to by contemporaries as a 'royal library', like Ptolemy's library at Alexandria, that not only contained extravagantly beautiful codices for display but – like copyright libraries today – offered a body of uncorrupted texts for public consultation.[31]

Although the Medici palace was becoming distinctly old-fashioned by the late Quattrocento, its books and collections of antiquities were not. Piero found himself acting as the learned cicerone, displaying its treasures to someone 'who seems intelligent and loves to see antiquities', according to Lorenzo, who told his son to show him everything in the garden and in the study, 'more or less whatever you think will give him pleasure'.[32] This was evidently Ermolao Barbaro, on his way to be Venice's ambassador in Rome via Florence and a quick visit to Lorenzo at the baths.[33] The occasion is famous for the guests Piero hastily assembled for a dinner party in the Medici palace at Barbaro's request. Apart from Barbaro's brother, Cardinal Marco Barbo's secretary and a doctor, they included the humanists Giovanni Pico della Mirandola, Ficino and Poliziano – to whom Piero added, as a representative citizen and a scholar within the family, Bernardo Rucellai: 'I don't know if we've done well or badly', Piero wrote to his father. After dining, he showed Barbaro the house, the medals, the vases and the cameos, 'in short everything, including the garden', 'in which he took great pleasure, although I don't think he knew much about the sculpture', 'and everyone marvelled at how many such good things there were, etc.'.[34]

Piero's comment has been taken to show his own superiority as a connoisseur of sculpture, but what is striking about his account of Barbaro's visit is his shrewd analysis of Barbaro's character. For what he spotted was the incongruity between Barbaro's life of scholarship and his life as a statesman that, a year later, caused a crisis in his life. He was very literate and elegant in his speech, Piero told his father,

> stealing witticisms and also speaking in Latin ... temperate in everything, as he needs to be, since he has a very weak and delicate constitution. He has the

---

[31] Dillon Bussi and Fantoni, 'Biblioteca', p. 137 (citing Valori: 'regiam illam Ptolomei bibliothecam', Kristeller, *Suppl.* I, p. 94).
[32] Lorenzo in Bagno to Piero, 9 May 1490, MAP 18, 19, ed. Fusco and Corti, *Lorenzo de' Medici*, p. 314, doc. 136 (with full bibliography); tr. Ross, *Lives*, 316–7.
[33] On Ermolao Barbaro 'the Younger' (1453–93), *DBI* 6, 1964 (Emilio Bigi).
[34] Piero to Lorenzo, 10 May, MAP 42, 59, fol. 59r–v (autogr), ed. Fabroni (*Laurentii ... Vita*, 2, pp. 377–9) and Roscoe (*Life*, 2, Append., pp. 96–7), extract in Fusco and Corti, p. 315, doc. 137, cf. 141; Gilbert, 'Bernardo Rucellai', p. 106; Bullard, *Lorenzo*, p. 32; Elam, 'Lorenzo...'s Sculpture Garden'; Beschi, 'Sculture antiche', esp. pp. 291–3.

reputation for being an expert in public affairs [*rebus agendis*] but these things don't seem to go together and are more for display than not.³⁵

As Piero understood all too well – perhaps not without a touch of *schadenfreude* – it was difficult to combine the public life of diplomacy with other interests, for by accepting from the pope the office of Patriarch of Aquileia counter to Venetian law, Barbaro, the eminent scholar and diplomat, died in exile in Rome only three years after his visit to Florence.³⁶

The other marvel that drew visitors from afar was the Medici villa at Poggio a Caiano. Lorenzo had acquired it from his brother-in-law Bernardo Rucellai in 1474, and although building did not begin until the late 1480s, he began planning its novel classicising design at once and it soon became the subject of widespread interest and praise. So, too, did the even more innovative model farm that Lorenzo developed on the site during his lifetime.³⁷ Something of the excitement the project generated can be seen in Piero's letter to his father in early May 1490, when he visited Poggio for the first time since his father had left for the baths, 'to inform myself of what you asked me to tell you about'. Poggio, he said, was 'very beautiful, the fields all green since the bad weather had prevented mowing them'; the silkworms (*bruchi*) were doing well, though a wolf had eaten a pair of peacocks; the guinea fowl appeared haphazardly, one here, one there; there were about thirty or thirty-four calves; the doves had a pair of chicks; the furnace couldn't be finished because of the weather; and there were cheeses in the dairy farm.³⁸ His reference three weeks later (on 27 May) to 'the Poggio things going well', despite a great downpour and continued rain that day, pre-dates a reference to work having begun on the *palazzo* on 12 July 1490. By September the building was well under way and what was emerging was already 'the most beautiful thing'.³⁹

During the following summer, admiration for the villa was no longer confined to Medici intimates but had spread to the wider world. In May

---

³⁵ Piero, letter of 10 May: 'Ha nome di experto in Rebus agendis, ma non pare consuonino queste cose insieme, che più presto pare da ceremonie che no' (fol. 59r).
³⁶ Bigi in *DBI*, p. 98, commenting too on 'questo acuto giudizio di Piero'.
³⁷ Fubini, 'Lorenzo...'s Regime', pp. 80–2; on the villa, Foster, *A Study;* on the farm, Foster, 'Lorenzo...'s *Cascina*', Kent, *Lorenzo de' Medici*, pp. 73–5, 135–45; Kent, *Princely Citizen*, pp. 128, 165–80.
³⁸ Piero in Florence to Lorenzo in Bagno, 8 May 1490.
³⁹ The same, 27 May 1490, MAP 42, 73, fol. 74r: 'le cose del Poggio vanno bene', Nelson, 'Filippino Lippi at ... Poggio', pp. 163–4 and nn. 15 and 16 (citing Filippo da Gagliano on 18 September: 'non vedesti mai la più bella coxa', etc.). On 6 November (MAP 56, 47), Dovizi reported to Lorenzo the completion of 'la quarta volta' and 'la prima tirata all'anitre'.

ambassadors from Milan were not only 'amazed' but 'stupefied' by what they saw: they thought the building was appropriate for the estate, 'and, in short, it pleased them immeasurably', while messer Branda da Castiglione didn't think he had ever seen anything like it: if Lodovico Sforza saw it, they opined, he wouldn't like it. The duke clearly felt challenged by it and the following year Piero was asked to send Lodovico a model of the villa.[40] It was Piero who oversaw the building of the front block with the vaulted loggia after Lorenzo's death (the only part of the villa completed by Giuliano da San Gallo before 1494), and although Lorenzo may have commissioned it, it was Piero who also oversaw Filippino Lippi's Laocoön fresco for the loggia in 1493 and who possibly commissioned the violent *Death of Meleager*, which may have influenced the striking imagery of his later poems in recalling the murder of Giuliano in 1478 and its legacy of fear.[41]

The villa at Poggio was very close to Piero's heart. He had frequently stayed there as a child and he and Alfonsina went there after their marriage instead of immediately entering Florence, due to his sister Luisa's death. So it was a place for enjoying the pleasures of family and countryside as well as showing off. Piero went to Poggio not only to report to his father on its progress but to visit Alfonsina and Contessina, for whom he carried a message from her husband (Piero Ridolfi) in Florence. His other sister Maddalena, in Rome, also sent messages to Piero for 'my two hearts, Alfonsina and Lucretia' (the eldest sister), as well as for Lorenzo and 'our mother, the countess [Alfonsina's mother, now evidently replacing Maddalena's deceased mother in that role] and all the others' – that is, 'the other brigade', Piero's brothers and cousin who were then with their tutors in Pisa and the nearby Medici villas.[42] It was also when Piero was in Poggio that we first hear about his lover, the anonymous 'R', whom he visited in or around Prato and to whom he remained in thrall for at least the next eighteen months, when he declared he was prepared to lose everything – the regime, Florence and Italy – in order to regain her love. On 28 August 1492 Piero wrote from Poggio to tell Dovizi that he had planned to stay there until returning to Florence

---

[40] Dovizi to Lorenzo, 26 May 1491, MAP 56, 11v, Kent, *Lorenzo de' Medici*, pp. 139, 141; Piero to Lodovico Sforza, 5 October 1492, ed. Heydenreich, 'Giuliano da Sangallo' (Kent, ibid., pp. 188–9); cf. p. 173 in this volume.

[41] Nelson, 'Filippino Lippi at ... Poggio', pp. 162–6.

[42] Maddalena to Piero, 16 April, 22 May 1490, Franco, *Lettere*, pp. 144–6 at 145; cf. Maldei in Pisa to Piero, 13 May, MAP 18, 23, Picotti, *Giovinezza*, pp. 251–2, and Append. 2, 19, pp. 678–9 ('Vita pisana'). Cf. Piero to Lorenzo, 23 May, 3, 5 and 9 June (MAP 42: 70, 83v, 88r, 95r) on Lorenzo's ailing sister Nannina Rucellai († 1493, aged 46) Pieraccini, *Stirpe*, I, pp. 147–8; Tomas, *Medici Women*, pp. 1, 17–18.

for one night, 'and then I would go with la R. etc.'; Dovizi was to try to find Giannozzo Pucci, who was to come to Piero the following day in Prato, for the celebration of the Virgin Mary:

> and I want him to return with me so he can learn en route the villa of R, which he knows about and not anyone else that I might trust, so understand what I want to say; if I'm lucky, I'll go to Prato tomorrow ... if I'm not, I'll be in Florence tomorrow evening. Tell Giannozzo that if he comes to Prato, he should find some reason for coming that isn't this one.[43]

So Poggio and nearby Prato were the source of personal as well as family pleasures for Piero. Poggio and his other country villas near Pisa, Agnano and Spedaletto were also his bases for enjoying riding, falconry and bird catching, the other passions – with footballing and jousting – that were an important feature of Piero's life.

Horses, Falcons and Footballers

The Medici children had all enjoyed horses and ponies as part of their upbringing in the countryside – especially Pierfrancesco, from the other branch of the family, who spent much of his day hunting and racing in and around his villa of Trebbio in the Mugello, in close contact with ducal families like the Gonzaga, the Este and the Sforza through buying and selling horses as well as racing them.[44] Although his young cousins Lorenzo and Giuliano had a more urban upbringing than Pierfrancesco, they too were brought up to love hunting in the Mugello, so Piero's affection for horses is unsurprising.[45] As an adult he founded the Ruota hunt, and even as a six-year-old he delighted in hearing his pony's 'joyous ncighs' resounding in the countryside when it was finally returned to him in Cafaggiuolo. Poliziano's image of what Piero would choose for a present is equally revealing: not the gelded horse or the pony he and little Giovanni would choose, but 'a Spanish horse with a golden saddle and tasselled reins'.[46] His parents, too, contrasted the characters of the two brothers, his mother saying Piero loved games (too busy skirmishing with clods of mud in 1485 to be given his brother's message) and that Giovanni should do the same sometimes, and his father calling Piero his

---

[43] Piero in Poggio to Dovizi in Florence, 28 August 1492, MAP 72, 40r: 'monstri qualche facienda che non paia quella'.
[44] Brown, *Medici in Florence*, pp. 79, 81–4; on Lorenzo's horses, Mallett, 'Horse-racing and politics', pp. 257–62.
[45] In fact, his first cousins once removed; on Lorenzo as a countryman, Kent, *Princely Citizen*, pp. 254–6, Rochon, *La Jeunesse*, pp. 263–6, Walter, *Lorenzo il Magnifico*, pp. 37–40.
[46] p. 32 in this volume.

'warrior son' compared with the 'good' Giovanni.[47] So it is unlikely Piero would have welcomed Innocent VIII's advice that Franceschetto offered him after his 'disaster' with a horse in March 1494, 'that one shouldn't run or ride a horse unless necessary'.[48]

As well as hunting, Piero enjoyed the urban sports of jousting and horse racing. Chivalric in origin, jousts became a civic entertainment in Florence in the fourteenth and fifteenth centuries, the commune contributing to the expense of public jousts on feast days to add to civic glory and fuse possibly discordant noble and popular forms of entertainment.[49] Similarly, although it was Italy's aristocratic elite who first owned the Arabian horses, or *barbieri*, used for racing, the early practice of betting on horses in the races celebrating saints' days made them a popular form of entertainment, too. So when Lorenzo started to collect Arabian *barbieri* in the 1470s and then win races with them, it strengthened his popularity with ordinary Florentines as well as his prestige with Italy's elite.[50] By then, the mercantile Medici had been participating in jousts and winning at least once as a rite of passage – Pierfrancesco had been victorious in 1454, Lorenzo in 1469 and Giuliano in 1475. Piero himself finally won his 'golden lance' as the first prize in July 1493, in a joust in which his cousin Lorenzo Tornabuoni won the second prize. Although his entrant had failed to win in 1490, Piero had organised a very prestigious joust the previous year, as we saw, in preparation for which he had broken two lances on the wall and was pronounced to be 'good on a horse' and becoming 'quite skilled and experienced'.[51] As well as enjoying a vaulting master (Vincenzio Pappacoda), Piero's passion for jousting is attested by the lists of armour, helmets and weapons in his rooms in the Medici palace. His *camera* contained four crested helmets given as jousting gifts, with figures respectively of Pallas, San Bartolomeo, a nude Cupid whose hands were bound behind a laurel tree, and a ship with a sail; and in the storeroom above the latrine (that contained various basins and shaving bowls) were two suits of jousting armour with helmets, breastplates and shields, all

---

[47] pp. 48 and 2, n. 3 in this volume.
[48] Cibo in Pisa to Piero, 12 March 1494, MAP 98, 598: 'lo dezastro ... ocorso de lo cavallo'.
[49] On the carefully calibrated levels of jousting for diplomatic visits, Otto Respons. 8, fol. 26v, 11 April 1491: for the French, 'poco di giostra ... cosa leggieri sanza proporvi alchuno segno di pregio'.
[50] Mallett, 'Horse-racing and politics', esp. pp. 256–8.
[51] pp. 83–4 in this volume, Maldei to Piero, 13 May 1490, MAP 18, 23, and Pandolfini to ser Andrea, 28 August (p. 102 in this volume); on the 1493 joust, Martelli, '*Libro delle Epistole*', p. 187; cf. Trexler, *Public Life*, esp. pp. 225–40, at 232–5, 423–4; Brown, *Medici in Florence*, pp. 81–2.

gilded, as well as Lorenzo's and Giuliano's breastplates covered in velvet. Piero had various additional breastplates *alla napolitana*, which were covered in green and Alexandrine velvet, others in white and red leather – and a mass of other accoutrements, all valued moderately except for one of the two suits of armour, which was valued at ninety florins.[52] When Bernardo Ricci was serving as the Florentine ambassador's secretary in Milan (the centre of the armaments industry) in 1493, he was instructed 'to give *maestro* Michele what he'll need to supply a small breastplate for Piero'; and in a revealing letter a year later, Ricci told Piero that *maestro* Michele's design for a new outfit would be 'something worthy of being with all the other beautiful and magnificent things you have; it would be a mortal sin for me to believe you'd have to refuse it for the cost, since the richer it is, the more certain I am that you'll love it'.[53]

Ricci's comment suggests jousting appealed to Piero's love of rich display and finery as well as to his competitiveness as a sportsman – what Parenti calls his dedication to body building and spear throwing 'in order to try to overcome his competitors, thinking it was a great glory to be considered bold and dextrous'. In November 1493, perhaps to prepare for his much-heralded joust the next year (but then cancelled, in deference to Ferrante's death), Piero enclosed a long stretch of public land running along the city walls (between the gates in Borgo Pinti and alla Croce, now in Piazza Beccaria) for riding and jousting – 'an unheard of thing to do, never before attempted by a private citizen', Parenti thought.[54] It was unpopular because it blocked free transit around the whole city, and since at the same time he reneged on his father's urban housing plan for the area west of Borgo Pinti, selling off the plots in 1493–94 and renting out the kiln for firing bricks and tiles, Piero seemed to be prioritising his own pursuits at the expense of his father's plan for urban regeneration.[55]

Horses were also useful as gifts and exchanges, oiling the wheels of diplomacy between Italian rulers. In late December 1491 Ferrante of Naples sent Piero a medium-sized dapple-grey, and another one two years later, 'a fine and noble animal', perhaps in return for Piero sending him the runner Garzerano; and when Duke Alfonso learnt that the

---

[52] *Inventario*, ed. Spallanzani and Bertelà, pp. 80–1, 88–92.
[53] Piero to Bernardo Ricci in Milan, 17 December 1493, *Ricordi di lettere* (2), p. 111; Ricci in Milan to Piero, 18 May 1494, MAP 50, 296, fol. 309r, appending on 310r 'Nota delle cose vanno in una Corazina del Magnifico …' totalling c. 63½ ducats.
[54] Parenti, *Storia*, I, pp. 55, 61–2; Najemy, 'Florentine Politics', p. 45; Brown, 'Piero in Power', pp. 122–3.
[55] Elam, 'Lorenzo's Architectural and Urban Policies', pp. 372–3. Only four of the 80–100 houses planned for the Via Laura project were built before Lorenzo died.

stables and horses at Poggio a Caiano had been burnt in 1493, his father King Ferrante promised to see Piero was mounted 'even better than before'.[56] He also received a *bella acchinnea* from the king of France, which Piero thought of sending to young Astorre Manfredi in Faenza (whose marriage he would soon be involved in brokering).[57] Other horses were procured for Piero in France through his bankers. In March 1493 Cosimo Sassetti in Lyon bought him three heavy horses (probably for jousting) and in June two more were despatched for him from Paris, one a young, beautiful and powerful Frisian, the other a somewhat lighter horse that would become a fine charger.[58] Sassetti and Franceschetto Cibo also procured horses for Piero's much-heralded joust; others were requested as loans from Giovanni and Annibale Bentivoglio, from his uncle, Rinaldo Orsini, and from Giacoppo Petrucci in Siena, who then presented him with a beautiful dapple-grey called Raona (adequate recompense would be a pair of hose for one of the men who brought it, the secretary Braccesi thought).[59]

Piero also loved falconry and hawking in the countryside. In 1488 he had said that a gift of some peregrine falcons from Francesco Gonzaga would be as welcome as horses from the marquis's famous stables, and after a visit from Lorenzo di Pierfrancesco's falconer Galletto when in Pisa, Piero told Dovizi that, without him, 'I would have no pleasure at all'.[60] The following year, as we saw, he left his pregnant wife in Florence in order to train some sparrowhawks that he had just received from Faenza.[61] The competition for the forty-eight highly prized falcons Piero sent to France in 1493 shows they were as valuable as horses for gift exchange: Philippe de Commynes wanted two, so did the Seneschal, and two were intended for Giuliano da Gagliano to give to the queen's

---

[56] Giuliano Ridolfi in Naples to Piero, 17 December 1491, MAP 14, 250, Bernardo Dovizi in Naples to Piero, 8 March 1494, ed. Grimaldi, 'Bernardo Dovizi', p. 231, Alamanni in Naples to Piero, 7 January 1493, *Correspondenza* 7, p. 213, and Baccio Ugolini in Naples to Piero, 7, 20 March, 12 April 1493, ibid., pp. 261, 265, 267. On Garzerano, pp. 121–2 following.

[57] Dovizi to Puccio Pucci in Faenza, 22 September 1493, SSX8LCMR 15, fol. 166; on the marriage, Brown, 'Piero in Power', pp. 119–20, and pp. 129–30 in this volume.

[58] Cosimo Sassetti in Lyon to Piero, 30 March 1493, MAP 14, 337 ('l'uno leardo et l'altro sagginato' bought 'per ordine di Vostra Magnificenza' and another 'assai più possente'); della Casa in Paris to Piero, 28 June 1493, ed. Can, p. 232.

[59] Piero, *Ricordi di lettere*, 13–19 January 1494, (2), pp. 114–15; Braccesi in Siena to Piero, 27 January, MAP 19, 209 ('uno paio di chalze solamente … gli basterà in segno ch'el Raona vi sia stato grato').

[60] Piero in Cafaggiolo to Dovizi, 30 July 1491, MAP 60, 50. The falconer also cared for Piero's horses in Pisa (Galletto to Piero, 11 June 1490, 8 December 1493, MAP 18, 31 and p. 140 in this volume); Kent, *Princely Citizen*, p. 258, n. 60.

[61] p. 84 in this volume.

treasurer, but the king wanted them all for himself and was delighted when he first viewed them by torchlight in the dusk.[62]

All these sports, like the Medici's cultural patronage, were politically useful as well as recreational, and the same is true of the plays, masques and triumphs that the Medici promoted in the last years of Lorenzo's life, which also lay on the delicate boundary between republican and royal enterprises. In 1489 Piero organised his own confraternity play in the Carmine, followed by a joust in late August,[63] and in the following years Lorenzo produced the *Seven Triumphs of Seven Planet*' for his company the Stella, a play for the company of St. John the Evangelist, the *Rappresentazione dei Santi Giovanni e Paolo* (in which Piero's twelve-year-old brother Giuliano took part) and the fifteen *Triumphs of Paulus Emilius* to celebrate Florence's patronal feast day, with five squadrons of horses and forty to fifty pairs of oxen pulling the carts – 'the best thing ever done for San Giovanni', one Florentine recorded.[64] Piero, meanwhile, was increasingly involved in the Company of the Magi, a confraternity based in San Marco whose annual pageant for Epiphany the Medici found irresistible in enabling them to dress up as kings (pausing in front of their own palace as they processed to San Marco), and yet was a communal event paid for by public funds.[65]

The only exception to these useful sports and shows was Piero's love of footballing in the streets. Football, or *calcio*, was beginning to be played as a team game in Florence, and in January 1491 the chronicler Cambi records a game played for three days on the frozen Arno by *giovani da bene*, who set little store by their lives – perhaps with Piero and his friend Alessandro Alessandri in mind.[66] Such was Piero's skill at playing both handball and football (*giuoco della palla, col pugno e col calcio*), according to Nardi, that outstanding players came to Florence from all over Italy to gain experience by playing with him. Piero also patronised a famous Spanish runner called Garzerano, who was so excellent 'in running and playing' that King Alfonso's eldest son Ferdinando wanted Piero to send

---

[62] Della Casa to Piero, 17 and 21 July 1493, ed. Can., I, pp. 238, 239–40; Pollini-Martin, *Banque*, pp. 166–9.
[63] pp. 82–3, n. 44 in this volume.
[64] Ventrone, *Feste*, pp. 29, 32, 33, citing Tribaldo's *Ricordanze*, pp. 271–2; on Lorenzo's *Rappresentazione* (pr. Buonaccorsi, c. 1485, de' Libri, 1498), Newbiggin, 'Politics in the *Sacre Rappresentazioni*", pp. 124–5, cf. Brown, *Florence* (2011), pp. 238–9.
[65] Hatfield, 'Compagnia de' Magi', Trexler, *Public Life*, pp. 422–4, 458–9 and in general, Trexler, *Journey of the Magi*, esp. pp. 89–92. On Piero and the Magi in 1492, p. 103 in this volume.
[66] Cambi, *Istorie*, 21, p. 57 (10 January 1491): 'da giovani da bene che rincresceva loro el vivere'. On snow in Florence in 1494 and Piero's snow sculpture, Marchand, 'Materials of Ephemeral Sculpture', pp. 261–3, and p. 111 in this chapter.

him to Naples, so he could run with the man whom his court awaited 'as though he were some prince'.⁶⁷ But although Nardi considered Piero unrivalled in riding and jousting – since he was 'robust in body, taller than average in stature, broad in chest and shoulders, agile and dextrous in all bodily sports and in the military art' – he thought his 'ball playing' (like his philandering) excessive, as did other Florentines, who especially condemned Piero for playing handball for money against a single opponent, which he was still doing four years later, when playing in the street against 'a wretched Spaniard'.⁶⁸ Nevertheless, Piero's wide cultural and sporting interests gave him standing and prestige with Italy's rulers and with his Guelf supporters in Florence's dominion and beyond. The Medici's links with towns outside Florence were long-standing, and they, too, contributed to the power and princely renown that the family was increasingly enjoying.

---

⁶⁷ Bernardo Dovizi in Naples to Piero, 15 February, 8 March 1494, ed. Moncallero, I, pp. 45–6, n. 14, and 65: 'come fussi qualche principe' Cf. Grimaldi, 'Bernardo Dovizi', p. 225.
⁶⁸ Nardi, *Istorie*, I, p. 21: 'troppo inclinato agli amori delle donne e al giuoco della palla col pugno e col calcio', cf. Alessandri to Piero, 4 May 1490 (p. 86, n. 55 in this volume), and Antonio Dovizi to ser Piero, 29 July 1493, p. 175, n. 29 in this volume.

9 Ruling as Patrons in Florence's Dominion and Beyond

Although Florence was where Piero lived and where his fate would be decided, he was nevertheless sustained by an extensive web of patronal, as well as banking, relationships that stretched outside Florence into its dominion and beyond, providing Piero with support from clients and supporters that helped to sustain him in his exile with a high price on his head. Through his great-grandmother Contessina, Piero was already in close contact with his Bardi relations in the Mugello and with old feudal families in Pistoia and Siena, and his father took care to nurture his role as patron and boss by introducing him early on to these client networks and teaching him through his own example. Like Lorenzo, Piero was called 'master of the workshop' to describe his role as boss – even if neither enjoyed the success of Giovanni di Bicci and Cosimo as bankers. Piero was appointed head of the Medici Bank in Pisa in 1489 (aged seventeen) under the aegis of his manager Giovanni Cambi, and he enjoyed a close relationship with his cousin Nofri Tornabuoni, who became manager of the Medici Bank in Rome, both cities of strategic and cultural importance that must have contributed to his political experience if not to his banking skills.

The strings of commendatory letters in the Medici's family archives show how extensive the family's web of patronal relationships was.[1] Piero's letter book, like his father's, is full of references to letters written 'for a friend', 'for the men of', 'recommendation for', which mingle with letters asking for personal favours and offering thanks for favours received. But perhaps because of the Orsini and the courtly influences on his upbringing, Piero adopted feudal gestures and the language of partisanship and revenge more freely than his father, not replying but 'biting his finger as a sign of vendetta' on being refused entry to

---

[1] Thanks largely to the work of F. W. Kent and his now classic essay 'Patron-Client Networks in Renaissance Florence', repr. in Kent, *Princely Citizen*, pp. 199–224, esp. 199–203, 212–14; cf. Kent and Simons, intro., *Patronage, Art and Society*; Kent, 'Ties of Neighbourhood', ivi, 79–98; Weissman, *Ritual Brotherhood*.

the government palace in 1494, and when angered with the behaviour of Francesco Soderini in June that year, threatening to wage open war on him and 'publish [him] as his enemy and treat [him] as an enemy everywhere'.[2] Chancery secretaries working for him called themselves his 'men' and in Florence's territory and border states Piero was the boss, working with clients for their mutual benefit, welcomed with old-fashioned family battle cries of 'Palle, Palle' in towns like Colle and Siena. Like a child who effortlessly moves from formal to demotic and back again, Piero's fluency in the city's language of republicanism and the territory's language of clientage suggests he was equally at home with both.

Patronage as a system of exercising political power worked on several levels: in cities it provided a bond linking factions or parties, rich with poor, and outside it linked urban lords with rural clients. Although it clearly survived the establishment of communal governments, enabling Lorenzo to be both a *gran maestro*, city boss, and a republican icon, *salus populi*, the system of bestowing favours to win political support and exercise private justice contradicted the city's republican ethos of impartial justice and awarding public offices for merit.[3] Lorenzo had shown himself to be adept at obtaining political offices for friends and clients, arbitrating marriage settlements and legal disputes and even circumventing due legal process by his personal intervention, despite considerable public outcry.[4] And although he retained the role of city boss until his death, effectively limiting Piero's patronage to the countryside, letters nevertheless show Piero acting as an arbitrator and being asked for political favours,[5] and in Lorenzo's absence in 1490 and after his death, Piero used 'the friends' to intervene in judicial cases as his father had done. Like Lorenzo, he was also ready to support his bodyguards and *bravi* when they got into trouble with the law – and to get his Bardi kinsmen to do the same, unwilling though one of them was to protect Piero's ex-retainer Papino, who had treated him as his 'mortal enemy'. When he asked Bernardo Dovizi to bring a certain Matheino back to Florence from Careggi after his 'misdeed', Bernardo wondered if Piero

---

[2] Cerretani, *Storia*, p. 206, 'morsesi il dito in segno di vendecta'; Brown, 'Piero in Power', pp. 121–2, and n. 50.
[3] Kent and Simons, *Patronage, Art and Society*; Brown, *Florence* (2011), intro., pp. xvi–xvii.
[4] On Lorenzo as arbitrator, Fabbri, 'The Magnificent Arbitrator'; Fabbri, 'Women's Rights', pp. 99, 101–2.
[5] E.g. Bernardo degli Alberti to Angelo Niccolini, 19 August 1494, Niccolini Archives, 14, 41.

still wanted him back in Florence, 'and, one could say, in prison', since the man he wounded might have died.[6] Far from adopting his father's tough stance on criminal justice in the city, Piero's street pastimes made people suspect (wrongly, it appears, in 1491) that he was himself involved in crime, and when the assassins of a young maker of paternosters in via de' Servi were allowed to escape a couple of years later, Dovizi warned Piero that unless he remedied crimes like this, 'one day this city will be quite unsafe'.[7]

Capo in Florence's Dominion

So it was not in Florence but outside, in the towns and cities in Florence's territorial state and on its liminal frontier where party feuds and vendettas abounded, that Piero's patronal influence was strongest.[8] In theory, the city's elected officials – its *podestà*, captains and commissaries – exercised impartial control over the territory, but patronage ties between its ruling factions and the subject towns undermined this by creating a three-way pull between the locals, the resident Florentine official and the patron.[9] In Prato, for example, the subject-city closest to Florence, Piero frequently used the wide powers inherited from his father to appoint to offices, telling the Florentine *podestà* in June 1493 to 'put the reformers in the palace and keep them there until they carry out the reform as agreed with Piero' – though still needing the *podestà*'s cooperation. And similarly it seems he 'sent a new *podestà* to Pistoia' for a year as a result of certain 'pacts' he had made there even before his father's death.[10] Nevertheless, Piero's position as territorial boss gave him greater status than the *podestà*, as we can see from Carlo Gherardacci's letter to Piero in July 1493 telling him that 'we want you to be lord of our persons and possessions, both in public and in private'.

---

[6] Tommaso Gualterotti de' Bardi de Vernio in Vernio to Piero, 9 June 1492, CS I, 3, fol. 146, cf. Kent, *Princely Citizen*, p. 257, n. 57. On Matheino, Bernardo Dovizi to Piero, [22] July 1493, ed. Moncallero, I, p. 24.
[7] Dovizi in Florence to Piero, 6 (January 1493), MAP 124, 23: 'un dì questa citta sarà pocha secura'.
[8] On feuds, Zorzi, '"Ius erat in armis"' and n. 15 in this chapter; on Guelf-Ghibelline labels, Ferente, *Gli Ultimi Guelfi*, esp. pp. 227–8, Gentile Becchi to Piero, 24 December 1493, ed. Buser, *Beziehungen*, p. 544, no. 22.
[9] Zorzi and Connell, ed. *Lo stato territoriale* (tr. *Florentine Tuscany*); on the officials, Guidi, *Il Governo*, 3 and 1, pp. 16–24, Connell, 'Il Commissario', Milner, 'Lorenzo and Pistoia', p. 237. On Piero as arbiter, Otto di Guardia rep. 95, fol. 55r.
[10] Piero, *Ricordi di lettere* (1), pp. 395, 428 (5 July 1492, 28 June 1493), 423–4 (recording c. 18 letters to the Reformatori in May–June 1493); cf. Kent, *Princely Citizen*, pp. 293–7.

Like many other rural clients, he needed Piero's support in a lawsuit, but by stressing that his family had supported the Medici in 1466 and had their arms mounted in his house, he clearly implied that they shared the deep patronal bonds that linked the countryside to political factions and parties in Florence.[11]

Piero similarly inherited his family's patronal interests in Pistoia, a town notoriously divided between the Cancellieri and the Panciatichi families, hence Lorenzo's reputed saying that Pistoia had to be held 'through its factions'.[12] Like Prato, it was close to his Bardi cousins' sphere of influence, and although earlier Medici had supported the Cancellieri faction while ensuring both factions participated in the political process, Lorenzo, like the Bardi, increasingly supported their rivals, the Panciatichi, replacing statutory procedures to make himself the city's indispensable patron and arbiter.[13] Piero found himself embroiled in Pistoia's unrest in 1490, during his father's absence from Florence, when – like his father – he was criticised by the Florentine commissaries there for opposing their strong measures to subdue the troublemakers.[14] In 1493 he was asked to protect some long-standing Medici 'friends and partisans' from a bann for a revenge murder issued by the Florentine Captain of Pistoia.[15] But Pistoia remained a dangerous place for the Medici and their supporters – despite the fact that Salvalaglio, one of their toughest bodyguards and devoted adherents, came from Pistoia, where the six-year-old Piero had delivered his first public speech while staying there on the outbreak of the Pazzi war. Even before 1494, the Medici needed the help of other members of the ruling group to control the city's factionalism, and after it, in the 'patronal vacuum' left by the Medici's exile, the city collapsed into full-scale civil war.[16]

---

[11] Carlo d'Andrea di Carlo [Gherardacci] in Prato to Piero, 29 July 1493, CS ser. I, 3, fol. 151, Kent and Simons, *Patronage, Art and Society*, p. 9.

[12] Machiavelli, *Il principe*, ch. 20: 'tenere Pistoia con le parte e Pisa con le fortezze'; Connell, 'Clientelismo' and 'I fautori delle parti'; Milner, 'Lorenzo and Pistoia', 'Rubrics and Requests'. On Pistoia, p. 91 in this volume

[13] Gori, *Una donna*, pp. 28–9; Connell, 'Clientelismo', pp. 538–42; Milner, 'Rubrics and Requests', pp. 319, 321–4.

[14] pp. 91–2 in this volume; letters to Piero from Pistoia in 1490 include MAP 81, 7 (Jacopo Conte, 17 April) and MAP 18, 10 (Andrea de Rossi, hospitalerius Ceppi, 29 April).

[15] A. Braccesi in Siena to Piero, 4 September 1493, SSX8LCMR 27, fol. 105v: 'amici et partigiani della casa vostra'.

[16] Milner, 'Rubrics and Requests', pp. 327–30 at 329; Connell, 'Clientelismo', pp. 540–2; Piero, *Ricordi di lettere* (1), p. 385, etc. On Salvalaglio, Kent, *Princely Citizen*, p. 257; B. Dovizi, *Epistolario*, ed. Moncallero, I, pp. 100–1, n. 7; Brown, *Florence* (2011), p. 109.

Faenza and the Romagna

Piero's patronal influence also extended into the Romagna, where it was mediated by Florentine commissaries, not by the city's captains and *podestà*.[17] One Romagna lord in contact with Piero was Pandolfo Malatesta of Rimini, who successfully used him to obtain offices, benefices and favours for his friends – enabling one to become judge of appeals in Florence and asking for another to be allowed to return with his family to Faenza.[18] But it was the two towns of Faenza and Forlì that were most strategically important to Florence for reasons that messer Puccio Pucci (who had replaced his uncle Dionigi in May 1493 as commissary) made clear.

Both towns lay on the Via Emilia, 'this Romagna highway', which is 'the most frequented in the whole of Italy and carries all the armies everywhere', messer Puccio told Piero. Little wonder that both Florence and Milan competed to protect these fortress towns after the murders of their rulers in 1488 – especially Faenza, now nominally ruled by Galeotto Manfredi's young son Astorre, but also Forlì and Imola, whose regent, Girolamo Riario's widow the 'virago' Caterina, despite being a Sforza and Lodovico's niece, was dependent on Florence's support (she was holed up in Forlì's fortress of Ravellino with her lover, its castellan, who was Lodovico's enemy).[19] Because of Forlì's importance in protecting Florence's frontier – as 'the walls of Florence' – messer Puccio strongly urged Piero to continue his father's protection and, if necessary, take over Caterina's state, in order to make:

the Florentine dominion very prosperous and glorify your [Florence's] name ... for you would dominate this Romagna highway ... And if you were the lords of this road, you would be the judges of Italy. So, Magnificent Patron, I urge and pray you to apply your intelligence to these affairs of the Romagna, since they can exalt the Florentine name more than all the others.[20]

---

[17] Whereas commissaries were hand-picked officials, the others were normally drawn (but see Rubinstein, *Government*, Append. 14, pp. 378–91), Connell, 'Il Commissario', p. 604.

[18] Pandolfo Malatesta in Rimini to Piero, 4 and 28 September 1492, MAP 60, 302 and 19, 161 (the latter ed. Masetti Zannini and Falcioni, *La signoria di Pandolfo IV*, pp. 237–8), and four letters in 1494 (MAP 138: 159–161, 100, 144).

[19] Pellegrini, *Congiure di Romagna*, Lorenzo, *Lettere* 12, pp. 195–7, 344–7. On Caterina's grief on Lorenzo's death, Pucci in Faenza to Piero, 25 May 1493, MAP 54, 168, fol. 167v ('lla Natura non produrrà mai più un simile huomo').

[20] Letter of 25 May, fol. 167 bis, r–v, urging Piero to support Caterina, secretly if not openly (since Lodovico and Cardinal Alessandrino opposed her liaison with Feo). On the virago Caterina, Pitkin, *Fortune Is a Woman*, pp. 249–50 and n. 53 (citing Machiavelli, *Disc.* 3, 6, *Principe*, ch. 20), Lev, *Tigress of Forlì* (but mistaking Pucci for his emissary il Bello on pp. 168–9).

Both states would become crucial to Piero and Florence when facing Lodovico's opposition during the Cibo crisis in 1493 and the French invasion in 1494 (when Piero was tasked with getting Caterina to join the allies' league); and because Florence's commissary there, messer Puccio, was a Medici intimate, it was to Piero rather than to the Otto di Pratica that messer Puccio wrote for advice: should Caterina be protected by some of the two hundred men-at-arms promised by Florence, should he reveal himself in Caterina's favour, do nothing – or what?[21] Although the authoritative messer Puccio claimed to have attended Caterina's marriage to Riario in 1473 and now offered her his personal support, 'as if you were the [male] lord of Forli', Piero was the boss and did not hesitate to criticise Puccio for over-interrogating her about Lodovico's visit to Ferrara, warning him never to mention Lodovico when writing to Caterina.[22] In the event, Caterina shrewdly refused to commit herself to Piero and Florence either in 1493 or in 1494, instead signing a treaty with Charles VIII and Lodovico, who promised to protect her state and pay her 20,000 ducats.[23]

Piero's patronal control was more direct in Faenza due to the minority of Astorre Manfredi, who had been supported by Lorenzo and the urban ruling elite in Faenza in 1488 against the claims of his cousin Ottaviano (backed by the popular party in the town and countryside and favoured by an earlier Florentine commissary).[24] So although Piero intervened frequently in its affairs, through the Pucci and with the cooperation of the castellan and Astorre's 'tutors', he did so within a traditionally partisan and clientage-based system that worked for the mutual gratification of all concerned – Piero, the commissaries and the locals. As messer Puccio told Piero in mid-June, he would gain credit himself from recommending someone to Piero for an office in Florence, and since his uncle Dionigi had been gratified by Piero's many favours, 'your Magnificence must also gratify me'. Piero in turn asked messer Puccio to support the Gondoni family in a dispute over a church by speaking 'modestly' on his behalf to

---

[21] Puccio in Faenza to Piero, 21 May 1493, MAP 54, 145, fols. 144r, 145r. On the offer of troops, Pucci to Caterina Sforza, 13 May 1493, MAP 54, 141.
[22] The same, 11 and esp. 13 May 1493, MAP 54, 138 and 141: 'chome se voi fussi signore'; Puccio to Piero, 25 May 1492, MAP 54, 168, fol. 167r; Puccio headed the 1492 embassy to Rome in which Piero was the youngest member. On road networks and changing routes to the east, Franceschi, 'Medici Economic Policy', pp. 131, 139.
[23] The same, 8 June 1493, MAP 54, 175, fol. 174r, cf. P. A. Soderini in Venice to Piero, 28 October 1494, MAP 73, 183.
[24] Pellegrini, *Congiure di Romagna*, pp. 120 (n. 58), 141; Cattani in *Faenza*, ed. Vasina, pp. 35–8 (the earlier commissary was G. B. Ridolfi), and p. 93, n. 26 in this volume; on Ascanio Sforza's rumoured plan to poison Astorre and Ottaviano, Puccio in Faenza to Piero, 12 June 1493, MAP 54, 180, fols. 179r–v, 179 bis^r.

the governor and castellan. In his – by now familiar – even-handed manner, he told his commissary he wanted an open and fair settlement that would please his friends and offend nobody, since 'on one hand, I willingly take trouble for my friends, as is customary in our family', but 'on the other, I don't want to upset anyone there'.[25]

The issues at stake in the granting and withholding of favours emerge more starkly in the affair of 'the men from Cirone'. These men had been 'given' to Piero by Astorre, so messer Puccio's failure to get them out of prison for a murder they had committed upset Piero more than he could say, since it was a slur on his honour and standing in Faenza as their boss, especially as their enemies were threatening to kill the men once they emerged. He then rejected messer Puccio's and the castellan's solution (safe conduct for the men from the brother of the victim, in order to restore the equilibrium) and was delighted when the men were released at the end of July, apparently without bloodshed.[26] When Piero failed to persuade the men from Cirone to relinquish a castle to the castellan the following year, he admitted to messer Puccio (in 'an aside for your ears alone') that the castellan should not be gratified at once but held 'on a tight curb chain' until they saw how things were going, in order to get better service from him.[27]

Much grander issues were at stake in Faenza than this, however, for which messer Puccio's favour was later rewarded with a cardinalate for his brother Lorenzo as one of Leo X's first appointments in 1513.[28] Messer Puccio was married to Girolama Farnese, sister of the beautiful Giulia, the pope's current lover, and it was through her and Lorenzo, then a cleric in Rome, that Piero got drawn into the Borgia pope's curial circle. The initial plan hatched in Rome was for Piero to act as broker in a marriage between the little Astorre Manfredi and Laura, the pope and Giulia's one-year-old daughter (who resembled the pope so closely, Lorenzo Pucci told his half-brother Giannozzo, that 'truly she can be

---

[25] Puccio in Faenza to Piero, 15 June 1493, MAP 54, 181, fol. 180v, Piero to Puccio, 20 June 1493, SSX8LCMR.15, fol. 104.
[26] Piero to Puccio in Faenza, 10 July 1493, SSX8LCMR 15, fol. 114r: 'con tanta molestia dello animo mio, che non vi potrei dire tanta'; Puccio to Piero, 25, 30 May and 2 June (MAP 54: 168, fol. 167r–v, 172, fol. 171r and 173, fol. 172r); Bernardo Dovizi to Puccio, received 26 July, SSX8LCMR 15, fol. 132; cf. Piero to Puccio, 16 July 1493, ibid., fol. 123 (and on the theft of the cardinal's silver *tazze* in Passignano, Braccesi to Giovanni on the 17th, SSX8LCMR.15, fol. 81r).
[27] Piero to Puccio, 2 January 1494, CS ser. 1, 340, fol. 107v, 'tenergli strecto el barbazale'.
[28] Lorenzo, *Lettere* 9, p. 388, n. 15. Lorenzo Pucci refused to head Cardinal Farnese's household without first 'satisfying' Piero, 'sanza voluntà del quale ... non piglierei partito alchuno', to messer Puccio (28 September 1493), CS I.340, fol. 13r–v.

said to have sprung from his seed').[29] His letter shows how intimate he had become with his sister-in-law, Giulia Farnese, whose unbound hair he described as more beautiful than he had ever seen it when he visited her and Lucrezia Borgia on Christmas Eve 1493. As a result, he was able to explain to Giannozzo that Laura's dowry would be large (since the pope liked to do well by his daughters, as he had done for 'madonna Lucrezia'), and that Piero could expect to get a third of the dowry's value for brokering it and become 'the patron of everything', with influence in the church and the Papal States.[30] Eventually the little Laura was betrothed neither to Astorre nor to Piero's brother Giuliano (whom Giannozzo proposed as a substitute, knowing the castellan of Faenza wanted Astorre to marry Piero's own daughter, Clarice), but to Pope Julius II's nephew, Niccolò della Rovere.[31] Once again the Pucci's ambition had outstripped Piero's, but the incident is revealing of the way they promoted him in Rome, Lorenzo Pucci going so far as to tell Cardinal Alessandrino (Giovanni di San Giorgio, 'l'Alessandrino') in late December 1493 that Piero's authority in Florence was tantamount to the pope's in Rome: together, he said, they had 'a God in the sky and a lord on the earth that was the magnificent Piero, who could dispose of the city of Florence as our lord [the pope] could dispose of the mitre, and more'.[32] He must have boosted Piero's self-esteem, if not his reputation.

Rome and the Medici Bank

Rome, of course, was neither in Florentine territory nor on its frontier, but it became part of the Medici's patronage network through the Pucci and through the influence of the Medici Bank there. Although the bank had been closed in the aftermath of the Pazzi conspiracy, it was reopened in 1481 by Piero's great-uncle Giovanni Tornabuoni, who was succeeded as manager in 1487 by his nephew Nofri. As a result of Lorenzo's commitment to pay the debts of Pope Innocent and his son Franceschetto Cibo, the bank incurred heavy losses in the late 1480s and the early 1490s, which continued under Piero, especially after his exile and the execution of his cousin Lorenzo Tornabuoni, when the

---

[29] Lorenzo Pucci to Giannozzo Pucci, 24 December 1493, CS I, 340, fol. 99r, Gregorovius, *Lucrezia Borgia*, pp. 42–4, and Mathew, *Life and Times*, p. 86: 'adeo ut vere ex eius semine orta dici possit'.
[30] The same, fol. 98v, Brown, 'Piero in Power', pp. 119–21 at 120, n. 39.
[31] Ibid., p. 120, nn. 40 and 41.
[32] Ibid., p. 121, n. 45 (26 December 1493). He added that 'Gianozo [Pucci] aveva data l'anima e il corpo' to Piero as the cardinal 'dice da aver dato a nostro Signore' (de Roover, *Banco*, p. 320 shows Gio. Tornabuoni using the same expression).

bank was declared bankrupt.³³ Nofri had quickly offered advice to Piero after Lorenzo's death, and after Innocent's death three months later, he warned Piero of a tough papacy ahead under Alexander VI, whom he shouldn't trust, since during his time in Rome, Nofri had never seen him do anything good for the Medici or for the Florentine nation – adding that he hoped he wouldn't be thought presumptuous in talking to Piero as freely as he used to talk to Lorenzo.³⁴ Although careful not to overstep his brief – especially after Valori's precipitous flight from Rome at the height of Cibo crisis – his growing intimacy with the pope nevertheless enabled him to mediate with him and offer Piero his advice.³⁵ So although a banker and not a resident secretary in Rome like Guidotti, Nofri nevertheless contributed an important thread to the web of the Medici's patronal power.³⁶

Siena as a Client State

Among the frontier towns on the southern boundary of Florence's dominion, Arezzo and the walled towns of Colle Val d'Elsa and San Gimignano all maintained close patronal ties with the Medici.³⁷ But there were two cities that were particularly important to the Medici, both formerly wealthy commercial and trading centres: Siena to the south and Pisa at the mouth of the Arno, due west of Florence. Whereas Pisa formed part of Florence's dominion only after 1406, valued especially as the gateway to the Mediterranean and its maritime trade, Siena remained independent until 1555, but because of its situation between Arezzo and Colle di Val d'Elsa, it too enjoyed very close clientage links

---

[33] Guidi Bruscoli, '1487 Medici-Cybo Marriage', esp. pp. 75–6, 81–3, Picotti, *Giovinezza*, pp. 84–6, 133–4, n. 74, 523–4, and 466–7 (nn. 4–6 on 523–4). On the bank's bankruptcy and the cardinals' protest, Signori respons. 10, fol. 57, 16 March 1498.

[34] Nofri in Rome to Piero, 8–9 September 1492, MAP 14, 300, fol. 311r: 'vegho apparecchiarsi un duro papato', etc.

[35] The same, 10–11 September 1492, MAP 14, 302, fol. 315r; 16 January 1494, MAP 18, 79, fols. 90r–91r; 27 April 1493, MAP 18, 99, fols. 111r–112r. In July Nofri helped Piero arrange a marriage within the Lapi family, Piero, *Ricordi di lettere*, 13 June 1493, (1), p. 427 and Nofri to Piero, 13 July, MAP 60, 601, Tewes, *Kampf um Florenz*, p. 160.

[36] Nofri returned briefly to news gathering in August 1493 (writing to Piero on 6, 16 and 27 August, MAP 18: 127–9, 133) during the hiatus before the secretary Guidotti's return; on Guidotti, Brown, *Florence* (2011), pp. 25–8.

[37] Piero, *Ricordi di lettere*, (1), pp. 384–90, 393, etc. (re: Arezzo, also pp. 93–4 in this volume), (2), p. 124 (re: Colle, also Muzzi, 'Social Classes', esp. pp. 280–9), and (1), pp. 408, 410 and 427 (re: San Gimignano, also Piero to its priors, 7 March 1491, ASF Acq. Doni 59, ins. 3, no. 4, the priors to Piero, 30 January 1493, CS I, 3, fol. 149).

with Florence and especially with the Medici.[38] Like Florence, the city was falling under the control of a single family in the late fifteenth century. When Piero first visited Siena on his way to Rome in 1484, the philo-Florentine popular regime favoured by his father was still in power. But when he returned en route to Rome in 1487, the Noveschi had just seized control, and on his third visit, in 1492, the Petrucci under Pandolfo were consolidating their grip on the Noveschi regime. Lorenzo had remained on outwardly friendly terms with this regime, especially with messer Antonio Bicchi and Giacoppo, Pandolfo's brother, and he was honoured with a lavish banquet in Siena en route to the baths in late April 1490.[39] When Alessandro Braccesi replaced Andrea da Foiano as Florence's resident secretary in Siena the following year, he – like da Foiano and Ricci – combined his official duties with personal service to the Medici.[40] Before leaving for Siena, Braccesi had received a 'very loving and necessary' memorandum from Lorenzo on his duties and why he was there, which he promised to learn by heart, also promising Piero (before Lorenzo died) that he would 'follow the rubric by writing to you about the more private matters, according to the memorandum you gave me'.[41]

So Braccesi provided the link that enabled Piero to exercise patronal influence in Siena. His letters show how beholden he was personally, as well as professionally, to his patron. On the birth of Piero's son in September 1492, he sent Piero fourteen lines of 'amateur verses' in Latin, which came – he wrote – from 'an unlearned man' but one 'totally dedicated to you'; two months later, when thanking Piero for the care he showed him during his illness, he said he was sure it must have upset Piero, 'since I belong to you'; and in 1494, when begging Piero for a loan of 250 golden ducats for the dowry of the second of his five daughters – 'for it's a bad and harsh thing to be born of poor parents' – he said he had

---

[38] On Pisa and Florence, Petralia, 'Fiscality, Politics and Dominion', esp. p. 84 (that 90,000 fl. was collected by Florence from Pisa shortly after 1406, reduced to a third by 1470).

[39] Dovizi and Andrea da Foiano to Piero, 28 April 1490, MAP 18, 9, and 18, 13. On Lorenzo's friendship with the Petrucci, *Lettere* 12, intro. n., pp. 83–5, and 16, p. 346, n. 3.

[40] On Braccesi, *DBI* 13, 1971 (A. Perosa), Brown, *Scala*, pp. 124, 139, 204; on his literary interests, Najemy, *Between Friends*, pp. 40–2 and n. 55. He, Gaddi and ser Francesco Baroni as secretaries of the Otto received 190 fl. o/o p.a., whereas Bernardo Ricci, Foiano and Antonio Guidotti as assistants received only 50 fl. p.a.

[41] Braccesi in Siena to Lorenzo de' Medici, 13 October 1491, MAP 60, 72; to Piero, 21 February 1492, MAP 19, 60: 'Seguiterò la rubrica scrivendo ad voi le cose più private, secondo il ricordo mi desti chosti.' Cf. Shaw, 'Politics', p. 244 (a succinct account of these years), Terziani, *Il governo di Siena*, Jackson, *Pandolfo Petrucci*, and Piero's *Ricordi di lettere*.

'always been helped and favoured by your family in my difficulties'. Like the other secretaries, he repaid his debt to the Medici with acerbic reportage in his often daily communications to Piero, who was equally indebted to Braccesi for carefully nurturing his relationship with Siena's leading citizens.[42]

Piero's 'favour', it slowly emerges from the letters, consisted of money payments of 200 ducats to various Sienese friends and soldiers, who were 'somewhat uneasy' after Lorenzo's death, not knowing what Piero's intentions were.[43] More than that, it consisted of a loan of 4000 golden ducats that Piero paid the regime secretly for their military expenses.[44] Its secrecy, and the fact that it was requested after a private lunch hosted by Piero in the Medici villa of Montepaldi, suggests this money and the retainers came, at least initially, from Piero and the Medici Bank. But since Piero later refused Siena's increasingly insistent demands for money on the grounds that he, too, was faced with huge expenses in this year of crisis – not only his current expenses but the additional cost of more than 36,000 ducats for new *condotte* and increased payments to *condottieri*, which he said would require raising taxes to great popular outcry – it is likely that the bulk of his contribution to Siena's military expenses was paid for with public money, not his own.[45]

Florence needed Siena on its side, especially after Siena was invited to join the new papal League of St. Mark in 1493, from which Florence was excluded, so Piero had to play the difficult game of refusing his friends' demands for money while keeping them sweet.[46] After another lunch at Montepaldi, during which Piero again charmed the Sienese leaders and then refused their inflated demand for a loan of 8000 ducats, Braccesi was left to 'entrance' Pandolfo 'like a snake with music' and arrange a

---

[42] Braccesi to Piero, 13 September 1492, MAP 19, 139r (celebrating the return of '*Laurentius heros*' after the pater-patriae's death); 3 November, MAP 19, 169, fol. 182r, and 23 January 1494, MAP 19, 202: 'È male et aspra cosa nascere di poveri parenti'. Also Braccesi to Guidotti, 13 September 1493, SSX8LCMR 27, fol. 110v.

[43] Braccesi to Piero, 30 April 1492, MAP 19, 83: 'che qualchuno di questi che hanno la provisione de 200 ducati ne stanno con qualche gelosia per essere manchato vostro padre'.

[44] Shaw, 'Politics', p. 247; on d'Appiano's contract, Braccesi to Piero, 17 December 1492 (MAP 19, 176, fol. 194r–v and 177, fol. 196r), 8 and 10 January 1493 (MAP 19, 14, fol. 18r, and 19, 17); cf. p. 137 following.

[45] Piero to Braccesi, *Ricordi di lettere* (1), pp. 386–7 (3 May 1492), Braccesi to Piero, 5 May, 1, 20 June 1492, MAP 19: 84, 90, 92 (fol. 102r). On the money payments, *Ricordi*, 23 December 1492, 24 December 1493, pp. 407, 112; Braccesi to Piero, 18, 19 January 1493 (MAP 19, 24, fol. 32r, and 26, fol. 34r); Shaw, 'Politics', pp. 249–52, who suggests that the secret loan was a private one.

[46] Braccesi to Piero, 24 (2), 25, 28 April and 6 June 1493 (MAP 19: 332–5, 338, 371, fols. 402–3).

further lunch at Montepaldi in early July, when total unity ('incarnation') was apparently achieved between the Sienese and Piero. On this occasion Piero was accompanied by two of his closest supporters in the regime, Pierfilippo Pandolfini and Piero Alamanni, who in view of the Italian situation agreed to engage Leonardo Bellanti's and Giacoppo Petrucci's sons to fight under Florence's captains, both sides – according to Braccesi – then returning home satisfied.[47] And after some small gifts of money were dispensed to Bellanti and to Giacoppo's father to soften them up, using 'first the syrup' and then 'the medicine given them through your letters', the Sienese raised the 8000 ducats they needed from their own taxes.[48]

This sequence of appeals for money and agreeable lunch parties in Montepaldi – during which Piero apparently overwhelmed his friends 'with love and affection' before later drawing back – was a pattern frequently repeated during the following two years, suggesting that Piero had lost none of his old power to charm people by his presence without following through on his promises, now perhaps toughened by his henchmen in Florence, Dovizi and the finance officer Antonio Dini. What Braccesi's letters reveal is the extent to which Piero was responsible for overseeing not only these financial 'loans' and gifts to members of the Noveschi regime, but their military contracts, too.[49] Soldiers appealed to Piero to serve under Florentine *condottieri* and, as we have seen, so did the leading citizens Giacoppo Petrucci and Leonardo Bellanti. Bellanti wanted his fifteen-year-old son Giulio to become a soldier under Piero's protection, 'because he knew you would be a good father and would treat him as a son'.[50] And far from being marginal to the discussions of Siena's ruling elite, Piero's approval of important decisions was sought through personal meetings (on his own or with some of his leading citizens) in Montepaldi or Passignano – as, for example, over the double marriage pact agreed between the Petrucci and Leonardo Bellanti in June 1494, or

---

[47] Piero to Braccesi, 14 June 1493, *Ricordi di lettere*, (1), p. 427, also 28 and 30 June, p. 428; Braccesi to Piero, 10 June–12 September 1493, SSX8LCMR 27, fols. 59v–110v passim (citing 3 July at 70v: 'chome la biscia allo incanto'), Braccesi to Dionigi Pucci in Naples, 4 July (74r–v): 'quasi uno incarnarsi'.

[48] Braccesi in Siena to Piero, 7, 11, 12, 17 July 1493, SSX8LCMR 27, fols. 75v, 76v, 77v, 81v (also in MAP 19: 39, 399, 404).

[49] On the payments, nn. 43, 45 in this chapter, also Braccesi to Piero, 18, 29 December 1492, MAP 19: 178 and 186. On 14 April 1494 Pandolfo asked for an advance of 400 ducats for property he had recently bought, MAP 19, 550.

[50] The same, 23 December 1492, 13 February, 17 April 1493, MAP 19: 182, 51, 320 (fol. 345r: 'gli saresti un buon padre et che lo arresti in luogho di figluolo'); on his conditions, the same, 13 May, 29 June, 3 July 1493, etc., MAP 19: 349, 389, 393 (and SSX8LCMR 27, fols. 70v–71r, 3 July). Cf. 30 April 1493, 1, 9 and 12 May 1494, MAP 19: 341, 560, 566, 567.

before soldiers were engaged and fiscal decisions taken.[51] When Braccesi demurred on Piero's behalf because of Piero's many occupations (and also because he knew Piero would be asked for money), the Sienese – he told Piero – reminded him that 'sometimes your late father did not wait to be summoned when there were important matters to discuss but went ahead and sent for one of them'. But since they eventually agreed to pay the 8000 florins themselves instead of borrowing it from Florence, Piero's tough approach evidently worked, even at the risk of destabilising the Noveschi regime.[52]

Piero's relationship with the Sienese was also characterised by the usual exchange of favours and recommendations for people and offices, reciprocal deals on border disputes and exiles, arbitrations and especially by public agonistic events like the Palio and bullfights with dogs, where victories and defeats impacted on Piero's standing and honour as much as they did in the Romagna.[53] For six weeks, from 23 July to 6 September, both were in the balance as magistracies and judges of appeal were called on to adjudicate whether Cesare Borgia's riderless horse or Piero's mounted steed had won the July Palio. The affair dominated Braccesi's letters to Piero in this period, and although Piero himself seems to have taken the eventual verdict against his horse's victory philosophically when the judge of appeal pronounced in favour of Cesare – 'perhaps because he had been an archbishop', Braccesi surmised – it nevertheless reflected badly on Piero and Florence, especially since 'all the people are enraged against us in favour of the pope'.[54] In Florence's eyes, the long saga revealed how untrustworthy the Sienese were, for not only had they broken the rules of gift exchange by not repaying Piero and Florence for Siena's victory in Florence's San Giovanni Palio in June, but in supporting the archbishop and his backers (the papal bankers Spannochi and the pope), they had shown – as Braccesi had once told Lorenzo – 'they are

---

[51] The same, 6, 10 June 1494, MAP 19: 584, 585 ('che prima se ne facci scriptura alchuna o che si manfesti, si intenda el parere della Magnificentia Vostra', 24 July 1494, MAP 19, 609, fol. 691r ('dove andrete voi, vogliono andare ancora loro'), 29 July, MAP 19, 612, fol. 695v ('Pandolfo non moverebbe un passo senza lui'), etc. On the marriages, Shaw, p. 270.

[52] Braccesi to Piero, 6 June 1493, MAP 19, 371, at fol. 403r. In response to their demand, Braccesi outlined Florence's new expenses of 36,000 fl., 27 June 1493, SSX8LCMR 27, fols. 67r–68v and MAP 19, 387.

[53] On the bullfight, the same, 17 August 1493, SSX8LCMR 27, fol. 94r–v. Important exiles were Agnolo Palmieri, Crescenzio Gori and Francesco Severini (a Popolano exile who returned in 1486 to form part of the Noveschi regime).

[54] The same, 23 July–6 September 1493, SSX8LCMR 27, fols. 83v, 84v, 92r–v, 106r–107r (MAP 19: 409, 412, 414, 416, 422), citing fol. 106r–107r (6 September): 'forse per essere stato arcivescovo [di Valencia] add. in marg. (om. MAP); Shaw, 'Politics', pp. 261–2, Mallett. The Borgias, pp. 119–20.

friends of fortune and measure friendship by its utility', especially 'the good Pandolfo, who is truly our simulated friend'.[55]

Nevertheless, Piero enjoyed considerable patronal influence in Siena, despite its frequent regime changes and an attempted uprising against his friends in October 1494. In retrospect, it is ironic that only a month before Piero's fall, Braccesi 'lovingly' explained to the rulers that they should govern with more popular support, 'because states that are held with hatred and by force don't last long'.[56] Perhaps Braccesi's message was also intended for Piero, to whom he frequently invoked 'the blessed memory of Lorenzo, your father', as a way of reminding him how Lorenzo had made Siena 'tremble' through his patronage and warmth, and who the friends were that he must cultivate: not only the Petrucci and Bellanti, but also Francesco Severini, a former exile.[57] After Severini complained bitterly to Braccesi in 1494 that, after all he had done to help Florence through his close friendship with Lorenzo, he no longer enjoyed the same position in Piero's affections, Braccesi reminded Piero that Francesco was someone 'of considerable importance in this city, a man of faction and a natural friend of your family'.[58] But despite his failings, Piero remained important to the Sienese in his own right (as Braccesi also reminded him), since he knew much more than they did about what was going on in Italy and outside – what Braccesi called 'the inner workings and basis of the Italian states and those outside' – and lacking other allies and friends, they would be in the dark without Piero and his reports.[59]

On this occasion, what they needed to know about was the pope's appointment of new cardinals and the threatened French expedition to Naples.[60] The latter was fast becoming a reality, especially when, two

---

[55] The same, 2 September 1493, MAP 19, 424, fol. 467: 'che costoro sono amici di fortuna et che misurano la amicitia dalla utilità' (*om.* SSX8LCMR 27, fol.104r–v). On the 1493 Florentine Palio, Jackson, *Pandolfo Petrucci*, p. 199 and n. 66.

[56] The same, 15 October 1494, MAP 19, 656, fol. 758v: 'perché gli stati che si tenghono con odio et per forza durono pocho' (cf. Cic. *De off.* II, vii, 23–4, reversed by Machiavelli, *Il principe*, ch. 17), adding 'ma perché ho veduto non *prebent benignas aures*, me ne ho inposto silentio'.

[57] The same, 30 April 1492, MAP 19, 83: 'sotto la protezione e chaldo del quale dice che faceva tremare Siena, usando proprie decte parole'; he also invoked Lorenzo's memory on 28 December 1492 (MAP 19: 184, fol. 207r), 21 April 1493 (MAP 19, 327r) and 8 October 1494 (MAP 19, 650, fol. 749v).

[58] Braccesi to Piero, 25 February 1493, MAP 19, 65: 'huomo di factione et amico naturale di casa vostra' (65v). On 24 December Piero sent him 200 ducats, totalling 1200 *ducati d'oro* in all, *Ricordi di lettere* (2), p. 112.

[59] The same, 28 September 1493, MAP 19, 432, fol. 477v: 'che sapete lo intrinseco et fondamento degli stati di Italia et di fuora'.

[60] Ibid., fol. 477r.

months later, Braccesi reported a secret visit to Siena of Piero's cousin Lorenzo di Pierfrancesco, who arrived alone and in disguise outside the northern gate, the Porta Camollia, in order to talk to Jacopo d'Appiano (his brother-in-law, the lord of Piombino) and the two men accompanying him. Since Siena was once again planning to dismiss Jacopo as their captain, 'having lost hope' of being subsidised by Piero, this visit was an ominous portent of what was to follow, for Jacopo then became involved in the conspiracy of Lorenzo di Pierfrancesco, who was married to Jacopo's sister Semiramide.[61] Although Jacopo had concluded a deal with Giovanni Cambi (later manager of the Medici Bank in Pisa) concerning the iron ore he controlled in Piombino and Elba, and in 1493–94 suggested marrying his little daughter to the 'reborn' Giuliano, Piero's brother (named after his murdered uncle), he was not trusted by Cambi and ended up working for the pope, not for Siena (and Florence) or for the conspirators.[62]

By September 1493 the growing reality of the French invasion revealed the weakness of Siena's 'incompetent and crippled government', which was ready to attach itself to whomever it thought would protect its interests, not only Florence and Naples, who were approached for military support and money, but also Lodovico Sforza, in order to have, as Pandolfo put it, 'a foot in both stirrups'.[63] A month later, in the course of an attempted uprising, someone from the popular party blamed the French threat on Siena's friendship with the Florentines, 'with whom we have a sort of servitude and do everything as they want', and he suggested that Siena should adopt a position of neutrality, pincered as it was between the church, the king of Naples and the Florentines.[64] In fact, Siena remained loyal to Medicean Florence, and although Piero was slow to pay the soldiers and unwilling to make them large loans, he cared for them and 'knew what was going on in that state', according to the pope, who said he too wanted to be 'governed by his opinion'.[65] After the

---

[61] Braccesi to Piero, 19 November 1494, MAP 19, 442: 'stravestito et solo'. Initially betrothed to Giuliano de' Medici, Semiramide married Lorenzo di Pierfrancesco in 1482, Centanni, *Fantasmi*, pp. 485–8.

[62] Cambi to Piero, 4 January 1493 ('d'età d'anni .5. istarebbe bene a G<i>uliano') and 19 March, MAP 56, 119, cf. Vaglienti, *Storia*, p. 9. On Jacopo, the same, 30 June 1492, MAP 56, 120 ('So bene che gl'à avuto senpre un soldo per lire di vantagg<i>o da voi'). On the conspiracy, Chapter 12 in this volume.

[63] Braccesi to Piero, 13 September 1494, MAP 9, 632, fols. 725r ('inhabile et impedito'), 725v–726r ('per tenere il piè in due staffe'); Shaw, *Popular Government*, p. 270.

[64] Braccesi to Piero, 27 October 1494, MAP 19, 668, fol. 782r (messer Bolgherino): 'quasi come una spetie di servitù et che noi facciamo in tucte le cose a modo loro'.

[65] The same, 25 September 1494, MAP 19, 641, fol. 736r; Puccio Pucci in Rome to Piero, 3 July, MAP 19, 456, fol. 511r ('havendo voi lo intrinsecho di quello stato, il papa se ne

threatened uprising in October 1494, Piero and the Otto di Pratica sent troops to man the frontier in Chianti and the Valdarno and to capture Sienese escapees to prevent them returning home. Braccesi concluded his last surviving letter to Piero from Siena – written just two weeks before Piero was himself chased from Florence – by urging him 'to think about how best to help and advise their Magnificences in these times'.[66] The best evidence of their relationship is Siena's support for Piero when he was an exile with a high price on his head.

Pisa and the 'Company of Piero de' Medici'

Piero's relationship with Pisa was more firmly based than his relationship with Siena, thanks to his family's possessions there and their bank and trading company. Cosimo de' Medici had acquired a palace and established a branch of his bank in Pisa in 1441–42, and in 1462 he succeeded in having a Medici appointed archbishop of Pisa, but it was Lorenzo who consolidated his family's influence through his extensive land purchases and through the university he reestablished there in 1472–73. Although initially an extension of Florence's *studium*, it rapidly reduced the *studium* to a liberal arts campus of Pisa's multifacultied university, which became a rich source of patronage as well as prestige for the Medici.[67] The family profited, too, from Lorenzo's land investments in the Pisan Maremma, where he developed four large estates of arable land and pastures to provide a cheese factory and an innovative company, the Magona dei bestiami, which reared cattle to hire out to local landowners. The villas and land at Agnano and Spedaletto were acquired from the master of Altopascio in 1486 to replace their lost Mugello villas and estates at Trebbio, Cafaggiolo and Castello, that had been given as compensation to the younger branch the previous year. They, too, served practical as well as pleasurable functions, since Agnano surveyed Pisa's maritime traffic at the confluence of the Arno and the sea, and Spedaletto was

---

vuol ghovernare secondo il parere vostro'); 15, 18, 24 and 26 October, MAP 19: 659, fol. 765r–v, 660, fol. 767r; 665, fol. 777r–v, 667, fol. 780r.

[66] The same, 15, 18, 24, 26 October 1494 (MAP 19: 655–6, 659, 665, 667); 27 October (MAP 19: 668, fol. 783r).

[67] Mallett, 'Pisa and Florence', esp. pp. 409, 433–41 on the Medici's 'sort of private patrimony based on Pisa and its contado' and on the acquisitions of other Florentines; Franceschi, 'Medici Economic Policy, pp. 141–3; Petralia, 'Pisa Laurenziana', pp 975–8 on the 'reti e clientele dello "stato"'; Davies, *Florence and Its University*, at pp. 71–7; Davies, *Culture and Power*, pp. 48–50.

near to Lucrezia Tornabuoni's baths at Bagno a Morbo and the copper sulphate mines in Volterra.[68] Although the Medici's involvement in the Pisan branch of the bank was minimal by the 1470s, they contributed to a company run by Giovanni Cambi, who acquired the right to mine as well as sell iron ore from Elba. In 1489 Cambi became manager of a new company, Piero de' Medici and Co., which administered the iron ore Magona of Pisa and Pietrasanta and the purchase of copper sulphate from mines near Volterra.[69]

So Piero had a special bond with Pisa not enjoyed elsewhere, or by his father, although both men shared a love of hunting and hawking in the Pisan countryside. Working under Cambi's guidance as manager, the bank and trading company not only gave Piero experience in his family's commercial interests but also trained him to deal with the wide variety of clients – scholars, soldiers, businessmen and engineers – who passed through Pisa in need of favour and money. He seems to have been less interested in the university than his father, partly, perhaps, because his brother Giovanni attended the university himself from 1489 to 1492; but he received appeals for support from its teachers and students, as well as from Francesco Cambini, a Florentine devoted to the Medici in Pisa, where he played an important administrative role.[70] Cambini worked principally in the Dogana (customs house), but he was also a procurator of the Studio and the Spedale Nuovo, in which Piero was also involved. In 1493–94, Piero helped his old family retainer, Matteo Franco (now working as chaplain and secretary to his sister Maddalena), to become its rector, and Franco in turn asked Piero to help to repair the dilapidated hospital and its 'miserable and abandoned' inmates.[71]

The Medici's 'house or rather palace' – originally owned by the Appiano rulers of Pisa – enjoyed a courtyard, loggia and stables. Behind it was another house with a loggia, large courtyard, stables, dovecote and rooms on the first and second floors, all for the use of the servants, and

---

[68] MAP 104, 42, fols. 418–27 (Cegino's 1492 Inventory, copied in 1509), Foster, *A Study*, esp. pp. 296–9 (on the Magona), and n. 892; Lillie, 'Lorenzo's rural investments', esp. pp. 65–6 (on the 'Magona di bestiame', Vicopisano and the villas; Kent, *Lorenzo de' Medici*, pp. 121–29.
[69] On Cambi, his father Bernardo and his cousin, *DBI* 17, 1974 (Luzzatti, Cruciani Troncarelli), at pp. 90–1, 96, 97–100, Lorenzo, *Lettere* 11, pp. 203–4, n. 9; on the bank, Tewes, *Kampf um Florenz*, pp. 173–6.
[70] Picotti, *Giovinezza*, pp. 235–94; on Cambini, Böninger, 'Francesco Cambini', esp. pp. 39, 40 (n. 81), 42–5, and the Pisa account book, GC 5 (n. 76 in this chapter), naming him on fol. 86 left as Cardinal Giovanni's *fattore*.
[71] Franco, *Lettere*, ed. Frosini, pp. 53–6 (and n. 5), and n. 93 in this chapter. On the Spedale Nuovo, Piero, *Ricordi di lettere* (2), p. 116 (23 January 1494), to Cambi, Cambino, etc. 'per le cose dello spedale nuovo di Pisa'; Franco to Piero, 22 March 1494, *Lettere*, p. 134, wanting 'maschio aiuto' for 'questi miseri et abandonati malati'.

next to it was another house used by Galletto, the Medici's falconer, where their devoted secretary Bernardo Dovizi stayed in 1496 when the palace was occupied by the visiting emperor.[72] The family also owned 'a warehouse used as an arsenal' (for Piero's ship?), a shop on the Arno facing the Piazza de' Cavoli rented from the Magona, as well as other small dwellings, shops in Pisa and a washhouse (*lavatoio*) outside the walls, which consisted of a complex of buildings that was rented out until 1497 before reverting to the Florentine commune. Then there were pastures for about 150 cows at Vico Pisano, with buildings for cheese making, extensive agricultural lands and pastures at Colle Salvetti and in the Maremma, and at Librafatta a fulling mill with three houses for millers, one of them for 'our residence' and one (with an oven) used as an inn.[73]

So the Medici's investment in Pisa and its environs was considerable, although Piero clearly left the running of his company in Cambi's capable hands.[74] Like Braccesi in Siena, Cambi called himself Piero's 'creature and servant', but as a businessman in his own right, his position was very different from Braccesi's. He required the Medici's capital for his company and their help with his niece's betrothal and his family's litigation, but as his letters show, the Medici needed him for his business skills and acumen as much as he needed them – perhaps more.[75] It was he who secured from Jacopo d'Appiano the rights to mine iron ore from Elba in 1489, despite regarding him as unreliable. We can see from a surviving (and incomplete) Pisa account book how profitable the mines were. On 24 March 1494 they contributed more than 7500 gold florins to the bank's profit, by far the largest source of profit for the Pisan branch, whose total profit (after deducting the losses) in the year 25 March 1493–24 March 1494 was about 9414 florins. By contrast, in dealings with the company of Piero de' Medici and Lorenzo Tornabuoni and

---

[72] Cegino, 1492 Inventory, MAP 104, 42, fol. 419r: 'una chasa o vero palazzo', etc., Foster, *A Study*, pp. 378–9 and n. 894; cf. p. 242 in this volume.

[73] Cegino, 1492, Inventory, fols. 419r: 'uno maghazzino a uxo d'Arzana'; 419v (on the *lavatoio* whose price 'non l'à anchora chiarito alle ragioni del chomune a ordine Antonio di Bernardo [Dini]'); 420r–422r (on Vico Pisano, Colle Salvetti and the Maremma); 423r (on the mill and houses); cf. Foster, *A Study*, pp. 299–302 and n. 939. On 'Piero's galley', p. 92 in this volume.

[74] Chapter 7 in this volume, esp. n. 23 citing his letter of 1–3 May 1490. Piero's surviving letters indicate he was certainly in Pisa in late November to early December 1493 (MAP 72, 68 and Mantua AS, busta 1085, no. 253), in Vico Pisano and Cascina nearby in early April 1494 (MAP 124, 105 and MAP 72, 71, fol. 77v).

[75] Cambi in Pisa to Piero, 14 December 1493, MAP 18, 183: 'creatura e servitore vostra', whom Piero, by helping him escape 'da questo laberinto', 'farà di morto vivo'.

Partners of Lyon, the Pisa company incurred losses totalling around 1450 florins between July 1493 and March 1494.[76]

As well as being responsible for the bank, Cambi was also manager of the Medici's estates. The most original of his initiatives concerned a 'fantasy for public and private benefit' that would create a proper outlet into the sea at Motrone for two of the three small streams near Pietrasanta, a fortress town that Florence had recovered from Genoa in 1484. Expecting to meet Piero in Pietrasanta, Cambi had hoped to explain his fantasy to him in person, but in his absence he described in writing his plan to drain a marsh that infected the air of Pietrasanta and create from the streams a river wide enough for boats to navigate, which would not only improve the town but also protect it in time of war; he had discussed it with experts (*maestri*), who agreed with him that it would be extremely useful and would cost no more than 600 ducats, so he was sending one of them to Piero with the plans.[77] Later that year he was fully involved in organising repairs to Piero's mill, which he once again regretted Piero had been unable to see for himself, in order to give advice and ensure everything went better.[78]

Perhaps this suggests a lack of interest on Piero's part in Cambi's business ventures, as well as in the wide range of clients seeking his favour whom Cambi was left to 'manage', especially the Milanese captain Francesco Secco, the learned jurist Bartolomeo Sozzini, and Piero's brother-in-law Franceschetto Cibo, but also many other needy people – such as soldiers who wanted employment, a Sicilian studying in Florence for six or seven years who wanted Piero to renew Lorenzo's letters recommending him to the king of Spain and his treasurer, a notary from Volterra who wanted Piero, like Lorenzo, to be his patron, and someone accepting Piero's mediation in the marriage being arranged for him and his cousin by Gabriele Malaspina.[79] Since Cambi thought Secco and

---

[76] 'Libro dei debitori e creditori [del Banco di Piero di Lorenzo de' Medici a Pisa], 1493–1521', GC 5, esp. fols. 248, 268 and 273 (Avanzi) for the 'Maghone delle vene di Pisa & Pietrasanta', 106, 131, 140, 161, 180, 210, 248, 81, 314, 344, 367, 370, and for the Lyon company, 62, 73, 145, 201, 250, 263, 283. It was not used by de Roover and needs careful analysis, cf. Guidi Bruscoli, '1487 Medici-Cybo Marriage', p. 82, n. 65 and Goldthwaite, 'Performance of the Florentine Economy', p. 258.

[77] Cambi to Piero, 13 March 1493, MAP 56, 128: 'una fantasia per util' publicho e privato'. One of the proposed reforms to Pisa's economy (which concerned the Seventeen Reformers in 1490–91) was opening the mouths of dried-up rivers and encouraging ship building, Misc. repubb. busta XI. no. 286, fols. 34r–35v, cf. Brown, *Medici in Florence*, pp. 163, 185–6.

[78] The same, 18 October 1493, MAP 18, 147 (referring to *maestro* Giovanni di Dimitri), 20 May 1493, MAP 66, 264.

[79] The same, 27 June and 22 August 1492, MAP 56, 122 and 60, 283; 28 May and 13 June 1493, CS I, 3, fols. 153, 150; on the Sicilian, 29 May 1492, MAP 56, 124; on the notary,

Sozzini would be valuable acquisitions for Florence, he had to ensure that Piero would accept the difficult negotiations he was conducting on his behalf – especially with Secco, because of the information he would provide about Lodovico Sforza's movements if he agreed to serve under Piero's protection.[80] Bartolomeo Sozzini would also be a catch for Florence if the terms were right, since his legal expertise was much in demand. So once again Cambi had to ensure that if Sozzini agreed to do what Piero 'ordered' in return for his conditions (which included a contribution towards the farm he was buying), Piero would accept this, 'for the benefit of the Studio'.[81]

It was Franceschetto Cibo who proved to be Cambi's (and Piero's) most demanding responsibility, however. Leaving Rome after his father Innocent VIII's death, he later spent much time in Pisa, even before acquiring through his wife the Medici villas of Agnano and Spedaletto in 1494.[82] In early May 1493 Cambi forewarned Piero that Franceschetto was coming to Florence and wanted a contract to serve with thirty or forty crossbowmen. Advising him to keep him happy 'with good words', he left it to Piero to 'decide what you think best'. A month later he reported that Franceschetto planned to spend the summer in Pisa with all his *brigata* because there was more room for him there than in Florence: his 'business' – Giovanni Cambi told Piero – 'is to play *ronfa* [a card game played by gamblers] for a good part of the day'.[83] Now it was Cambi, not Nofri in Rome, who had the invidious task of coping with Cibo's financial demands and the continuing crisis over his disputed land – finally succeeding in getting the proxy demanded by Virginio only with the help of Maddalena and her chaplain and secretary Matteo Franco.[84]

Cambi was still battling with Franceschetto's affairs in 1494, first over a tax favour his friend in Pietrasanta had failed to obtain, then over the design of the galley he was planning to build, which Cambi thought was

---

20 July 1492, MAP 56, 117; on Panico Panichi, 5 June 1494, MAP 56, 114; cf. 28 December 1493, MAP 124, 156, on Piero's orders re: Carlo Bardi.

[80] The same, 15, 18, 20 May 1493, MAP 73, 455; 60, 621; 66, 264. On Lodovico, 3, 10, 20 June, MAP 56: 130, 110, 108.

[81] The same, 18 May 1493, MAP 60, 621: 'Essi farà quanto ordinerete… per utile dello Studio, assodiate esso messer Bartolomeo ci dimora più d'un anno', the same, 28 December, MAP 124, 156. On his property plans, 13 March (MAP 56, 18), 18 May and esp. 14 December 1493, MAP 18, 100.

[82] CS 3, 177, fols. 212r–213v (copy), 2 July 1494.

[83] Cambi in Pisa to Piero, 8 May 1493, MAP 60, 504: 'lo'ntrattenerlo chon buone parole lo terrebbe chontento …'; the same, [2] June, MAP 56, 126: 'Suo esserczio è di fare a rronfa buona parte del g<i>orno' (cf. p. 72, n. 4 in this volume).

[84] The same, 3, 10, 11, 15 (2), 17 June 1493, MAP 56: 130, 110, 112, 129, 115, 109. Cf. Franco, *Lettere*, p. 53.

beautiful but impractical. Far better for navigating Porto Pisano would be two smaller vessels, at little more cost, Cambi told Piero, as he deterred him from underwriting the enterprise.[85] Before Franceschetto left for Genoa in February, Cambi refused to pay him 600 ducats 'for that business' and then refused to make good the cheque he had withdrawn from the Sauli bank for this amount, causing Franceschetto to expostulate to 'my Piero, these things should be dealt with by you and not by your ministers'.[86] Perhaps this was why Franceschetto bestowed generous presents on all the family when he and Maddalena returned from Genoa in February – two boxes of Neapolitan *copeta* (a sweet based on almonds) as a special treat for Alfonsina; fireworks and a hat for Giuliano; for Piero a pot of oil, 'but be careful not to overdo it!'; also Genoese shoes and slippers and a pair of slippers for Piero's 'ladies' (*dame*); and a golden chain that Cambi forwarded to Piero.[87] He also provided Piero with the loan of his horse Diamante for the planned joust in January.[88] But Piero still failed to engage him as a soldier as promised, and in April Maddalena was forced to write movingly to her brother about their desperate plight, urging him – knowing Franceschetto as he did – to use his brains on Franceschetto's behalf, for her sake, as his sister, and for the sake of their children, who were Piero's nephews and nieces.[89] 'Poor little Francesco' remained a liability, not only for Piero and his siblings, but also for Cambi and the Medici Bank in Pisa.

Cambi's letters show why Piero valued having him as manager in Pisa, which was 'the eye' of Florence and a hub of maritime activity. He described to Piero in September 1492 the arrival of a Genoese galley in the port, which was laden with about two hundred Jews from Sicily, including many women who would be sold off if their ransom price was not recovered. The following year he reported the arrival of a large Portuguese ship in Genoa that had left Cadiz a month earlier, then the arrival in Pisa of a Spanish ship from Barcelona en route for Naples and

---

[85] Cibo in Pisa to Piero, 5 January 1494, MAP 18, 385, Maddalena to the same, 16 January, MAP 18, 227; Cambi in Pisa to Piero, 1 February 1494, MAP 18, 89.
[86] Cibo in Pisa to Piero, 7 March, 1494, MAP 19, 494: 'Piero mio, voria avere a fare queste cosse con voi e non con vostri ministri', and from Genoa, 14 February, MAP 19, 463, urging payment, 'aciò io non ve recepa vergogna, dico de la fede'.
[87] The same, 15 March 1494, MAP 19, 506: 'doe scatole di copeta di Napoli', 'certe candele da focho per Juliano ... una anpoleta ... per untare ... ma avertite non untati tropo', etc.; also on 12 March 'uno chatena d'oro', MAP 98, 485.
[88] Piero, *Ricordi di lettere* (2), pp. 114 (14 January 1494): 'che serva Piero del suo cavallo decto il Diamante' (also to Tagliacarne), and 115 (21 January), Piero's 'risposta grata et amorevole' to Cibo.
[89] Maddalena in Pisa to Piero, 1 April 1494, MAP 100, 135, ed. Pieraccini, *Stirpe*, I, pp. 235–6: 'Bisongna che voi, Piero mio, habiate del cervello ancora per lui.'

Syria, with many passengers bound for Jerusalem, and finally the news that the king of Portugal was sending armed caravels to 'the new islands', which he predicted would cause trouble with the king of Spain.[90] Genoa remained in a state of latent war with Florence, despite Lodovico Sforza's earlier promise to resolve their differences – so, faced with the impending crisis over the Cibo lands (when Lodovico deserted Florence and Naples for the papal League of St. Mark in April 1493) and hearing that the famous sea captain Villamarino had broken with Genoa, Cambi attempted to procure his services for Florence.[91] He also advised Piero on Florence's galleys, telling him that the two small galleys (*fuste*) he had seen would be as good as one large galley, and the money spent on the crew would 'remain with your men', many of whom would come from Livorno.[92] The following year Pisa, like Siena, was on the front line as the French expedition assembled in Genoa as the base for its maritime campaign. Although Piero was fully involved in the situation there, giving daily briefings to Marino Tomacelli in Florence and writing from Pisa to Dionigi Pucci in Naples at the end of May 1494, Cambi, too, was busy providing Piero with information, telling him to 'think of a solution' to the overflowing hospital, and – as one of his last preparations before the arrival of the French – ordering armour and saltpetre, for which he wanted Piero's authorisation to pay for them from the Medici Bank.[93]

After the Medici's exile, Piero's company was taken over by the Ufficiali dei Ribelli, and the iron ore Magona was acquired by the Buonvisi company of Lucca. But before the transfer took place, on the very day of Piero's flight from Florence on 9 November 1494, the cashier Donato Capponi handed 4960 florins over to Cambi, who then passed the money on to several people – including a friar from the Carmine, who was captured by the Pisans with a bag containing 671 florins. This was the beginning of a 'clandestine operation' by Cambi,

---

[90] Cambi in Pisa to Piero, 8 September 1492, MAP 56, 125; 24 May 1493, MAP 60, 523; [2] June 1493, MAP 56, 126 ('in sul tal nave molti vanno in Ierusalem', and that he understood 'il re di Portoghallo was sending armed caravels 'alle nuove isole trovatesi da mandata del re di Spagna, doverrà nascere fra lloro disensione').

[91] Cambi in Pisa to Piero, 13 March 1493, MAP 56, 128; 20 and 24 May, MAP 66, 264 and 60, 523. On Genoa, p. 73 and n. 9 in this volume; and on Bernardo Villamarino, count of Bosa, who worked mainly for Ferrante but also for Florence, Genoa and the pope, Lorenzo, *Lettere* 12, pp. 482–4, n. 1. The Cibo crisis is discussed in Chapter 11 in this volume.

[92] Letter of 24 May 1493: 'innoltre al rimanere negli uomini vostri, vi farebbe tanti soldati al Livorrno'.

[93] Piero in Pisa to Dionigi Pucci in Naples, 29 May 1494, MAP 138, 255, fol. 250r–v, and in Florence, 3 July, SSX8LCMR 65, fol. 70r (copy); Cambi to Piero, 21 June 1494, MAP 100, 145, 20 August, MAP 56, 127 ('tanti infermi che sson pieno le lette e pe' tutto lo spedale') and 27 September 1494, MAP 73.143.

Lorenzo Tornabuoni and a bank employee to recover the exiled Medici's possessions (including jewels and medallions) and redeem them for cash for the exiles, as we shall see – for which Cambi's and Tornabuoni's reward was death by execution two and a half years later.[94]

Cambi's fate as Piero's 'creature and servant' raises the question of how to define the nature of Piero's power in Florence's dominion. It has been suggested that instead of ruling through a coalition of equals using elected officials, the Medici ruled with an executive team of devoted personal agents.[95] This describes quite well Piero's government in Florence, which depended on loyal personal secretaries like the Dovizi and chancery secretaries like Braccesi, as well as on the support of families like the Pucci and some of the ruling elite. Although the term 'clientage' seems inappropriate to describe Piero's relationship with bankers and managers like Giovanni Cambi and Nofri Tornabuoni, the patronal and family bonds he enjoyed with such men strengthened his web of power throughout the state – and even extended it to Rome. Despite this, Piero was unable to claim hereditary succession in republican Florence and it remains to be seen how he would fare there when his father died.

---

[94] Libro di debitori e creditori, GC 5, fol. 358 left; 'Nota che de £4950.15. che si trovava Donato Chapponi in quel tempo chassiere, li chonsegnò a Giovanni Chambi addì viiii di novembre' (see pp. 259, n. 16, and 268 in this volume); Troncarelli in *DBI*. On the Buonvisi, Tewes, *Kampf um Florenz*, pp. 165, 168–71, etc.

[95] Bullard, *Lorenzo*, pp. 226–7, and on Nofri Tornabuoni as a 'kind of super-agent and proxy' rather than 'a classic example of a toady, or agent underling', Bullard, 'Hammering Away', p. 396.

Part III

Piero in Power

10 Lorenzo's Death and Its Aftermath, 1492

The much-feared event of Lorenzo's death happened on 8 April 1492, heralded ominously by a bolt of lightning striking the cupola of the Duomo in the direction of the Medici palace.[1] Piero's years of apprenticeship were over and everyone awaited his response to the challenges ahead. 'Who would Piero side with', Parenti wondered, 'and how would he be treated, as the boss, the equal or the inferior of the others?'[2] Uncertainty about Piero's reaction to the new, upside-down world that confronted him was widely shared, not least by Lorenzo's secretary, ser Niccolò Michelozzi, who found himself isolated in Naples as his patron lay dying, consoled only by the letters he received from Florence. One of the most heartfelt was from Piero himself on the day of Lorenzo's death:

I am in such turmoil and distress [he wrote] that I don't know where I am because of the news I'm about to give you: and this is that Our Lord God just now, at seven hours, has pleased to call my late father Lorenzo to himself, leaving us in such grief and bitterness that we are out of our minds, because you, in your wisdom, know how much he mattered to the regime and to my affairs.[3]

He must indeed have felt bereft on the death of his father, who had never relinquished the reins of control, even when ill and away at the baths in the summer of 1490 and after his return. Piero alone of the brothers was in Florence when his father died and was present at Lorenzo's deathbed to receive the traditional last words of a father to his son, which included advice as well as his blessing. Lorenzo died half an hour later after kissing

---

[1] Poliziano to Jacopo Antiquario, 18 May 1492, *Letters*, ed. and tr. Butler, pp. 226–51 at 246–9; Cerretani, *Storia*, pp. 184–5; Parenti, *Storia*, pp. 21–2; Kent, *Princely Citizen*, pp. 299–320 ('The Death of Lorenzo') at 305–6.

[2] Parenti, *Storia*, I, pp. 28–9; Najemy, *A History*, pp. 375–6. 'The world upside down' is Michelozzi's expression (to Dovizi, 1 March, MAP 124, 182, Kent, p. 304); Martelli (*Studi laurenziani*, pp. 216–23) charts his illness through letters.

[3] Piero to Michelozzi in Naples, 8 April 1492, secr. hand (Dovizi?), ed. De Marinis and Perosa, *Nuovi documenti*, pp. 76–7, also 5 April re: Naples and Milan, asking Michelozzi to modify and correct him 'se … io mi movessi presumptuosamente', ibid., pp. 75–6. Cf. Poliziano to Jacopo Antiquario, 18 May, pp. 242–7 on Piero.

all his servants and ministers, fully conscious until the end. The body was then taken from Careggi to San Marco, where it lay uncovered before being taken in the evening of the 9th to Lorenzo's patronal church of San Lorenzo for a simple burial 'like Cosimo's', as Lorenzo had apparently requested in his last words to Piero.[4] That day Piero was at home to receive people's condolences, and in the evening he followed the bier as it was carried down Via Larga by the Company of the Magi. Shops and businesses were closed, and everyone flooded on to the streets and into the Piazza of San Lorenzo, 'to show love to this Holy family': 'if they had carried him uncovered, I think the weeping would have been heard in heaven', ser Pace Bambello told Michelozzi; 'as it was, all one could hear was sobbing'. Following an autopsy in San Lorenzo, thousands of black-clad citizens came to pay their respects before the burial service on 10 April.[5] Another secretary, ser Francesco Baroni, reported to Piero Guicciardini in Pisa that everyone was united in wanting to preserve Piero, who was responding to everyone 'like a Solomon', and Filippo da Gagliano confirmed that everything was going well and to the credit of Piero, Lorenzo's remaining 'branch', in whom everyone had great hopes and who seemed to be behaving well towards the regime and everyone else in these ceremonies.[6]

The only untoward event was the apparent suicide of Lorenzo's doctor, Pier Leone, in a well on the Martelli estate outside Florence a day after Lorenzo's death. There were many rumours about it: that he had poisoned Lorenzo, that he had been killed by Lorenzo's servants, that he had been removed by Piero to the Martelli estate to protect him and to allow him to rest. But one little-recorded piece of evidence comes from the employee of Virginio Orsini, Bartolomeo da Bracciano, who had heard about the incident from Piero's autograph letter to his brother Giovanni, which Giovanni had passed on to Rinaldo Orsini. According to Bartolomeo, the letter described how Piero had made a fuss of Leone and tried to dissuade him from going to Spoleto, his home town; when he insisted, Piero suggested he should first go to the Martelli garden to rest and have supper, which he did; then, having eaten, he walked through the

---

[4] Francesco Baroni to Piero Guicciardini in Pisa, 10 April 1492, ed. De Marinis and Perosa, pp. 76–7, cf. Kent, p. 309, nn. 40, 42: 'semplice e sanza pompa'; Filippo da Gagliano to Michelozzi, 8 April 1492, GC 29, 69, fol. 40r (8 April) (om. Martelli, *Studi*): 'non si faccia altrimenti che quello si fecie per Coximo, parendomi che così li fussi ricordato a bocha dal padre'.

[5] Pace Bambello to Michelozzi, 11–12 April 1492, ed. Brown, *Florence* (2011), Append. 2, pp. 64–5.

[6] Baroni to Guicciardini, 10 April 1492; Gagliano to Michelozzi, 9 April 1492, GC 29, 69, fol. 41r: 'Confidiamo in questo bronchone rimasto di lui del quale si fa grandissima stimazione', etc. On the *broncone*, p. 104 in this volume.

garden with his servants and, seeing the well, suddenly, without saying anything, threw himself into it and drowned. This seems to confirm that Piero was responsible for sending Leone to the Martelli and thus why he felt it necessary to explain the drowning to his brother, even if it remains – as Bartolomeo commented – 'quite a strange thing to happen'.[7]

Despite Poliziano's and the secretaries' confidence about Piero's succession, it was potentially more fraught than they suggested. Aged twenty, he was well below the statutory age for holding office, and in inheriting his father's position as de facto head of the Medici regime, he gained no privileges that other members of the regime did not also possess. The Wool Guild was quick to replace Lorenzo with Piero as one of their governors on the day before the funeral, and the Merchants' Guild (the Calimala) followed suit. Three days later, Bambello (Michelozzi's assistant in the Wool Guild) was clearly relieved to be able to report, in a postscript, that the councils had approved unanimously (*nemine discrepante*) that 'Piero should succeed his father in everything'. In fact, there had been one vote cast against him in the Seventy on 12 April, 'which although small, may seem too much to you', Gagliano wrote to Michelozzi, 'considering the status of the Seventy' (as the hand-picked, supreme agency of control), and although the legislative council of Cento approved the law by a large majority, the small number of hostile votes was not surprising 'in view of who has the vote'.[8] This meant that Piero replaced Lorenzo in the Council of Seventy (from which the Otto di Pratica and the Dodici Procuratori were drawn), that he could attend meetings of the legislative council, the Cento, and be an electoral scrutineer. He was also appointed a supervisor of government building works in Lorenzo's place.[9] But it was much more difficult to replace Lorenzo in his pragmatic role as pivot of Italy's balance of power, the acrobat who juggled simultaneously three incompatible sets of alliances: with the pope, with the pope's enemy Ferrante of Naples and with Ferrante's enemy Lodovico Sforza (who at the time was aiming to replace his nephew Gian Galeazzo, Ferrante's son-in-law, as duke of

---

[7] Bartolomeo da Bracciano to Virginio Orsini, 10 April, 1492, 'Lettres', ed. Boüard, p. 323: 'lo quale caso pare assai strano'. The other conflicting evidence for his death is discussed by Kent, *Princely Citizen*, pp. 316–19.

[8] Gagliano in Florence to Michelozzi in Naples, 13 April 1492, GC 29, 69, fol. 43r: 'intendo fu una biancha che, ancora sia poca coxa, parrà forse troppo a voi considerato la condizione de' 70' (the negative vote in the Cento is not recorded; on the others, Rubinstein, *Government*, p. 264, n. 6, and on the Seventy, 230). On Bambello, p. 14, n. 23 in this volume.

[9] Bambello to Michelozzi, 11–12 April 1492, p. 65. Piero replaced Lorenzo as an Operaio del Palagio in May 1492 (*praepositus* for six months on 30 June 1492 and 1494), Opera del Palagio 4, fols. 14r–v, 31r; 15v.

Milan, with Lorenzo's secret support). According to Guicciardini – who more than anyone else has influenced our view of Piero – everything was in his favour on his father's death, in view of his inheritance and support in Florence and Italy, especially from the pope, Naples, Milan and other princes. But his downfall and the ensuing 'ruin' of Italy he blamed almost entirely on Piero's 'lack of intelligence' and on his 'tyrannical and proud' nature, failing not only to take the advice of his father's friends but 'totally alienating' Milan and the Sforza by 'throwing himself', instead, 'into the arms of the king [Ferrante]' – charges, as we shall see, that were untrue.[10]

Parenti is less judgemental than Guicciardini and imagines Piero weighing up in his mind the burden of his inheritance on Lorenzo's death.[11] On one hand, he suggests, Piero had inherited wealth and greatness and he was beginning to enjoy exercising power, with the warm support of powerful friends and the intimates and functionaries of his father – especially ser Piero Dovizi – all of whom feared ruin without him.[12] On the other hand, his father, with all his foresight and authority, had scarcely been able to survive and keep the restless citizens and his rivals in check; his uncle had been chopped to pieces and Lorenzo had lost power and credit, only managing to save his life with armed support, which left him always fearful, unable to trust anyone or enjoy any peace of mind or body. Moreover, Parenti continued, despite the outpouring of grief on Lorenzo's death, many citizens had welcomed it: the leading citizens because they hoped (like himself) that republicanism would be restored, many others, from all classes, because they had suffered from his devalued currency and heavy taxes.[13] No lover of Medici power himself, Parenti's sensitive assessment reminds us that Piero's inheritance was far from easy. Nor was his initial reception in Florence, despite receiving support from the many visiting foreign ambassadors and showing great tact himself towards the citizens by appointing a new Signoria with the other scrutineers and curtailing unnecessary expenditure – such as his numerous Barbary horses, his falcons 'and similar accoutrements'. For when Piero and Giuliano (back from Rome) with other family and

---

[10] Guicciardini, *Storie*, pp. 83–4, 87–8. Manfredi reported that Ercole d'Este 'molto ne rimase ben satisfatto' with Piero in early April 1492, 'per essere giovine di buono spirito e di prudenza assai', *Lettere*, ed. Cappelli, p. 312.

[11] On Parenti, *DBI* 81, 2014 (Arrighi), Matucci, intro. to Parenti's *Storia* I, vii–xlvi, esp. xvi–xxi; cf. Phillips, *Memoir of Marco Parenti* (Piero's father, his *Ricordi storici* are ed. by Doni Garfagnini).

[12] Parenti, *Storia* I, pp. 25–6. On Lorenzo's functionaries and new men, Brown, *Florence* (2011), pp. 1–38.

[13] Parenti, *Storia* I, p. 25; Brown, *Florence* (2011), pp. 87–8; Najemy, *A History*, p. 343.

friends paid a ceremonial visit on 16 April to the Annunziata, the Signoria and 'the orators', Piero 'churned the stomachs of all the city' by being accompanied by armed guards – like Lorenzo, and as the leading citizens wanted – and also by limiting access to the Signoria's audiences.[14]

So despite the support Piero received from other rulers and from the Florentine councils, the presence of even a few negative votes in the Cento was a cause for concern, as were growing signs of dissension within his own family and within the ruling elite. Initially, it was his sixteen-year-old brother Giovanni who challenged Piero's authority by becoming not only a cardinal but papal legate to Tuscany. The brothers' different professions may always have encouraged some rivalry between them. In 1490, when complaining to Dovizi about the young cleric's life as a student in Pisa in 1490, Gentile Becchi said he thought Giovanni was perhaps modelling himself on Piero and others, without realising that his profession was quite different from Piero's; so although Giovanni assured Piero on Lorenzo's death that 'it will be for you to rule, for me to carry out your orders', his attitude changed when he was appointed a cardinal legate.[15] After angering Piero by disobeying his somewhat equivocal voting instructions in the papal conclave following Innocent VIII's death in late July, Giovanni responded with equal anger to remind Piero that in Rome he knew 'as much as anyone else about carrying out our business'; as well as being Piero's brother, he was 'also a cardinal, towards whom you should have some consideration when you get me to do things – at least you should respect my dignity'.[16] But Giovanni was deceived in the conclave by both Ascanio Sforza, Lodovico's brother, and by his own relative, Cardinal Orsini.[17] The election on 26 July of Rodrigo Borgia (Ascanio's secret favourite) as Pope Alexander VI – the 'Catalan

---

[14] Parenti, ivi, pp. 25–9: 'stomaco a tutta la città ... mosse' (28); Gagliano to Michelozzi, 16 April 1492, GC 29, 69, fol. 44r: 'mena 6 o 8 staffieri come faceva Lorenzo, che così vogliono questi dello stato'. Picotti, *Giovinezza*, pp. 360–5.

[15] Becchi to Dovizi, 1 April 1491, ed. Picotti, ivi, p. 677 (Append. 2, 18); Giovanni to Piero, 12 April 1492, ivi, p. 622 (Append. 1, 8): 'Tuum erit imperare, meum vero iussa capessere'; Parenti, *Storia* I, pp. 30–1.

[16] The same, 21 August 1492 (autogr.), ed. Picotti, *Giovinezza*, pp. 626–8 (Append. I, 20), 439–40; on Piero's anger, Piero to Dovizi, 1 August 1492, ibid., pp. 700–1 (Append. II, 30), Piero to Michelozzi, 3 August [dated 2 August in his *Ricordi di lettere* (1), p. 397], GC 29 35, fol. 14r; cf. Dovizi to Michelozzi, undated note, GC 29, 62, fol. 111r ('non vidi mai Piero peggio disposto et lo sdegno lo fa scrivere così'). On Lorenzo's acrobatics and 'doppio patto con due nemici reciproci', Pellegrini, *Ascanio Sforza*, 1, p. 318, cf. p. 67, n. 61 in this volume; Picotti, *Giovinezza*, pp. 414–15.

[17] Pellegrini, *Ascanio Sforza*, p. 391; Picotti, *Giovinezza*, pp. 94–5 (and n. 114 on the benefice of Calenzano, etc., acquired in 1492 on the death of his great-uncle, Carlo), cf. 504–5, and 499 ff. on losing the legation to 'el Pharnese poverissimo'.

simoniac, father of many children and great voluptuary of dubious faith', as Parenti called him – meant that Giovanni lost face in Rome, as well as the favour of the Sforza and the Borgia families, and he immediately left the city, to be later replaced as papal legate in the Patrimony by Alessandro Farnese. Moreover, both brothers lost the prestige and influence that their *parentado* with Innocent VIII had recently won for them.[18]

Before Giovanni left Rome he met his cousin, Lorenzo di Pierfrancesco, who was already at odds with the elder branch of the family. What passed between them is not known, except that it involved the soldier and Lucretian scholar Michele Marullo, who became part of the plot organised by the Prince of Salerno in France that Lorenzo di Pierfrancesco was about to join. As the most senior member of the Medici family in age but not in status, Lorenzo di Pierfrancesco proved a much more serious threat to Piero's authority than his brother Cardinal Giovanni, especially when he was supported by members of Florence's ruling elite on joining Salerno's conspiracy, which under the aegis of the French king was plotting to bring down both the Medici regime and the Aragonese King Ferrante in Naples.[19]

Piero and the Ruling Elite in Florence

If his own family challenged Piero's authority, so did some of the leading citizens, despite the support they initially gave him. For although Lorenzo had consolidated his regime after the crises of 1466 and 1478, family and Guelf–Ghibelline rivalries soon reopened old fissures after his death.[20] The clearest evidence of this was a report, forwarded to Piero from Faenza in May 1493, that Florence was divided into three groups: one consisting of his alienated relations by marriage, Bernardo Rucellai and Pagolantonio Soderini; a second group formed by Bernardo del Nero, Niccolò Ridolfi and Pierfilippo Pandolfini; and a third by Piero and a few young friends.[21] This last group was ill defined, perhaps including Giannozzo Pucci (whom Piero called his 'alter ego') and Bernardo Dovizi, as well as some of the friends who accompanied Piero to Rome in 1492, like Antonio Serristori, Alessandro Nasi, Pierantonio

---

[18] Picotti, *Giovinezza*, pp. 509–11; Parenti, *Storia* I, p. 34: 'catelano e tenuto di non perfetta fede ... publico simoniaco', 'molti figiuoli e sempre ... vissuto voluttuosissimamente'.

[19] Discussed in Chapter 12 in this volume. On Marullo, patronised by both Lorenzo di Pierfrancesco and Antonello Sansevarino, Prince of Salerno, Kidwell, *Marullus*, Brown, *Florence* (2011), pp. 119–20, esp. n. 13; Brown, *Return of Lucretius, ad ind.*

[20] p. 125, n. 8 in this volume.

[21] Puccio Pucci in Faenza to Piero, 25 May 1493, MAP 54, 168, Rubinstein, *Government*, p. 266.

Carnesecchi and Jacopo Gianfigliazzi.²² Although the report was written in 1493, a year after Lorenzo's death, we know it represented divisions that were already evident the previous autumn, when Bernardo Rucellai and Pagolantonio Soderini found themselves excluded from the all-important body of electoral scrutineers (*accoppiatori*), to be replaced by Piero and some other partisans. According to Parenti, the reform 'broke Lorenzo's order' – that is, the constitutional *Ordine del Settanta*, according to which twenty-five scrutineers were appointed in February 1489 to serve for the following five years (ten to be chosen every two years to serve in groups of five per year, the remaining five to serve in 1494). By appointing ten new scrutineers two years before the twenty-five had all enjoyed office, it enabled Piero and his partisans to preempt the choice of the next year's officials by reappointing himself (now in his own name and not as his father's replacement), as well as supporters like del Nero and Francesco Valori, while ruling out other members of the original twenty-five, like Bernardo Rucellai and Pagolantonio Soderini. Since this happened on the very same day – 26 September 1492 – that Piero and five others were elected as ambassadors to Rome, the reform seems intended to purify the regime and ensure its stability during the ambassadors' absence.²³ According to Guicciardini, Rucellai (married to Lorenzo's sister) and Soderini (Lorenzo's first cousin) both tried to modify some of Piero's habits that irked the citizens, Bernardo doing so even in Lorenzo's lifetime, and when they failed, they betrothed their children to the Strozzi without consulting Piero.²⁴ So despite efforts to reconcile both men by appointing them to the Otto di Pratica in January 1493, the divisions got stronger. Pagolantonio's brother Francesco, the bishop of Volterra, joined Lorenzo di Pierfrancesco's conspiracy, and so did Bernardo's son Cosimo, and according to Giovanvettorio Soderini (the youngest brother), Pagolantonio, Bernardo del Nero and others wanted to replace Piero with Lorenzo di Pierfrancesco even before 1494, in order 'to have an idol more to their taste'.²⁵

---

[22] On Giannozzo and on Piero's young friends, pp. 159, n. 39, and 162 following.
[23] Otto Respons. 9, fol. 26 (to Filippo Valori, 26 September 1492); on the reform, Cento 3, fols. 15v–16v (26 September) etc.; cf. Parenti, *Storia*, I, pp. 37–8: 'rottosi el dato da Lorenzo ordine ... per tôrre lo stato ad alquanti Principali e stretti parenti di Piero', etc.); Rubinstein, *Government*, pp. 239–41 (on the 1489 reform and its renewal in '1493', not mentioning 1492 at all), 266–7, 279–80 (listing five *accoppiatori* per year from 1489 to 1494, selected biennially).
[24] Parenti, *Storia* I, pp. 41 and 43 (on Piero and Cosimo Rucellai), Guicciardini, *Storie*, pp. 84–5.
[25] Bertelli, '*Ricordi* di G. V. Soderini,' p. 366: 'per havere idolo più a loro modo', cf. Bertelli, 'Di due profili mancati', p. 584; on Rucellai, p. 53, n. 3 in this volume.

Bernardo del Nero in fact headed the second group in the 1493 report that represented the *stato* – that is, the inner ruling group of ten people, according to Parenti, 'on whom the whole weight of the regime rested': Piero let them govern and they used him 'as their *capo* to keep themselves in power'.[26] Although Bernardo changed his position after Piero's exile, he was initially a key figure in the regime who rose from lowly origins to become a leading statesman, thanks to Medici support – for which he, like Giovanni Cambi, was executed in 1497, despite being by then regarded as head of 'that sect in the middle', loved by some and loathed by others.[27] As well as Piero himself and del Nero, this inner ruling group included most of the 'intimates' listed by Dovizi in 1490 (that is, the lawyer Angelo Niccolini, Niccolò Ridolfi and the functionaries Antonio di Bernardo Dini, Giovanni Guidi and ser Piero Dovizi).[28] The group also included three upstanding statesmen: Pierfilippo Pandolfini, Piero Alamanni and Francesco Valori. Because of their importance and frequent appearance in the events that follow, they need some introduction to explain their role in the structure and workings of the Medici regime.

Among them, Pierfilippo Pandolfini was probably Piero's most important adviser and loyal supporter after the death of Jacopo Guicciardini in 1490. During Lorenzo's lifetime, Pierfilippo had been described by the Este ambassador as 'the heart of his Magnificence Lorenzo in the council and the first citizen of the city', and he had helped Jacopo to initiate Piero into politics in 1489.[29] When he accompanied the young Cardinal Giovanni to Rome for his triumphal entry in 1492, the ambassador Filippo Valori praised him unreservedly as 'everyone's godfather': 'in everyone's opinion, there's no one like him in Florence apart from Lorenzo ... *upright of life and free from vice.*' Still in Rome when Lorenzo died, he sent Piero important advice about strengthening the bank there with extra funds, and he always reported fully to both the Otto di Pratica and to Piero on his repeated embassies abroad.[30] During Dovizi's

---

[26] Parenti, *Storia* I, pp. 46–7, at 47: 'In questi .X. consisteva tutto il pondo dello stato, benché PIero de' Medici da lloro governare si lasciassi, e essi lui come capo per la loro conservazzione usassino.' Cf. Najemy, *A History*, p. 376.

[27] On del Nero and 'quella secta che fu facta di mezzo', pp. 262 and 270 in this volume.

[28] p. 89 in this volume. Dovizi's list of 'questi vostri' included the lawyer, Giovanni Serristori, Francesco Dini and Bernardo Rucellai. On Niccolini as the 'Dottore de' primi, che non vo' per honestà fargli quella vergogna meritava', Cambi, *Istorie*, 2, p. 44; Guicciardini, *Storie*, pp. 85 (named with 'alcuni altri maligni'), 91, etc.

[29] On Pierfilippo, second son of Giannozzo Pandolfini, *DBI* 80, 2014 (E. Plebani), Boschetto, 'Letteratura, arte e politica'; on his library, Verde, 'Nota d'archivio'.

[30] Kent, *Princely Citizen*, p. 235, n. 33; Filippo Valori to Dovizi, 24 March 1492, MAP 98, 539, fol. 541v: 'si è detto compare di tutti, non cede a nessuno cittadino excepto el magnifico Lorenzo a g<i>udicio d'ongnuno ... *integer vir et scelerisque puru*s [Hor. *Od.* 1.22]';

absence in Milan in July–August 1493, Pierfilippo actively supported Piero with help and advice; in July he advised Piero about the French ambassador Péron de Basque's visit to Florence ('if I were Piero', he told Bernardo Dovizi, 'I would return tomorrow, let him [Péron] know I had arrived, and after lunching I would talk to him for a bit to delay him somewhat, and when Piero thought the moment right, I would tell the Frenchman ... what you've said to me').[31] The following year he similarly suggested how Piero should deal with trouble within the ruling elite. He survived Piero's exile and remained a frequent speaker in consultative meetings (now critical of Piero), in 1496 visiting Gianvettorio Soderini 'for the public [and private] good', he said, to warn him of gossip about Francesco Soderini's 'great enmity' with the Capponi that would damage the city.[32]

Piero Alamanni, too, was close to Piero, one of the very few diplomats to address him with the familiar *tu* instead of the more formal *voi*, choosing him, with Pierfilippo Pandolfini and Poliziano, as godparents to his expected child in June 1494, 'to give him a little of the faith I have for so long given to the walls of your house, not to mention its people'.[33] We have seen him helping to train Piero when he visited Milan for Gian Galeazzo's wedding in 1489, encouraging him then – and more crucially in 1494 – to enjoy Lodovico's friendship, but at the same time insisting that Piero's initial visit to him as ambassador in 1489 should be open and not secret (as Lorenzo had wanted). Like Pandolfini, Alamanni was also an eloquent spokesman for Florence as its ambassador, delivering a long homily to Lodovico in 1494 in praise of the republic's free and popular government.[34]

Other members of the ruling elite changed from being loyal supporters to critics of Piero when they thought he was overstepping the boundary between public and private interest. Piero Capponi was one of them. As a

---

Pandolfini in Rome to Piero, 12 April 1492, MAP 18, 46: 'Et in vero, Piero, sforzatevi di farlo'.

[31] Bernardo Dovizi to Piero, n.d. (21 July 1493), ed. Moncallero, I, p. 24.

[32] The same in Spedaletto to his brother ser Piero Dovizi, 19 July 1493, ivi, I, pp. 20–1; p. 256, n. 8 in this volume); G. V. Soderini, *Ricordi*, ed. Bertelli, p. 375 (7 September [1496]:'per ben publico ... et etiam privato, che amava ciascheduno').

[33] Alamanni in Milan to Piero, 28 June 1494, MAP 50, 280, fol. 292v: 'um poco di quella fede che io ho tanto tempo data alle mura di casa tua non che alle persone'. Alamanni was born in 1434 'to one of oldest and most distinguished Florentine families', *Corrispondenza* 7, pp. ix-xi. His letters mix affectionate advice with confidentiality, e.g. MAP 74, 96 (to Piero, 23 April 1494), which Piero was not to discuss 'con anima nata'.

[34] pp. 76–7, 80–1 in this volume; Alamanni to Piero, 25 April 1494, MAP 50, 288, fol. 301, bis-sex ('un volume'), esp. 301 bis^r: 'ch' el popolo è in libertà et non si fa cosa alchuna se non co' modi antichamente consueti, et è tucto concorde allo stato presente'. He remained a Medicean moderate after 1494, Butters, *Governors*, pp. 168, 185, 191.

Francophile, he initially served Piero loyally as an ambassador to France and then as Gonfalonier of Justice in 1493, but he became increasingly critical of him as the French expedition to Italy gathered momentum, deserting him in November 1494 to become, with Francesco Valori, competing supporters of the republican regime.[35] Francesco Valori's nephew Filippo Valori was another. He served as Florence's ambassador in Naples during the revolution in November and died there the following month before his loyalty was put to the test; but despite being reconciled with Piero as a godfather to his son after their falling-out during the 1492 papal conclave, he maintained a critical stance as ambassador in Rome and Naples and was awarded a public funeral by the republican government on his death in December.[36]

These families could be – and have been – accused of 'having a foot in both stirrups', but the case of Piero Soderini suggests that self-interest is insufficient to account for his reputation as an impartial, civic-minded citizen – and chosen, as such, as Florence's first life Gonfalonier of Justice in 1502 – despite his support for Piero in the face of his brothers' defection to Lorenzo di Pierfrancesco. He served Piero with total loyalty as an ambassador to France with Gentile Becchi in 1493–94 (as Becchi confirmed to Piero) and even after Piero's exile he was considered to be his friend. In 1497, he was held in the government palace with around fifty other Medici 'friends and supporters' to prevent him making contact with Piero during Piero's attempted return to Florence in 1497, and in 1501 he and Alamanno Salviati were distrusted as possible envoys to Cesare Borgia for being 'men belonging to the old regime and close friends of Piero de' Medici'. When he was chosen as Florence's first life

---

[35] On Capponi, *DBI*, 19, 1976 (M. Mallett), Brown, *Florence* (2011), p.129, and p. 223 in this volume. Della Casa had warned Piero on 17 April 1494 that the Capponi bankers in Lyon 'secretamente aggravono il male nostro' and hoped Piero Capponi as ambassador would not be influenced by them (ed. Can. p. 291). On the Valori, Pesman Cooper, *Pier Soderini*, p. 292 and n. 20 (303); Polizzotto, *Memorie di casa Valori*, pp. 9–48 (intro.); on Francesco, Parenti, *Storia* I, pp. 37–8 and 59–60.

[36] Signori Delib. ord. aut. 96, fol. 109v (awarding Filippo a public funeral with sixteen 'torcibus et una filza drappellonorum sumptibus et expensis communis flor'). On events in August 1492, Picotti, *Giovinezza*, pp. 417–21; Filippo Valori in Rome to Bernardo Dovizi, 23 August 1492, MAP 124, 306 ('Io te ringrazio assai dell'opera hai fatto a Piero e di farmi suo chompare'). He told Bernardo Dovizi on 19 April 1493 that he would never refuse to 'servire lo stato e Piero di tutto quello che in benifizio e commodo suo venissi e io potessi' (MAP 55, 44). But Piero claimed to see for himself when in Rome that Valori, as ambassador there, 'non faccia per le cose nostre publiche e private quello che richiede la intelligentia nostra et la servitù di questa casa', Piero in Rome to Angelo Niccolini in Milan, 21 November 1492, Niccolini Archives, 315, ins. 54; the same, 4 October, ibid.; cf. Valori to Giannozzo Pucci, 17 July 1493 (SSX8LCMR 15, fol. 122).

head of state in 1502, it was for his noted impartiality.³⁷ With such men as his friends and mentors, Piero may – even unwittingly – have imbibed some of their republicanism and ethos of public service.

According to the historian Nardi (though not mentioned by Parenti), Piero also received support from two of the 'wisest' leading citizens in Florence, Francesco d'Antonio Taddei and Francesco di Gherardo Gherardi. Gherardi, he said, was especially fond of Piero and deterred him from laying his hands on his own kith and kin, Lorenzo and Giovanni di Pierfrancesco, when their conspiracy was discovered in April 1494.³⁸ In addition to these citizens, Piero was also supported by long-standing Medici partisans like the Pucci, who from being minor guildsmen at the time of Cosimo had risen to become important members of the regime. Antonio's brother Dionigi served both Piero and his father as commissary in Faenza and from April 1493 as ambassador in Naples, where he died fifteen months later. He was replaced in Faenza by his nephew messer Puccio, who became ambassador in Rome in June 1494 (also dying in office only three months later). Messer Puccio's half-brother Giannozzo was one of Piero's closest friends, called by Piero his 'alter ego', for whom he also suffered execution in 1497.³⁹

Of course these men knew that their own standing depended on the Medici's success and standing abroad. In 1483 the Ferrarese ambassador in Florence had explained to Duke Ercole that Lorenzo's reputation consisted in the esteem in which he was held by 'the powers of Italy and lords from outside', without whom 'he would lack the esteem he enjoys here [in Florence], and if those in power didn't have this idol (*hiidolo*), they would be just like everyone else'. Piero, too, was regarded as the ruling elite's idol for the same reasons – until he was replaced by his cousin Lorenzo di Pierfrancesco as 'an idol more to their taste' – and

---

[37] pp. 193 and 245 in this volume; Parenti, *Storia*, 2, p. 435 ('sì come homini dello stato vecchio, e intrinseci amici di Piero de' Medici'); Pesman Cooper, *Pier Soderini*, esp. 1–41, at 33, 43–98 and her fundamental essay, 'The Florentine Ruling Group under the *governo popolare*' (ibid., pp. 141–251); Butters, *Governors*, pp. 45–6, and now Baker, *Fruit of Liberty* and Append. I (pp. 235–53); Bertelli, 'I *Ricordi* di G. V. Soderini' (p. 406, 9 July [1498] on his brother Piero's advice always to recommend what was for the good of the city and not the opposite, cf. pp. 365–6).

[38] Nardi, *Istorie*, 1, p. 23 ('uomo grande e molto affezionato al detto Piero'). Gherardi was Gonfalonier in September–October 1494 and again in 1499, highly regarded for resolving the tax crisis, Guicciardini, *Storie*, pp. 178–9.

[39] Piero to Michelozzi in Rome, 26 November 1491, GC 29, 35, fol. 8: 'Giannozo Pucci mio, el quale (se gl'è vero che *amicus est alter ego*) fia costì [Rome] io'; in 1493 Lorenzo Pucci said Giannozzo had given his body and soul to Piero, p. 130, n. 32 in this volume. On the Pucci, D. Kent, *Rise of the Medici*, esp. pp. 122–3; Rubin, *Images and Identity*, pp. 229–71.

he similarly needed to be successful abroad.⁴⁰ This explains the importance of his visit to Rome in late 1492 as one of six Florentine ambassadors to congratulate the new pope. It was his first public engagement abroad after his father's death, through which he hoped to regain the ground lost by the humiliation of the papal conclave.

The Embassy to Rome, November–December 1492

Piero was confident of success when he set out for Rome in November 1492 as part of the Florentine embassy to honour the new pope and offer him the city's obedience. Two months earlier, on 12 September, Alfonsina had given birth to their second child, Lorenzo, the grandson that his namesake, Piero's father, had hoped for. There was great rejoicing as the news was spread through the dominion by Medici retainers. Piero's colleagues in the Otto di Pratica were among the godparents, together with fra Mariano da Gennazzano from San Gallo, the prior of San Lorenzo and 'some others' (including Filippo Valori, as a sign of restored favour); and on 28 September one of the Otto was authorised to spend ten gold ducats and £600 on a present for Alfonsina.⁴¹ From his castle in Vicovaro, Virginio Orsini wrote to tell Piero of his 'incredible pleasure' at the news, which was just what the family needed, and he hoped that his and Alfonsina's fecundity would go from good to better.⁴² So Piero's election as the youngest of the six ambassadors to Rome on 26 September must have contributed to his happiness (when he was in Rome, he sent kisses to 'la Cice [his daughter Clarice] et Lorenzino', as well as a letter to Alfonsina reminding her to write to him sometimes).⁴³

Piero had in fact been chosen because he was young and Florence's counterpart to the young princes being sent by Naples and Milan in what

---

⁴⁰ Antonio Montecatini to Ercole, 17 December 1492, ed. Cappelli, p. 265, Lorenzo, *Lettere* 7, p. 157 ('... quando non havesseno quello hiidolo, seriano come gli altri'); cf. G. V. Soderini's *Ricordi*, n. 25 in this chapter.

⁴¹ Opera del Duomo, Registri battesimali 6, fol. 16 'Lorenzo Francesco et Ro<mo>lo ... a dì 12 [1492], hore 18, ba<ptizato> a dì 13'; Parenti, *Storia* I, p. 36; Otto di Pratica 5, fol. 65v; Filippo Valori to Bernardo Dovizi, 23 August 1492, n. 36 in this chapter; cf. 2 September, MAP 124, 353, fol. 397r (on his and Dovizi's 'opera ... per me appresso a Piero').

⁴² Virginio to Piero, 14 September 1492, MAP 137, 526: 'acciò possiate fecondare da bene in meglio'. Bernardo mentions (to Piero, 20 February 1494, ed. Moncallero, I, p. 56) a third child, 'Luisa' after Piero's dead sister, who, as a 'femina è più secondo el desiderio vostro' (females are unrecorded in the 1489 register, when Clarice was born, or in 1494).

⁴³ Piero in Rome to Michelozzi in Florence, 4 December 1492, GC 29, 35, fol. 27: 'Baciate la Cice et Lorenzino per amore mio'; Dovizi to Michelozzi, 15 November, GC 29, 62, fol. 101r, forwarding Piero's letter to Alfonsina, to whom he says 'scriva qualche volta a Piero'. On Piero's election, Parenti, *Storia* I, p. 36, and p. 155 at n. 23 in this chapter.

was intended to be a joint embassy (don Federigo was King Ferrante's grandson and Ermes Sforza was Duke Giangaleazzo's brother).[44] So for the first time he could play the prince as part of a republican delegation, indulging his love of fine clothes without his father's constraint and including in his retinue three of his chapel singers, among them the famous Heinrich Isaac, and two viola players.[45] Despite his confidence, Piero's departure for Rome caused considerable consternation. His brother Giovanni warned him of the dangers of Rome.[46] And his friends were worried about his absence from Florence at a time of heightened tension, his prolonged stay awaiting Virginio Orsini in Bracciano making 'the hair of more than one of them rise up', according to ser Francesco Baroni.[47] But Piero had been reassured by Sforza Bettini (who had visited Rome as a peacemaker in September) that the Borgia pope was very affectionate towards him and his family, promising them and the regime total support if needed; and since he was on friendly terms, too, with the pope's son Cesare, who had been a student in Pisa before his father's elevation, he found Giovanni's warning 'untimely and unreasonable'.[48] So Dovizi, travelling to Rome with Piero, told Michelozzi not to worry, Piero had his father's spirit, didn't plan to stay there long,

---

[44] Parenti, *Storia* I. Lodovico later blamed Piero for the allies' failure to appear together ('per potere monstrare la pompa tua', Alamanni to Piero, 22 November 1492, *Corrispondenza* 7, p. 168). Piero's letters to Niccolini in Milan show him initially delaying their departure to have time 'nell'ordinarsi et nel vestire, etc.' and later helping to thwart Ascanio's 'nuovo modo' of a joint audience (4, 6 and 26 November 1492, Niccolini Archives, 315, ins. 54; but letters in Otto Respons. 8 and 9 (18 August–16 November 1492) suggest Naples and Milan also caused delays and that Ferrante was willing for Florence to go ahead alone.

[45] D'Accone, 'Lorenzo and Music', p. 279 and n. 54 (the viola players were the famous Cardiere and il Campare, cf. MAP 104, 57, fol. 583). Not part of Piero's retinue, Giorgio Benigno Salviati also accompanied him to Rome to promote his campaign against the General of the Franciscan Order in which Piero was later embroiled (pp. 166-7 following.).

[46] Michelozzi to Dovizi, 12 November, MAP 72, 122 (Giovanni's letter has not survived, Picotti, *Giovinezza*, p. 505), Dovizi's reply from Bracciano on the 15th, GC 29, 62, fol. 101 ('Piero si maravigliò grandemente del ricordo del cardinale et vostro et li parse iudicio inconveniente et pocho ragionevole'). Cf. Piero in Rome to A. Niccolini in Milan (that after the arrest of Nofri Tornabuoni in Rome, 'li più si sono maravigliati che Io stessi in proposito di venire ad Roma'). In the absence of Giovanni's initial letter, see his letter to Michelozzi, on the 16th, GC 29, 39, fol. 10.

[47] Baroni to Dovizi in Rome, 17 November 1492, MAP 72, 98r: 'tucti li amici antichi del padrone monstrano molto desiderare la tornata sua con prestezza et questo vostro soprastare a Bracciano fa arricciare il pelo a più di uno'.

[48] Sforza Bettini to Piero, 29 September 1492, MAP 18, 63, 'né mai ... udii le più amorevoli et eficaci parole da cuore ... in dimostratione di amore et affectione paternale verso di voi e di tutta la Casa vostra' (on Bettini, Lorenzo, *Lettere* 10, p. 61, n. 1); Cesare to Piero, 5 October 1492, Gregorovius, *Lucrezia Borgia*, p. 30, and Picotti, *Giovinezza*, pp. 268–9.

wouldn't talk to anyone about his business, nor go as a guest to any banquets or wear any of the fine things he had had made in Florence; the pope would cite Franceschetto Cibo for the conflict over his lands, not Piero, and Piero he would 'caress and honour greatly'. All the *brigata* were very well and Piero better than the others.[49]

Four days later they arrived in Rome in drenching rain, but even so the loyal Dovizi reported that they had all made a fine showing:

> and the boss has moved the hearts of everyone again, cheering up all the friends, who think that although the first boss is dead, he's left behind a green branch that is alive and well, and strong enough to support the city.[50]

The ten-page account book of 'the Magnificent Piero's' *Gita di Roma* shows that 1312 florins were spent on Piero's clothes, nearly a third of which (488 florins), was for his 'large gown of black velvet used as a cloak with large sleeves lined with silver brocade', the rest on other gowns, big robes, little robes, jackets, stockings and so forth; another 1432 florins was spent on clothing his large retinue, which included the two secretaries Piero and Bernardo Dovizi, two chaplains (one of them Matteo Franco), the purse keeper (Francesco della Casa), three singers and Cardiere the viola player, as well as a barber, two stewards, two men 'for the mules' (one of them, Golpino, listed separately), a trombonist, grooms, six crossbowmen and four lackeys. The listed relatives and friends who accompanied them – Piero's cousin Lorenzo Tornabuoni, his brother-in-law Piero Ridolfi, Antonio Serristori and Alessandro Nasi – had to pay for their silver adornments, and Pierantonio Carnesecchi, Giannozzo Pucci, Jacopo Gianfigliazzi, Lorenzo Martelli, Antonio Ricasoli and Count Gabriele da Bolgheri had to pay for dressing their retinues like Piero's.[51] The largest expenditure by far was 3530 florins spent on paying merchants supplying materials and goods – especially gold and silver for clothes and jewelry – and on the craftsmen who made

---

[49] Dovizi to Michelozzi, 15 November 1492: 'costui [Piero] ha-l'animo del padre, né sa perché Virginio maxime lo dovessi fare villania, et del papa non dubita ... fa male et dice bene, che vedrà, charezzerà et honorerà Piero grandemente'.
[50] The same, 19 November, 1492, GC 29, 62, fol. 102r: 'Siamo stati tenuta una bella cosa ... Et il padrone ha facto rintenerire ognuno, et rallegrato ha tucti gl'amici, parendo loro che se bene il primo patrone è morto, ci sia restato bronchone verde, vivo, sodi et da appogiarli cotesta città.' On the *broncone*, p. 104, n. 78 in this volume.
[51] 'Ritratto della ispeza della Gitta di Roma', MAP 104, 57, fols. 580r–585v (581v and 584 blank), Frosini, *Lettere di Matteo Franco*, p. 51; 582r, 'Spesa delle veste del Magnifico Piero fatosi per la gita di Roma', 583r–v: 'Spesa per vestire la famiglia del Magnifico Piero', 584v ('Debitori per chonto della Gita'), etc., 281r and 585r on Alfonsina (did she accompany Piero or join him later?). Cf. MAP 88, 234 listing Piero's *famiglia* in two groups: first, the servants (Salvalaglio and Golpino among the fourteen *staffieri*); second, Piero, his first four friends and relatives, then the others named in the accounts.

them, as well as on the horses for the journey to Rome (acquired by Antonio Pappacoda, the brother of Piero's jousting master).[52]

All the ancient curialists agreed that the coronation of Alexander VI on 26 August was 'the most ostentatious and sumptuous ceremony' they had ever seen, so perhaps Piero's extravagance was excusable. The Florentine ambassador in Rome, Filippo Valori, reported home on the equally showy embassies that arrived, one by one, to offer obedience to the Borgia pope, and they must have raised the game in Florence, whose republican government offered its ambassadors a modest 100 florins each for extraordinary expenses and a salary of 4.5 florins *per diem* while away (for the bishop Gentile Becchi and the doctor, messer Puccio, this totalled 330 florins; for Piero and the others, 270 florins for two months' absence), plus a supplement of eighty florins for the embassy's other expenses and tips.[53] Among the other republics visiting Rome, only Lucca got away with rhetoric rather than sartorial splendour, with a well-delivered oration praising the liberty Lucca had enjoyed (with papal help) for 123 years, while Siena, although dressing its ambassadors sumptuously, disgraced itself oratorically when Bartolomeo Sozzini dried up, 'through losing his nerve or forgetting his words'.[54] At least Gentile Becchi's oration for the Florentines was said to have been well received by the College of Cardinals (although Becchi himself refers to being 'stoned' for it, perhaps for wanting, with Piero, a separate ceremony in order that he, not the others, could deliver the oration).[55] Piero himself was honoured by holding the papal train during the ceremony, as the youngest of the six ambassadors, and afterwards he enjoyed a private audience with the pope.

The embassy nevertheless served to mark the difference with his father's more 'republican' visits to Rome. In 1471 Lorenzo had visited Rome, like Piero in 1492, as a member of Florence's embassy to offer obedience to the new pope Sixtus IV, but instead of arriving with his own cultured entourage, he had used the occasion to tour the city with Leon Battista Alberti and to lay the foundation of his own collection of

---

[52] MAP 104, 57, fol. 580r–v.
[53] Signori, Collegi, Condotte e Stanziamenti 16, fols. 66v-67r: 'fl. 100 per uno per più spese extraordinarie in decta gita ... Et a lloro decti fl. octanta larghi di grossi per tucti loro per supplemento di più altre spese et Benandate che anno a fare.'
[54] Valori to the Otto, 27 October 1492, Otto Respons. 9, fol. 49r, 'havendosi preservata Lucha la libertà già 123 anni col favore *solum* del Pontifice'; the same, 14 October, fol. 45: 'o che l'animo o la memoria gli manchasse, si perde'.
[55] The same, 28 November 1492, 'per essere stata aprobatissima et detta accuratamente et con buona gratia, da tutti è stata commendata', Tribaldo de' Rossi, *Ricordanze*, p. 280; cf. Becchi, *La congiura della verità*, ed. Simonetta, p. 47: 'Io fui sì lapidato d'una bona opera a Roma'; Guicciardini, *Storia*, pp. 86–7.

antiquities from Paul II's collection and as papal gifts.[56] Piero was already familiar with the city thanks to his earlier visits, especially in 1487 when he was shown the sights by his brother-in-law, Innocent VIII's son, who was now in conflict with the new Borgia pope over his lands. Moreover, in retaliation for the large sums Franceschetto had withdrawn from the Apostolic Camera, Alexander was now refusing to repay money owed to Florence's merchants in Rome. So instead of returning home in glory like his father, laden with gifts from the pope, Piero left Rome on 13 December before most of the Florentine contingent, alienated from the pope and angry with his brother-in-law Franceschetto Cibo.[57]

The Cibo Lands and Religious Disputes in Florence

Far from being caressed and honoured by Alexander VI (as he had been by Innocent VIII), Piero found himself engaged in a long and acrimonious audience with the pope about 'this blessed sale' of the Cibo lands, during which Piero learnt that Franceschetto had accused him of keeping him in Florence by force and being the cause of the whole affair.[58] In fact, Piero was initially involved in the dispute over the Cibo lands only as Franceschetto's brother-in-law and as a relative by marriage of Virginio Orsini. It had been his father Lorenzo's idea that Innocent VIII should give Franceschetto some lands in the Papal States (Anguillara and Cerveteri, as well as Montorano and Viano) in order to make him self-sufficient, and it was Ferrante's idea that he should sell them on his father's death to Virginio Orsini, Ferrante's *condottiere* – to 'be a bone in the throat' of their rival, the new Borgia pope and his ally, Ascanio Sforza.[59] Piero had been protecting them at Cibo's request since the pope's death, and he had evidently agreed to bring Franceschetto Ferrante's contribution to Virginio's payment for the lands – for which

---

[56] Rochon, *La Jeunesse*, p. 204, Fusco and Corti, *Lorenzo de' Medici*, esp. pp. 6–10.
[57] Signori, Coll. Cond. Stanz. 16, fol. 67r (the others left between 15 and 22 December, Becchi staying on until January 1493). In 1488, when the pope was ill, Lorenzo himself suggested Franceschetto should 'ponere mano su qualche somma di quelli sono in cassa', Bullard, *Lorenzo*, p. 148 and n. 54.
[58] Piero in Rome to Michelozzi, 24 November 1492, GC 29, 35, fol. 24: 'venimo a questa benedecta vendita' and during 'molti discorsi et dibattiti', the pope showed 'che io lo tengo di costà [Florence] per forza et ... et che da me nasce tucta questa cosa'. Cibo also blamed Piero 'che ... Io mi trovo senza el mio stato', 10 April 1493, MAP 100, 118r (autograph).
[59] Alamanni in Naples to Piero, 31 October 1492, *Corrispondenza* 7, pp. 152–3, they want to *'fare questa cosa secretamente* et ... *coprire quello che non si può tenere occulto'* (decoded); cf. the same, p. 115, that we must ensure 'il signor Virginio a ogni modo habbi lo stato del signor Francesco', etc. On the sale, Shaw, *Julius II*, pp. 87–8.

Virginio thanked Piero as the person responsible for bringing all this about.[60] But far from achieving his plan for a settlement of the affair in Rome by means of a military contract for Franceschetto, Piero learnt on his arrival there on the 19th that Alexander had reignited the flames by prohibiting the sale altogether, declaring that as pope he demanded obedience, not the law, from Franceschetto; and since Piero also learnt that Franceschetto had broken his word to him, he in turn declared that since Virginio 'wants the lands ... has the money, and I can't get him to change his mind, it's now up to Signor Francesco to decide whether to accept – as seems reasonable'.[61]

The anger and sense of betrayal in his letters both to Angelo Niccolini in Milan and to Michelozzi in Florence are palpable. Piero's clear grasp of the danger of the situation, even at this early stage, emerges from his letters to Niccolini, in which he describes what he had attempted to do to resolve the crisis of the Cibo lands – even to the extent of 'shamefully' going back on his father's and Innocent's agreement about the lands by altering the contract of sale – but to no avail, because of the stubbornness of Franceschetto and Virginio, who became even more uncooperative when Ferrante promised to provide him with most of the money for the lands (destroying in a hour, Piero said, what he had been trying to achieve in a month).[62] His letter to Michelozzi accused Franceschetto of 'losing his brain' and 'betraying' him (carefully toned down by Dovizi), but what he resented most was being accused of ingratitude by

---

[60] Virginio to Piero, 4 January 1493, MAP 18, 69, fol. 79r; ASF Notarile antecos. 10200, fol. 362r-v, 6 November 1492 (Cibo makes Piero his procurator to receive Virginio's money , 'che comprende la vendita di queste terre' to 'dare perfectione al contracto'); Piero to Michelozzi, 16 November, GC, 29, 35, fol. 18r; and Alamanni in Milan to Piero, 2 January 1493, ed. Can, pp. 444–45 (reporting Ferrante's payment to Cibo of 40,000 duc. and Piero's refusal to pay him anything).

[61] Piero in Rome to A. Niccolini in Milan, 4 October 1492, Niccolini Archives, 315, ins. 54, fol. 1v: 'Io ho facto pensiero in questa mia andata ad Roma accozarmi con Virginio et poi col Papa ... et vedere se per mezo d'una condocta nel S. Fr<ancesco> si potessi adormentare questa cosa'; to Michelozzi, 19 November 1492, GC 29, 35, fol. 20r: 'che non voleva legge dal Signor Francesco ma essere obedito, etc' (according to Dovizi, Piero wrote this letter 'con assai alteratione').

[62] Piero to Niccolini, 4 October 1492, fol. 1r-v ('io cerco di alterare quello che fu facto fino a tempo di Innocentio et di mio Padre ... et è pure il vero che lo alterare questa cosa è con ignominia et charicho ... et di mio Padre che ne fu auctore'; 'due teste le più dure et pertinaci del mondo'; 'credo certamente che il Re [Ferrante] guasti più in una hora che io non acconciò in uno mese, perché intendo ha dato speranza a Virginio di servirlo de' denari o della maggiore parte, et questo debbe fare Virginio più renitente ... che non vorrei spronassi el Re al favore di Virginio' etc.; 'io non desidero mancho del Papa che questo contracto si rompa'. As he had said, 'sarebbe più l'utile del S. Fr<ancesco> tenere queste Terre per sè, le quali ha vendute assai mancho che le vaglino et de' danari che gli venissino in mano in pocho tempo non se ne vedria el fumo' (fol. 1r-v), but cf. his letter of 21 November, n. 65 in this chapter.

Franceschetto, a charge that Piero totally rejected, adding that Franceschetto should be aware of what Piero had suffered by being involved in this latest business, and of the patience he needed to cope with the burdens and infamy it had given him. For him, 'poor little Francesco' – 'weak in everything, especially judgement', as the Florentine ambassador Lanfredini had described him in 1488 – was becoming an unwelcome responsibility.[63] For although Lorenzo had been responsible for the deal, as Piero said, and for agreeing that the Medici Bank should pay for the pope and his son's expenses, it was Piero and the bank who now suffered from the great financial burden placed on them by Franceschetto's passion for gambling and the good life, exacerbating the crisis that now confronted Piero.[64] In April 1493, angered by Cibo's attempted sale to Virginio Orsini of lands within the Papal States, the pope created a new league to recover them, the League of St. Mark, which by excluding Florence and Naples left Piero and Florence isolated in northern Italy. As Piero's worried letters to Niccolini in 1492 show, he was initially as keen as the pope to break the contract of sale of the Cibo lands, foreseeing – quite rightly – that Ferrante's support for his *condottiere* Virginio (by helping to pay for the lands) would encourage Lodovico to change sides to support the pope, and further spur on Ferrante's support for Virginio.[65] The changing gist of Piero's letters to Niccolini once he arrived in Rome shows that his fears were justified. The visit that had begun so well ended with Piero's rebuff and the beginning of a shift in power that in the following year threatened to destabilise Italy's old equilibrium.

There was trouble for Piero in Florence, too, in the year following his embassy to Rome. He had been accompanied to Rome by his former philosophy teacher, Giorgio Benigno Salviati, who hoped to become the

---

[63] Piero in Rome to Michelozzi, 19 November 1492, cit. and 30 November, GC 29, 35, fol. 26r: 'che la casa mia, né mio patre o io non furono mai, né sono o sarò ingrato de' benefici', etc. Lanfredini in Rome to Lorenzo, 12 December 1488, Picotti, *Giovinezza*, p. 169

[64] Lorenzo, *Lettere* 12, pp. 43–7; Bullard, *Lorenzo*, pp. 145–8, cf. 165–85; and now on the bank, Guidi Bruscoli, 'Medici-Cybo Marriage'.

[65] Despite his letter to Niccolini on 4 October (n. 62 in this chapter), on 21 November, when in Rome, he regretted being unable to help Virginio as he should, 'ma io so che se il S. Lodovico ci penserà bene, lascierà più tosto ire inanzi questo contracto et ne conforterà Nostro Signore.' This long letter, with its many altered and deleted passages, also sought to persuade Lodovico that the Medici were not threatening or ambitious: Lorenzo 'non hebbe in pugno Papa Innocente ... et restò solo contento de havere obtenuto mio fratello Cardinale', and Piero too 'mi contento molto di quello che ho, et mi pare havere uno bello et uno sicuro stato', Niccolini Archives, 315, ins. 54.

new general of the Franciscan Order.⁶⁶ But when he failed to be elected in April and then refused to relinquish his office as provincial minister of Tuscany, the local populace of S. Croce rose up in arms with shouts of 'Hang!', 'Murder!' and 'Sack!' to prevent Salviati from cutting the newly elected general to pieces. He and his supporters were rescued only thanks to the intervention of the government, who removed them to the safety of the palace, but their cries of 'Palle!' as they went can have done little to endear Piero to the Franciscans and the local populace.⁶⁷

So although Piero won the favour of the rival Dominican Order in Florence in May by supporting Savonarola's campaign to withdraw the convent of San Marco from the Lombard congregation, rivalries continued to divide the citizens.⁶⁸ After Lorenzo's Order of the Seventy had been renewed by the councils in September (despite considerable opposition), a seemingly small reform proposed by Francesco Valori when Gonfalonier of Justice in September–October 1493 showed that the old divisions were still alive and well. The reform – preventing the Signoria's domestic servants from taking food home to their families and selling their jobs in order to augment their salaries – was aborted by Piero at the request of some of the inner circle who resented Valori's authority and then refused to agree to Valori's choice of Pagolantonio Soderini as his successor. Since both Valori and Pagolantonio Soderini later changed from being Piero's supporters to being his critics, these tiffs were indicative of deeper divisions within the ruling elite.⁶⁹ And because, as we saw, this elite depended for its standing on Piero's standing with 'the powers of Italy and lords from outside', Piero's success or failure would ultimately depend on his relationship with these powers and his ability to maintain the precarious balance of power between them that had contributed so much to his father's renown.

---

[66] See n. 45 in this chapter. As Piero's 'creatura, vostro huomo', he was offered by Piero in recompense a readership in theology in the University of Pisa (Salviati to Piero, 15 January 1493, Verde, *Studio* 2, p. 278). On the attempt to move the Franciscans' general chapter from Siena to Grosseto, Braccesi in Siena to Piero, 23–29 April 1493 (MAP 19: 331–9); Piero, *Ricordi di lettere* (1), pp. 419–20 (28 April); Vasoli, *Profezia e Ragione*, p. 55.

[67] Parenti, *Storia* I, pp. 51–4; Vasoli, *Profezia e Ragione*, pp. 52–7.

[68] Weinstein, *Savonarola*, p. 99 and n. 15 (p. 334), quoting Savonarola's letter of thanks to Piero of 26 May 1493.

[69] Parenti, *Storia* I, pp. 60–1; Rubinstein, *Government*, pp. 266–7.

11 Balancing Power in Italy, 1493

Francesco Guicciardini, as we saw, famously attributed Italy's 'ruin' after 1494 to Piero upsetting the balance of power between Milan and Naples by 'throwing himself into the arms of Ferrante' and 'totally alienating Milan'. He was, of course, judging Piero in the light of what happened after the event, when Lodovico Sforza's alliance with the king of France seemed to be a determining factor in the king's victory and the overturning of the Medici regime. But before the French arrived in Italy, the situation was more fluid and Piero more concerned with preserving the balance held by his father than Guicciardini suggests. He was in fact wary of Ferrante and was in close contact with Lodovico, but since his diplomacy was often secret, like his father's, hidden even from ambassadors like Piero Guicciardini in Milan, it is likely that Piero Guicciardini's son, Francesco the historian, was unaware of it. Although the dispute over the lands had spoilt Piero's visit to Rome, it only threatened Italy's balance of power after the pope created the League of St. Mark to recover the lands from Virginio Orsini in April 1493. By following Piero's moves in the face of this threat, we can understand better his secretive strategy to keep the old balance alive.[1]

Piero, Virginio and the Pope

Even before the League of St. Mark was signed, Piero sent the accomplished Baccio Ugolini to visit Virginio Orsini in Bracciano in order to persuade him (with the gift of a horse) to modify his behaviour and dispel 'the doubts and suspicions of prudent and cautious men' about him.[2]

---

[1] p. 152 in this volume. Grimaldi ('Bernardo Dovizi', pp. 229, 236) importantly contrasts Piero's attempt to continue Lorenzo's 'sistema d'equilibrio', his indecisiveness, subterfuges and double politics (see p. 190, n. 3 in this volume), with the traditional account of his 'abbandono ... in braccia agli Aragonesi'.

[2] Ugolini in Bracciano (en route to Naples as interim ambassador) to Piero, 20 February 1493, MAP 19, 57 ('una cavalla', 'li dubii et sospecti che per li homini prudenti et cauti si proponeano') and to the Otto di Pratica, 25 February, Otto Respons. 9, fol. 260r: 'Per

After another emissary, Francesco Cambini, had failed to move the obdurate Virginio, Piero then contributed his own private instructions to the chancery secretary Francesco Gaddi's public mission to Virginio and to the pope in Rome.[3] It was in one of his lengthy private letters to Piero that Gaddi – after warning him about the 'duplicity and guile' in Rome and the need to 'cover his tracks' – told him that Alexander wanted Piero to act as mediator between himself (the pope) and Ferrante:

> for he knew your father had often been a good intermediary between the king and Lord Lodovico, and you should be the same between his Holiness and the king if the need arose ... he appears to think that all the good that has happened in this business is largely due to you.[4]

The pope evidently wanted Piero to support his plans for a marriage relationship with the Aragonese (as eventually agreed in the settlement in August that year). But despite the intimacy of these talks with the pope, conducted one evening from the papal bed – during which Gaddi assured him that there was no difference between the public interest in Florence and Piero's – Gaddi remained cautious about the pope's intentions, and after sharing everything with Florence's ambassador (Filippo Valori), he returned home when he thought it would damage Florence's 'public dignity' to stay on in the face of Virginio's obduracy.[5]

Piero and Naples

Piero was more closely involved in Naples, where he attempted to exert his influence by ensuring that his friend Dionigi Pucci was appointed ambassador there in April 1493 – to enable him, as he put it, to continue

---

ordine del Magnifico Piero de' Medici feci la via per Bracciano'. As well as serving the republic, Baccio, a singer, was a trusted friend and envoy of the Medici, serving as Giovanni's administrator in San Germano, *Corrispondenza* 7, pp. xi–xii, Kent, *Princely Citizen*, pp. 218–19, Lorenzo, *Lettere* 10, p. 13, n. 8, etc. on his death, p. 207, n. 40, in this volume.

[3] Piero, *Ricordi di lettere*, (1), p. 423 (21 May 1493), Cambini in Bracciano to Piero, 24 May, MAP 18, 101, fol. 114r: 'absolutamente ... lo acordo suto egli proposto pella Maestà del re non lo piglieria mai' (Lorenzo, *Lettere* 10, p. 255, n. 1). Gaddi, *Ricordi*, 22 May (Laur. Acq. Doni, 213, fol. 95): 'mandato dal publico' to Virginio and the pope, 'per comporre le differentie infra loro', writing to the Otto and to Piero, Otto Respons. 9, fols. 334–5, MAP 28, 103–9 (27 May–6 June).

[4] Gaddi in Rome to Piero, 19 June 1493, MAP 18, 116, fol. 138v, and 11 June 1493, MAP 18, 111, fol. 132r ('pieno di duplicità et arte ... andar molto cauto et vedere di nettare ogni segno'), Pellegrini, *Ascanio Sforza* I, p. 434, at n. 104. Cf. p. 131 in this volume, on Nofri's earlier discussions with the pope.

[5] Gaddi to Piero, 11 June, fol. 130v: 'voi e il publicho eri in tal modo coniuncti che quello si desiderava per l'uno si desiderava per l'altro'; the same, 28 June, MAP 18, 121r: 'potrebbe in qualche parte offendere la degnità publicha'.

his old practice of communicating with Dionigi 'everything we learn about' and 'return to the discussions we had together on the road to Fiesole' as though they were taking place in Naples.[6] By using a series of duplicitous ploys to keep the king from going back on his word, he then misdated some of his letters and wrote others that were either 'readable' or 'non-readable', 'showable' and 'non-showable', since 'it's not good always to mix a salad in the same way'.[7] On 23 May he sent Dionigi two letters about his negotiations with Lodovico with different dates: 'As you will see, I pretend they were written one after the other but in fact they were written on the same day ... I think you will understand my purpose.'[8] Later it emerged that he disapproved of Dionigi's growing support for Ferrante and Virginio, so he added a codicil to his 'readable' letter, criticising him for encouraging Ferrante to back Virginio (for which he said he, Piero, would bear more responsibility than Ferrante): Dionigi was not to use Piero's name, but talk of it 'as something you have thought about and recorded yourself'. In an undated note from this time, he also told Dionigi to 'warm up Ferrante in all possible ways', 'away from the stinginess of states and of the conventions of Virginio's money and similar messes', in order to get the pope to withdraw from his old alliance (with Lodovico and Venice) and be in their hands.[9]

Despite initially suggesting that Naples and Florence should 'draw close together', Piero soon showed his independence by being as hostile as his elders in the Otto di Pratica to Ferrante's plans for sharing military contracts with Florence.[10] Commenting shrewdly on Ferrante's inconsistency in wanting both a settlement and military escalation against the pope, he told Dionigi that the more he thought about sharing contracts with Ferrante, the more he agreed with the citizens that they should be separate, 'because they would contribute to our reputation and wouldn't

---

[6] Piero to Dionigi Pucci in Naples, 26 April 1493, MAP 138, 276, fol. 271r and MAP 138, 248 (undated, enclosing his cipher); on 6 July (MAP 49, 312, fol. 520r–v), Dionigi acknowledged that Piero ('capo della città') 'per havermi mandato quà voi', would bear responsibility for what he did in Naples.
[7] Piero to Dionigi in Naples, 1 July 1493, MAP 138, 245, fol. 240r: 'questa volta la presente lettera non sarà mostrabile, perché non è bene sempre dare per insalata una medesima mescolanza'.
[8] The same, 23 May 1493, MAP 138, 258r: 'fingo essere scripta dopo l'altra ... Credo intendiate il fine nostro.'
[9] The same, n.d., MAP 138, 302: 'Riscalderetela in tutti e' modi possibili et sopratutto si lievino da queste pidochierie ... et simili imbracti.'
[10] The same, 23 April 1493, MAP 138, 279, fol. 274v:'per hora el fine nostro è diritto a stringere insieme', and 6 May 1493, MAP 138, 260, fol. 255r, that 'questi miei maggiori et Padri' opposed 'questa del conducere a comune'.

be provocative in the way that sharing them might be'.[11] This suggests Piero was far from 'throwing himself into Ferrante's arms', as Guicciardini suggests, but was working to recover the old structure of power that would destroy the pope's alliance with Lodovico and Venice by restoring Florence's old, 'natural' relationship with Milan as well as Naples.

Piero and Milan

Piero had been in secret contact with Lodovico Sforza about renewing the old Triple Alliance since at least the spring of 1493 and possibly earlier. A note in Piero's letter book – that Dionigi was 'not to tell the king [Ferrante] of the paragraph in his instructions concerning Lodovico's discussions with Angelo Niccolini about us colleagues returning to our union and trust in each other' – was confirmed during Dionigi's audience in early April with the pope and Filippo Valori as he passed through Rome. When Valori told the pope that there was no need for his new league (the League of St. Mark) since he could become 'head of ours' (the old Triple Alliance), it emerged that Lodovico had said it would be good 'to reinstate our league' (though without telling the pope). Dionigi, writing from Rome, linked this to 'what you [Piero] did here to unite with Milan, etc.', suggesting that Piero may have broached the idea during his embassy in Rome in late 1492.[12] Since Piero Guicciardini was apparently out of the loop after succeeding Niccolini as ambassador in Milan, his son the historian perhaps knew as little about these discussions and events as his father in describing them.[13]

Piero, in fact, was negotiating with Lodovico not through Guicciardini, the ambassador, but through the ambassador's secretary, Bernardo Ricci. Ricci was the first of the new chancery secretaries serving ambassadors abroad who was not qualified as a notary (like Piero, he had been a student of Poliziano's). After working in Naples, he was posted to Milan, where he had established a certain independence as

---

[11] Ibid., fol. 255v: 'Quanto più penso ...tanto più m'accordo col parere di questi cittadini et più mi piace questo modo di soldare di parte.'
[12] *Ricordi di lettere*, 6 April 1493, (1), p. 416; Dionigi in Rome to Piero, 8 April 1493, MAP 49, 268: 'Parmi questa risposta tolta da quella facesti voi qui del unirsi con Milano, etc.'. Cf. Pandolfini to Piero, same day, SSX8LCMR 65, fol. 9v. On Piero's letters to Milan from Rome, see pp. 165–6 and n. 65 in this volume.
[13] A later ambassador, Alamanni, had to deny that 'noi havamo lasciato P. Guicciardini' (to Piero, 25 April 1494, MAP 50, 288, fol. 301 quat.ʳ) and Guicciardini himself complained that his predecessor, Niccolini, had not written to him as promised and as was customary: 'benché da un mese in qua per essere suto più vicino il S. Lodovico a voi che a noi, ne harete inteso più di me', etc. (12 June 1493, Niccolini Archives, 14, ins. 43, autogr.).

Piero's 'creature' while working for the then ambassador Francesco Valori in 1490. When sent by his successor, Piero Guicciardini, to accompany Lodovico from Ferrara to his castle at Torrechiara in May 1493, his official brief was to discuss the situation in Genoa but, unbeknown to Guicciardini, Ricci was also providing Piero with a private conduit to Lodovico, after Lodovico deserted his old allies to join the pope's new league.[14]

Ricci's confidential memorandum to Dovizi on 24 May reveals that Lodovico blamed Dovizi for encouraging Piero to think too highly of himself, 'as suggested by the reputation and ways of the late Lorenzo'. Despite this, Piero's double-level politics were being encouraged by Lodovico's friends at court, Galeazzo and his brother Gian Francesco, count of Caiazzo, the sons of the Milanese *condottiere* Roberto Sanseverino. For in a letter to Dovizi, Ricci described how they were angling for someone to act as Piero's confidant in Milan whom they could talk to 'with less reserve' than to the ambassador – and to whom Piero could sometimes write with more freedom.[15] Ricci had already bypassed the ambassador Piero Guicciardini ('a good and honourable man', he called him) in sending Dovizi information that Guicciardini thought inappropriate to send, and since he called himself 'a loyal servant of Piero's' who would serve Galeazzo and his brother well, he was clearly the go-between they had in mind.[16]

Ricci throws light on another ruse of Renaissance diplomacy, its use of astrology and the occult to influence politics. In August 1492 he had been sent by Guicciardini's predecessor, Angelo Niccolini, to discuss Piero's unpropitious birth chart with Lodovico's court astrologer, 'that devil *maestro* Ambrogio' (da Rosa), thanks to whom Lodovico was rising high in the court.[17] Ambrogio had grilled Ricci about Piero's stature, his nature and his body: had he been ill in fourteen or fifteen years or shown any untoward signs? What was the hour of his birth? When the ambassador Niccolini was told a few days later that Piero was in some danger, he immediately countered by stating the chart was invalid because Piero

---

[14] Brown, 'Florentine Diplomacy', pp. 304–6; cf. Ricci [in Ferrara] to Dovizi, 24 May 1493, MAP 72, 51r: 'Ma venendo come servidore, anzi vero servo di cotesta casa, stimo sarà iudicato da amore e non da presumptione questo poco che dico.'
[15] Ricci to Dovizi: 'in quella alterigia e suggeritoli la reputatione et modi della fe<dele> me<moria> di Lorenzo', and the postscript on fol. 52v. Brown, 'Florentine Diplomacy', p. 306, n. 14). The Milanese Sanseverini are not to be confused with the Neapolitan Antonello Sanseverino, prince of Salerno.
[16] Brown, 'Florentine Diplomacy', pp. 305, n. 13 and 306, n. 14.
[17] Ricci to Dovizi, 24 May 1493, fol. 51r: 'promesso da' Cieli, et da Maestro Ambruogio, o dal Diavolo'; on Lodovico and Ambrogio Varesi da Rosate, Azzolini, *The Duke and the Stars*, pp. 167–209 passim, esp. 200.

was not twenty-one years old, as it suggested, but twenty – later shrewdly suggesting to Piero that it would be worth paying *maestro* Ambrogio something to get a favourable prediction.[18] Not long afterwards, Ricci was also sent by Niccolini to accompany the architect Giuliano da San Gallo to Lodovico with Piero's propitiatory offering of a model of the Medici villa at Poggio a Caiano, which 'pleased him a lot, and he thanks you warmly for it, saying that nothing at the moment could have given him more pleasure'.[19]

Now, in mid-May 1493, Piero despatched another mollifier (at Lodovico's request, conveyed by his ambassador): twenty-seven buffaloes, which Lodovico found quite beautiful when he saw them in Pavia on his return to Milan in June.[20] This was the moment when the pope was assembling an army to defend himself and his new league from Virginio. As one of its members, Lodovico was himself gathering troops in the Romagna, causing consternation to the rulers of Faenza and Forlì and their protectors, especially the Florentine commissary in Faenza, messer Puccio Pucci (Dionigi's nephew), who tried to find out 'the truth of what they're doing, that is, whether they're staying, going, where, to do what and when'.[21] In fact, Virginio Orsini's change of heart over the castles between Piero's letters to Lodovico of 5 and 8 June (in accepting the judicial verdict of the Ruota instead of attempting to defend himself by force of arms) made it unnecessary for Ferrante or Piero to 'plant mortars in Virginio's house', as Lodovico had initially wanted them to do; but ser Francesco Baroni's careful listing of the pope's forces in his *Memorie di varie guerre d'Italia* attests to the reality of the 'new war' being planned against Virginio 'for the lands he bought from Cibo against the pope's wishes'.[22]

It was now that the crisis of the castles (seemingly resolved in the settlement described later) was overtaken by a much graver threat to Italy's peace that Lodovico heard about during Ricci's visit to his court: Charles VIII of France had decided to claim the throne of Naples, with Lodovico as his ally in charge of his Italian expedition. This was the

---

[18] Niccolini in Milan to Piero, 20 August 1492, ed. Buser, *Beziehungen*, pp. 534–5.
[19] Niccolini to Piero, 25 October 1492, ed. Heidenreich, 'Giuliano da S. Gallo', p. 323, n. 2.
[20] Piero, *Ricordi di lettere* (1), p. 422 (14 May 1493) and Lodovico to Piero, 26 June, MAP 61, 91: 'havendole vedute a Pavia m'è parso de vedere una cosa belissima'.
[21] Puccio Pucci to Caterina Sforza, ruler of Imola and Forlì, 28 May 1493 (copy), MAP 54, 169v: 'cioè dello stare, andare, dove, a che effecto, et quando'. On Caterina, pp. 127–8 in this volume.
[22] BNF Magl. 25, 161, fol. 16v, listing Alexander VI's troops in the 1493 league with Venice and Milan, 'atorno la practica di nuova guerra al S. Virginio Orsino per le terre lui havea comperate dal Signor Francesco Cibo contra la voglia del Papa'.

bombshell that so shocked Piero when he heard it from Ricci that he spent a whole day and a night imagining what Lodovico meant by scaring and threatening them with the ruin of Italy: 'it seems to me that what's happening in France is becoming terrifying'.[23] The news transformed the distant threat of a French expedition to Italy into a reality, and it must have contributed to Piero's decision – made apparently with Ferrante's approval – to send his secretary Dovizi himself to visit Lodovico in Milan in late July. Under the pretence of attending the marriage of Lodovico's niece to the emperor Maximilian, Dovizi was in fact representing Piero on a secret mission to reestablish their old relationship, 'as the best and most effective witness I could draw from this city, having been raised like me in my house and together with me'.[24]

Piero's strategy to restore the Medici's old friendship with Milan is illustrated by his two surviving letters to ser Piero Dovizi. The first was a long autograph letter clearly intended for Lodovico's eyes that spoke grandiloquently of his happiness in having regained the trust of his 'lord and protector' (lost, he said, through no fault of his own) and acknowledged his family's ancient obligation 'towards the illustrious blood of the Sforza and his Excellency'. The second letter was a much more practical assessment of the political problems ahead, for which Piero left 'the remedy' in Dovizi's hands, ending with the anxious hope of hearing 'if my autograph letter has borne great fruit with signor Lodovico'.[25] In fact, Lodovico told Piero that he had initially intended to return to the old alliance with Florence but drew back after hearing about Florence's and Naples' intended alliance with the pope, or what he called this 'plastering-over job' (*rimpiastramento*) for which he suspected Piero had been responsible.[26] There is confirmation that this was Piero's strategy in

---

[23] Brown, 'Florentine Diplomacy', esp. pp. 303, 307–9 at 308, n. 22 (Piero to Dionigi, 11 June 1493).

[24] Ibid., p. 309 and n. 23, citing Piero to Dovizi, 26 July 1493, MAP 72, 55, fols. 58–59 (autogr., *Ricordi di lettere* (1), p. 431:'scripse et dectò Piero', dated 27th); [Piero] to Dionigi in Naples [mid-March 1494], MAP 124, 435, fol. 480r: 'quando mandai ser Piero ad Milano, che 'l Re Ferrando me ne decte auctorità'.

[25] Both referred to in Brown, 'Florentine Diplomacy', p. 309, n. 23; 26 July (fol. 58r–v, autogr.) and 29 July (63r, secr. copy) referring to 'la variatione *preter spem* delli accordi et mente del papa' that made them agree to 'comportare el Re a fare lo accordo *quomodocumque*'. Dovizi had been instructed to 'participare tucto quello che Piero de' Medici li scrivessi', Otto to Piero Guicciardini, 9 August, SSX8LCMR 28, fol. 42, cf. Guicciardini to Dovizi, 3 August, MAP 72, 65r, n. 16.

[26] Lodovico Sforza to Piero, 5 August 1493, autogr. signature, MAP 72, 67 ('la venuta di ser Piero a me è stata di Grande satisfactione', 'tanta satisfactione quanta dire potesse') until hearing of the 'intelligentia particulare' being sought by Naples and Florence with the pope (the same, 10 August 1493, CS Append. 3, ins. 3, fol. 15, confirmed by Alamanni in Vigevano to Piero, 7 April 1494, MAP 138, 289, fol. 284 ter^v): that

Becchi's message to him in October, that the French had reacted badly to 'that letter in your hand urging a general league to withstand the ultramontanes'.[27] Moreover, the following spring, after asking Alamanni, 'do you think I can trust Piero?' and 'do you think he'll be upset to hear that I want the state for me and my sons?', Lodovico went on openly to declare his ambition to become duke of Milan, hoping that Piero would support him or at least guarantee his neutrality as middleman – 'in the middle' – between him and Alfonso, if Lodovico was attacked by Alfonso or his sons. Far from observing the secrecy enjoined by Lodovico, Piero at once copied and despatched Alamanni's letter to Dionigi Pucci in Naples, who also ignored his instructions to 'tear it up once read and share it with no living creature'. Thanks to them, the letter survives to document Piero's double game in supporting Lodovico's ambitions while being part of a league to frustrate them.[28]

The Cibo Settlement in Rome

Before the agreement between Rome, Naples and Florence was signed in August 1493 and confirmed as an alliance the following March, Piero was busy jousting and footballing in Florence. In mid-July he had won the golden lance in a joust in which his cousin Lorenzo Tornabuoni won the second prize, and later that month he spent two days losing money ('perhaps fifty florins') in a game of football with a 'wretched Spaniard'.[29] He may also have continued playing the lyre and singing, since in March that year he had been urged by his friend Baccio Ugolini to continue to practise his lyre playing and singing in his absence, since he depended on him 'in versifying and in everything else'.[30] But although Parenti thought

---

Lodovico had decided to 'tornare in fede et unione con noi' during Dovizi's visit before drawing back, fearing Dovizi had been sent 'per fare questo rimpiastramento'.

[27] Becchi to Piero, 8 October 1493, MAP 18, 142, that the prince of Salerno 'afermocci ch'el male raporto di quella lettera di vostra mano [of 26 July, n. 24 in this chapter], confortante a lega generale per obviare a' oltramontani nasceva dal papa'.

[28] Alamanni in Milan to Piero, 13 March 1494, MAP 124, 434 ('Copia'): '"Credete voi che io mi possa fidare di Piero? ... Credete voi che ad Piero dispiacirà Io voglia questo stato per me et mia figliuoli?" ... replicò "Io voglio questo stato per me"', 'starli di mezzo', 'Stracciatela subito che è letta et ... non conferite questo adviso con creatura che vive', cf. MAP 124, 435, fol. 48r (covering letter to Dionigi) and p. 192–3 in this volume.

[29] Antonio Dovizi in Florence to his brother ser Piero in Milan, 29 July 1493, MAP 72, 61: 'El Padrone è in Firenze, et hieri buon pezo et hoggi ha giucato alla palla con uno sciagurato spagnuolo, el quale gli ha vinti forse cinquanta ducati'.

[30] Picotti, *Ricerche*, p. 110, n. 3 ('una lanza indorata'), Martelli, 'Libro dell Epistole', pp. 187–9; Parenti, *Storia* I, p. 55; Ugolini in Capua to Piero, 3 March 1493, *Corrispondenza* 7, pp. 258–9, at 259, that in Rome 'trovai el Corso [Jacopo Corsi, poet and musician] morto et suo Adriano [the medallist and sculptor] semi-morbato' (258 and n. 3).

Piero's 'juvenile activities' and body building betrayed indifference to politics, this was far from the truth. A day or two after the joust, he sent letters to Florence's ambassadors in Rome and Naples, evidently supporting 'an agreement [over the Cibo lands] with the pope' but not Ferrante's more extended plans for a league and marriage with him as well. But just before this agreement between the three powers was signed in early August, the Florentine ambassador Filippo Valori and his secretary, ser Antonio Guidotti da Colle, galloped out of Rome and home to Florence.[31] It was said that Filippo's cook had fallen ill with the plague, but people suspected Filippo had left in order to avoid signing the document, especially since he was known to be opposed to Florence helping Virginio to purchase the lands. Piero soon sent Guidotti back to Rome to deny the rumour: if this had been their intention – he later wrote to Dionigi – why send 'a public servant back there, who serves just as well as an ambassador?'[32] The joint agreement (over the Cibo lands as well as the papal-Neapolitan marriage contract) was then stipulated in Rome on 16 August, 'in the presence of the pope, don Federigo, the Spanish ambassador staying in your house, and ser Antonio da Colle our chancellor' (ser Francesco Baroni informed messer Puccio Pucci).[33]

The question of who was to pay for the lands, however, remained a vexed issue that reveals Piero being more public-spirited than Dionigi, his friend and factotum. As Nofri Tornabuoni explained to Piero in early August, 'the pope wanted to be certain of the money before signing', but since Florence was refusing to pay anything (despite its generous promises), Virginio would have to rely on being paid by Ferrante.[34]

---

[31] Bernardo Dovizi initially reported the good news ('BUONE', MAP 18, 123v) to Piero in Poggio that the contracts were all but signed, before countermanding it with the bad news, brought by *staffetta*, of the ambassadors' sudden departure, 3 August 1493, *Epistolario*, ed. Moncallero, I, pp. 28–30, which Sante, Virginio Orsini's man in Rome, told Piero on 6 August (MAP 18, 125r), 'è stato molestissima ... e dolemo insino al core'.

[32] Piero to Dionigi Pucci in Rome, 21 August 1493, MAP 138, 239, fol. 233v: 'un grande mormorare della partita dello imbasciadore ... uno secretario publico che in facto non serve mancho che un oratore'. Cf. Nofri to Piero, 8 August 1493 (MAP 18, 126, fol. 149r, that Ser Santi told Virginio: 'la partita sua era suta con arte et per non si trovare unitamente con lui alla finale conclusione di queste cose'). On Guidotti ('Antonio da Colle'), p. 207 and nn. 41 and 42 in this volume.

[33] Baroni in Florence to Puccio Pucci in Rome, 19 August 1493, SSX8LCMR 15, fol. 151, also Guidotti in Rome to Piero, 16 August. MAP 60, 604. The pope's youngest son, Giuffrè, was to marry Sancia, the duke of Calabria's natural daughter.

[34] Nofri in Rome to Piero, 6 August 1493, MAP 14, 367, fol. 386r: 'perché el papa voleva avanti che venissi alla stipulatione essere sicuro del denaio'; the same, 8 August, MAP 18, 126, fol. 149v, that Florence 'non haveva obligo alcuno con Virginio di servirlo più che la si volesse' (on the 6th, fol. 387r, Nofri had urged Piero to send Guidotti or someone 'per intratenere queste vostre cose publiche').

Piero evidently agreed with Valori that public money should not be used for the lands – unlike Dionigi (by now a firm partisan of Ferrante's), who urged Piero to get Florence to contribute several thousand ducats: 'I say, those of the community, under the name of the bank or some other merchant, with whatever security they can have'. Enclosing a letter that Piero could either give to the Otto di Pratica or destroy, he added ruthlessly that to satisfy both Virginio and the king, it would perhaps be 'no bad thing to make the city suffer a bit of hardship, if not damage'.[35] When he learnt two days later that Piero would rather pay several thousand ducats himself to Virginio than ask his colleagues to use public funds, Dionigi urged him 'to pay up, if you haven't already done so, and under whatever name seems best to you'.[36] On 19 August, the Otto di Pratica (with eight coopted members) agreed after lengthy discussion to help Virginio pay for the lands, and so did the Seventy, who reportedly agreed to add 10,000 ducats to Ferrante's 35,000, under the guise of paying for Virginio's military service, not for the castles. Nevertheless, it was evidently the Medici Bank that was later debited for almost the entire amount paid by Virginio to the pope for the lands.[37] Although this outcome might seem to support Guicciardini's verdict on Ferrante's (and Virginio's) influence on Piero, Guicciardini oversimplifies a complex situation in which Piero was vainly attempting to balance the conflicting interests of the three major powers as well as his own conflicting public–private interests in Florence. Although he was told that the pope had signed the agreement at Piero's prompting, since he trusted him and Florence, Dionigi more realistically told him how untrustworthy the

---

[35] Dionigi Pucci to Piero, 1 August 1493, MAP 49, 310: 'qualche migliaio di ducati, dico quelli della communità, socto nome del banco o di qualche altro mercatante ... non saria forse male la città patisse un poco di sinistro, non dico danno'.

[36] The same, 14 August 1493, MAP 49, 326, fol. 538r ('Vedete pure, Piero, ... di servire Virginio di x mila fiorini ... e li potete addirizzare al banco vostro di Roma, e' quali quando s'haranno ad pagare al Papa si paghino in nome del S. Virginio ... Et potete fare anche per via d'altro banco se non volete s'intenda che né la S<ignoria> né voi lo serviate'); 16 August, MAP 49, 327, fol. 541r: 'più presto subvenire voi Virginio in questi suoi bisogni di qualche migliaio di ducati che persuadere cotesti cittadini al farlo la communità'; cf. Guidotti to Piero, 13 and 15 August, MAP 60: 600, fol. 605r, and 602, fol. 607r.

[37] Otto Delib. 5, fol. 198r (19 August 1493); Dionigi to Piero, 30 August, MAP 49, 333, fol. 554v: 'M. Marino schrive essersi obtenuto ne' lxx^{ta} [Settanta] il prestare ad Virginio . x. mila ducati et che Virginio dice li vuole per substenare le genti d'arme et non perché servino al pagamento delle xxxv'; Guidotti to Piero, 13 August, MAP 60, 600, fol. 605 bis^r: that on the 10th ser Santi promised to repay Alfonso 35,000 ducats 'obrigando ... tutti li stati del Signor Virginio, la persona sua et de' figliuoli'. On Virginio's debt of 39,204 ducats to the Medici Bank, Shaw, *Political Role*, p. 160, n. 33, Sapori, 'Il "bilancio"', p. 194: 'Virginio Orsini. Questi sono danari et robe che noi lo servimo per ordine di Piero nostro maggiore, de' quali non si può sperare di cavarne uno zero.'

pope was. By December, Becchi concluded that the agreement that Piero thought 'had settled everything' in fact had done the opposite.[38]

While Dovizi was still away in Milan, in late July–early August 1493, a curious incident took place in Florence that revealed how complicated the political situation had become there. Pierfilippo Pandolfini with two of the other leading elders, Angelo Niccolini and Niccolò Ridolfi, took the initiative in apparently pressing for a quick agreement with the pope and Naples in view of the French threat. They accosted Dovizi's younger brother Antonio (standing in as a secretary in the Medici palace) and ordered him to follow the French ambassadors to Rome. Antonio was upset because he had no money and didn't want to go, so he at once visited Piero, his boss, to find out if this was what he wanted and if Piero would support him if he refused to go. But Piero's enigmatic reply was simply, 'you must drink this cup', perhaps meaning that Antonio, too, must suffer what Piero had suffered in accepting the elders' decision to accompany the ambassadors to Rome.[39] Since the brigata – according to Antonio – still knew nothing about the real purpose of his brother ser Piero's mission to Milan – that is, rapprochement with Lodovico[40] – it seems that three different agendas were being pursued at this time: Piero's and his secretaries' secret negotiation to renew the old Triple Alliance with Lodovico in Milan; the elders' negotiation, in Piero's name, for an alliance with the pope and Ferrante; and the Francophiles' support for the French expedition and Péron de Basque's embassy to Rome.

It was the last that was most dangerous for Piero. For during Péron's visit to Florence in late July 1493 – with Dovizi still in Milan and Piero in his villa at Poggio – Bernardo Dovizi appended to his letter of advice from Pandolfini a warning to Piero that his 'relative and neighbour' was hanging around the ambassador and had given Salerno's secretary 100 golden ducats.[41] The relative and neighbour was his cousin Lorenzo

---

[38] Guidotti in Rome to Piero, 13 August 1493, fol. 605 bis^r: 'El [the pope] dice essere venuti a questi termini per ricordi vostri et per la speranza ha nella Città et in voi'; Dionigi Pucci to Piero, 26 August, MAP 49, 332, fol. 553r: 'non conobbe mai, per i tempi passati, né amicitia né fede, né è da credere ... habbi mutata natura'; Becchi to Piero, 9 December 1493, ed. Can. p. 355: 'come dello accordo di Roma, che credesti accordasse qua ogni cosa, e discordò'.

[39] Antonio Dovizi to ser Piero in Milan, 'come padre', 29 July 1493: 'mi ferono chiamare in piaza et mi dixono che a ogni modo bisognava che io venissi drieto a cotesti imbasciadori ..."è bisogna che tu bea questo calice"' (Matth. 20: 23, Mark 10: 39).

[40] Ibid.: 'perché anchora che la brigata non sappi apuncto le cagioni della gita vostra'.

[41] Bernardo Dovizi to Piero, [21 July 1493], ed. Moncallero, I, pp 23–5, at 25, Brown, *Florence* (2011), p. 121, n. 16.

di Pierfrancesco, and 'Salerno' was Antonello Sanseverino, prince of Salerno, the Neapolitan exile who was already in France plotting the French expedition to Italy. Their friendship posed the greatest threat to Piero, as we shall see in the following chapter, since together they plotted to use the military might of France to provoke revolutions against Piero's regime in Florence and Ferrante's in Naples.

12 'The Viper with Its Tail in Florence', 1493–1494

If the news Piero had received from Ricci and Lodovico Sforza in the summer of 1493 of Charles VIII's threatened invasion of Italy was a bombshell, he received a second one, and one much closer to home, the following October when his cousins Lorenzo and Giovanni di Pierfrancesco were appointed French officials.[1] A few weeks earlier, Piero Soderini had told Gentile Becchi, his fellow ambassador in France – alluding to Lorenzo di Pierfrancesco's emblem of a coiled snake – 'this viper has its tail in Florence, and he's not going to give it to you'.[2] The brothers' appointment was the first open challenge to Piero's power and it provides the subtext of his downfall.

Piero cannot have been totally unprepared for the news that his cousins were plotting against him in conjunction with France. Blame fell on him for not taking effective action against his cousins before it was too late, but despite persistent rumours of trouble between them, it is unclear how much he knew about the details and extent of their conspiracy. There had been inklings of trouble soon after Lorenzo's death. Piero had been told by Cosimo Sassetti in mid-April 1492 of Lorenzo di Pierfrancesco's friendship with Antonello Sanseverino, the exiled prince of Salerno, then in France plotting against Ferrante (and similarly by Bernardo Dovizi over a year later).[3] In August 1492 there were reports of quarrels between the cousins and of Piero's brother, Cardinal Giovanni, meeting Lorenzo di Pierfrancesco in Rome. The following year the rumours of a 'forthcoming revolution' in Florence were more specific. In mid-March

---

[1] n. 17 in this chapter. Although often called 'Lorenzino' to distinguish him from il Magnifico, Piero's father, he will be referred to as Lorenzo di Pierfrancesco in what follows.

[2] Becchi in Tours to Piero, 28 September 1493, ed. Can, p 329: 'questa serpe abbi la coda costì in Firenze, e che non sia per dare a voi', discussed by Nelson, 'Filippino Lippi's *Allegory*', esp. pp. 244–5 and fig. 8.

[3] Cosimo Sassetti in Paris to Piero, 15 April 1492, MAP 14, 270, fol. 277v; Brown, *Florence* (2011), pp 119–20, n. 12, also p. 178 in this volume; on Sassetti, a partner in the Medici Bank in Lyon, de Roover, *Banco Medici,* pp. 447–9.

1493 Piero was warned by Baccio Ugolini in Naples about a six-page letter being sent to messer Marino in Florence by the secretary of Giuliano della Rovere ('Vincula'): he was to be careful about mentioning it to the Otto di Pratica, Ugolini wrote, because it involved the bishop of Volterra (Francesco Soderini), which might upset someone, 'so open your eyes wide!'[4] A month later Baccio sent Piero an extract from the secretary's letter, warning him again to be alert 'and not make a joke about the things that can happen' since the pope was waiting for 'this revolution' in Florence, which the Pazzi had already been told about. This was followed by a coded letter from France from one of the two Florentine ambassadors there, Piero Capponi, that Cardinal San Malo had asked him 'who would be willing to change the regime' in Florence[5] Despite these warnings, Piero apparently remained unperturbed, although he did send Francesco della Casa to France as his private envoy in May, followed in the summer by the public embassy of Gentile Becchi and Piero Soderini.[6] It was not until the following year, in April 1494, that the full extent and danger of his cousins' involvement was revealed by the confession of one of the conspirators, Zanobi Acciaiuoli.

Zanobi Acciaiuoli's Confession

Zanobi lived in Lorenzo's and Giovanni di Pierfrancesco's household as their secretary before eventually becoming librarian of the Vatican Library in 1518.[7] His father Raffaello and grandfather Angelo Acciaiuoli (brother of Laudomia, Lorenzo and Giovanni's mother) had both been exiled in 1466, so the Acciaiuoli shared the cousins' resentment towards the elder Medici branch, especially now that they were senior in age but not in rank to Piero and his brothers.[8] This is shown by Zanobi's long and literate confession, which describes the ambitions of the younger

---

[4] Ugolini in Palma Campania to the Otto di Pratica, 15 March 1493, *Corrispondenza* 7, pp. 261–2, and to Piero, same day, pp. 263–4, at 263. Pagolantonio, Francesco's brother, was then a member of the Otto (Otto, Delib. 4, fol. 12r). 'Vincula' was pro-French and later joined the conspirators in France, Shaw, *Julius II*, p. 93, Mallett, *Borgias*, p. 121.
[5] Ugolini in Aversa to Piero, 18 April 1493, *Corrispondenza*, 7, p. 269, and Allegato A (pp. 269–70, the secretary's letter): 'questa mutazione de stato in Fiorenza'; Piero Capponi to Piero, MAP 35, 47, deciphered from letter dated 29 April, Brown, *Florence* (2011), p. 120, n. 14: 'chi fussi contento mutare lo stato'.
[6] On della Casa's mission, Can, I, p. 221 (on his 'anticha servitù et ardente affectione' towards Piero, MAP 15, 103, 17 April 1492). On the official embassy, Dovizi to Puccio Pucci 15 June 1493, ibid., pp. 321–5.
[7] Parenti, *Storia*, 1, p. 68; on Zanobi, *DBI*, 1, 1960 (A. Redigonda).
[8] Lorenzo (b. 4 August 1463) was nine years older than Piero, and Giovanni (b. 21 October 1467) was five years older.

182   Piero in Power

branch as a mirror image of the elder branch's achievements. According to Zanobi, they planned to achieve:

> two things, one a relationship with the pope by marrying a daughter of his Holiness to Lorenzo's son Pierfrancesco, and with this a cardinalate for Giovanni [di Pierfrancesco], the other renting from the chapter of St. Peter's certain gardens and houses in Rome with the idea of having somewhere to stay for part of the year and do business, especially at the time of the Jubilee.[9]

Angered by the verdict in a lawsuit that went against Raffaello in June 1492, Lorenzo di Pierfrancesco left for Rome on the death of Innocent VIII on 25 July and quickly 'struck up a bit of a friendship' with the new Borgia pope, evidently to further his ambitions.[10] He must also have been profiting from the coded message – sent from Rome by fra Lauro de' Bossi – that Piero was unhappy with the new pope and would rely on Ferrante; nor was he liked by the college for being too pompous.[11]

Without following all its twists and turns, Zanobi's narrative reveals how closely the conspirators' ambitions mirrored those of Lorenzo for his children: marriage to the pope's offspring, a cardinalate and the acquisition of property in Rome, where he could rival the status of the elder Medici. Their movements, too, shadowed Piero's without ever colliding with them. At the time when Piero and Puccio Pucci were in close contact with Caterina Sforza, for instance, she was apparently considering employing the cousins to fight for her, using fra Lauro to contact them in Florence (alerted by two of Caterina's horsemen, who were accompanying the friar from Forlì to Rome, Giovanni di Pierfrancesco leapt on his horse, with Zanobi riding pillion, to meet fra Lauro outside Florence).[12] Fra Lauro was also wooing Lodovico Sforza on Lorenzo di Pierfrancesco's behalf, through whom Lodovico would have known of the conspiracy at the time when he was also being assiduously courted by Piero.[13] Meanwhile, in Rome, the pope simultaneously received letters

---

[9] *Confession*, CS, Appendice 3, inserto 5, fols. 185r–v: 'Et qui cominciorono alcune pratiche di due cose', etc.

[10] Ibid., fol. 185r. On the lawsuit with Angelo Niccolini, one of the stalwarts of the regime, and Raffaello's failed appeal, ASF, Atti del Podestà 5421, fols. 461r–465v, 1 June 1492; cf. Florence, Niccolini Archives, 14, ins. 22.

[11] *Confession*, fols. 185r–190v: 'ambiguo dello animo del nuovo Pontefice', 'superchia pompa et fasto' (185v). Fra Lauro de' Bossi, an Augustinian friar, became the conspirators' principal messenger and go-between, cf. n. 13 in this chapter.

[12] Ibid., fols. 185v–186r. Caterina would marry Giovanni di Pierfrancesco as her third husband in September 1497.

[13] Ibid., fols. 185r (on fra Lauro's mission to Milan in April 1492 on behalf of Raffaello's wife, evidently to win Lodovico's and Galeazzo Sanseverino's support for Lorenzo di Pierfrancesco). Zanobi was distrustful of fra Lauro, especially his later story of Ferrante and Piero plotting to 'poison or murder' Lodovico (186v).

from Piero and Lorenzo di Pierfrancesco promoting their rival candidates for a Florentine cardinalate, Gentile Becchi and Francesco Soderini.[14] Soderini had been coopted in place of Giovanni di Pierfrancesco, whose secular status was now thought to be a drawback, and in a document that Giovanni and Cosimo Rucellai drew up in late November in Cosimo's 'ground floor room' in the Rucellai palace, it was stated that the whole Soderini family shared a 'common cause' with Lorenzo di Pierfrancesco and, as a cardinal, Francesco would always vote with Ascanio Sforza (despite the *condottiere* Jacopo Conti's later opinion that, once elected, Francesco would be reconciled with Piero).[15] Lorenzo himself wrote out the letter recommending Soderini to the pope, after destroying Cosimo Rucellai's first draft because of its style, and by the end of the year, even Cardinal Giovanni de' Medici supported Soderini's cardinalate in opposition to his brother Piero's wishes.[16]

What gave the conspiracy momentum was Lorenzo's and Giovanni di Pierfrancesco's appointment as French barons in early October. Although Piero's emissary in France, Francesco della Casa, claimed 'they are only letters and seals' that would bring no profit to Lorenzo and his brother (Giovanni being similarly honoured by the king), it was perhaps more worrying that the Pazzi had also been considered for this honour.[17] The immediate outcome of the news was the despatching of fra Lauro to France to thank the king on their behalf, which enabled him to whip up support for the cousins and their conspiracy in Ferrara, Parma and Milan en route. He left Florence around 11 December, meeting Jacopo Acciaiuoli in Ferrara (Raffaello's brother, also exiled in 1466 and resident in the Este court, who was seemingly unwilling to participate), Cosimo Rucellai in Parma and Lodovico Sforza and Galeazzo Sanseverino in Milan, finally arriving in the French court in Tours on 5 or 6 January 1494. There the conspirators intended to persuade the king to engage both Jacopo Conti and Jacopo d'Appiano as his soldiers,

---

[14] Piero, *Ricordi di lettere* (2), p. 106; Zanobi, Confession, fol. 186v: 'erano in comune fortuna con Lorenzo'.

[15] Ibid., fols. 186r: 'pareva cosa dificile essendo egli secolare' and 188v. On Conti, n. 18 in this chapter.

[16] *Confession*, fol. 186v: 'Ma non piacendo lo stile a Lorenzo'. On Giovanni's support for Soderini, Picotti, *Giovinezza*, pp. 510, 545, n. 131; Soderini to Piero, 22 December 1493, MAP 18, 206, to Cardinal Giovanni, MAP 49, 403; cf. Guidotti to Dovizi, 20 November, MAP 55, 98, fol. 146r–v, to Piero, 7 January 1494, MAP 55, 121, fol. 195r.

[17] Della Casa in Tours to Piero, 19 October 1493, MAP 14, 382v: 'ch'el *principe di Salerno et Perone* pochi dì sono hanno facto *expedire lettere* per le quali *il Re di Francia fa suo cianberlano Lorenzo di Pierfrancesco* il quale ha promesso *el principe di Salerno* di cinque mila ducati' (decoded); repeated on 21 October but referring now to '500 mila' ducats (MAP 18, 151, fol. 177r–v, Brown, *Florence* (2011), pp. 121, n. 16, 124, n. 28).

Conti to serve as a link with Rome and d'Appiano with Siena, 'through the proximity of his state [Piombino] and the port of Elba'.[18] On reaching the court, fra Lauro was questioned closely by the king and Beaucaire about Piero and his cousin Lorenzo di Pierfrancesco: who was more powerful in terms of partisans and friends, and who was richer?

> Lorenzo [fra Lauro replied] was more loved, but the magnificent Piero was richer through enjoying political power, which also gave him a greater following, for all that Lorenzo had nearly 30 thousand francs from trade and from his landed income, as well as cash in hand.[19]

At the mention of money and Lorenzo di Pierfrancesco's loans to Lorenzo il Magnifico, Beaucaire suggested to the king that the younger Lorenzo could also help to pay the king's debts with that sum of money. And to the question of how Lorenzo would make himself great, the friar responded:

> There are different ways of raising men up, according to the different conditions prevailing in different places. In Genoa you need arms but in Florence the reputation and warm support of lords from outside is sufficient. If your Majesty provided this for Lorenzo, he would easily become great.[20]

Fra Laura also ingratiated himself with the Florentine ambassadors at the court (Piero Soderini and Becchi), to the dismay of Sanseverino, the exiled prince of Salerno; for when the friar told them about the offices granted to Lorenzo and Giovanni di Pierfrancesco by the king, Piero Soderini responded that it would be a great sign if they had been granted, but Lorenzo must look for them by proper means, and when told they had been granted, both Soderini and Gentile Becchi objected and asked whether other Florentines had received similar honours. Fra Lauro returned to Florence on 5 March, where he was debriefed by Zanobi Accaiuoli in the cousins' villa at Cafaggiolo, 'partly by the fireside, partly while suppering together'.[21]

The French were evidently taken aback by the ambassadors' hostile reaction to the honours and by 'other difficult things', and as a result they

---

[18] *Confession*, fol. 189v: 'servendo l'uno alle cose di Siena per la vicinia dello stato et porto della Helba, l'altro alle cose di Roma'. On Conti, a Lazio baron and leading *condottiere*, employed by Florence and then France, Lorenzo, *Lettere* 15, esp. pp. 11–12 (nn. 21, 22), 120; Puccio Pucci in Rome to Piero, 18 July 1494, MAP 139, fol. 26r.

[19] *Confession*, fol. 187v.   [20] Ibid., fols. 187v–188r.

[21] Ibid., fol. 187v ('parte a fuocho, parte cenando'). Cf. Alamanni in Vigevano to Piero, 30 April 1494, MAP 50, 289, fol. 302v, naming as Lodovico's informers 'Marullo, fra Manuele, Paulo et degli altri', as well as 'frate Lauro'. Cf. Cosimo Sassetti to Dovizi, 28 April, MAP 73, 30r: 'uno Merullo, homo del principe di Salerno' was in Lyon, who was formerly 'in casa Lorenzo di Pierfrancesco'.

warned Lorenzo and Giovanni di Pierfrancesco to be careful and to delay Giovanni's departure for France, 'in order not to lose the magnificent Piero'.[22] In mid-December, when told by Salerno that Piero was 'doing everything to break the expedition', the king evidently excused Piero's 'temporising and neutrality', though saying that he would soon have to make up his mind. This suggests that the die was not yet cast and that, despite appearances, the French were still hoping for Piero's support.[23]

By the beginning of February, however, the French expedition was becoming a reality. The three Florentines in France – the ambassadors Soderini and Becchi and Piero's envoy della Casa – were ordered to guarantee that Florence would help the king to recover the kingdom of Naples and provide three hundred lances, one hundred foot soldiers and six galleys in return for his protection when he arrived in Italy.[24] A month later, news reached Rome that Giovanni di Pierfrancesco and Cosimo Rucellai had fled Florence, 'with many young men from leading families', and had gone to France to establish themselves with the king, due to their discontent with Piero; reporting this, the secretary-envoy Guidotti intensified fears of a repetition of the 1478 conspiracy by adding that a Florentine had just been decapitated in France for opening Guglielmo Pazzi's letter urging the king's expedition.[25] At the same time, the king issued an ultimatum in Lyon, giving Florence five days to confirm in writing the Signoria's oath of loyalty to the French king on taking office. Unless it did so, Becchi told Piero, the city would be considered Aragonese and Piero could send all the lilies in his house to Lorenzo di Pierfrancesco's home. Becchi appealed to Piero for protection, not – he said revealingly – 'to honour your words or your status, which you show you're so keen about', but to save his and Soderini's lives. Four days later he informed Piero that revolution and a change of regime were imminent.[26]

---

[22] Foreign honours needed to be approved by the councils in Florence, hence Soderini saying 'sarebbono grande segno quanti fussino ordinati ma che bisogna che Lorenzo cerchi queste bo' vie', etc., *Confession*, fol. 187r.

[23] Della Casa in the French court to Becchi in Tours, 11 December 1493, MAP 60, 668r ('fa ogni cosa per rompere questa impresa') and to Piero on the 19th (MAP 18, 201v): the king 'sapea bene bisogniava temporeggiassi et vi mantenesse neutrali, ma che presto verrebbe tempo che sicuramente vi harete a scoprire, etc.'; Brown, 'Piero in Power', p. 120, n. 43.

[24] Becchi, Capponi and della Casa to Piero, 2 February 1494, ed. Can I, pp. 362–3.

[25] Guidotti in Rome to Piero, 3 March 1494, MAP 55, 155, fol. 255v: 'con molti giovani de' principali di Firenze'.

[26] Becchi to Piero, 8 and 12 March 1494 (MAP 75: 139 and 144r: 'Le minacci sono hor sul mutare dello stato', Martelli, 'Il *Libro*', pp. 201–2, 195–6. Cf. the same (n.d., MAP 18, 371): 'Il dì di Pasqua [30 March] habbiamo da uno che sa le cose che s'atende al mutare costì lo stato', Martelli, pp. 194–5.

The Unmasking of the Conspiracy

Although regime change had been threatened since March and early April 1494, nothing happened until the arrival in Florence of the two French envoys, returning from Rome on 20 April – dangerously close to the date of the earlier conspiracy on 26 April 1478. It was then that the parallel developments in France and in Florence converged. The French envoys had already left Florence (without meeting Piero) en route to France; they were accompanied to the border by Lorenzo and Giovanni di Pierfrancesco, with whom they had been staying in the Mugello instead of in the inn provided for them by the government. The brothers returned home to find themselves summonsed before the Signoria – where, to general amazement, they explained that because they were the king's paid retainers (each receiving 2000 scudi a year from him), they had to honour his envoys. After refusing them permission to go to the king in France, the government decided to discuss the situation not in an open meeting of citizens but secretly within the Seventy, who on 25 April ordered the brothers to be sequestered in the government palace, together with their secretary Zanobi Acciaiuoli and a few of their servants.[27] The following day, Piero urgently summoned his close supporters Niccolini and Pandolfini back from Naples, on account of 'quelli di Pierfrancesco'.[28]

The details of what happened next are opaque, since the Seventy's records were secret, the Otto di Guardia's records silent about the whole event and the chroniclers discordant. Like earlier threats to the regime, it was apparently dealt with by three non-judicial, political insiders – according to Parenti, by Bernardo del Nero, Piero Guicciardini and Antonio Dini, 'as well as the Otto [di Guardia]'. Parenti then describes how the brothers were first held in one of the prior's rooms and then in the captain of the infantry's room (their food provided by their servants, 'for fear of poison'), but when they were separated on 26 April, that 'unhappy day, sixteen years' earlier', Lorenzo di Pierfrancesco feared that the chancellor of the Otto was going to kill him when he appeared six hours after sunset. Despite refusing to make a general confession to the Gonfalonier of Justice (but 'only' – he reportedly said – 'before Him who

---

[27] Parenti, *Storia* I, pp. 67–70, at 68 (the French envoys were the bishop of Lodena, St. Malo's son, and abbot Benoit de St. Moris, Delaborde, *L'expédition*, p. 365; on the dates, Tribaldo de' Rossi, *Ricordanze*, pp. 291–3, Martelli, p. 190; Brown, *Florence* (2011), pp. 122, 124.

[28] Piero to Niccolini and Pandolfini, 26 April 1494, Niccolini Archives, 315, ins. 54, 'Cito, cito', 'con più prestezza potete'. He reports his cousins' request to the Signoria, their detention in the Palace on the 25th, and also that 'la Città è quieta et sanza movimento'.

should judge all'), he did confess, without torture, most of what had happened. This was well-enough founded to give Piero and others in the government food for thought, since it involved all the people we know about from Zanobi's confession – that is, Cosimo Rucellai and Francesco Soderini, as well as Giannozzo, grandson of messer Giannozzo Manetti, Piero di Jacopo Ridolfi and three servants, and from outside, Charles VIII and Lodovico Sforza, as well as the marquis of Mantua and (according to Parenti, though not Zanobi) Jacopo Acciaiuoli. Lodovico apparently asked Alamanni if Piero intended to 'chop off Lorenzo and Giovanni's heads', but the government decided to limit the damage by forgiving what had happened and reuniting the families through marriages, in order to break their links with outside contacts.[29]

Parenti's detailed narrative credibly reconciles Piero's initial anger and desire for retribution with his later clemency towards his cousins, which according to Nardi was due to the advice he received from Francesco Taddei and Francesco Gherardi.[30] Unmentioned by Parenti or Nardi is an incident described by Cerretani that suggests that either Piero or the regime's tough men knew about the conspiracy from at least December 1493 and planned to forestall it by persuading three successive Gonfaloniers of Justice to behead the cousins and three others; the Gonfaloniers refused to act without authorisation from Piero and the leading citizens, who eventually decided to call a *pratica* and summonsed the cousins before the Signoria.[31] There is support for Cerretani's account in a letter to Dovizi in March from 'your Tommaso in the palace' – evidently Tommaso Minerbetti, then Gonfalonier of Justice (following Piero Capponi and Filippo Taddei), who told Dovizi he wasn't ready to move where there was any danger to their common patron, but he would try to carry out what he was told to do by the government, despite finding it a very tough and dangerous assignment: 'and since it matters so much to the Magnificent's honour, I can't rest until I speak to you to tell you more about it'.[32] According to Zanobi's confession, the conspirators believed

---

[29] Parenti, *Storia* I, pp. 70–1; Alamanni to Piero, 30 April 1494, MAP 50, 289, fol. 320v: 'Ricercòmmi poi se io credevo che voi tagliassi [*sic*] la testa a' prefati Lorenzo et Giovanni o che deliberatione ne piglieresti'; the same, 5 May, MAP 50, 291, fols. 304, bis-sex, relating Jacopo Acciaiuoli's account of events at 304v–bis^r.

[30] p. 159, n. 38 in this volume. On these divergent accounts, Brown, *Florence* (2011), pp. 122–4; Martelli, citing Poliziano's propagandistic account, 'Il *Libro*', pp. 190–3.

[31] Cerretani, *Storia fiorentina*, pp. 190–1: 'in modo che Piero tenttò, ma non a bochcha ma per mezzo di chancellieri, tre ghonfalonieri a la fila di fare tagliare la testa a cimque di loro et de' primi de la ciptà' (191).

[32] 'Tommaso in Palagio' to Dovizi, n.d. MAP 124, 213r: 'io ci vegho manifestissimo pericolo et importando tanto allo honore del Magnifico, non mi posso quietare infino che io non vi parlo ... Vostro Tommaso'. Minerbetti was Gonfalonier of Justice in

that Paolo Orsini's troops had been lodged at the city's gates at the end of December not for Piero's forthcoming joust but 'to put his hands on us', so it is possible that Piero or his partisans did consider forestalling the conspiracy in this way, though through the government, and that it was Minerbetti and the two friends named by Nardi who deterred him from 'laying his hands on his own blood'.[33]

What happened instead was that the Seventy – after meeting, without Piero, until late on the 28th – decided to condemn Lorenzo and Giovanni to life imprisonment with confiscation of goods, informing the brothers of their verdict before leaving the palace; then Piero arrived and for about an hour he and the cousins vented their feelings as they talked together. Whereas Piero showed himself ready to pardon them if they agreed to reunite through marriage agreements, the cousins insisted on their position as King Charles's men and tried to persuade Piero to desert Alfonso and support the French king as Florence's benefactor – a response that Piero found hostile. As a result, when people came the following morning to congratulate Piero at home and in the piazza on the expected reconciliation, the cousins' liberation failed to take place; instead, they (but not their children) were confined for life to their villas – that is, to a mile's distance from Florence but within its territory. On the same day, the 29th, Cosimo Rucellai was cited to appear before the Signoria within a month, before being condemned to life exile in Prato and its territory on 30 June, a soft punishment for his crimes and disobedience, the Signoria said, 'treating him not as he deserved but with humanity'.[34]

According to Alfonso, the Signoria and 'those wise leading citizens of the state' wanted to keep them imprisoned for some time – as he and Virginio Orsini also wanted – but Piero, influenced by some of his friends, decided to let them go free.[35] He came to the palace to escort his cousins as far as his home – Lorenzo, the eldest of the three, in the middle, Giovanni to the right and Piero himself, as the youngest, to the

---

March–April 1494, the others in November–December 1493 and January–February 1494, Cambi, *Istorie*, pp. 76–7.

[33] Zanobi, *Confession*, fol. 188v: 'dubitavano non fussi chiamato socto nome di giostra a mectere loro le mani adosso'.

[34] Parenti, *Storia* I, pp. 71–2; Signori Delib. ord. aut. 96, 29 April 1494, fols. 25r ('extra civitatem florentinam et utrum unum miliare circum … prope dictam civitatem' but within Florentine territory) and 25v, 47v–49v (30 June) on Cosimo Rucellai, exiling him for life 'in terra Prati',volentes procedere non secundum … merita sed cum humanitate'.

[35] Dionigi Pucci in Naples to Piero, recd. 10 May 1494, MAP 138, 296, fol. 291r: that to Ferrante and Virginio Orsini, 'parea molto più aproposito la deliberatione facta per quella Excelsa Signoria et di quelli primi et savi cittadini dello stato che non è suta la vostra'.

left, followed by a large crowd of people supporting the cousins. In the fifteen days before they had to leave for exile in their villas, they assiduously courted Piero at home to please him, despite behaving with their friends as if nothing had happened, and on the 14th they duly left for Castello and Cafaggiolo, where they lived happily, surrounded by friends and riding hither and thither while awaiting help and support from the king – whom they eventually joined in Vigevano outside Milan in October that year, breaking the terms of their confinement.[36] This is the moment when the two disasters threatening Piero converged and revolution in Florence became increasingly certain.

---

[36] Parenti, *Storia* I, pp. 72–3, 75, 104–5; Signori Delib. 96, fol. 25r (their arrival on 15 May at their places of exile); Tribaldo de' Rossi, *Ricordanze*, pp. 294–5 (a marginal addition on events in October, see pp. 214–5, nn. 2 and 4 in this volume).

13 The Crux, 1494

Piero's behaviour in the months before the denouement of the cousins' conspiracy in late April showed the two contrasting sides of his nature: lazy and hyperactively scheming. Both were pinpointed by Becchi's idiosyncratic turn of phrase when he criticised him – on one hand – for letting ser Piero Dovizi govern Italy as his boss while he rested on his oars, 'allowing some wind to blow the boat where the oars can't arrive, it wears you out to use your arms', and on the other for restlessly moving in a rocking gondola: 'keep still, for God's sake, for you can't see everything and you shouldn't help the side opposite to yours'.[1] Outwardly, at least, Piero seemed unworried either by his cousins or by the French expedition. He stood high in the pope's esteem as the broker of a possible marriage for little Laura (the pope's daughter) and, indeed, as Florence's St. Peter, 'the rock on which our city is now rising up'.[2] He was also as 'ambiguous' as the pope, 'temporising in order to see whom to please'. After receiving despatches from France, Milan, Rome and Naples in November 1493, with news of 'Ferrante's trepidation, the pope's instability and the general state of affairs in Milan', Piero told Dovizi he had little to reply except that he was waiting to hear more before writing to Becchi in France, so that, 'well informed, [Becchi] can ... temporise or do as he thinks fit'.[3] In the meantime, he was busy organising the joust

---

[1] Becchi to Piero, 23–26 January 1494, MAP 75, 130, fol. 197r ('perché riposiate ser P<ier>o dalla tutela d'Italia et stiate sotto ... volli dire qualche vento conduca la barca dove non possono e' remi, che chotesto vostro menare di braccia affatica voi et chiarisce altri'); 197v: 'Siate in su una ghondola che continuamente ondegia et pur vi movete. State fermo per l'amor di Dio, che il tutto vedere non potete, et la parte altro che la vostra non dovete per anchora aiutare').

[2] Becchi's draft oration to Charles VIII, in which he referred to 'Magnificus ipse Petrus, in cuius petra nunc urbs nostra consurgit', ed. Can, 1, p. 337; cf. p. 130 in this volume.

[3] Zanobi, *Confession*, fol. 189v, describing the pope as 'ambiguo, temporeggiava per vedere chi havessi a compiacere'; Piero in Pisa to Dovizi, 24 November 1493, MAP 72, 68, fol. 73r: 'della trepidantia del Re Ferrante, instabilità del papa et generalità di Milano', 'temporeggiare o lasciarsi andare come gli parrà di bisogno'. Cf. Grimaldi, 'Bernardo Dovizi', p. 229, describing Piero as 'gingillandosi in mezze misure ... per la smania di tenersi sempre aperta una scappatoia'.

that he and his friends had long been practising for – probably on the large tract of public land along the walls he had enclosed in November as a jousting yard. In Piazza S. Croce the stockades had been built and the seating was being constructed.[4] Then, at the end of January, everything came to an abrupt halt, not because of the cousins or news from France, but because of the death of Ferrante of Naples on 25 January 1494.

Realignment on Ferrante's Death

Piero responded to Ferrante's death by immediately cancelling his joust as a mark of respect. He then sent his intimate friend and secretary Bernardo Dovizi to Alfonso, Ferrante's son and heir, together with two leading members of the regime as ambassadors, Pierfilippo Pandolfini and Angelo Niccolini – a signal in itself of a new start in the regime's relationship with the young king, who was 'less used to dissimulating and more powerful' than his unpopular father.[5] There was the usual exchange of princely gifts – horses for Piero, and for Alfonso the loan of Piero's trophy athlete Garzerano. But the seriousness of the embassy emerged only in late March when news trickled out of a new 'agreement, alliance and pact' agreed in Rome on 28 March between the pope and King Alfonso, with Florence as a secret third participant.[6] Confirmed by the meeting (or 'Diet') between Alexander VI and Alfonso at the Orsini castle of Vicovaro near Rome in July 1494, the pact established the framework for the allies' campaign against France and Milan in the months until Piero's expulsion from Florence in November.

Although the pact seemed to do no more than confirm the alliance of powers that had settled the Cibo affair the previous August, in fact – unbeknown to King Alfonso or Florence's ambassadors in Naples – Piero and his Dovizi secretaries had agreed to one of two secret clauses in the treaty, promising that Florence would contribute 15,000 florins to

---

[4] Rossi, *Ricordanze*, pp. 286–7: 'la giostra che Piero facieva e facieva fare, cioé Piero de' Medici', which had been announced for 6 February, about a week before news of Ferrante's death reached Florence on 27 January; cf. Parenti, *Storia* I, p. 63.
[5] Becchi to Piero, 29 January 1494, MAP 18, 368v: 'chostui è giovene, meno uso a dissimulare, più potente'; Zanobi, Confession, fol. 189r: 'Giovanni interpretava el mandare sì grandi huomini a Napoli era per assodarsi col Re nuovo in una perfecta amicitia'. Cf. Parenti, *Storia* I, p. 63, and Grimaldi, 'Bernardo Dovizi' (he arrived in Naples on 9 February, p. 219).
[6] The 'intelligentia, confederatio et pactum' was signed in Rome on 28 March 1494, MAP 138, 287, fol. 282r–v and bis, Parenti, *Storia*, 1, p. 66. Excluded from the pact, Lodovico criticised Italy's frivolity in the face of crisis, Alamanni in Vigevano to Piero, 19 March; Brown, *Florence* (2011), p. 115.

the *condotta* of Juan, duke of Gandia, the pope's second surviving son (the other clause promised that Virginio and the third son, Giuffrè, would enforce della Rovere's obedience to the pope).[7] It is another illustration of Piero's double-level politics, for he had ordered Bernardo Dovizi to leave Naples on a private mission to the pope, in order to counter the 'diabolic suggestions' that he lacked respect for Alexander – but without divulging the involvement of ser Piero Dovizi, Bernardo's brother, 'in the 15,000 ducats'.[8] Despite the fact that the signatories wanted the pact, and especially the extra clauses, to be secret, by the end of March all were being 'talked about everywhere in Rome by everyone'.[9] Since Virginio Orsini had signed the treaty on behalf of both Alfonso and Piero, the Milanese at once accused Alfonso 'of doing what the Orsini want, and the Orsini of doing what they want with Piero', and although the Florentine ambassadors in Milan en route for France quickly denied this, saying Piero wanted to pull the Orsini, not vice versa, the accusation was repeated in June by one of Piero's own intimates, messer Puccio Pucci.[10]

Despite Milan's displeasure at being excluded from an alliance between the other powers, it was now that Piero was entrusted by Alamanni with Lodovico's secret wish to become duke of Milan, encouraged too by Ascanio Sforza, who urged Piero to follow his father's example and reestablish 'a secret understanding' with Lodovico.[11] As we know, Lodovico was already committed to supporting the French expedition to Italy and he was also giving encouragement to Piero's cousins, so by temporising with all the players in the game, Piero was suddenly confronted with a stark choice: to support Lodovico – and Charles VIII? – or adhere to the new alliance with the pope and

---

[7] Niccolini, Pierfil. Pandolfini and Dionigi Pucci in Nola to Piero, 6 April 1494, MAP 138, 301, fol. 296 and bis at 296r (the king 'si maravigliava che Virginio fussi transcorso in tale obligatione sanza sua saputa et contro a la voluntà sua et nostra'); Dionigi to Piero, s. d, MAP 138, 290r: 'quello atiene a noi' was 'molto disforme dal pensiero vostro per quello mi scriveste'.

[8] Piero de' Medici, instruction to Bernardo Dovizi (who arrived in Rome from Naples on the 20th), n.d., MAP 72, 128: 'a me basta satisfare a Quella [Sua Santità] ... et in effetto obedirla et chiarire quelli che mettono tali suggestioni diaboliche'.

[9] Guidotti in Rome to Piero, 29 March 1494, MAP 19, 535, fol. 593r: 'la stipulazione del accordo il papa vuole sia secreta et per Roma se ne parla per tutto'. On Bernardo's urging, Virginio had agreed to 'ingannarne il papa per salvare voi' (ser Piero), 'et che di voi non si faria alcuna mentione ne' xv mila ducati', Bernardo to his brother, 21 March 1494, postscript, MAP 72, 108 bis^r, ed. Moncallero, I, pp. 78–9; cf. p. 63 (to Piero, 8 March) and Grimaldi, 'Bernardo Dovizi', pp. 234–6.

[10] Vespucci and Capponi in Vigevano to Piero, 12 April 1494, ed. Can. 375: 'el Re fa quello che vuole degli Orsini, e li Orsini dispongono di Piero quello che vogliono', 'voi [Piero] voevate tirare gli Orsini, e non che gli Orsini tirassino voi'.

[11] p. 175, n. 28 in this volume; Pellegrini, *Congiure di Romagna*, p. 169, n. 42.

Alfonso.[12] Whereas Bernardo Dovizi understood this, Alfonso thought the new alliance would help to achieve a reconciliation with Lodovico and was amazed when Bernardo told him that 'it would have completely the contrary effect'.[13]

Piero's Crisis

It is at this moment that Becchi's letters to Piero from France provide a sense of the desperation of Piero's position. The idiosyncratic 'scrappy notes' (*cartuggie*) of his father's old tutor are a counterpart to Zanobi Acciaiuoli's confession in documenting the other side of the story in these months. They were written, he said, 'in bursts', as confidential memoranda, not to be shown to anyone else, excusing them as an old man's unwillingness to trust others that also enabled him to evade the protocol of official letters. Piero's great-grandfather, grandfather and father (Cosimo, Piero and Lorenzo) had all liked them, he told Piero, but if Piero didn't, he would 'abbreviate' them.[14] Many are undated and difficult to decipher, but this allowed him not only to criticise Piero in the way we have seen, but also to write freely about others. He praised his colleague Piero Soderini for giving his loyalty and affection to Piero and not to Lodovico Sforza (*non Ludovicheggia*) – unlike his brother Francesco, bishop of Volterra, or Piero's cousins – and Charles VIII he characterised pithily in four words, skilled in 'hunts, dogs, birds, horses', interested in the kingdom of Naples only as a hunting ground.[15] Soon after his arrival at the French court, Becchi had told Piero that Lodovico was honoured there only because he sent the king gold, not birds (alluding to the falcons Piero had sent Charles in July), and later that Piero was criticised in France for 'not living like Lorenzo' (his father) and for writing an autograph letter urging a general league to obstruct the ultramontanes.[16] In December Becchi warned Piero not to be deceived,

---

[12] Mallett, 'Personalities', pp. 158–60.
[13] Bernardo to Piero, 13 March 1494, ed. Moncallero, I, pp. 69–70: 'maraviglarsi di questa risposta mia perché aspectava il contrario di quello havevo decto'.
[14] Becchi to Piero, 28 September 1493, ed. Can, I, p. 330: 'Scrivovi queste a balzelloni perché non mostriate ad altri che a voi proprio'); 4 October, pp. 337–8 (on his 'raguagli in cartucce' that 'serve anche al non essere poi littere mostrabili'); 16 October, p. 338 (*'uno piccolo cenno me abbrevierà'*, decoded). On Becchi's 'giocosità idiomatica, l'allusività ironica dello stile personalissimo', Simonetta, *Rinascimento secreto*, pp. 176–81 (177), Simonetta, ed., *La congiura della verità*, pp. 17–24, 39–48.
[15] Becchi to Piero, undated fragments, ed. Can, p. 340: '*Caccie, cani, uccelli, cavalli … il Re voleva venire in persona per iscacciare e che per altro non voleva il Reame*' (decoded); also 28 September and 3 November, pp. 330 and 342.
[16] Becchi in Tours to Piero, 29 September 1493, ed. Can, p. 331: 'non vivete come Lorenzo'; the same, 8 October, MAP 18, 142, p. 175, n. 27 in this volume.

as he had been about 'the Rome agreement', which Piero thought would 'settle everything' instead of 'unsettling' things (here evidently referring to the agreement of mid-August with the pope and Ferrante over the Cibo castles).[17] And at the end of January 1494 (before he would have heard of Ferrante's death five days earlier), he warned Piero not to make himself 'the tutor of Italy': 'You can't do everything. Think of your role ... for God's sake, tread carefully.'[18] Becchi seems to be anticipating Piero's subsequent alliance with Naples and Rome, which as a Francophile (his love of France imbibed, he said, from his many years living in the Medici palace), he would not have welcomed.[19] So when Becchi and Soderini failed to respond to King Charles's demand for support and guarantees in February and March, things rapidly spiralled out of control.[20] Piero was already alarmed by 'playing a game' in which there were 'so many uncertainties on the gaming board'; by early April it was clear that his tactics had brought him to the brink of a nervous crisis.[21]

On 4 April 1494, a week after the papal pact was signed in Rome, Piero sent Dovizi three letters (the first and last autograph) from different places in the countryside around Pisa where he was bird hunting. Whereas the first two letters concern matters in Florence, the third letter, written at the end of the day, is about Piero himself and his deeply depressed state of mind.[22] Had he not been out riding all day (as we know from the other letters he had been), his condition, he told Dovizi, would have been noticed by everyone; and since his horses were now unrideable, he had to stay at home to avoid others seeing him doing nothing but stare into the void. Although triggered by a crisis in his affair with his beloved 'R', Piero's vivid and convincing account of his symptoms suggests they reflect a deeper breakdown, stemming both

---

[17] The same, 9 December 1493, p. 178, n. 38 in this volume. Dovizi's 'dubio solo' was 'se fussi da dubitare dello animo del papa verso la città, poiché non fa el breve a voi come al Re' (to Piero, 3 September 1493, MAP 18, 137).

[18] Becchi to Piero, 23–26 January 1494 (n. 1 in this chapter), Martelli, 'Il *Libro*', p. 200; the same, 29 January, MAP 18, 368v: 'Non vi movete. Non vi fate da voi tutore d'Italia. Non potete al tutto ... Siché, per l'amor di dio, andate acortamente.'

[19] Becchi to Dovizi, 29 September 1493, ed. Can, p. 332: 'la via larga dove sono alievato'. On his Francophilism, Becchi to Piero, recd. 21 December 1491, MAP 19,187: Tre cose ve ho mosse poi ch'io rimasi vostro: Il parentado di Giuliano. Il *quamquam*, et la via di Francia ...'

[20] p. 185 in this volume.

[21] Piero to Dionigi Pucci, 16 February 1494, MAP 138, 253, fol. 248r, Brown, *Florence* (2011), p. 83, n. 60.

[22] Piero to Dovizi, 4 April 1494, from Vaiano, MAP 124, 316 (autogr.), Pieraccini, *Stirpe* I, p. 171 (for whom these letters reveal Piero's 'debolezza spirituale'), from Vico Pisano, MAP 124, 105, and from Cascina, MAP 72, 71 (autogr.), cf. Brown, 'The Poems of Piero', forthcoming.

from his unstable temperament and from the wider crisis that confronted him at this time.

The evening letter opens by promising to follow the suggestions Dovizi had drafted for Piero when replying to 'R', lest he lacked words to express his own feelings towards his lover. He was on the verge of madness and might explode with grief:

> I am so depressed that I speak and write as though in a dream, I don't think anyone in my state can live, I am so melancholic. I hope, God willing, there is a good outcome, since I do nothing all day long but stare out fixedly.[23]

More ominously, Piero then urged Dovizi to stop at nothing – from threats or worse – in order to restore his spirits 'with that gentle presence', 'because my life depends on your expedients'. If Dovizi didn't succeed, Piero had no wish to think about saving the regime, the good of the city or the peace of Italy, nor would he be moved by his children or his friends: he would rise higher or lower, assuredly not staying in the middle where 'la R' wanted him to be satisfied. In short, he would play recklessly, for better or for worse. He concluded this outburst by saying he would write to 'la R' and would now not return to Florence directly, but would leave Cascina on Sunday to come back via Poggio a Caiano, where he would await a reply from Dovizi, or hopefully one from his lover – and even if she failed to come to see him, he would be thankful if she remained as she used to be. Dovizi was to tell the *brigata* that he expected to be away for several days. A shaft to his heart, he ended dramatically, would kill him, so he hoped for a 'good' reply to keep him alive.[24]

Written 'one or two hours after sunset', the letter testifies to Piero's desperation. For although it may represent no more than an exaggerated Petrarchan response to an unhappy love affair, its mixed pathos and bombast are not only consistent with what we know of Piero's character but also, perhaps, typical of a volatile, bipolar nature. This is true, too, of two undated autograph notes that he wrote to Dovizi, probably around the same time or slightly later. The first brief and highly allusive note is not autograph and again describes a state of depression: 'I do nothing, nor do I think of anything except wearing out my life'; 'Unless "R"

---

[23] Piero in Cascina, 4 April 1494 (MAP 72, 71), fol. 77r: 'sono su lo impazzare et credo scoppio di dolore ... et parlo et scrivo in sogno ... mi si è <desto> uno humore melancolico ... che mai fò altro el dì che affisare'.

[24] Ibid., 'negli expedienti vostri consiste la vita mia ... non voglo pensare a salvatione di stato o bene della cipta o quiete d'Italia ... *aut longe altiora aut inferiora <co>gitabo ... non sono da quella mediocrità a che .R. mi faceva stare contento et infine giucherò del disperato'.

changes', it ends abruptly.²⁵ The second, like his autograph letter of 4 April, opens by bewailing his unhappy fate that had persecuted him from the time of his birth in all he did and had now led him into an error that would require all the remedies recommended to him to cover it up – possibly to do with a servant or companion Ramon, whom his friends Giannozzo, Giovanni, Jacopo and others seemed willing to remove from the house. The one thing he didn't want to happen was losing 'Francesca', 'the repose from all my woes and source of all my hope':

> whom I love more than my life and would put before everything else, especially because she is something neutral in everything else that is happening.²⁶

The letter then goes on to refer to a visit to Gino's house that evening (where he had never been before) as a chance to remedy his father's – and to a lesser extent his own – grievance against him, so he hoped Dovizi would not prevent him from going, for 'everything else is nothing and this is everything'. If he did prevent him, he would think his ill fortune and loss were irremediable and would be convinced that he would 'never be content' – as he thought Dovizi knew, whose response would bring the 'yes' or 'no' to his life.²⁷

There is much that is unclear in these melodramatic letters, but as well as showing his closeness to Dovizi as his confidant, they also show how perceptive Piero was about himself and his unhappy and unstable nature that women helped to keep in balance. 'Francesca' (a new lover?) is described as 'neutral' in the midst of all his other troubles, in the same way that 'la R' was described in the 4 April letter as wanting Piero to be satisfied with staying in the middle, instead of recklessly seeking to rise higher or sink lower. Piero's father, Lorenzo, also had 'a sensual and amorous nature' and enjoyed extramarital relationships with women from upper-class Florentine families, and he, too, was volatile, prone to frequent uncontrollable rages, like his son.²⁸ Piero's letters suggest his seemingly erratic behaviour – now bold and confident ('ballsy', as one of

---

²⁵ The same, n.d., MAP 72, 155 (autogr): 'né io fo o penso a nulla se non a logarare la vita mia ... Se già .R. non si muta.'
²⁶ The same, n.d., MAP 72, 156r (autogr.): 'la mia mala sorte che da che io naqqui in qua mi ha in tucto le mie cose perseguitato ... il riposo di tucti e' mia dolori et *ubi spes mea*: la Francesca ... cosa neutrale in queste altri occurrentie'.
²⁷ Ibid., fol. 156r-v: 'aspecto risposta dal sì o no della vita mia'. 'Casa Gino' might refer to the home of Gino di P<iero> Capponi, who failed to get Piero's help in 1493, when 'per la Vostre occupationi non potè parlarvi' (MAP 14, 338, 1 April). Gino di Lodovico Capponi is referred to as Piero's friend in 1497, p. 269 in this volume.
²⁸ Kent, *Princely Citizen*, pp. 41–66, referring to the youthful Lucrezia Donati and the older Bartolommea Nasi as his *dame* (51, 59–60); on his rages, Lorenzo, *Lettere* 1, p. 177, n. 3 ('in tanta passione che may non vidi homo alchuno de sua conditione in simile'), 9, p. 328, nn. 2 and 10, p. 18, nn. 6 and 11, p. 580, intro. n.

his secretaries called him), now frightened and in retreat – might be the result of mood swings rather than incompetence or cowardice.[29]

It is interesting to compare the letters with Piero's poems and with the letter he drafted to Dovizi after the death of Poliziano later that year, which show similar insight into himself and into his character as something fixed and unchanging, according to his 'unhappy fate' since he was born. Dovizi was upset to hear that, according to Poliziano, he ruled Piero, to which Piero had replied, no, he ruled Dovizi. So in his draft letter to Dovizi, Piero told him not to worry about hearsay (what Piero had heard through his 'pulled and lewd ears, which you know were never closed to anyone'), but instead to watch what he did and said ('my hands and mouth') since 'you being what you are and I what I am, we won't change', and nor would Poliziano's recalcitrant and volatile nature: better not to probe too deeply into things, he wisely concluded, 'because if I catch fire, I show it, because as you know I'm not good at hiding my anger'.[30]

Although Piero's fortunes continued to fluctuate, this moment of crisis and self-examination nevertheless marked a turning point for him. For the closer he drew to his Italian allies and their campaign to combat the French (which was confirmed in Vicovaro in July), the more alienated he became from his Francophile colleagues in Florence's government, as well as from the populace at large, as the summer was to show.

---

[29] p. 209, n. 49 in this volume.
[30] On the 1494 draft letters, Picotti, *Ricerche*, pp. 123–4, and p. 38 in this volume (letter to Dovizi at n. 51): 'alle mie mane et bocca che a mia sbracati e puttani orecchi ... sendo voi quello siate et io quello sono né per mutarsi nessuno ... che sapete non sono buono celatore di stiza'.

14 The French Descent

The pope's support for the new king of Naples in the 'agreement, alliance and pact' signed in Rome on 28 March 1494 changed the balance of power in Italy – and with it, Piero's importance as a mediator. It had been the pope's long years of conflict with his recalcitrant vassal Ferrante that had enabled Lorenzo de' Medici to mediate between Italy's rulers as the needle of the balance, but the new alignment meant that Piero had lost his father's role, and once the French expedition was confirmed, the months of temporising were also over. But Lorenzo had not called Piero his 'warrior son' for nothing, and when the war was decided on, he entered energetically into its planning, offering forth ideas as his father used to do, who liked to share his fantasies or *ghiribizzi* with his colleagues as a form of thinking aloud.[1] So although the events of the next few months are well known in outline, Piero's own role – which, as usual, combined bursts of action with periods of inaction or escape – is less familiar.[2]

One of his early suggestions was that the Italian powers should send ambassadors to the Spanish monarchs, Ferdinand and Isabella, who being 'extremely religious' would prohibit the French expedition. It may have been intended as a delaying tactic to avoid decisive action, but the idea was not as fanciful as the secretary Guidotti and the pope thought (to whom fra Giovanni had duly transmitted Piero's idea), in dismissing it as a 'fantasy' and one of Piero's 'castles in the air'.[3] By the end of June the Spanish monarchs were indeed becoming worried about the expedition (they reminded the Sicilians of the Vespers in 1282, when an uprising was provoked by the rape of a Sicilian woman by the French

---

[1] On Lorenzo's 'disegni in aria' or *ghiribizi*, Lorenzo to Jacopo Guicciardini, 22 June 1486, *Lettere* 9, p. 342.

[2] On the French expedition, Delaborde, *L'expédition*; Canestrini and Desjardins (Can), *Négotiations*; Denis, *Charles VIII*; and essays in *The French Descent*, ed. Abulafia.

[3] Guidotti in Rome to Dovizi, 1 June 1494, MAP 124, 212: that fra Giovanni [da Prato, p. 113 in this volume] 'conferimmi ... certi disegni in aria, che tutte le potentie d'Italia mandassino ambasciatori in Spagna ... sua Santità ha mostro pocho ghustarlo'.

invaders), and by early July King Ferdinand of Spain told Charles to 'abstain from this expedition' for the sake of Christianity (just as Piero had suggested he should do), and then offered Alfonso his support.[4]

Another idea that Piero pondered with Alamanni in Milan was a crusade against the infidel, which Alamanni told Lodovico Sforza would be more glorious than the infamy of introducing barbarians into Italy. Alamanni said it was his idea and, 'like Piero', he had spoken without any commission, suggesting the two men saw it as a means of controlling Lodovico, who one moment was threatening Piero and Florence with the French invasion and another lulling them with offers of friendship. Alamanni agreed with Piero that it was better to remain a step ahead (by continuing their military preparations) and thought they could adopt this diversionary plan of attacking the Turks without renouncing their preparations – and this, too, reemerged in later plans to avert Charles's expedition.[5]

The military preparations that he referred to began to gather pace after the middle of May, when news of French troops crossing the Alps and its armada spurred the allies 'to spend, not to save', for things were so far advanced (Dovizi warned Dionigi Pucci in Naples) that it would be shameful to do nothing and say, like Scipio Africanus, 'I wouldn't have believed it!'[6] Piero had been about to go hawking in the countryside around Pisa in late May when he decided to combine his trip with a review of the coastal defences in the company of the commissaries Pierfilippo Pandolfini and Piero Corsini.[7] But it was only after receiving a terrifying report of the power of French firearms from Guidantonio Vespucci and Piero Capponi in France that Piero and the allies fully woke up to the danger they faced. Quoting Virgil's *Aeneid*, the ambassadors described to Piero the French artillery's ability to pierce thick city

---

[4] Puccio Pucci to Piero, 27 June 1494, SSX8LCMR 65, fol. 140r: 'che si ricordassino del vespro syciliano'; 3 July, MAP 19, 456, fol. 511v ('abstenire da questa impresa'), and 6 August, MAP 18, 263, fol. 313r (that Ferdinand had decided to 'scoprirsi' in Alfonso's 'favore'); also Gentile Becchi to Piero, 4 September, ed. Buser, *Beziehungen*, p. 554.

[5] Alamanni in Vigevano to Piero, 1 June 1494 (MAP 50, 300, fol. 315ter^r: 'procede interamente di me et, come Piero, ho parlato e sanza alchuna commissione'; 25 May (MAP 50, 298, fols. 312 bis^r, on Lodovico's *aggiramenti*) and 28 May (MAP 50, 299, fol. 313 ter^v: *'anticipare giova'* (decoded); Piero could 'sventare la impresa' without 'intralasciando'). On the later plans, pp. 208–9 in this chapter.

[6] Dionigi Pucci in Naples to Piero, 19 May 1494, MAP 138, 291, fol. 286r ('ora vi paiono tempi da spendere') and Dovizi to Dionigi, 31 May 1494, MAP 138, 249: 'non è da dormire, *quia turpe est dicere non putaram*' (quoting Val, Max. 7. 2). On Florence' *condotte*, Alamanni to Piero, cit. (fol. 315 quattro^r).

[7] Piero in Empoli and Pisa to Dovizi in Florence, 22, 25 May 1494, MAP 96: 258 and 124, 116; Parenti, *Storia* I, p. 75.

walls and bring them down by constant pounding by day and night, *'allowing neither pause nor respite, thick as the hammering hailstones hurled down by a storm'*. Only two responses were possible to the frightening things their friends had seen with their own eyes: not to fight, or to respond in kind (Capponi adding, as evidence that Italy, too, had master engineers, that he had once seen La Ceccha mounting artillery in Livorno).[8]

This evidently encouraged Piero's third initiative at this time. Florence, unlike Naples, had never withdrawn its ambassadors from Milan, so what Piero suggested was an overt attempt, with the Neapolitans, to win over Lodovico and draw Venice into their alliance as well. Forwarding Vespucci's and Capponi's letter to the Pucci in Rome and Naples, he instructed messer Puccio to behave as if off his own bat, not according to instructions from Florence, by 'warming up the pope to remedies'.[9] Despite it being 'late, and I'm very tired', Piero told Dionigi about a meeting he had had that evening (17 May), with the Neapolitans in Florence, Marino Tomacelli and Jacopo Pontano – ostensibly to discuss Genoa and other matters at the suggestion of the leading citizens.[10] What Piero described to Dionigi (in language suggesting Alamanni's influence) was 'the virile enterprise' of sending a leading citizen quickly to Milan, to ensure 'we don't have to remain in the dark, uncertain if we're being led by the nose'.[11] Although many consultative meetings and debates were held at this time, they have left virtually no record, but the fact that Parenti, as a citizen, evidently knew nothing of this meeting suggests the initiative for it may have come from Piero, encouraged by Alamanni.[12] It is consistent with Piero's continuing ambition to mediate between Naples and Milan, and since Alfonso was

---

[8] Vespucci and Capponi in Lyon to Piero, 8 June 1494 (MAP, 138, 282, fol. 277r–v and bis, ed. Can. pp. 400–4), citing Virgil, *Aen*, V, 458–9; Capponi continued (fol. 277v, om. Can.): 'sono pure de' maestri ingegnieri in Italia, et io, Piero Capponi, mi ricordo essendo a Livorno che la Ceccha', etc.). On French firepower, Pepper, 'Castles and cannon'.

[9] Puccio Pucci in Rome to Piero, 17 June 1494, SSX8LCMR 65, fol. 51r: 'Et intendo come volete mi ghoverni ... come da me et non come per commissione havuta di costà. Et ch'io riscaldi el papa a' rimedii,' cf. 18 June, MAP 18, 252, fols. 52v, 64v.

[10] Piero to Dionigi Pucci in Naples, 17 June 1494, MAP 138, 243r: 'Per essere l'hora tarda et io molto stracco, non vi posso scrivere più a longo', 'habbiamo del tutto deliberato mandare uno di questi primi presto ad Milano ...'

[11] Ibid., 'né voliamo stare più in queste tenebre et accertarci se siamo menati al buio', 'temptare virilmente queste experientie et poi mostrare a tutto el mondo che non habbiamo perduto né lo animo né le forze.' Cf. Alamanni to Piero, 4 June (MAP 50, 316 bis^r): 'il dimonstrare *tu virilità*' (decoded), etc.

[12] Puccio Pucci refers to the Neapolitan ambassadors' approval of 'questa vostra decisione' (to Piero, 20 June 1494, SSX8LCMR 65, fol. 58v, cf. MAP 18, 253, fol. 294v). Otto di Pratica Delib. 4 records nothing between 29 January and 6 August (reply to the French ambassadors), then a final discussion on 16 October (fols. 19v–20r).

very worried that Piero would be let down by the untrustworthy Lodovico, the idea is unlikely to have come from him.[13] Moreover, the envoy chosen for Milan in late July was a Medicean intimate (Angelo Niccolini), whereas the envoys chosen for Venice (Pagolantonio Soderini and Giovanbattista Ridolfi) were not, raising the possibility that they and the embassy to Venice were proposed by the *savi* as a counterbalance to Piero and Niccolini's embassy to Milan.[14]

The mission to Milan represents a late and abortive attempt to draw Lodovico back into an alliance of Italian powers before the French advance made it impossible. In mid-June Charles VIII had expelled Florence's ambassadors from France, together with all the personnel of the Medici Bank in Lyon, around the same time that Milan and Naples withdrew their resident ambassadors from each other's cities.[15] Although the bank's manager, Cosimo Sassetti, hoped the damage would not be as great as feared, the worst damage was inflicted on Piero at home, where according to Parenti he began to lose 'reputation and credit': whereas earlier in the month many debates and public advisory meetings had been held until the French plans were clearer, now (he said) Piero shut himself up with a few advisers and decided to give all his support to Alfonso – and therefore also to Alfonso's captain, Virginio Orsini.[16] It was Virginio who had negotiated the pact between Alfonso and the pope in March 1494, with the secret clause committing Piero to paying 15,000 ducats towards Juan's *condotta* (which messer Puccio pretended to know nothing about when arriving in Rome in June as Florence's ambassador).[17] Puccio then told Piero that Virginio promised too much

---

[13] Dionigi Pucci to Piero, 20 June 1494 (MAP 19, 592, fol. 661r: 'la Maestà Sua lo danna') and 23 June (MAP 19, 597. fol. 668r: 'Dite a Piero che non si lasci dondolare al Signor Lodovico').

[14] Their commissions are dated 21 July 1494 (ed. Can, pp. 497–9, with biographies on 495–7); according to Alamanni (in Vigevano to Piero, 4 July , MAP 50, 282, fol. 295 quatt.ʳ) the decision was made much earlier; in September Ridolfi joined Niccolini in Milan, leaving Soderini in Venice (Can, pp. 510–31), cf. Parenti, *Storia* I, p. 93.

[15] De Roover, *Banco*, p. 449, Buser, *Bezierungen*, pp. 547–9; cf. Vespucci and Capponi in Lyon to Piero, 19, 22 June, ed. Can. pp. 407–9. On 20 July Angelo Niccolini reported to Piero that Florentines from four leading families '*tengono questa praticha in Lione col Re di Francia et che hanno ordinato scoprirsi come il Re avvicina*' (decoded), MAP 74, 97, fol. 222r.

[16] Cosimo Sassetti in Chambery to Piero, 22 June 1494, ed. Buser, pp. 547–50; Parenti, *Storia* I, pp. 80–1.

[17] Puccio Pucci in Rome to Piero, 13 June 1494, SSX8LCMR 65, fol. 36r [*add. in marg.*], that when the pope referred to 'quello obligho fece con Sua Santità el Signor Virginio della cipta vostra', 'non risposi parola et finxi non intendere', etc. On Puccio and Piero, pp. 128–9 in this volume, also Puccio to Piero, 21 June 1494, SSX8LCMR 65, fol. 125r (that if he overdid it, 'non lo imputate ad arrogantia né ambitione, ... ma [al]la servitù et

on his behalf, and since it was thought 'you depend totally on Virginio and that he does with you what he wants', he urged Piero 'to use your customary skill in showing that *you* want to be acknowledged as Master of the Workshop'.[18] Whereas Alfonso and the pope were contributing men to the military campaign as well as to the armada against France, Piero alone would be accused of temporising (Puccio told him) if he failed to play his part by engaging Giovanni Bentivoglio and Caterina Sforza.[19]

If messer Puccio wanted Piero to exert his patronal influence, other Florentines accused him of abusing it by including too many of his foreign friends and clients in the one thousand men-at-arms he was raising, 'who will bring you no benefit at all'; instead, he was told by Nofri Tornabuoni to engage the excellent Florentine, Carlo da Pian di Meleto, since spending the republic's money on his military skills would benefit the public interest, and as he would keep his money in Medici banks, it would also benefit Piero.[20] It was the return from Rome of two of the four French ambassadors that finally brought the ruling elite's differences out into the open – one of the ambassadors, after initially being refused passage through Florence, was allowed to stay in a villa outside Florence, 'not to provoke the king of France into totally being our enemy'.[21] What was contentious was the French request that Florence support not only the king's expedition but also Lorenzo and Giovanni di Pierfrancesco. Bernardo del Nero, then one of the Otto di Pratica, evidently drafted a proposal that Piero's cousins should remain under French protection, to which Piero responded from Poggio a Caiano, via Dovizi, that he wanted to see in writing what 'those wise men, as they're called [the *savi*, in the Otto di Pratica], who support me

---

sincera fede mi stringe e forza ad scrivervi ciò che intendo'), 29 June 1494, 145v (thanking Piero as his 'Mancipium et factura tua' for his election to the Seventy).

[18] Puccio Pucci in Rome to Piero, 16 June 1494, ed. Can at p. 494 (my italics), cf. Shaw 'Lorenzo and Virginio', p. 40: 'dimostrare di volere essere recognosciuto per el Maestro della Bottegha'. On Virginio's loans from the Medici Bank, Piero to Nofri, 3 July 1494, *Ricordi di lettere* (2), p.132 ('per 4000 ducati che sua signoria vuole in presto') and p. 177, n. 37 in this volume.

[19] The same, 20 June 1494, SSX8LCMR 65, fol. 58v (much corrected draft, copied in MAP 18, 253, fols. 294–5): 'indutiando o faccendo dilatione nel mandare parrebbe che voi andassi temporeggiando et trovando scuse al facto vostro'.

[20] Ibid., (27 June 1494), fol. 141r–v (cf. MAP 18, 254, fol. 296r–v): 'per la utilità publica non potete spendere più utilmente li danari di cotesta republica ... Deinde da lui in privato voi ne trahete utile'.

[21] Parenti, *Storia* I, p. 82, 'per totalmente non ci si provocare el re di Francia inimico', Landucci, *Diario*, p. 69. The two ambassadors were d'Aubigny and Matheron; their instructions (dated 11 June 1494) and Florence's verbal reply on 14 July, are ed. Can, I, pp. 414–17.

and the regime, reply'; he was sorry not to reply himself, but he would be equally sorry to accept del Nero's proposal: 'in short, they should reply at all costs and without me, that's enough'.[22]

Piero's perfunctory response to one of the most revered elders marked a new stage in his deteriorating position in Florence. For although it concerned his cousins, it nevertheless marked a wider rift between him and the *savi*, to which Pierfilippo also alludes in a letter to Dovizi soon after the arrival of the French ambassadors at the end of June. Referring to the malign consequences of 'the talk of those leading citizens' that could lead many to err and sully the regime's reputation abroad and at home, he told Dovizi to remind Piero to use his prudence, since he was sure that everyone would eventually settle down: 'Take a little time and help him – as I'm sure, however, that you do.' He wished he was in Florence so he could be of use (he was still serving as a commissary in Pisa), but he trusted Piero to overcome these difficulties, which were perhaps among the greatest they had ever had:

Piero must think carefully about them. I'm confident that if we don't fail, the end will be good and honourable – and if we're victorious here, we will be everywhere, and soon there will be a great revolution in favour of our affairs.[23]

Pandolfini's careful advice to Piero hints at the seriousness of the situation. For although as one of Piero's most trusted advisers Pierfilippo retained confidence in him, support was ebbing, and by the end of the month the Mantuan envoy in Florence reported that Piero was as hated there as if he were a Turk.[24] When another French (and Milanese) delegation arrived in Florence to demand the same privileges for themselves that had been granted to the Neapolitan fleet in Livorno, Piero was absent in Borgo Sansepolcro, meeting Alfonso's son Ferrandino.[25] As a result, the Signoria's reply (after consulting the Otto di Pratica) was perhaps more favourable than it might have been had Piero been in Florence, offering not to fail in its duty to the French despite denying

---

[22] Piero in Poggio to Dovizi in Florence, 14 July 1494, 'cito, cito, cito', MAP 72, 75: 'cotesti savi, *ut aiunt* ... In summa, che omnino si risponda et sanza me et basta'; Parenti, *Storia* I, pp. 83–8. On Del Nero, p. 156 in this volume.

[23] Pierfilippo Pandolfini in Pisa to Dovizi in Florence, 3 July 1494, CS I, 3, fol. 155r: 'Mettevi un pocho di tempo et voi ne lo aiutate come sono certo però che fate ... Bisognia Piero ci pensi bene. Io sto di buono animo ... et presto si sarebbe fatto in Italia una grande mutatione a beneficio delle cose nostre.'

[24] Picotti, *Giovinezza*, p. 560, Brown, *Florence* (2011), p. 84, n. 62. Gonzaga, mentioned in Zanobi's confession, had been tempted by French offers in April 1494 (p. 187 in this volume and Chambers, 'Francesco II Gonzaga', p. 221).

[25] Parenti, *Storia* I, p. 90; on Piero's visit to Borgo, n. 30 in this chapter.

the Genoese, as their enemies, entry to their ports.[26] These French visits provided a counterpoint to the allies' campaign against the French expedition, a barometer of the strength of Francophilism in Florence.[27] Little surprise, then, that Piero now devoted his energies to the allied campaign being planned at Vicovaro, 'this Diet of the pope', as messer Puccio called it, which met under papal auspices in mid-July.

The Meeting at Vicovaro

The Orsini castle of Vicovaro lay within papal territory, so when King Alfonso arrived on 14 July, Alexander VI was already there, enthroned and surrounded by six cardinals as he waited for his vassal to kiss his feet. Although not present himself, Piero was well represented by messer Puccio (one of two ambassadors in the papal retinue) and by Puccio's uncle, Dionigi (who with Baccio Ugolini was part of Alfonso's retinue, until falling ill en route and dying on 26 July). Dionigi's place was then taken by Baccio Ugolini and two secretaries, ser Antonio Dovizi (ser Piero's and Bernardo's younger brother) and ser Francesco Cappelli.[28] Messer Puccio provides a revealing glimpse of the absent Piero making his influence felt by going over the heads of his ambassadors, suggesting (through Marino Tomacelli in Florence) that Ferrandino, duke of Calabria, should lead the army in the Romagna in his father Alfonso's place – forcing Puccio 'to stay silent and not want more than you yourself'. By telling him and the others 'nothing about this change of yours', he complained to Piero, 'you make us look like men who don't know what our superiors want'.[29]

This change of plan may have been disastrous for the Romagna campaign, since Ferrandino's slow arrival in the camp at Cesena removed the element of surprise from the campaign and enabled the French to arrive

---

[26] Parenti, p. 91; the Otto's reply was more non-committal (Delib. 4, 6 August 1494, fols. 16v–19r; the *aggiunti* included the lawyers G. A. Vespucci and Malegonnelle, as well as Tommaso Minerbetti, Francesco Valori and Antonio Dini, 18v); Virginio later blamed Piero and Florence for the 'ruina del Re' (Puccio to Piero, 23 August, MAP 18, 264, fol. 319r).

[27] Florentine Francophilism is exemplified by Vaglienti, *Storia*, p. 100, cf. p. 215 in this volume.

[28] Dionigi in Celano to Piero, 11 July 1494, MAP 19, 605 (6 pages) at fol. 683r; messer Puccio to his 'Magnifico Padrone', 18 July, MAP 139, fols. 24r–27v at 27r (on Dionigi) and to the Otto (Respons. 10, fols. 83r, 85r–v); Antonio Dovizi in Vicovaro to Piero, 17 July, MAP 13, 162, fol. 174r.

[29] Puccio in Vicovaro to Piero, 18 July 1494, fol. 25r: 'che ci fate parere homini che non sappiamo la volontà de superiori nostri' (writing four pages to Piero, three to the Otto). On the esteem felt for Piero's 'ricordi', the same, 3 July 1494 (MAP 19, 456, fol. 511–12), Dionigi to Piero, 1 July (MAP 19, 601, fol. 677r) and 11 July, fol. 683r.

in the Romagna first.³⁰ Nevertheless, it demonstrated Piero's standing with King Alfonso, who already treated him 'as if he was his son' before the conference opened, asking Antonio Dovizi about Piero's love of horses and his way of life, and warning him (as his father Ferrante had done) to be very careful, 'especially when riding and at night, because he's in the greatest danger'.³¹ The king's eldest son, Ferrandino, was just five years older than Piero and three years older than Piero's envoy in the Romagna, Bernardo Dovizi, who would have met Ferrandino on his embassy to Naples earlier that year. The close friendship that developed between the three young men during the Romagna campaign provides an interlude that must have contributed to Machiavelli's critique of Renaissance warfare, as we shall see.

The main work of the allies at Vicovaro was to produce a plan of campaign, with agreed lists of the companies to be involved, their *condotte* and shared costs.³² But the occasion was also used to discuss the forthcoming appointment of new cardinals, as Puccio reported to Piero in his long letter of 18 July. Although Alfonso had been assured by the pope that one would be a Florentine – he wrote – the pope had also said that if Piero wanted 'the person who went to France' (Gentile Becchi), the cardinals found him lightweight and whimsical and preferred the bishop of Volterra. To this, Alfonso had responded that if he (the pope) was giving Piero a cardinal to please him, then 'the person who went to France' was the person he wanted, a learned, sharp and witty man who was certainly worthy of a cardinal's hat, whereas to appoint Soderini would be to appoint an enemy, the opposite of what was desired (as messer Puccio himself knew well, having just attacked Soderini in Rome for being Piero's enemy).³³ When Puccio thanked Alfonso for this, the king added that he shouldn't think the pope's 'wanting to make Soderini a cardinal springs from affection for him, or from wanting to offend you', 'it only comes from a thirst for money, since he'd hope to draw 30,000 or

---

³⁰ According to Landucci (*Diario*, p. 69) Piero left on 5 August to go 'in quello d'Arezzo, a vicitarlo [the duke of Calabria] come si va a vicitare un gran maestro, un signore'. Clough implies Ferrandino rode from Cesena to meet him, where his camp had arrived by 19 July, 'The Romagna Campaign', p. 109.

³¹ Antonio Dovizi in Celano to Piero, 8 July 1494, MAP 18, 258: 'maxime quando chavalcha et la nocte, che porta grandissimo pericolo'.

³² Puccio Pucci in Rome to [Piero], 18 July 1494, fol. 27v: 'Le gente d'arme che andranno del S. Re <in> Romagna saranno queste, *videlicet*' (listing them).

³³ Puccio in Rome to Piero, 18 July 1494, fol. 26r: 'per homo leggiera [*sic*] et fantastico', 'la Maestà sua replicò che ... [Becchi] era homo docto, acuto et faceto', 'fare il Soderino ... sarebbe il contrario effecto di quello che si desidera' (cf. Bertelli, '*Ricordi* di G. V. Soderini', p. 394; Brown, 'Piero in Power', pp. 121–2, for Pucci's attack on Soderini in June).

more [ducats] from him, creating someone the court would be happy with'.[34] Filippo Valori had commented caustically in April 1493 that 'since the pope has had no scruples in buying the papacy, one shouldn't think he has any fewer in selling cardinalates'.[35] So unsurprisingly Becchi never got his cardinalate, being not only poor but also disliked in Rome for his *Synodus Fiorentina* attacking Sixtus IV's involvement in the murder of Giuliano de' Medici in 1478; for similar reasons, neither did Poliziano, Piero's alternative candidate for a cardinalate at this time.[36]

The meeting in Vicovaro was followed by Piero's four-day meeting with Ferrandino in Borgo in August, a month (according to Parenti) that Piero devoted to 'bird hunting and playing football publicly in the streets as though nothing was important to him'.[37] It is true that he had combined his business trip to Borgo with hunting for partridges in the surrounding countryside with his cousin Lorenzo Tornabuoni, but he would have considered his meeting with Ferrandino serious work, not play, and he also devoted time before and after his visit to Borgo to a boss's traditional work of election fixing in Florence and mediating marriages and festering disputes.[38]

The events of the summer nevertheless showed the balance of power was shifting. Although Piero's standing was growing outside Florence, within the city he was losing support among the elders and its Francophile populace. He also suffered the loss of important supporters and friends. Dionigi Pucci's death in July was followed a month later by the death in Rome of his nephew, messer Puccio.[39] In September both

---

[34] The same, fol. 26v: 'solo procede da sete di danari'.

[35] Filippo Valori, 18 April [1493], MAP 138, 303: 'Copia d' uno capitolo di lettera' without addressee: 'Et non havendo havuto la Santità Sua respecto a comprare il Papato, era da credere che manco l'harà a vendere e' cappelli.'

[36] On Poliziano, Chapter 3 in this volume and Parenti, *Storia* I, p. 100; he, too, attacked Sixtus in his *Coniurationis Commentarium*, ed. Simonetta, *Congiura della verità*. According to Antonio Dovizi (in Rome to Piero, 1 July 1494, MAP 55, 186, fol. 305r–v), Virginio had asked 'come la Magnificentia Vostra si contenterebbe del Conte Giovanni della Mirandola'.

[37] Parenti, *Storia*, 1, p. 92.

[38] Tornabuoni in Florence to A. Niccolini in Milan, 20 August 1494 (Niccolini Archives, 14, ins. 41: Piero 's'è stato parecchi dì fuori e affacendo e alle starne'); on elections, Bernardo de' Albertis to Niccolini, 19 August 1494, ibid. and Niccolini to Piero, 18 August, MAP 14, 430r; on mediation, Piero to Tomè [Bardi] da Vernio, 22 July 1494, ASF Bardi BI, 1, fol. 8; and on marriages, Ricci to A. Niccolini, 11 October 1493, Niccolini Archives, 14, ins. 41.

[39] King Alfonso wrote a formulaic but affectionate letter to his widow on 31 July 1494 (MAP 96, 265r). On his illness and death, Puccio Pucci to the Otto, 26 and 27 July, Otto Respons. 10, fols. 90r and 91r. On messer Puccio's death, Guiducci in Rome to Piero, 31 August 1494, MAP 55, 187, fol. 307r: 'In questa hora a messer Puccio si è data la extrema untione, lui parla pocho, ha grande affanno et è in tal termine ch' e' medici al più lungo giudicano non passerà domani dassera.'

Matteo Franco and Angelo Poliziano died, and in early October so did the 'loving and gentle' Baccio Ugolini, who had been 'an effective and charming agent' for Piero – Antonio Dovizi wrote – and a 'great supporter' of the Dovizi brothers: 'may his soul rest in peace'.[40] With their deaths, Piero had lost three of his most devoted political aides, as well as two close friends, leaving him almost entirely in the hands of his unpopular Dovizi secretaries – especially ser Piero, who according to both Poliziano and Gentile Becchi 'ruled Piero' and was widely disliked for his arrogance and pretensions, which were thought to have hastened Piero's fall. The secretary Antonio Guidotti was similarly disliked, regarded by Filippo Valori as unfit for his role in Rome, for as he told Dovizi in mid-September, there must be 'an ambassador of authority' there, someone like Angelo Niccolini or Pierfilippo Pandolfini, who would be capable of the top-level diplomacy needed, since 'that man [Guidotti] longs to be esteemed' and at times he lacked courage and confidence.[41] Valori reflects the shift in power within the government at a time, when, as he said, 'able men' (*uomini sofficienti*) were urgently needed in the top positions. He himself replaced the defunct Dionigi Pucci in Naples, two similarly able (and republican) statesmen were sent to Venice, Pagolantonio Soderini and Giovanbattista Ridolfi, the latter then replacing Alamanni and Niccolini in Milan.[42] Although Piero still retained support in Florence, he presented the city with a 'calamity' – as Parenti put it – whether the French expedition went ahead or not, since Florence would either lose its freedom to an outside power or to 'a proud and rash young man', keen to secure himself in power.[43]

---

[40] Antonio Dovizi in Bologna to his brother Bernardo, 8 October 1494, MAP 124, 344: 'nostro amorevole et dolce messer Baccio Ugolini ... El patrone ha perso un sufficiente et gentile instrumento et noi altri, et maxime tu, un grande partigiano.' Franco died on 9 September (n. 61 in this chapter) and Poliziano on the 24th (Bernardo Dovizi to Piero, 2 October, ed. Moncallero, I, p. 149).

[41] On Piero Dovizi, Brown, *Florence* (2011), pp. 8–9. On Guidotti, ibid., pp. 16–17, 25–8, and Filippo Valori in Rome to Dovizi, 16 September 1493, MAP 124, 148r ('chostui' lacked the authority of an ambassador and 'apetisce essere anche stimato et anche ha bisongno alle volte d'animo et d'essere isp<in>to').

[42] Ibid. (fol. 148r): 'questi tempi ricerchano huomini sofficienti, perché s'à a praticare *de summa rerum*'. On these appointments, n. 14 in this chapter. Lorenzo Tornabuoni told Niccolini on 20 August (n. 38 in this chapter) that 'questo nostro stato e ghoverno ha carestia de vostri pari'. On Piero and the Soderini, Nardi, *Istorie* I, pp. 22–3.

[43] Parenti, *Storia* I, p. 77: 'alla discrezione d'un giovane baldanzoso e altiero', 'E in tale calamità condotti eravamo.'

Piero the Strategist in His Study

Piero was well represented at the meetings in Vicovaro, even if not present, and subsequently Alfonso instructed his eldest son, Ferrandino, to consult with him and the Florentines during the campaign, in view of his own and the pope's distance from the fighting – even though Bernardo Dovizi (Piero's commissary in the camp) dissuaded Ferrandino from doing so on one occasion to save Piero being held responsible for the outcome.[44] Piero was busy not only attempting to procure money for the campaign but also procuring delicacies and wine for Ferrandino, whose *affaire amoreuse* during the campaign he tried to share with Piero, as we shall see. He was doubtless in Machiavelli's mind when famously criticising Italian rulers before 1494 for conducting wars from their studies and love affairs from the battlefield – sleeping and eating well and bestowing honours for favours, while being parsimonious and condescending towards their subjects.[45]

But Piero was more seriously engaged in less publicised attempts to mediate peace through truces and agreements between the antagonists. Ever since the summer, he had been suggesting strategies to hinder the French expedition, as we have seen, including the plan in June to send new ambassadors to Milan and Venice to discuss terms for a truce. In late August we know from the letters of Lorenzo Spinelli, who did business for the Medici in Lyon as well as for the French, that two of Piero's other ideas for averting the French expedition were under discussion with men who both professed to be very 'affectionate' and friendly with Piero. One was Philippe de Commynes, a long-standing friend of the Medici's who now offered to act as mediator or go-between in offering Charles VIII a large sum of money through Spinelli. The other was Mons. de Bresse ('Brescia'), who wanted Piero to use his influence with Alfonso and the pope to gain their support (with money and galleys) for a crusade against the Turks, drawing in Milan and Venice too, in order to ruin San Malo's Italian plans.[46] In the middle of the month

---

[44] Bernardo to Piero, 26 September 1494, ed. Moncallero, I, pp. 138–9 (postscript); the same, 20 ('ditene, per vostra fè, il parere vostro'), 23 and 25 September ('ho deliberato seguire lo designo della Magnificenza Vostra'), pp. 123, 128 and 134v).

[45] Machiavelli, *Arte della Guerra*, bk. 7, ed. Bertelli, p. 518; Najemy, 'Arms and letters'. The *affaire* is discussed later in this chapter.

[46] Spinelli in Chambery, 26 August [1494], copied in MAP, 88, 266, fols. 324r–325, partly ed. Buser, *Bezierhungen*, pp. 552–3: Commynes 'è afezionato a Piero ... et se il Magnifico venissi aproxpoxito di fare qualche acordo col re, desiderrebbe essere mezano', similarly Philippe, count of Bresse (later duke of Savoy, Labande-Mailfert, *Charles VIII*, pp. 60, 222, Parenti, *Storia*, 1, p. 138: 'uno de' principali governatori del Re ... et di Piero de' Medici grandissimo partigiano'). Cf. Commynes to Spinelli, 6 August, Can, I,

Piero had written to Lodovico via Florence's ambassadors in Milan, Alamanni and Niccolini, to suggest a joint mediation by the pope, the emperor and the king of Spain to deter the French expedition. Lodovico promised to consider it, and had gone on to say 'it would be a great thing if Piero came to visit the king' (Charles was about to meet Lodovico himself in Alessandria, midway between Milan and Genoa). Although the ambassadors wondered if it would be safe for Piero, or acceptable for the ambassadors, to meet him after the Florentines had been 'chased out of Lyon', it may have planted a seed in Piero's mind that influenced his decision to go himself to seek peace from the king in October.[47]

Despite the military plans agreed on in Vicovaro for a quick victory over France and Milan, the duke of Calabria's long delay in reaching the Romagna and Piero's diplomatic plans to avoid the war altogether meant the allied forces failed to arrive there before the French. Nor was Piero able to fulfil his responsibility for engaging Giovanni Bentivoglio and Caterina Sforza, or for arranging the former's payment to the pope of 18,000 ducats for a cardinalate for his son, the protonotary Anton Galeazzo.[48] The pope distrusted Giovanni, withdrawing his promise of a cardinalate until Giovanni had signed the *condotta*, and Giovanni distrusted the Medici after Lorenzo failed to reward him with one of the Pazzi's palaces for his help in 1478 (it was now that Antonio Dovizi commented on Giovanni not being 'ballsy like Piero', he needed to be led little by little).[49] So although Bentivoglio's sons and the populace supported the Medici – as Antonio discovered, when hailed by Annibale and Alessandro in Bologna's square and led by them, arm in arm, to the public palace, to shouts of 'Han, Han,' 'Alexandro' and sometimes, to Antonio's amazement, 'Palle, Palle,' too – Giovanni refused to commit

---

pp. 417–19, and Lettenhove, *Lettres* 2, pp. 98–101, 106–7, 123–4, 126–36, 139–43; on the Medici Bank's role in funding the French, Pollini-Martin, *Banque*, pp. 166–70.

[47] Alamanni and Niccolini in Vigevano to Piero, 30 August 1494, MAP 50, 276, fols. 287-bis: 'il modo proponi del temperare la caldeza del re di Francia', etc.(287r), 'sarebbeli, però, così gran facto che Piero venissi a visitare il re ... almeno vi mandare imbasciadori ... havendoli chacciati di Lione, non sapevamo come si li fussino accepti' (287bis^r).

[48] Puccio Pucci in Rome to Piero, 18 July 1494, fols. 25r–26r, Dionigi Pucci in Celano, ditto, 11 July, fol. 683r–v, and Antonio Dovizi in Bologna to Piero, 31 July, MAP 16, 383r. On the campaign, Clough, 'The Romagna Campaign', and letters to Piero from Bernardo Dovizi in the camp (ed. Moncallero, I, pp. 82–235), from Antonio Dovizi in Bologna in MAP, and Filippo Valori in Naples (4–28 October, ed. Can, I, pp. 451–83).

[49] Antonio to ser Piero Dovizi, 29 August 1494, MAP 16, 399 ('gli fu promesso la casa di Messer Jacopo o di Renato ... et poi non ne fu nulla'); the same, 8 September, MAP 16, 406, fol. 435r ('Costui non è Piero, che habbi e' coglioni grossi!'). On the pope and Bentivoglio, 29 August, fol. 399v; Filippo Valori in Naples to Piero, 4 October, ed. Can, I, p. 454–5.

himself to Piero and the allies.[50] Caterina Sforza was playing similarly hard to get, promising support to her uncle Lodovico at the same time as demanding more money from the allies.[51] As a result, Piero was unable to secure either contract and the French army and artillery streamed across the Reno river unimpeded, 'all fine men' in Antonio Dovizi's fascinated eyes.[52]

Equally fatal to the campaign was Piero's inability to contribute his full share of the expenses of the campaign – for which he was no more to blame than for the failed *condotte*. For unlike the rulers of Naples and Milan (as his father Lorenzo had complained in 1487), the Medici could not use their own money for public expenses like war that had to be approved by the councils in Florence.[53] This involved Piero in equivocations and deceptions in Florence that further undermined his position there while not helping his allies. Two of Piero's letters to Bernardo Dovizi (who had arrived in the camp as paymaster on 2 September) illustrate this particularly well. A week after Bernardo's arrival, Piero wrote ordering him to pay Ferrandino the 2000 ducats he had been given, in return for a receipt and a letter of exchange.[54] Having signed but not despatched the letter, Piero then received two letters from the camp: one from duke Ferrandino (asking for his 'opinion and advice' about pressing on and wanting money to do so), the other from the marquis of Pescara (Alfonso d'Avalos) about the terms of his engagement. Squeezed on to the bottom of Piero's letter were instructions about an additional 1000 ducats (or £4000) for Ferrandino and for Bernardo's needs, which Bernardo was simply to tell the duke about, instead of showing him this disordered letter that Piero wanted him to 'destroy completely, all of it', once its instructions had been carried out.[55]

---

[50] Antonio to Piero, 23 August 1494, MAP 16, 393, fols. 409r–411v ('continuamente gridava, chi Hann, Hann, et chi Alexan<dro>, et qualche volta Palle, Palle, che quando senti questo, mi maravigliai', fol. 410r).

[51] The same, 4 August, MAP 16, 384, fols. 390v–391r.

[52] The same, 25, 27 August 1494, MAP 16: 394, fols. 412r–413r, and 395, fol. 414r–v: 'tutti bella gente', 'Non viene carraggio che non havessi la femmina sua, che è segno vengono per stare' (in contrast to the ducal camp that Bernardo described as like 'una sacrestia. Le femine non ci stanno', to Piero, 3 September, ed. Moncallero, I, p. 91).

[53] Brown, 'Piero in Power', p. 115, n. 13.

[54] Piero to Bernardo in the camp, 9 September 1494, MAP 124, 335, fol. 379r, and on his arrival, Bernardo to Piero, 2 September, ed. Moncallero, I, p. 82: 'dolorosissimo tempo, la via pessima, li cavalli non buoni'.

[55] Letter of 9 September, fol. 379r ('Circa la richiesta ne fa el Marchese di Pescara, rispondi a Sua Signoria quello dico di sopra de' fanti et de' danari') and 379 bis[r]: 'Dirai: "Piero mi scrive', etc. 'Hai una buona informatione da me, exequita questa lettera, stracciala tucta.' This, it seems, fully satisfied the duke, Moncallero, I, pp. 97, 10 (9, 11 September).

This was followed a day later by a similarly equivocal letter, in which Piero told Bernardo to pay the 2000 ducats to the duke at once as instructed – though Bernardo had acted very wisely in asking Piero what he wanted him to do; that day, Piero continued, he had just received 12,000 ducats from the king in cash and 5000 ducats in letters of exchange. But again the message was undermined, this time by ser Piero Dovizi, who added a note at the bottom of the page to his brother: 'Bernardo, if you can save the other 2000 ducats, do so, despite what "P" wrote to you yesterday, your brother P[iero].'[56] The following day the exhausted ser Piero ordered his brother to return at once to Florence, but Bernardo was back in the camp by the 15th (after visiting Bologna), asking his boss to have 2000–3000 ducats ready to send him when requested – as they were, two days later.[57] The letters demonstrate the difficulty Piero faced in raising money to support the Romagna campaign. When Bernardo wanted more money to pay for the infantry in mid-October, he told Piero to keep it ready or send it 'by your post secretly through the Medici Bank so no one knows until it's needed' – and if it wasn't, he'd spend nothing so no one in Florence would hear about it through the bank. Although it was not unusual for public money to be funnelled through private banks, the need for secrecy and the fact that Bernardo expected to be criticised for it by Antonio Dini, Florence's tight-fisted finance minister, suggest the payments were being made on Piero's personal authority.[58] Bernardo later explained to Alfonso that the Florentines had refused to grant Piero money to support him because he, Piero, was blamed by them all for the cruelty inflicted by the French army.[59]

There seems no doubt that Florence's difficulty in paying for troops contributed to the retreat of the ducal army to the strongholds of Luga and Massa and its eventual defeat after the cruel massacre at Mordano on

---

[56] Piero to Bernardo in Faenza, 10 September 1494, MAP 124, 336r (on the arrival of the money), *in fundo*, 'Bernardo, se tu puoi salvare li altri 2 mila ducati, fallo nonobstante quello ti scrivessi hieri P<iero> perché farai una spesa buona. Fr. P.'

[57] Ser Piero to Bernardo in Imola, 'fratri meo', 11 September 1494, MAP 124, 338: 'alla havuta di questa tu torni', and, after a coded passage, 'similmente hacci salvato 2 mila ducati'; Bernardo in the camp to Piero, 15 September ('habbiate in ordine ad ogni richiesta mia due o tre mila ducati') and the 17th ('subito, subito mi mandiate due o tre mila ducati'), ed. Moncallero, I, pp. 107, 114, cf. n. 60 in this chapter.

[58] The same, 16 October 1494, ed. Moncallero, pp. 201–2: 'ma fatelo secretamente ... pure che di costà per via del bancho non s'intenda', ending 'mi paiono bene spesi li danari, benché Antonio di Bernardo mi riprenderà'; Piero also instructed Bernardo to keep counterfoils of payments to the troops, the same, 19 September, p. 117.

[59] See p. 213 in this chapter.

20 October.[60] But although Dovizi professed to 'feel so sorry for those two young men' (Piero and Ferrandino) after the Neapolitan armada was defeated at Rapallo on 8 September and Ostia was lost to the Francophile Colonna ten days later, the young men themselves were less troubled than the worn-out secretary.[61] Soon after arriving in the camp, Ferrandino had embarked on an amorous dalliance with a Caterina family which Bernardo described to Piero a month later. The affair is well known, partly because it served as the basis for Bernardo's play *La Calandra* that shocked nineteenth-century historians.[62] Its interest now lies in the relaxed, laddish culture it describes as Piero, his secretary and the king's son exchanged trophies and portraits with great glee. When Ferrandino with noble generosity offered to share his trophy with Piero, Bernardo responded that Piero had seen Caterina the previous year in Florence and if he had wanted her, he would have had her then.[63] The surprise came three days later, when Piero replied with a letter enclosing a portrait of Caterina as proof of his success with her, which Ferrandino and Bernardo, shut up in a room together, read and reread with great hilarity, repeated when they then read it to the marquis of Pescara, whose wife had died only two days earlier. As Bernardo said, they were reverting to the 'old practices of boyhood' – and of camp soldiers deprived of their wives? – especially when they planned to send Caterina off to be King Charles's *bella madama* with the 1500–2000 ducats proffered by Lodovico, which they would then steal from her en route. All this, Bernardo said, was very enjoyable and, 'with some pleasing additions, it would make a fine novel'. So, pleasure combined with profit: a book out of it for Bernardo and for Piero 'a thousand good fruits' from this fun with the duke, which would make them closer to each other than brothers.[64]

[60] Bernardo also requested money from Piero on 9 and 11 October 1494, etc., *Epistolario* I, pp. 183, 188; cf. Piero to Bernardo, 10 October, MAP 124, 345–6, and to Soderini in Venice, 11 October, ed. Can, I, p. 522.
[61] Dovizi to his brother Antonio in Bologna, n.d. (after the loss of Ostia on 18 September), MAP 124, 273, wanting the General of the Servites, Antonio Alibanti, to pray God 'pel Duca e per Piero, che ho compassione per questi dua giovani'. Due to his exhaustion, he said, he envied Bertoldo and Franco (who died in 1491 and on 9 September 1494).
[62] Before Moncallero's edition, the letter was published by Isidoro Del Lungo in 1862 and then, without cuts, by G. G. Ferrero in 1948, v. *Epistolario* I, p. 161, n. I (identifying Caterina as the daughter of Giorgio di Novellara and Paola Sciantesci della Faggiuola, cf. Moncallero, *Il Cardinale*, pp. 118–19).
[63] Bernardo to Piero, 4 October, *Epistolario* I, pp. 155–63.
[64] The same, 7 October, pp. 163–71, 'per tornare alla sua vechia usanza de' garzoni' (164); 4 October, p. 161: 'una bella novella'. On their exchange of gifts of wine and food, ibid., pp. 84, 126, 142, 181, 203 (2, 20, 28 September, 9, 16 October 1494). According to Salvalaglio (one of Piero's armed guards then fighting for the duke), Ferrandino intended to marry one of his daughters to Bernardo Dovizi, 7 October, pp. 168–71, n. 23.

But the reality of war now disrupted this enjoyable dalliance. The same letter that began by describing Ferrandino's and Bernardo's laughter on receiving Caterina's picture from Piero ended in a sobering account of the military situation. On 20 October a mixture of French, Milanese, Swiss and Scots infantry and one thousand French archers and artillery sacked Mordano (near Imola in Caterina Sforza's territory), and the French, who were in the lead, 'murdered I don't know how many women and children' and 'used such cruelty that everyone is totally sickened'.[65] Since late August, Spinelli had warned Piero that the king and San Malo were predicting he would soon be dead, he should beware of his cousin, and the king had been promised that, when he reached Modena, 'the Florentines would get rid of the Magnifico [Piero]'.[66] So when Lorenzo and Giovanni di Pierfrancesco broke their exile by joining the king at Vigevano (between Alessandria and Milan) on 13–14 October, followed two weeks later by the retreat of the allied army from their camp and the brutal sacking of Florence's frontier town of Fivizzano, the predicted revolution appeared inevitable.[67]

---

[65] Bernardo to Piero, 21 October 1494, ed. Moncallero, I, pp. 218–19. On the sack, which created 'grandissimo odio a' franzesi', Clough, 'The Romagna Campaign', p. 211 and n. 84.

[66] Spinelli in Chambery to Piero, 26 August 1494, ed. Buser, *Beziehungen*, p. 552 ('che in breve Piero abbia a essere morto', etc.); the same to Cosimo Sassetti, recd. 4 September, ivi, p. 553. Piero's *balestriere* and his friends had also warned Piero to 'guardare da quelli di casa vostra', Antonio Dovizi in Bologna to Piero, 14 August, MAP 16, 390, fol. 403r.

[67] Bernardo to Piero, 24 October 1494, ed. Moncallero, I, p.231; Lorenzo di Bernardotto Medici, commissary in Faenza, to Piero, 25 October, MAP 18, 356. According to the Otto, Ferrandino left for Castrocaro on the 28th (Missive 25, fol. 30v, 29 October). On the sack of Fivizzano, Guicciardini, *Storie*, p. 94.

15 Revolution in Florence

The departure of Lorenzo and Giovanni di Pierfrancesco from their villas at Olmo and Cafaggiolo on 13–14 October had been triggered by yet another French deputation that had arrived in Florence ten days earlier. This time the envoy was met by Piero (with a present in hand) and Domenico Bonsi, and after later lengthy discussions with Piero and his secretary Dovizi, he and the French ambassador already in Florence were officially received by the Signoria on 7 October.[1] Not awaiting an official reply, they both left on the 11th to join the king in Parma, with permission, however, to talk to Lorenzo and Giovanni di Pierfrancesco en route – who then fled their villas two or three days later.[2] On 16 October, 'having heard of the departure of Pierfrancesco's sons', the Otto di Pratica, with ten coopted citizens including Piero – the residual core of the inner elite – were summoned to what turned out to be their last recorded meeting to discuss what to do and what security measures should be taken.[3]

It was Piero Alamanni who recommended on their behalf that an ambassador should be sent to the king of France and to the duke of Ferrara, Piero Corsini should go to Lucca to ensure its loyalty, and commissioners should be sent to the mountains of Pistoia and Barga to safeguard the passes. As for the cousins, since Lorenzo di Pierfrancesco had left his wife and children behind with 150,000 ducats in money and valuables, Alamanni's advice was to guard the children diligently

---

[1] He possibly joined Matheron, Delaborde, *L'expédition*, p. 422 and n. 4; Parenti, *Storia* I, pp. 101–4. Bonsi, later a prominent Savonarolan, was a member of the Settanta but not the Otto di Pratica.

[2] They left on the 13th or 14th (Tribaldo de' Rossi, *Ricordanze*, p. 295, Berardino de Bernardo, 18 October, Orsini Archive, 102 (3), fol. 694). Guidotti (in Rome to Piero, 20 October, MAP 55, 196r) told the pope, who feared revolution, that Florence would swiftly defend itself, 'dandoli lo exemplo di Sisto contro di vostro padre'.

[3] Otto Delib. 4, fol. 19v, 16 October 1494, listing with 'Petrus Medices' nine others (Alamanni, Niccolini, Malegonnelle, Davanzati, Domenico and Pierfil. Pandolfini, Niccolò Sacchetti, Francesco Valori and Bernardo Rucellai – half of them named by Guicciardini as Piero's 'pratica stretta', *Storie*, p. 91).

'outside, or here inside their own house, to prevent them from fleeing', and also 'to investigate what possessions they have left behind, without proceeding further'. Although Parenti thought that it was both surprising and worrying that the rebels had left so valuable a pawn behind, Virginio Orsini's agent in Florence opined that Piero intended to do little about their flight to avoid causing trouble.[4]

Piero had been warned of a possible revolution involving his cousins and the arrival of the king in late August, and although an unreliable source had reported in September that he had exiled many leading citizens who were his friends, it is unclear if his inaction towards the cousins was due to respect for them, cowardice or laziness.[5] Alfonso's immediate response was that if Piero had followed his advice in April, this would never have happened.[6] Nevertheless, the damage was done. Leaflets criticising the Medici and asking the king to free them from the tyrant were circulated and there was fear of popular agitation. On the day the French left, an anonymous Florentine wrote to Pagolantonio Soderini in Venice that he hoped Florence would return to its allegiance to France, 'which is our natural custom and especially my family's'. And at exactly the same time the famous Michelangelo suddenly left Florence for Bologna and Venice without saying a word to Piero, his patron and host.[7]

In the face of these signs of disaffection, the caucus remained loyal to Piero in its attempt to secure the regime against the threat of an uprising. The surge of letters recorded in October to commissaries and other officials in towns in the dominion is evidence of the government's heightened concern to protect the frontiers, with Piero still in charge. Since Piero had been closely involved in these towns, as well as in hiring Florence's soldiers, it is not surprising to find officials like the Florentine commissary in Faenza and the podestà of Prato following his orders rather than those of the Otto and advising him to use his friends (*amici*

---

[4] Otto, Delib. 4, fol. 20r, Parenti, *Storia* I, pp. 104–5; Berardino to Virginio, 18 October: 'per potere fare poco offensione'.
[5] Antonio Dovizi in Bologna to Piero, 15 [September, not 'August'] 1494, MAP 16, 410, fol. 422v (re: a report from Florence, 'che voi havevi facto confinare molti di cotesti Primi amici vostri', cf. Otto di Guardia, rep. 98, fol. 65r.
[6] Filippo Valori in Terracina to Piero, 21 October 1494, ed. Can, p. 479 ('se ve ne fussi governato *iuxta* il consiglio e parere suo, non vi sarebbe intervenuto questo'), cf. the same, 16 October, p. 466, cf. p. 188, n. 35 in this volume.
[7] Parenti, *Storia* I, p. 103; anon. to P. A. Soderini in Venice, 11 October 1494, MAP 75, 24, fol. 29r. On Michelangelo, Elam, 'Lorenzo's Sculpture Garden', p. 58, n. 126, cf. Rubin, 'Vasari, Lorenzo', p. 435, n. 24.

vostri) as *capi*.⁸ The choice of Gentile Becchi as the ambassador to France also suggests Piero's influence, and it was he who sent Gentile his instructions and credential letters.⁹ Yet at the same time divisions were appearing within the government after letters from Giovanbattista Ridolfi in Milan reported the French plans for an uprising in Florence and the news that, following Giangaleazzo Sforza's death (due, it was widely believed, to his uncle Lodovico himself), Lodovico was now duke of Milan. Whereas the Otto wanted Piero to yield instead of standing firm, and Ridolfi urged him to be prudent and get together with the citizens – since, he said, to see Piero loved and cherished by them 'would be worth more than a good army' – Piero himself 'spat out' as he left their meeting, 'One man must die for the people' (others said his words were 'Each man for himself').¹⁰ As a result, according to Parenti, he decided to go to the king before he intended to, in order to achieve an agreement with greater safety and reputation to himself.¹¹

Nevertheless, Piero – as we have seen – was already involved in plans to negotiate a peace with France, not only with the banker Lorenzo Spinelli and Philippe de Bresse in France, but in Venice with Pagolantonio Soderini and the Medici's old friend Philippe de Commynes. In mid-October King Alfonso told Filippo Valori how pleased he was with what Piero was doing to coordinate these two plans, 'so one doesn't wreck the other'.¹² And the pope came to agree with him. Whereas he had thought Piero shouldn't try so hard for an agreement with the king of France, by the 20th (after the cousins' flight) he was persuaded of the danger of an uprising in Florence and the need for a truce.¹³ So Piero's apparently sudden decision to meet the king may have been less unpremeditated

---

⁸ The letters are listed in the *Carteggio ... Missive*, II* (Missive 24); Lorenzo di Bernardetto de' Medici in Faenza to Piero, 20 October, MAP 18, 343, and Tommaso Antinori, Podestà di Prato, to Piero, 19 October 1494, MAP 73, 173.

⁹ Piero to Gentile Becchi, 24 October 1494, MAP 18, 214 (dated by Piero's *Ricordi di lettere* (2), p. 140) enclosing 'una lettera mia di credentia in voi al Re di Francia di mia mano', whereas Lorenzo Spinelli, 'che domane parte di qui', 'porterà mie lettere ad V. S. informato di mia intentione'; ed. Can, I, pp. 420–2, 22 October; Parenti, *Storia*, 1, pp. 106–7.

¹⁰ Ibid., p. 113: 'Onde lui, turbato, nello uscire sputò: "Oportet quod unus moriatur pro populo" (altri dissono che sue parole furono: "Ciaschuno facci per sé").'

¹¹ Ibid.: 'forse prima che suo concetto non era'; Ridolfi to Piero, 22 October 1494, ed. Can, pp. 585–6: 'Per dio, Piero, siate prudente et restrigneretevi co' vostri cittadini', etc., reporting that Charles rejected Piero's offer of 300,000 francs, 'che non ha bisogno di denari'.

¹² Filippo Valori in Naples to Piero, 13 October 1494, ed. Can, I, p. 461: 'perché l'una non guasti l'altra'; the same, 21 October, p. 479 (the king welcomed 'questa modo servatosi da voi' with the pope, 'per indurlo a pensare di accordo').

¹³ Guidotti in Rome to Piero, 9, 20 October 1494, MAP 18: 333 and 344.

than it has appeared. According to Parenti, at the time when most Florentines wanted to give in to the king:

> Piero alone shouldered most of the burden of this undertaking, saying that he knew very well what he was doing and they shouldn't fear, for he would always be in time to throw himself into the arms of the king [of France], and they shouldn't allow themselves to be so easily upset, because they would get a better deal doing that [going to the king] than not.[14]

In early September Becchi had encouraged Piero to persuade the king of Spain to divert Charles from the Italian expedition, and 'removing the war, you would remain the arbiter between these two princes, the best thing that could possibly happen to Florence, let alone to your family, and serve all Italy!'[15] If Piero was encouraged by Becchi to imitate his father in acting as arbiter or mediator, he also imitated his father's behaviour in 1479 – as he reminded the Otto – in waiting until he was outside Florence before informing the government of his unauthorised peace mission.[16]

The French Coup De Grâce

Piero had evidently planned his visit to the French king by the time he informed Becchi on 24 October that he would receive his letter (with a letter of credence for Charles VIII) via Spinelli, who had been 'informed of my intention', and that he should await Spinelli in Ferrarese territory. On the same day he told Antonio Dovizi that Alfonso 'doesn't blame us', since the campaign against Charles had been undertaken by everyone without enthusiasm, and he asked him to thank the General of the Servites for his 'wise, truly wise, and loving' letter (Antonio Alabanti had advised Piero two days earlier to employ five hundred armed soldiers to guard himself, as other rulers did, in view of the unprotected and disorderly state in which he found the Medici palace on his last visit).[17] On the following day, he wrote the last four letters recorded in his letter book – credential letters for Spinelli to the king of France, to Bernardo and Antonio Dovizi, and to Antonio Guidotti, 'to entreat King Alfonso'.

---

[14] Parenti, *Storia*, 1, p. 97 (mid-September).
[15] Becchi to Piero, 4 September 1494, ed. Buser, *Beziehungen*, p. 554: 'restate l'arbitro tra questi due principi'.
[16] Lorenzo to the Dieci and the Signoria, 7 December 1479, *Lettere* 4, pp. 257–8, 265–70; Guicciardini, *Storie*, p. 95: 'seguitando adunche ... l'esemplo del padre Lorenzo quando andò a Napoli'.
[17] Piero to Becchi, 24 October 1494 (n. 9 in this chapter), and to Antonio Dovizi, same day, MAP 18, 214r–v: 'la Maestà del Re non ci da colpa, et altri non so'; on Alibanti's letter to Piero on 22 October, Brown, *Florence* (2011), pp. 84–5 and n. 66.

And on the 26th he set off for Empoli – according to Parenti, after 'the new [and more hostile] Signoria had been drawn in the *palace*'.[18]

Piero's banker Filippo da Gagliano provides the most vivid account of Piero's movements that day in a letter to Niccolò Michelozzi, who was in his villa at Quinto (five Roman miles from Florence). In the morning, he wrote, he happened to encounter Piero in the Duomo, who summoned him and asked him 'about that business' (buying the king off with money, according to Spinelli's plan?). After lunch, when Filippo set about organising it, he found Piero had ridden off at once, 'almost alone', with the *brigata* following behind, one by one; he had ordered the chests to be sent on and had left without conferring with a soul, 'least of all with any of the leading citizens'. The friends were mostly optimistic, some thinking it was planned and that Spinelli was involved: 'however it is, pray God it ends well!'[19]

The friends who followed him, one by one, included his cousin Lorenzo Tornabuoni, Jacopo Gianfigliazzi and Giannozzo Pucci, and a secretary, probably Antonio Dovizi. Once in Empoli, Piero wrote to the elders with a covering autograph letter to ser Piero Dovizi, who as usual had been left to hold the fort at home. Explaining that he thought it would be arrogant of him to write to the Signoria, Piero asked Dovizi to present the letter to 'those citizens' (presumably the Otto di Pratica) and then report to him what happened, enclosing a cipher if necessary. He also asked Dovizi to comfort his family, especially Alfonsina – the first mention of his wife for a long time – and guiltless little Lorenzo; so far, he was well and optimistic, '*Sed Tiphis in bonaccia fata*': 'Pray God for me and *la Cice* [his daughter]'. And on finding his brother-in-law Franceschetto in a disordered state when he reached Pisa the next day, he 'removed' him to Florence, urging Dovizi to make as much fuss of him as possible in order to prevent him returning to Pisa too quickly.[20]

---

[18] *Ricordi di lettere* (2), p. 140; Parenti, *Storia* I, 111. The new Signoria was now headed by Francesco dello Scarfa in the place of Piero's friend Francesco Gherardi, Cambi, *Istorie*, pp. 88–9.

[19] Gagliano in Florence to Michelozzi in his villa a Quinto, 26 October 1494, GC 29, 69, fol. 58: 'quella faccenda', 'È preso da Piero e che non è conferito con anima nata, maxime di questi principali ... con qualche intelligienza da la banda di là e qualchuno dicie essere questa praticha dello Spinello.'

[20] Piero in Empoli to Dovizi, 26 October 1494, MAP 72, 79, autogr., ed. Can, pp. 588–9 (but omitting the reference to Tiphys and transcribing 'la Cice' as 'la Citta'); the same, from Pisa, 27 October, MAP 72, 80, fol. 94r–v, secr. copy, ibid., pp. 589–90. The reference to Tiphys, fearless steersman of the Argos, suggests Piero may have seen himself as Tiphys, praying for calm seas as he boldly set out on his equally dangerous mission, Seneca, *Medea*, lines 301–49, cf. Val. Flaccus, *Argonautica*, 5, 102, etc.

In his letter to the Otto, Piero justified his sudden departure as the best way to achieve peace for his patria with the least hindrance and danger to everyone, himself included, since offering himself in person to the king of France would help to quell the king's anger and hatred towards the city and its territory for adhering to its (treaty) obligations, and he, as the person responsible, would take the punishment, not the republic. Although his family had already done something similar (referring to his father's solo peace mission to Naples in 1479), he was more obliged to suffer than his predecessors, since he had been more honoured, undeservedly, than they had been – and so on, with rising emotion, until he asked them, on account of the trust and affection they owed 'to the bones of our Lorenzo, my father, and the love you have kept for me', to pray God for him, his brothers and his children, whom he commended to them in case he didn't return.[21]

The following day, 27 October, he left Empoli – not for 'Piacenza or beyond' (to find the king), as he wrote to the Otto, but for Pisa, where he arrived in the evening, 'absolutely worn out, what with the journey, my thoughts, ceaseless rain and my bad bed the previous night'.[22] The next day he withdrew money from his personal account in the Medici Bank to equip himself 'for the visit to the king of France': sixteen pairs of heraldic stockings (*a divisa*) and various fabrics and cloths (his other clothes and provisions he had asked to be sent on from Florence).[23] In his letter of the 27th he gave Dovizi the embarrassing task of informing Marino Tomacelli what he had done without consulting his principal ally and supporter, King Alfonso, for reasons he explained in another rhetorical outpouring of self-pity:

Abandoned by all the Florentine citizens, my friends and enemies, and finding that my reputation, my money and my credit are no longer sufficient to sustain the war I freely accepted on my home ground, I have taken the decision – since I am unable to serve his Majesty King Alfonso through strength (which is now lacking) – to serve him at least with desperation by putting myself in the power of the king of France, vulnerable, with no standing, or hope, or any good whatsoever

---

[21] Piero in Empoli to [the Otto di Pratica, 'Magnificis Patribus', not the Signoria, as in Can, I, pp. 589–90], 26 October 1494, MAP 137, 578, fol. 586r–v: 'alle ossa del vostro Lorenzo, mio padre, et lo amore havete conservato inverso di me' (588). Despite ending 'Piero de' Medici manu propria', the letter and signature are in his secretary's hand.

[22] Piero in Pisa to ser Piero, 27 October, Can, p. 289.

[23] Parenti, *Storia* I, p. 111; GC, ms 5, fol. 350 (Piero's 'conto proprio', paid 8 August 1495): 110 lire piccoli for 'paia xvi di chalzze a ddivisa date nella sua andata al re di Francia', also fl. 110 and fl. 90 o/o, 'per più panni e drappi avuti ... per detto Piero in la sua andata al re di Francia', and fl. 21 'per tanti ... avere speso a Pietrasanta per bisogna di detto Piero'.

except for giving my life, after my other possessions, to the person to whom I have considered myself, and will consider as long as I live, most indebted.[24]

After apologising for not explaining his idea before leaving, since he had never imagined losing faith in 'so many friends and in a city like Florence', he added – with a flash of insight into his difficult situation – that perhaps he would be more useful serving the French king in a lowly position 'than in the top position of state that is so weak in Florence'.[25]

This, of course, was the problem that Piero's current situation illustrated so well, his unconstitutional status as Florence's unofficial *capo*. The prosecution of the war needed money and, as Parenti explains in his *History*, the expulsion of the Florentine bankers in Lyon had led to a restriction in the flow of money in Florence's money markets, which in turn led to difficulty funding the increasing costs of the war through the councils. Parenti presents this as the issue that divided the city, after 'a good citizen and lover of the public' dared to raise the question of whether a grant of 50,000 or 100,000 ducats would be enough to resist the king of France, winning wide support for his bravery in speaking out in favour of his city and against the present regime, which 'in the face of imminent ruin shrugged their shoulders and let themselves be led by a child'.[26] By contrast, Luca Landucci, describing how Piero 'was a bit blamed' when he sent Lorenzo Tornabuoni back to Florence to report his surrender to the king, nevertheless excused him because 'he did it as a young man and perhaps with a good result, since he remained a friend of the king's, praise God'.[27]

Predictably, Piero fluctuated between confidence and fear. Reaching Pietrasanta on the evening of the 28th, he immediately wrote to Pisa, and the following day to Dovizi in Florence, describing the dire situation he found there, which initially fired him with enthusiasm to strengthen its resistance. Specifying precisely how many men and exactly what types of weapons were needed for the town's defence, he also said the men-at-arms needed disciplining with a firm leader after he left; Barga, too,

---

[24] Letter of 27 October, Can, p. 589: 'abandonato da tutt' i cittadini fiorentini, amici et nimici miei ... non potendo servire con le forze (le quali *iam defecerunt*) alla Maestà del signor Re Alfonso, servirgli almanco con la desperazione'.

[25] The same, ed. Can, p. 590: 'forse li sarò più utile servitore in vile conditione appresso Re di Francia che nel primo luogo dello stato, che è sì debole a Firenze'. According to Nardi (*Istorie* I, p. 27), the French called Piero 'il gran Lombardo, per non avere egli in Fiorenza alcuno legitimo titolo di signoria', 'Lombardo' being what they called all Italians at that time.

[26] Parenti, *Storia* I, pp. 110, 111, describing the speech of Lorenzo Lenzi, 'come buono cittadino e amatore del publico'.

[27] Landucci, *Diario*, p. 71: 'Piero fu un poco biasimato. E' fece come giovanetto, e forse a buon fine, poiche si restò amico del Re, a lalde di Dio.'

needed arms – fifty rifles, four mortars and ten arquebuses, so 'for the love of God ... ensure that supplies arrive'.[28] His active response suggests that he was preparing for peace negotiations through strength, not weakness. But at the same time he was fearful about reaching the king without a safe conduct, since the French were besieging the fortress of Castelnuovo on the inland road, midway between Florence's maritime fortresses of Sarzana and Pietrasanta. Both fortresses would be lost without further supplies, so would Pisa and also Barga, lying south of Castelnuovo on the road the French would take. Because of the danger, Piero was urged by the Otto to return to Pisa since he lacked a safe conduct, and the following day, the 30th, he was ordered to do so 'absolutely at once, without a moment's delay', while they tried to raise men and money.[29]

But before Piero would have received these orders from the Otto, the situation changed again, and with it, Piero's mood. For it was also on 30 October that the king's herald arrived in Pietrasanta asking for a safe conduct for Briçonnet, the cardinal of San Malo, and two other French lords to come ahead to receive Piero on behalf of the king. Overjoyed (and relieved) by this honour, Piero wanted Dovizi to rejoice with him and pass on the news to the Otto, Alfonsina and his brothers Giovanni and Giuliano.[30] He was even happier to be told by San Malo that the king was coming to Pisa and then to Florence in four or five days, and he hastened to write to Dovizi to ensure that 'those wise citizens', in their prudence, made the necessary preparations in Florence and Pisa to honour so great a king.[31] So when Dovizi's brother Bernardo returned to Florence from the Romagna that same day, the 30th, he found Florence 'so changed and so different from how I left it, I don't know where I am', upset for himself, and even more for Ferrandino, because 'this city is completely French'.[32] The regime responded by electing citizens to discuss the problem of raising 30,000 ducats to honour the

---

[28] Piero in Pietrasanta to Dovizi, 29 October 1494, MAP 72, 81, fol. 95r–v, ed. Can, pp. 591–2: 'Fate per l'amore di Dio et del honore di cotesta [nostra Can] Città et anche per *la sicurtà mia* ci si provegga' (592), 'Non ci è *molto che mangiare ma ce ne* per tanto che crederrei havere tempo a fare *li patti* honorevolmente' (om. Can; decoded).

[29] Otto di Pratica to Piero in Pietrasanta, 29 and 30 October 1494, Otto, Missive 25, fols. 25r–v ('ti ricordiamo e confortiamo', 33r–v ('subito subito et sanza interporre una minima dilatione, et così ti confortiamo ad fare. Et quando il confortare non basti, te lo comandiamo').

[30] Piero in Pietrasanta to Dovizi, 30 October 1494 at 19 hours, MAP 72, 82, 'Cito, cito, cito', ed. Can, p. 593.

[31] The same, 30 October 1494 (in the evening), MAP 72, 83, ed. Can, p. 592; Otto Missive 25, fol. 41v–42r (1 November).

[32] Bernardo Dovizi in Florence to the duke of Calabria, 31 October 1494, ed. Moncallero, I, p. 235: 'franzese tucta'.

king and appointing eight ambassadors (including Piero) to receive Charles in Sarzana.[33] Then letters were despatched to all the captains and commissaries in the dominion, initially to those on the front line in Castrocaro and the Mugello, where the danger of the new situation was reflected in the Otto's note of caution – which they hoped would prove unnecessary in view of the king's arrival, 'as a friend', in Florence in a few days' time.[34]

But the city's 'great happiness' quickly turned to tears when Tornabuoni returned with news of Piero's meeting with Charles on 31 October. Far from it being a meeting of monarchs on a Field of the Cloth of Gold to cement a friendship, the meeting at St Stefano (near Sarzana) turned out to be a parley between conqueror and suppliant. For all his high hopes and fine apparel, Piero was unexpectedly asked to cede possession of the fortresses of Pisa, Livorno, Pietrasanta and Sarzanello to Charles, as well as 200,000 ducats, as security for the king's visit to Florence. Despite resistance from Pietrasanta, Piero finally agreed to cede the castles – all of them proudly acquired and refortified at great public expense in the course of the fifteenth century – which were handed over to the king 'without any mandate from Florence or countersign, such was the authority attributed to Piero de Medici'.[35] After this, the end came quickly.

The Fall of Piero and the Medici Regime

Already alienated by Piero's high-handed behaviour and by the order to let their houses be requisitioned by the French, the Florentines began to express open hostility to Piero and his ministers.[36] On the evening of 4 November, at an 'emergency *pratica*' of all the elected officials together with former Gonfaloniers of Justice, it was decided to send new

---

[33] Parenti, *Storia* I, p. 114; ASF, Signori, Leg. e Comm. Elez. Istruz. Lett. 21, fol. 133r–v (2 November 1494), despatching the ambassadors Alamanni, Bonsi, Niccolini, Franc. Valori, Braccio Martelli, Giuliano Salviati, Piero Soderini, 'simul cum Petro Medici' (misinterpreted by Nardi I, pp. 26–7) with two letters of credence, one including Piero, the other 'senza la persona di Piero', to be used as they thought best. Cf. Otto Missive 25, fols. 41v–42r, 43r–v.

[34] Ibid., fols 43v–54r (1–5 November 1494). On the 5th, the Otto informed their 'orators and commissaries' of the decision to send 'nuovi inbasciadori' to the king: fra Girolamo (Savonarola), with Tanai de' Nerli, Pandolfo Rucellai, Piero di Gino Capponi and Giovanni Cavalcanti (55r–v).

[35] Parenti, *Storia* I, p. 114. On the agreement on 31 October, Delaborde, *L'expédition*, pp. 436–7, Labande-Mailfert, *Charles VIII*, p. 288. The penultimate letter in Missive 25 (to Filippo dell'Antella, commissary of Castrocaro, 8 November, fol. 62v) commends his decision 'del non andare in campo franzese se tu non hai la sicurtà'.

[36] Parenti, *Storia* I, pp. 116–17, Landucci, *Diario*, p. 72.

ambassadors to the French king, to include fra Girolamo Savonarola. So the following day the five new ambassadors set off on the heels of the citizens elected as ambassadors only three days earlier.[37] There could not have been a more symbolic transfer of power from the old to the new order. With the exception of the two commissaries who were to join them as a link between the two regimes (Pierfilippo Pandolfini and Piero Guicciardini), the new ambassadors – 'that is, fra Girolamo, Tanai de' Nerli, Pandolfo Rucellai, Piero Capponi and Giovanni Cavalcanti' – were all committed republicans and supporters of the friar. Moreover, in the course of the meeting on the 4th, some of the speakers had dared to speak out against Piero and the old regime. They included not only the two young men who later prevented Piero from entering the palace – Luca Corsini and Jacopo de' Nerli, both trembling and tongue-tied from nervousness – but also the valiant patriot Piero Capponi. In a long speech, Capponi defined Piero's mistakes, 'as an inexperienced youth', as failing to reconcile Lodovico and King Alfonso, failing to consult with the citizens when Charles VIII arrived in Italy, and – worst of all – 'throwing himself like a broken tool into the hands of the king' and giving away the best part of the state. It was he who suggested sending Savonarola as one of six new ambassadors to the king in Pisa, and if they met Piero en route, they were not to speak to him or tell him anything.[38]

So when Piero reentered Florence 'with many horses' four days later, on 8 November, he found himself greeted at the gate with fireworks and shouts of 'Palle' by only a few supporters. Once he reached the Medici palace, where his brothers and one or two close relatives were awaiting him, he tossed some confetti to the crowd of lowly workers and people below, followed by some bread and alms to keep them 'well disposed'. Taken aback by his cool reception, Piero decided to take measures to protect himself.[39] On Sunday the 9th, accompanied by his usual bodyguard of about twenty men and a few 'little soldiers', he attended mass as usual in the Duomo and then went to the government palace, where the Signoria were having lunch. Only two priors came to the head of the stairs to tell him not to worry, he should go home to lunch and

---

[37] n. 34 in this chapter; Parenti, *Storia* I, 117–18; Landucci, *Diario*, 72–3 (misnaming Piero Capponi as Piero Soderini), cf. Najemy, *A History*, p. 378.

[38] Cerretani, *Storia fiorentina*, pp. 197, 198–9 (Piero Capponi):'gitato come ferro rotto nelle mani del re'. According to Parenti (*Storia* I, p. 118), the election of new ambassadors followed the 'ordine di città libera'. Cf. Luigi Guicciardini's incomplete and untitled account of this meeting, BNF. Magl. XXV, 636, fols. 15r–v.

[39] Parenti, *Storia* I, pp. 121–2 (Piero secretly sent arms 'al giardino suo di San Marco' and asked Paolo Orsini to come to Florence with his gente d'arme), cf. Cerretani, *Storia fiorentina*, p. 205, Landucci, *Diario*, pp. 73–6, and Luigi Guicciardini, MS, fol. 15v.

return later. He did so, accompanied by more armed men and some relations and supporters. By now it was known that Paolo Orsini had arrived with his men-at-arms at the city gates, so the Signoria closed the raised palace doors giving on to the piazza, which were guarded by the two young men who had criticised Piero a few days earlier, Jacopo de' Nerli and Luca Corsini. After one of his bodyguards was refused entry, Piero himself knocked on the door and shouted, 'Open!', to which Jacopo replied that if he wanted to enter, he must do so alone by the little door. 'To this, Piero said nothing but bit his finger as a sign of vendetta and retreated.' Accounts differ over what happened next. Did he turn tail because of stones hurled down from the palace and its call to arms of 'popolo, popolo', or was it the derision of the unarmed people and children in the square that unmanned him, by telling him to 'get the hell out' (*andar con Dio*) and throwing stones at him?[40] Both probably played a part, but Jacopo Nardi's account of the impact on Piero of the people's derision is convincing, in view of what we know about his nature:

So although Piero was by nature feisty and bold, he suddenly – I don't know how it happened – became so frightened ... that these shouts from a few disarmed men made him more afraid than their words, their faces, their gestures and the pointed hoods of their cloaks, and it was this, more than anything else, that made him leave the piazza.[41]

He describes a familiar trait in Piero: boldness followed by retreat. The same bystanders then disarmed the police official, the Bargello, who had come to help Piero, and this emboldened the Signoria to ring the great bell that called the people to arms. Although the government portrayed the sequence of events as the principled overthrow of Piero by the citizens and the nobility, then supported by the people, the interaction between Piero and the ordinary bystanders in the square must also have played its part.[42] To a man used to deference and loved as a child by the populace for his sayings and good looks, the ridicule and hostility of these same people must have been even more upsetting than the growing alienation of his peers.

---

[40] Cerretani, *Storia fiorentina*, pp. 205–6: 'non respose Piero ma morsesi il dito in segno di vendecta' (206); Luigi Guicciardini, MS, fol. 16r: 'con forse 20 staffieri che era la sua solita guardia, si morse el dito et tirossi adrieto', adding 'et in un subito sentì gittare sazi [= sassi] dalle finestre del palazo et gridare' [incompl.].

[41] Nardi, *Istorie* I, p. 33, discussed by Brown, 'Between the Palace and the Piazza', p. 41.

[42] Ibid., p. 42 (the Signoria to the marquis of Mantua) and Legazioni e Commissarie, 22, fol. 26r (the same to Alessandro Braccesi), 9 November 1494: 'tucta la cittadinanza e nobilità della terra, conseguito di tucto il popolo, si opposono'.

By the time Piero reached the safety of his home in Via Larga, most citizens had flooded to the Piazza della Signoria, leaving few to support him in his palace – especially after the government had issued a bann that no one was to give him or his family any help. So sending Alfonsina and her mother to the convent of S. Lucia in Via San Gallo, Piero quickly left his palace on horseback and made for the San Gallo Gate.[43] According to the prior of San Lorenzo, Lorenzo Guiducci, it was only after one of Piero's supporters threatened to kill the banner bearer of the *gonfalone* Drago, crying 'Popolo', that a price was placed on the heads of Piero and Cardinal Giovanni – 5000 florins for their capture and 2000 florins for killing them – although no bounties were recorded officially until 20 November, and they were then revoked five days later (according to the terms of Florence's peace treaty with Charles VIII that instead exiled him one hundred miles from Florence and its 'imperium').[44] Cardinal Giovanni experienced more violence than Piero when sent by his brother to pacify the Signoria. He was on his way to the government palace on foot, preceded by the steward of his household, Andrea Cambini, when Cambini was attacked and left for dead in the piazza; a Tornabuoni was also badly wounded (he escaped only by sheltering in Orsanmichele), and the son-in-law of Antonio Dini was wounded, too, but the only fatality (according to Guiducci) was someone wearing Piero's device on his leg. Faced with this violence, Giovanni rapidly made for home; then, disguising himself as a Franciscan friar, escaped like Piero through the San Gallo Gate, which was still being held open by their brother Giuliano with the help of Paolo Orsini and his men-at-arms.[45]

This suggests that Piero and his brothers were not exiled and condemned as tyrants because of any bloodshed they caused on 9 November, but rather because Piero's behaviour had alienated public opinion. Once

---

[43] Parenti, *Storia* I, p. 125 (cf. Cerretani, *Storia*, p. 208 (the two women were taken there by order of the Signoria, after being stripped of their jewels). On the bann, Signori Delib. ord. aut. 96, fols. 86v–87r (9 November 1494), also ordering Piero to appear before them within an a hour and revoking his cousins' decree of exile; cf. Guiducci, *Diario*, pp. 73–4, Pitti, *Istoria*, pp. 50–1, Landucci, *Diario*, pp. 74–5.

[44] Guiducci, *Diario*, p. 74, citing on 76–8 the terms 'in volgare, acciò che ognuno gli intenda'; Parenti, *Storia* I, p. 125; Signori Delib. ord. aut. 96, fol. 96v, 20 November 1494). On 15 October 1495 (after Alfonsina and her children's flight from Florence) a fl. 4000 bounty was offered for Piero, dead or alive (later extended to his heirs), and on 26 November fl. 2000 for Giuliano, Provvisioni 186, fols.120r–121r, 142r–v. Cf. pp. 233, n. 7 and 239, n. 32 in this volume.

[45] Parenti, *Storia* I, p. 124; Guiducci, *Diario*, p. 74. Giovanni (with Giuliano) was en route for Rome on 22 October when urged back to Florence; arriving on the 27th, he vainly advised Piero not to meet the French king, Moncallero, *Il Cardinale*, pp. 132–3, Picotti, pp. 569–70, Parenti, pp. 110, 111; Landucci, *Diario*, p. 75 (who was moved to see the young Giovanni 'alle sue finestre colle mani giunte ginocchioni').

the popular tide was seen to flow towards the public piazza (which had been secured by Francesco Valori, Piero Vettori and Bernardo Rucellai, all former supporters of Piero), the Medici palace was quickly left high and dry, public opinion speaking more loudly than force. It is true that Piero had vainly attempted to enter the public palace with his armed retinue, but when he was eventually declared a rebel on 20 November, it was for his disobedience (in failing to obey the Signoria's order on 9 November to appear before them). Of more immediate concern to the government was confiscating the Medici's and their intimates' possessions (*omnes res et masseritiae*) on 10 November and dismantling their regime the next day, when the Otto di Pratica, the Seventy and the Cento were all abolished. The regime's unpopular legislative and the financial officials, ser Giovanni Guidi and Antonio Dini, were executed; Salvalaglio, one of Piero's special bodyguards, was quickly declared a rebel; the Dovizi fled (bounties of 1000 and 500 florins were offered for handing in ser Piero and Bernardo unharmed, ser Piero going to Venice, where he remained a staunch supporter of the exiled Medici); and most of the chancery secretaries were sacked.[46]

What Piero had done was unforgivable, whatever way we look at it. As a citizen, he went to meet the king of France and surrendered to him four of Florence's major castles without a mandate and without legislative consent. As an ally of the king of Naples and the pope, he had broken their trust and acted without consulting them. He may have seen his visit to the king as a prelude to the truce he had been negotiating – as well as a way (according to Parenti) of escaping from Lodovico Sforza's control – only to be taken unawares by the king's sudden demand for Florence's castles.[47] He may also have thought that gifts and his elegant apparel would be enough to persuade the king to favour him, or even that he was engaged in a sort of gift exchange, undertaken for the honour of receiving him. Bernardo Dovizi tried to assuage Ferrandino by explaining that the cruelty and the damage done by the French made everyone discontented with Piero, his patron, who was alone in fighting for Alfonso, and because of this he couldn't get the citizens to pay for the war out of their own pockets – 'to take the necessary measures to face up boldly to the French fury' – forcing him, out of despair, to attempt some kind of a settlement

---

[46] Signori Delib. ord. aut. 96, fols. 87r, 88v, 96r–v and 102r–v (90r on Salvalaglio, 96v on the Dovizi, 10–12, 20 November, 2 December 1494). On the fate of their possessions, Fusco and Corti, *Lorenzo de' Medici*, pp. 159–77 and 353–64 (Append. II, iii); on the dismissals, also Brown, *Scala*, p. 117, and in general, Parenti, *Storia* I, pp. 125–32.

[47] Parenti, *Storia* I, p. 116: 'el non volere allo arbitrio del signor Lodovico rimettersi'.

with the king, 'for which we should feel great compassion for him'.[48] But although he was condemned by the government as a tyrant who had 'tried to invade and suppress our liberty', which became the republicans' rallying cry throughout Piero's years of exile,[49] Piero himself was right to feel aggrieved by this label. His failure, as Parenti put it, was to have 'lost through his rashness the regime that had lasted for sixty years since the time of his great-grandfather [Cosimo]', freeing the city 'more thanks to God than to men'.[50]

---

[48] Bernardo Dovizi to the duke of Calabria, 31 October 1494, pp. 235–6; Moncallero, *Il Cardinale*, pp. 129–30: 'gran conpassione ad lui'.

[49] E.g. the Signoria's letters cited in n. 42 in this chapter, also the law of 15 October 1495, Provv. 185, fol. 120r (referring to Piero's 'tirannico appetito' and many deeds 'contro lo stato et libertà di questa vostra città vostra'); Brown, *Florence* (2011), p. 239 (on the giant female figure of 'Libertas' that welcomed Charles VIII to Florence). On Piero as a tyrant, p. 243, and Chapter 20 in this volume.

[50] Parenti, *Storia* I, p. 125: 'più per opera di Iddio che delli uomini'.

Part IV

Piero in Exile

16   Perambulating Italy, 1494–1497

'The great rebel', as Machiavelli now called Piero, was a fugitive for the nine years between his escape from Florence on 9 November 1494 to his death by drowning on 28 December 1503. It was a time of great turbulence. The two French expeditions to claim the kingdom of Naples in 1494 and 1499 not only exiled the Medici from Florence and the Aragonese from Naples, but also destabilised the whole of Italy as they came and went. As the Florentines predicted, Piero 'threw himself' wherever Florence had enemies, and these enemies in turn used the Medici as 'instruments and, as they say, a lure', in order to foment trouble in the city and uprisings in its territory.[1] Like a matador who wears out his victim by endless prodding from different flanks, Piero constantly threatened Florence as he crossed and recrossed Italy – moving from Venice to Pitigliano, Bolsena and Narni to Rome; back to Venice, then to Milan and Pisa, before returning to Rome; to Perugia, Viterbo and Bracciano, Naples and back to Rome. His relatively few surviving letters from this period initially reflect shock and self-pity for what had happened to him, then anger and alienation. More revealing of his state of mind are the poems he wrote during his exile. The two opening poems allude more obviously to his grief, his face 'washed with tears' as he thinks 'of what I am and what I was' and his one hope, if not allowed to return, of being buried in Florence with his father, 'who once made the city so glorious and eminent'. It is the third poem, 'Cruel, unhappy day and full of grief', that shows the extent of his bitterness in using the unexpected images of the two exiles Thyestes and Medea (the father who ate his children and the mother who slaughtered hers) to depict the depths to which they sank and the fate of their unhappy children – perhaps with his own children in mind. Instead of returning to Florence, he died far away in southern Italy, and all 'the great rebel' achieved, according to Machiavelli, was 'the burial of five citizens', his

---

[1] Machiavelli, *Decennali*, I, p. 126, l. 152: 'el vostro gran rebel'; p. 278, n. 37 in this volume, and Guicciardini, *Dialogo del Reggimento*, p. 164, tr. p. 160.

most loyal supporters in the city, who were executed after his failed attempt to return to Florence in 1497.[2] These years offer a sad but revealing coda to his early years in power.

In Venice and Central Italy, 1494–1495

The Medici brothers initially escaped to their villa in Careggi and thence over the Apennines to Bologna, where they hoped to be protected by Giovanni Bentivoglio, despite his prevarication over his *condotta*. Clothes were foremost in Piero's mind when he asked the government to send him some linen and woollen garments (which he was allowed, in order to 'quieten him down'). According to Parenti, he also wrote to the Signoria apologising for what he had done, believing he had been abandoned by his friends; all he wanted was for the people to enjoy liberty, as he had declared when sending his brother, Cardinal Giovanni, to pacify the crowds, so he was particularly upset to be called a tyrant, since he had never thought of such a thing; but even if he was rejected, at least his brothers should be respected by them.[3]

Since Bentivoglio was still employed by Milan, he was less welcoming than Piero had hoped. Fearing he might be imprisoned if he remained in Bologna, Piero left for Venice, where – according to the Milanese envoy there, Taddeo Vicemercato – he arrived with thirty to forty people on 17 November. He was put up by one of the grand banking families in Venice, the Lippomani, and a day later he was visited there by Commynes and by an envoy with royal letters telling him belatedly to remain in Bologna – both King Charles and Lodovico being very vexed to hear what had happened.[4] Commynes, however, told Piero not to lose heart, and in his memoirs he enlarged on Vicemercato's report by saying that he wanted to help Piero (in the absence of instructions to the contrary) and that he attributed his flight to fear of the people, not to fear of the king, for although the Venetians were afraid of displeasing the king, they would put Piero up and treat him honourably. Comforting him

---

[2] On the poems in Laur. 41, 38, fol. 68r–v, pp. 109–10 in this volume (no. 1 is ed. Pieraccini, *Stirpe*, 1, p. 169, no. 2 is ed. and tr. Roscoe, *Life*, 1, pp. 274–5: 'che già ti [la patria] fè sì gloriosa et degna'; no. 3, 'Crudo, funesto giorno et di duol pieno', is on fol. 68v.

[3] Parenti, *Storia* I, pp. 130 ('concessonsili per quietarlo'), 132 ('sopratutto li dolea tiranno essere chiamato, imperò che mai pensò tal cosa').

[4] On Piero's visit to Giovanni Bentivoglio (who bought the Medici's sculpture garden at auction a year later), Elam, 'Lorenzo's Sculpture Garden', pp. 51–2; Taddeo Vicomercato to Lodovico Sforza, 18 November 1494, tr. Lettenhove, *Lettres*, 2, p. 146. On Vicomercato (or Vimercato), ivi, 118–21, 137–8; on the Lippomani, 'gentili uomini, antiqui amici insino di Cosimo', Vettori, 'Vita di Lorenzo', *Scritti storici*, pp. 262–3; Goldthwaite, *Economy*, pp. 450, 181.

again 'to the best of my ability' when listening to his long account of his travails, Commynes nevertheless thought Piero was 'not a man to regain his force'.[5]

A week later, Piero wrote from Venice to his cousins Lorenzo and Giovanni di Pierfrancesco in Florence, who by a total reversal of fortune found themselves (with Cosimo Rucellai) released from their exile on the very same day that Piero fled the city, Giovanni arriving in Florence on 14 November to popular acclaim. Piero's letter spoke bitterly of this 'persecution' of his person and estate: if his cousins felt no compassion for him, all he asked of them was justice and to be allowed to see his wife and poor children – and, if nothing else, at least to be able to enjoy 'the dowry', something that was always permitted, he said, even to the lowest and worst of scoundrels. If his cousins wanted him to die of hunger, they shouldn't want his brothers and little babies to suffer, and if their shared blood and the exile of their own kith and kin left them unmoved, then – in a crescendo of self-pity – God and his justice should move them. He ended gnomically by quoting Terence, that 'there is change in all things'.[6]

On 25 November Florence's treaty with Charles VIII rescinded Piero's condemnation as a rebel and the confiscation of his possessions, enabling him to return to Florence if the people decreed it, but until then he and his brothers had to stay a hundred miles from Florentine territory and his wife and family had to reside in the Medici palace in Florence.[7] Two days later Piero visited the Venetian government, encountering Taddeo Vicomercato on the steps of the Doge's Palace. From their conversation in the antechamber, we can reconstruct Piero's movements and state of mind at this time. Charles VIII had apparently invited Piero to return to Florence with an armed escort (according to Parenti, the king and his advisers had been bribed in Florence by 'some beautiful and upstanding women', Piero's wife Alfonsina and his Tornabuoni relations).[8] To Vicomercato,

---

[5] Lettenhove, ivi, cf. p. 145, quoting Commynes, *Mémoires*, 2, p. 360, 'il me sembla bien. qu'il n'estoit point homme pour respondre'.
[6] Signori Delib. ord. aut. 96, fol. 87r (9 November 1494); Parenti, *Storia* I, pp. 130, 132; Piero to his cousins in Florence, 24 November 1494, ed. Kennedy, 'Some unpublished letters', p. 74, citing Terence, (*Eun.* 2.2): 'omnium rerum vicissitudo est'.
[7] Capitoli, ed. G. Capponi, *ASI* 1 (1842), pp. 362–75 (doc. 3) at 372–4: §17 'ex nunc ita revocant', §18–19, §20, pp. 372–4; confirmed on 2 December, Signori, Delib. ord. aut. 96, fol. 102v; cf. Parenti, *Storia* I, pp. 143, 155–6. On 28 December five syndics were appointed to recover Medici property, Merisalo, *Collezioni Medicee*, cf. Brown, *Florence* (2011), pp. 132–3 and n. 60.
[8] Parenti, *Storia*, i, pp. 135–40 at 139, cf. Tomas, *Medici Women*, p. 107; on the role of Philippe de Bresse, Labande Mailfert, *Charles VIII*, p. 295, Guicciardini, *Storia d'Italia*, I, 16.

however, Piero said that he had no intention of leaving Venetian territory until the 150 promised crossbowmen had arrived and he had received a safe conduct; he sought only to live in peace and tranquillity in his native city with his son and his wife and the small inheritance left to him by his father. During the time of prosperity, he had never been anything other than a good citizen and lover of his country, of liberty and the common good, for the preservation and defence of which he had been reduced to his present condition; he had never wanted 'supereminence' over other citizens and even less now, when his condition could only arouse compassion and pity in those who understood it.[9] After these 'formal words', Piero went on to bewail his situation (again), explaining to Vicomercato, 'almost in tears', that he had written to inform Lodovico of his visit to Venice and ask for money 'to clothe himself and pay his expenses', which Lodovico had refused to provide, although he did invite him to visit (by April it seems he was keen to support Piero as a means of constraining Charles VIII).[10]

Piero rapidly changed on receiving Lodovico's 'brusque and acerbic' reply. Responding in equal measure, he blamed him for his exile from Florence and told him that, since his life was all that was left to him, he did not intend to place it in Lodovico's hands. Money was what he needed, and he would have gone begging but for the hospitality of these Venetian nobles. This all-too-familiar Piero – quickly moved to tears for lack of suitable clothing (as in 1485) and as quickly moved to anger – defiantly insisted on his patriotism as a good citizen and as a republican 'lover of liberty and the common good', attributing his exile to outside events, especially Lodovico Sforza's invitation to the French to invade Italy, not to himself.

Between the League and Florence

The interest of the confused years of Piero's perambulations lies in his restless search for safe havens in an Italy under pressure from the French, which he combined with unremitting attempts to return to a hostile but unstable Florence. Because the king wanted Piero and the Orsini with him as he advanced on Rome in late 1494, Piero left Venice for Città di Castello in Umbria accompanied by a French envoy. From Città di Castello, Piero sent the Signoria a letter asking if Alfonsina could join him, but whose real purpose, Parenti surmised, was to alert his friends

---

[9] Vicomerato to Lodovico Sforza, 27 November 1494, ed. Buser, *Bezierhungen*, pp. 557–9, at 558.
[10] Ibid., pp. 557, 558 ('cum parole quasi lacrimevole [sic]'; Parenti, *Storia* I, pp. 205–6.

(emboldened by Savonarola's desire for amnesty) to his whereabouts.[11] So Florence was understandably worried about Charles's return through Tuscany in the summer of 1495, after conquering Naples. Five extra citizens were appointed to guard the territory and the city, and suspected Francophiles and Medici partisans were sent away to prevent them making contact with the French or with Piero. Fourteen citizens were appointed to spy on the royal court and two commissaries were appointed to accompany the king once he entered Tuscany, to prevent any trouble with Piero's partisans; the king would meet Savonarola at Poggibonsi and return to France via Pisa without reentering Florence.[12]

The discovery in May of a cache of arms to provoke an uprising when the king returned to Florence shows the city's fears were well founded, especially as one of the two men involved, Lamberto dell' Antella (with his brother, the priest Alessandro) was implicated more seriously with Piero two years later.[13] At this fraught moment of heightened security, a lackey of Piero's called 'il Pentolino' was caught in San Casciano carrying a letter from Piero (who was by now in Pitigliano, the home of Niccolò Orsini) to a leading Florentine citizen, Piero Corsini. Once in Florence, Pentolino was tortured and an authenticated copy of Piero's letter was sent to the French king (the original and the copy are both carefully preserved in the Florentine archives today).[14]

Piero Corsini had been a close friend of Lorenzo's, as the letter says, working beside Piero in 1490 to clear Lorenzo's name in Lucca. So in appealing to Corsini's great humanity and compassion for the sons of his dearest old friend, Piero was confident of his support.[15] He wanted Corsini to know that he, Piero, was coming to Florence with the king of France and the help of some friends, and was writing to ensure that his opponents – who included two of Corsini's relations – would not cause

---

[11] Piero to Passerini in Bolsena, ASF Acq. e Doni 142, ins. 8, 15 May 1495 (autogr), a rare letter expressing fear of showing himself; Parenti, *Storia* I, p. 163. Savonarola's amnesty law was not passed until 19 March 1495 (Cadoni, *Provvisioni* I, pp. 108–18), but he was preaching the need for universal peace from mid-December 1494.

[12] Piero in Bolsena (where he arrived from Pitigliano), 'al mio caro Bernardo Bibbiena', 10 June 1495, autogr., SSX8LCMR 66, fol. 11r: 'io non sono per star qui oltra hoggi, che andrò apresso Sua Maestà'; Parenti, *Storia* I, pp. 224–34, 237–9, cf. *Consulte*, ed. Fachard, pp. 29–34 [31 May].

[13] Parenti, *Storia*, 1. pp. 221–2, 277. On Lamberto dell'Antella and his *Processo*, n. 67 in this chapter.

[14] Ibid., p. 235; Piero in Pitigliano to Piero Corsini, dated 7 June 1495, SSX8LCMR, 66, fol. 8r-v (chancery copy of the autograph original on fols. 102r–103r, authenticated on 8v–9r).

[15] pp. 97–8, esp. n. 46, and 214 in this volume; Lorenzo, *Lettere* 16, p. 340 (29 January 1490): 'la affectione che io porto a Piero Corsini' (who was married, however, to Ginevra di Tanai de' Nerli).

trouble, particularly Corsini's brother, the lawyer messer Luca,[16] and Jacopo di Tanai de' Nerli, both of whom had criticised Piero and blocked his entry to the palace in November 1494:

> I only want to return home without offending anyone who wants to be my friend, believing, perhaps, that everyone will have a more secure and contented life and higher status than those you seem to think deserve it ... You know I am peace-loving and never wanted to play the tyrant.[17]

Thanks to the government's security measures, Piero nevertheless found himself unable to draw any closer to Florence, and the end of June found him in Rome, writing one of a series of letters to the papal commissary in Bolsena, Silvio Passerini, the Medici's former secretary.[18] Three months earlier the Orsini had joined the rest of Italy to form a general league against France, so for once Piero found himself isolated.

It was only after the French retreated north that Piero rejoined the Orsini in rallying support for the league against the French before they left Italy in November. In mid-September he accompanied Virginio and Carlo Orsini and the Venetian captain Bartolomeo d'Alviano to Perugia, in order to force the city to support the league – and, with the Sienese, assist the Medici return to Florence.[19] The abstract of letters compiled by Marcello Adriani as chancellor of the Dieci di Balìa (before becoming first chancellor in 1498) reflected on the 'amazing' situation, whereby 'every power, great and small, wanted the favour of the Medici': the Venetians had sent 10,000 ducats to the Orsini to help them; Milan encouraged them and so did Siena; Giovanni Bentivoglio offered them thousands of horses and foot soldiers and urged Giuliano de' Medici to come via the Mugello; and the pope had ordered Perugia and the Baglioni to support the Medici, not Florence, 'because the Florentines now ruling the republic [as Francophile Savonarolans] are stumbling blocks and enemies of Italy's liberty'.[20] Despite this, Adriani was right to conclude that 'experience shows how little nerve there is in things in which many participate and how weak exiles are', for the months that

---

[16] On Luca Corsini, Guicciardini, *Storie*, p. 95, Rubinstein, *Government*, p. 269.
[17] SSX8LCMR 66, fol. 102r–v, (cf. 8r): '... Voi sapete sono pacifico, né mai volsi tiranneggiare ...' Cf. Chapter 20 in this volume.
[18] Piero in Rome to Passerini in Bolsena, 27 June 1495, ASF Acq. doni 142, ins. 8 (with other letters dated 15 May, 30 November 1495, March–July 1496, February 1498). On Passerini (cardinal of Cortona in 1517), *DBI*, 81, 2014 (G. Brunelli).
[19] Adriani, *Sumpto*, SSX8LCMR 4, fol. 81r, mid-September [1495]. According to Parenti (*Storia* I, p. 177, cf. 162), Piero had been with Carlo in January as the king passed through Orsini lands north of Rome.
[20] *Sumpto*, fols. 82v: 'Era cosa mirabile quanto ogni <po>tentato grande et piccolo aspirava al favore de Medici', 83r: 'quanto pocho nervo habbino le cose in nelle quali participino molti et come sieno deboli e' fuoruscti'.

followed proved both to be true. Initially, the army being raised by Piero and the Orsini in October 1495 was successful in winning the support of the Orsini's Guelf supporters as they moved towards Perugia.[21] It would consist of thirty squadrons and four hundred light cavalry, not counting the Sienese, who would provide Paolo and Lodovico Orsini and their other soldiers, and he hoped the numbers would increase as they proceeded. All that they needed was money, for although the Orsini had been quick to offer help and some Florentines had sent Piero money, he had used what little he had left to raise troops, and now urgently needed a loan of 5000 ducats from the Doge of Venice – for which the only security he could offer was his little son in Siena, 'the dearest thing I have in the world'.[22]

In November Virginio sent his son Carlo to force Perugia to adhere to the league in the name of the pope, and on the 22nd Piero was to be found with him, Virginio and Gian Giordano Orsini, Bartolomeo d'Alviano and Giorgio di Santa Croce at Panicale (just south of Lake Trasimene).[23] Later that month, when the Dieci di Balìa in Florence asked a consultative meeting why 'all the Italian powers' were favouring the Orsini and Piero against Florence, the reply was that the Italian powers wanted to turn France against Florence and they were also using Piero as an instrument to overturn Florence's government and acquire its territory.[24]

Although Piero Capponi countered these fears by declaring in December that 'Piero has no friends in this city' and would never return, outside Florence the Medici's former secretary, ser Piero Dovizi, was telling Lionardo Bartolini in Rome that things 'couldn't be going better'.[25] Milan had decided to restore Piero to power, he wrote; in Bologna Giovanni Bentivoglio had been given money by Venice to raise three hundred men-at-arms, three hundred light cavalry, three hundred *provigionati* and five thousand infantry, and Caterina Sforza, ruler of Forlì,

---

[21] Piero in Narni to Dovizi in Venice, 7 October 1495, accompanying a letter of credence to the Doge, ed. Buser, *Bezierhungen*, pp. 555–7. All the Orsini except for Giulio were in Narni with him.

[22] Piero to Dovizi, 7 October, p. 556. To offer up his son may have been a token gesture, but Lorenzo was then living with the Lippomani (n. 4 in this chapter), who could have held him as a hostage as the Medici held Niccolò Orsini's son in 1489 (p. 82 in this volume).

[23] *Consulte 1495–1497*, s.d. [24 October–7 November] 1495, pp. 53; Adriani, *Sumpto*, fol. 84r (22 November): 'et per Piero fu ricordato loro e' meriti di Casa sua con minacciare che se ne riavrebbe'.

[24] *Consulte 1495–1497*, pp. 64, 67 (27 November 1495) and 83 (24 December 1495).

[25] Ibid., p. 83 (24 December 1495): 'Piero non è per tornare mai a Firenze'; Dovizi in Venice to Lionardo Bartolini in Rome, CS, ser. I, 336, fol. 154v (11 December 1495).

and others would follow; money would also be sent from Venice to Annibale Bentivoglio; and since his father Giovanni still wanted his clerical son to be made a cardinal as a condition of his help, the pope was being urged to do everything that would facilitate Piero's restoration. Dovizi also reported the unconfirmed news from Ferrara that many placards had been found by night (in Florence), saying, 'If you don't give us grain, we'll recall Piero and Giuliano', and that in Siena they were keeping the gates shut.[26]

The seriousness of the threat posed by Piero and the Orsini at the time of this letter is reflected in the citizens' discussion in Florence about increasing their defences at Vaiano and Cortona, 'in view of the preparations of the Sienese, Orsini and Piero de' Medici against us' (yes, they all agreed, and Piero's possessions should be seized to pay for it, also the Perugians should be buttered up to make them 'good and loyal friends').[27] A week later, on 10 December, when they were asked 'how to remedy the tumult of people coming with Piero de' Medici', the answers ranged from 'guarding the palace and the city in some secret way' to sending a company of constables and light cavalry to restrain the Sienese, and talking to the Colonna, 'even with a sweetener' (*beveraggio*). The Bolognese, like the Perugians, needed a soft touch, for although Giovanni Bentivoglio was thought to be friendly ('though he wasn't'), he should be written to as though he were Florence's friend, and at the same time spies should be sent to Bologna, 'where Piero was said to have sent money to raise troops'. Anyone found lending money on Medici jewels should be caught and punished and a decision should be made about the Medici's possessions, 'since they would raise a lot of money'.[28] And in view of Piero's credit, or support, in Florence, guards were to seize letters in order to discover its source and its thinking.[29] This must be the moment described by Cerretani when Piero came to Perugia supported by the reputed *condottieri* Paolo and Virginio Orsini, and after waiting in

---

[26] Ibid. Although Dovizi wrote 'di Piero non s'intende cosa alcuno', Piero's letters to Passerini in ASF Acq. Doni 142, ins. 8, show he was in Chianciano on 30 November (autogr.), in Balneo Rapolano on 25 December 1495, in Rome on 4 March, 4, 10, 3, 25, 27, 30 June, 19 July and in Bracciano on 8 [May?] 1496.

[27] *Consulte 1495–1497*, pp.39–44, 2 October 1495: 'et fare loro ogni carezza et amorevolezza per farsili fidati et buon amici' (43).

[28] On the Medici syndics, n. 7 in this chapter. From July onwards, Florence held auctions of Piero's possessions in Orsanmichele, Fusco and Corti, *Lorenzo de' Medici*, pp. 166–7.

[29] *Consulte, 1495–1497*, pp. 44–8 (10 October), at 47. On 31 December the Otto di Guardia (Otto rep. 102, fol. 341r) paid five gold florins 'per una spia per andare e stare drieto a Piero de Medici in quello di Lucignano' (south of Siena), and in 1495 two men were hanged for wanting to give him Montecatini, Rondoni, '"Giustiziati"a Firenze', p. 224.

vain for a conspiracy in Cortona to reveal itself in their favour (thanks to the 'diligence' of the Florentine government), they returned disgruntled to Rome, thus ending the first of Piero's abortive attempts at repatriation.[30]

Adriani's experience proved right in detecting a 'lack of nerve in things in which many participate' and also the weakness of exiles. For if Piero enjoyed some success with the Orsini and their Guelf adherents, by 1496 his allies in the Italian league proved as unreliable as Adriani predicted. Despite a meeting held in Rome in the spring to plan action, the league was fracturing. Both Lodovico Sforza and the Orsini frequently changed sides according to their own changing interests, and the pope, who initially wanted to attack Florence because of his hostility to Savonarola, vacillated too, from fear of Venice's growing power. And so, as Parenti put it, 'the affairs of Italy moved from perfidy to perfidy'.[31] At the same time, Florence demonstrated how difficult it could make life for exiles. After Alfonsina fled Florence with her children on 20 September 1495, Piero had his decree of exile reimposed and doubled for breaking the terms of his exile, and in November it was extended to his heirs, when a bounty of 2000 florins was also imposed on Giuliano.[32] As Piero said in his letter to Dovizi on 7 October, the government 'appeared to make quite a fuss about it'.[33] The Otto di Guardia immediately issued letterspatent ordering her capture and return to Florence under guard, and three days later it issued a bann citing Averardo de' Medici to appear before them (for accompanying Alfonsina out of Florence), while another punished anyone who failed to report helping Alfonsina before she left or who received any of her or her mother's possessions of any kind, including their jewels, clothes, money and documents.[34] On 25 September the Otto, supported by twenty-two named citizens, imposed a bounty of 4000 florins on Piero's head for breaking the limits imposed by his exile, which – they spelt out – pardoned any two men who killed him and

---

[30] Cerretani, *Storia*, p. 231: 'malcontentti si ritornò in Roma'.
[31] Pellegrini, *Ascanio*, 2, pp. 566–80, Sanudo, *Diarii*, I, 8–9 (January 1496); *Consulte, 1495–1497*, p. 106 (18 January 1496) and Parenti, *Storia*, 2, p. 17 (p. 29 on fear of Venice becoming 'signori d'Italia' in July 1496), cf. Bernardo Dovizi in Pisa to Piero and Giovanni, 13 November 1496, SSX8LCMR 66, fol. 180r (decoded on 196r).
[32] 15 October 1495, Provvisioni 186, fols. 120r–121r, approved by 62/21 in Ottanta, 600/99 in the Great Council; 26 November 1495, ibid., 142v–143r. The law of 15 October also states that 'secondo e' nostri statuti può essere morto sanza alcuna pena, la quale cosa etiam dale sacre leggi permesso' (120r).
[33] Piero in Narni to Dovizi in Venice, 7 October 1495, Buser, *Bezierhungen*, p. 557: 'monstrano far caso assai'. Cf. Parenti, *Storia* I, pp. 219, 269, Lamberto dell'Antella's confession, CS. Appendice 3, 1, fols. 77r–82v, 98r–99r, ed. Villari, *Storia*, p. v.
[34] Otto di Guardia repubb. 102, fols. 67v, 74v–75r (20 and 23 September 1495).

rewarded them with 2000 florins and the privilege of bearing arms. The bann was then circulated widely to the captains of all the frontier cities of Florence's state – Arezzo, Borgo San Sepolcro, Pistoia, Volterra, San Gemignano and Castrocaro, and also to the vicar of San Giovanni and the commissaries in the camp.[35]

So life for the exiled Medici became increasingly difficult, scattered as they were in March 1496 between Milan (where Cardinal Giovanni and Giuliano were to be found) and Rome and Bolsena, where Piero was facing problems over money and the safety of his mail.[36] In June, Piero asked Passerini to apply 'another tug of the rope' to a courier he had already examined under torture for the theft of mail – and what, he wondered, had happened to the mail he had despatched with Carlo Orsini's chancellor to Milan in April? His letters to Passerini graphically describe the problem he faced in securing the safety of his friend Francesco Nero's two strongboxes and mailbag, which Passerini was to open, inventory (with a copy for himself), relock and put somewhere secure, removing nothing without Piero's autograph letter or signature. The following day Piero repeated all this in a letter to his cousin Giulio de' Medici, telling him to send Giuliano (Piero's brother) to Bolsena to open the chests with Passerini, but to tear up his letter and tell no one about it or about Giuliano's trip. Two weeks later he told Passerini to hand everything over to Nero, including some of his own things.[37]

The letters also illustrate the money problems faced by exiles and Piero's petty control of detail, at least where the expenses of his employees were concerned: not for nothing did he come from a family of bankers.

> I'm not sending the money you asked for [he wrote to Passerini on 17 July] because I haven't the means and also I think you can very well pay yourself for any necessary expenses there. For when I tot it all up, that is, what you've received up to now as ordinary and extraordinary income, it seems to me that you can pay for everything without bothering me in these times.[38]

---

[35] Ibid., fols. 80v–84v (25 September 1495), listing the names of twenty-two citizens 'qui soprascripta consultatione interfuerunt', headed by five doctors, Bonsi, Pepi, Gualterotti, G. V. Soderini and Luca Corsini, On the 28th, Averardo de' Medici was fined and punished with loss of office and exile (fol. 88r–v).

[36] Sanudo, *Diarii* I, 138 (early March 1496), 203 (early June).

[37] Piero in Rome to Passerini in Bolsena, 30 June, 13 July 1496 (autogr. signatures), to Giulio de Medici in Bracciano, 1 July 1496, Acq. Doni 142, ins. 8. On the Lombard Nero, *al*. Piero Negri, initially Piero's friend, then his enemy, pp. 208 and 257–8 in this volume.

[38] The same, 17 July 1496: 'mi pare trovare che cumulatissimamente possiate satisfare a tutto sanza molestare me in questi tempi'.

He, too, had financial problems, he continued, and to show he wasn't talking in the dark and knew 'how to draw up an account', he proceeded to list Passerini's income since Giulio (Monsignore) left eight months ago, which totalled some 177 florins (including the 100 florins paid as Giulio's monthly subsidy of 9 florins a month), 25 florins from a Jew for Ricci's account, 16 florins from Tibaldo on Cardinal Giovanni's departure, plus the money that Giovanni had sent him from Milan, his ordinary salary and extraordinary payments. This was more than enough to sustain the family with something left over, nor did he believe Passerini was as broke as his letter suggested; so instead of receiving more money, he could and should pay off the debts in Piero's account.[39]

Piero was evidently attempting to raise larger sums of money at this time from the banker Lionardo Bartolini in Rome, as well as a loan from Agostino Chigi. So money may well have been the motive behind his attempt, at Cardinal Federigo Sanseverino's request, to reconcile Passerini and Bartolini, 'who one could say is one of ours'. As Piero told Passerini, he was obligated to Cardinal Sanseverino as well as to Bartolini.[40] As well as being his generous host in Rome, Sanseverino was also the person spearheading Piero's repatriation at this time by hosting discussions about it in Rome with the Venetian ambassador and the pope, who was 'their axis'. Siena, too, was drawn in, and for his part Piero promised Venice that he would leave Pisa in liberty and allow Montepulciano to be under the control of Siena, not Florence: 'all of which was put into effect at the end of April'.[41]

The Emperor-Elect in Italy, 1496

In November Piero was still in Rome, engaged in discussions with his brother Giovanni and the Medici bankers and factors Nofri Tornabuoni,

---

[39] Ibid.: 'né sono in credere vi troviate cosi al verde ... Et però io non darò ... e' danari mi scrivete ...'
[40] Piero to Passerini, 10 June 1496, ibid. On the Bartolini in Florence, Brown, *Florence* (2011), pp. 28–31, and *Delizie*, 24 for the family tree; in Lyon, where with Giuliano da Gagliano they helped to provide the Medici with money in Rome, Pollini-Martin, *Banque, négoce et politique*, pp. 169–70. On money owed to the Medici for Gonzaga's unpaid debts that Piero hoped to raise from the Chigi, Chambers, *Cardinal Francesco Gonzaga*, pp. 126–7, Fusco and Corti, *Lorenzo de' Medici*, doc. 215 (17 May 1496), pp. 340–1 (p. 74 in this volume).
[41] Adriani, *Sumpto*, SSX8LCMR 4, fol. 88v: 'il perno di tutt' i ragionamenti'; Ridolfi, 'La Spedizione', p. 133, n. 13, Lamberto dell'Antella's confession, ed. Villari, pp. xvii–xviii; *Consulte, 1495–1497*, discussing Siena's support for Piero on pp. 93–7, 120, 123, 124 and 190 (7 January, 5 February and 22 April 1496). Bertelli, 'I *Ricordi* di G. V. Soderini', pp. 367 and 370 (25 June).

Lionardo Bartolini and Domenico Alamanni.[42] This is the moment when a new player enters the Italian stage, the German emperor-elect Maximilian. He had been invited by Lodovico Sforza and the league to help them defeat France, with Florence encouraged to join them. So for the second time Piero and his brothers found themselves competing with their native city for the favour of the same patron, not the French king this time but Maximilian. The new hub of activity, 'the place on which all the actions of Italy today depend', was Pisa. After being conquered by Florence in 1406, Pisa was now engaged in a bitter struggle to retain its independence, so it found itself the focus of attention, as the anti-French league and the emperor fluctuated between attacking Pisa in order to win Florence's support against France and supporting it in order to attack Florence.[43]

This was why the peripatetic Bernardo Dovizi found himself in Pisa in November, in disguise to avoid being seen by the Florentines as they competed for the emperor's favour. Although he found Maximilian well disposed towards the Medici – Maximilian was staying in their palace in Pisa, while Bernardo inhabited the falconer Galletto's house nearby – Bernardo was afraid Florence would woo him by providing the money the emperor desperately needed, which the Medici would have to equal, and for this reason he wanted one of the brothers to come to Pisa to disrupt Maximilian's rapport with Florence.[44] This meeting never happened, however. For after Bernardo had enjoyed three encounters with Maximilian, attempting to persuade him 'with infinite reasons' to reenter Florence with the Medici – first, with the Sforza count of Caiazzo on 9 November, then in the antechamber of the Medici palace, and last riding with him on the 13th to Vico Pisano (near Pisa) – an unexpected event dramatically changed the situation.[45] A massive storm arose that destroyed several ships belonging to Venice and the league that had

---

[42] Domenico (called Lorenzo Tornabuoni's 'ministro' in Cegia's 'Ricordi segreti', pp. 212, 205, 206) was sent to Rome in mid-November 1496, Lamberto dell'Antella's confession, ed. Villari, p. xii. Giuliano was with the duke of Milan in September 1496-April 1497 (Sanudo, *Diarii*, 1, 309, 613), then in Bologna. On Nofri and Lionardo, de Roover, *Banco Medici*, p. 319, and on Alamanni, Fusco and Corti, *Lorenzo de' Medici*, p. 305, doc. 99, n. 3.

[43] Bernardo Dovizi in Pisa to Cardinal Giovanni and Piero, 13 November 1496, SSC8LCMR 66, fol. 180r (decoded on 199r): 'essendo in loco donde dependono hoggi tucte le actioni de Italia.' On Pisa, Mallett, *The Borgias*, pp. 130–1.

[44] Bernardo Dovizi to Giovanni and Piero, 7, 10–13 November 1496, ibid., fols. 205r-v, 179–183v (decoded on fols. 186r–191r, v. 187v and 188r), 14 November (178r and 196r).

[45] The same, 14 November 1496, fols. 178r (decoded on 196r–v): 'faccendo la impresa con la Casa de Medici, con la quale haria gloria, stato, gente et danari, et sanza, vedevo sua Maestà andare ad manifesto danno et vergogna', etc'.

invited Maximilian to Italy, while most of the French fleet had already escaped towards Provence, so feeling unsupported and let down, the emperor returned home in ignominy.[46]

At the Gates With Sword in Hand, 1497

What seemed to the Florentines an act of God, predicted by Savonarola, was to the Medici another cruel blow of fate that struck at their chances of returning to Florence. Moreover, in January the following year, 1497, Francesco Valori was elected Gonfalonier of Justice with the popular support of the followers of fra Girolamo. Savonarola had gained political influence after Piero's flight from Florence in November 1494, leading to a revolution that replaced Medici control with something much more radical: the creation of a vast legislative council, the Great Council, that consisted of all the citizens who were eligible to hold office in Florence. The wave of enthusiasm for this new way of doing things greatly helped the republican government to carry out its concerted campaign against Piero as an enemy of freedom, the 'tyrant' whom Savonarola repeatedly attacked in his sermons and writings. However, Savonarola in turn created enemies among the elite, and the large majorities needed to win the vote in the Great Council rapidly led to the formation of factions and sects that Savonarola's peace-and-forgiveness campaign only served to exacerbate.[47] By 1497, there was a group of citizens, the Bigi – called by Cerretani 'a compact Medicean seed' – who wanted Piero back to counterbalance the influence of Savonarola, and although weakened by ambition for honours and office and by popular fear of the old regime, the Bigi's promise of cheap grain and bread (no circuses as yet) gave it popular appeal at this time of famine and hardship.[48] So Francesco Valori's election as Gonfalonier of Justice in January 1497 came at a critical moment. Opposed to both the Bigi and the faction that favoured the league, he introduced a programme of reform with the popular support of Savonarola and his party. Among the measures introduced to reform the Great Council on 25 January was one aimed specifically against the Medici and the citizens he thought were plotting secretly to restore 'the horrible Piero' ('Pieroaccio', Parenti calls him) through

---

[46] Ibid. (14 November), fol. 185r: 'el più terribile vento del mondo et il mare grossissimo' (and to Giacoppo Petrucci, fol. 204); Parenti, *Storia*, 2, pp. 57–58; Guicciardini, *Storie*, p. 129.
[47] Najemy, *A History*, pp. 381–400, at 397–8; Weinstein, *Savonarola*, esp. pp. 121–31, 157–63, 205, 219, Polizzotto, *Elect Nation*, esp. pp. 20–49, Martines, *Scourge and Fire*, pp. 176–82.
[48] Cerretani, *Storia*, p. 234: 'era un seme stretto palescho benché debole'.

contact with his brother, Cardinal Giovanni, in Rome. The law condemned as rebels anyone in Florence or its territory who served the Medici now or later, or were the companions of the Medici brothers and failed to return to Florence within a month; and any father or brother who failed to report these absentees after a month was deprived of office and exiled from Florentine territory for life.[49]

Although the law was passed on 24–25 January, with more than the necessary two-thirds majority in both the Council of Eighty and the Great Council (confirming what Parenti says about Valori's success in ruling as *capo* with the support of the Savonarolans), there nevertheless remained a consistent opposition on which the Medici must have placed their hopes.[50] So when Valori's two-month term of office came to an end and he was replaced by a Signoria that included three Medici supporters – the Gonfalonier of Justice Bernardo del Nero and the priors Battista Serristori and Francesco Davanzati – the Medici's hopes were once again rekindled. The new government served as Piero's call to action. In early March the Florentine ambassador in Rome, Ricciardo Becchi, was already reporting that Piero and Cardinal Giovanni were emboldened and were telling the whole papal court that the corn repository in Florence had been sacked to cries of 'Palle, Palle,' and that they hoped to return there within the next two months.[51] A flurry of letters between Florence and Rome (using various friars as couriers, as we shall see in the following chapter) transmitted coded messages in which 'Lino' (Piero's alias) proposed he should be recalled by the Gonfalonier legally, as a private citizen. But the fact he also wanted money and outside help indicates that he did not rule out the use of force.[52]

Initially delayed by the unexpected truce between France, Spain and the league that made Siena seek reassurance before agreeing to support

---

[49] Provv. 187, fol. 168r–v, 25 January 1497: 'fussi al servigio in alchuno modo o in compagnia appresso del cardinale de' Medici o di Piero o di Giuliano ...', Parenti, *Storia*, 2, p. 71, cf. Guicciardini, *Storie*, pp. 130–1. Other laws passed on 25 January are ed. Cadoni, *Provvisioni*, I, pp. 333–43.

[50] The votes were 70/30 in the Eighty and 718/347 in the Great Council; Parenti, *Storia*, 2, p. 71 (on Valori as 'capo di quella setta' and 'un'altra parte a lui opposita ... massime quella che con la Lega teneva').

[51] Ricciardo Becchi to the Dieci, 7 March 1497, ed. Gherardi, *Nuovi documenti*, pp. 146–7, also describing discussions in Rome between the Medici and a fra Santi, who had a secret commission from Savonarola, though not part of his sect.

[52] *Consulte, 1495–1497*, 17 March 1497 (pp. 439: 'per levare 'l caldo che Piero de' Medici si vede havere da' potentati d'Italia', 442 and 443); 28 March (453, 454: 'observare suo andamenti et veghiarlo continuamente', 456–8), 4 April (462). Cf. Sanudo, *Diarii*, 1, 548, 640 (that Lorenzo di Pierfrancesco was in Florence in March, 'pur era senza majestrato et in pocha auctorità', and by June the 'popolo menuto vol che Piero di Medici ritorna ... ma non vene a effecto'.

Piero, Piero finally arrived in Siena with about forty horses and on 23 April confirmed the guarantee negotiated five days earlier by Cardinal Federigo Sanseverino: that fifteen days after reentering Florence, Piero would hand over to Siena Florence's fortress at Ponte a Valiano – its bridge, tower, the entrance to the fortress and the rampart. With little time left before the election of a new priorate in Florence, Piero and Bartolomeo d'Alviano set off quickly with 120 men-at-arms, 300 light cavalry and 1500 foot soldiers.[53] Travelling via Castellina and San Casciano, they captured a Florentine courier en route to prevent news reaching Florence before they arrived there. But quick though his journey from Siena had been, a torrential downpour at Tavarnelle on the 27th delayed his arrival just long enough to allow a new and hostile government to be chosen before he reached the walls the next day. Moreover, news of his arrival in Siena on the 23rd had reached Florence in time for preparations to be made to limit its impact. Commissaries had been despatched to the Chianti and to Poggio Imperiale, and the sixteen standard-bearers had told the men in their *gonfaloni* (subdivisions of the quarters of the city) to lay in food and arms. About fifty of Piero's old friends and partisans (including Piero Soderini) and a few others were summoned to the government palace and kept there until Piero had left, in order to prevent an uprising – and mingling with them was the public executioner, armed with a chopper, shackles and large quantities of rope. No one was allowed to enter or leave the city, and supporters of the regime were ordered to arm local militias to prevent the workers from rising up and rioting.[54]

The government may by then have received an anonymous letter from Rome urging it to take the threat from Piero very seriously, 'since your enemy thinks only of returning home and he's going around stirring up trouble everywhere', while at the same time Florence (it said) was surrounded by unfriendly neighbouring states, each of whom wanted to weaken the city and 'play with the abacus' in his own way 'without following the rule of counterbalancing Venice'.[55] The news from Siena

---

[53] Siena, AS, Colle 1081 (Notarile), fol. 471, 23 April 1497 (signed on the 26th by Giacoppo Petrucci, with Pandolfo and a notary as witnesses and D'Alviano as guarantor, fol. 471v); Ridolfi, 'La spedizione', esp. pp. 130–9; Sanudo, *Diarii*, 1, 613.

[54] Parenti, *Storia*, 2, pp. 96–9 listing twenty of the ca. fifty names, including Piero Alamanni, Piero Soderini and Giannozzo Pucci (who commented in his *Examina*: 'né havevo in casa mia che e' coltellini da tavola et uno famiglio zoppo', CS I, 360, fol. 15r); Cerretani, *Storia*, pp. 234–5; Bertelli, '*Ricordi* di G.V. Soderini, pp. 381–2: 'questi dello stato vecchio stimansi ingiuriati per essere stati chiamati in palagio et vedersi el manigoldo in su gli occhi'.

[55] Anon. letter from Rome to the Signoria, April 1497, SSX8LCMR 66, fol. 304r: 'el vostro nimico non pensa mai ad alttro che a ttornare in casa e va nuttrendo ogni possibile

would also have prepared the city for Piero's arrival. So when Piero reached the outskirts of Florence on 28 April, he awaited a call to enter the gates that never came, his friends locked up in the palace and the populace controlled by armed militias. The newly elected government gathered together the leading citizens most opposed to Piero – people like Pagolantonio Soderini, Tanai de' Nerli and his children, Lorenzo di Pierfrancesco (now renamed Popolano) and Alfonso Strozzi – and despatched them to the Roman Gate, accompanied by many armed men and two of Florence's captains, Ercole Bentivoglio and Paolo Vitelli, both conveniently in Florence. Another captain, Rinuccio Farnese, was ordered to come from Pisa to encircle Piero. And to make him all the more frightened, they read out to him the public bann imposing a bounty of 4000 florins on his head. For about four hours he and his forces stood their ground outside the gate. Then, when Piero finally asked to parley, he was told by Paolo Vitelli that no one supported him and that he was encircled. So Piero turned his back on Florence and was setting off to Siena by an indirect route when he heard that Rinuccio Farnese's forces were in fact much weaker than expected. So he rejoined the main road but continued his ignominious retreat whence he had come, closely protected by his men.[56]

Parenti's account of this dramatic day leaves many questions unanswered: was Piero once again unlucky in being initially delayed by the truce and then by bad weather? Was he misled about the amount of support he enjoyed in Florence and thwarted by the government's firm measures? Or was he a coward, unwilling to press on when his considerable forces might well have been enough to topple the government? An anonymous letter reporting Piero's return to Siena on 1 May, evidently sent by one of the Orsini from their enclave of Monte Giordano in Rome, was not surprised that 'the thing hadn't succeeded', because Piero's friends in Florence hadn't wanted to reveal themselves – unsurprisingly, since many were shut up in the palace and others deterred by the danger of failure. It would have been a great thing for the Orsini, had it succeeded – the letter continued – since they would have recovered all their

---

cattivo omore per tutto'. Braccesi, called inexperienced compared with the writer, was sent to Rome on 3 March 1497 (*DBI*, 13, 1971: A. Perosa).

[56] Parenti, *Storia*, 2, p. 97, cf. Ridolfi, 'La Spedizione di Piero', pp 137–40. According to Sanudo (*Diarii*, 1, col. 613) 'stete a porta Romana da hore 13 … fino a hore 22, che fo 9 hore', then, after spending three days at the Certosa, 'si tirò a Siena'.

losses, but they should be patient and not despair since the friends would not have changed their minds.[57]

There is no doubt about the political instability at this time, due as much to Savonarola's growing unpopularity as Piero's. The Milanese ambassador in Florence, Paolo Somenzi, reported (in June) that 'about three months ago', to everyone's great surprise, Lorenzo di Pierfrancesco had begun to send away his household possessions and had sent his children to Forlì, removing himself with all his band to live in the Mugello, for which the only possible explanation was that he wanted to make himself a grandee and head of the city, like Piero, 'which would never be tolerated because this city doesn't want a head'.[58] This is perhaps supported by what Somenzi wrote about the creation of the 'Paciali' in April – a new magistracy representing a coalition of 'friends of Piero's and of the friar' – that it showed times had moved on and Piero's friends 'wanted to be free and their own bosses rather than work for Piero's return'.[59] Similarly, Lamberto dell'Antella wrote in his confession that Bernardo del Nero was lukewarm on hearing news of Piero's planned arrival, saying that he was 'a good friend of the Medici' and would always remain their friend, but that one must await the right time for such things. And in his confession in August, Niccolò Ridolfi stressed Bernardo's criticism of Piero's 'bad government' and underplayed his support for him.[60] Nevertheless, Parenti thought that, but for the storm that had delayed his arrival, Piero might well have succeeded in entering the city and caused a great disturbance there, since he had offended no one, and by befriending the peasants had won great support; some were upset that so many people had been detained in the palace (he names twenty of the fifty detained), others thought the government was using the occasion to increase its power, and many sat on the fence. He thought, too, that Piero might have had support from the north, since Tommaso Bardi, Piero's relation, had arrived in Vernio ready to fight but went home when he heard of Piero's retreat, and Giuliano de' Medici and Bernardo Dovizi had both appeared in Bologna – confirming what was reported before Piero's arrival, that Piero was coming via Siena with many troops and he was being supported by Perugians and Vitelleschi, and similarly by many from the direction of Bologna and the Romagna.

---

[57] SSX8LCMR 66, fol. 309r, 1 May 1497: 'et certo saria stata una gran cosa *per tucta casa Orsina con lo restauramento di tucti li danni ricevuti* (decoded)'.

[58] Somenzi to the duke of Milan, 29 June 1497, ed. Villari, *Storia*, pp. xxx–xxxi: 'questo populo non vole capo' (xxxi); n. 52 in this chapter.

[59] The same, 2 April 1497, ivi, pp. xxvi–xxvii: 'che questi tali vorano più presto stare liberi et essere patroni loro ch'a operare la ritornata de Piero' (xxvi).

[60] Discussed on pp. 261–2 in this volume, on Bernardo, cf. p. 156.

All this suggested that the conspiracy was more extensive than at first appeared, but despite support for it within the city, Pagolantonio Soderini thought 'more was gained than lost' by it, 'especially with the outside powers'.[61]

These events were not the end of what Guicciardini called 'this year of the greatest movements and changes'.[62] Piero's attempted return in late April was followed by Savonarola's excommunication in June, and then in August by the momentous repercussions of the recapture and confession of the rebel Lamberto dell'Antella. A letter found in Lamberto's bag when recaptured told his brother-in-law, Francesco Gualterotti, that he wanted to print and circulate throughout the world all he knew about Piero's doings in Rome and elsewhere.[63] The letter and his later confession under torture helped to incriminate five leading Mediceans – initially Giannozzo Pucci, Piero's intimate friend, and Giovanni Cambi, the manager of the Medici Bank in Pisa, then another three citizens, Lorenzo Tornabuoni (Piero's cousin), Niccolò Ridolfi (his sister Contessina's father-in-law) and Bernardo del Nero (as Gonfalonier, guilty of not revealing to his colleagues Piero's letter shown to him by Ridolfi). Piero's brother-in-law Jacopo Salviati was not one of them, since he was said to disapprove of his wife Lucrezia's involvement ('a proud and fearless woman', according to Parenti) and he may also have been protected by Francesco Valori. On 17 August the Otto di Guardia read out the confessions to the Signoria and both colleges.[64] So desperate was Valori to secure the death penalty, despite the five's appeal to the Great Council (supported by their lawyer, Guidantonio Vespucci, and five members of the Signoria, including Piero Guicciardini), that he summoned ever larger groups of citizens – initially 20, then 160, then 200 – to discuss whether the appeal should be allowed or not. Finally, on 21 August, after the last group had been debating for five to seven hours, Valori strode to the rostrum and forced a decision. Such was the furore

---

[61] Bertelli, '*Ricordi* di G. V. Soderini, p. 382: 'pur s'era acquistato più che perduto, maxime colle potentie di fuora', also pp. 379 and 384–5; Parenti, *Storia*, 2, pp. 98–9; Lamberto, *Processo*, CS. Append. 3, I, fol. 99v.

[62] Guicciardini, *Storie*, p. 132; Soderini, *Ricordi*, pp. 383–7.

[63] Lamberto, *Processo*, ed. Villari, p. vii, §10 (CS. Append. 3, I, fol. 79v): 'la quale si potrà mandare per tutto il mondo, et vogliamo si getti in forma che conterà molte cose'; Martines, *Scourge and Fire*, pp. 182–200.

[64] Guicciardini names all the sixteen Gonfaloniers and twelve good men (and the Guelph party captains) with the speeches of their spokesmen, CS I, 360, fols. 10r–11r; cf. his *Storia*, p. 141; on his autograph transcript, Ridolfi, 'Spedizione', p. 128, n. 1, and n. 67 in this chapter; Parenti, *Storia*, 2, pp. 119–20; Jacopo Pitti (*Storia fiorentina*, pp. 59–62, that 136 people attended the meeting, plus its *ex officio* members; others 'restati a casa, per diversi rispetti', 61). On Piero's letter, p. 262 in this volume.

that some dissident members of the Signoria – notably Piero Guicciardini (according to his son), as the most 'authoritative' of the dissidents – were seized by their clothing and threatened with defenestration; had one of the dissenting lawyers been there, Cerretani said, he would certainly have been flung from the windows to the piazza below.[65]

The five men were immediately executed in the Bargello, from where their families were allowed to remove the bodies for private burial. Only Lorenzo Tornabuoni and Giannozzo Pucci were defended by their families, both of them signed-up supporters of Savonarola (apparently Lorenzo's young, well-brought-up son won the Signoria's compassion). The other three belonged to the opposing party and made little attempt to defend themselves according to Parenti, who also records the punishments meted out to their accomplices. Some were expelled from Florence and confined to Florentine territory (to prevent them joining up with Piero, from families like the Pitti, Corbinelli and Martelli). Others were deprived of office and exiled to specific places for a certain time, like Andrea de' Medici (il Butto), Jacopo Gianfigliazzi, Cosimo Sassetti and Gino Capponi.[66]

If the reaction against the deaths of these notable citizens and the overriding of the law of appeal contributed to Savonarola's fall, the revelations in Lamberto's confession about Piero's dissolute life in exile and the retribution he and his brother intended to inflict on many leading families on their return to Florence also made this a turning point in the Medici's fortunes.[67] Perhaps it was now that the idea was seeded that some of the family could return, but not Piero, thanks to Lamberto's letter and confession. The letter in his bag was clearly intended to protect himself if captured, and although he was called by Parenti one of Piero's 'closest intimates', Lamberto was a friend only too happy to denounce

---

[65] Cerretani, *Storia*, pp. 236–9; Guicciardini, *Storie*, p. 142 (that his father Piero with two priors alone stood firm in favour of the appeal); cf. Parenti, *Storia*, 2, pp. 123–5, Pitti, *Istoria fiorentina*, pp. 62–5; Cambi, *Istorie*, pp. 105–15. On the trial, Martines, *Lawyers and Statecraft*, pp. 442–8.

[66] Parenti, *Storia*, 2, pp. 124–42, Cambi, *Istorie*, pp. 109–10, listing eight citizens implicated in the confessions (including Piero Alamanni and his son, Sforza Bettini, Piero and Luigi Tornabuoni) who were punished more lightly, cf. Sanudo, *Diarii*, 1, 710, 711–12, 714–15, and p. 256, n. 6 in this volume. According to the records of the company del Tempio (Rondoni, 'I "Giustiziati" a Firenze', p. 224), all but Tornabuoni were decapitated at 7 hrs and 'sepolti tutti nelle loro sepolture'.

[67] Cerretani, *Storia*, pp. 238–40; the *Processo* (with Lamberto's letter to Gualterotti and his further confession to the Otto), is ed. Villari, *Storia*, 2, Documento I, pp. iii–xxv, based on the C17 copy in BNF, MS II.IV.309, fols. 19–39v; cf. BNF MS G. Capponi 93, fols. 94r–101v. I cite CS. Append. 3, 1, fols.77r–82v, 98r–99r when it offers a fuller or variant version and for the testimonies of the five and others, also CS I, 360, fols. 10r–18 (Guicciardini's transcript).

Piero's decadence in exile, either – Guicciardini speculated – because he disliked what he saw or because he was malevolent and hoped to use his confession as a means of returning to Florence.[68]

As promised in his letter to Gualterotti, Lamberto also described under examination the Medici's network of contacts in Florence, among whom he himself had played an important role as go-between.[69] More revealing, if tendentious, is his account of Piero's 'way of life and behaviour and customs and thoughts'. In Rome, Lamberto reported, Piero would get out of bed at lunchtime, and if there was not enough to eat at home, since he loved his food, he went to Cardinal Sanseverino's house, where they ate and drank well, before retreating to rooms where there would be a beautiful courtesan or even a beautiful boy. After spending the day having a good time, he would perhaps gamble and then after supper go out on the town to visit courtesans and take them, and sometimes a boy, out to eat, drink, gamble and so on, before returning shortly before daybreak to his wife, 'who remained fresh, the poor thing'.[70] Lamberto went on to describe Piero's dissolute companions and his unpleasant treatment of loyal servants and of upstanding citizens like himself and his brother Alessandro, a priest, which he ascribed to Piero's belief that everyone owed him service as a form of tribute.

One of the servants named by Lamberto was Francesco Nero from Lombardy, a man of some standing who left Florence with Piero and, after looking after him with great devotion, clothing, feeding and even finding money for him, was treated disgracefully by Piero – who, according to Lamberto, wanted him killed: 'imagine how he would treat someone who served him badly when this is how he treats someone who has served him so faithfully!'[71] Two friars and a mace bearer were treated even worse; and as for Lamberto and his brother Alessandro, there was too much to say and much of it about public matters – but he did add 'another fine thing', that Piero wanted frog poison from Lamberto's brother Alessandro, and it was only when Alessandro led him on by persuading him that he could make counterfeit money that Piero realised

---

[68] Guicciardini, *Storie*, p. 139; Parenti, *Storia*, 2, pp. 119 and 133–4 (on his reward); his alienation may be explained by Piero's treatment of his brother Alessandro's benefice, Lorenzo, *Lettere* 16, pp. 275–6, n. 2.
[69] *Processo*, ed. Villari, pp. xiii–xxv, and Chapter 17 in this volume.
[70] Ibid., Villari, pp. xvii–xviii (cf. CS. Append. 3, 1, fols. 98v–99r). On Piero's love poems, possibly written during his exile, Brown, 'Piero de' Medici's Poems'.
[71] *Processo*, ed. Villari, p. xix.

it wasn't true. 'So you see what a man this is, he's not good enough to govern a castle, let alone a city.'[72]

We know enough about Piero's gambling and womanising habits, probably picked up during his second visit to Rome in 1487–88, to detect some truth in Lamberto's revelations about his lifestyle there. His letter criticising Passerini's accounts shows how niggling and ungenerous Piero could be towards his loyal servants and administrators, and Lamberto's account of Francesco Nero's treatment by Piero is confirmed by two secret encounters that Alessandro Braccesi had in Rome with Nero in October 1497.[73] What would have been more disturbing to the Florentine elite were Lamberto's revelations about the revenge the Medici would wreak on their return to Florence. In order not to feel obliged to their peers, he said, they would return with the support of the outside powers, Venice, Milan, the pope and, of course, the Orsini, bringing back with them administrators like the Dovizi brothers from Bibbiena. When the Medici brothers, Alfonsina, Lionardo Bartolini and others were talking in Rome about the future government and someone had proposed a fine state with a mature council of some twenty-five to thirty citizens for advice, Piero made a rude gesture and said he wanted advice from no one.[74] Nor was Cardinal Giovanni any better, for Lamberto reported that in Bolsena, during the emperor's visit to Pisa in 1496, the cardinal had said that if they returned, the slaughter in 1478 and the exiles in 1434 would be nothing compared with what they would do. They would destroy all the Nerli, most of the Capponi, the Nasi, the Gualterotti, the Bardi, Pagolantonio Soderini and his son (Tommaso), all the Giugni and the Corsi, part of the Rucellai, Scarfi, Valori and Pazzi, one or two Albizzi and selected others, especially Girolamo Martelli. They would take all the possessions of Lorenzo and Giovanni di Pierfrancesco, according to clauses in Cosimo's agreement with his brother (Lorenzo, their grandfather), and all the revenues of the commune would go towards paying the Orsini and Bartolomeo d'Alviano, as well as Giacoppo Petrucci's son and some of the Corsi.[75] After damning Piero as brainless and mad, penniless and indebted, with no reputation

---

[72] CS. Append. 3, 1, fol. 99r (abbreviated in Villari, p. xxii, § 46): 'Siché vedete che homo costui è, che non che fusse sofficiente a governare una cipta, non sarebbe sofficiente a governare uno chastello.'

[73] On the meetings in Rome, pp. 257–8 in this volume.

[74] *Processo*, ed. Villari, p. xix–xx, §37 (*om.* CS): 'egli fè dua fiche in sul viso'; Bertelli, 'Machiavelli e la politica estera', p. 37. Dovizi was described by Sanudo (*Diarii*, 1, 726) as one of Piero's secretaries, who, when Piero was in Florence 'haveva gran poder'; 'spesso va a la Signoria' (in Venice), especially now, after the beheading of the five.

[75] *Processo*, ed. Villari, pp. xxi–xxii, §§ 38–42, cf. CS. Append. 3, 1, fol. 99r.

and no friends, Lamberto ended by making a formal declaration that he was Piero's mortal enemy, *nimico capitale* – something that accorded badly, perhaps, with his plea to be forgiven by the Signoria as Christ forgave St. Paul. Yet it seems to have worked, for according to Parenti, Lamberto was pardoned as a reward for his revelations; he was awarded the privilege of carrying arms, had his tax debts cancelled and, with his brother, was granted other favours.[76]

Even before these revelations in August 1497, however, a harsh reaction to the Medici was taking place. Wherever the arms or insignia of Lorenzo de' Medici and his children and heirs were painted or sculpted – in homes, in all public or private, secular as well as ecclesiastical places within Florentine territory and jurisdiction – they were to be chiselled out, destroyed and replaced by the insignia of the Florentine people, that is, 'a red cross on a white ground'. The symbolism of Piero's defeat by the Florentine commune could not have been clearer.[77] The price on his head still made him vulnerable to bounty seekers – not least the Colonna family, the Orsini's inveterate enemies, whose cardinal was quick to offer Braccesi (then Florence's special envoy in Rome) his family's support in 'getting [Piero] out of the way'.[78] But although Piero and Giovanni wanted to retreat to Giovanni's benefice of Montecassino for some weeks, their supporters in Rome – the cardinal, the Orsini and others – had been heartened by his arrival at the walls of Florence 'with a lance on his hip' and now regarded Venice as their best support, where they had been promised arms and horses.[79]

Then the events of August intervened, and afterwards the Medici suffered further humiliations. In mid-September some rooms in their palace in Via Larga were commandeered by the Officials of the Abbondanza for storing grain; in October Maddalena was ordered to leave Florentine territory and not return; and two days later the Officials of the Rebels were ordered to hand over to the king of France's envoy two books from Piero's and his brothers' former library, Ptolemy's

---

[76] Ibid., p. xxxiii, §§ 48–9, and n. 68 in this chapter. His enmity towards Piero is explained in his letter to Gualterotti (pp. iii–iv).

[77] Signori, Delib. ord. aut. 99, fol. 37r, 9 May 1497: 'videlicet insignia + rubee in campo albo' (the cost of which was to be borne by the Officiales Rebellium and the Medici syndics, 14 May, fols. 38v–39r).

[78] Braccesi in Rome to the Dieci in Florence, 20 and 31 May 1497, ed. Guidi, *Segretario militante*, pp. 441–2, 444–5 (Append. 3, nos. 1 and 4, cf. 98–9), which Braccesi welcomed, even though the cardinal's syphilis delayed immediate action (441).

[79] The same, 24 May 1497, ed. Guidi, pp. 443–4: 'con la lancia in sulla coscia'(443). Florentines like del Nero and Vespucci wanted the city protected by armed forces outside, not by armed guards within, *Consulte 1495–1497*, at p. 506 (28 July 1497).

Cosmographia and Seneca's *Opera*.⁸⁰ December saw the beheading in the Bargello of the Medici's devoted agent Francesco Cegia, after the government had retrieved everything they could of Piero's that Cegia had so zealously tried to protect.⁸¹ With his closest friends in Florence beheaded and his reputation seriously weakened, Piero's chances of return once again seemed increasingly remote.

---

⁸⁰ Signori Delib.ord. aut. 99, fols. 84r, 90r–v, 19 September, 13, 15 October 1497). The envoy was Niccolò Alamanni.
⁸¹ Parenti, *Storia*, 2, p. 130; on Cegia, Fusco and Corti, *Lorenzo de' Medici*, p. 353, doc. 233; *DBI*, 23, 1979 (R. Ristori); Pampaloni, ed., Cegia's 'Ricordi segreti'; Kent, *Princely Citizen*, p. 196, and pp. 260–1 in this volume.

17 'Contamination in the Labyrinth'
Networking in Exile

Lamberto dell'Antella's confession and the execution of five leading Florentines in August 1497 marked a watershed in Piero's years of exile. Before that, Piero's friends met in Florence to discuss plans to bring him back to Florence, with Lamberto as a go-between carrying messages to and fro. In the early years of his exile, Piero had described himself in letters to the government and to his cousins as a good citizen who only wanted to be treated fairly and allowed to return home. But after 1497 everyone was afraid of contagion and we have to rely on the reports of ambassadors, merchants and spies to discover his movements. They show how high the stakes were in a conflict that pitted the leading families of Florence against each other.

Anonymous letters to the government and to Piero's friends also show how the screws were tightening on Piero, even before August 1497. The long letter of warning sent from Rome as Piero approached the walls in April that year was addressed to the Signoria and written in very small, neat characters that give it the anonymity of a printed text. It explains that, although its writer knew the government was well informed and that the envoy in Rome (Alessandro Braccesi) was a sensible man, he couldn't know what went on outside and in secret, whereas he himself (the writer), as well as dealing in high places with men of authority, also enjoyed domestic relationships with people who might be useful to the government. And warning of Piero's 'incredible malignity' and his skill in trying to entice people to him whom he then discarded, it continued: 'Don't be surprised I don't reveal my name. I need to carry out some business affairs of mine here and I don't want to be discovered. You will know who I am one day.' At the foot of the page the writer left his counterseal in case he wrote again.[1]

---

[1] SSX8LCMR 66, fol. 304r, anon. to the Signoria, inc. 'amice carissime' (cf. pp. 245–6, n. 55 in this volume): 'So io che e' vorrebbe con ogni arte tirare a se certi che spera avere con animo di saziarsi poi di loro.'

A second anonymous letter from Rome a year later (dated 26 March 1498, at the height of the Savonarola crisis) was written by someone connected with business and banking circles there. The writer was also hostile to Piero, but addressed his letter not to the Signoria but to a friend who would know with whom to share it. It reports news from two sources (the banker Jacopo Rucellai and a friend from Siena sent by Piero): that according to Piero his affairs were going well and this time he wouldn't need arms, and that he wanted to tell one of his friends he was well disposed towards him and wanted to give good for evil. Although the writer drove his friend (Piero's emissary) away, he returned the next evening to talk again, only to be told that the writer didn't want to hear him, to avoid entering into matters that could lead to trouble, etc.' The 'etcetera' meant one of three things, he explained, that Piero was trying to make trouble for him, that 'by contaminating' him Piero wanted 'to place him in some labyrinth' or that he was simply using him to gain profit and reputation with the pope (since Piero had told the pope recently that support for him in Florence was increasing, due to the Savonarola conflict). The writer didn't want to show his letter to the ambassador (Domenico Bonsi) because that would have required a public letter with his name in it, and since he knew such things were never kept secret, he had chosen the more secure option.[2] This man's refusal to be contaminated by entering the labyrinth resembles closely what Bonsi told the Dieci on 4 April, that he avoided meeting Piero because Piero would use it to his advantage with the pope. And since the writer knew what was going on in Milan – where he had learnt that the duke was fantasising about creating 'some Idol in Florence, either Piero or someone else' – and also knew about what the 'big men', *gran maestri*, were up to in Rome, with the pope 'listening and helping', he may have been the ambassador's secretary or a man of affairs in close touch with what was going on.[3]

The Florentines' fear of contact with exiles abroad continued. In 1501, when Piero asked the ambassador in Rome (by then Francesco Pepi) if he could talk to him, even with others present, Pepi replied no, it wouldn't

---

[2] Signori Respons. 10, fol. 35r, 26 March 1498: 'non lo volli udire, per non havere da entrare in pratiche da poterne conseguire noia, etcetera. Hora l'amico intendendo "etcetera", dà a questa cosa tre commenti: el primo che forse Piero cerchava metterlo in qualche travaglio, o veramente contaminandolo metterlo in qualche laberyntho. Tertio', etc.

[3] . Bonsi to the Dieci, 20 April 1498, SSX8LCMR 30, fol. 43v: 's'andava vantando per acquistare credito et favore apresso di chi l'udiva'; Signori Respons. 10, fol. 35v: 'che'l Duca di Milano sia in fantasia d'ingegnarsi creare costì qualche Idolo, o Piero o altri', '*auscultante Pontefice et annuente*'.

help Piero and he, Pepi, would incur blame for it – adding that he had refused in order to protect himself ('it would be safer for me') and that he wouldn't change unless instructed to do so by the government.⁴ Piero de' Medici himself had been told by his father to be careful whom he talked to in Rome in 1487, and even Machiavelli was fearful he might end up in gaol if he visited Rome in 1513 and talked to the Soderini exiles.⁵ Even so, 'contamination' and 'labyrinth' are strong words to evoke the dangers of networking with exiles. They perhaps owe something to what the earlier letter described as Piero's skill in enticing people to him whom he then discarded. They owe much more, however, to the events of August 1497. It was then that the confessions, or testimonies, of leading members of the elite demonstrated publicly how their meetings in Florence had been contaminated by contact with go-betweens like Lamberto dell'Antella, or through the betrayal of friends, leading them into a maze of interrogations – who said what, to whom and when – that, unless they escaped by fleeing the city, ended in death by execution, slain by the minotaur of the state.⁶

Lamberto's confession also throws light on the role of letters and couriers in exile networks. We know, of course, from the records of the Otto di Guardia that the government paid spies as part of its rigorous system of criminal justice, and when the Otto enjoyed *balìa* (as it always did, by this time), it could exercise summary punishment on its victims. It could also issue preemptory bulletins and banns to extend its web of control throughout its territory, like the ones issued after Alfonsina's unauthorised departure from Florence in September 1495.⁷ We have seen it appointing citizens to spy on the king of France and on Piero earlier that year and using merchant communities (especially in Rome) to provide the government with information.⁸ Most ambassadors and local

---

⁴ Pepi to the Signoria, 8 March 1501, SSX8LCMR 34, fols. 8v–9r: 'Piero de Medici hieri mi mandò a dire che harebbe caro visitarmi et parlarmi ... ho facto cosi credendo essere a me più sicuro.'
⁵ Brown, *Florence* (2011), pp. 198–9.
⁶ In September 1497, when the government summonsed other 'colpevoli, impuniti' citizens, including Piero Alamanni, messer Luigi and Piero Tornabuoni, they were exiled and deprived of office when they failed to appear, Parenti, *Storia*, 2, p. 127. On Lamberto's *processo*, p. 249, n. 67 in this volume, and what follows in this chapter.
⁷ Stern, *Criminal Law System*, pp. 193–8, Zorzi, *L'amministrazione della giustizia penale*, pp. 67–82, and pp. 239–40 in this volume.
⁸ p. 238, n. 29 in this volume, *Consulte e pratiche, 1495–1498*, p. 53 [October–November] 1495: 'per mezo di mercatanti di Roma o di qualche persona secreta' (Pierf. Pandolfini), 454, 455 (28 March 1497): 'tenergli ascolte dietro et observare suo andamenti et veghiarlo continuamente', 'tenere spie et observare Piero de' Medici'; Pepi in Rome to the Signoria (4 November 1501), SSX8LCMR 34, fol. 175r, that although most rumours were false, 'qui ... 20 lettere private di costì in vostri mercanti ... dicono affirmative che

officials had 'friends' who bravely supplied them with information, like the 'trustworthy person' from Montepulciano who visited the Florentine commissary in Brolio when he learnt about a raid on Florentine territory, and 'the friend' who was prepared to work for Florence provided he could be remunerated for what he lost by leaving his work to do so.[9] Couriers and mailbags were regularly captured that provide us, as well as the government, with letters we would otherwise know nothing about. We saw the worry it caused Piero in 1496 when he thought his mail had been stolen, and vice versa, the Florentine government was equally upset when its couriers were attacked and its mailbags stolen by Piero and his supporters.[10] And sometimes, alienated by Piero's treatment, people volunteered information to the government, as in 1497 when Francesco Nero approached the Florentine envoy in Rome, Alessandro Braccesi.

Nero was a former soldier of the Milanese captain Francesco Secco. He became Piero's 'most faithful friend and most privy to all his secrets' after Charles VIII's arrival in Serezzano in 1494, but now he professed to be Piero's mortal enemy and wanted safe conduct to give the Signoria important information. Understandably worried that he might be a spy, Braccesi asked Nero for a sample of what he would reveal, before concluding that, since he was determined to come to Florence in any case, the Signoria should probably trust him as 'someone very judicious, who is evidently well informed about these humours, having been for a few weeks in on the discussion of these things'.[11] Meeting secretly in the cloister of S. Maria sopra Minerva in Rome, Francesco Nero was able to warn Braccesi and Antonio de' Pazzi – as a sample of his wares – that Piero might be inciting Castrocaro to rebel against Florence. Then he told them a lot about the Orsini: the money they had recently acquired to set their affairs in order, their support for Jacopo Conte and their wish to improve their conditions with the French, or else with the Venetians.

---

questi Medici hanno a tornare', etc. On exiles and merchant communities, Guicciardini, *Dialogo*, pp.168–9, tr. Brown, pp. 164–5.

[9] Bindaccio Ricasoli in Brolio to the Dieci, 10 June 1496, Dieci Respons. 48, fol. 148r–v: 'sono advisato da una persona degno di fede', 'Questo dì mi è venuto uno amico mio ... ha buona volontà di servire alle Vostre Signorie', etc.

[10] E.g. Bonsi in Rome to the Dieci, 9 February 1498, SSX8LCMR 30, fol. 9r–v: 'da Bacchano li furono tolte tucte la lettere da due benissimo a chavallo armati et stravestiti ... è interpretata ... che sia stata per ordine del Vinetiano col mezo di questi Orsini o vero di Piero de' Medici', pp. 240, 271–2 and 284 in this volume.

[11] Braccesi to the Dieci, 6 October 1497, SSX8LCMR 66, fols. 325r: 'ha sempre seguito Piero et è suto il più fedele amico et il più conscio d'ogni suo secreto che huomo di suo pari ...'; 325v: 'hoggi capitale inimico a Piero'; 326r: 'persona molto sensata', etc., 328r, the same, 18 October 1497. On Braccesi, formerly in Siena (p. 132, n. 41 in this volume), now a secret envoy in Rome to assist the ambassador Becchi, Gherardi, *Nuovi documenti*, p. 148, n. 1.

He also said that Florence shouldn't trust Carlo Orsini when he said he didn't support Piero, since the two men enjoyed an incredibly close relationship, with Gian Giordano (the illegitimate Carlo's half-brother) in tow, for stupid though he was ('a man of few words, less intelligence and a beast'), Carlo treated him like wax, and unless the Orsini had trouble in Rome or from the French, 'they will give all their support to Piero'; and as they were very close to Anton Maria Sanseverino, Florence should be on the alert if he came to Siena, since that city would always do what he wanted.[12]

When Braccesi and Antonio de' Pazzi met Nero some ten days later 'at the Minerva' again, he had more useful information to give them about Piero's contacts in and around Bracciano, like fra Lauro and Giulio Bellanti, who had arrived in disguise from Siena. From Giulio, Nero was able to learn about Sienese movements and their threat to Florence, and also that the Orsini, especially Carlo and Gian Giordano, would always do everything possible for Piero, whose quarrel with his brother Cardinal Giovanni was still unhealed.[13]

Informants like Francesco Nero and Lamberto dell'Antella were, of course, invaluable in revealing the Medici's networks of communication inside and outside Florence. Fulfilling the promises made on his capture, Lamberto revealed in the first of his legal testimonies that the courier who took letters to Alfonsina in Siena and then on to Piero was Luca Speranzini. He was initially sent to Alfonsina by Giovanni Cambi, with instructions to get the Buonvisi in Lucca to pay 400–500 ducats (secured by jewels taken to the Buonvisi by Naldini) to the Venturi Bank in Siena. But instead of Speranzini receiving the money for the Venturi, Alfonsina confirmed that it had been paid to Giuliano de' Medici.[14] Speranzini then carried Piero's brief reply in his saddlebags to Florence. It read:

My Fathers, you urge me to forge ahead and I will; but I want to understand clearly from you, if I come, what you will do.

And then, according to Cambi's testimony, Piero had long discussions with Lionardo Bartolini and Luca Naldini, with the conclusion that

---

[12] Braccesi to the Dieci, 6 October 1497, SSX8LCMR 66, fols. 326r: 'è cosa incredibile la intrinsecha benivolentia che hanno inseme', 325r 'di pocho dischorso et di mancho ingegno et una bestia'. On Antonio Pazzi, a merchant in Rome whom the Dieci used as an informant, Gherardi, *Nuovi documenti*, p. 149, n. 1.
[13] Braccesi to the Dieci, 18 October, ibid., fol. 328r–v. on Giulio, p. 134 in this volume.
[14] Lamberto, *Processo*, ed. Villari, pp. v, viii–ix (cf. Cambi in CS. Append. 3, 1, fol. 99r. On Speranzini, Fusco and Corti, *Lorenzo de' Medici*, p. 356, n. 8, Tewes, *Kampf um Florenz*, pp. 332–3, etc.

nothing would happen unless helped by God, the Medici and 'the sect in the middle' (led by Bernardo del Nero).[15]

Giovanni Cambi had initiated the clandestine operation to distribute money from the Medici Bank to the exiles on the day of Piero's escape from Florence, when he handed on to various couriers the 5000 florins he had been given by the bank's cashier in Pisa.[16] The Medici were also given money from the Rome branch of the bank by Nofri Tornabuoni. According to Lamberto, Nofri took 500–600 ducats to Piero in Rome before his attempted return in 1497, which was carried to Siena by the protonotary Raffaello Petrucci (to give to Silvio Savelli and others).[17] He also revealed the names of two people who talked to Piero on 10 May 1496 in Galera (one of them was Francesco di Domenico Naldini, employed by the Medici Bank). Although he didn't know what they talked about, the secret memoirs of the Medici's confidential agent in Pisa and Florence, Francesco Cegia, make it clear that Cegia was at the centre of what has been called 'an underground movement', involving not only Alfonsina and her mother but bankers like the Tornabuoni and the Bonvisi in Lucca and their factors, Giovanni Cambi, and also friars attached to Medici convents, all of whom conspired to recover Medici possessions and provide the exiles with money.[18] In August 1496 Naldini was given 184 florins 'to send to Piero', and he also took silver and gold medals to the Bonvisi bank in Lucca as security for their loan of 300 florins to Giovanni Cambi – 'that is, 48 gold medallions, 200 silver ones and an emerald set in gold' – and he went to Piombino for business concerned with the alum mines there. Another banking clerk used as an agent between Florence and Rome was Domenico Alamanni, who talked to Piero and Cardinal Giovanni on arriving in Rome in mid-November 1496 and later spent many days shut up with them and the Medici bankers Nofri Tornabuoni and Lionardo Bartolini.[19]

---

[15] Lamberto, *Processo*, p. ix, citing Cambi in CS. Append. 3, 1, fol.99r: 'et portò la lectera nel posolino della cavalla ... et recò la risposta la quale diceva "patri mia"', etc. (Piero was in Rapolano in December 1495). On Naldini and Bartolini, CS. Append. 3, fol. 99r and Tewes, *Kampf*, pp. 167–9. On 'the sect in the middle', n. 25 in this chapter.

[16] Libro di debitori e creditori, GC 5, fol. 358 left (cf. p. 144 in this volume), that Cambi gave the money to several people, including 'Fratande di uno frate del Charmine al quale ne fu da Pisano tolto un sachetta di fl. 671'.

[17] *Processo*, ed. Villari, p. x. On Nofri and banking *fattori* as special agents, Bullard, *Lorenzo*, pp. 221–7, cf. Bullard, 'Hammering Away', pp. 394–5; on Nofri and Lorenzo 'doctoring' the bank's accounts in Rome, Fusco and Corti, *Lorenzo de' Medici*, pp. 170–1.

[18] Fusco and Corti (ibid., pp. 167, 170) refer to many of these agents.

[19] *Processo*, ed. Villari, pp. ix, x, xii; Cegia, 'Ricordi segreti', intro. (pp. 188–96) and 223, etc.; Fusco and Corti, *Lorenzo de' Medici*, pp. 168–9. On Naldini, Tewes, *Kampf um Florenz*, pp. 162–3, etc., and CS. Append. 3, 1, fols. 88r, 100r-v.

Piero's network of contacts included the wife of Donato Benci, who ordered two trunks of delicate objects to be despatched from Florence; after being hidden for a time, they were then taken to Carlo Altoviti's house in Orvieto. A peasant from Quinto outside Florence carried letters from Piero to his father's old secretary, Niccolò Michelozzi, before Piero's attempted return in 1497, and other letters to Giovanni Cambi were carried by an employee of Siena's government, sewn into his stirrup strap: after being accompanied across the Arno at the Porta San Frediano to the Pazzi loggia by a saddlemaker, he dismounted at the inn, dug the letters out and gave them to a woman in Franceschetto Cibo's house (nearby) on Easter Saturday. They were said to be from Alfonsina's mother, but Lamberto thought they were from Piero.[20]

Members of religious orders, especially friars, were also valuable as messengers and middlemen thanks to their peripatetic lifestyle and their status as confidants, which enabled them to carry letters to and fro and make payments without comment. Fra Mariano da Gennazzano, General of the Augustinian Order, and the friars Serafino and Cherubino from the Augustinian church of San Gallo appear frequently in the testimonies. This church was closely associated with the Medici, but members of other orders are also mentioned. They include a Carthusian monk 'with a long beard', fra Michele, a Carmelite who carried a bag of money for Cambi from Pisa before being captured by the Pisans, an Olivetan who reported on Piero in Siena – and even fra Lauro turned up in Piero's service after acting as his cousins' emissary in 1493–94.[21] So by using a mixture of couriers, friars, banking clerks and government and family employees, Piero was able to send letters in and out of Florence and secure money – from the bank and from his wife's jewels – to pay for the fighting around Ossaia and Rapolino in late 1495–96 and for the 1497 expedition against Florence.

If captured, these men might be tortured for evidence – like Cegia, who provides a vivid account in his secret memoirs of how a messenger of the Signoria summonsed him before the Otto di Guardia in August 1496 to discuss a letter he had written to Cardinal Giovanni. The Otto then sent him to the Bargello, where he said yes, he had written to the cardinal about some Medici jewels he needed to be told about, but nothing else, because he knew his letter had been captured at Firenzuola

---

[20] Parenti, *Storia*, 2, p. 105; *Processo*, ed. Villari, pp. vi–vii, x.
[21] On San Gallo as Lorenzo's, Kent, *Princely Citizen*, pp. 187–93, at 193, on fra Mariano and the other friars, see the testimonies that follow and n. 31 in this chapter. Alamanni to Piero (1 April 1494, MAP 50, 264r) describes a possible spy of Lorenzo di Pierfrancesco's in Forlì, who *'non è piu de' frati di Sangallo, che se ne è uscito et ha preso habito di monaco nero'*, cioè, di queste anguille dicadute *di San Benedecto'* (decoded).

by a courier and taken to the government. At the urging of some leading citizens, the Otto then told him to write down everything that had happened from the Medici's expulsion until now, and when he refused, they tortured him with the rope, telling him that 'in the days of the other [Medici] regime' they would at least have chopped off his head or hanged him and that Lorenzo de' Medici wrote to Turkey to get people murdered and take revenge.[22] Cegia claimed he had merely 'written about some business matters' in a letter sent by Francesco Scarfi to Cardinal Giovanni, but his suggestion that Giovanni was sending the letter back (through a priest) either as a reminder of the business, 'or to harm me', shows that the cardinal was considered just as capable of contaminating his devoted servants as Piero, and just as vengeful in promising the destruction of his enemies in Florence. Cegia was in the end fined 200 florins and ordered to stay twenty miles outside Florence for a year and then inside Florence for three years; and on returning home, he wrote down this cautionary tale to explain the payment to his descendants and also to warn them how nearly he lost his life. The following year, however, he was implicated again by Lamberto's confessions, and although not executed with the five Mediceans in August 1497, he was held for prolonged questioning before being finally beheaded on 16 December that year.[23]

The five citizens beheaded in August were – with the exception of Cambi – all members of Florence's ruling elite who had been contaminated by Lamberto dell'Antella's confession.[24] Their confessions, describing their meetings with each other in their homes, in churches, in piazzas and in the government palace, provide an unrivalled source of information about networking circles, especially within the city. The most outstanding of the five was Bernardo del Nero, whose election as Gonfalonier of Justice in March 1497 was the trigger that set in motion Piero's most serious attempt to return. But although Piero relied on his support, del Nero himself had moved to a more neutral position (perhaps after his contretemps with Piero in 1494), and when he was Gonfalonier he created an innovative magistracy, the Paciali or 'peacemakers', composed of twelve members of opposing sects. His mediatory role seems

---

[22] Cegia, 'Ricordi segreti', p. 230: 'a tenpo dell'altro stato', referring to the capture in Constantinople and repatriation of Baroncelli in 1479 to be hanged in Florence, Lorenzo, *Lettere* 3, p. 103, n. 11, and 4, p. 108. n. 1.

[23] Pampaloni, intro. to Cegia's 'Ricordi', p. 196, Parenti, *Storia*, p. 130, cf. 38, describing Cegia as one of the 'cancellieri e fattori' of Cardinal Giovanni.

[24] CS. Append. 3, 1, fol. 82v: 'Per causa della qual lettera et esamina fatte da detto Lamberto furono decapitati li appié: Niccolò Ridolfi, Giannozzo Pucci, Lorenzo Tornabuoni, Bernardo del Nero, Giovanni Cambi.'

confirmed by Giovanni Cambi's description of him as 'one of that sect in the middle' who, because they had been helped by the Medici, felt they 'had to do them some good'. He was a controversial figure, as we have seen, so his testimony is of the greatest interest.[25] Tornabuoni quoted Alamanni as saying that Bernardo didn't talk much about Piero [de' Medici] and seemed worn out and uncertain of his end, although he did say that Florence 'couldn't live without a head'.[26] Del Nero himself initially confessed that he had had no dealings with Piero and always hated him, with evidence to support this, before adding, under torture:

> I understand Nicolò [Ridolfi] has said, also in my presence, that while I was Gonfalonier, he read me a letter from Piero to Lorenzo Tornabuoni, which Lorenzo ordered Nicolò to read to me and, trusting him, I confess that he read it to me without it ever leaving Nicolò's hands, nor do I remember ever sharing it with my companions [in the Signoria].

This was Piero's letter to Tornabuoni in which he said he would be happy to relinquish power ('let himself be governed') if he returned. After hearing the letter, Tornabuoni recalled Bernardo saying: 'he counts without the host', which he thought was true and seemed appropriate – in other words, he agreed with Bernardo that Florence would not receive Piero gladly, and interestingly this terse reply is what Parenti chose to record in his *History*. Under torture, Bernardo confessed his error in not reporting the letter to the government and asked God to forgive Niccolò for putting him in this spot.[27]

Niccolò Ridolfi, the 'authoritative and noble' father-in-law of Piero's sister Contessina, didn't remember Bernardo's reply, but he recalled discussing Piero's bad government with Bernardo, adding that 'in truth it seemed to me he [Bernardo] held him in low esteem and alien to himself'. He claimed he had never been interested in Piero's affairs, not in his return or anything else, and when told a letter had been received from Piero in Rome, he wanted to hear nothing about it; when given it, he did however hand it over to Bernardo (without remembering his reply). He also showed Bernardo a coded letter sent by Giacoppo

---

[25] On 'quella secta che fu facta di mezo', *Processo*, CS. Append. 3, 1, fol. 99r–v; on the Paciali, Brown, *Florence* (2011), pp. 208–10; on del Nero, Guicciardini, *Dialogo*, tr. Brown, pp. xi, xii–xiii, 180–1; Parenti, *Storia*, 2, pp. 82 and 87, pp. 156 and 247 in this volume and *ad ind*.

[26] CS. Append. 3, 1, fols. 83v–89r, 100v–102r (Tornabuoni): 'li pareva che li avessi logoro la<s>ciato e che non sapeva giudichare el fine suo. Le conclusioni di Bernardo erono che qui non si potessi stare senza capo'; cf. Villari, pp. xii–xiii.

[27] CS. Append. 3, 1, fol. 102v (*om*. Villari): 'di poi con tormento disse "io intendo"', etc. [cont. *in marg*]. Cf. Bertelli, '*Ricordi* di G. V. Soderini', p. 395, citing Bernardo Rucellai, who said del Nero deserved to die but that he had been deceived by Niccolò Ridolfi.

Petrucci in Siena to Giovanni Cambi about 'Lino' (Piero de' Medici). Despite this non-committal evidence, Ridolfi asserted that on another occasion Bernardo said he would become twenty years younger if Piero returned.[28]

Another topic in Ridolfi's testimony concerned his views on the Medici's chances of returning: little would happen without Milan, he told Lorenzo Tornabuoni, but Tornabuoni thought the duke and some citizens wanted Lorenzo di Pierfrancesco as head, not (as the Milanese ambassador reported) Piero. In 1496 Ridolfi had been asked to contribute money for Piero to return 'as a respected citizen' (*uomo da bene*) by the Medici's favourite friar, the Augustinian Mariano da Gennazzano, who wanted to know what people in Florence thought of Piero. Niccolò replied that he heard fra Mariano willingly but could not give him money, and when asked if he had any messages for Piero (since the friar was about to return to Rome), only that Piero should husband himself by behaving well. Ridolfi also had two meetings with fra Serafino in San Gallo and Santo Spirito, who told him from fra Mariano that Piero had considerable support in Rome: the pope, the Orsini and others were offering to raise men-at-arms and infantry to fight in the Val di Lamona and the Romagna. When asked again what people thought of Piero in Florence, since he was much loved in Rome, Ridolfi replied that unless he was loved more in Rome than here, he couldn't be much loved. And when asked to return to Alfonsina a book of hers, he was equally unforthcoming, saying that he only knew the book as part of his daughter-in-law Contessina's dowry and now wasn't the time to talk about it. Yet despite the terseness of his replies, when asked under torture if he wanted Piero's return, he replied affirmatively: 'yes, yes, yes' (*sì, sì, sì*).[29]

Unlike Niccolò Ridolfi and Bernardo del Nero, Giannozzo Pucci was not an office holder. He was, however, one of Piero's closest personal friends and although his name is frequently mentioned in all the other testimonies, his own testimony in the Strozzi manuscript is the shortest of them all, simply confirming what Lorenzo Tornabuoni had said about discouraging Piero's attempts to return through friars from the Certosa and San Gallo. The surprise is that in Francesco Guicciardini's transcript, Giannozzo's testimony is by far the longest, with a particularly interesting account of his extensive encounters with fra Mariano da

---

[28] CS. Append. 3, 1, fol. 102r (Ridolfi) '... dice che e' conta senza l'oste ... che possa esser vero, parendomi risposta conveniente in quel tempo dello uficio di Bernardo', cf. Parenti, *Storia*, 2, pp. 124–5.

[29] *Processo* (Ridolfi), fol. 102v: 'a fare masseritia e a portarssi bene'. Guicciardini in CS I, 360, fol. 14r adds that on 13 August Ridolfi said he'd been 'uno pazo essere ito drieto a una fungaia di fanciulli ... e confessò havere errato'.

Gennazzano, whom he describes as an intimate friend with whom he often chatted about the city and the bad state it was in.³⁰ In his first day's testimony, Giannozzo also elaborated on the curious visit he received from 'a Certosan friar with a very long beard' (fra Michele, whom he got his wife's relative, Luigi Bini, to track to see where he went and whom he talked to); sent to him by Giacoppo and Pandolfo Petrucci in Siena, he produced a golden rod or stick for Giannozzo to use as a countersign, his own sign being a simple golden thread of gold that he carried underneath a ruby or sometimes a diamond.³¹

Four days later, on 8 and 9 August, Giannozzo went much further in describing his recent contact with fra Mariano in the summer of 1497, when the friar was very ill. Initially they talked about Giannozzo's clerical (half-)brother in Rome, Lorenzo, before turning to Piero, who hoped Giannozzo hadn't forgotten their old friendship – no, he replied to fra Mariano, but it would serve only to make him pray to God for him, as he urged fra Mariano to get all his friars to do, too. Fra Mariano started to tell Giannozzo that he had found Piero in a much better state of mind than he had expected, promising not to upset anyone if he ever returned to Florence and admitting he'd made many mistakes – and then the friar was too tired to continue. When Giannozzo returned two days later, it was the state of Florence that dominated their discussion, fra Mariano saying that no one he had talked to liked the present way of governing and he knew for sure that all the leading citizens were unhappy. He particularly wanted to talk to Francesco Valori, who used to love him; he didn't want to displease Savonarola, but he wanted to reassure Valori about Piero. As for Pierfilippo Pandolfini, Niccolò Ridolfi and Bernardo del Nero, how were they and was Giannozzo close to them? They were all well, but stretched by doing what was necessary for the commune; he, Giannozzo, regarded them as his fathers, but now was not the time to be any closer. What about Lorenzo Lenzi, who fra Mariano had heard was completely Francophile, and what did Giannozzo think about the French situation? 'I replied that if it weren't for Fra Girolamo, I'd have lost all hope.' At this fra Mariano began to discuss the Italian powers, that France had no place among them and everything would be fine if they could settle the state of Florence, which the league could do by restoring Piero; a long debate ensued between them about Venice and the danger

---

[30] Guicciardini, CS I, 360, fols. 14v–17v (4, 8, 9 August 1497) at 14v (4th): 'essendo molto suo dimesticho et spesso confabulando seco più volte venimo in discorso della cictà et dei suo male essere' (cf. *Processo*, ed. Villari, fol. 100r–v). Guicciardini, *Storie* (p. 142) on Giannozzo as a 'giovane di grande ingegno e molto d'assai ... ma tutto di Piero', etc.

[31] Guicciardini, CS I, 360, fols. 14v: 'uno frate Certosino con una gran barba', 15r: 'si cavò una verghecta di filo d'oro di oro', etc. On the Bini, Rubin, *Images and Identity*, p. 248.

of its ambition to rule Italy, which fra Mariano thought might be unavoidable as protection against France; and about Milan, which would not agree to restore Piero unless he put himself in its hands.[32]

A further encounter took place in Santo Spirito (where fra Mariano had himself carried), in which he reported his conversation with Ridolfi about Bernardo del Nero having turned to Lorenzo and Giovanni di Pierfrancesco with a good number of citizens. Then, because Giannozzo had been seen talking to Cegia before his capture, the spectre of contamination deterred further encounters until one last meeting, when the friar reported that even Jacopo de' Nerli might easily be won over to support Piero. After he left, it was fra Serafino who brought Giannozzo news from Rome. Sitting in the garden at San Gallo, he drew out from a bag under his tunic a letter (from Piero) and a note in which he jotted down the details of the people engaged by the league 'for Piero's expedition' – which made Giannozzo laugh, for surely such a large force was unnecessary if the league was for real. More details of Piero's commitment emerged, but when fra Serafino said the pope was sending someone to represent the league to whom the friends should entrust themselves, both Giannozzo and Niccolò Ridolfi responded that they would certainly not do so and that Piero should in no way return to the city by force. And so things slowly cooled down, especially when Piero wanted to be sent 7000–8000 ducats, as well as ser Francesco Baroni or il Butto to update him on affairs in Florence.[33]

What this testimony demonstrates is the strength of Piero's support outside Florence and equally the steadfastness of the republican opposition inside, linked by fra Mariano weaving his way between the two worlds. Another strand in this interlocking network is provided by the bankers and businessmen Lorenzo Tornabuoni and Giovanni Cambi. The repeated interrogations of Lorenzo Tornabuoni reflect his importance, not only as Piero's cousin but as the person in charge of the Medici's financial affairs after Piero's exile.[34] Together with his Tornabuoni cousin Nofri, manager of the bank in Rome from 1487, Lorenzo was responsible for settling the Medici's debts in Rome and Naples and for supervising the division of goods between family

---

[32] CS. I, 360, fols. 15v–16v: 'Risposigli se non fussi le cose di Fra Hieronomo n'harei perduto ogni speranza' (16r). Giannozzo, like Lorenzo Tornabuoni, was a signed-up Savonarolan, Polizzotto, *Elect Nation*, pp. 16, 456, 459.

[33] Ibid., fols. 16v–18v: 'a uso di figure di abacho' (17r).

[34] De Roover, *Banco Medici*, pp. 320 and (on the Naples branch, similarly taken over by a company in Giovanni's name), 372–3; Bullard, 'Hammering Away', pp. 394–5; Guidi Bruscoli, '1487 Medici-Cybo Marriage', p. 82, n. 66. On Ridolfi's alignment in 1493, p. 154 in this volume.

members. So he inevitably got drawn into the labyrinth, contacted by everyone who wanted the Medici's return, forced to make payments or accept Nofri's payments to the exiled Medici in Rome, as well as settle affairs with the Medici women at home in Florence. Although he had legitimate reasons to remain in contact with the exiles, he struggled, like Ridolfi, to avoid being entirely enmeshed in the web that was tightening around him, as his lengthy and repeated interrogations demonstrate. He admitted Giannozzo Pucci was a close friend with whom he often talked about the day's affairs. It was Giannozzo who drew him into reading Piero's letters and writing to his banking cousins in Rome about Bernardo's appointment as Gonfalonier; on one occasion Giannozzo even pursued him to the Church of Santo Spirito to get him to agree to write – which he did, since he had to write anyway about the Orsini's debts with the bank.[35]

Lorenzo Tornabuoni was crucially involved in reading two letters from Rome. One was the transcript of a letter from Piero to fra Serafino in San Gallo, in which Piero asked the friar to organise his return together with Lorenzo, Bernardo, Niccolò Ridolfi and Giannozzo (explaining that although he, Piero, could return with the help of the league, he would need to enter into many contractual obligations, whereas if his friends helped him with 6000 florins, he could return peacefully via the favourable Signoria).[36] The second was a letter to the same effect, brought from Rome to Lorenzo by the courier Ungherotto. Lorenzo had been careful to change the names of Bernardo and Niccolò when transcribing it for Giannozzo, in case it fell into the wrong hands and implicated them too much when read by the Signoria, who were shortly to discuss the matter.[37] Meeting Ridolfi in the piazza after his visit to the Gonfalonier Bernardo del Nero, Lorenzo asked him what the Gonfalonier thought about it, to which Niccolò replied (as we saw) that Bernardo said Piero 'counted without the host'. After that, he told his interrogators, 'you must understand that speaking for myself I heard nothing more whatsoever about the plans' – apart from telling Nofri not to get involved in any such business; and if they read his ordinary letters to Rome, they would see how far he was from wanting to help Piero. He also said that although he got involved in the Medici accounts for business reasons, he cut off all conversation with Lucrezia about Alfonsina or Medici affairs, since he

---

[35] *Processo* (Lorenzo Tornabuoni), CS. Append. 3, 1, fol. 83v, also fol. 101r.
[36] Ibid., fols. 83v: 'in chasa mia che Io avevo fatto alla palla', 85v and 101r (cf. Preyer, 'Palazzo Tornabuoni', p. 58, fig. 10), 86r.
[37] Ibid., fol. 84r ('Io tramutai ... el nome di Nicholo e Bernardo mettendovi dua vari nomi'), cf. 101r.

didn't want to be involved in affairs of state, even though it was only about her dowry.[38]

Lorenzo was evidently persuaded by Giannozzo that there was nothing wrong in taking Piero's letters to the Signoria, where responsibility lay with Bernardo as Gonfalonier to respond to them.[39] Subsequent meetings in late March 1497 – in the Church of SS. Annunziata ('the Servi'), in the piazza (with Giannozzo and Jacopo Gianfigliazzi) and in the Duomo – concluded with the men deciding to send fra Serafino away and not to participate any longer 'in the affairs of Piero', since it was madness to get involved.[40] In another meeting with Cambi, Lorenzo Tornabuoni was told about a visit by him – or possibly by Massimo Corbinelli – to Jacopo Salviati and Lucrezia the previous day, when he was told that Anton Maria (Sanseverino) had been refused permission to pass through Florentine territory en route to Siena, because he was going to help Piero. Lucrezia (Lorenzo continued in his testimony) had once visited his wife and signed an agreement about the bank and the Medici jewels (there was one jewel he had received from the syndics administering the Medici's affairs that Lucrezia very much wanted), and how Piero was drawing money from the Rome branch to which he was not entitled, and so on. He also talked about the people who had discussed Piero's return: Tincha (Francesco Martelli), il Butto (Andrea de' Medici), Piero Pitti, Gino Capponi and Pandolfo Corbinelli, and when asked by Tincha what he thought about Piero's return, he replied that the matter had been dealt with and the less said, the better. This is consistent with what Lorenzo said in later examinations, that he had received no letters or embassies from Piero since his exile, only a cipher that he had passed on to the Gonfalonier of Justice, Francesco di Martino Scarfa. Also, that he'd told the young Cambi not to play the role of God, he should let things take their course; he himself wanted to get on with his own affairs, leaving God to deal with the rest – and He wouldn't be bothering with Piero.[41] After mentioning other people involved in helping Piero – including Galeazzo Sassetti, son of the former manager of the Medici Bank, messer Agnolo da Tivoli and Piero Alamanni, who

---

[38] Ibid., fols. 84r and 100v. Although implicated by Alessandro dell'Antella's confession in May 1495, he was found to have no arms in his house, Parenti, *Storia*, 1, p. 222.
[39] *Processo* (Tornabuoni), fols. 84r and 101r: '... concludemo non ne potere essere molto inputati andando la lectera alla Signoria alla quale stava poi il deliberare'.
[40] Ibid., fol. 101r: 'non più travagliarci de' casi di Piero'; cf. 86r: 'che lla nostra era pazia'. On Jacopo di Bongianni Gianfigliazzi, Piero's young friend (b. 1470) who married Pierfilippo Pandolfini's daughter, *DBI*, 54, 2000 (V. Arrighi), Piffanelli, "*Libro Rosso seghreto*", esp. pp. 88, n. 43, 121–2, and p. 162 in this volume.
[41] Ibid., fols. 84v, 86v ('Lui non troverebbe atendere a chose di Piero'); 101v. On 'Francesco di Ruberto Martelli detto el Tinca', Guicciardini, *Storie*, p. 139.

apparently knew nothing of what was going on, but was very well disposed towards Piero's affairs – he concluded by saying that he, Giannozzo and Jacopo Gianfigliazzi decided around Easter (26 March 1497) 'not to torment ourselves any longer with Piero's affairs, so about a month before he finally reached the gates I was as much in the dark about them as any man in Florence'.[42]

Giovanni Cambi, last of the five men, was the manager of the Medici Bank in Pisa and general administrator of their coastal estates, and the person who headed the clandestine operation to distribute the bank's money to the exiles.[43] Like Niccolò Ridolfi, he discussed Piero's return with fra Serafino in San Gallo, including the plan for the Sienese to restore Montepulciano and provide grain, and for the despatch of clothes and luxury goods for the Medici in Siena. With Francesco Martelli (Tinca), il Butto and Giannozzo, he discussed 'lightweight matters that everyone in the city was talking openly about', and around 24 April 1497 he was one of this close network to be told of Piero's imminent arrival from Siena, with men and support from the Perugians and the Vitelleschi, as well as from Bologna and the Romagna. He in turn circulated this information to the sceptical Niccolò Ridolfi, whom he found at the Canto de' Biliotti; and on his way home, to Galeazzo Sassetti at the entrance to his house, who was equally dismissive in saying, 'God, perhaps, will want to help these poor young men trying to do their duty.' When Naldini told him Piero wanted the names of some citizens who were his friends, Giovanni suggested himself, il Butto and Gino Capponi, although they thought his expedition would fail. Naldini then passed on to him the code Giacoppo Petrucci would use to signal Piero's arrival by calling him 'Lino': 'Lino will be here [in Siena] on Wednesday and there [Florence] on Friday or Saturday.' Telling Niccolò Ridolfi, il Butto and Galeazzo Sassetti, their reply to Giacoppo was, 'that Lino isn't wanted here and if they wanted him, they would send and ask for him'.[44] He shared with the same friends information from a friar from Monte Uliveto (fra Francesco da Bologna) that Piero was in Siena ready to return to Florence. And Naldini also told him that the lord of Piombino's greatest wish was for his daughter to marry Giuliano de' Medici (Piero's brother) publicly.[45]

---

[42] *Processo*, fols. 88r–v, 101r ('di non più travagliarci de' casi di Piero ... ero di così al buio quanto homo di Firenze'.
[43] pp. 144-5, n. 94 in this volume.
[44] *Processo* (Cambi), fol. 99v. Galeazzo was a son of Francesco Sassetti, the bank's general manager; Cosimo, his brother, worked in the Lyon branch and then in Chambéry, De Roover, *Banco Medici*, pp. 440, 448–9.
[45] *Processo* (Cambi), fols. 99r–100r. On the planned marriage, p. 137, n. 62 in this volume.

Other information about Piero in Giovanni Cambi's testimony concerned messer Luigi Tornabuoni, newly returned to Florence from Rome. Encountering Gino di Lodovico Capponi and Pandolfo Corbinelli on his way home, Luigi told them that Piero sent his greetings, especially to Gino, 'and he wanted to behave like Christ with his apostles and have supper with you one evening'.[46] On another occasion he told Cambi and Francesco Martelli (Tinca) in the Duomo: 'Prepare yourselves to celebrate, for they hope to return shortly', then 'he said "that bloody shit Piero hasn't entirely got rid of his harshness, although I wouldn't say it to others"', at which point Cambi left him with Francesco.[47] After Piero's failed attempt to return, Cambi regretted what he had done for the Medici, telling Niccolò Ridolfi that he wanted to liberate himself, to which Niccolò replied that he would see Francesco Valori and that Cambi should come clean and in the future think of other things.[48] In his testimony, he also referred to talking to the archbishop (Rinaldo Orsini) and Francesco Niccolini, and to the parish priest of Cascina, who urged Lorenzo and Giovanni di Pierfrancesco to unite with their cousins. He concluded on 14 August that what he had done for Piero's return had been in his own interest, as he thought, without considering other consequences; that he couldn't go on and hadn't confessed earlier in order not to harm other people.[49]

The written testimony of Cegia (who was executed in December 1497) added more details about the people involved, that Bartolini wrote to Piero in code, calling his friends 'creditors' and his enemies 'debtors'; he named Giovanni Cambi and Galeazzo (Sassetti) as people he could talk to about what the citizens were doing; he said that Antonio de' Medici had a brother in Rome who wrote to Lucrezia in cipher, and that he found Lucrezia well informed about why, or how, Piero came to the walls and about the people who would help him in Florence, Siena and Rome. The three remaining testimonies came from people who were punished but not put to death. Piero di Luca Pitti had been shown letters by Giovanni Cambi and told in general about Piero's plans to return, and when he went to Siena on business he was used by Cambi and Francesco

---

[46] *Processo*, fol. 99v: 'et desiderebbe fare come Christo colli apostoli cenare una sera con voi'.
[47] Ibid.: 'et disse "questo caca sangue di Piero non ha lasciato interamente la sua dureza, benché non lo direi con altri."' They were among those who failed to appear when cited, Guicciardini, *Storia*, p. 139. Luigi Tornabuoni was Piero's cousin once removed, brother of Pietro, captain and commissary in Sarzana in 1490 (p. 100 in this volume).
[48] Processo, fol. 99v, continuing on 100r: 'et tu disobrighati da' sindachi in poterti poi exercitare in qualche cosa per non mi consumare'.
[49] Ibid., fol. 100r 'era perché existimava esse a benefitio suo ... e prima non have confessato per non far male a altri'.

Naldini to communicate with Piero in Bracciano and to negotiate a deal over medallions (valued at 800 florins) through Giacoppo Petrucci.[50] Tommaso Corbinelli testified to hearing from Lucrezia about Piero's plans to return with the help of Milan and Anton Maria Sanseverino, who was seeking passage through Florentine territory to help Piero in Siena.[51] And finally Lucrezia herself testified to her involvement with her brothers' return and to the difficulties of navigating the treacherous waters of life as an exile, once her husband (Jacopo Salviati) had shown her letters to the Otto di Guardia.[52]

The value of these testimonies lies in the detail they provide of networks and contacts inside and outside the city – especially the role played by peripatetic friars like fra Mariano da Gennazzano, the Medici's favourite preacher, who more than repaid his debt to them for his monastery of San Gallo by his loyalty to Piero after Lorenzo's death. The caution that hedges their evidence about Piero makes Luigi Tornabuoni's reference to 'that bloody shit Piero', who hadn't entirely got rid of his harshness, stand out for its frankness in expressing what many of Piero's friends and relatives must have felt towards the increasingly stubborn and resentful exile. Even so, the corroboration of so many testimonies suggests he enjoyed a compact group of loyal supporters at least until the five most outstanding friends were executed without appeal, after which confidence in him seriously waned. The young Cambi's remorse and the fact that two friends were followers of Savonarola is telling evidence of the new direction that republican politics was taking in Florence. So is the ambivalence of Bernardo del Nero, who declared in his testimony that he hated Piero but that he would also be rejuvenated by his return, before finally admitting that Florence needed a head. His role in 'the sect in the middle' and his pragmatism – so admired by Guicciardini – offered a third way of thinking about politics that came to fruition after Piero's death.[53] Before that happened, Piero made two more attempts to return until his deteriorating health and disposition lost him the support not only of the Florentines but of his military allies in Italy, too.

---

[50] *Processo* (Piero di M. Luca Pitti), fol. 103r.   [51] *Processo* (Corbinelli), fol. 103r–v.
[52] *Processo* (Lucrezia), fols. 103v. On Sanudo's view of Lucrezia as 'donna molto saputa, copiosa di nuove de lì' (Florence), p. 274, n. 13 in this volume.
[53] On Del Nero, n. 25 in this chapter; on Florence's need for a head, Brown, 'Piero in Power', pp. 124–5, and pp. 306–7 in this volume.

18   The Last Years, 1498–1503

As Bernardo Dovizi had said, as long as there was fighting in Italy, Piero was not without hope. So although the new year, 1498, opened with Piero enjoying 'little reputation and less credit', renewed fighting in Italy kept his hopes alive for the remaining years of his life.[1] Two events helped to change the political scene, principally the succession of Louis of Orleans to the French throne in April, but also the execution of Savonarola the following month. With claims on Milan as well as Naples, King Louis XII forged new alliances in Italy, most notably with Venice and Pope Alexander VI, who used France to further his son Cesare Borgia's attempts to build a state for himself in central Italy. The destabilisation they created encouraged Piero's military adventurism, while the final unravelling of Savonarola's life – his attack on the pope, his last defiant sermons and the aborted Trial by Fire in March and early April 1498 – also helped to revivify Piero by discrediting the Florentine government at home and abroad.[2] So Piero's little-known movements in these years provide a novel outside-in view of Florence's crisis that helps to explain the threatened *coup d'état* in 1500 and the life Gonfaloniership two years later.

When Piero visited the pope in late March, he seemed 'more hopeful than ever' of his return to Florence, cheered by the theft of Florentine mail ordered by Venice and carried out by 'these Orsini, or indeed by Piero de' Medici', as well as by an attempted break-in at the Florentine ambassador's residence in Rome by someone wearing the insignia of the

---

[1] Bonsi in Rome to the Dieci, 1 February 1498, SSX8LCMR 30, fol. 5r: 'Di Piero de' Medici, il quale si truova qui, ho ritracto lui ... essere in pocha reputatione et mancho credito.'

[2] Najemy, *A History*, pp. 400–7, Weinstein, *Savonarola*, pp. 250–76; anon. to the Signoria, 'Amice carissime', dated 26 March 1498, Signori Respons. 10, fol. 35r (copy), on Savonarola's trial and his fear lest 'le discordie nostre, intra li mali portano seco, non rimettino Piero in Firenze' (and following note).

Petrucci of Siena on his leg.³ Piero was often with Pandolfo Petrucci's man, 'the little devil' Guido da Castello, as well as in Cardinal Sanseverino's house in Rome, from where it was reported that the duke of Milan entertained the fantasy of creating in Florence 'some Idol, either Piero or someone else'.⁴ So he had many irons in the fire. Perhaps for this reason he was keen to talk to Domenico Bonsi (Florence's ambassador) in Rome, although Bonsi repeatedly refused to get involved, partly from fear of contamination and partly (he said) to deprive Piero of the chance of boasting about it.⁵

Fighting in the Casentino, 1498–1499

So the old cycle began again of speculation and sightings in constantly changing locations – the 'perambulations' that later so annoyed the pope. Piero's hopes must initially have been dashed by the heavy defeat of the Orsini by the Colonna in early April 1498, when their army of eight hundred cavalry and two thousand infantry was 'smashed to pieces' in a four-hour battle involving all the leading Orsini. Piero's close friend Carlo was captured, and Piero himself (as a 'brother-in-law of the Orsini') was sent with Cardinal Sanseverino to attempt to pacify them on behalf of the pope, in order to avert war.⁶ In late June Piero was reported to be in the Romagna and, with the 'protonotary Petrucci' (Raffaello, bishop of Grosseto), in part of the Orsini camp. A Florentine poem sent to Venice in July suggested Piero was uncertain whether to return or not; in Bologna one voice replied, 'Piero in Florence will say yes'; another was uncertain but wished the day might come 'that I have him here'.⁷

---

³ The same, fol. 35r; Bonsi in Rome to the Dieci, 9, 22 February, 7 March 1498, SSX8LCMR 30, fols. 9r–v (p. 257, n. 10 in this volume), 16r ('il quale è sanese o vero da Montepulciano ... con la divisa de' Petrucci in ghamba'). On Piero's 'venuta' to Siena in April and the impact of Louis XII's accession, G. V. Soderini's *Ricordi*, at pp. 392–6, 400–1.

⁴ Bonsi, 7 March 1498, also SSX8LCMR 30, fols. 27r, 28v, 32r, 35v, 46r (16, 19, 27 March: 'con quel Ser Guido da Città da Chastello ... essere molto alle strecte'), 4 and 25 April (on the 22nd 'fu veduto in casa dicto Cardinale di San Severino et hieri in casa sua'); Signori Respons. 10, fol. 35v (20 April: 'lo spirito di Pandolfo Petrucci et suo diavolino').

⁵ SSX8LMR 30, fol. 43v (20 April 1498), cf. 32r and 46r (27 March, 25 April).

⁶ Prospero Colonna to Cardinal Colonna, 12 April 1498 (copy), Signori Respons. 10, fol. 78 (cf. Bonsi to the Signoria, 12, 13 April, fols. 83, 77); Sanudo, *Diarii*, 1, 939–40, 16 April, 'per esser cugnato di caxa Orsina', etc. Cf. Bonsi to the Dieci, 6 March, SSX8LCMR 30, fol. 21v.

⁷ The same, 23 and 30 June, SSX8LCMR 30, fols. 76r and 79r; Eubel, *Hierarchia*, 2, p. 179; Sanudo, *Diarii*, 1, 1021: 'Soneta facto a Fiorenza: "... Piero sta del tornar fra el no e 'l si"', and the 'Risposta facta in Bologna: "Piero a Fiorenza farà dir de sì." Altra risposta facta in questa terra: "De Pier hor non so; ma venga un dì l'ho qui."'

For the rest of that year, 1498, it was Piero's close relationship with Venice that dominated his fortunes. In early August the Venetian government discussed making Piero a captain in their army for the campaign in the Romagna and the Casentino, planned to divert the Florentines from their campaign to recover Pisa. Piero was then in Bracciano, using Dovizi to get 5000 ducats from Venice for an uprising against Florence with Sienese help. Although the Sienese had by now changed sides (bribed by the same promise Piero had made to them a year earlier), Venice gave Piero money to support this new diversionary initiative, engaging its own soldier Bartolomeo d'Alviano, as well as Piero and Giuliano de' Medici, Carlo Orsini, Astorre Baglioni and the duke of Urbino.[8] The plans were delayed until late September – partly due to Cesare Borgia and partly due to an all-too-familiar sequence of events nearer home: Piero suddenly demanding more money from Venice, then falling ill, then being prevented by the pope from receiving the seven hundred Spanish soldiers he had engaged in Rome, then both Carlo Orsini and Bartolomeo d'Alviano falling ill ... and so on.[9] Finally, on 24 September, Giuliano de' Medici informed Dovizi in Venice that he had entered the Florentine frontier fortress of Marradi in the Mugello to cries of 'Marco, Marco, Palle, Palle' ('which is the name of the Medici', Sanudo helpfully explains), 'and no one wanted to move against the Medici, which is an excellent sign that the Medici will enter Florence'.[10]

The news encouraged Piero to dream of 'eating figs and grapes in Florence' again; and although he failed to join his brother in Marradi as planned, Giuliano was briefly successful in capturing the fortress there before being forced to retreat towards Faenza.[11] Fighting then moved to the Casentino, where Bernardo Dovizi had by guile captured the castle of Bibbiena, his home town, and Bartolomeo d'Alviano the hill at La Verna.[12] In mid-October Piero visited the Doge in Venice and over two days secretly addressed the council and then the College and the Ten, in order to win support for his campaign. Sanudo's reports show how successfully he kept up the pressure on Venice through his letters to the government or to his secretary Dovizi, who then read them out to the

---

[8] Ibid., 1030–1 (8 August 1498).
[9] Ibid., 1030–110 (8–27 August , 1–24 September 1498).
[10] Ibid.,1109–10 (24 September 1498): 'et niun contra Medici si voleano muover. Et questo è optimo signal, che Medici intrerano in Fiorenza.'
[11] Ibid., 1112–14 (23 September 1498): 'andar a manzar fige et uva in Fiorenza', and 27 September.
[12] According to Parenti, *Storia*, 2, pp. 192–202, esp. 201; cf. Guicciardini, *Storie*, 166–70, Vaglienti, *Storia*, pp. 63–7. On reports of Piero's renewed attack (dismissed by some as *spaurachi*), *Consulte 1498–1505*, I, pp. 100–2 (18, 28 August 1498). On Venice's support for Piero, Cerretani, *Storia*, pp. 257–9 and the deleted passage on 257, n. 247.

government, and also through his feisty sister Lucrezia's letters from Florence.[13] As a result, Venice decided to capture Bibbiena rather than Forlì because that was what the Medici (and some others) wanted.[14] When the castle of Lierna was stormed and sacked by the duke of Urbino, the cruel massacre of all its inhabitants, including children, was attributed by Parenti to Piero's desire to frighten everyone from further resistance (even though, according to Sanudo, it was d'Alviano who was keener to attack than the duke or Piero).[15] What followed showed that Piero saw his role as a provisioner, organiser and mediator rather than a fighter, even when his friend Carlo Orsini urgently appealed for his help.[16]

Before that, declaring again that 'the hour has come for me to return home', Piero proposed a meeting in early December with Florence's captain, Paolo Vitelli (Alfonsina's relation by marriage) and with its commissary Jacopo de' Nerli. Piero's sister Lucrezia had urged this meeting by telling Piero that although Vitelli would initially be resistant – like Jacopo de' Nerli – he would support Piero's return, and that Florence was being ruled by twenty tyrants (the name given to the twenty electoral scrutineers appointed, after Piero's fall, to fill offices until the new electoral bags were ready; despite resigning in June 1495 because of their unpopularity, the name evidently survived to describe this core of ambitious citizens).[17] Piero had again promised that he would not reenter Florence 'as lord, but as a citizen', and that he would not take the city from the Florentines to give it to Venice, but would ensure the peace was endorsed by Venice and by its captain: 'and if I do, I will always be the slave of that most illustrious Signoria'.[18] But Vitelli would meet Piero only in the company of the Milanese commissary, and since the Venetians were unwilling for Piero to do this, Piero was forced to concur, saying 'he would rather be dead than act against their will'. Meanwhile Nerli was heavily criticised for acting without the Florentine

---

[13] Sanudo, *Diarii*, 2, 46 [16–18] October 1498 ('questa cossa fo tratata molto secretissima'); 49 (Lucrezia as a 'dona molto saputa', her letter of 18 October 'copiosa di nuove de li'), 60, 64, 65 (Piero asks for supplies), 145, 155, 159, 163–8, 171, 173, etc. Cf. Parenti, *Storia*, 2, p. 201.

[14] Sanudo, *Diarii*, 2, 72–3. Bibbiena was captured on 24 October by d'Alviano.

[15] Parenti, *Storia*, 2, p. 210, Sanudo, *Diarii*, 2, 168 ('posto a sacho e fato gran crudeltà', 170 (26–29 November 1498).

[16] Ibid., 180 ('Piero vol andar in persona a trovar 200 cavali per condur le victuarie ...', cf. 194 (3 December 1498) and what follows in this chapter.

[17] Ibid., 177, 179 (reports from Bibbiena, 29, 30 November, 2 December 1498), 182–83 ('et 20 tirani governa quel stato'). On the Twenty, Najemy, *A History*, pp. 381–2, 387; on Vitelli, p. 279 and nn. 42 and 43 in this chapter.

[18] Sanudo, ivi, 195, citing Piero's typically clear, well-articulated words from the Provisor's letter of 4 December.

government's knowledge and was recalled to Florence, to be replaced as commissary by Piero's nemesis, Piero Corsini, who immediately republished the bann against 'our rebels', Piero and Giuliano, and, by recapturing many castles in the Casentino, virtually imprisoned Giuliano, with the duke of Urbino, Astorre Baglione and the Venetian commissary, in the castle of Bibbiena.[19]

A stalemate had been reached in which neither side could make headway in the restricted Tiber Valley, and in early December Carlo Orsini warned that the castle of Montalone was about to be lost and La Verna too would quickly fall without more support.[20] There was resentment within the motley Venetian army over 'some people being made into idols' (evidently referring to Piero and Giuliano de' Medici), while the duke of Urbino felt neither esteemed nor believed.[21] Meanwhile, Piero had again absented himself from the fray and was in the castle at Elci when, on Christmas Day 1498, Carlo Orsini wrote him a desperate letter from Montalone:

I think you'll have heard from a thousand sources, especially me, about the difficulties that have arisen here and the state we're in. This is to tell you that the problems are constantly increasing, so that unless you come with quick and substantial help and supplies, it's *all over for you and for all of us at last*, to put it in a word.

Summing up the military situation, he reminded Piero that they were undergoing great danger for love of him – as well as for their duty to Venice – which they were happy to do, provided Piero acted speedily, time being of the essence, otherwise their undertaking would have achieved nothing.

Indeed, if you don't act this time you will lose all hope of ever returning to your home. And if our honour and standing are endangered, you can never again put your trust in us. So see to it that this time you uphold and preserve the name of Magnificent ... if you unite with us, we'll not only wipe out the enemy and recover what we've lost, but you'll be able to say, "I'm in Florence and back home."[22]

---

[19] Ibid., ('et Piero fu contento non andar'), 201, 217–18; Parenti, *Storia*, 2, p. 212.
[20] Piero Marcelli, Provisor Venetorum in Bibbiena, to Marco da Sanctis, his secretary, 7 December 1498, Signori Respons. 10, fol. 318 (and 319, 8 January 1499).
[21] Sanudo, *Diarii*, 2, 242–3 (also 179–80, 194–5, 201, 220–1 on other complaints about the campaign).
[22] Signori respons. 13, fol. 316r–v (autogr.?), copy in vol. 10, fol. 314: '*actum est de te et de omnibus nobis tandem* a dirlo ad una parola ... porrai dire "sono dentro di Fiorenza in Casa mia"'.

'This time' suggests earlier disgrace, highlighting the contrast between Piero and the professional soldier Carlo, 'unafraid of the enemy', whom even now Piero did not hurry to save (it seems he remained in Castel d'Elci, in the company of Annibale Bentivoglio and visited by Franciotto Orsini, until 17 January).[23]

At this juncture, the situation was transformed by Venice's two unexpected treaties: a peace settlement with Florence (signed in April 1499) and a treaty with the new French king, Louis XII (published on 25 March that year).[24] The agreement with Florence had been made through the mediation of the duke of Ferrara, the only condition being that no mention should be made in it of Piero and his brothers.[25] It pardoned the inhabitants of Bibbiena, and on 24 April Florence regained control of the castle, which was razed to the ground in June – after releasing its Venetian prisoners and Giuliano de' Medici.[26] Its destruction marked the humiliating end of the Romagna campaign and with it the Medici's hopes of returning home via the Mugello, their old heartland.

'Piero's Mask' After the French Return, 1499–1500

The new French king's claim to the duchy of Milan as well as to the kingdom of Naples forced all the Italian states to recalibrate their strategies in response to the new situation, like chess players – to adopt the metaphor used by the Florentines themselves at this time – who have to change their whole game in response to a single move. And it was the kings from outside Italy, Louis XII of France and Ferdinand of Spain (with his queen, Isabella) and their knights, Cesare Borgia and Ferdinand's Captain Gonsalvo (Gonsalo) da Còrdoba, who now dominated the game in which Piero (and Florence) found themselves reduced to the role of pawns – even in the last game he played, when he died fighting for the French against the great Gonsalvo.

The first person to react to the new French king was Pope Alexander VI and his son Cesare, who, having renounced his cardinalate, was given

---

[23] Sanudo, *Diarii*, 2, 316, 326, 330 ('el signor Carlo esser disposto starve et non teme inimici, do volte li ha dato la bataia'), and 350. Parenti, *Storia*, p. 228, Vaglienti, *Storia*, p. 66 and Nardi, *Istorie*, I, pp. 151–2.
[24] Guicciardini, *Storie*, p. 171: 'fuora della opinione di tutti essersi fatto accordo e lega tra el re di Francia, papa e viniziani'.
[25] Parenti, *Storia*, 2: pp. 207–9, at 209; Vaglienti, *Storia*, p. 69, *Consulte, 1498–1505*, 1, pp. 118–20 (25 January 1499); Sanudo, *Diarii* 2, 342, Guicciardini, *Storie*, pp. 170–1. Venice was demanding repayment to include 6000 ducats that Dovizi claimed it paid annually to Piero and Giuliano (Signori Respons. 10, fol. 324v).
[26] Parenti, *Storia*, 2, 228–9, 255, 262; on the settlement, ibid., 242–3, 250–1 (listing its terms); Cerretani, *Storia*, pp. 260–1; Guicciardini, *Storia*, pp. 175–7.

the county of Valence in France and married to Charlotte d'Albret, with the agreement that he would help the French drive the Sforza out of Milan in return for their help in establishing a state for himself in the Romagna. After evicting Duke Lodovico, they adopted a pincer movement in their advance south, Louis taking a westerly route to Naples via Pisa and southern Tuscany (after securing Florence's support), and Cesare an easterly one. Helped by a large and well-equipped French army and by his father's spiritual powers (used to excommunicate the Romagna vicars), Cesare quickly conquered Imola and Forlì in 1499, before moving on to conquer Rimini, Pesaro and Faenza, and then, after treating with Florence at Campi Bisenzio, moving through Tuscany to capture Piombino before returning to Rome.[27]

It was after the defeat of the Sforza in Milan that Guicciardini commented on how 'the three great families who had acquired power in Italy, the Aragonese, the Sforza and the Medici', all lost it 'at almost at the same time' – that is, the Medici in 1494, the Aragonese in 1501 and the Sforza now, in 1499.[28] This was the moment when there was talk of a *coup d'état* and the creation of a life Gonfalonier in Florence. From late 1498 onwards, popular resentment of high taxes and the city's failure to recover Pisa showed itself in the council chambers as well as in the streets.[29] On Christmas Day 1498, the very day of Carlo Orsini's dramatic appeal for Piero's help in the Casentino, Florentine youths had driven a horse round the choir of Florence's cathedral and forced the congregation out of SS. Annunziata by placing a stinking plant in the church. In the streets, rival gangs of young Savonarolans and Mediceans attacked each other, and in the Great Council chamber the Gonfalonier of Justice, Guidantonio Vespucci, was subjected to ridicule – later, bunches of rope were attached to the grating outside his home to the accompaniment of ribald comments.[30] From the middle of 1499 until September 1500, the Great Council refused to reappoint the Dieci di Balìa, initiating the crisis that led to the creation of a life head of state in 1502. The desire for a permanent leader at this time of crisis might equally well have led to Piero's return, however, as the febrile debates in Florence at this time demonstrate.[31]

---

[27] Guicciardini, *Storie*, p. 193, cf. Mallett, *The Borgias*, pp. 153–7, 165–70, Najemy, *A History*, pp. 403–7.
[28] Guicciardini, *Storie*, p. 197.
[29] Brown, 'Between the Palace and the Piazza', pp. 42–4.
[30] Parenti, *Storia*, 2, p. 217, and Nardi, *Istorie*, 1, pp. 152–5 and Brown, 'Between the Palace and the Piazza', p. 43, nn. 26–8.
[31] *Consulte, 1498–1505*, I, pp. 119 (25 January 1499); Parenti, *Storia* I, p. 389 (August 1500): 'polize per la terra: diceano … richiamassimo Piero de' Medici', etc.), cf.

278   Piero in Exile

But where was Piero? It was in July 1499 that Florence's ambassador in Venice, Giovanbattista Ridolfi, talked of 'the Mask of Piero de' Medici' to describe the continual sightings that he thought were used to annoy the Florentines. When he asked the French ambassadors in Venice about 'the mask' in order to draw them out, Dumont only smiled and said, 'Piero has no breath.'[32] It is only from reports of assiduous Florentine ambassadors like Ridolfi, Antonio Malegonnelle and Francesco Pepi in Rome, and the secretary Antonio Guidotti in Siena, that we have any idea of Piero's whereabouts.[33] Piero and Giuliano were still in Murano in May, hoping for Venice's support since their companions in arms, Carlo Orsini and Bartolomeo d'Alviano, remained on its payroll.[34] Giuliano had apparently asked to join Ercole d'Este's court in Ferrara, and although unlikely to be successful, he enjoyed more sympathy in Venice than Piero, according to the Florentine ambassador.[35] It was there, in late May, that Piero received a visit from his brother-in-law, Franceschetto Cibo, who had come to Venice from Genoa to recover some money from the emperor's ambassador. The ambassador had just left, but finding his brothers-in-law were in Venice, Franceschetto visited them to recover 3000 ducats he said he was owed by Piero – which may be why, shortly afterwards, Piero was forced to sell four goblets, or *tazze,* in order to survive, since the Venetian government hadn't yet given him any money and the French remained his last resort if their plans to come to Italy went ahead.[36] Bernardo Dovizi, en route from Venice to Rome via Siena, agreed that 'Piero was in misery', but 'as long as there is fighting in Italy' – as the Florentine ambassadors in Rome put it – 'Piero will throw himself where you [the Florentines] show yourselves to be opposed'.[37] So was he in France, people wondered, in Siena, Perugia,

---

Cerretani, *Storia*, p. 287: 'volevano fare un capo' (with Lorenzo di Pierfrancesco in mind, however, who refused).

[32] Ridolfi in Venice to the Signoria, 27 July 1499, Signori respons. 12, fol. 37v (cf. n. 39 in this chapter): 'era chi temptava darvi qualche noia con la Maschera di Piero de Medici ... Bel Monte se ne rise et dixe Piero non ha del fiato.'

[33] Braccesi in Rome to the Dieci, 24 May 1497, ed. Guidi, *Segretario militante*, p. 443 (reporting 'da chi mi tiene raguagliato delli andamenti di Piero'; cf. Malegonnelle's commission to Rome, 15 May 1499 (Signori respons. 11, fol. 242r). On Malegonnelle's appointment, Parenti, 2, p. 234, cf. Vagliente, *Storia*, p. 68.

[34] P. A. Soderini in Venice to the Dieci, 2 and 15 May 1499, SSX8LCMR 32, fols. 50r, 57r; cf. 62v (Ridolfi to the same, 25 May).

[35] Soderini, 2 May, fol. 50r ('questa Signoria è più inclinata per compassione verso Giuliano che di Piero').

[36] Ridolfi to the Signoria, 15 June 1499, ivi, fol. 68r: 'vendere 4 taze delle sue per vivere che dimostra necessità ... di gittarsi là e far ultima experientia'; Malegonnelle in Rome to the Signoria, 6 July 1499, Signori respons. 12, fol. 185r.

[37] Malegonnelle with Gualterotti in Rome to the same, 28 June 1499, Signori respons. 11, fol. 267r–v (postscript): 'si gitterà in quello luogho dove si scoprirrà Vostre Excellenti

Rome, or on his way to meet up with his brother Giovanni in S. Maria del Loreto?[38]

In fact, Piero was still in Venice, or rather in Murano, in late July, where Cardinal Giovanni came to find him and Giuliano.[39] Two weeks later the cardinal was still there, devoting himself to sightseeing, disguised as a German, and he was still wearing secular dress when he set off shortly afterwards with a few companions for France (going via Germany to avoid Lombardy, then under French assault, only to be captured and held there a month later).[40] Giuliano left for a few days, probably for Ravenna where the Medici kept their horses, but was soon back. Piero was ill towards the end of the month but had recovered by early September, when the brothers rented a house for 100 ducats a year, where Alfonsina would join them – a sign that they expected to stay there for some time.[41]

It is now that Piero's fortunes begin to rise while those of Florence sank, thanks initially to Florence's execution of its captain general, Paolo Vitelli, on 1 October 1499.[42] Without French help, Florence was failing in its attempt to recover Pisa and blamed Vitelli, who was suspected of secretly supporting Piero. Although repeated torture got nothing out of him, one of his constables revealed that Paolo had indeed plotted with Venice and the pope to restore Piero to Florence and give Pisa to Cesare Borgia.[43] So whereas Florence 'had no friends left in Italy' by March 1500 (according to Parenti), Piero had regained the friendship of King Louis XII of France and Paolo Vitelli's brother Vitellozzo, as well as

---

Signorie essere opposite'; Antonio Guidotti in Siena to the Signoria, 20 July, ibid., fol. 108v.

[38] Ridolfi in Venice to the Signoria, 13 July 1499, Signori respons. 12, fols. 115r ('sono per andare alla volta di Francia'); Malegonnelle in Rome to the same, 147v (11 and 13 July), 151r–v (15 July): that Bernardo Dovizi, in Siena, then Rome, 'hora ha menato il Cardinale ad accozzarsi con Piero verso Sancta Maria dello Oreto', 102r–v (20 July): that Piero 'è stato ad Siena, et di poi qui [in Rome], et poi ad Perugia, et iterum tornato ad Siena'.

[39] Ridolfi as in n. 38, 27 July 1499, fol. 37v: 'Non è vero che Piero ... sia stato a questi giorni verso Roma ... perché lui et Giuliano sono stati al continuo e sono ancora di qua a Murano, et due giorni fa è venuto a trovarli il Cardinale.'

[40] The same, 9, 17 August 1499, fols. 339v ('et non s'intende che facci altro che ire veggiendo a sollazo sconosciuto in habito alla Thodescha'); 312r ('sconosciuto in habito secolare').

[41] The same, 27 August and 8 September 1499, ibid., fols. 264v, 468v.

[42] Parenti, *Storia*, 2, pp. 302–5; *Consulte, 1498–1505*, 1, p. 228–32 (1 October 1499). Cf. Vaglienti, *Storia*, pp. 90–1, 128–9. Florence's captain general, Paolo, was a 'parente di Piero de' Medici et delli Orsini' (married to Alfonsina's sister) and it was feared that, as well as going slow in the Pisa campaign, he would turn against the city 'et stato populare' when his *condotta* ended (Cerretani, *Storia*, p. 259 and Signori respons. 11, fol. 38v, 18 January 1500).

[43] Parenti, *Storia*, 2, p. 307.

Giulio and Paolo Orsini, who were all angered by Paolo's execution. Piero met Vitellozzo in Milan in October (who had already met Giuliano in Venice), and in February he and Giuliano were being entertained in Milan by Lodovico, his brother Ascanio and Federigo Sanseverino (these two cardinals having fled Rome together) – all of them going out riding in the countryside as in the good old days.[44] Moreover, in early October Piero was also sighted in the French court in Pavia (but as yet making 'no noise'), and in March the following year, according to Parenti, Louis 'spat out' that once his affairs were settled, he would restore Piero to Florence and massacre his enemies.[45]

So by 1500 Piero had won the support of powerful allies, the king of France and the battle-hardened Vitelli and Orsini who were fighting for Cesare Borgia. No wonder Malegonnelle warned Florence's government in January that year: 'Open your eyes, my lords and be careful!'[46] The pope added to the pressure. Not only had he called the Florentines 'not *Fiorentini* but *Fraudentini*' (little fraudsters), now he condemned Florence's treatment of the Pisans, provocatively reading out to Malegonnelle Florence's 'authentic letter' of 7 August to Paolo and Vitellozzo Vitelli, ordering them to 'sack the land [of Pisa], imprison its citizens, make free with its women and put its peasants to the sword'.[47] The Florentine ambassador's revealing rejoinder – that it was 'necessary at that time to use every possible form of cruelty towards those who rejected clemency' – anticipates Guicciardini's famous justification of murdering Pisan prisoners on the grounds of reason of state, not Christian morality. So does a later letter, in which Malegonnelle adjured the government to 'calculate and counter-weigh carefully every part' before advising that to deal with the pope's duplicity, it would be necessary to 'use methods

---

[44] Fr. Soderini and Pepi in Milan (with Charles VIII) to the Signoria, 29 October 1499, Signori respons. 13, fol. 19r: '*che il prefato Vitellozo si ristrigne assai con Piero de Medici*' (decoded), from Ridolfi in Venice, 11 October, fol. 81v; and Benedetto Portinari in Milan, 11 February 1500, fol. 130r; also *Consulte, 1498–1505*, I, pp. 301, 305–6 (6, 14 February 1500), recording Piero's visits to the Malaspina in Fosdenovo ('pe' entrare in Pisa') and to Milan.

[45] Cosimo Pazzi and Piero Soderini in Pavia to the Signoria, 2 and 8 October 1499, Signori respons. 13, fols. 122v ('anchora no<n> fa romore alchuno'), and 109r; Parenti, *Storia*, 2, p. 342.

[46] Malegonnelle in Rome to the Signoria, 5 October 1499, Signori respons. 13, fol. 110r (on the Orsini's wish to avenge Paolo Vitelli's 'ingratitudine ... contro alla Casa de' Medici' by supporting Piero); the same, 29 January 1500, Signori respons. 11, fol. 29r: that Paolo Orsini had warned 'voi fiorentini', '"Fate pensiero ... Vitellozzo è disperato."'

[47] The same, Signori respons. 13, fol. 178r (8 November 1499, decoded) and 11, fol. 36r–v (18 January 1500): 'Dare la terra ad saccomano et li cittadini prigioni, le donne al loro libera volontà et li contadini al filo delle spade' (the Signoria's 'lettera autentica' was given by the Pisans to the pope as evidence that Florence 'è d'intentione spegnere al tucto il sangue pisano').

other than the simple dissimulation used up to now'.⁴⁸ The old diplomacy and morality of Italy's carefully balanced states were becoming outmoded in the new world that confronted Florence – as well as Piero, whose allies were no longer armchair strategists but soldiers like the Vitelli, the Orsini and Cesare Borgia, as well as a Borgia pope and ultramontane France.⁴⁹

Cesare Borgia's Campaign, 1500–1501

Of these allies, ultramontane France may have been Piero's principal supporter during the summer and early autumn of 1500, but from October until the fateful events at Magione and Sinigaglia in December 1502, it was Cesare Borgia's prolonged campaign to build himself a state in Italy that promised Piero the most effective support against Florence. After helping Louis XII to defeat Lodovico in Lombardy, Cesare rapidly captured Rimini and Pesaro and by October was advancing on Faenza and Bologna, helped by the Orsini and the Vitelli, and with them Giuliano de' Medici. Giuliano's name alarmed the Florentines and helped to spread the rumour, reported by Machiavelli's friend and chancery colleague Agostino Vespucci, that 'with his sword he will clear a path for Piero de' Medici to exercise lordship over our great city as more than a citizen (*plus quam civis*), a great crime'.⁵⁰ Cesare had got to know Piero as a student in the University of Pisa, and on moving to Spoleto in October 1492 (by now, the bishop of Valencia), he wrote to Piero 'as his brother', but whether or not he nursed a long-standing grievance against him, as Guicciardini suggests, his support for Piero proved to be less than wholehearted, and it was Piero's relatives by marriage who proved more reliable until slaughtered by Cesare in 1502–03.⁵¹

---

⁴⁸ Malegonnelli to the Signoria, 18 January 1500, Signori respons. 11, fol. 36v: 'onde pare molto conveniente a chi non vuole la clementia usarla ogni crudeltà'; the same, 13 February (fol. 102r–v, decoded): '*che credo bisognerà usare altri termini che semplice dissimulare usato infino a qui*', '*et computeranno e contra peseranno bene ogni parte*'; cf. Guicciardini, *Dialogo*, p. 163, tr. p. 159; Cerretani, *Storia*, p. 338, 'di non pigliare prigioni ma amazargli' (1505).
⁴⁹ On Piero and the Vitelleschi, Malegonnelle to the Signoria, 20 February, 4 and 14 March 1500, Signori Respons. 11, fols. 135r and 179r.
⁵⁰ Vespucci to Machiavelli, 20 October 1500, Machiavelli, *Lettere*, ed. Gaeta, p. 62 (tr. pp. 32–3): 'velit ferro aperire iter Petro Medici, ut hic plus quam civis (facinus magnum) tante civitati imperitet', Klein, 'Note in margine', p. 224. On Giuliano, Cerretani, *Storia*, p. 275; Machiavelli, *Legazioni*, I, pp. 177–8 (21 October); on Borgia's intention to restore Piero, Vaglienti, *Storia*, p. 161.
⁵¹ Cesare to Piero, 5 October 1492, Gregorovius, *Lucrezia Borgia*. p. 58; Guicciardini, *Storia d'Italia*, bk. 5, ch. 5 , cf. Vettori, *Scritti storici*, p. 293, and pp. 290–1 in this chapter.

282 Piero in Exile

According to Machiavelli, Piero arrived in Pisa from France (via Genoa) in October 1500. Since his brother Giuliano was in the Romagna as a valued member of Cesare's army, the Florentines found his arrival there very sinister, since it was feared he was on his way to join his brother.[52] Although he quickly set sail again for Rome, fear of his return to Florence stimulated a group of young anti-Mediceans in December to organise themselves at a supper party as *vigilanti*, in order 'to keep an eye on things and on Piero's friends' in their local districts; and his return was then the subject of discussion in consultative meetings in Florence in January and February 1501.[53] In early March Paolo Orsini set off for a new season's campaigning, determined to make a big push to take Faenza, after which (it was rumoured in Rome) the army would restore the exiles to Florence, where more than two-thirds of the city were said to want them back.[54] When Piero pressed for an interview with the new Florentine ambassador in Rome, Francesco Pepi, Pepi refused for fear of being criticised, 'and I couldn't and wouldn't do it'.[55]

Once Piero reached Rome, all the talk in the papal court was of the viability of the Medici's repatriation. As Cesare's father, the pope had a personal interest in his son's campaign and the help he was giving to the Medici. He disapproved of the Medici's 'perambulations' and their 1497 attempt to return to Florence, he told Pepi, so he wanted to know how much support they enjoyed in Florence, especially after Florence's new agreement with the king. He then asked Pepi, 'And you, what do you want? They [the Medici] speak well of you.'[56] He couldn't speak well of them, Pepi replied, since they grieved the whole city that he represented, and the pope should reflect on how much better his son Cesare would be served by a republican government (where honours and offices were

---

[52] *Consulte, 1498–1505*, I, pp. 492, 494 (24 October 1500): 'sia di grandissimo misterio', 'sia misterioso', cf. Cerretani, *Storia*, p. 277: 'non fussi sanza misterio', Cerretani, *Ricordi*, p. 9; Machiavelli, *Legazioni*, I, pp. 204 (Tours, 21 November 1500), 143 and 208 (8 September, 24 November); Parenti, *Storia*, 2, p. 397, October 1500.

[53] Cerretani, *Storia*, pp. 277, 280, and *Ricordi*, p. 13; *Consulte 1498–1505* (6 January, 10 February 1501), 2, pp. 547, 568.

[54] Pepi in Rome to the Signoria, 8 and 10 March 1501, SSX8LCMR 34, fols. 8v–9r, 11r ('desiderati da più che 2 Terzi della Città'); cf. fol. 25v (27 March): 'qui si persuade al papa che [in Florence], excepti pochi, tutto lo universale delli huomini da bene li desidera', 'De Petro Medice', *in marg* . (on Vespucci's marginal notes as a 'commento personale', Klein, 'Note in margine', p. 216 and n. 24); Parenti, *Storia*, 2, pp. 431 (May 1501): if the enemy approached 'con Piero de' Medici o sanza, qui dal popolo si tumulterebbe', 435.

[55] p. 256 in this volume. On Pepi, Klein, 'Note in margine', pp. 212–13, 219, 223, Pesman, *Pier Soderini*, p. 103, and p. 303 in this volume.

[56] Pepi in Rome to the Signoria, 15 and 23 March 1501, SSX8LCMR 34, fols. 13r and 21r: 'subiunxemi, "et voy, che vorresti? loro dicono bene di voi."'

distributed by the Great Council, affairs of state by a smaller council with the Signoria and its colleges, and more secret matters by the Ten) than by a regime like Lorenzo and Piero de' Medici's, where one person was easily swayed by an outside prince or ruler – as Lodovico Sforza had once conceded.[57] His reports throw interesting light on their political dialogue about the relative merits of republics and the Medici's government and how the counter-arguments of the French ambassador in Rome, Trans, undid in one hour – Pepi said – what he himself had taken four days to achieve.[58] Pepi also reported that Carlo Orsini had been engaged by the pope with a hundred men-at-arms and that Carlo, Piero and Cardinal Giovanni were often seen in discussion with Cardinal Orsini, the previous day for as long as five hours.[59] By the end of April the idea had been floated, first by Trans and then by the pope, that if Piero was not wanted in Florence, at least the other brothers should return – but as private citizens, not what they were before.[60] This must be what Cerretani refers to when he describes a letter from the pope saying that if Piero de' Medici had committed any errors, the Florentines should restore Giuliano, his brother, 'to which we replied, after careful discussion, that we wanted neither of them, nor any other bosses (*capi*), and that through justice we planned to defend ourselves from the snares and traps set by evil men'.[61]

Despite this, the plans for Piero joining Cesare's army in order to return to Florence went ahead. On 27 April Piero told Pepi that he had Pisa in his hands and could hand it over to Florence in exchange for his return.[62] On the following day Pepi reported that a meeting of the consistory had discussed Medici affairs at some length, and although the discussion itself was inaudible to his source, the gestures of Cardinal Giovanni suggested he was greatly pleased by it, for at the end he thanked the pope 'with happy gestures and once almost on his knees', using 'new and quite inappropriate forms of behaviour for your cardinal'.[63] The next day Piero had a long meeting in Cardinal Sanseverino's house with Carlo

---

[57] The same, 23 March 1501, fols. 21v–22r: 'che il distribuire li honori e li officii della città e del dominio era bene nel Consiglio grande', etc., 'più approposito ... che uno come quando vi era Lorenzo o Piero ... el Signore Lodovico mi concedeva questo medesimo per aver trovato Lorenzo e Piero non ad sua voglia'.

[58] Ibid., 29 March 1501, fol. 28r.   [59] Ibid., 26 March 1501, fol. 24v.

[60] Ibid., 30 March 1501, fols. 29v ('e se non Piero *saltim* li altri .2. che non vi sono con quello odio di luy') and 51v (30 April), fol. 51v.

[61] Cerretani, *Ricordi*, p. 17.

[62] Pepi to the Dieci, 27 April 1501, SSX8LCMR 34, fols. 48v, and 44r (15 April) on the Pisans' offer to restore Piero to Florence as their 'padrone'.

[63] The same, 28 April 1501, fol. 49r: '*tamen* a gesti loro coniecturava che tutto il colloquio era in sul caso de Medici', 'con gesti lieti et una volta quasi *flexis genibus* con modi et acti nuovi e non conveniente ad vostro Cardinale'.

Orsini and the French ambassador and then with the pope alone, when it was evidently agreed that he would ride to join Cesare Borgia's camp, now that Cesare had captured Faenza.[64] Florence – Pepi warned again – should be prepared.

Piero left Rome on 8 May with Raffaello Petrucci, the bishop of Grosseto, having spent the previous week raising as many *bravi* as possible to ride with him, and stealing mailbags from Rome and later from Bolsena.[65] After being sighted in Montefiascone on the day he left, and then in Perugia, Cafaggiuolo, Prato and Pistoia, Piero's progress, according to Pepi's reports, seemed unstoppable.[66] At the same time a Florentine citizen, Geri Grazzini, was prosecuted for wanting to restore the exiles, saying in public:

> the people are boiling and everyone, it seems, is calling for Piero de' Medici. You have the Gonfalonier who has the authority to restore him or whoever. Now is the time if you want to acquire this people's favour. Recommend me to him.[67]

Yet Piero got no closer to Florence than Cesare Borgia's camp in Loiano, just north of Bologna's border with Florence. 'The Florentines' – the Bolognese humanist Sabbadino degli Arienti said wittily – 'are cured and have no further need of doctors (*medici*).' So, apparently, was Cesare Borgia. Despite persistent rumours that he was going to force the Florentines to reinstate Piero, he 'left Piero de' Medici in Logliano' and after acquiring Castel Bolognese (but not Bologna itself), he moved with Vitellozzo Vitelli and the Orsini from the Florentine fortress of Firenzuola to Barberino, which they sacked.[68] The first three of the five conditions he proposed to the Florentine envoys who came to parley were the restoration of the Medici to Florence or the creation of a restricted government (*uno stato di pochi*), his appointment as Florence's captain with three hundred lances, and the restoration of the Orsini's and

---

[64] The same, 30 April 1501, fol. 50v: 'e per molti si afferma che Piero debbe cavalcare in campo del Duca'.

[65] The same, 6 and 8 May 1501, fols. 60r and 62r (*in marg.* 'Discedit Rom<am> P. Medices etc.'). On the theft of mail, 8 and 15 May, SSX8LCMR 34, fols. 62r and 73v.

[66] The same, 13 and 14 May, ibid., fols. 70v, 71v: 'dello essere di Piero ad Perugia', 72v: 'si dicono nuove in favore de' Medici e quando è posto in Cafagguolo et quando che ha preso Prato e Pistoia'.

[67] 'Questo popolo rughia et pare che tutto chiami Piero de Medici ...', Otto di Guardia, rep. 120, fol. 6r (6 May 1501), copied in CS. Append. 3, ins. 3, fol. 20r; Parenti, *Storia*, 2, p. 445.

[68] Arienti to Ercole d'Este, 17 May 1501, *Letters*, ed. James, p. 155 (cf. Machiavelli in Imola to the Dieci, 7 October 1502, *Legazioni*, I, p. 339: 'né [Cesare] aver mai voluto che Piero venisse in campo suo'); Guicciardini, *Storie*, p. 212: 'lasciato Piero ... a Luiano in bolognese', Bertelli, 'Petrus Soderinus', p. 1.

Vitelli's lost possessions. They were immediately rejected by the Council of Eighty and a consultative meeting of citizens, and commissaries were despatched to prevent Cesare from increasing his already large army as it proceeded towards Florence, burning and stealing as it went. On reaching Campi Bisenzio just outside the city, Cesare reduced his terms to one: that he be made their captain with three hundred lances and 36,000 ducats a year, bound to serve wherever he was ordered.[69]

Although to accept them would save the city from the danger of attack, it would also risk bringing the Medici back or a change of government without Piero. For although Cesare seemed unwilling to have Piero fighting with him, he was evidently still committed to restoring his family to Florence. That Cesare was untrustworthy was shown by his behaviour as he burnt and sacked his way through southern Tuscany after agreeing these terms, leaving his army to capture Piombino as he returned to Rome. Nevertheless, in view of the threat of an uprising in Florence, to have him as their captain seemed to the government the lesser of two evils, shocking though most Florentines – as well as Vitellozzo and Paolo Orsini, Cesare's allies – found it. Piero himself, according to Parenti, was left 'totally crushed and done in'.[70] In Rome, news of the agreement and yet another Medici debacle had contrasting results. The pope could not have been more delighted by his son's agreement with Florence, and, angered with 'these beasts, the Medici' for capturing his mail at Bolsena, he threatened to deprive Giovanni of his land when speaking to him after Vespers in the Camera del Pappagallo.[71] But within Cardinal Giovanni's household, still confident that support in Perugia, Siena and Città di Castello would secure their return, the news transformed their 'contentment and happiness' to shock and horror. Having the previous evening run to the ambassador Pepi's house, shouting the Medici battle cry of 'Palle, Palle', the following morning the cardinal and his supporters were 'ashen-faced, dumbfounded and stunned'.[72] Two months later — following an incident in which the cardinal's servant had been taken to court by Paolo and killed for wounding his page – Giovanni was evicted

---

[69] Parenti, *Storia*, 2, pp. 436–2; Cerretani, *Storia*, pp. 288–90; Guicciardini, *Storie*, pp. 212–14, Mallett, *Borgia*, pp. 168–9.
[70] Parenti, *Storia*, p. 442: 'al tutto rimase anichillato e spacciato'.
[71] Pepi in Rome to the Dieci, 19 May 1501, SSX8LCMR 34, fol. 76v: 'Monstrommi dispiacerli e dixe "Queste bestie di questi Medici mi vanno intraversando. Io torrò quella terra al Cardinale de Medici"', etc.
[72] The same, 15, 17 May 1501, fols. 73r ('in casa sua crescere il contento et allegreza'), 75r ('Sono ... questa mattina bianchi, cheti, e sbigoctiti ... che la sera di nocte mi venivono ad gridare Palle, Palle intorno a casa').

from the house he had been lent by Paolo Orsini in the Orsini stronghold of Monte Giordano.[73]

As for Piero, he was accompanied from Viterbo by a courier for two miles and then travelled to Rome 'as a huntsman, with a sparrowhawk in his fist and three horses', arriving on 26 May on foot, escorted by only six bodyguards.[74] So ended Piero's second serious attempt to return home, the Medici brothers now deserted not only by friends in Florence but by their allies outside.

The Last Turn of Fortune's Wheel, 1501–1503

Only four months after this debacle, the Medici were, astoundingly, 'happier and more contented than usual', thanks once again to events outside their control. After keeping a low profile in Rome, Piero had retreated with Alfonsina and their children to Bracciano, where in June the Orsini were preparing to receive the French army on its way to Naples (which it captured in August) with the greatest show and expense.[75] This enabled Piero to reattach himself to the French. He left Rome on 30 June to follow Ubigny (Béraut Stuart, lord of Aubigny) to Naples, where he arrived on 11 August, 'though not very honourable' – having (it was rumoured) recovered on the way Giovanni's benefice of San Germano with its fortress 'and an alum mine'.[76] More important for the Medici after Piero's loss of honour was the continuing loyalty of their long-standing retainers. On the same day that Pepi reported Piero was little to be seen in Rome, he told the Dieci that the Medici's doughty bodyguard, the Pistoian Salvalaglio, was in the city, locked in discussions with Cardinal Giovanni, and two months later Bernardo Dovizi also visited Giovanni (and the Orsini) on his brief return from France.[77] Perhaps encouraged by these visits, the pope once again wanted the Medici's return to Florence, helped by the arms of Vitellozzo and the

---

[73] The same, 15 July 1501, fol. 120r: 'intendo che il cardinale non tornerà più per habitatione in Monte Giordano'.

[74] The same, 25 and 27 May 1501, fols. 85v ('con uno sparbiere in pugno e tre cavalli con sè', *in marg.* 'P. Medi. redit Romam In morem aucupantis'), 87v ('con 6 staffieri ad piè, sanza altra compagnia').

[75] The same, 1 June 1501, fols. 92r–v (though Pepi mentions only 'la donna e figlio', who left with Piero for Bracciano), 95v (7 June). The new French expedition left Milan in June, Mallett and Shaw, ed., *Italian Wars*, pp. 58–61.

[76] Pepi to the Dieci, 30 June, 15 July, 11 August 1501, SSX8LCMR 34, fols. 110v, 119v ('qui è fama che habbia obtentato da luy [Ubigni] san Germano con ogni sua forteza ... con la badia e più una lumiera'), 137v. On Ubigny as 'scozeso, glorioso, nutrito nell'arme', 'franco huomo che vada d'uno pezo', Martelli, 'Il *Libro*', p. 190, quoting Becchi.

[77] Pepi to the Dieci, 1 June, 3 August 1501, SSX8LCMR 34, fols. 92v and 131v.

Orsini, but although he recalled Piero from Naples, Piero was 'a shadow of his former self' on his arrival, due to his recurrent tertian fever.[78]

It was at this time that Pepi reported the presence in Rome of a skilful and clever Florentine rebel, who was used by the Medici and wanted to be pardoned 'within the eight months allowed by law', since he was tired and would willingly leave Rome; if he did, the Medici would be left without a compass, and since creating rebels only served to provide the Medici with companions, Pepi recommended lifting his sentence. The Signoria replied by asking Pepi for 'the name of the person who is such a good and skilled instrument for the Medici'. 'He is Lionardo Bartolini', he replied, 'and to remove him from here would be no less significant than removing all the Orsini because of the skilful and loyal service he gives them, and he is even more of a friend of Sanseverino.'[79] He had worked for the Medici Bank in Rome as a very young man and came from a Florentine banking family with close financial links to the Medici and the government. But although Pepi suggested Lionardo was tired of the way he was treated and eager to rejoin his family and cousins, who were happily integrated into Florence's civic regime, did he also, as a banker, know of the financial deal about to be struck between the Medici and the French king, which might have made it a propitious moment to return with the Medici to Florence?[80]

Once more the tide had turned in the Medici's favour, and on 4 November Rinaldo Orsini informed Pepi in Rome about this deal between France and the Medici, with papal support. King Louis would give the Medici 25,000 ducats – to be procured from Genoese or Florentine banks in Rome – as well as eight hundred lances and six thousand foot soldiers, if money was insufficient, and also Pisa, once

---

[78] Ibid., 17 September 1501, fols. 155v, 161r (to the Signoria, 29 September), adding: 'Piero de Medici è arrivato qui ... è schalmanato et più tosto con qualche reliquia di epsa che altrimenti', 162r (the same, 3 October), 'chiamato dal papa per volere che facci la inpresa di tornare, se non lui, il cardinale e Iuliano'; 166v (the same, 14 October): 'malato non poco et sta continuo in lecto. Ha .2. terzane').

[79] Ibid. fol. 167r (14 October 1501): 'L<eonar>do ille est' [*in marg.* 'Leonardus Bartholinus'], evidently omitted from the letter sent to Florence, for on 21 October (fol. 171v) Pepi provided the name they wanted of 'quello che è sì buon instrumento et apto per il Medici: lui è Lyonardo Bartolini'.

[80] Ibid. (21 October). On Lionardo di Zanobi, *Delizie*, 24, p. 250 (b. 1464, eligible for offices in 1508, first exercised them in 1512); Tewes, *Kampf um Florenz*, p. 124, Bullard, *Lorenzo*, pp. 157–8, n. 11, Bullard, *Filippo Strozzi*, esp. pp. 76, n. 49, 96; on the family and bank, p. 241, n. 40 in this volume; he and Nofri had been declared rebels on 11 August 1497, Cambi, *Istorie*, pp. 109–10. On the family's standing in Florence, Lingohr, 'Palace and Villa', pp. 245–6, 269–70.

the Medici had returned to Florence.⁸¹ It emerged on the 12th, after discussions between the pope, his son and cardinals Giovanni de' Medici and Giovanbattista Orsini, that Giovanni and Giuliano hoped to return to Florence within a month or two with the help of the cardinal of Rouen, while Piero was to stay away for three or four years.⁸² Although Rinaldo Orsini confirmed that surety for the payment of 25,000 ducats had been sent to the French court, Pepi discovered from spies that only 10,000 ducats had been promised to Rouen by the Sienese bankers Spannocchi and Agostini Chigi, to be paid after the Medici's return.⁸³ Apologising for the harm done to Florence by these Medici, 'although they were his nephews', Rinaldo warned Pepi that their return with the help of the Orsini family would entail Florence's destruction, since the Orsini were 'mad and bad and more avid for blood than for wine'. Affirming that these were his very words, Pepi went on to describe the dangerous divisions among them, due to the illegitimate Carlo being excluded from their division of the Savelli lands.⁸⁴

Worse was to follow for the Florentines. Not only would the city have to pay an additional 300,000 ducats to the French after the Medici's return (100,000 ducats a year for three years), but three cardinals – Lisbon, Siena and Alexandrino, who had been Florence's friends – were now its enemies, due to Florence's reprisals for their debts to the city. Once again the pope condemned the Florentines as fraudulent and their merchants in Rome as bankrupt, making the disheartened ambassador wish he were in the Florentine prison of the Stinche rather than in Rome. Moreover, Pepi's reports to the government were leaking out, since someone who was not a member 'of any of the Three Major Offices nor the Eighty' had nevertheless sent an extract from one of Pepi's confidential letters (about the terms for the Medici's return) to a friend in Rome.⁸⁵ Although Piero was still suffering from fever in late November, he was overheard by one of Sanseverino's household discussing with cardinals Orsini and Sanseverino the French ambassador's plan 'on the

---

[81] Pepi to the Dieci, 4 November 1501, SSX8LCMR 34, fol. 175r; cf. *Consulte, 1498–1505*, 2, p. 704, 16 November 1501, 'che e' Medici speravano presto ritornare et che havevano apuntato col Re et davanli 25 mila ducati', etc.

[82] The same, 8 November 1501, fols. 176r (*in marg.* 'Cavendum'); 12 November, 177v, on the Medici's 'certa speranza del ritornare costi infra uno mese o 2 almeno … et che Piero stia fuori 3 o 4 anni' (*in marg.* 'Spes vana').

[83] The same, 13 and [14–16] November 1501, fols. 178r-v, 179r.

[84] Letter of 13 November, fol. 178r, Shaw, *Political Role*, p. 84: 'più avidi di sangue che di vino, e pazi e tristi, usando le sue formali parole', cf. p. 75.

[85] Pepi to the Signoria, 16 and 20 November 1501, SSX8LCMR 34, fols. 179v–180r, 184r-v at 184v: 'tutto quello che io scripse … che dovea o meritava essere secreto' (enclosing the extract from the Florentine's letter of 13 November).

old design', and in December discussions continued about money and other details.[86] Once the plan was ratified by the king and executed with the arms of Cesare Borgia, Vitellozzo and the Baglioni (with Città di Castello, Perugia and Siena), Giuliano de' Medici would come to Pisa – but if Florence fell behind in its payments to the king, Louis was no longer obliged to return Pisa, 'and ordered us to restore the Medici'.[87]

This was the prelude to the last and potentially most successful of Piero's and his brothers' attempts to return to Florence, despite its dramatic conclusion. In May 1502 two secretaries from Pandolfo Petrucci and from the Orsini confessed, after torture, that they had come to Florence 'to restore Piero de' Medici', although not – as initially thought – let in by citizens. What was worse was to hear that the Medici had not changed at all and were still determined to return to profit from the city, helped by citizens who, though cautious, were of the same mind.[88] At the beginning of June an uprising against the Florentine officials in Arezzo heralded its successful capture by the Vitelli, the Orsini (Paolo and his son Fabio) and Piero de' Medici, supported by the Baglioni and the Petrucci.[89] By the 5th, Piero had reportedly left Rome, and by the 15th, as the Vitelli and one of the Baglioni were making their way to Arezzo, he had reached Città di Castello, though again delayed by his tertian fever.[90] According to Vaglienti and Cerretani, Piero entered the citadel of Arezzo on the 18th to shouts of 'Palle, Palle' and 'Vitello, Vitello', and having taken it, Piero and Cardinal Giovanni placed their cousin Giulio there.[91] Two days later, Piero was sleeping with an armed guard in the fortress of Marciana (south of Arezzo) after the castellan's departure and was expected with Vitellozzo in Castiglione Fiorentino. Then Cortona surrendered to him, and by July he, Vitellozzo and

---

[86] The same, 23 November 1501, ivi, fol. 188v. The plan included a payment to the pope, and the gift to Cardinal Borgia of the Abbey of Montecassino with all its lands, which Giovanni de' Medici would renounce in his favour.

[87] The same, 4 December 1501, ivi, fol. 198r-v ('dato il suo consenso in nel farlo poy con la forza ... Et Juliano de Medici facto la ratificatione per il re, viene ad Pisa'; *Consulte, 1498–1505*, 2, p. 716 (9 January 1502):'et il Re Christianissimo comanda et pregha si rimettono i Medici'; Guicciardini, *Storie*, pp. 216–17.

[88] Cerretani, *Storia*, pp. 299–300: 'l'umore de' Medici non era spentto ... non manchando un numero di ciptadini benché cauti a' quali non era altro in animo che questo'.

[89] Piergiovanni Ricasoli, commissary general in Montevarchi to the Signoria, 4 June 1502, Dieci Responsive 67, fol. 201r: 'uno a chavallo volando dicendo che Arezzo ha facto novità et hanno preso il Capitano e commissario'.

[90] *Consulte 1498–1505*, 2, p. 788 (5 June 1502): 'quella terra [di Arezzo] si è levata in arme ... et come Piero de' Medici è partito da Roma'; Antonio del Vigno, captain and commissary in Borgo [San Sepulcro] to the Signoria, Dieci Responsive 67, fol. 244 (15 June 1502).

[91] Vaglienti, *Storia*, p. 155; Cerretani, *Ricordi*, pp. 47–8; cf. Najemy, *A History*, p. 404.

290   Piero in Exile

Baglione were holding a circle of surrounding strongholds, Borgo and Anghiari as well as Cortona and Arezzo itself.[92]

While Piero was at last enjoying a successful campaign, his brother Cardinal Giovanni was in the vicinity of Siena, where a second front was opening up.[93] The key figure there was Pandolfo Petrucci, the Medici's old ally, who was attempting to broker a deal between Vitellozzo Vitelli and the Florentines (represented by the dedicated republican Francesco Gualterotti). However, Antonio Guidotti had omitted to report from Siena that Vitellozzo wanted Piero restored to Florence, which should 'unite and embrace the Medici with all the other exiles', and when he learnt this, Gualterotti broke off all discussion of a deal with Vitellozzo.[94] Despite this contretemps, by the beginning of August Piero was confident enough to attempt to treat with Florence himself. He sent Antonio del Vigna, the former commissary in Borgo (whom he had freed from imprisonment in Arezzo), to convey to the Signoria his own offer of restoring everything he had taken since 1494 if he could return as a citizen. Although del Vigna spoke 'with great affection', the government listened scornfully and made no response except to pass him on to the Dieci, at the same time imposing exile on the castellans at Borgo, Cortona and elsewhere for giving their fortresses to Piero.[95]

However, Piero's and his allies' success soon raised the spectre not only of the Medici's return to Florence but also of Cesare Borgia's conquest of Tuscany. It was at this juncture that Louis XII changed sides (once again) and in mid-June agreed – at Piero Soderini's request – to help Florence recover Arezzo. And three months later, on 22 September, Soderini was chosen by Florence as its first permanent head of state (*Gonfaloniere di Giustizia a vita*) in the attempt 'to restore some good form of government'.[96] Since this provided a popular solution to Florence's need for a *capo* that avoided recalling Piero, both Soderini's election and the French help he obtained for Florence boded ill for Piero. They were followed later that year by the third rebuff: the conspiracy of Cesare Borgia's captains and former allies against Cesare at the Diet of Magione in late September to early October. Cesare's quick

---

[92] Dieci Respons. 67, fol. 324v (Niccolo Bonc<i>ani, commissary in Foiano, to Dieci, 20 June 1502).
[93] Ibid., fols. 250 (Francesco Gualterotti in Staggia, 16 June 1502), 212 (Piergiovani Ricasoli in Castellina, 13 June) and 272 (Piero Martelli in Castelfiorentino, 17 June).
[94] Gualterotti in Villa Marciani outside Siena to the Dieci, 16 June 1502, ibid., fols. 257r ('li ruppi il parlare') and 309r (20 June): Vitellozzo said 'le cose erano in termini che non poteva abandonare Piero de' Medici'.
[95] Cerretani, *Ricordi*, p. 54, 'con molta affetione', and Cerretani, *Storia*, p. 305.
[96] Pesman Cooper, *Pier Soderini*, p. 21; Najemy, *A History*, pp. 406–7 (the law creating the new office was passed on 26 August).

response – as Machiavelli famously reported – initially encouraged the conspirators to seek reconciliation before he wrought his revenge at Senigallia on 31 December 1502, strangling Vitellozzo Vitelli on the spot and later killing Paolo and Francesco Orsini as he recovered Città di Castello, Perugia and Siena from the control of the remaining leaders. The pope then imprisoned other Orsini in Rome, including the cardinal Giovanni Battista, Rinaldo, the archbishop of Florence, and Piero's close friend Carlo.[97] Since Cesare's victims were all related to Piero by marriage or his loyal supporters, like the Baglioni of Perugia and the Petrucci in Siena, their death and defeat was a final blow to his fortunes.

This was the last of Piero's attempts to return to Florence before his death. Having been with the French army for its successful capture of Naples from its Aragonese rulers in 1501, he had now rejoined it – taking his wife Alfonsina and the children with him to Gaeta, according to Francesco Vettori – and was fighting with his old comrade-in-arms Bartolomeo d'Alviano against the Spanish monarchs and their captain, Gonsalvo, in southern Italy.[98] Stopped and forced to retreat by the great Gonsalvo, Piero suffered the unheroic death of drowning with the artillery train as he attempted to flee across the swollen Garigliano on 28 December 1503.[99] His fate, Cerretani reported, 'pleased many and displeased some, but what people talked more about in Florence was the defeat of the French, because factional passions were still very fresh'.[100] As a last indignity, Piero's body failed to be recovered from the Garigliano, making it uncertain if the bones in Piero's grandiose tomb in the Abbey of Montecassino are his own: a fitting memorial, perhaps, to the powerful 'Mask of Piero' that had galvanised Italy during his long years of exile.

---

[97] Machiavelli, *Il principe*, ch. 7, *Descrizione del modo tenuto dal duca Valentino nello ammazzare Vitellozzo Vitelli*, ed. Bertelli, and letters to the Dieci in *Legazioni e commissarie*, 1, esp. 7 October, 31 December 1502 and 1 January 1503, pp. 338–44, 506–10; Cerretani, *Storia*, pp. 314–15.

[98] Vettori, 'Life of Lorenzo', in *Scritti storici*, ed. Niccolini, p. 263: Lorenzo 'benché fanciullo' went with Piero to Montecassino, 'et quando Piero annegò nel Garigliano ... egli era in Gaeta con la madre e sorella'.

[99] Ibid., pp. 268–9.

[100] Cerretani, *Storia*, pp. 329–30, cf. Cerretani, *Ricordi*, p. 97; Guicciardini, *Storie*, pp. 288–9.

19 Piero's Burial and Legacy

It was not until mid-January 1504 that Cardinal Giovanni made his first apparent reference to his brother's death. Concerned by the fate of his commend of Montecassino, which was now in Spanish hands, he explained to Silvio Passerini on 15 January that distress over Piero, as well as 'a certain indisposition', had prevented him from replying fully to his letters before then.[1] Nine days later, he wrote again to his 'dearest treasurer', mainly about Montecassino, but also expressing his amazement that Piero's body hadn't yet been found, which he blamed on fra Leo's and others' lack of diligence in searching for it: Piero should surely be found if the other bodies had been recovered, and similarly 'that little horse of ours that Piero had', which he wanted back at a reasonable price: 'you know what it cost, apply yourself to the matter'.[2]

Renewed searching evidently produced some bones, which were placed in 'a little brick urn' on the right-hand side of the nave of the Abbey of Montecassino, near the choir. Despite the fact that the commend of the abbey belonged to Cardinal Giovanni, who within a decade was to become pope, neither Giovanni – nor Alfonsina, Piero's widow – seem to have felt it necessary to commemorate him more fittingly. In 1531 it was their cousin Giulio, as Pope Clement VII (acting with the abbey's protector, Cardinal Cesi), who was responsible for commissioning the magnificent funerary monument filling the wall adjacent to the abbey's high altar, an impressive memorial not only to Piero but to the whole family after its final return to Florence the previous year. Giulio also wanted to recover some of the 16,000 ducats he claimed he

---

[1] Cardinal Giovanni in Rome to Passerini, 15 January 1504, Acq. Doni, 142, ins. 8 (autogr): 'oltre allo affanno del caso di Piero, semo stati molestati da certa indispositione'; on 27 December 1503, the day before Piero's drowning, he had asked Passerini to declare his and Giuliano's devotion to the Spanish monarchs (ibid.).

[2] Ibid., 24 January 1504 (autogr.): 'Assai ci maraviglamo che fra Leone et li altri non habino ritrovato el corpo di Piero, siché voglamo vi rimandi un altra volta ... Tu sai quello ci costò, usaci solicitudine.' The same letter professed to approve the destruction of Montecassino's fortresses and promised to send a governor to San Germano shortly.

was owed by the monks (after Leo had resigned the commend), whom he made responsible for paying 3000 scudi for the tomb, as well as providing food and lodging for the architects and seven apprentices from Florence.[3]

So it was a typical Medici commission that combined *onore et utile*, and although Piero's drowned figure dominates the monument, all the family, including Duke Cosimo, are commemorated in the concave inscription on the tomb itself:

For Piero de Medici, son of Lorenzo the Magnificent, brother of the pontifex maximus Leo X, cousin of Clement VII, who died aged 33 in a shipwreck at the mouth of the Liri after defeat in a battle while fighting with the French, erected in 1552 thanks to the help of Cosimo de Medici, duke of Florence.[4]

The work was to be completed within three years, but Clement's death in 1534 caused initial delays, which were then protracted until the 1550s (perhaps because extensive work to enlarge the monastery was being undertaken at the same time), and on 10 December 1559 a celebratory mass was finally held to welcome Piero's 'remains and bones' into their new home.

According to the initial contract drawn up between the monks and Antonio da Sangallo the Younger and his brother Battista on 13 June 1531, it was planned to inter Piero in a little chapel to the left of the entrance to the church. Of the two alternatives offered by Antonio the following year – a wall tomb on the right of the high altar, or a grandiose mausoleum modelled on the baths of Diocletian and Caracalla to the left of the portico abutting the church's atrium – the first was adopted in the contract concluded that year. In it, Antonio and his son Francesco were made responsible for designing and executing the tomb (with a naturalistic statue of the dead Piero, 'un morto al naturale', statues of saints Peter and Paul, curtains and Christ's resurrection); Battista was to produce the model, and Antonio Solosmeo, helped by Lante from Fiesole, the wall decoration. So apart from the bas-reliefs by the Neapolitan Matteo Quaranta, it was a very Florentine enterprise, with Battista supervising the work in Montecassino and the others evidently working mainly from Florence.

Piero's slumped but sitting figure is remarkable, his head resting on his shoulder, his eyes closed, his right leg splayed. Dressed as an ancient Roman general, his inertia evokes not simply the sleep of death but his

---

[3] For what follows, Giovannoni, 'Rilievi ed opere architettoniche', pp. 307–32, pls. 1–9, Caraviti, *I codici e le arti*, pp. 80–115, at 80–7.
[4] Transcribed by Mario Cesari, cf. Caravita, p. 86 (the River Liri becomes the Garigliano when it joins the Gari).

futile years of combat as an exile, for whom, nevertheless, the resurrected Christ above offers the hope of another, better, afterlife.[5] Equally remarkable is the statue's survival after the bombardment of Montecassino in 1944, for although the monument itself must have been reconstructed, the statues are authentic. If Piero failed to be buried, as he had hoped, with his father in Florence (together with his brother Giuliano and his son Lorenzo, the two dukes, also in ancient military dress, commemorated in Michelangelo's famous statues in the New Sacristy in the Church of San Lorenzo, Florence) – or with his papal sibling Giovanni and their cousin Giulio in S. Maria sopra Minerva in Rome – his tomb is as distinctive as theirs and close to the revered founder of Italy's oldest monastic order, St. Benedict, who is buried with his sister Scholastica just beneath him in the crypt of Montecassino.

The Medici's Return to Florence

After Piero's death at the end of 1503, the Medici's fortunes in Florence slowly revived – helped by the death of the fickle Borgia pope Alexander VI on 18 August 1503 and the succession (after a brief interlude) of Giuliano della Rovere as Pope Julius II on 26 November, with whom Cardinal Giovanni rapidly established a friendly relationship. They were helped, too, by growing hostility towards the new head of state in Florence, Piero Soderini, which encouraged the rapprochement of some leading families with the Medici. Less than a year after Piero's death, Giovanni and Giuliano brazenly celebrated the feast day of their family's patron saints (Cosmas and Damian) with a banquet attended by most of the Florentine community in Rome – despite the laws against having contact with them.[6] These laws were then challenged in a variety of ways in Florence itself, especially by the betrothal of Piero's eldest child Clarice ('la Cice') to Filippo Strozzi in July 1508, after a failed attempt to marry her to a Pitti two years earlier.[7] Cardinal Giovanni had

---

[5] Among the influences and models for the tomb suggested to me by Charles Robertson are Michelangelo's early design for Julius II's tomb (1516–17) in the Casa Buonarrotti, his seated Medici statues in the New Sacristy of San Lorenzo, for the resurrection theme, Bandinelli's early design for Clement's tomb (1534–36, in RISD Museum, Prints, Drawings and Photograph 4956) and for a model of an ancient Roman general, Giovanpietro Birago's painting of Francesco Sforza. On Piero's 'riposo e l'inerzia che mette il sonno nelle membra', Caraviti, p. 84.

[6] Butters, *Governors*, pp. 74–8; Tomas, *Medici Women*, p. 110 and n. 4; Najemy, *A History*, pp. 415–18. Alexander VI died on 18 August 1503, succeeded briefly by Pius III (Piccolomini) and on 26 November by Julius II.

[7] Cerretani, *Ricordi*, pp. 119–20 and 176–77; cf. Bullard, 'Marriage Politics', at p. 677; Butters, *Governors*, pp. 129–34.

personally discussed the betrothal with the pope and the 'very generous dowry' he had offered his niece (which a Florentine marriage would 'keep within the city'); he also discussed with the pope his hope of being pardoned and allowed to return to Florence with Giuliano, although 'not through force' (despite the brothers' repeated attempts to do so before Piero's death). The Florentine government refused to consider it, but the fact that the marriage took place the following year, with only limited repercussions, shows that support for the Medici was growing.[8] So, too, does Soderini's attempt to smash all the terracotta pots bearing the Medici coat of arms on sale in shops, which according to Parenti were symbols of 'the growth of devotion to the Medici in the city', even among the lower classes, since 'manual workers ... are happy to keep in their homes the arms of the magnates on whom they depend or are attached'.[9]

Cardinal Giovanni also assumed responsibility for recovering his sister-in-law Alfonsina's dowry and the money owed to her deceased mother, perhaps sharing Alfonsina's view that it was Piero's stubbornness that had kept them out of their ancestral 'house' for nineteen years (since 1494).[10] Although Giovanni claimed Alfonsina 'found herself in need' when he wrote in May 1503 to urge the repayment of her mother's loan of 3000 ducats to the Medici Bank, the repeated demands for this and the dowry repayments were probably also part of the Medici's strategy for returning to Florence.[11] If so, the strategy worked, although only through the brutal use of force that Giovanni had promised to renounce. After their return in 1512, the family reestablished all the restrictive institutions of their former regime, the Cento, the Settanta,

---

[8] Parenti, *Storia fiorentina*, BNF II, IV, 171 (the third, as yet unpublished volume), fol. 5r–v (June 1508): 'Ricusò il cardinale volere tornare per forza ne la sua Città', 'tale sua dota grandissima resterebbe nella città'; cf. Cerretani, *Ricordi*, p. 177; Cerretani, *Storia*, p. 359; Bullard, 'Marriage Politics', pp. 672–81.

[9] Parenti, *Storia fiorentina*, fol. 5v: 'la devotione de' Medici [oltre a con i loro assai parenti, ancora *add. in marg.*] multiplicare nella città et fino a nelli huomini bassi', 'quella divotione et inclinatione de' manuali, e' quali volentieri soglono tenere in chasa l'arme de' magnati di cui dipendono o a cui adheriscono'.

[10] Alfonsina to Lorenzo, 16 August 1515 (MAP 137, 652v), Devonshire-Jones, 'Lorenzo de' Medici', p. 303, Tomas, *Medici Women*, p. 171 and n. 51, cf. p. 105. The context was the danger of alienating France, for which Alfonsina also blamed Bernardo Dovizi, now Cardinal S. Maria in Portico. On 'Alfonsina's Dowry Wars', Tomas, *Medici Women*, pp. 113–15.

[11] Antonio Malegonnelle in Rome to the Signoria, 21 December 1499, Signori respons. 13, fol. 239r–v; Cardinal Giovanni de' Medici to the same, 27 May 1503, Signori respons. 26, fol. 102; Cerretani, *Storia*, p. 358; cf. Tomas, *Medici Women*, pp. 113–15; Reiss, 'Widow, Mother', pp. 127–9. Sanudo (*Diarii*, 2, 331) greatly exaggerates Alfonsina's dowry as 'ducati 50 milia' (according to a letter of Dovizi's) instead of 12,000 ducats.

the Otto di Pratica, and so on – and yet three years later Giovanni (by now Pope Leo X) opposed Florence's first visible step on the road to lordship, the appointment of Piero's son Lorenzo as the city's captain general.

Lorenzo di Piero as Florence's New Head

Leo X may have opposed the idea of the Medici becoming lords of Florence, or he may simply have resented his nephew Lorenzo (and Alfonsina) assuming control in Florence, where he himself had been managing the family's interests from Rome. It is equally unclear what Lorenzo's own intentions were.[12] Some Florentines assumed that he wanted to become absolute ruler of Florence in 1515 or on his marriage to his French bride three years later, whereas according to the political realist and diplomat Francesco Vettori (who had negotiated the marriage in France), it was unnecessary for Lorenzo to seize power in this way, since he 'already disposed of the city as he wanted without being its lord'. In fact, Vettori claimed that after Lorenzo returned from France in 1518 (where he became betrothed to Madeleine de la Tour), he wanted to renounce his position as Florence's captain (and duke of Urbino) and 'return to govern the state of Florence as a citizen, as had always been his intention', but that Alfonsina stepped in and by feigning mortal illness aborted his plan.[13] Alfonsina was undoubtedly ambitious for her son. She had governed Florence during his absence in 1515 when he was fighting abroad, and her unpopularity – both as a female ruler and for the qualities that Jacopo Salviati had mocked at the time of her betrothal and marriage in 1487–88 – makes it likely that the republicans' fear of Medici ambition was directed towards Alfonsina as much as towards Lorenzo.[14]

Lorenzo's death in 1519, only a year after his marriage to Madeleine de la Tour, makes the question of his political ambition difficult to answer.

---

[12] On Lorenzo's situation, Devonshire Jones, 'Lorenzo de' Medici', citing Giorgetti; cf. Baker, *Fruit of Liberty*, p. 83 (that he took it upon himself to remind Leo X and Cardinal Giulio not to ignore the civic republicanism of Florence).

[13] Vettori, *Scritti storici*, p. 184 ('lasciare lo stato di Urbino alla Chiesa e non volere essere più capitano de' Fiorentini e tornare a tenere lo stato di Firenze come cittadino, come sempre era stato il suo disegno'), Devonshire-Jones, 'Lorenzo de' Medici', pp. 299–300 and Devonshire-Jones, *Francesco Vettori*, p. 136; on Lorenzo's practical power in Florence in terms of offices and patronage, Stephens, *The Fall*, pp. 80–8.

[14] On Alfonsina as a female ruler, Tomas, *Medici Women*, pp. 167–85, esp. 181–5; on her and Lorenzo's Francophilism (to avoid Piero's mistakes), Devonshire-Jones, 'Lorenzo de' Medici', pp. 301–5; cf. Stephens, *The Fall*, pp. 74–5.

What we do know is that only six months after his uncle's election as pope, in October 1513, Lorenzo wrote to Cardinal Giulio about the dangers for 'brothers and nephews' of popes who lacked the insurance of offspring, like his uncle Giuliano and himself. This made him determined not only to marry but to acquire the lordship of a secure block of territory in an enlarged Tuscany ('presumably with Florence as its nucleus' and including Piombino, Siena or Lucca) or in the Romagna, which he deemed preferable to a state like Urbino (which he did acquire in June 1516), which was 'easy to gain but even easier to lose'.[15] He must, of course, have been thinking about the fate of Cesare Borgia, who lost his new state in the Romagna after his father Pope Alexander's death in 1503, famously exemplified by Machiavelli in *The Prince*, which he dedicated in 1515 to Lorenzo, by then a more appropriate dedicatee than Machiavelli's first choice, the pleasure-loving Giuliano de' Medici. Although this might provide evidence of Lorenzo's unscrupulous intentions (if we accept the view that *The Prince* was a handbook for tyrants), it is more credible that *The Prince* merely intended to offer him practical (if expedient) advice on how to acquire and govern a state as a new prince, given the strength of republican feeling in Florence.[16]

Lorenzo was exactly the same age as his father, Piero, and his grandfather il Magnifico when they became unofficial *capi* of Florence in 1492 and 1469, and it is as difficult to define his status and political ambition as it is to define theirs.[17] Piero demonstrated by his exile the danger for the Medici of acting as princes in republican Florence, and it is no easier to know if he wanted to govern Florence 'as a citizen' (as Vettori suggested Lorenzo wanted to do) or to become the ruler of an enlarged territorial state. As we have seen, Piero was closely involved in the places his son later wanted to include in his state, especially Piombino, Siena and the Romagna, and he might have had a territorial state in mind before losing power in 1494. His experience as patron would have been good preparation for this, and so would his later experience fighting with the Orsini, when he drew support from many of

---

[15] Devonshire-Jones, ibid., pp. 313–15: 'come quello stato era facile a pigliare, così era facilissimo a perdere' (314). On 'Lorenzin' as 'un animo gajardo ... fiol del magnifico Piero', Sanudo, *Diarii*, 24, 90.

[16] For a recent full summary of interpretations of *The Prince* (including Busini's account in 1549 of why everyone hated Machiavelli for it), Pedullà, ed. *Il Principe*, pp. v–xviii (at xviii); on 'principe/tiranno', xxxix–lvii, and on its relevance to Lorenzo, lxxxviii–ix, citing esp. chs. 7 and 9 (on pp. 72–91, 104–119). On its dedication, see now J. Barthas, 'La composizione del *Principe* di Machiavelli e la restaurazione dei Medici', forthcoming.

[17] As Baker reminds us (*Fruit of Liberty*, p. 82): it is 'a false dichotomy' to distinguish between republican and Medicean government before 1532.

Florence's subject cities, especially in 1502. Equally, he may have preferred to follow his father's example of enjoying princely power while living as a citizen in Florence. But times had moved on and this would scarcely have been feasible without the revolution in political thinking that had also taken place during the span of Piero's lifetime. What this was and how it relates to Piero's life remains to be discussed in the concluding chapter.

Conclusion

20 Power and Legitimacy in Renaissance Italy

Piero's life has been a missing chapter in the history of Florence during its transition from republic to principate, considered irrelevant, except by its failings, to the crisis of Italian states at this time. As with any biography, the importance of his life lies in providing a witness to events as they happened – in his case the threat to Italy's, and especially Florence's, stability in the face of foreign invasions. Piero was very articulate in expressing himself and the pressure he suffered in his unofficial role as Florence's *capo*, neither powerful enough to rule nor free enough to indulge his talents and pleasures as a prince. He enables us to appreciate the situation faced by republics like Florence that had become territorial states without the military power or the permanent leadership to withstand foreign armies – except at risk of being accused of tyranny. This, of course, was Piero's fate, and it again raises the question of whether he was the ambitious tyrant that his reputation suggests or whether, instead, his temperament and experience would have qualified him to be the new type of civilian ruler that political realists like Machiavelli, Francesco Vettori and Guicciardini were proposing for Florence after the unexpected death of Piero's son in 1519.

Traditionally, tyranny was defined as ruling illegitimately or behaving despotically.[1] According to Francesco Guicciardini's *Florentine Histories*, Lorenzo may have wanted to legitimate his own rule by becoming life Gonfalonier of Justice when he was forty-five, had he not died before then. Although this left Piero without a legal title to rule, there is no evidence he intended to seize power in order to become an absolute ruler by force. Guicciardini's reason for condemning Piero as a tyrant was his despotic behaviour, not his lack of a title.[2] It is true Piero had a

---

[1] On the jurists' definition of tyranny, Cavallar, 'Il tiranno', pp. 310–11, 336 (citing Bartolo da Sassoferrato, *De tyranno*, 'ex defectu tituli' and 'ex parte exercitii'); Marrara, 'Il problema della tirannide'.
[2] Guicciardini, *Storie*, p. 71, Fubini, *Politica e pensiero politico*, pp. 187–203 at 193, 236. On Lorenzo as a tyrant, Cavallar, 'Il tiranno', pp. 298–300, 311, and on Giovanni Guidi (the

reputation for being involved in violent incidents, often caused by his *bravi* (as in his father's day). But although he enjoyed an armed bodyguard in Florence on his father's death – which Cerretani regarded as a sign of behaving 'like a tyrant, doing things by force and against the law', when Savonarola adopted one without consent – the privilege had in fact been granted to the Medici by the ad hoc powers of the Otto di Guardia after the Pazzi conspiracy, and thereafter regularly renewed to Lorenzo, the cousins and then to Piero. When the General of the Servites, Antonio Alabanti, tried to visit Piero on the eve of the revolution in Florence and found the Medici palace open and unguarded, he advised Piero to employ 'five hundred trusted soldiers' as protection, but Piero, seemingly unconcerned about his safety, rejected his advice – unless the presence of 'a few soldiers' accompanying him on 9 November, with Paolo Vitelli's troops at the gate, was his response to Alabanti's letter.[3] Piero also rejected Alfonso's offer of an estate in the kingdom of Naples in May 1494, telling him that his ancestors had always lived as citizens and he intended to do the same.[4]

We may not necessarily believe him, but the character traits revealed by the life we have been following show that Piero was very different from the savage and bestial tyrant portrayed in Guicciardini's *Florentine Histories*, where he condemns Piero as 'tyrannical and arrogant', 'arrogant and bestial', wanting to be feared rather than loved, 'savage and cruel', 'foolhardy' and 'not a Medici in his behaviour but following the customs of the Orsini'. Since Guicciardini wrote the *Histories* in 1508, just after his marriage to a Salviati, when he was embarking on a political and legal career – and when Cardinal Giovanni was planning an unwelcome return through the marriage of Piero's daughter to a Strozzi – its vehement criticism may reveal as much about Guicciardini as about Piero.[5] Viewed through the spectrum of his life and writings, Piero emerges as a diffident or unwilling political leader, happy to assume the trappings of power without involving himself too deeply in the political process; and although he was outgoing and confident as a sportsman, he lacked

---

legislative draftsman)'s allusion to Lorenzo's 'belli et grandi disegni' in November 1490, Brown, *Florence* (2011), p. 3, n. 7.

[3] Ibid., pp. 84–5, and p. 217 and n. 17 in this volume; Kent, *Princely Citizen*, p. 257: the bodyguards 'were violent men, often in trouble with the law and yet duly protected by the Medici'; Cerretani, *Storia*, p. 240. On the Medici practice of summoning military allies to defend their regime, as in 1466 and 1478, Gori, 'La crisi', pp. 813–20, Lorenzo, *Lettere* 3, pp. 3–6 and n. 4,

[4] Brown, 'Piero in Power', pp. 123–5.

[5] Guicciardini, *Storie*, pp. 84, 94, 100, 164, 321. As we have seen (pp. 152 and 171 in this volume), the *Storie* was biased against him in other ways.

confidence at moments of crisis and failed to strengthen his position when the opportunity arose.

Piero had been brought up as a republican citizen by his father, who had imposed the city's strict dress code on his children; and when Piero set out for Rome aged twelve, he was told by Lorenzo that being his son didn't make him different from other Florentine citizens. His translation into Latin of Bruni's analysis of Florence's republican constitution would also have instructed him in the republican tradition, and so would his political education in the hands of leading citizens like Jacopo Guicciardini and Pierfilippo Pandolfini five years later.[6] Although their support for Piero was self-interested, since – as they admitted themselves – their own standing in Florence depended on the Medici's upright behaviour, they nevertheless advised Piero throughout his period in power as loyal members of a cadre of public officials dedicated to the service of the state. The ethos of these officials was well expressed by Francesco Pepi's defence of popular government to the pope in 1501, when he praised the republican system of putting the distribution of honours and offices in the hands of the popular Great Council, affairs of state into the hands of the Council of Eighty, the Signoria and its colleges, and more secret matters into the hands of the Dieci di Balìa (much better, he said, than the Medici government of Lorenzo and Piero, where decisions were made by one person who was often influenced by another prince or Italian ruler without respect for loyalty or friendship).[7]

How far Piero was influenced by these ideals as a young man is unclear. His attitude towards politics was certainly laconic, and temperamentally he lacked the enthusiasm and dedication of his father – 'Piero is not Lorenzo', as people rightly said. But he nevertheless impressed ordinary citizens, as well as Italy's rulers, with his intelligence and his shrewd judgement of people and situations. The people were entranced by the way he talked to them, and so evidently was the young Alfonsina, whom Jacopo Salviati revealingly describes spending all day with him when they first met in Monte Rotondo, 'discussing and arguing about so many things I don't know where they all come from!' Particularly telling is his great-uncle Giovanni Tornabuoni's early account of Piero's contrasting spirit and modesty, which tempered 'that innate ardour of his so one can't tell which is stronger' – an early sign, perhaps, of the contradictions that presaged the later crises of nerve that made the naturally

---

[6] pp. 45, n. 27; 40; 36; 84–6 in this volume.
[7] pp. 282–3 in this volume. On Pepi's suggestion for a large popular council for tax legislation, Butters, *Governors*, p. 44.

'feisty and bold' Piero suddenly turn and flee instead of fighting in 1494, similarly in 1497, when he was at the city gates, and again in 1498 when Carlo vainly summoned him to his aid.[8] They suggest that far from being empowered by his position, Piero may have been incapacitated by it, fleeing when a more courageous stance might have enabled him to prevail and reassert his authority.

The political life in Florence was not Piero's principal concern during his father's lifetime, although what happened there would be crucial to his fate. He had been introduced by Lorenzo to other ways of life that would be important to his survival in exile, as well as to his possible future as head of a territorial state. His early visits to Rome in 1484 and to Milan in 1489 had taught him the art of being a successful courtier, and he was soon treated as an equal by princely rulers, thanks to his sporting, literary and musical talents and his Orsini blood. As a result, after his father's death he was entrusted by Alfonso of Naples and the pope with the role of mediator to organise a truce with France and Milan.[9] At the same time, he was being taught the role of tough *capo* or boss of Florence's rural clients in the dominion and its bordering cities – like Faenza, where he combined charm and shrewd manipulation to control its castellan, or Siena, which valued him for his superior knowledge of what was going on in Italy and in France.[10] His influence in Faenza in turn gave him standing in the papal curia through the negotiations for him to broker the marriage of the pope's daughter by a Farnese, related by marriage to Puccio Pucci (Piero's envoy in Faenza), while in Pisa the Medici Bank and its control of the university gave him money and a source of patronage.

The importance of the Medici's patronal control of Florence's surrounding territory became apparent during Piero's exile and after his death, when his brother Giuliano and his son Lorenzo became the first members of the family to aspire to ruling small territorial states – Giuliano as governor of Parma and Piacenza, before becoming duke of Nemours; Lorenzo as duke of Urbino – for whom Machiavelli famously wrote *The Prince*. Lorenzo thought that ruling such a state would offer him more security than living as an untitled head of republican Florence, with its family rivalries and restless populace. Florence's ruling families, especially the Medici, had well-established patronal relationships with its subject cities, and as the podestà and captains of these cities they had long experience of controlling them as administrators. Piero died too soon to share his son's awareness of how fragile states like his Duchy of

---

[8] pp. 46–7, 62, 43 and 224, 246, 275–6 in this volume.
[9] pp. 169, 208–9 and 216 in this volume.   [10] See Chapter 9 in this volume.

Urbino were for papal sons (like Cesare Borgia) and nephews (like himself) when the pope died. But he had experienced the power struggle in Florence and as an exile he benefited from his strong bonds with subject states. In exile, he had also become a battle-hardened soldier who shared with *condottieri* like the Orsini and the Vitelli the new morality that justified the use of force and 'every kind of cruelty'. So in many ways he would have been better equipped to rule the new territorial states than his father or his republican peers.

Piero had also learnt for himself the lessons of the new political morality that grew out of Italy's crisis. Formulated in the early decades of the sixteenth century by men actively engaged in politics like Machiavelli, Francesco Guicciardini and the Vettori brothers, Paolo and Francesco (the friend of Machiavelli and Piero's son Lorenzo), it challenged the traditional Christian morality underpinning politics. For example, Paolo and Francesco Vettori both justified the use of force to govern Florence after 1512. Machiavelli, too, advised the young Medici princes, Giuliano and Piero's son Lorenzo, to be prepared to use force and fraud as new rulers. And Guicciardini also admitted that 'deception is very useful', and (like earlier Florentines) he justified using every form of cruelty against the Pisans, by adopting – as he put it in his *Dialogue* – 'reason of state', not Christian morality, in dealing with their prisoners. Another novelty that grew out of these destabilised years was emphasis on the important role of fortune in influencing events, which was something Piero had also frequently experienced for himself during his exile. By making flexibility a key virtue, it too contributed to the new political morality.[11]

It also contributed to Guicciardini's realistic description of the powers exercised by Piero and his father in his *Dialogue on the Government of Florence*. Written in the early 1520s, fifteen or so years after the *Florentine Histories* and more than a decade after the Medici's first return to power in 1512, it now called Piero and his father not tyrants but Florence's bosses, who ruled in as civilised a way as possible and exercised power through 'signals', without ever resorting to the 'blood and violence' of rulers elsewhere – a much better description of Piero during his two years in power than as the arrogant tyrant of Guicciardini's earlier *Histories*.[12] If constrained on one hand by Florence's republican tradition, Piero

---

[11] On 'the new political realism', Brown, 'Rethinking the Renaissance', pp. 254–9 (citing the Vettori); also Machiavelli, *The Prince*, esp. chs. 18 and 25, Guicciardini, *Dialogue*, p. 163, tr. 157–8, *Ricordi*, C 105, and pp. 280–1 in this volume. On Vettori's friendship with Machiavelli, Najemy, *Between Friends*.

[12] Guicciardini, *Dialogo*, 25, 32, 75, tr. pp. 23–4, 31, 72, and n. 5 in this chapter.

happily adopted his father's legal sophistry and manipulative politics and used the same devotees to execute them – like the Pucci and the Dovizi brothers. Piero also shared many of the vices Guicciardini ascribed to his father in his famous two-faced portrait of Lorenzo, and especially his competitiveness, pride and vindictiveness, rages and lust.[13] Guicciardini's fluctuating reflections on princes and tyrants in his later *Ricordi* and the fact that he welcomed Piero's putative grandson Alessandro as duke in 1532 (five years before Alessandro was murdered as a tyrant), makes it likely he would have accepted the fait accompli of Piero as prince or as the 'superhead' he thought Florence needed – belying his earlier violent condemnation of him that has been so influential in blackening Piero's later reputation.[14]

It is in the *Dialogue*, too, that Guicciardini defines the new and flexible head of state he thought republican Florence required. Through the mouth of his alter ego, Bernardo del Nero, he argued that what was needed was

> a boss or patron, he does not have to be a lord who rules but someone who, being a fixture, will necessarily devote the thought and care to the city's affairs that bosses give to their own affairs, or to put it better, like a loving and faithful administrator.[15]

Guicciardini had already referred to people's need of someone to 'fear or revere' when writing about the chaos shortly before a life Gonfalonier was elected in 1502, and Machiavelli agreed with him. He commented in his *Discourses* on how a grave and magisterial man could successfully quell a rioting crowd, as Francesco Soderini had done in 1498 by donning his robes and episcopal rochet; and in the *Discursus*, his proposal for how Florence should be governed in the vacuum following the sudden death of Piero's son Lorenzo in 1519, he acknowledged the need for the head of state to enjoy 'majesty and reputation'.[16] Although, as a republican, he

---

[13] *Storie*, pp. 73–80: 'di natura molto superbo', 'libidinoso e tutto venereo', 'tenuto da qualchuno di natura crudele e vindicativo', 77–8), etc.; cf. Brown, 'Lorenzo and Guicciardini'.

[14] *Ricordi*, ed. Spongano, pp. 110–13 (C 98, 99–101), 232 (C 220 on tyrants), 139 (C 128), 183–5 (C 170–2), 207–8 (C 195, 196), 215 (C 203 on princes); Brown, 'Lorenzo and Guicciardini', esp. 289–93. On Alessandro, *Dialogue*, tr. Brown, pp. xii, xxiv, and the bibliography in Dall'Aglio, *Duke's Assassin*, p. 201, n. 14).

[15] Guicciardini, *Dialogo*, cit., p. 104, tr. 101: 'E però ci bisogna uno padrone, non dico che sia signore e che domini ... sia come uno fattore amorevole e fedele'; cf. Guicciardini, *Storie*, p. 178, 'uno sopracapo chi e' temino o riverischino'.

[16] Machiavelli, *Discorsi* I, 54 (ed. Walker, 2, p. 84, n. 2); *Discursus*, p. 270, tr. Gilbert, I, p. 109: 'esserli renduto la maestà e la reputazione al capo dello stato'. Cf. his *Sommario delle cose della città di Lucca* (1520), ed. Bertelli, p. 241: 'Sta ben male un capo di republica senza maestà, come sta in Lucca.'

placed this authority not in a single figure but in a group of older citizens appointed for life, his proposal acknowledged Florence's need for a head of state with the *maestà* lacking in the elected and constantly changing Signoria and its two colleges, or in the popular Great Council. The image that immediately springs to mind is of Hobbes's *Leviathan*, a single majestic figurehead with a crown and sceptre, whose body is composed of all the people – who still enjoy a role in Machiavelli's proposal.[17] Like the *Leviathan*, the *Discursus* was a compromise solution to suit the times, but it clearly acknowledged that even a republic needed someone to play the role of 'idol' and 'master of the workshop' in the wake of Lorenzo il Magnifico and his son Piero. Although Piero had been condemned by Agostino Vespucci as a 'more than citizen' (*plus quam civis*), 'a great crime', the appointment of a life Gonfalonier of Florence in 1502 acknowledged the need for such a figure. Even though it was not the hereditary position that the Medici eventually achieved, it nevertheless helps to explain the support that sustained Piero, especially in the dominion, both before and after his exile, as well as his family's later success.[18]

There is no doubt that Piero's character deteriorated during his exile, even though the poems he wrote as an exile remind us of the reflective scholar he once was. The turn taken by politics and political thinking after his death suggests he might have been better qualified for the new model of leadership than the old one he inherited. Nevertheless, his frequent assertions of patriotism and his wish to be buried in Florence beside his father, who had once made the city 'so glorious and eminent' – like his craving to return 'to eat figs and grapes in Florence' in the autumn of 1498 – shows he still loved the city of his birth and longed to return to it.[19] He was a more complicated and multifaceted person than his critics suggest, and so too was Florence in these years of change.

---

[17] Machiavelli retained the Great Council to distribute honours and offices, the sixteen standard bearers to act as Rome's tribunate in controlling the senate, and the Gonfalonier of Justice to govern with the sixty-five, jointly enjoying *maestà e reputazione* (plus a legislative life senate of two hundred and an appeal court), *Discursus*, pp. 269–75, Najemy, 'Machiavelli's Florentine Tribunes', Barthas, 'Pensiero costituzionale', and Pedullà, *Machiavelli in Tumult*, pp. 109–10.

[18] Vespucci to Machiavelli, 20 October 1500, p. 281, n. 50 in this volume. On constitutional reforms at this time, Fubini, 'Innovazioni costituzionali', repr. in Fubini, *Politica e pensiero politico*, pp. 165–203, esp. 180–3, Barthas, 'Pensiero costituzionale', and Brown, 'Between Constitution and Government', esp. 100–2; cf. Stephens, *The Fall*, pp. 154–5.

[19] pp. 231 and 273, n. 11 in this volume.

Bibliography

Abulafia, D. ed. *The French Descent into Renaissance Italy, 1494–95. Antecedents and Effects*, Aldershot: Ashgate, 1995.
Anzilotti, A., *La crisi costituzionale della Repubblica fiorentina*, Florence: Seeber, 1912.
Arrighi, V. and Klein, F., 'Strategie familiari e competizione politica alle origini dell'Archivio Mediceo', in Scritture e governo dello stato a Firenze, pp. 243–64.
Aubert, A., *La crisi degli antichi stati italiani, I (1492–1523)*, Florence: Le Lettere, 2003.
Azzolini, M., *The Duke and the Stars. Astrology and Politics in Renaissance Milan*, Cambridge, MA: Harvard University Press, 2013.
Baker, N., *The Fruit of Liberty. Political Culture in the Florentine Renaissance, 1480–1550*, Cambridge, MA: Harvard University Press, 2013.
Bandini, A. M., *Catalogus codicum latinorum Bibliothecae mediceae laurentianae*, 5 vols., Florence, 1774–78.
Barsacchi, M., *Cacciate Lorenzo! La guerra dei Pazzi e l'assedio di Colle Val d'Elsa (1478–1479)*, Siena: Protagon, 2007.
Barthas, J., 'Il pensiero costituzionale di Machiavelli e la funzione tribunizia nella Firenze del Rinascimento', in *Il laboratorio del Rinascimento*, ed. Tanzini, pp. 239–56.
Becchi, G., *Il synodo fiorentino* in *La congiura della verità*, ed. Simonetta.
Belluzzi, A., 'Chiese a pianta centrale di Giuliano da Sangallo', in *Lorenzo il Magnifico e il suo mondo*, ed. Garfagnini, pp. 385–406.
Bertelli, S., 'Arcana Savonaroliani. I *Ricordi* di Giovanvittorio Soderini (1495–1498)', ed. R. Mancini, *Memorie domenicane*, 132 (2015): 347–414.
  'Di due profili mancati e di un bilancino con pesi truccati', *ASI*, 145 (1987): 579–610.
  'Machiavelli e la politica estera fiorentina', in *Studies on Machiavelli*, ed. Gilmore, pp. 29–72.
  'Petrus Soderinus Patriae Parens', *Bibliothèque d'Humanisme e Renaissance*, 31 (1969): 93–114.
Beschi, L., 'Le sculture antiche di Lorenzo il Magnifico', in *Lorenzo il Magnifico e il suo Mondo*, ed. Garfagnini, pp. 291–317.
Black, R., 'Arezzo, the Medici and the Florentine Regime', in *Florentine Tuscany*, ed. Connell and Zorzi, pp. 293–311 (tr. *Lo Stato territoriale*, ed. Zorzi and Connell, pp. 329–57).

Black, R., *Humanism and Education in Medieval and Renaissance Italy*, Cambridge University Press, 2001.
'Lorenzo and Arezzo', in *Lorenzo the Magnificent*, ed. Mallett and Mann, pp. 217–34.
Black, R. and Law, J., ed. *The Medici: Citizens and Masters*, Florence: I Tatti, 2015.
Bloch, A., James, C. and Russell, C., ed. *The Art and Language of Power in Renaissance Florence: Essays for Alison Brown*, Toronto: CRRS, 2019.
Böninger, L., 'Francesco Cambini (1432–1499): doganiere, commissario ed imprenditore fiorentino nella "Pisa Laurenziana"', *Bollettino storico pisano*, 67 (1998): 21–55.
Böninger, L., ed. Medici, Lorenzo, *Lettere*, 15–16 (2010, 2011).
Bornstein, D. ed., see Peterson, D., *Florence and Beyond*.
Boschetto, L., 'Letteratura, arte e politica nella Firenze del Quattrocento. La collaborazione tra Vespasiano e Manetti per l'*Oratio funebris* di Giannozzo Pandolfini', in *Palaeography, Manuscript Illumination and Humanism in Renaissance Italy: Studies in Memory of A. C. de la Mare*, ed. R. Black, J. Kraye and L. Nuvoloni, London: Warburg Institute, 2016, pp. 23–37.
Botto, C., 'L'edificazione della chiesa di Santo Spirito in Firenze', *Rivista d'arte*, 14 (1932): 23–53.
Bratchel, M., *Lucca, 1430–1494. The Reconstruction of an Italian City Republic*, Oxford University Press, 1995.
de Broüard, A., 'Lettres de Rome de Bartolomeo de Bracciano a Virginio Orsini (1489–1494)', *Mélanges d'archéologie et l'histoire*, 33 (1913): 267–331.
Brown, A., *Bartolomeo Scala, 1430–1497, Chancellor of Florence. The Humanist as Bureaucrat*, Princeton University Press, 1979.
'Between Constitution and Government: The Problem of Defining the Medici Regime', in *Il laboratorio del Rinascimento*, ed. Tanzini, pp. 89–102.
'Between the Palace and the Piazza: Locating Power and Agency in Bill Kent's Florence', in *Studies on Florence*, ed. Howard and Hewlett, pp. 35–51.
'Florentine Diplomacy on the Banks of the Po', in *Mantova e il Rinascimento italiano. Studi in onore di David S. Chambers*, ed. P. Jackson and G. Rebecchini, Mantua: Sometti, 2011, pp. 301–14.
'Insiders and Outsiders. The Changing Boundaries of Exile', in *Society and Individual in Renaissance Florence*, ed. W. J. Connell, Berkeley: University of California Press, 2002, pp. 337–83.
'Lorenzo and Guicciardini', in *Lorenzo the Magnificent*, ed. Mallett and Mann, pp. 281–96.
Medicean and Savonarolan Florence. The Interplay of Politics, Humanism and Religion, Turnhout: Brepols, 2011.
The Medici in Florence. The Exercise and Language of Power, Florence: Olschki, 1992.
'Piero de' Medici's Poems in the Context of His Life and Letters', in the volume in honour of Letizia Panizza, forthcoming.
'Piero in Power, 1492–1494. A Balance Sheet for Four Generations of Medici Control', in *The Medici*, ed. Black and Law, pp. 113–25.

'Rethinking the Renaissance in the Aftermath of Italy's Crisis', in *Italy in the Age of the Renaissance*, ed. J. Najemy, Oxford University Press, 2004, pp. 246–65.
Brucker, G., 'The Medici in the Fourteenth Century', *Speculum*, 32 (1957): 1–26.
Bryce, J., 'Performing for Strangers: Women, Dance, and Music in Quattrocento Florence', *Renaissance Quarterly*, 54 (2001): 1074–107.
Bullard, M., *Filippo Strozzi and the Medici. Favor & Finance in Sixteenth-Century Florence and Rome*, Cambridge University Press, 1980.
'"Hammering Away at the Pope": Nofri Tornabuoni, Lorenzo de' Medici's Agent and Collaborator in Rome', in *Florence and Beyond*, ed. Peterson and Bornstein, pp. 383–98.
'In Pursuit of *onore* et utile. Lorenzo de' Medici and Rome', in *Lorenzo il Magnifico e il suo Mondo*, ed. Garfagnini, pp. 123–42.
Lorenzo il Magnifico. Image and Anxiety, Politics and Finance, Florence: Olschki, 1994.
'Marriage Politics and the Family in Florence: The Strozzi-Medici Alliance of 1508', *American Historical Review*, 84 (1979): 668–87.
Bullard, M., ed. Medici, Lorenzo, *Lettere*, 10–11.
Buonarroti, Michelangelo, *Il Carteggio*, ed. P. Barocchi and R. Ristori, Florence: Sansoni, 1965.
Buser, B., *Die Beziehungen der Mediceer zu Frankriech während der Jahre 1434–1494, in ihrem Zusammenhang*, Leipzig: Duncker and Humblot, 1879.
Butters, H., 'Florence, Milan and the Barons' War (1485–1486)', in *Lorenzo de' Medici Studi*, ed. G. C. Garfagnini, Florence: Olschki, 1992, pp. 281–308.
Governors and Government in Early Sixteenth Century Florence, 1502–1519, Oxford: Clarendon Press, 1985.
Butters, H., ed. Medici, Lorenzo, *Lettere*, 8–9 (2001, 2002).
Cadoni, G., ed. *Provvisioni concernenti l'Ordinamento della Repubblica Fiorentina 1494–1512*, Rome: Istituto storico Italiano per il Medio Evo, 1 (1994); 2, ed. with F. di Sciullo (2000).
Cambi, Giovanni, *Istorie*, in *Delizie degli eruditi toscani*, 23, 1785.
Campana, A., 'Per il carteggio di Poliziano', *La Rinascita*, 6 (1943): 469–72.
Canestrini, G. and Desjardins, A., *Négotiations diplomatiques de la France avec la Toscane*, 6 vols., Paris: Impr. nationale, 1859–66, I (1859).
Cantone, R., 'Il Castello Orsini di Bracciano', in *Bracciano e gli Orsini nell '400. Tramonto di un progetto feudale. Catalogo della mostra*, ed. A. Cavallaro et al., Rome: De Luca, 1981, pp. 39–48.
Cappelli, A., 'Lettere di Lorenzo de' Medici ...con notizie tratte dai carteggi diplomatici degli oratori estensi a Firenze', in *Atti e Memorie delle RR. Deputazioni di Storia Patria per le Provincie Modensei e Parmensi*, I, 1863, pp. 231–320.
Caraviti, A., *I codici e le arti a Montecassino*, III, ii, Montecassino: della Badia, 1870.
Carteggio delle magistrature dell'etá repubblicana. Otto di Pratica, I* *Legazioni e commissarie*, II* *Missive*, Florence: Olschki, 1987.
Carte Strozziane del R. Archivio di Stato in Firenze, I, Florence: Galileiana, 1884.

Cattani, G., 'Politica e religione: Vicende e ordinamenti politici' in *Faenza nell'età dei Manfredi*, ed. A. Vasina, Faenza Editrice, 1990, pp. 13–36.

Cavallar, O., 'Il tiranno, i *dubia* del giudice, e i *consilia* dei giuristi, *ASI*, 155 (1997): 265–345.

Cavallaro, A., 'Musica, danza e svaghi di corte in un ciclo di figure femminili nel Castello Orsini di Bracciano', in *Donne del Rinascimento a Roma e dintorno*, ed. A. Esposito, Rome, 2013, pp. 105–31 and pls. II–VIII.

Cegia, Francesco, 'I ricordi segreti del mediceo Francesco di Agostino Cegia (1495–1497)', ed. G. Pampaloni, *ASI*, 115 (1957): 188–234.

Centanni, M., *Fantasmi del antico. La tradizione classica nel Rinascimento*, Rimini: Guaraldi, 2017.

Cerretani, Bartolomeo, *Ricordi*, ed. G. Berti, Florence: Olschki, 1993.

Storia fiorentina, ed. G. Berti, Florence: Olschki, 1994.

Chambers, D., 'A Cardinal in Rome. Florentine and Medici Ambitions', in *The Medici*, ed. Black and Law, pp. 205–17.

'Francesco II Gonzaga, marquis of Mantua, "Liberator of Italy"', in *The French Descent*, ed. Abulafia, pp. 217–29.

A Renaissance Cardinal and his Worldly Goods: The Will and Inventory of Francesco Gonzaga (1444–1483), London: Warburg Institute, 1992.

Chittolini, G., 'Dominant Cities. Florence, Genoa, Venice, Milan and their Territories in the Fifteenth Century', in *The Medici*, ed. Black and Law, pp. 13–26.

Ciardi Dupré Dal Poggetto, G., 'I dipinti di Palazzo Medici' in *La Toscana*, I, pp. 131–61.

Clough, C., 'The Romagna campaign of 1494: a significant military encounter', in *The French Descent*, ed. Abulafia, pp. 191–215.

Colucci, Benedetto, *Scritti inediti*, ed. A. Frugoni, Florence: Olschki, 1939.

Comanducci, R., 'Bernardo Rucellai', *DBI*, 89, 2017.

'Bernardo Rucellai e L'"Accademia Neoplatonica" di Careggi', *Rinascimento*, 33 (1993): 223–51.

Il Carteggio di Bernardo Rucellai. Inventario, Florence: Olschki, 1996.

'Impegno politico e riflessione storica. Bernardo Rucellai e gli Orti Oricellari' in *I ceti dirigenti in Firenze dal gonfalonierato di giustizia all'avvento del ducato*, ed. E. Insabato, Lecce: Conte, 1999, pp. 153–70.

Connell, W., 'Clientelismo e stato territoriale. Il potere fiorentino a Pistoia nel XV secolo', *Società e storia*, 14 (1991): 523–43.

'Il Commissario e lo stato territoriale fiorentino', *Ricerche storiche*, 18 (1988): 591–617.

'"I fautori delle parti". Citizen interest and the treatment of a subject town, c. 1500', in *Istituzioni e società in Toscana nell'età moderna*, Ministero per i beni culturali, 1994, pp. 118–47.

Connell, W., ed. with A. Zorzi, *Florentine Tuscany. Structure and Practices of Power*, Cambridge University Press, 2000 (tr. of *Lo Stato territoriale*, Zorzi and Connell).

Consulte e Pratiche della repubblica fiorentina, 1495–1497, ed. D. Fachard, Geneva: Droz, 2002.

1498–1505, ed. D. Fachard, 2 vols., Geneva: Droz, 1993.

Corrispondenza degli ambasciatori fiorentini a Napoli, ed. M. del Treppo, 2nd. ser., 8 vols, Naples: Istituto italiano per gli studi filosofici, 2006, citing 3 (ed. Meli, 2013), 5 (ed. Trapani, 2010), 7 (ed. Figliuolo, 2012).

Cortese, D., 'Noterelle Medicee: Un epigramma per Simonetta Cattaneo e otto lettere di Claricia Orsini al Magnifico', in *Medievo e Rinascimento*, etc. *Lazzarin*, 2 vols., Padua: Antenore, 1979, I, pp. 529–39.

D'Accone, F., 'Lorenzo the Magnificent and Music', in *Lorenzo il Magnifico e il suo Mondo*, ed. Garfagnini, pp. 259–90.

Dall'Aglio, S., *The Duke's Assassin. Exile and Death of Lorenzino de' Medici*, 2011, (tr. D. Weinstein, New Haven: Yale University Press, 2015).

Davies, J., *Culture and Power: Tuscany and Its Universities, 1537–1609*, Leiden: Brill, 2009.

Florence and Its University during the Early Renaissance, Leiden: Brill, 1998.

Delaborde, H.-F., *L'expédition de Charles VIII en Italie. Histoire diplomatique et militaire*, Paris: Firmin-Didot, 1888.

De La Mare, A., 'New Research on Humanistic Scribes in Florence', in *Miniatura fiorentina del Rinascimento, 1440–1525*, ed. A. Garzelli, I, Florence: La Nuova Italia, 1985, pp. 383–476.

Del Corno Branca, D., *Sulla tradizione delle Rime del Poliziano*, Florence: Olschki, 1979.

Delizie degli eruditi toscani, ed. I. di San Luigi, 24 vols., Florence: G. Cambiagi, 1770–89.

Del Lungo, I., *Florentia. Uomini e cose del Quattrocento (1897)*, repr. Montepulciano: Le Balze, 2002.

Gli amori del Magnifico Lorenzo, Bologna: Zanichelli, 1923.

Prose volgari inedite e poesie latine e greche edite e inedite di Angelo Ambrogini Poliziano, Florence: Barbèra, 1867.

'Tra lo Scala e il Poliziano', *Miscellanea storica della Valdelsa*, 4 (1896): 179–80.

Del Piazzo, M., *Il carteggio "Medici-Este" dal Sec. XV al 1531: regesti delle lettere conservate negli archivi di Stato di Firenze e Modena*, Rome 1964.

Protocolli del carteggio di Lorenzo il Magnifico per gli anni 1473–74, 1477–92, Florence: Olschki, 1956.

Del Piazzo, M., ed., see Medici, Piero, 'I ricordi di lettere'.

De Marinis, T. and Prosa, A., ed. *Nuovi documenti per la storia del Rinascimento*, Florence: Olschki, 1970.

Dempsey, C., *The Portrayal of Love. Botticelli's* Primavera *and Humanist Culture at the Time of Lorenzo the Magnificent*, Princeton University Press, 1992.

Denis, A., *Charles VIII et les Italiens: histoire et mythe*, Geneva: Droz, 1979.

De Robertis, D., 'Supplementi all'epistolario del Pulci', *Giornale Storico della Letteratura Italiana*, 134 (1957), pp. 548–69.

De Robertis, D., ed. Pulci, Luigi, *Morgante e lettere*.

De Roover, R., *Il Banco Medici dalle Origini al Declino (1397–1494)*, Florence: La Nuova Italia, 1970.

Devonshire-Jones, R., *Francesco Vettori, Florentine Citizen and Medici Servant*, London: Athlone Press, 1972.

'Lorenzo de' Medici, duca d'Urbino, "Signore" of Florence?', in *Studies on Machiavelli*, ed. Gilmore, pp. 297–315.

Dillon Bussi, A., 'Le bibliotheche di Mattia Corvino e di Lorenzo il Magnifico', in *Italy & Hungary. Humanism and Art in the Early Renaissance*, ed. P. Farbaky and L. Waldman, Florence: I Tatti, 2011, pp. 231–65.

Dillon Bussi, A., with Fantoni, A., 'La biblioteca medicea laurenziana negli ultimi anni del Quattrocento', in *All'Ombra del Lauro*, ed. A. Lenzuni, Florence: Silvana, 1992, pp. 135–47.

Dovizi, Cardinal Bernardo, *Epistolario*, see Moncallero, ed.

Elam, C., 'Lorenzo de' Medici's Sculpture Garden', *Mitteilungen*, 36 (1992): 41–84.

'Lorenzo's Architectural and Urban Policies', in *Lorenzo il Magnifico e il suo Mondo*, ed. Garfagnini, pp. 357–84.

Eubel, C., *Hierarchia Catholica medii Aevi*, 8 vols., Regensburg: Monasterii, 2 (1901), 3 (1910).

Fabbri, L., 'The Magnificent Arbitrator: Lorenzo de' Medici and the Patrician Families in Florence', in *Studies on Florence*, ed. Howard and Hewlett, pp. 95–113.

'Women's Rights according to Lorenzo de' Medici: the Borromeo-Pazzi Dispute and the Lex de testamentis', in *Art and Language of Power*, ed. Bloch, James and Russell, pp. 91–115.

Fabroni, A., *Laurentii Medicis Magnifici Vita*, Pisa: J. Grazioli, 1784.

Magni Cosmi Medicei Vita, Pisa: A. Landi, 1789.

Fachard, D., 'Dietro le quinte della cancelleria premachiavelliana', in *Storiografia repubblicana fiorentina*, ed. Marchand and Zancarini, pp. 267–82.

Fachard, D., ed., see *Consulte e Pratiche*.

Feeney, D., Review of A. Rogerson, Virgil's Ascanius, in *The London Review of Books*, 39 (15 June 2017).

Ferente, S., *Gli Ultimi Guelfi. Linguaggi e identità politiche in Italia nella seconda metà del Quattrocento*, Rome: Viella, 2013.

Ficino, Marsilio, *The Letters*, 10 vols., 1975–2015, 5, London: School of Economic Science, 1994.

Figliuolo, B., ed., *Corrispondenza degli ambasciadori fiorentini a Napoli*, 7, 2012.

Foster, 'Lorenzo de' Medici's Cascina at Poggio a Caiano', *Mitteilungen*, 14 (1969): 47–56.

A Study of Lorenzo de' Medici's Villa at Poggio a Caiano, 2 vols., New York: Garland, 1978.

Fournel, J.-L., 'L'ennemi dans l'histoire florentine selon Machiavel et Guicciardini' in *Storiografia repubblicana Fiorentina*, ed. Marchand and Zancarini, pp. 31–49.

Franceschi, F., 'Medici Economic Policy', in *The Medici, Citizens and Masters*, ed. Black and Law, pp. 129–54.

Franco, Matteo, *Lettere*, ed. G. Frosini, Florence: Accademia Della Crusca, 1990.

Frosini, G., '"Honore et utile": vicende storiche e testimonianze private nelle lettere romane di Matteo Franco (1488–1492)', in *Reti Medievali Rivista*, 2009, www.retimedievali.it, 1–17.

Fryde, E., *Humanism and Renaissance Historiography*, London: Hambledon Press, 1983.

'Lorenzo's Greek Manuscripts', in *Lorenzo the Magnificent*, ed. Mallett and Mann, pp. 93–104.

Fubini, R., 'The Italian League and the Policy of the Balance of Power at the accession of Lorenzo de' Medici', in *The Origins of the State in Italy*, ed. Kirshner, pp. 166–99 (tr. of 'Lega italica', repr. in Fubini, *Italia Quattrocentesca*, pp. 185–219).

Italia Quattrocentesca. Politica e diplomazia nell'età di Lorenzo il Magnifico, Milan: FrancoAngeli, 1994.

'Lorenzo the Magnificent's Regime. Aims, Image, and Constitutional Framework', in *The Medici*, ed. Black and Law, pp. 61–84.

Politica e pensiero politico nell'Italia del Rinascimento. Dallo Stato teritoriale al Machiavelli, Florence: Edifir, 2009.

Fubini, R., ed., Medici, Lorenzo, *Lettere*, 1–2, 1977.

Fusco, L. and Corti, G., *Lorenzo de' Medici, Collector and Antiquarian*, Cambridge University Press, 2006.

Ganz, M., 'Paying the price for political failure. Florentine women in the aftermath of 1466', *Rinascimento*, 34 (1994): 237–57.

Garfagnini, G. C., ed. *Lorenzo de' Medici Studi*, Florence: Olschki, 1992.

ed. *Lorenzo il Magnifico e il suo mondo*, Florence: Olschki, 1994.

Garin, E., 'L'ambiente del Poliziano', in *Il Poliziano e il suo tempo*, Florence: Sansoni, 1957, pp. 17–39.

Gavitt, P., *Charity and Children in Renaissance Florence. The Ospedale degli Innocenti, 1410–1536*, Ann Arbor: University of Michigan Press, 1990.

Gentile, M., 'Tuscans and Lombards. The Political Culture of Officialdom', in *The Medici*, ed. Black and Law, pp. 101–12.

Gentile, M., ed. *Guelfi e ghibellini nell'Italia del Rinascimento*, Rome: Viella, 2005.

Gentile, S., 'Lorenzo e Giano Lascaris. Il fondo greco della Biblioteca Medicea privata', in *Lorenzo il Magnifico e il suo Mondo*, ed. Garfagnini, pp. 177–94.

Gherardi, A., *Nuovi documenti e studi intorno a Girolamo Savonarola*, Florence: Sansoni, 1887.

Gilbert, F., 'Bernardo Rucellai and the Orti Oricellari', *JWCI*, 12 (1949): 101–31.

Gilmore, M. F., ed., *Studies on Machiavelli*, Florence: Sansoni, 1972.

Giorgetti, A. 'Lorenzo de' Medici, capitano della repubblica fiorentina', *ASI*, ser. 4, 11 (1883): 194–215.

Giovannoni, G., 'Rilievi ed opere architettoniche del Cinquecento a Montecassino', in *Casinensia. Miscellanea di Studi Cassinesi*, Montecassino (Monastery), 1929, pp. 305–36.

Godman, P., *From Poliziano to Machiavelli. Florentine Humanism in the High Renaissance*, Princeton University Press, 1998.

Goldthwaite, R., *The Economy of Renaissance Florence*, Baltimore: The Johns Hopkins University Press, 2009.

'Performance of the Florentine Economy, 1494–1512: Moneys and Accountancy', *ASI*, 176 (2018): 245–73.

Gori, O., 'La crisi del regime mediceo del 1466 in alcune lettere inedite di Piero de' Medici', in *Studi in onore di Arnaldo d'Addario*, 3, Lecce: Conte, 1995, pp. 809–25.

'Per un contributo al carteggio di Lorenzo il Magnifico: lettere inedite ai Bardi di Vernio', *ASI*, 154 (1996): 253–378.
Una donna del Rinascimento. Contessina Bardi, Vernio: Accademia Bardi, 2012.
Gregorovius, F., *Lucrezia Borgia*, 1874 (tr. J. L. Garner, London: Phaidon, 1948).
Grendler, P., *Schooling in Renaissance Italy. Literacy and Learning, 1300–1600*, Baltimore: Johns Hopkins University Press, 1989.
Griffiths, G., Hankins, J. and Thompson, D., ed. *The Humanism of Leonardo Bruni. Selected Texts*, Binghamton: MRTS, 1987.
Grimaldi, G., 'Bernardo Dovizi alla Corte d'Alfonso II d'Aragona', *AS per le province napoletane*, 25 (1900): 218–37.
Guicciardini, Francesco, *Dialogo del Reggimento di Firenze*, in *Dialogo e discorsi del Reggimento di Firenze*, ed. R. Palmarocchi, Bari: Laterza, 1932, pp. 3–172 (ed. and tr. A. Brown, Cambridge University Press, 1994).
Ricordi, ed. R. Spongano, Florence: Sansoni, 1951.
Storia d'Italia, ed. F. Catalano, 3 vols., Milan: Mondadori, 1975.
Storie fiorentine, ed. R. Palmarocchi, Bari: Laterza, 1931.
Guidi, A., *Un segretario militante. Politica, diplomazia e armi nel Cancelliere Machiavelli*, Bologna: il Mulino, 2009.
Guidi, G., *Il Governo della Città-repubblica di Firenze del primo Quattrocento*, 3 vols., Florence: Olschki, 1981.
Guidi Bruscoli, F., 'Politica matrimoniale e matrimoni politici nella Firenze di Lorenzo de' Medici: uno studio del ms. Notarile antecosimiano 14099', *ASI*, 155 (1997): 347–98.
'The 1487 Medici-Cybo Marriage and Its Implications for the Medici Bank in Rome', in *Art and Language of Power*, ed. A. Bloch, C. James and C. Russell, pp. 65–89.
Guiducci, Lorenzo, 'Diario (1492–1496)', ed. M. Simonetta and L. Giorgetti, *Rivista di letteratura storiografica italiana*, 1, 2017, pp. 47–81.
Hatfield, R., 'The Compagnia de' Magi', *JWCI*, 33 (1970): 107–44.
Hewlett, C., ed. with Howard, P., *Studies on Florence*.
Heydenreich, L. H., 'Giuliano da Sangallo in Vigevano, ein neues Dokument', in *Scritti di storia dell'arte in onore di Ugo Procacci*, 2, Milan: Electa, 1977, pp. 321–3
Hicks, D., 'The Sienese Oligarchy and the Rise of Pandolfo Petrucci, 1487–97', in *La Toscana*, 3, pp. 1051–72.
Hirst, M., *Michelangelo. The Achievement of Fame*, New Haven: Yale University Press, 2011.
The Young Michelangelo: the Artist in Rome, London: National Gallery, 1994.
Howard, P. and Hewlett, C., ed. *Studies on Florence and the Italian Renaissance in Honour of F. W. Kent*, Turnhout: Brepols, 2016.
Hurtubise, P., *Une famile-témoin, les Salviati*, Città del Vaticano: Biblioteca apostolica vaticana 1985.
Ianziti, Gary, *Humanistic Historiography under the Sforzas. Politics and Propaganda in Fifteenth-Century Milan*, Oxford: Clarendon Press, 1988.
Jackson, P., *Pandolfo Petrucci. Politics and patronage in Renaissance Siena*. Doctoral dissertation, Warburg Institute, University of London, 2006.

James, C., 'Florence and Ferrara. Dynastic Marriage and Politics', in *The Medici*, ed. Black and Law, pp. 365–78.
The Letters of Giovanni Sabadino degli Arienti (1481–1510), Florence: Olschki, 2002.
'Marriage by Correspondence: Politics and Domesticity in the Letters of Isabella d'Este and Francesco Gonzaga, 1490–1519', *Renaissance Quarterly*, 65 (2012): 321–52.
James, C., ed. with Block, A. and Russell, C., *The Art and Language of Power*.
Jones, P., 'Communes and despots: The City State in Late-Medieval Italy', 1965, repr. in *Communes and Despots*, ed. Law and Paton, pp. 3–24.
Kennedy, W., 'Some unpublished letters of the Italian Renaissance from the Collection of Harold C. Bodman', *Studies in the Renaissance*, 7 (1960): 67–75.
Kent, D., 'I Medici in esilio: una vittoria di famiglia ed una disfatta personale', *ASI*, 132 (1976): 3–63.
The Rise of the Medici. Faction in Florence, 1426–1434, Oxford University Press, 1978.
Kent, F. W., *Lorenzo de' Medici and the Art of Magnificence*, Baltimore: Johns Hopkins University Press, 2004.
Princely Citizen. Lorenzo de' Medici and Renaissance Florence, Turnhout: Brepols, 2013.
'Ties of Neighbourhood and Patronage in Quattrocento Florence', in *Patronage, Art and Society*, ed. Kent and Simons, pp. 79–110.
Kent, F. W., ed. with P. Simons, *Patronage, Art and Society in Renaissance Italy*, Oxford University Press, 1987.
Kidwell, C., *Marullus. Soldier Poet of the Renaissance*, London: Duckworth, 1989.
Kirshner, J., ed. 'Introduction', in *The Origins of the State in Italy, 1300–1600*, Chicago University Press, 1995, pp. 1–10.
Klapisch-Zuber, C., *Retour à la Cité. Les magnats de Florence, 1340–1440*, Paris: Ècole des Hautes Etudes, 2006.
'San Romolo: un vescovo, un lupo, un nome alle origini dello stato moderno', *ASI*, 65 (1997): 3–48.
Women, Family and Ritual in Renaissance Italy, Chicago University Press, 1985.
Klein, F., 'Note in margine a/di Agostino Vespucci, cancelliere nella repubblica soderiniana. Una Storia prima delle Istorie?', in *Il laboratorio del Rinascimento*, ed. Tanzini, pp. 211–38.
Scritture e governo dello stato a Firenze nel Rinascimento. Cancellieri, ufficiali, archivi, Florence: Edifir, 2013.
Kraye, J., 'Lorenzo and the Philosophers', in *Lorenzo il Magnifico*, ed. Mallett and Mann, pp. 151–66.
Kristeller, P. O., *Supplementum ficinianum*, 2 vols., Florence: Olschki, 1937.
Labande-Mailfert, Y., *Charles VIII e son milieu, 1470–1498: Jeunesse au pouvoir*, Paris: Klincksieck, 1975.
Landucci, Luca, *Diario fiorentino dal 1450 al 1516*, Florence: Sansoni, 1883, repr. 1985.
Law, J. and Paton, B., ed., *Communes and Despots in Medieval and Renaissance Italy*, Farnham: Ashgate, 2010.

ed. with Black, R.,*The Medici*.
Lazzerini, I., 'The Words of Emotion: Political Language and Discursive Resources in Lorenzo de' Medici's *Lettere* (1468-1492)', in *Emotions, Passions, and Power in Renaissance Italy*, ed. F. Ricciardelli and A. Zorzi, Amsterdam: Amsterdam University Press, 2015, pp. 91–110.
de Lettenhove, K., *Lettres et négociations de Philippe de Commines*, Brussels: Academie royale, 1867–74.
Lev, E., *Tigress of Forlì. The Life of Caterina Sforza*, London: Head of Zeus, 2015.
Lillie, A., 'Lorenzo de' Medici's rural investments and territorial expansion', *Rinascimento*, 33 (1993): 53–67.
Lingohr, M., 'The Palace and Villa as spaces of Patrician Self-definition', in *Renaissance Florence*, ed. R. J. Crum and J. T. Paoletti, Cambridge University Press, 2006, pp. 240–72.
Machiavelli, Niccolò, *Arte della Guerra e scritti politici minori*, ed. S. Bertelli, Milan: Feltrinelli, 1961.
  The Chief Works and Others, tr. A. Gilbert, 3 vols., Durham: Duke University Press, 1989.
  'I Decennali' in *Il teatro e tutti glli scritti letterari*, ed. F. Gaeta, Milan: Feltrinelli, 1965, pp. 233–66.
  'Descrizione del modo tenuto dal duca Valentino nello ammazzare Vitellozzo Vitelli', in *Arte della Guerra*, ed. S. Bertelli, pp. 33–48.
  Discorsi sopra la prima deca di Tito Livio, ed. S. Bertelli *Il Principe e Discorsi*, Milan: Feltrinelli, 1960 (tr. L. J. Walker with full notes, 2 vols., London: Routledge and Kegan Paul, 1975).
  'Discursus Florentinarum rerum post mortem iunioris Laurentii Medices', in *Arte della Guerra*, ed. S. Bertelli, pp. 245–77.
  Legazioni e commissarie, ed. S. Bertelli, 3 vols., Milan: Feltrinelli, 1964 (legations to Cesare Borgia tr. Gilbert in *Chief Works*, I, pp. 120–60).
  Lettere, ed. F. Gaeta, Milan: Feltrinelli, 1961 (tr. and ed. J. B. Atkinson and D. Sices, *Machiavelli and His Friends. Their Personal Correspondence*, DeKalb: Northern Illinois University Press, 2004).
  Il Principe, ed. G. Pedullà, Rome: Donzelli, 2013 (ed. S. Bertelli, with *Discorsi*).
  'Sommario delle cose della città di Lucca', ed. S. Bertelli in *Arte della Guerra*, pp. 229–44.
Maîer, I., *Ange Politien. La Formation d'un poète humaniste (1469–1480)*, Geneva: Droz, 1966.
Mallett, M., *The Borgias.The Rise and Fall of a Renaissance Dynasty*, London: Paladin, 1969.
  'Horse-racing and Politics in Lorenzo's Florence', in *Lorenzo the Magnificent*, ed. Mallett and Mann, pp. 253–62.
  'Personalities and Pressures: Italian Involvement in the French Invasion of 1494', in *The French Descent*, ed. D. Abulafia, pp. 151–63.
  'Pisa and Florence in the Fifteenth Century: aspects of the period of the first Florentine domination', in *Florentine Studies. Politics and Society in Renaissance Florence*, ed. N. Rubinstein, London: Faber, 1968, pp. 403–41.
  'The transformation of war', in *Italy and the European Powers*, ed. Shaw, pp. 3–21.

Mallett, M., ed., with Mann, Ni. *Lorenzo the Magnificent. Culture and Politics*, London: Warburg Institute, 1996.
  ed. Medici, Lorenzo, *Lettere*, 5–7 (1989, 1990, 1998).
Mallett, M., ed. with Shaw, C., *The Italian Wars, 1494–1559*, Harlow: Pearson, 2012.
Marchand, E., 'The Materials of Ephemeral Sculpture in Renaissance Italy', in *Art and Language of Power*, ed. A. Bloch, C. James and C. Russell, pp. 251–69.
Marchand, J.-J. and Zancarini, J.-C., ed., *Storiografia repubblicana Fiorentina (1494–1570)*, Florence: Cesati, 2003.
Marrara, D., 'Il problema della tirannide nel pensiero di Francesco Guicciardini e di Francesco Vettori', *Rivista di storia del diritto italiano*, 39 (1966): 99–154.
Martelli, M., *Angelo Poliziano. Storia e metastoria*, Lecce: Conti, 1995.
  'Il *Libro delle Epistole* di Angelo Poliziano', *Interpres*, 1 (1978): 184–255.
  Studi Laurenziani, Florence: Olschki, 1965.
Martines, L., *Lawyers and Statecraft in Renaissance Florence*, Princeton University Press, 1968.
  Scourge and Fire. Savonarola and Renaissance Florence, London: Jonathan Cape, 2006.
Masetti Zannini, G. L. and Falcioni, A., ed. *La Signoria di Pandolfo IV Malatesta (1482–1528)*, Rimini: B. Ghigi, 2003.
Mathew, A., *The Life and Times of Rodrigo Borgia, Pope Alexander VI*, London: S. Paul and Co, 1912.
Mazzalupi, M., 'Signorelli, the Vitelli and the Medici', *Burlington Magazine*, 159 (2017): 442–44.
Mcgann, M., 'The Medicean dedications of books I–III of the *Hymni Naturales* of M. Marullus', *Res Publica Litterarum*, 3 (1980): 87–90
Medici, de', Lorenzo, *Lettere*, 1–12, 15–16, dir. N. Rubinstein, F. W. Kent, Florence: Giunti-Barbèra, 1977 <2011>, 1–2 (ed. Fubini, 1977), 3–4 (ed. Rubinstein, 1977, 1981), 5–7 (ed. Mallett, 1989, 1990, 1998), 8–9 (ed. Butters, 2001, 2002). 10–11 (ed. Bullard, 2003, 2004), 12 (ed. Pellegrini, 2007), 15–16 (ed. Böninger, 2010, 2011).
  Canzoniere, ed. T. Zanato, 2 vols., Florence: Olschki, 1991.
Medici, de', Piero, 'I ricordi di lettere', ed. M. Del Piazzo, *ASI* (1) = 112 (1954), pp. 378–432 (April 1492–July 1493); (2) = 113 (1955), pp. 101–41 (August 1493–October 1494).
Meli, P., 'Un episodio dell'espansione fiorentino in Lunigiana: le lenta aquisizione del marchesato di Verrucola', *ASI*, 165 (2007): 665–97.
Meli, P., ed. *Corrispondenza degli ambasciatori fiorentini a Napoli*, 3, 2013.
Merisalo, O., *Le Collezioni Medicee nel 1495: Deliberazioni degli Ufficiali dei Ribelli*, Florence: Amici del Bargello, 1999.
Miglio, L., *Governare l'alfabeto. Donne, scrittura e libri nel Medievo*, Rome: Viella, 2008.
Milner, S., 'Lorenzo and Pistoia: Peacemaker or Partisan?', in *Lorenzo the Magnificent*, ed. Mallett and Mann, pp. 235–52.
Milner, S., 'Rubrics and Requests: Statutory division and supra-communal Clientage in fifteenth-century Pistoia' in *Florentine Tuscany*, ed. Connell

and Zorzi, pp. 312–32 (tr. in Zorzi and Connell, *Lo Stato territoriale*, pp. 405–29).
Mommsen, T., 'Petrarch and the Story of the Choice of Hercules', *JWCI*, 16 (1953): 178–92.
Moncallero, G., *Il Cardinale Bernardo Dovizi da Bibbiena, umanista e diplomatico (1470–1520)*, Florence: Olschki, 1953.
Moncallero, G., ed. *Epistolario di Bernardo Dovizi da Bibbiena*, 2 vols., Florence: Olschki, 1, 1955.
Moulakis, A. 'Civic Humanism, realist constitutionalism, and Francesco Guicciardini's *Discorso di Logrogno*', in *Renaissance Civic Humanism*, ed. J. Hankins, Cambridge University Press, 2000, pp. 200–22.
'Leonardo Bruni's Constitution of Florence*'*, *Rinascimento*, 26 (1986): 141–90.
Najemy, J., 'Arms and letters: the Crisis of Courtly Culture in the Wars of Italy', in *Italy and the European Powers*, ed. C. Shaw, pp. 207–38.
Between Friends. Discourses of Power and Desire in the Machiavelli-Vettori Letters of 1513–1515, Princeton University Press, 1993.
'Florentine Politics and Urban Spaces', in *Renaissance Florence. A Social History*, ed. R. Crum and J. Paoletti, Cambridge University Press, 2006, pp. 19–54.
A History of Florence, 1200–1575, Oxford: Blackwell, 2006.
'Machiavelli's Florentine Tribunes', in *Renaissance Studies in Honor of Joseph Connors*, Florence: I Tatti, 2013, 2, pp. 65–72.
Nanni, P., *Lorenzo Agricoltore. Sulla proprietà fondiaria dei Medici nella seconda metà del Quattrocento*, Florence: Accademia dei Georgofili, 1992.
Nardi, Jacopo, *Istorie di Firenze*, ed. A. Gelli, 2 vols., Florence: Le Monnier, 1858.
Nelson, J., 'Filippino Lippi e i contesti della pittura a Firenze e Roma (1488-1504)' in Zambrano, P. and Nelson J., *Filippino Lippi*, Milan: Electa, 2004, pp. 367–555.
'Filippino Lippi at the Medici villa of Poggio a Caiano', in *Florentine Drawing at the Time of Lorenzo the Magnificent*, ed. E. Cropper, Bologna: Villa Spelman Colloquia, 1994, pp. 159–83.
'Filippino Lippi's *Allegory of Discord*: A Warning about Families and Politics', *Gazette des Beaux-Arts*, 128 (1996): 237–52.
'Leonardo e la reinvenzione della figura femminile: Leda, Lisa e Maria', *Lettura Vinciana*, 46 (2006): 5–24.
Newbiggin, N., *Feste d'Oltrarno. Plays in Churches in Fifteenth-Century Florence*, 2 vols., Florence: Olschki, 1996.
'Piety and Politics in the feste of Lorenzo's Florence', in *Lorenzo il Magnifico e il suo mondo*, ed. Garfagnini, pp. 17–41.
'Politics in the Sacre Rappresentazioni of Lorenzo's Florence', in *Lorenzo the Magnificent*, ed. Mallett and Mann, pp. 117–30.
Orvieto, P., *Poliziano e l'ambiente mediceo*, Rome: Salerno, 2009.
'Religion and Literature in Oligarchic, Medicean and Savonarolan Florence', in *The Medici*, ed. Black and Law, pp. 189–203.
Palmarocchi, R., 'Lorenzo de' Medici e la nomina cardinalizia di Giovanni', *ASI*, 110 (1952): 38–54.

Pampaloni, G., 'I Tornaquinci, poi Tornabuoni, fino ai primi del Cinquecento', *ASI*, 126 (1968): 331–62.
Pampaloni, G., ed. Cegia, Francesco, 'I ricordi secreti'.
Parenti, Marco, *Lettere*, ed. M. Marrese, Florence: Olschki, 1996.
  Ricordi storici, 1464–1467, ed. M. Doni Garfagnini, Rome: Edizioni di storia e letteratura, 2001.
Parenti, Piero, *Storia fiorentina*, ed. A. Matucci, 2 vols., Florence: Olschki, 1994, 2005.
Pedullà, G., *Machiavelli in Tumult. The Discourses on Livy and the Origins of Political Conflictualism*, rev. Cambridge University Press, 2018.
Pedullà, G., ed. Machiavelli, *Il Principe*, Rome: Donzelli, 2013.
Pellegrini, M., *Ascanio Maria Sforza. La parabola politica di un cardinale-principe del rinascimento*, 2 vols., Rome: Istituto storico per il medioevo, 2002.
  Congiure di Romagna. Lorenzo de' Medici e il duplice tirannicidio a Forlì e a Faenza nel 1488, Florence: Olschki, 1999.
Pellegrini, M., ed., Medici, Lorenzo, *Lettere*, 12.
Pepper, S., 'Castles and cannon in the Naples campaign of 1494–95', in *The French Descent*, ed. D. Abulafia, pp. 263–93.
Pesman Cooper, R., *Pier Soderini and the Ruling Class in Renaissance Florence*, Goldbach: Keip Verlag, 2002.
Peterson, D. and Bornstein, D., ed. *Florence and Beyond. Culture, Society and Politics in Renaissance Italy. Essays in Honour of John M. Najemy*, Toronto: CRRS, 2008.
Petralia, G., 'Fiscality, politics and dominion in Florentine Tuscany at the end of the Middle Ages', in Connell and Zorzi, *Florentine Tuscany*, pp. 65–89 (tr. in Zorzi and Connell, *Stato territoriale*, pp. 161–87.
Petralia, G., 'Pisa Laurenziana: una città e un territorio per la conservazione dello "stato"', in *La Toscana*, 3, pp. 955–80.
Phillips, M., *The Memoir of Marco Parenti. A Life in Medici Florence*, Princeton University Press.
Piccolomini, E. 'Inventario' and 'Ricerche intorno alla libraretia medicea', *ASI*, ser. 3, 20 and 21 (1874–75): 51–94, 282–98.
Picotti, G. B., *La Giovinezza di Leone X*, Milan: Hoepli, 1928.
  Ricerche umanistiche, Florence: Nuova Italia, 1955.
Pieraccini, G., *La Stirpe de' Medici di Cafaggiolo*, 3 vols., I, Florence: Vallecchi, 1924.
Piffanelli, L., *Il "Libro Rosso Seghreto" di Bongianni Gianfigliazzi. Famiglia, affari e politica a Firenze nel Quattrocento*, Rome: Edizioni di storia e letteratura, 2014.
Pitkin, H., *Fortune is a Woman. Gender and Politics in the Thought of Niccolò Machiavelli*, Berkeley: University of California Press, 1984.
Pitti, Jacopo, *Istoria fiorentina*, ed. A. Mauriello, Naples: Liguori, 2007.
Poliziano, Angelo, *Della congiura dei Pazzi (Coniuratione commentarium)*, ed. A. Perosa, Padua: Antenore, 1958; ed. and tr. M. Simonetta in *La congiura della verità*.
  Detti piacevoli, ed. T. Zanato, Rome: Istituto Poligrafico e Zecca dello Stato, 1983.

Letters, ed. S. Butler, Cambridge MA: ITRL, 2006.
Liber Epigrammatum Graecorum, ed. F. Pontani, Rome: Edizioni di storia e letteratura, 2002.
Opera omnia (Basel, 1553), repr. Turin: Bottega d'Erasmo, 1971.
Poesie, ed. F. Bausi, Turin: UTET, 2006.
Polizzotto, L., *The Elect Nation. The Savonarolan Movement in Florence, 1494–1545*, Oxford: Clarendon Press, 1994.
'Introduction', in *Memorie di casa Valori*, ed. with C. Kovesi, Florence: Nerbini, 2007, pp. 9–56.
Pollini-Martin, A., *Banque, négoce et politique. Les Florentins à Lyon au moment des guerres d'Italie*, Paris: Garnier, 2018.
Preyer, B., 'Palazzo Tornabuoni in 1498. A palace "in progress" and its interior arrangement', *Mitteilungen*, 57 (2015): 42–63.
Preyer, B., with Zervas, D., 'Donatello's "Nunziata del Sasso".
Pulci, Luigi, *Morgante e lettere*, ed. D. De Robertis, Florence: Sansoni, 1962.
Reiss, C., 'Widow, Mother, Patron of Art: Alfonsina Orsini de' Medici', in *Beyond Isabella. Secular Women Patrons of Art in Renaissance Italy*, ed. S. Reiss and D. Wilkins, Kirksville: Truman State University Press, 2001, pp. 125–57.
Ricchioni, V., *La costituzione politica di Firenze ai tempi di Lorenzo il Magnifico*, Siena, 1913.
Ridolfi, R., 'La spedizione di Piero de' Medici nel 1497 e la repubblica senese', *Bullettino senese di storia patria*, 70 (1963): 127–44.
Prolegomeno ed aggiunte alla Vita di Girolamo Savonarola, Florence: Sismel, 2000.
Vita di Francesco Guicciardini, Rome: Belardetti, 1960 (tr. London: Routledge and Kegan Paul, 1967).
Rinuccini, Alamanno, *De libertate dialogus*, ed. F. Adorno, in *Atti e Memorie dell' Accademia Toscana di scienze e lettere 'La Colombaria'*, 22, 1957, pp. 270–303.
Rochon, A., *La Jeunesse de Laurent de Médicis (1449–1478)*, Paris: Les Belles Lettres, 1963.
Romby, G., 'Novità documentarie sulla villa di Spedaletto', in *La Toscana*, 1, pp. 173–81.
Rondoni, G., 'I "Giustiziati" a Firenze (dal secolo XV al secolo XVIII)', *ASI*, 28 (1901): 209–56.
Roscoe, W., *The Life of Lorenzo de' Medici Called the Magnificent*, 2 vols., London: Strahan, Cadell and Davies, 1796.
Ross, J., ed. and tr., *Lives of the Early Medici as Told in Their Correspondence*, London: Chatto and Windus, 1910.
de' Rossi, Tribaldo, *Ricordanze*, in *Delizie degli eruditi fiorentini*, 23, 1786, pp. 236–303.
Rubin, P., *Images and Identity in Fifteenth-Century Florence*, New Haven: Yale University Press, 2007.
'Vasari, Lorenzo and the myth of magnificence', in *Lorenzo il Magnifico e il suo Mondo*, ed. Garfagnini, pp. 427–42.
Rubinstein, N., *The Government of Florence under the Medici (1434 to 1494)*, 2nd. ed. Oxford: Clarendon Press, 1997 (tr. G. Ciappelli, Milan: RCS libri, 1999).

The Palazzo Vecchio, 1298–1532. Government, Architecture, and Imagery in the Civic Palace of the Florentine Republic, Oxford: Clarendon Press, 1995.

'Politics and Constitution in Florence at the end of the fifteenth century', in *Italian Renaissance Studies*, ed. E. F. Jacob, London: Faber, 1960, pp. 148–83.

'Il Poliziano e la questione delle origini di Firenze', in *Il Poliziano e il suo tempo*, Florence: Sansoni, 1957, pp. 101–10.

Rubinstein, N., ed. Medici, Lorenzo, *Lettere*, 3–4 (1977, 1981).

Rucellai, Bernardo, *De bello italico*, Florence: University Press, 2011.

Salvadori, P., 'Florentines and the communities of the territorial state', in *Florentine Tuscany*, ed. Connell and Zorzi, pp. 207–24 (tr. *Lo Stato territoriale*, ed. Zorzi and Connell, pp. 477–97).

Salvadori, P., ed. Tornabuoni, Lucrezia, *Lettere*.

Santoro, M., *Fortuna, ragione e prudenza nella civiltà letteraria del Cinquecento*, Naples: Liguori, 1967.

Sanuto (Sanudo), Marino, *I Diarii (1496–1533)*, ed. R. Fulin, Venice: Visentini, 1879–1903 (repr. Bologna: Forni, 1969–70, 58 vols.).

Sapori, A., 'Il "Bilancio" della filiale di Roma del Banco Medici del 1495', *ASI*, 131 (1973): 163–224.

Scala, Bartolomeo, *Humanistic and Political Writings*, ed. A. Brown Tempe, Arizona: MRTS, 1997.

Scarton, E., *Giovanni Lanfredini, uomo d'affari e diplomatico nell'Italia del Quattrocento*, Florence: Olschki, 2007.

Schiera, P., 'Legitimacy, Discipline, and Institutions: Three Necessary Conditions for the Birth of the Modern State', in *The Origins of the State in Italy*, ed. Kirshner, pp. 11–33.

Shaw, C., *Julius II. The Warrior Pope*, Oxford: Blackwell, 1993.

'Lorenzo de' Medici and Niccolò Orsini', in *Lorenzo de' Medici Studi*, ed. Garfagnini, pp. 257–79.

'Lorenzo de' Medici and Virginio Orsini', in *Florence and Italy. Renaissance Studies in Honour of Nicolai Rubinstein*, ed. P. Denley and C. Elam, London: Westfield College, 1988, pp. 33–42.

The Political Role of the Orsini Family from Sixtus IV to Clement VII, Rome: Istituto Storico Italiano per il Medio Evo, 2007.

'Politics and Institutional Innovation in Siena, 1480–1498', *Bullettino senese di storia patria*, 104 (1997): 194–307.

Popular Government and Oligarchy in Renaissance Italy, Leiden: Brill, 2006.

'The Roman barons and the French descent into Italy', in *The French Descent*, ed. Abulafia, pp. 249–61.

Shaw, C., ed. *Italy and the European Powers. The Impact of War, 1500–1530*, Leiden: Brill, 2006.

Shaw, C., ed. with Mallett, M., *The Italian Wars, 1494–1559*.

Simonetta, M., *Rinascimento Segreto. Il mondo del Segretario da Petrarca a Machiavelli*, Milan: FrancoAngeli, 2004.

Volpi e leoni: i misteri dei Medici, Milan: Rizzoli, 2017.

Simonetta, M., ed. Angelo Poliziano, Gentile Becchi, *La congiura della verità*, Naples: La scuola di Pitagora, 2012.

Simonetta, M., ed. Guiducci, 'Diario'.
Simons, P., 'Giovanna and Ginevra: Portraits for the Tornabuoni Family by Ghirlandaio and Botticelli', *I Tatti Studies*, 14–15 (2011–12), pp. 103–35.
'Patronage in the Tornaquinci Chapel, Santa Maria Novella, Florence', in *Patronage, Art and Society in Renaissance Italy*, ed. Kent and Simons, pp. 221–50.
Simons, P., ed. with Kent, *Patronage, Art and Society*.
Soderini, Giovanvittorio, *'I Ricordi* [1495–1498]', under Bertelli, 'Arcana Savonaroliani'.
Spallanzani, M. and Bertelà, G., *Libro d'Inventario dei beni di Lorenzo il Magnifico*, Florence: Associazione 'Amici del Bargello', 1992.
Stern, L., *The Criminal Law System of Medieval and Renaissance Florence*, Baltimore: Johns Hopkins University Press, 1994.
Stephens, J., *The Fall of the Florentine Repubic, 1512–1530*, Oxford: Clarendon Press, 1983.
Strocchia, S., 'Death Rites and the Ritual Family in Renaissance Florence', in *Life and Death in Fifteenth-Century Florence*, ed. M. Tetel, R. Witt and R. Goffen, Durham, N.C Duke University Press, 1989, pp. 120–45.
Tanzini, L., ed. *Il laboratorio del Rinascimento. Studi di storia e cultura per Riccardo Fubini*, Florence: Le Lettere, 2015.
Terziani, R., *Il governo di Siena dal Medioevo all'età moderna: la continuità repubblicana al tempo dei Petrucci, 1487–1525*, Siena: Betti, 2002.
Tewes, G.-R., *Kampf um Florenz: die Medici im Exil (1494–1512)*, Köln: Böhlau Verlag, 2011.
Tomas, N., 'Alfonsina Orsini and the "Problem" of a Female Ruler in Early Sixteenth Century Florence', *Renaissance Studies*, 14 (2000), pp. 70–90.
The Medici Women. Gender and Power in Renaissance Florence, Aldershot: Ashgate, 2003.
Tommasi, G., *Sommario della storia di Lucca*, 1847 (repr. Lucca, M. Pacini Fazzi, 1969).
Tornabuoni, Lucrezia, *Lettere*, ed. P. Salvadori, Florence: Olschki, 1993.
La Toscana al tempo di Lorenzo il Magnifico. Politica, Economia, Cultura, Arte, 3 vols., Pisa: Pacini, 1996.
Trapani, F., ed. *Corrispondenza degli ambasciadori fiorentini a Napoli*, 5, 2010.
Trexler, R., *The Journey of the Magi. Meanings in History of a Christian Story*, Princeton University Press, 1997.
Public Life in Renaissance Florence, New York: Academic Press, 1980.
Vaglienti, Piero, *Storia dei suoi tempi, 1492–1514*, Pisa: Nistri-Lischi e Pacini, 1982.
Varanini, G. M., 'Medicean Florence and Beyond. Legitimacy of Power and Urban Traditions', in *The Medici*, ed. Black and Law, pp. 27–37.
Vasoli, C., *Profezia e ragione. Studi sulla cultura del Cinquecento e del Seicento*, Naples: Morano, 1974.
Vatovec, C. V., 'Lorenzo il Magnifico e i Gonzaga: due 'viaggi' nell'architettura', in *La Toscana*, 1, pp. 73–101.

Ventrone, P., 'Feste e spettacoli nella Firenze di Lorenzo de' Medici', in *Le tems revient'l tempo si rinuova. Feste e spettacoli nella Firenze di Lorenzo il Magnifico*, ed. P. Ventrone, Florence: Silvana, 1992, pp. 21–53.

Verde, A., 'Nota d'archivio. Inventario e divisione dei beni di P.F. Pandolfini', *Rinascimento*, s. II, 9 (1969): 307–24.

Lo Studio fiorentino, 1473–1503: Ricerche e Documenti, 5 vols., 1, 2, 4, 5 (Florence: Istituto sul Rinascimento, 1973, 1985, 1994), 3, pts. 1 and 2 (Pistoia: Memorie Domenicane, 1977).

'Un terzo soggiorno romano del Poliziano', *Rinascimento*, ser. 2, 22 (1982): 257–562.

Vettori, Francesco, *Scritti storici e politici*, ed. E. Niccolini, Bari: Laterza, 1972.

Villari, P., *La Storia di Girolamo Savonarola e de' suoi tempi*, Florence: Successori Le Monnier, 1887–88, 2 vols., in vol. 2, appendix, doc. 1: *Processo di Lamberto dell'Antella*, pp. iii–xxv.

Viti, P., 'Lettere familiari di Federigo da Montefeltro', in *Federico di Montefeltro. Lo Stato, le arti, la cultura*, ed.G. Cerboni Baiardi, G. Chittolini, P. Floriani, Rome: Bulzoni, 1986, I, pp. 471–86.

Walter, I., *Lorenzo il Magnifico e il suo tempo*, 2003 (tr. Rome: Donzelli, 2005).

Weinstein, D., *Savonarola: The Rise and Fall of a Renaissance Prophet*, New Haven: Yale University Press, 2011.

Weissman, R., *Ritual Brotherhood in Renaissance Florence*, New York: Academic Press, 1982.

Wilson, B., 'Sound Patrons. The Medici and Florentine Musical Life', in *The Medici*, ed. Black and Law, pp. 267–80.

Wright, A., 'The Myth of Hercules', in *Lorenzo il Magnifico e il suo Mondo*, ed. Garfagnini, pp. 323–39.

The Pollaiuolo Brothers: The Arts of Florence and Rome, New Haven: Yale University Press, 2005.

Zervas, D. and Preyer, B., 'Donatello's "Nunziata del Sasso": The Cavalcanti chapel at S. Croce and its patrons', *Burlington Magazine*, 150 (2008): 152–65.

Zorzi, A., '"Ius erat in armis". Faide e conflitti tra pratiche sociali e pratiche di governo', in *Origini dello Stato*, ed. G. Chittolini, A. Molho, P. Schiera, Bologna: Mulino, 1994, pp. 609–29.

L'Amministrazione della giustizia penale nella Repubblica Fiorentina. Aspetti e problemi, Florence: Olschki, 1988.

Zorzi, A., ed. with Connell, W., *Lo Stato territoriale fiorentino (secoli XIV–XV). Ricerche, linguaggi, confronti*, Pisa: Pacini, 2001 (tr. ed. Connell and Zorzi, *Florentine Tuscany*).

Index

Abbondanza officials, 252
Acciaiuoli family, 181
Acciaiuoli, Angelo, 31, 71, 181
Acciaiuoli, Jacopo, 183, 187
Acciaiuoli, Laudomia, 181
Acciaiuoli, Raffaello, 181–2
Acciaiuoli, Zanobi, 181–8
accoppiatori. *See* scrutineers
Adriani, Marcello, 236, 239
Aesop, *Fables*, 28, 36
Africa, trade with, 93
Agnano, 72, 94, 98, 117, 138, 142
Alabanti, Antonio, 217, 302
Alamanni, Domenico, 242, 259
Alamanni, Piero, 56, 76–81, 134, 157, 192, 199, 214, 267
Aldobrandini, Giovanni, 10
Alessandri, Alessandro, 90, 107, 121
Alexander VI, pope, 131, 153–4, 206, 216, 239, 271, 276, 280
  and Cibo lands dispute, 164–6
  and daughter Laura, 129–30, 190
  and Piero, 161, 169, 190, 192
  at Vicovaro, 191, 204–6
  coronation, 163
  death, 294
Alfonso I of Naples, 5, 107, 175, 188, 191–3, 198–202, 208, 211, 215–17, 219, 223, 226, 304
  at Vicovaro, 204–6
  on D. Pucci's death, 206n39
alliances, leagues. *See under* Italy, alliances
Altoviti, Carlo, 260
Alviano, Bartolomeo d', 236–7, 245, 251, 291
  and Venice, 278
  in the Casentino, 273
Ambrogini, Angelo, da Montepulciano. *See* Poliziano, Angelo
Ambrogini, Tommaso, da Montepulciano, 27, 33
Angelico, fra, 110

Antiquario, Jacopo, 37
Apelles, 29
Appiano, Jacopo d', 137, 140, 183, 268
Appiano, Semiramide d', 137
Aragon, House of, 277
Aragon, Alfonso I. *See* Alfonso I of Naples
Aragon, Federigo di Alfonso, 161, 176
Aragon, Ferdinando (Ferrandino), duke of Calabria, 121, 203–6, 221, 226
  and Piero, 208, 210–12
  and the Romagna campaign, 208–13
  dalliance, 1494, 212
Aragon, Ferrante (Ferdinando) I of Naples. *See* Ferrante I of Naples
Aragon, Isabella
  in Pisa, 1488, 75
  marriage, 74, 79–80
Aragona, fra Francesco da, 72
Arezzo
  and the Medici, 93, 131
  uprising, 1502, 289
Arienti, Giovanni Sabbadino degli, 74, 284
Aristophanes, 33
Aristotle, *Politics*, 36
astrology, 172
Attavante, miniaturist, 112
Avalos, Alfonso d', marquis of Pescara, 210, 212

Baglioni family
  fighting and defeat, 1502–3, 289–91
Baglioni, Astorre
  and Venice, 273
Bagno a Filippo, 49
Bagno a Morbo, 11, 14, 20, 22, 44, 50, 139
Bagno a Vignone, 94
balance of power. *See under* Italy, balance of power
Bambello, ser Pace, 14, 24, 33–4, 150

325

Barbari, Bartolomeo, 203
  visit to Florence, 1490, 35, 92, 112, 114–15
Barbaro, Francesco, 19
Bardi family, 16
Bardi family, di Vernio, 16, 18, 20, 123–4, 126, 251
Bardi, Contessina, 12, 17, 19, 123
  death, 19
Bardi, Gualterotto, 17–18
Bardi, Tommaso, 18, 247
Barga, 214, 220–1
Bargello, police official, 224
Baroni, ser Francesco, 61–2, 102, 150, 265
  cited, 161, 176
  Memorie di varie guerre d'Italia, 173
Bartolini Bank, in Florence, 93
Bartolini, Lionardo, in Rome, 237, 241–2, 251, 258–9
  coded letters, 269
  described, 287
Bartolus, of Sassoferrato, 6
Basque (Baschi), Péron de, 157, 178
battle cries, 23, 124, 167, 209, 223–4, 244, 273, 285, 289
Beaucaire, seneschal. *See* Vesc, Etienne
Becchi, Gentile, 6, 24, 30, 57, 59, 64, 104, 153, 158, 163, 175, 178, 180–1, 184–5
  and cardinalate, 183, 205–6
  and Piero, 185, 190, 193–4, 207, 216–17
  described, 205
  oration in Rome, 1492, 163
  oration to Charles VIII, 190n2
  Synodus fiorentina, 206
Becchi, Ricciardo, 244
Bellanti, Giulio, 134, 258
Bellanti, Leonardo, 134
Bellincioni, Bernardo, 109
Bentivoglio, Alessandro, 209
Bentivoglio, Annibale, 78–9, 81, 84, 120, 209, 238, 276
Bentivoglio, Anton Galeazzo, 209
Bentivoglio, Ercole, 246
Bentivoglio, Giovanni, 45, 57, 81, 95, 120, 202, 209, 232, 236, 238
Bertoldo di Giovanni, 110
Bettini, Sforza, 161
Bevilaqua, in S. Fiore, 107
Bibbiena castle, 273–6
Bibbiena, Bernardo, later cardinal. *See* Dovizi, ser Bernardo
Bible, 98
Bicchi, Antonio, 132
Big men, *gran maestri*, 255

Bigi, 243
Bini, Luigi, 264
Bolgheri, Gabriele da, count, 162
Bologna, 43, 45, 49, 209, 232, 238, 247, 272, 284
Bonsi, Domenico, 214, 255, 272
Borgia, Cesare,
  and Romagna campaign, 281–5
  in Italy, 271, 276–7, 279–80, 284–5, 289–91, 297
  Palio in Siena, 135
Borgia, Giuffrè, 192
Borgia, Juan, duke of Gandia, 192
Borgia, Lucrezia, 130
Borgia, Rodrigo, see Alexander VI, pope
Bossi, fra Lauro de', 182, 183–4, 258, 260
Botta, Giacomo, bishop, 59
Botticelli, Sandro, 110
Braccesi, ser Alessandro
  and the Medici, 132–3, 145
  in Rome, 251–2, 254, 257–8
  in Siena, 132–8
Bracci, Giovanbattista, 92
Bracciano, Bartolomeo da, 150–1
Bracciano, Orsini castle, 20, 24–5, 44, 49, 59, 62–3, 168
  Piero's visits to, 63–4, 66–8, 161, 273, 286
Bresse, Philippe de, count, later duke of Savoy, 208, 216
Briçonnet, Guillaume, cardinal of S. Malo, 181, 208, 213, 221
broncone. *See* Medici family:emblems, insignia
Bruni, Leonardo
  On the constitution of Florence, 34, 36, 303
Buonvisi company, Lucca, 144, 258–9
Burchard, Johan, 59

Cafaggiolo, 10, 13, 18, 28–9, 31, 33, 138, 184, 189, 214
Calderini, Benedetto, 98
Calenzano, benefice, 153n17
Cambi, Giovanni, chronicler, 121
Cambi, Giovanni, manager of Medici Bank in Pisa, 123, 137, 139–45, 258–9
  and the Medici, 140, 145, 258–60
  and Piero, 145
  execution, 248–9, 261
  in testimonies, 263, 265, 267–9
Cambini, Andrea, 225
Cambini, Francesco, 139, 169
Campofregoso al. Fregoso, Paolo, 43
Cappelli, ser Francesco, 204
Capponi Bank, in Lyon, 158n35

Index

Capponi family, 157
Capponi, Donato, cashier, 144
Capponi, Gino, 196, 249
Capponi, Gino di Lodovico, 267, 269
Capponi, Guglielmo, 42
Capponi, Piero, 157, 223, 237
   in France, 181, 199
   speech, 1494, 223
Caradosso Foppa, 82
Cardiere, viola player, 108, 162
cardinals, appointment, in 1494,
   205–6
Careggi, 11–12, 29–30, 84, 101, 232
Carnesecchi, Pierantonio, 75, 155, 162
Casentino campaign. *See under* Medici,
   Giuliano and Piero di Lorenzo
Castello, 189
Castello, Guido da, 272
Castello, ser Niccolò da, 65
Castelnuovo, fortress, 221
Castiglione, Branda da, 98–9, 116
Castrocaro, 257
Cavalcanti family, 16
Cavalcanti, Ginevra, 12, 19
Cavalcanti, Giovanni, 223
Cegia, Francesco
   memoirs, 260–1
   networking, 259, 265
   testimony and death, 253, 269
Cento (One Hundred), council, 151, 153
   abolished, 226
   reestablished in 1512, 295
Cerretani, Bartolomeo,
   cited, 2, 187, 238, 243, 249, 283, 289,
      291, 302
   Storia fiorentina, 6
Cesi, Federico, cardinal, 292
Charles VIII. of France, 4–5, 128, 184, 187,
      189, 201, 208, 220
   and Florence, 221, 225, 233–5, 284–5
   and Piero, 192, 233–4
   described, 193
   Italian expedition, 173, 180, 213–14
Chigi, Agostino, 241
Ciampolini, Giovanni, 42
Cibo lands. *See under* Cibo, Franceschetto
Cibo, Franceschetto, 71, 84, 101–3, 108,
      118, 120, 142–3, 218
   and Apostolic Camera, 164
   debts, 130
   entry in Florence, 1488, 69
   gambler and womaniser, 72, 142
   in Venice, 278
   lands, dispute and settlement, 162,
      164–6, 175–8

   marriage to Maddalena, 52, 56, 58–61,
      63–4, 67–8, 71–2
Cibo, Marco, 68
Cibo, Niccolò Bucciardi, archbishop, 59
Cicero, 29
Cimabue, 111
Città di Castello, 234
Civita Castellana, 44
clientage, 92, 128, 131, 145
   language of, 124
Colle Val d'Elsa, 22–3
   and the Medici, 131
Colonna family, 212
Colonna, Giovanni, cardinal, 252
Coltibuono, abbey, 101
comet, 1484, 24n39
Commedia, Martino della, 31
Commynes, Philippe de,
   120, 208, 216, 232–3
Conte, Jacopo, 183–4, 257
Corbinelli, Massimo, 267
Corbinelli, Pandolfo, 267, 269
Corbinelli, Ruggieri, 99
Corbinelli, Tommaso, 270
Corsini, Luca, 223–4, 236
Corsini, Piero, 214, 235–6, 275
   in Lucca, 1490, 97–8
   in Pisa, 199
Cortesi, Alessandro, 61
Corvinus, Matthias, king, 35, 112
countersign, 222, 264
couriers, 240, 245, 256–60, 266, 286
   friars as, 260
Cristofano di Antonio, 12
crusade, proposed, 1494, 199, 208

Dante Alighieri, 28
Davanzati, Francesco, 244
de la Tour, Madeleine, 296
death rites, in Florence, 70
Dei, Benedetto, 74
del Nero, Bernardo, 89–90, 96, 154–6, 186,
      248–9, 264–5, 306
   and Piero, 202–3, 247
   Gonfalonier in 1494, 244, 266
   head of the 'sect in the middle', 156, 259,
      262, 270
   testimony, 261–2, 270
del Pace, Zanobi, 95, 99
del Vigna, Antonio, 290
dell'Antella, Alessandro, 235, 250
dell'Antella, Lamberto, 235
   Confession, 247–52
della Casa, Francesco, 162
   in France, 181, 185

328 Index

Dieci di Balìa, 33, 236–7, 277, 303
Dini, Antonio di Bernardo, 72, 89, 93, 134,
    156, 186, 211
  executed, 226
  his son in law, 225
Dini, Francesco, 89
Dio Cassius, *History of Rome*, 50
Dodici (Twelve) Procuratori, 151
Donati, Lucrezia, 21
Dovizi, ser Antonio, 178, 204–5, 207, 218
  in Bologna, 209–10
Dovizi, ser Bernardo, later cardinal, 66, 124,
    154, 157, 162, 180, 205, 221, 247
  and Piero, 178, 226, 278
  bounty and exile, 226
  commissary in the Romagna, 205,
    208–13
  in Bibbiena, 273
  in Naples and Rome, 191–3
  in Pisa, 140, 242
  La Calandra, 212
Dovizi, ser Piero, 24, 38, 74–5, 79, 88, 99,
    103, 134, 162, 191–2, 199, 211,
    218–19
  and Piero, 84–6, 152, 162, 172, 174,
    190–2, 194–7, 207
  bounty and exile, 226
  embassy to Milan, 1493, 174
  in Venice, 237–8, 251n74, 273
dowries
  in Florence, 132
  papal, 130 *See also under* Medici,
    Maddalena; Orsini, Alfonsina

education in Florence, 26, 28–9, 46
Eighty (*Ottanta*), council, 244, 285
Empedocles, 110
Este family, 117
Este, Ercole d', 28, 50
Este, Isabella d', 108
Éstouteville, Girolamo d', 61, 63, 68, 72

Faenza, 90–1, 215–16, 284
  and Piero, 127–9, 304
falconry and hawking. *See under* Medici,
    Piero di Lorenzo, sports
Farnese, Alessandro, cardinal, 154
Farnese, Girolama, 129
Farnese, Giulia, 129–30
Farnese, Rinuccio, 246
fate, 196
Ferdinand and Isabella of Spain, 198–9,
    217, 276
Ferrante I of Naples, 5, 48–9, 52, 68, 71,
    73, 119, 169–71, 174, 179

and Cibo lands dispute, 164–6
  death, 191
Ficino, Marsilio, 30, 35, 85, 113–14
Filarete, 110
Filetto, 100
Fivizzano, 76, 79, 213
Flaccus, Valerius
  Argonautica, 218n20
Florence, position in Italy, 5
  and republicanism, 124
  bankers in Lyon, 220
  churches
    S. Croce, 167
    S. Gallo, 167, 260, 263, 265–8, 270
    S. Lorenzo, 294
    S. Lucia, 225
    S. Paolo, 27
    S. Spirito, 111, 263, 265–6
    SS. Annunziata, 267
  citizen meetings (*consulte, pratiche*),
    201, 222–3, 238, 248, 282, 285
  Council of, 1439, 34
  crisis, 1498–1502, 277
  Duomo, 149, 267, 269
    Piero in, 101, 218, 223
  embassy to Charles VIII, 222–3, 235
  exercise of justice, 96–9, 125, 186–8
  Feast of S. Giovanni, 10, 69, 102, 135
  Francophilism, 158, 178, 185, 194,
    197, 204, 206, 215, 221, 236, 264
  galleys, 144
  head of state
    capo, sopracapo, boss, 244, 263, 283,
      290, 297, 301, 306
    for life (*Gonfaloniere a vita*), 158,
      277, 290, 307
  merchants in Rome, 164
  money markets, 220
  public officials, 303
  regime of 'Twenty Tyrants', 1498,
    274
  reprisals for cardinals' debts, 288
  revolution, 1494, 180, 214–27
  Roman origins, 36
  ruling elite, 84–6, 88–9, 154–60
  social ascent in, 184
  sumptuary laws, 45
  treaty with Charles VIII, 233
  treaty with Venice, 1499, 276
Florentines as fraudsters (*fraudentini*),
    280, 288
Foiano, ser Andrea da, 132
football (*calcio*), handball, 121, 175, *See
    also under* Medici, Piero di
    Lorenzo, sports

Forlì, 90
  and Piero, 127–8
fortune, role of, 305
Fracassini, Francesco, 97
France
  ambassadors to Italy, 202–3, 214
  army, 1494, 210
  expedition to Italy, 136, 144, 185, 198–9, 231, 286
Francesco da Bologna, Olivetan friar, 268
Franco, Matteo, 14, 23, 35, 38, 46–7, 69, 103, 139, 142, 162
  death, 207

Gaddi, Francesco, 51
  public-private mission to Rome, 1493, 169
Gaeta, 291
Gagliano, Filippo da, 150–1, 218
Gagliano, town, 11
Galeazzo, lord of Correggio, 63
Galletto, falconer, 120, 140
Garzerano, runner, 107, 119, 121
Gaza, Theodore, 28–9
Gellius, Aulus
  cited, 64
Gennazzano, fra Mariano da, 160, 260, 263–5, 270
Genoa, 48, 73–4, 76, 80, 103, 143
  and Florence, 40, 144
  social ascent in, 184
gestures, 224
  Cardinal Giovanni's, 283
  Piero's, 123, 251
Gherardacci, Carlo, in Pisa, 125
Gherardi, Francesco, 159, 187
ghiribizzi, 198
Ghirlandaio, Domenico, 20
Gianfigliazzi, Jacopo, 155, 162, 218, 249, 267–8
gift exchanges, 18, 74, 107, 119, 191, 226
Giovanni da Prato, fra, 113, 198
Gita di Roma. See under Medici, Piero di Lorenzo
Golpino, groom, 62–3, 162
Gonsalvo (Gonsalo) da Còrdoba, 276, 291
Gonzaga family, 117
Gonzaga, Caterina, 212
Gonzaga. Federigo, cardinal, 241
Gonzaga, Francesco, cardinal, 74
Gonzaga, Francesco, marchese, 52, 74, 187
  horse racing, 101
Gonzaga, Ridolfo, 81

Grazzini, Geri, 284
Great Council, 243–4, 277
  appeal to, 248
Gualterotti, Francesco, 248
Guelfs, Ghibellines, 4, 93, 154, 239, 283, 307
  networks, states, 4
Guicciardini family, 20
Guicciardini, Francesco, 6, 20, 171, 270
  and reason of state, 280
  cited, 3–4, 53, 152, 155, 248, 250, 277, 281
  Dialogue on the Government of Florence, 305–6
  Florentine Histories
    and the Medici, 301–2, 305
    political morality, 305
    portrait of Lorenzo, 306
  Ricordi, 306
  transcript of 1497 testimonies, 263
  view of Piero, 168, 171, 177, 302
Guicciardini, Jacopo, 33, 74
  and Piero, 84–6, 89, 303
  death, 1490, 89
Guicciardini, Luigi, 223–4, nn. 38,40
Guicciardini, Piero, 3, 150, 172, 186, 223, 248–9
  in Milan, 168, 171–2
Guidi, ser Giovanni, 156
  executed, 226
Guidotti, ser Antonio, da Colle, 198
  described, 207
  in Rome, 131, 176, 217
  in Siena, 278, 290
Guiducci, Lorenzo, calim, 225
Guilds
  Merchants' (Calimala), 151
  Moneychangers (Cambio), 16
  Wool (Lana), 151

head of state, in Florence. *See under* Florence
Hercules, Choice of. See Prodicus
Herodian
  Lives of the Caesars, 42
Hobbes, Thomas, *Leviathan*, 307
Homer, 29, 35, 49
  Iliad, 26, 36
horse racing, 101, 107

Idol (*hiidolo*), role in Florence, 307
  and the Medici, 6, 155, 159, 255, 272, 275
Imola, 127, 177

Innocent VIII, pope, 39, 42, 55–6, 58–61, 66–7
  Medici parentado, 55–6, 58–61, 66–7, 71–2, 154
  and Florence, 66
  debts, 130
  sayings, 86, 118
iron ore, in Piombino and Elba, 137, 139, 140: *see also Magona*
Isaac, Heinrich, 108–9, 161
Isocrates, 29
Italy
  alliances
    against France, 236–9, 242, 244, 264–6
    League of St. Mark, 73, 133, 144, 166, 170–1, 173, 268
    pope, Naples, Florence, 175, 178, 191–4, 198, 201
    Triple Alliance, 5, 73, 171, 178
  balance of power, 4, 166–8, 198, 245, 281
  and Lorenzo, 5, 67, 151, 171, 198
  invasions, 4–6
  'ruin of', 55, 174
  states and communes, 1, 136
    as chess players, 276
    crisis, 301
  territorial states, 297, 301, 304

Jerusalem, passengers to, 144
Jews, from Sicily, 143
John II, king of Portugal
  new islands, 144
jousts, jousting, in Florence, 83, 118, *See also under* Medici, Piero di Lorenzo
justice, in Florence. *See under* Florence

La Ceccha, engineer, 200
labyrinth, 140n76, 255–6
Landino, Cristoforo, 92
Landucci, Luca, 48
  on Piero, 220
Lanfredini, Giovanni, 10, 58, 60, 67, 81, 166
Lante from Fiesole, 293
Lascaris, Janus, 107, 112–13
League of St. Mark, *See under* Italy, alliances
Lenzi, Lorenzo, 220n26, 264
Leone, Pier, 101n61
  death, 150–1
liberty, 163, 227, 232, 234
  and Italy, 236
Libri regionum, 36
Lippi, Filippino, 116

Lippomani, bankers in Venice, 232
Livorno, fortress, 222
Livy, 28, 36, 113
Louis XII of France
  alliances in Italy, 271, 281
  and Florence, 1502, 290
  and Piero, 279
  and the Medici, 1501, 287
  treaty with Venice, 1499, 276
Lucca, 97–8
  oration in Rome, 1492, 163

Machiavelli, Niccolò, 256, 291
  and military leaders, 205, 208
  and Piero, 2, 231
  politics and morality, 305–7
  writings
    Discourses on Livy, 306
    Discursus, 306, 307n17
    The Prince, 297, 304
Magi, company, 103, 121, 150
Magione, Diet of, 290
Magona dei bestiami, 138
Magona of iron ore in Pisa and Pietrasanta, 139, 144
mail, 240, 271, 284
Malaspina, Gabriele, marchese, 100–1
Malatesta, Pandolfo, lord, 127
Maldei, ser Stefano, da Castrocaro, 75, 78–80, 84
Malegonnelle, Antonio, in Rome, 5n11, 278, 280
Malgra (Malgrate), 100–1
Mammola, company, 85
Manetti, Giannozzo, the younger, 187
Manfredi, Astorre, 120, 127–8, 130
Manfredi, Ottaviano, 128
Marradi, fortress, 273
marriage ritual, in Italy, 54–5
Martelli estate, 150–1
Martelli, Carlo, 42
Martelli, Francesco, 'Tincha', 267
Martelli, Lorenzo, 162
Marullo, Michele, 154
mask, masks, 71
  Mask of Piero, 278, 291
Maximilian 1, emperor, 242–3
May Day songs, 65, 108
medallions. *See under* Medici family
Medea, 231
Medici Bank, 13, 17, 20, 28, 40, 42, 52, 74, 92, 133, 166, 177, 202, 209n46, 211, 287, 295

Index

in Lyon, 103, 140–1, 201
in Pisa, 103, 123, 137, 139–41, 143–4, 219, 259, 304
in Rome
  losses and bankruptcy, 130–1, 267
Medici family, 9, 15–16, 31
  after Piero's death, 294–6
  in 1501, 287
  armed guards, 94, 153, 217, 302
  as merchants, 71
  as princely rulers, 1, 304
  emblems, insignia, 23, 80, 104, 112, 295
    destroyed 1497, 252
  jewels, medallions, 145, 238–9, 258–9, 260, 267, 270
  law against 1497, 243–4
  library, 35–6, 50, 108, 112–14, 252
  money in exile, 258–9
  music, 108–9
  palace in via Larga, 18, 70, 84, 92, 107, 110–11, 114, 217, 223, 225–6, 252
    Piero's rooms, 110, 118
  patronage networks, 74, 123–4, 130, 145
  repatriation, 288
  return, 1512, 295
  revenge planned, 251
  territorial rulers, 304
  villas. *See* Agnano, Cafaggiolo, Careggi, Castello, Montepaldi, Poggio a Caiano, Spedaletto, Trebbio
  wealth, 2
Medici, Alessandro di Lorenzo, duke of Florence, 306
Medici, Andrea, 'il Butto', 249, 265, 267–8
Medici, Averardo al. Bicci, 16
Medici, Averardo di Bernardetto, 239
Medici, Averardo di Francesco, 16
Medici, Bernardetto, 31
Medici, Bianca di Piero, 11–12
Medici, Clarice (Cice) di Piero, 130, 160, 218
  betrothal, 294
  birth, 86
Medici, Contessina di Lorenzo, 11, 13, 72, 75–6, 84, 116, 263
  betrothal, 56
Medici, Cosimo di Giovanni, 2, 16
  and Pisa, 138
Medici, Cosimo I, duke, 293
Medici, Francesca di Giovenco, 19
Medici, Giovanni di Bicci, 16, 78
Medici, Giovanni di Lorenzo, later Pope Leo X, 109, 139, 150, 161, 183, 221, 232, 294–6, 302
  and Lorenzo di Pierfrancesco, 154, 180, 183
  and Piero, 153–4, 180, 258, 292
  benefices, 42, *See* Calenzano, Coltibuono, Montecassino, Passignano
  bounty and exile, 225
  cardinalate, 2, 17–18, 48, 81–2, 102, 153, 251
  character, 260–1
  childhood, 10–11, 13, 14, 23, 29, 31–3, 35, 41, 47–8, 76
  exile
    Milan, 1, 240
    Rome, 283, 285
    Siena, 290
    Venice, in disguise, 279, 283, 285–6, 288
  tomb, 294
Medici, Giovanni di Pierfrancesco, 12, 61, 75, 83, 182, 233
  and cardinalate, 182–3
  betrothal in 1488, 56, *See also* Medici, Lorenzo and Giovanni di Pierfrancesco
Medici, Giuliano di Lorenzo, later duke of Nemours, 11, 13–14, 23, 45–6, 72, 75, 84, 121, 130, 137, 143, 152, 225, 268
  and *The Prince*, 297, 305
  bounty, 239
  Casentino campaign, 236, 273–6
  epithet, 2
  escape and exile, 225, 247, 258, 268, 276, 283, 288–9, 295
    Milan and Venice, 240, 278–9, 280
  governor of Parma and Piacenza, 304
  tomb, 294
  with Cesare Borgia, 1500, 280–1
Medici, Giuliano di Piero, 12
  murder of, 2, 12, 206
Medici, Giulio di Giuliano, later Pope Clement VII, 23, 76, 102, 240–1, 289
  and Piero's tomb, 292–3
  tomb, 294
Medici, Lorenzo and Giovanni di Pierfrancesco, 159, 202
  conspiracy, 37, 180–9, 213–14
  French barons, 180
  return to Florence, 233, 251, 265, 269
Medici, Lorenzo di Pierfrancesco, 12–13, 45, 69, 120, 202, 214–15, 251
  as *capo*, 247, 263

Medici, Lorenzo di Pierfrancesco (cont.)
  conspiracy, 154–5, 159, 180–9
  emblem, 180
  in Siena, 1493, 137
  renamed Popolano, 246
  threat to Piero, 213
  wealth and status, 184
Medici, Lorenzo di Piero, il Magnifico, 2, 9,
    13, 17–19, 68–9, 76, 83, 94–9,
    101, 102–3, 111
  and Ferrante, 48–9, 52, 73
  and Franceschetto Cibo, 164–6
  and Piero, 3, 45, 50, 84–6
  and Pisa, 138
  and Poliziano, 26–7, 30
  and Siena, 132, 136
  and the papacy, 55–6, 66
  balance of power, 3, 5, 151, 198
  character, 3, 196
  death, 94, 149–50
  instructions to B. Dovizi, 1488, 66
  instructions to Piero, 1484, 21,
    39–41
  marriage, 9
  marriage strategies, 55–7
  plays, 1490–91, 121
  politics and political role, 3, 124
    double politics, 66–7, 73, 90, 94
  rages, 51, 55
  revenge in 1479, 261
  Rome, 1471, 163–4
  to Naples, 1479, 219
  voice, 47
Medici, Lorenzo di Piero, later duke of
    Urbino, 160, 218, 237
  birth, 86, 132, 160
  death, 1519, 296
  death, as duke, 306
  dedicatee of Machiavelli's *Prince*, 304
  status and ambition after 1512,
    296–8
  territorial ruler, 304
  tomb, 294
Medici, Lucrezia di Lorenzo, 10–13, 31,
    74–5, 116, 248, 266–7, 274
  betrothal, 56, 60
  birth, 9
  letters to, 269
  testimony, 270
Medici, Luisa di Lorenzo, 11, 13, 68
  betrothal, 56
  death, 18, 116
Medici, Luisa di Piero, 160n42
Medici, Maddalena di Lorenzo, 10, 12–13,
    25, 101, 116

  and Franceschetto, 142–3
  betrothal and marriage, 52, 55–61,
    64–5
  expulsion, 252
Medici, Nannina di Piero, 12, 23
Medici, Pierfrancesco di Lorenzo, 13, 117,
    118
Medici, Piero di Cosimo, 18
  death, 9
Medici, Piero di Lorenzo,
  alias 'Lino', 244, 263, 268
  and Milan, 171–5
  and Naples, 169–71, 191, 205, 302
  appearance and character, 46–7, 86,
    102, 121, 190, 196–7, 209,
    224, 302–4, 307. *See also under*
    temperament
  armed guard, 223
  banker, in Pisa and Rome, 123
  birth, 9
  birth chart, 172–3
  bounty, 225, 239, 246, 252
  epithets and roles, 2
    capo, sopracapo, boss, 156, 220, 301,
      304, 307
    early modern sovereign, 6
    idol, *See under* Idol
    lord, 281
    republican head, 301–3
    tyrant, 5, 215, 227, 232, 236, 243,
      301–2, 305
  childhood, 9–15
  Cibo lands, 164–6
  clothes, 45, 80, 219, 226, 232
    in Rome, 1492, 161n44, 162–3
  confraternity play, 1489, 82
  conspiracy against, 180–9
  criticism of, 190, 193–4, 203, 207,
    226–7, 254–5, 269
  death and burial, 292–4
  education, 26–38
  emancipation, 1488, 69
  emblems, insignia, 225
  exile
    locations, 232
    Bolsena, 240
    Borgo S. Sepolcro, 203, 206
    Casentino, 272–6
    Gaeta, 291
    Milan and Pavia, 280
    Pisa, 282
    Pitigliano, 235
    Romagna, 272
    Rome, 236, 241, 250, 255, 271, 282
    Siena, 245

Index 333

Venice, 273, 278–9
money supply, 237–8, 240–1, 265–7, 278
repatriation attempts, 239, 244–7, 268, 274–5, 282–6, 289–91
supporters, 236–8, 268
Ferrandino, 210–12
funerary statue, 293–4
galley, 92
Gita di Roma, 162
Golden Lance, 1493, 118, 175
intimates, listed, 89, 156
letters
  as child, 12–13
  as exile, 231
  authorship, character, etc., 166, 170, 174
  from Empoli, 1494, 219–20
  to A. Niccolini, 165
  to B. Dovizi, 210–11
  to fra Seraphino, 266
  to his cousins, 233
  to his father, 88–95
  to friends in Florence, 1497, 258
  to N. Michelozzi, 165
  to P. Corsini, 235–6
  to P. Dovizi, 194–7, 202
  to S. Passerini, 240–1
  to the Otto di Pratica, 218–19
  to the Signoria, 232, 234
love affairs, lovers, 104, 109, 116, 194–6, 212
love of books. *See under* Medici family, library
marriage, 52–70
marriage broker in Rome, 129–30, 304
mediator, 5, 169, 198, 208–9, 216–17, 272, 304
meeting with Charles VIII, 209n47, 209, 216–20, 222, 226
Milan, visit to, 1489, 76–81
music, singing, 35, 65–6, 108–9, 175
on Lorenzo's death, 149–50
patron, cultural patronage, 110–16
patron, *mezzadro*, master of the workshop, 3, 33, 74, 93, 123–6, 202
perfumes, 103
poems, 2, 104, 109–10, 197, 231, 307
politics and political role, 72–4, 88–104, 198–213, 217–27, *See also under* Otto di Pratica
  double politics, 66, 172, 175, 192
power and status, 6, 37, 40, 84–5, 130, 145, 151, 184–5, 204, 219–20, 222, 275–6, 297

prince, princely rule, 4, 6, 161, 304, 306
rebel, 226, 231, 233
Romagna, the
  campaign, 1494, 208
  expenses, 210–12
  Piero as strategist, 208–13
Rome, visits to
  1484-85, 21, 34, 39–44, 49, 71
  1487, 57–61, 71
  1488, 65–8
  1492, 155, 160–4, 171
Siena, 131–8
speech, speeches, 28, 100, 129, 216
sports, 32, 48, 72, 107–8, 117
  bird hunting, 194, 206
  body building, 119, 176
  falconry, hawking, 74, 82, 84, 93, 103, 107, 117, 120–1, 199
  football, handball, 3, 86, 107, 117, 121–2, 175, 206
  horses and hunting, 28, 62, 72, 77, 84, 107, 117–18, 205
  jousting, 118–19, 122, 150, 163, 175, 191
temperament, 3, 193–7, 303–4
witticisms, 46
Medici, Salvestro, 16
Medici, Veri di Cambio, 16
merchants, in Rome, 256, *See also under* Florence
Michelangelo Buonarroti, 111, 215, 294
Michelangelo di Viviani, 112
Michele, Certosan friar, 264
Michele, fra, Carmelite, 260
Michele, armourer in Milan, 119
Michelozzi, Bernardo, 31, 44, 47
Michelozzi, ser Niccolò, 24, 26–7, 30, 34, 74–5, 88, 102, 149
  and Piero, 1497, 260
  villa at Quinto, 218
Minerbetti, Baccia (Bartolomea), 65, 86
Minerbetti, Tommaso, 187–8
Mirandola, Galeotto, lord of, 77–8, 81
Monte Giordano, Orsini enclave in Rome, 58–9, 64, 246, 286
Monte Rotondo, Orsini castle, 20, 43–4, 49, 62–4, 67, 303
Monte Scalari, abbey, 66
Montecassino, abbey, 48, 50, 56, 252
  and Cardinal Giovanni, 292
  and San Germano, 104, 286
  Piero's tomb and funerary monument, 291–4
Montefeltro, Federigo da, duke, 9
Montefeltro, Guidubaldo, duke, 273–5

Montepaldi, 102, 133–4
Mordano, massacre, 211, 213

Naldini, Francesco, 92, 95, 259, 268, 270
Naldini, Luca, 258
Naples
   and Piero, 169–71
   armada, defeat of, 212
   captured by France, 1501, 286
Nardi, Jacopo, 47
   cited, 121–2, 159, 187–8, 224
Nasi, Alessandro, 75, 154, 162
Nerli, Jacopo de', 223–4, 236, 246, 265, 274
Nerli, Tanai de', 223, 246
Nero, Francesco, 240, 250–1, 257–8
networking in exile, 250, 254–70, *See also* couriers and spies, informers
Niccolini, Angelo, 85–6, 89, 99, 156, 165, 171, 178, 186, 207
   in Milan, 172, 201
      Piero's letters to, 165
   in Naples, 191
Niccolini, Francesco, 269

Organi, Francesco degli, 107
Orsini family, 15, 20–1, 40, 52, 63, 68, 72, 78, 257, 287–9
   and Cesare Borgia, 281, 284, 291
   and Charles VIII, 234, 236
   and Piero, 192, 236–7, 258, 302
   debts, 266
   defeat by Colonna, 1498, 272
   divisions, 49, 288
   emblem, 23
   letter, 1497, 246–7
   Monte Rotondo and Bracciano branches, 49, 67
Orsini, Alfonsina, 1, 22, 51, 57, 72–3, 74–5, 82, 84, 108, 116, 143, 160, 218, 221, 225, 233–4, 239, 258, 263, 286, 291, 292, 296, 303
   appearance, 53–4
   dowry, 25, 52, 54, 64–5, 295
   marriage, 52–69
   portrait, 110
Orsini, Carlo, 236–7, 283, 288, 291
   and Piero, 258, 275–6
   and Venice, 278
   Casentino campaign, 272–6
   in Rome, 1501, 283
   letter to Piero, 1498, 275–6
Orsini, Clarice, 9–13, 20–5, 28, 44, 47–8, 57–9, 61, 63–5, 108
   and Poliziano, 26, 27, 29–30
   death, 70
Orsini, Francesco
   death, 1503, 291
Orsini, Franciotto, 72, 75, 276
Orsini, Gian Francesco di Niccolò, 82
Orsini, Gian Paolo, 49
Orsini, Giovan Battista, cardinal, 21, 40, 43, 63, 81, 153, 283, 291
Orsini, Gian Giordano, 67–8, 237, 258
Orsini, Giulio, 43, 49, 63, 280
Orsini, Lodovico, 237
Orsini, Napoleone, 63
Orsini, Niccolò, count of Pitigliano, 20–1, 49, 58, 67, 82, 235
Orsini, Organtino, 62–3, 68
Orsini, Paolo, 58, 63, 82, 84, 188, 224–5, 237, 280, 282, 285–6
   death, 1503, 291
Orsini, Rinaldo, archbishop, 21, 25, 39–40, 44, 53, 56, 71, 269, 287, 291
Orsini, Roberto, count, 52
Orsini, Virginio, 20–1, 25, 44, 49, 51–4, 58, 62, 67–8, 73–5, 82, 160, 164–9, 173, 176, 188, 192, 201, 236–7
   and Cibo lands dispute, 164–9, 173
   and Piero, 168–9
   condotta, 82
   in Pisa, 73
   loans from Medici Bank, 202n18
Ostia, 61, 212
Otto di Guardia, 91, 95–6, 186, 239, 248, 256, 260, 270, 302
Otto di Pratica, 56, 74, 92, 96–7, 103, 128, 151, 155, 160, 177, 181, 214, 218, 221, *See also under* Medici, Piero di Lorenzo, letters
   abolished, 226
   aggiunti, 89, 177, 204n26, 214
   and Lorenzo, 102–3
   and Piero, 99–101, 102
   defined, 88, 89
   elders, 170, 202
   reestablished, 1512, 296

Paciali, 247, 261
Palio, in Siena, 1493, 135
Pallavicino, Antoniotto, 59
Pandolfini, Domenico, 89
Pandolfini, Pierfilippo, 56, 74, 99, 134, 154–7, 178, 186, 207, 223, 264
   and Piero, 84–6, 203, 303
   in Naples, 191
   in Pisa, 199
   in Rome, 88
Pannochieschi, family, 17

Index

Papal States, 49, 55
Pappacoda, Antonio, 95, 163
Pappacoda, Vincenzio, 95, 118
Parenti, Piero, 200, 246
    cited, 21, 119, 149, 154, 186–7, 201, 206–7, 215–18, 220, 226–7, 232–4, 239, 243–4, 247–9, 252, 262, 274, 279, 280, 285, 295
    on Lorenzo's death, 152–3
    political views, 220
    Storie fiorentine, 6, 262
Passerini, Silvio, later cardinal, 236, 240–1
    letters from Cardinal Giovanni, 1504, 292
Passignano, abbey, 23, 48, 84, 134
patron, patronage, 306
patronage as political power, 124, *See also under* Medici, Piero di Lorenzo
Pazzi conspiracy, 2, 11, 41, 60, 186
    and war, 18, 123
Pazzi family, 181, 183, 251
Pazzi palace(s)
    and Cibo, 69, 102
    and G. Bentivoglio, 209
Pazzi, Antonio, in Rome, 257
Pazzi, Cosimo, 61
Pazzi, Guglielmo, 41, 185
Pentolino, il, 235
Pepi, Francesco, in Rome, 255–6, 278, 282–4, 286–8
    on Florence's republican government, 303
    reports leaked, 288
Pescia, ser Giovanni, 65
Petrucci family, of Siena, 132
    fighting and defeat, 1502–3, 289–91
    insignia, 272
Petrucci, Giacoppo, 120, 132, 134, 262–4, 268, 270
Petrucci, Giulio, 134
Petrucci, Pandolfo, 58, 132–3, 136, 137, 264, 289
    as broker, 1502, 290
Petrucci, Raffaello, protonotary, 259, 272, 284
Pian di Meleto, Carlo da, 202
Pico della Mirandola, Giovanni, 35, 37, 50, 114
Pietrasanta, fortress, 220–2
Piombino, alum mines, 259
Pisa, 131, 242
    and Piero, 72, 123, 138
    and the Medici, 138–45
    fortress, 222
    maritime affairs, 143–4

Medici clients in, 139, 141–2
Medici house, property and estates, 139–41
Spedale Nuovo, 139
university, 138–9
Pistoia, 28, 88, 91, 126
    and Piero, 125–6
Pitti, Piero, 267, 269–70
    testimony, 269
Plato, 30
Pliny, 98
Poggio a Caiano, 11, 14, 49, 68, 94, 96, 98, 103, 112, 115–17, 195, 202
    Laocoön and *Death of Meleager* frescoes, 110, 116
    model farm, 107, 115
    model of villa, 173
    stables, 120
political morality
    realism, 301
    reason of state and duplicity, 280–1
    revolution in, 297, 305
Poliziano, Angelo, 1, 11, 13, 20, 24, 42, 57, 59, 63, 66, 76, 104, 108, 109, 112, 114, 157
    and cardinalate, 206
    as Piero's tutor, 157, 26–37
    character, 38, 64, 197
    death, 37, 207
    writings
        Apologia, 1480, 30
        Commentary on the Pazzi Conspiracy, 30
        Detti piacevoli, 46
        Latini, 32
        Libro delle Epistole, 37
Pollaiuolo, Antonio, 110
Pontano, Jacopo, 200
Porretta, baths, 44
Prato
    and Piero, 125–6
    podestà, 215
prince, princely rule, 297
Procurators, Twelve, 89
Prodicus, *Choice of Hercules*, 71
Ptolemy
    Cosmografia, 252
    library at Alessandria, 114
public and private interest, 84, 86, 91–2, 157, 169, 177, 202, 210–11
public opinion, 225
Pucci family, 145, 159
    ambition, 130
    settlement, 93
Pucci, Bartolomeo, 92

Pucci, Dionigi, 159, 171
  at Vicovaro, 204
  death, 204, 206
  in Faenza, 91, 127–8, 175, 176–8
  in Naples, 144, 169–71, 175, 176–8, 200
Pucci, Giannozzo, 117, 129–30, 162, 196, 218, 266, 268
  and Piero, 154, 159
  execution, 248–9
  testimony, 263–5
Pucci, Lorenzo, later cardinal, 129–30
Pucci, Puccio, 159, 163, 173, 182, 192, 304
  at Vicovaro, 204–6
  death, 206
  in Rome, 200–2
  in the Romagna, 127–9
Pulci, Luigi, 10, 20, 22

Quaranta, Matteo, from Naples, 293

Ragonoro, Vincenzo. *See* Raimo da Gaeta
Raimo da Gaeta, 95–7
Rapallo, 212
reason of state. *See under* political morality
republicanism, republican government, 36, 152, 159, 265, 270, 303
  compared with Medici government, 282–3
  in Florence, 303
Riario, Girolamo, 127
Ricasoli, Antonio, 162
Ricci, Bernardo, secretary, 91, 109, 119, 162, 171–4
Ridolfi, Giovanbattista, 91
  in Milan, 207, 216
  in Venice, 201, 207, 278
Ridolfi, Niccolò, 89, 96, 154, 178, 243, 264–6, 268–9
  execution, 248–9
  testimony, 247, 262–3
Ridolfi, Piero di Jacopo, 187
Ridolfi, Piero di Niccolò, 162
  betrothal, 56
Romagna, the 127–9, 173
  and Piero, 127
  and Via Emilia, 127
  campaign, 1494, 204–5, 208–13
  campaign, 1498–99, 263, 270, 272–6, *See also under* Medici, Piero di Lorenzo
  murders, 1488, 73
Rome
  and Florence, 41
  and the Medici Bank, 130
  churches
    S. Maria sopra Minerva, 257–8, 294
  triumvirate, 36n43
Rosa, Ambrogio da, astrologer, 172
Rossi, Tribaldo de', 83
Rovere, Giuliano della, later Pope Julius II, 57, 66, 67, 181
  accession, 294
Rovere, Niccolò della, 130
Rucellai palace, 183
Rucellai, Bernardo, 35, 53, 54, 62, 89, 114–15, 154–5, 226
  De bello italico, 5n12
Rucellai, Cosimo, 12, 155, 183, 185, 187–8, 233
Rucellai, Jacopo, 255
Rucellai, Pandolfo, 223
Ruota, La, hunt, 72, 75, 117

Salvalaglio, bodyguard, 126
  rebel, 226
Salviati, Alamanno, 158
Salviati, Giorgio Benigno, 166
Salviati, Jacopo, 57, 59–64, 66–7, 72, 74, 88, 248
  and Alfonsina, 296, 303
  and Lucrezia, 267, 270
  betrothal, 56
  in Pisa, 102
San Germano. *See* Montecassino, abbey
San Gimignano
  and the Medici, 94n28, 131
San Giorgio, Giovanni di, 130
Sangallo, Antonio, Battista and Francesco da
  and Piero's tomb, 293
Sangallo, Giuliano da, 116, 173
Sanseverino, Anton Maria, 258, 267, 270
Sanseverino, Antonello, prince of Salerno, 154, 184–5
  and conspiracy, 179–80
Sanseverino, Caterina, countess, 25, 55, 61–2, 64, 116, 225, 239, 295
Sanseverino, Federigo, cardinal, 241, 245, 250, 272
  and Lionardo Bartolini, 287
  in Milan, 1500, 280
Sanseverino, Galeazzo, 83, 172, 183
Sanseverino, Gian Francesco, count of Caiazzo, 172, 242
Sanseverino, Roberto, 43, 45, 172
Sant'Agnese, company of
  and Piero, 82

Index

Santa Croce, Giorgio di, 63, 68, 237
Sanudo, Marin, 2, 273
Sarzana, Sarzanello, fortress, 221–2
Sassetti, Cosimo, 120, 180, 201, 249
Sassetti, Galeazzo, 267–8
Savelli family, lands, 44, 288
Savonarola, fra Girolamo, 235, 243, 247–8, 264, 270–1
  ambassador, 223
  and Piero, 167, 243
  execution, 271
Scala, Bartolomeo, 34, 38, 39, 92
  in Rome, 1484, 42
  Writings, *Centum Apologi*, 34
Scipio Africanus, 199
Scorciati, Camillo, 92
scrutineers, electoral (*accoppiatori*), 155
Secco, Francesco, 141, 257
Seneca
  Medea, 110, 218n20
  Thyestes, 110
Senigallia, 291
Serafino, friar in S. Gallo, 260, 263, 265–8
Serristori, Antonio, 154, 162
Serristori, Battista, 244
Serristori, Giovanni, 66, 68, 89, 99
Seventeen Reformers, 102, 141n78
Seventy (*Settanta*), 89, 151, 177, 186, 188
  abolished, 226
  Ordine del, 155, 167
  records, 186
  reestablished, 1512, 295
Severini, Francesco, 136
Sforza family, 117, 277
Sforza, Alessandro, 77
Sforza, Ascanio, cardinal, 81, 153, 164, 183, 192
  in Milan, 1500, 280
Sforza, Caterina, ruler of Forlì and Imola, 91, 127–8, 182, 202, 209–10
Sforza, Ermes, 161
Sforza, Giangaleazzo, duke
  death, 216
  marriage, 71, 74, 76–81, 90, 92
Sforza, Lodovico, duke, 71, 73–4, 90, 99, 144, 168, 182–3, 187, 199–201, 210, 239
  and Piero, 76–81, 100, 116, 171–5, 192, 226, 234, 280
  and the Triple Alliance, 174, 178
  as duke of Milan, 151–2, 175, 192, 216
  on Medici regime, 283
  and the Romagna, 127–8, 173

Siena, 39, 43, 45, 48, 58
  and the Medici, 131–8
  and Piero, 132–3, 245–6, 304
  financial gifts and loans, 133–4
  military contracts, 134
  oration in Rome, 1492, 163
Signorelli, Luca, 111
Signoria of Florence
  bann, 225
  palace, 223–6
  and piazza, 225–6
Sinibaldi, Antonio, 34
Sixtus IV, pope, 40, 163, 206
Soderini, Francesco, later cardinal, 59, 124, 155, 157, 181, 187, 306
  and cardinalate, 183
  and Lodovico Sforza, 193
  described, 205
Soderini, Giovanvettorio, 155, 157
Soderini, Pagolantonio, 74, 154–5, 167, 246, 248, 251
  in Venice, 201, 207, 215–16
Soderini, Piero, 158, 245
  as Gonfalonier a vita, 290, 294
  in France, 1493–94, 180–1, 184, 193
Solosmeo, Antonio, 293
Somenzi, Paolo, 247
Sozzini, Bartolomeo, 141, 163
Spannochi, bankers, 135
Spedaletto, 72, 84, 117, 138–9, 142
Speranzini, Luca, courier, 258
spies, informers, 238, 254–6, 288
Spinelli, Lorenzo, 208, 213, 216–18
Statius, *Achilleis*, 29
Strozzi family, 155
Strozzi, Alfonso, 246
Strozzi, Filippo, 111, 294
Stuart, Béraut, lord of Aubigny (Ubigny), 286

Taddei, Francesco d'Antonio, 159, 187
Tanaglia, Michelangelo, 111–12
tazze (goblets), 80, 112, 129n27, 278
Terence, *Eunuchus*, 233
Thyestes, 231
Tiphys, 218 and n20
Tivoli, Andrea da, 267
Tomacelli, Marino, 90, 96, 144, 200, 204, 219
Tornabuoni family, 16, 225, 233
  ex Tornaquinci, 20
Tornabuoni, Francesca, wife of Giovanni, 10n8
Tornabuoni, Francesco di Filippo, 21

Tornabuoni, Francesco di Simone, 20
Tornabuoni, Giovanni, 20–1, 28, 39–43, 60, 71, 74, 130
  and Piero, 303
Tornabuoni, Lorenzo, 20, 37, 118, 130, 145, 162, 175, 206, 218, 220, 222
  execution, 248–9
  testimony, 262–3, 265–8
Tornabuoni, Lucrezia, 10–12, 19–21
Tornabuoni, Luigi, 269–70
Tornabuoni, Nofri, 59, 65, 123, 130–1, 176, 202, 241, 259, 265
  and Piero, 145
  arrest in Rome, 161n46
Tornabuoni, Pietro, 100
Tornaquinci family. *See* Tornabuoni family
Torrechiara, castle, 172
Tortona, 77
torture, 96
Trebbio, 12, 19, 117, 138
Triple Alliance. *See under* Italy, alliances
Trivulzio, Giacomo, 57
tyranny, 6, 301–2, 306, *See also under* Medici, Piero di Lorenzo

Ugolini, Bartolomeo, *al.* Baccio, 44, 55, 64, 67, 168, 175, 181, 204
  described, and death, 207
  in San Germano, 1492, 104

Vaglienti, 289
Vaglienti, Piero, 289, 204n27
Valori, Filippo, 131, 156, 158, 160
  in Naples, 207, 216
  in Rome, 163, 169, 171, 176
  on papal simony, 206
Valori, Francesco, 91, 155–6, 158, 167, 226, 248, 264, 269
  Gonfalonier, 1497, 243
  in Milan, 89

vendetta, 224
Venice, 237–8
  alliance with Louis XIII, 271
  ambition and power, 239, 245, 264–5
  and Piero, 232–4, 252, 273–6, 278–9
  treaties with Florence and Louis XII, 1499, 276
Venturi Bank, in Siena, 258
Vesc, Etienne, seneschal of Beaucaire, 184
Vespers, Sicilian, 198
Vespucci, Agostino
  and Piero, 281, 307
Vespucci, Guidantonio, 42, 89, 100, 248
  Gonfalonier, 277
  in France, 199
Vespucci, Marco, 74
Vettori, Francesco, 291
  and Lorenzo di Piero, 296
  political morality, 301, 305
Vettori, Paolo
  political morality, 305
Vettori, Piero, 91, 226
Vicemercato, Taddeo, 232–4
Vicovaro, Orsini castle, 62, 160
  Diet, 1494, 191, 197, 204–6
Virgil, 28
  Aeneid, 27, 29, 36, 199
  Eclogues, 35, 49
Vitelli family, 111
Vitelli, Paolo, 246, 274, 280, 285–6
  execution, 1499, 279
Vitelli, Vitellozzo, 279, 280, 284–6, 289–90
  death, 289, 291
Vittorini, Sante, 92
Volterra
  copper sulphate mines, 139
  rebellion, 1472, 2

wet nursing in Tuscany, 10, 12

Milton Keynes UK
Ingram Content Group UK Ltd.
UKHW021536270923
429388UK00021B/135